INTERMEDIATE ACCOUNTING

J R Dyson

B.A., M.Soc.Sc, F.C.A., M.B.I.M.

DP PUBLICATIONS LTD
Aldine Place
142/144 Uxbridge Road
Shepherds Bush Green
London W12 8AA

1989

A CIP catalogue record for this book is available from the British Library

ISBN No: 1 870941 29 2

First published in Great Britain, 1989
Copyright J R Dyson © 1989

PageSet by Kai Typesetters in Times on a Macintosh IICX

Printed by: The Guernsey Press Co Ltd
             Braye Road Vale
             Guernsey
             Channel Islands

ACKNOWLEDGEMENTS

I am grateful to the following examination bodies for permission to use questions from past papers:

Association of Accounting Technicians (AAT)

Institute of Chartered Accountants of Scotland (ICAS)

London Chamber of Commerce and Industry (LCCI)

Royal Society of Arts (RSA).

In accordance with the wishes of the above examination bodies, any change made to a question has been kept to a minimum. The solutions are entirely my responsibility.

I am also grateful to all of my colleagues in the Department of Accounting at the Napier Polytechnic of Edinburgh for much sound advice, active encouragement, and a great deal of help in the preparation of this book. In particular, my thanks are due to David Young, Douglas Sievewright, and Ken Gill (now at the Chartered Institute of Public and Finance and Accountancy's Education and Training Centre), as well as to Mrs Margaret Lang, Mrs Jan McNeil and Mrs Winnie Wallace for typing most of the examples, questions and solutions.

PREFACE

AIM

The aim of this book is to provide all the support needed for basic and intermediate courses in financial accounting.

It is assumed that the principles of the subject have been taught. The book only contains, therefore, the EXTRA material needed by students, that is, a summary of the main points, course notes, examples, exercises and case studies. Detailed solutions are provided for all examples and exercises. Specific solutions are not provided for the case studies, partly because some of the tasks do not have specific solutions, and partly because it is expected that students will be encouraged to devise their own solutions. Where appropriate, however, some brief guidelines are provided for the benefit of tutors.

NEED

The need was seen for a book which did not DUPLICATE the teaching of the lecturer. Whilst students may understand the principles explained by the lecturer, they often have problems in remembering the key points and in applying their knowledge to practical examples.

SYLLABUS

The book is aimed at the following syllabuses:

Association of Accounting Technicians:
> Certificate in Accounting
> Paper A - Basic Accounting

Association of Accounting Technicians:
> Preliminary Examination
> Paper 1 - Basic Accounting

Association of Accounting Technicians:
> Intermediate Examination
> Paper 5 -Accounting

London Chamber of Commerce and Industry:
> First Level - Book-keeping
> Second Level - Book-keeping and Accounts

Royal Society of Arts:
> Book-keeping Stage I - Elementary
> Book-keeping Stage II - Intermediate

Some chapters in the book will also be useful to students taking more advanced papers set by the above bodies, as well as being of benefit to candidates taking the first stage of the various professional accounting body examinations, for example:

Chartered Association of Certified Accountants:

Paper 1.1 - Introduction to Accounting

Chartered Institute of Management Accountants:

Stage 1 - Accounting

Institute of Chartered Accountants in England and Wales:

Foundation Examination - Accounting

In addition, the book will be helpful to those accounting and non-accounting students in colleges, polytechnics and universities who are required to take a basic course in accounting as part of their certificate, degree or diploma studies. By using the book, such students will gain considerable experience and expertise in the APPLICATION of basic principles to practical accounting problems.

APPROACH

The book sets out to achieve its aim in a number of ways:

1. **Summary**. Each chapter contains a summary of a particular topic. This summary enables students to check that they understand the basic principles covered in that particular chapter.

2. **Examples and Exercises**. Worked examples (with solutions) and a number of exercises are included in each chapter. Detailed solutions to the exercises are contained at the end of the book. The examples and exercises are generally graded in order of difficulty, so that students can check their progress as they work through them.

3. **Common Errors**. The same mistakes are frequently made by students in EVERY topic in accounting. Each chapter contains a LIST of the common errors relevant to that chapter. This list enables students to spot their mistakes and to correct them.

4. **Case Studies**. The book contains four case studies. These case studies include material from various chapters in the book. Each case study requires student to undertake a number of tasks. Some of these tasks require a considerable amount of library research. Specific solutions have not been provided for the case studies, as students are recommended to put forward their own ideas and to be able to justify them. The case studies may be undertaken individually or as a group, and they are suitable for both verbal and written presentation.

CONTENTS

STUDY AND EXAMINATION HINTS

STUDY HINTS

This book has been written to enable you to pass your accounting examination. The following hints will help you to make good use of your study time.

Accounting is not an easy subject to learn, but it is even more difficult if you leave it all to the last moment. You must set aside a regular period of study well in advance of the examination date. By the time that the examination comes around, you should have covered every aspect of your syllabus, and you should also have left about three of four weeks for a thorough revision of all that you have learnt.

Obviously you must know what your syllabus contains. Often it is progressive, that is, what has been covered at an earlier stage is sometimes examined at a subsequent stage, although usually at a more advanced level.

The real key to success in accounting examinations is practice. The more questions that you tackle, the more successful that you are likely to be. Once you have gained some experience, try and do some more questions in examination conditions, that is, without reference to any text books and in the time allowed for the question. Resist the temptation to look at the answer unless you are absolutely stuck. Auditing a solution will teach you virtually nothing. You are only deluding yourself if you think that you are learning this way.

It is assumed that those students using this book have no prior knowledge of accounting, apart from any background explanation given by a lecturer before work is begun on a particular chapter.

In this book, the earlier questions in each chapter are the slightly easier ones, with the later ones being more difficult.

If you are studying the subject at the preliminary stage, you will not need to tackle all the questions in each chapter. You should be able to tackle those questions variously described as Basic, Certificate, Elementary, First Level, Part 1 and Preliminary.

However, if you are taking the subject at intermediate level, you should aim to do all the questions in each of the relevant chapters.

Note that some topics may be included in (say) a basic level syllabus by one accounting body, and in an intermediate syllabus by another body.

EXAMINATION HINTS

Success in an examination depends mainly on how well you have prepared for it. Many candidates do poorly because of bad examination technique. The following hints will help you make the best out of your examination.

1. *Read the question carefully*

   Very many marks are lost by candidates who have misunderstood a question. Not only do they lose marks for that question, but they also lose time, because the question often becomes more complicated as a result of their mistake.

2. *Best questions first*

   Do your best questions first, but make sure that you do all of the compulsory questions. Try to get as many marks as possible before you tackle the optional or more difficult questions.

3. *Sectionalised questions*

   If a question has several parts, then each part probably has a connection with the next part. Part (a) helps you with part (b), part (b) with part (c), and so on. Make sure that you do each part of the question. Sometimes the second or third part requires a written response. If you are stuck on the earlier part, you may be able to do the written part without reference to the calculative parts.

4. *Rigid timing*

   Do not spend too much time on one question. There is no point in spending a third of the examination time on a question which carries a twentieth of the marks. It is a good idea in accounting examinations to stick rigidly to the time allocation given to each question. When that time is up, leave the question. If you have some spare time at the end of the examination, you can always come back to it.

5. *Workings*

   It is important that you show your workings. If you obtain the wrong answer just because of a slight slip, then provided that you have shown your workings, you will not lose many marks. If you put down the wrong answer without any explanation, then you will not get any marks at all.

6. *Sensible answers*

   Make sure that your answer is sensible, especially if you are using a calculator. You should be a little puzzled, for example, if your net profit is in excess of your turnover. Go through your workings again, but do not spend too much time checking a question that is only worth a couple of marks.

7. *Presentation*

   Try to make your solutions neat, tidy and legible. Do not use pencil, (examiners find solutions in pencil difficult to read), corrector fluid (it is messy), or different coloured inks (it wastes time). Amendments should be made by neatly crossing out the error and inserting the correct item above it. If you leave a space between the various parts of your answer, it will look presentable and it leaves you room to insert any corrections.

8. *Careful preparation*

   During the months that you are preparing for your examination ensure that each hour of learning or revision is well spent. Do not pretend that you are working when in reality you are dreaming. It is far better to cut your losses, go for a walk, and then come back to your studies when you are able to concentrate.

PART 1

BASIC ACCOUNTING

1 THE BACKGROUND TO ACCOUNTING

MAIN POINTS

1. Purpose of Accounting

The purpose of accounting is to collect and record economic information about an entity, and to report upon its resources and performance to interested parties.

2. Branches of Accounting

There are two main branches of accounting:

    (a) Financial accounting (dealing primarily with external reporting, such as to shareholders); and

    (b) Management accounting (mainly concerned with INTERNAL reporting, such as to management).

3. Entities

An entity may be a private individual, a profit making business, such as a limited liability company, or a not-for-profit making organisation, such as a charity.

4. Accounting Practices

The amount of economic information that could be collected, recorded and reported upon is so enormous that a limit has to be placed upon it.

There are a few formal or legal limits in accounting, although there are many recognised practices and procedures that have been widely adopted over many centuries.

Such limits are variously known as assumptions, axioms, concepts, conventions, practices, principles, procedures and rules. There is no generally agreed definition of these terms, but for convenience, they may collectively be referred to as ACCOUNTING RULES.

5. Accounting Rules

There are at least 150 fairly common accounting rules, but the most important ones are as follows:

    (a) entity: information is restricted to that which relates directly to the entity;

    (b) going concern: it is assumed that the entity will continue in operation for the foreseeable future;

    (c) periodicity: the information will be collected and summarised at defined and regular intervals;

(d) money measurement: the information will be restricted to that which can be easily quantified and expressed in monetary terms;

(e) historic cost: the information will be recorded and reported upon at its original (or historic) cost;

(f) realisation; goods and services will be treated as bought or sold when the legal title to them is transferred between the respective parties, and not just when the cash for them is paid or received;

(g) accruals: the income received for goods and services will be matched against the cost of making goods and services, irrespective of when the cash for them is exchanged;

(h) Dual aspect: each transaction should be recorded twice in order to record the giving and receiving effect of ALL transactions;

(i) prudence; if there is some doubt about how to treat a particular transaction or event, then the entity's profit should be understated or its losses overstated;

(j) objectivity: irrespective of individual feelings, personal bias should be put to one side, and an objective view adopted;

(k) consistency: the application of a particular accounting rule should be applied consistently in each period of account; and

(l) materiality; a recognised accounting rule may be ignored if the effect of doing so does not make any noticeable difference to the overall result.

6. Statements of Standard Accounting Practice

Although there are few formal accounting rules, the accountancy profession has attempted to narrow the areas of accounting practice. It has set up an Accounting Standards' Committee (ASC) which issues Statements of Standard Accounting Practices (SSAP's).

SSAP's lay down the accounting treatment and disclosure requirements on a wide range of problem areas in accounting. Professionally qualified accountants are expected to follow such recommendations, and their professional body can discipline them if they do not do so.

7. Fundamental Accounting Concepts

SSAP 2 (a standard requiring the disclosure of accounting policies) refers to four FUNDAMENTAL ACCOUNTING CONCEPTS: going concern, accruals, consistency and prudence.

The standard suggests that these particular concepts have general acceptability. It is assumed that these concepts have been followed, unless the accounts state otherwise.

Example 1. The observance of the following concepts is presumed in financial statements unless otherwise stated:

(a) going concern
(b) accruals
(c) consistency and
(d) prudence

Required:

Explain each of the above concepts giving examples of how each is observed in conventional financial statements.

(AAT Preliminary)

Solution

The requirements of SSAP 2 (Disclosure of accounting policies) are such, that unless a clear statement is made to the contrary, four fundamental accounting concepts are generally assumed to have been adopted in the preparation of financial statements.

Fundamental concepts are the broad basic assumptions which underlie the periodic financial accounts of business enterprises. Four such concepts are listed in SSAP 2:

(a) Going concern

   This concept means that it is assumed that the enterprise will continue in operational existence for the foreseeable future.

   Examples

   1. Fixed assets are listed in the balance sheet at their historical cost less the accumulated depreciation based on the historical cost. If the business was not a going concern, they would be listed at their net realisable value, that is, at their estimated selling price less any disposal costs.

   2. Debtors will be included in the balance sheet at the amount due from the debtors less any provision for bad and doubtful debts. If the going concern concept was not adopted, they would be included at an amount negotiated with the debtors.

(b) Accruals

   The accruals' concept means that revenue and costs are recognised in financial statements at the time that they are earned or incurred, and not at the time that a cash transaction takes place.

   Examples

   1. If an entity has paid three quarterly electricity bills during the year, it will make an estimate of the fourth quarter's electricity charge. That amount will be included in the year's accounts, even though it may not be paid until the next year.

   2. An entity may have paid for some services during the current year that relate to the next accounting period. The cost of these services will be deducted from the total amount paid during the current year. Thus only those costs that relate to the current year will be included in that year's accounts.

(c) Consistency

   This concept means that the accounting treatment adopted should not be changed in different accounting periods. Accounting methods should not be revised without good reason, otherwise it becomes difficult to compare the results for different accounting periods.

   Examples

   1. If stock is valued on a first-in, first-out (FIFO) basis in period 1, it would not normally be charged out in period 2 on (say) a weighted average basis.

2. Assets being depreciated on a straight line basis would continue to be depreciated on that basis, unless the circumstances altered so that a change in the depreciation method became necessary.

(d) Prudence

The concept of prudence means that revenue is only included in the accounts when it is reasonably certain that a cash transaction will take place.

Similarly, expenses should be included in the accounts if it is reasonably certain that they will have to be paid.

The prudence rule effectively means that in preparing accounts, when in doubt, treat an item so that it has either the effect of reducing profits or of increasing losses.

Examples

1. An order place for some goods is not normally treated as a sale until the legal title for the goods has changed hands.

2. If it is known that a customer has gone into liquidation, then his debt should be written off to the profit and loss account in the period that his liquidation is confirmed.

Example 2. In preparing the accounts of the Blake Manufacturing Company, the accountant has had to decide how to deal with a number of problems which have risen during the year. These are as follows:

1. The proprietor wishes to include his private dwelling as part of the fixed assets on the company, since the company bank overdraft is secured on the dwelling.

2. The company has capitalised some significant expenditure on research being undertaken on a new and highly speculative product.

3. The results for the year have not been good and a change to a different method of valuing closing stocks has been suggested.

4. The company has a stable and loyal work-force which is considered to be a great asset to the company.

5. The company's net profit for the year would be improved if the Provision for Bad Debts was reduced to only a small proportion of bad debts, even though most of the debts are long outstanding.

6. Small stocks of stationery have not been included in the closing stock.

Required:

State which rule the accountant would normally follow in dealing with each of the above problems, explain briefly what each rule means, and how each should be applied in the case of the Blake Manufacturing Company.

(AAT/IAS Part 1)

Solution

1. Business entity

Matters that relate to the PRIVATE affairs of the proprietor should not be accounted for as though they were the responsibility of the entity as opposed to the individuals who own the entity.

The Blake Manufacturing Company does not own the dwelling (even though it has been used by it as collateral), so it should be not be included in Blake's accounts.

2.   Prudence

This rule means that revenues should not be included in the accounts if they are not likely to be realised, whereas costs that are likely to be incurred should be included in expenses.

It would be prudent to write off the research expenditure to the profit and loss account, as it is unlikely that any revenue will be earned on such a speculative product.

3.   Consistency

Once an accounting method has been adopted, it should not be changed, unless the circumstances alter in such a way that it becomes necessary to adopt another accounting method.

Indifferent results are not a good enough reason for changing the stock valuation method, so Blake should continue to use the existing method.

4.   Quantification and Money Measurement

It is difficult to quantity and value the benefits which a stable and loyal work-force gives to an entity. Hence such an intangible asset would not normally be included in traditional financial statements.

However, Blake might perhaps include a note in its annual accounts drawing attention to its excellent work-force.

5.   Objectivity, Consistency and Prudence

Accounts should be prepared in such a way that they avoid as much personal bias or prejudice as possible. In other words, they should be prepared OBJECTIVELY.

In this example, the accountant should make a careful estimate of the debts that are likely to arise from the remaining debtors, and the provision for bad and doubtful debts increased (or decreased) accordingly.

No account should be taken because of a desire simply to increase profit for the year.

Both the consistency and prudence rules are also relevant in this example.

6.   Materiality

In some instances, the effect of following a recognised accounting rule may be quite insignificant, and out of all proportion to the work and cost involved. If this is the case, the materiality rule may take precedence over any other accounting rule.

Hence the cost of immaterial amounts of stock should be written off to the profit and loss account during the period in which they were purchased, instead of being carried forward to the next accounting period.

EXERCISES

1.1   Accounting is concerned with the quantification of economic events in money terms in order to collect, record, evaluate and communicate the results of past events and to aid in decision-making.

Explain.

(AAT Level 1)

1.2   Financial statements are normally prepared upon the basis of a number of accounting concepts.

Required:

State what you understand by each of the following accounting concepts, and how they are applied in the preparation of financial statements:

  (i)   entity;
  (ii) going concern;
  (iii) accruals (or matching);
  (iv) conservatism (or prudence);
  (v)   consistency.

(AAT Level 2)

1.3   In preparing the accounts of Fruit and Nut for the year to 31 March 19X5 a number of problems were encountered. These were as follows:

1. The partnership had paid both Fruit and Nut's personal income tax for the year to 5 April 19X4.

2. Fruit and Nut employed an excellent manager who had worked for the firm for 25 years. He was regarded as just a valuable asset as the premises in which he worked, and the partners are insisting that his worth be included on the balance sheet.

3. Specialist equipment had cost £10,000 to build, but if the partnership went into liquidation, it would probably have no value.

4. Certain stocks are valued on a FIFO (first-in, first-out) basis, but it was believed that less tax would be paid by the partners if the stocks were valued on a LIFO (last-in, first-out) basis.

5. At 31 May 19X5, there were only two gallons of petrol in the firm's delivery van. The partners are not sure how this should be recorded in the books of account.

6. The partnership owed £2,000 for outstanding rates as at 31 March 19X5.

7. It was believed that one of the firm's customers had gone into liquidation. The customer owed Fruit and nut £500.

8. Although some goods had been sold to a customer, it was not expected that the cash for them would be received until the end of June 19X5.

Required:

    (a) State which accounting procedure you would adopt in dealing with each of the above problems, outlining briefly the reasons for your choice; and

    (b) explain briefly how Statements of Standard Accounting Practice (SSAP's) help accountants prepare accounting statements.

(AAT Level 2)

1.4   In preparing the accounts of your company, you are faced with a number of problems. These are summarised below:

1   The managing director wishes the company's good industrial relations to be reflected in the accounts.

2   The long-term future success of the company is extremely uncertain.

3   Although the sales have not yet actually taken place, some reliable customers of the company have placed several large orders that are likely to be extremely profitable.

4   One of the owners of the company has invested his drawings in some stocks and shares.

5   At the year end, an amount is outstanding for electricity that has been consumed during the accounting period.

6   All the fixed assets of the company would now cost a great deal more than they did when they were originally purchased.

7   During the year, the company purchased £10 worth of pencils; these had all been issued from stock and were still in use at the end of the year.

8   The company has had a poor trading year, and the owners believe that a more balanced result could be presented if a LIFO (last-in, first-out) stock valuation method was adopted, instead of the present FIFO (first-in, first-out) method.

9   A debtor who owes a large amount to the company is rumoured to be going into liquidation.

10   The company owns some shares in a quoted company which the accountant thinks are worthless.

Required:

State which accounting rule the accountant should follow in dealing with each of the above problems, and explain briefly what each rule means.

(AAT Level 2)

1.5   Mr A., a client who has traded as a builder's merchant for the last four years, has told you that he finds difficulty in understanding the draft profit and loss account for the year ended 31 May 19X7 which has been prepared by your assistant. Mr A's main concern is that, although the accounts show a profit, the bank overdraft at 31 May 19X7 was significantly higher than it was a year earlier.

Required:

Outline your response to Mr A.

(ICAS Part 1)

COMMON ERRORS

Most examination questions at the basic or intermediate level will probably illustrate a problem that an accountant might be facing in the preparation of a set of accounts.

The type of errors that students make in dealing with this type of problem are as follows:

1. Lack of knowledge

Many students cannot recall the basic accounting rules.

2. Understanding

Such rules that are recalled are not understood.

3. Irrelevance

The question will usually ask the student to name a specific or an over-riding rule that should be used in a particular situation. Whilst it may not be inappropriate to mention other rules, it is most important to outline only ONE specific rule, and to state briefly the reason for choosing it.

4. Easy Option

When students are not sure which rule to recommend, they usually fall back on the prudence rule. Be on the look-out for a more specific rule that appears to meet more closely the particular requirements of the question.

2 DEBIT AND CREDIT TRANSACTIONS

MAIN POINTS

1. The Dual Aspect Rule

All transactions have a giving and a receiving effect. If a company repays a loan, for example, the effect is as follows:

    (a) the bank account balance goes down (the bank gives) ; and

    (b) the amount owed also goes down (the loan account receives).

This two-fold effect of ALL transactions gives rise to what is known as DOUBLE-ENTRY BOOK KEEPING.

2. Benefits

It is useful to know what the effect of the transaction is on both the giver and the receiver, so that it is possible to check what the entity owes and what is owing to it. In addition, if the two entries are recorded separately, the accuracy of one entry can be checked against the accuracy of the other.

3. Accounts

An ACCOUNT is simply a history or record of a certain type of transaction, such as the cost of electricity, sales of goods to customers, or wages paid to employees. In double-entry book-keeping, each transaction is recorded twice: once in one account, and once again in another account.

Accounts are usually classified according to the nature of the different types of transactions, for example, sales made to customers, goods purchased for resale, and rent paid to the landlord. If there is some doubt about which account to adopt, open ANOTHER account, and give it an appropriate title.

4. Debit and Credit Entries

In a manual recording system, it is customary to record each transaction on the left hand side of the folio (or page) in one account, and on the right hand side of the folio in another account.

The left hand side of the account is known as the DEBIT side, and the right hand side is known as the CREDIT side.

These terms come from the Latin. Debit means to receive or value received. Credit means to give or value given.

The basic rule in deciding whether to debit or credit an account is as follows:

      DEBIT the account which RECEIVES; and

      CREDIT the account which GIVES

Although many book-keeping systems are now computerised, the principles remain the same. Each transaction will still be recorded twice: once in one account, and once again in another account. When the information is printed, however, the format will probably be different from that used in a manual system.

Example 1. Shoot commenced business on 1 January 19X2. The following is a list of his transactions for the first month that he was in business.

(a) Shoot introduced some capital in cash into the business;
(b) he bought a van paying for it in cash;
(c) he purchased some goods for resale paying for them in cash;
(d) he sold some of the goods for cash;
(e) he paid the quarter's rent in cash;

Required:

State for each of the above transactions which account should be debited and which account should be credited.

Solution:

	Account	
	Debit	**Credit**
(a)	Cash	Capital
(b)	Van	Cash
(c)	Purchases	Cash
(d)	Cash	Sales
(e)	Rent payable	Cash

Example 2. Match had been in business for some years. The following is a list of his transactions for February 19X2:

(a) Match introduced further capital into the business in cash;
(b) he paid the cash into his business bank account;
(c) he bought some goods for resale paying for them in cash;
(d) he bought some goods for resale on credit terms for Sunny;
(e) he sold some of the goods for cash;
(f) the remaining goods were sold on credit terms to Grime;
(g) some business expenses were paid by cheque.

Required:

State for each of the above transactions which account should be debited and which account should be credited.

Solution

	Account	
	Debit	**Credit**
(a)	Cash	Capital
(b)	Bank	Cash
(c)	Purchases	Cash
(d)	Purchases	Sunny
(e)	Cash	Sales
(f)	Grime	Sales
(g)	Business expenses	Bank

Example 3. Game commenced business on 1 March 19X3. The following is a list of his transactions for the first year that he was in business:

- (a) Game introduced capital into the business by cheque;
- (b) he drew a cheque to open a petty cash account;
- (c) he paid the rent for the use of his business premises by cheque;
- (d) he bought a van for use in the business paying for it by drawing a cheque on the bank;
- (e) he bought goods for resale paying for them in cash;
- (f) Game paid the heating and lighting expenses of the business by cheque;
- (g) he sold some goods on credit to Tong;
- (h) he purchased goods for resale on credit from Odd;
- (i) Tong returned the goods previously sold to him on credit;
- (j) Game sold some goods for cash;
- (k) he returned the goods previously purchased from Odd on credit;
- (l) he paid van expenses in cash;
- (m) Game withdrew some cash for his own personal use.

Required:

State for each of the above transactions which account should be debited and which account should be credited.

Solution

	Account	
	Debit	**Credit**
(a)	Bank	Capital
(b)	Petty cash	Bank
(c)	Rent payable	Bank
(d)	Van	Bank
(e)	Purchases	Cash
(f)	Heating and lighting	Bank
(g)	Tong	Sales
(h)	Purchases	Odd
(i)	Sales returns	Tong
(j)	Cash	Sales
(k)	Odd	Purchases returns
(l)	Van expenses	Cash
(m)	Drawings	Cash

EXERCISES

2.1 The following is a list of transactions which a new sole trader might incur:

- (a) The sole trader introduces some cash into the business;
- (b) he pays some of the cash into a business bank account;
- (c) he purchases goods for resale paying for them in cash;
- (d) he sells some of the goods for cash;
- (e) he pays office expenses in cash;

Required:

State for each of the above transactions which account should be debited and which account should be credited.

2.2 Hopp buys and sells goods on cash and credit terms. The following is a list of some of his transactions:

- (a) Hopp introduced further capital into the business in cash;
- (b) he paid some of the cash into a business bank account;
- (c) he bought some goods for resale paying for them in cash;
- (d) he bought some goods for resale on credit from Pope;
- (e) he sold some goods to Lynn on credit terms;
- (f) he returned some goods previously purchased from Pope;
- (g) Lynn returned the goods sold to him;
- (h) Hopp opens a Petty Cash Account by drawing a cheque on the bank;
- (i) he pays rent by cheque;
- (j) Hopp pays the electricity bill in cash.

Required:

State for each of the above transactions which account should be debited and which account should be credited.

2.3 Major has been in business for many years. The following is a list of his transactions for the year to 31 March 19X3:

- (a) Major received a long term loan from Minor in cash;
- (b) Major introduced further capital into the business by cheque;
- (c) he drew a cheque on the bank in order to open a petty cash account;
- (d) some goods for resale were purchased on credit terms from Law;
- (e) gas expenses were paid in cash;
- (f) Minor was paid his loan interest in cash;
- (g) some goods were sold on cash terms;
- (h) Major took some cash out of the business for his holiday;
- (i) he drew a cheque out of the bank to pay his employees their wages;
- (j) some goods were sold on credit terms to Moor;
- (k) a car was purchased for use in the business by drawing a cheque on the bank;
- (l) Major incurred some travelling expenses which were paid for out of petty cash;
- (m) he returned some goods to Law;
- (n) Major paid his wife's dress account in cash;
- (o) Moor returned the goods previously sold to him on credit;
- (p) Major paid his garage expenses by cheque;
- (q) he bought some office stationery on cash terms;
- (r) he paid office expenses by cheque;
- (s) Major used some of the goods purchased for resale for his own personal use;
- (t) he purchased some goods for resale paying for them in cash.

Required:

State for each of the above transactions which account should be debited and which account should be credited.

2.4 The following is a list of ten transactions entered into by R Lapp who has just set up in business as a sole trader.

1   R Lapp starts up in business by opening a business bank account with £60,000.
2   Equipment for the business costing £37,500 is purchased and paid for by cheque.
3   Purchased goods costing £13,000 for resale on credit from Lapp Supplies Ltd.
4   Withdrew £180 from the bank for the till.
5   Sold some goods for £5,674 on credit to C Trewar.
6   Paid the rent on the business premises by cheque for £1,600.
7   Paid motor expenses of £77 in cash.
8   The owner of the business withdraws £100 from the till for personal use.
9   Some of the goods sold to C Trewar were returned and an allowance of £120 was made.
10   Paid Lapp Supplies Ltd by cheque in full settlement of their invoice for £13,000.

Required:

For each transaction identify clearly:

(a) the name of the account to be debited; and
(b) the name of the account to be credited.

(AAT Certificate)

2.5   The following transactions took place during the month of August 19X5, in the business of V Kohn, a sole trader:

19X5

(1)   5 August   Kohn paid rent of £150 by cheque.
(2)   10 August   J Chisholm, a debtor, paid to Kohn £165 in full settlement of the amount owed by £170. This cheque was banked on the same day.
(3)   15 August   P Burrows was declared bankrupt. He owed Kohn £112. Kohn, discovering that Burrows was unable to contribute anything towards settling his debt, wrote the amount off as a loss.
(4)   20 August   On 13 August Kohn paid by cheque £78 to settle a telephone bill. Unfortunately his book-keeper posted the transaction to the Electricity Account. Kohn corrected the error on 20 August.
(5)   31 August   The book-keeper had totalled the Purchases Day Book for the month correctly, amounting to £1,340. Unfortunately he had posted this to the Purchases Account as £1,430 in error. This was now discovered and corrected.

Required:

Set out the following columns for each of the above transactions the names and amounts of the accounts concerned:

Transaction:	Account to be debited	Account to be credited

(LCCI Elementary 1987)

2.6 The following table shows the cumulative effects of a succession of separate transactions on the assets and liabilities of a business

Transaction		A	B	C	D	E	F	G	H	I
	£000	£000	£000	£000	£000	£000	£000	£000	£000	£000
Assets										
Land and Buildings	500	500	535	535	535	535	535	535	535	535
Equipment	230	230	230	230	230	230	230	200	200	200
Stocks	113	140	140	120	120	120	120	120	119	119
Trade Debtors	143	143	143	173	160	158	158	158	158	158
Prepaid expenses	27	27	27	27	27	27	27	27	27	27
Cash at bank	37	37	37	37	50	50	42	63	63	63
Cash on hand	9	9	9	9	9	9	9	9	9	3
	1,059	1,086	1,121	1,131	1,131	1,129	1,121	1,112	1,111	1,105
Liabilities										
Capital	730	730	730	740	740	738	733	724	723	717
Loan	120	120	155	155	155	155	155	155	155	155
Trade Creditors	168	195	195	195	195	195	195	195	195	195
Accrued expenses	41	41	41	41	41	41	38	38	38	38
	1,059	1,086	1,121	1,131	1,131	1,129	1,121	1,112	1,111	1,105

Identify clearly and as fully as you can what transaction has taken place in each case. Give TWO possible explanations for transaction I. Do not copy out the table but use the reference letter for each transaction.

(AAT Preliminary)

16

COMMON ERRORS

1. Choice of Account

Make sure that the most appropriate account is chosen in which to enter the transaction. The nature of the transaction will determine the account to be used, for example, rent payable will go to a Rent Payable Account, payments for rates will go to a Rates Account and payments for wages to a Wages Account.

2. Purchases

The cost of purchasing goods should only be included in the Purchases Account if those goods have been bought with the primary purpose of selling them to customers. Thus a van purchased for long term use within the business would be recorded in the Van Account and not in the Purchases Account.

3. Sales

Only those transactions which relate to the type of sales ordinarily made to customers would be included in the Sales Account. It follows that if a van originally purchased for long term use in the business was eventually sold for cash, the cash received would be credited to the Van Account and not to the Sales Account.

4. Reversing Entries

The most common mistake is to reverse the transaction. Instead of debiting an account, the account is credited, and the corresponding account is then debited.

Remember that the account which RECEIVES a transaction is debited, and the account which GIVES the transaction is credited.

3

DOUBLE-ENTRY BOOK-KEEPING

MAIN POINTS

1. Ledgers

A ledger is a book in which accounts are kept. In a small entity there may only be one book of account, and all the accounts may be kept in that one ledger.

Even in the smallest of businesses, however, it is customary to keep the Cash and Bank Accounts in a separate ledger, because there are usually a lot of entries to go in such accounts. This separate ledger would be referred to as the CASH BOOK. All the other accounts would then be kept in one or more other ledgers.

2. Folio Lay-Out

The design of particular ledger folios varies greatly, even in the most simple of manual systems. The folio will usually be divided into two sections: the left hand side representing the debit entries and the right hand side representing the credit entries.

A BASIC folio will appear as follows:

3. Design of a Basic Ledger Folio

DEBIT SIDE   CREDIT SIDE

Date	Narration*	Folio+	Value	Date	Narration*	Folio+	Value

* narration: this usually refers to the account in which the opposite entry will be made;
+ folio: this again usually refers to the folio number of the opposite account.

18

4. Balancing an Account

Each transaction will be entered in the appropriate column according to whether it is a debit or credit entry. At periodic intervals each account will be balanced. The procedure is as follows:

(a) Balancing date 31 December 19X2: if the debit side exceeds the credit side:

			£			£
			100			50
			150			
			250	31 12 X2	Balance c/d	450
			£500			£500
1 1 X3	Balance b/d		450			

(b) Balancing date 31 December 19X2: if the credit side exceeds the debit side:

			£			£
			40			600
						400
31 12 X2	Balance c/d		1,160			
			£1,200			£1,200
				1 1 X3	Balance b/d	1,160

Note: the above accounts have not been written up in detail.

5. Reasons for Balancing Accounts

The accounts will be balanced regularly for two main reasons:

(a) to have up-to-date information about the overall state of each account; and
(b) to enable a trial balance to be prepared.

6. The Trial Balance

A trial balance is a listing of all of the balances in each ledger account. It us usually prepared at the end of each accounting period. A trial balance does not form part of the double-entry system.

A trial balance has two main purposes:

(a) to provide an arithmetical check on the accuracy of the ledger; and
(b) as the first stage in the preparation of the final accounts.

The arithmetical accuracy of the ledger is proved if the total of all the debit balances equals the total of all of the credit balances.

7. Errors Not Disclosed by a Trial Balance

A trial balance only confirms the arithmetical accuracy of the ledger. The following errors will not be disclosed by the preparation of a trial balance:

(a) Omission: omission errors occur when transactions have not been recorded anywhere within the books of account.
(b) Reversal of entry: these errors occur when transactions have been entered as debit entries instead of credit entries, and the corresponding entries have been similarly reversed.

(c) Principle: these errors occur where transactions have been entered in the wrong TYPE of account, such as the sale of a fixed asset being entered in the Sales Account.

(d) Commission: these errors occur when transactions are entered into the wrong personal account, such as in Song's Account instead of Wong's Account.

(e) Compensating: compensating errors occur when a mistake is made in one account but they are compensated by a mistake in another account, such as entering £120 as £20 in the debit of one account, and £200 instead of £300 on the credit side of another account.

(f) Original entry: these errors occur when transactions are entered incorrectly in both accounts, for example, £60 entered on both the debit and credit sides of the respective accounts, instead of £600.

Example 1.   Andy commenced business on 1 January 19X3. The following is a list of transactions for the first month that he was in business.

	Date	Transaction
(a)	1 1 X3	Introduced £50,000 into the business in cash.
(b)	3 1 X3	Transferred £45,000 of the cash into a business bank account.
(c)	5 1 X3	Paid three months' rent of £4,500 by cheque.
(d)	6 1 X3	Bought goods costing £20,000 paying by cheque
(e)	12 1 X3	Sold goods for cash amounting to £20,000.
(f)	16 1 X3	Paid general office expenses of £2,000 in cash.
(g)	20 1 X3	Purchased £6,000 of goods for cash.
(h)	25 1 X3	Andy withdrew £1,000 in cash for his own personal use.
(i)	31 1 X3	He transferred £11,000 of cash to the Bank.

Required:

(a) Enter the above transaction in appropriate ledger accounts, balance the accounts as at 31 January 19X3 and bring down the balances as at 1 February 19X3; and

(b) extract a trial balance as at 31 January 19X3

Solution

(a)

Cash account

		£			£
1 3 X3	Capital	50,000	3 1 X3	Bank	45,000
12 1 X3	Sales	20,000	16 1 X3	General office expenses	2,000
			20 1 X3	Purchases	6,000
			25 1 X3	Drawings	1,000
			31 1 X3	Bank	11,000
			31 1 X3	Balance c/d	5,000
		£70,000			£70,000
1 2 X3	Balance b/d	5,000			

20

Capital account

		£			£
			1 1 X3	Cash	50,000

Bank account

		£			£
3 1 X3	Cash	45,000	5 1 X3	Rent payable	4,500
31 1 X3	Cash	11,000	6 1 X3	Purchases	20,000
			31 1 X3	Balance c/d	31,500
		£56,000			£56,000
1 2 X3	Balance b/d	31,500			

Rent payable account

		£		£
5 1 X3	Bank	4,500		

Purchases account

		£			£
6 1 X3	Bank	20,000	31 1 X3	Balance c/d	26,000
20 1 X3	Purchases	6,000			
		£26,000			£26,000
1 2 X3	Balance b/d	26,000			

Sales account

		£			£
			12 1 X3	Balance c/d	20,000

General office expenses

		£		£
16 1 X3	Cash	2,000		

Drawings

		£		£
25 1 X3	Cash	1,000		

(b)

Andy
Trial balance at 31 January 19X3

	Dr	Cr
	£	£
Cash	5,000	
Capital		50,000
Bank	31,500	
Rent payable	4,500	
Purchases	26,000	
Sales		20,000
General office expenses	2,000	
Drawings	1,000	
	£70,000	£70,000

Example 2   Butt has been in business many years. The following balances were bought down in his ledger accounts as at 1 February 19X4:

	Dr £000	Cr £000
Bank	8	
Capital		80
Cash	10	
Motor vehicle (at net book value)	12	
Trade Creditors		50
Trade debtors	100	
	£130	£130

The following transactions took place during February 19X4:

	Date	Transaction
(a)	2 2 X4	Purchases of £4,000 in cash.
(b)	6 2 X4	Paid motor expenses of £2,000 by cheque.
(c)	10 2 X4	Credit sales of £35,000 made to customers.
(d)	14 2 X4	Cheques of £75,000 received from trade debtors.
(e)	18 2 X4	Paid £40,000 trade creditors by cheque.
(f)	20 2 X4	Paid £3,000 for office expenses in cash.
(g)	24 2 X4	Cash sales of £20,000.
(h)	26 2 X4	Goods purchased on credit amounting to £32,000.
(i)	27 2 X4	Office expenses of £7,000 paid by cheque.
(j)	28 2 X4	Goods worth £6,000 sold on credit terms returned by customers.
(k)	28 2 X4	Butt returned goods purchased on credit of £14,000.
(l)	28 2 X4	£18,000 of cash transferred to the bank.

Required:

(a) Enter the opening balances as at 1 February 19X4 and the transactions for February 19X4 in appropriate ledger accounts, balance the accounts as at 28 February 19X4, and bring down the balances on each account as at 1 March 19X4; and

(b) extract a trial balance at 28 February 19X4.

Solution

(a)

Butt
Bank account

		£000			£000
1 2 X4	Balance b/d	8	6 2 X4	Motor expenses	2
14 2 X4	Trade debtors	75	18 2 X4	Trade creditors	40
			27 2 X4	Office expenses	7
28 2 X4	Cash	18	28 2 X4	Balance c/d	52
		£101			£101
1 3 X4	Balance b/d	52			

22

Cash account

			£000				£000
1 2 X4	Balance b/d		10	2 2 X4	Purchases		4
24 2 X4	Sales		20	20 2 X4	Office expenses		3
				28 2 X4	Bank		18
				28 2 X4	Balance c/d		5
			£30				£30
1 3 X4	Balance b/d		5				

Capital account

		£000			£000
			1 2 X4	Balance b/d	80

Motor vehicle account

	£000		£000
1 2 X4	12		

Trade creditors account

		£000			£000
18 2 X4	Bank	40	1 2 X4	Balance b/d	50
28 2 X4	Purchases returns	14	26 2 X4	Purchases	32
	Balance c/d	28			
		£82			£82
			1 3 X4	Balance b/d	28

Trade debtors account

		£000			£000
1 2 X4	Balance b/d	100	14 2 X4	Bank	75
10 2 X4	Sales	35	28 2 X4	Sales returns	6
			28 2 X4	Balance c/d	54
		£135			£135
1 3 X4	Balance b/d	54			

Purchases account

		£000			£000
2 2 X4	Cash	4			
26 2 X4	Trade creditors	32	28 2 X4	Balance c/d	36
		£36			£36
1 3 X4	Balance b/d	36			

Motor expenses account

		£000		£000
6 2 X4	Bank	2		

Sales account

		£000				£000
			10 2 X4	Trade debtors		35
28 2 X4	Balance c/d	55	24 2 X4	Cash		20
		£55				£55
			1 3 X4	Balance b/d		55

Office expenses account

		£000			£000
20 2 X4	Cash	3			
27 2 X4	Bank	7	28 2 X4	Balance c/d	10
		£10			£10
1 3 X4	Balance b/d	10			

Sales returns account

		£000		£000
28 2 X4	Trade debtors	6		

Purchases returns account

	£000			£000
		28 2 X4	Trade creditors	14

(b)

Butt
Trial balance at 28 February 19X4

	Dr	Cr
	£000	£000
Bank	52	
Cash	5	
Capital		80
Motor vehicle	12	
Trade creditors		28
Trade debtors	54	
Purchases	36	
Motor expenses	2	
Sales		55
Office expenses	10	
Sales returns	6	
Purchases returns		14
	£177	£177

EXERCISES

3.1 W Flower commenced business on 1 March 19X8 paying £200 into a business bank account. During the next two months the following transactions took place. All payments are made by cheque.

			£
March	1st	Paid one month's rent	100
"	4th	Purchased goods for resale	500
"	18th	Paid vehicle insurance premium	50
"	24th	Banked shop takings for month	800
"	28th	Paid heating bill	40
"	30th	Cash drawn for self	100
April	1st	Paid one month's rent	100
"	4th	Purchased goods for resale	800
"	7th	Paid for repairs to motor vehicle	60
"	27th	Banked shop takings for month	950
"	28th	Paid heating bill	50
"	29th	Purchased new suit for self	100

Required:

(a) Write up the bank account (balancing at the end of each month) and all other accounts (use one account only for all motor vehicle expenses), total and balance the accounts at the end of the two month period; and

(b) extract a trial balance as at 30 April 19X8. *(RSA Elementary)*

3.2 On November 19X7 Peter House set up in business on his own account as an Estate Agent. The following transactions occurred during the month of November.

November 2	Peter House paid £10,000 into a bank account for the business.
November 2	Peter House withdrew £200 from the business bank account for the business petty cash box.
November 3	An office was rented for the business and the rent of £750 for November was paid by cheque.
November 4	Office furniture costing £2,400 was purchased from Grunwicks plc under their "interest free" credit scheme. A down payment of £600 was paid immediately by cheque. The balance is to be paid in three equal monthly instalments.
November 13	Peter House received a cheque for £600 as commission in respect of the sale of a client's home.
November 19	The home of another client, Jacob Podmore was sold. The commission on this sale was £875 but it will not be received in cash until later in December.
November 25	Advertising bills totalling £410 were paid by cheque of which £110 was incurred advertising the home of Jacob Podmore. This amount is recoverable from the client.
November 28	Peter House transferred £604 from his business bank account to his private bank account, £84 of which was to reimburse himself for motor expenses incurred on business use. The remaining £520 was withdrawn for private purposes.

Required:

(a) (i) Show by means of ledger accounts how the above transactions would be recorded in the books of Peter House;

     (ii) balance off the Bank Account as at 30 November 19X7 entering the correct balance in the account and closing off the account as at 30 November 19X7; and

(b)   extract a trial balance as at 30 November 19X7.

(AAT Certificate, adapted)

3.3   Charles opens a shop on 1 July 19X2, and during his first month in business, the following transactions occurred:

1 July	Charles contributes £20,000 in cash to the business out of his private bank account.
2 July	He opens a business bank account by transferring £18,000 of his cash in hand.
5 July	Some premises are rented, the rent being £500 per quarter, payable in advance in cash.
6 July	Charles buys some second-hand shop equipment for £300 paying by cheque.
9 July	He purchases some goods for resale for £1,000 paying for them in cash.
15 July	Seddon supplies him with £2,000 of goods on credit.
20 July	Charles returns £200 of the goods to Seddon.
23 July	Cash sales for the week amount to £1,500.
26 July	Charles sells good on credit for £1,000 to Frodsham.
28 July	Frodsham returns £500 of the goods to Charles.
31 July	Charles receives a cheque for £250 from Frodsham.
31 July	Cash drawings for the month amount to £150.

Required:

(a) Enter the above transactions in Charles' ledger accounts, balance off the accounts and bring down the balances as at 1 August 19X2; and

(b) extract a trial balance as at 31 July 19X2.

(AAT/IAS Part 1)

3.4   Connie has been in business for some years. The following balances have been extracted from her ledger accounts as at 1 April 19X4:

	£000
Plant and machinery (net book value)	75
Trade debtors:	
Abe	26
Burke	10
Crane	5
Bank	12
Cash	2
Capital	49

£000

Trade creditors:
Winnie 6
Yule 15
Zara 60

During the three months to 30 June 19X4, the following transactions took place:

Month	April £000	May £000	June £000
(1) Cash Sales	300	272	250
(2) Cash purchases	90	150	68
(3) Cash drawings	12	15	20
(4) Credit sales:			
Abe	20	22	16
Burke	4	8	6
Crane	3	4	1
(5) Credit purchases:			
Winnie	5	7	10
Yule	17	18	19
Zara	64	56	61
(6) Bank receipts:			
Abe	19	16	18
Burke	9	3	7
Crane	4	2	3
(7) Bank payments:			
Winnie	6	5	7
Yule	15	14	16
Zara	60	64	56
(8) Sales returns:			
Abe	8	-	-
Crane	1	2	-
(9) Purchases returns:			
Yule	2	3	1
Zara	-	-	4
(10) Office expenses:			
Cash	22	27	16
Bank	11	14	32
(11) Rents received:			
Cash	5	5	5
(12) Connie: withdrawal of goods for own use	2	3	4
(13) Sales of surplus plant:			
Cash	-	5	-
(14) Transfers of cash to bank	170	80	140
(15) Connie - payment of income tax:			
Bank	-	-	8

Required:

(a) Write up Connie's ledger accounts for each of the three months to 30 June 19X4, balance off each account (except where there is a single entry in an account) as at 30 June 19X4, and bring down the balances as at 1 July 19X4; and

(b) compile Connie's trial balance as at 30 June 19X4.

3.5 Andrew Flint is a part-time sole trader. His son, who has recently begun to learn book-keeping, prepared the following draft Trial Balance in respect of his father's business as at 31 January 19X7. In his father's absence, he was unable to enter the amount of the Capital Account at 1 February 19X6:

	Dr £	Cr £
Rent and rates	560	
Discount received	170	
Purchases	8,340	
Sales		16,530
Drawings		840
Stock 1 February 19X6	3,610	
Provision for doubtful debts	200	
Office furniture, at cost	900	
Discount allowed		460
Sundry debtors	3,820	
Sundry creditors		3,540
Sales returns		210
Cash in hand	130	
Wages and salaries	7,620	
Bad debts written off	490	
Bank overdraft	1,320	
General expenses	280	
Capital account		
	27,440	21,580

When Andrew Flint reviews his son's work he quickly realises that, whilst the amounts are correct, certain entries have been shown on the wrong side.

Required:

Prepare the correct Trial Balance, including the opening balance of the capital account. (Trading Account, Profit & Loss Account and Balance Sheet are not required.)

(LCCI Elementary 1987)

3.6 D Malt, a sole trader, extracted the following incomplete Trial Balance from his books at the close of business on 31 December 19X6:

	Dr £	Cr £
Freehold premises	50,000	
Sundry creditors		2,980
Drawings		4,160
Purchases	28,200	
Sundry debtors	3,600	
Provision for depreciation of office furniture	1,040	
Stock at 1 January 19X5	2,280	
Bad debts		240
Rent receivable	1,600	
Sales		42,300
Office furniture	5,200	
Provision for Bad/Doubtful debts	150	
General expenses	310	
Returns inwards		370
Discounts received	210	
Wages and salaries	8,150	
Bank overdraft	3,130	

The accounts mentioned above are all correctly described, with correct amounts, but some of them are in the wrong column, while the capital account has been omitted.

Required:

Draw up the Trial Balance, using the above figures, entering all the accounts in the correct column. Insert the correct balance of the Capital Account as at 1 January 19X5.

NOTE: A Trading, Profit and Loss Account and Balance Sheet are NOT required.

(LCCI Elementary 1986, adapted)

COMMON ERRORS

1. Incorrect Account

An incorrect account is chosen to record a particular transaction because the nature of the transaction is not understood.

2. Reversal of Entries

A transaction is entered as a debit instead of a credit with the corresponding entry similarly being reversed.

3. Presentation

Insufficient care is given to entering the transactions carefully, so that mistakes are made in entering either the date, the narration, the corresponding folio number, or the amount of the transaction.

4. Different Amounts

The corresponding debit shows a different amount from the corresponding credit. INVERSION errors are particularly common, for example, £291 entered as £921. It is also quite common to enter the transaction in one account and forget to complete the double-entry procedure by entering the transaction in a corresponding account.

5. Arithmetical

Numerous arithmetical and related errors may occur. The following are some of the more common ones:

(a) miscalculating the total of either a debit or a credit column;
(b) miscalculating the balance in an account;
(c) inserting the incorrect closing or opening balance in an account;
(d) the omission of an opening balance;
(e) bringing down the opening balance on the wrong side of an account;
(f) the extraction or omission of a balance in the trial balance;
(g) the entry on the wrong side of the trial balance; and
(h) the incorrect totalling of the trial balance.

6. Hidden Errors

Be very careful to watch out for those errors NOT revealed by the trial balance, for example, errors of omission, principal, commission, compensating and original entry.

4 DISCOUNTS

MAIN POINTS

1. Types of Discount

There are two main types of discount:

(a) trade discounts: these are usually deducted from the normal selling or purchase price; they are given to favoured customers, or for ordering in large amounts; and

(b) cash discounts: these are given as reductions from the amount due to creditors or from debtors for settling the amount within a specified period.

2. Trade Discounts: Accounting Treatment

Trade discounts should be deducted from the normal purchase or selling price. Only the NET amount of purchases or sales should be included in the books of account. Details about trade discounts are not normally recorded in a conventional double-entry book-keeping system.

3. Cash Discounts: Accounting Treatment

(a) Purchases should be recorded in the purchases account at the amount payable, and sales in the sales account at the amount receivable BEFORE any deduction is made for cash discounts.

(b) The book-keeping entries for discounts RECEIVED (that is, given TO the entity) are as follows:

    (i) During the accounting period
        Dr   Trade creditor's account
        Cr   Discounts received account
        With the amount of discount given by the particular trade creditor.

    (ii) At the end of the accounting period
        Dr   Discounts received account
        Cr   Profit and Loss account
        With the total amount of discounts received during the particular accounting period.

(c) The book-keeping entries for discounts ALLOWED (that is, given BY the entity) are as follows:

    (i) During the accounting period
        Dr   Discounts allowed account
        Cr   Trade debtor's account
        With the amount of discount allowed by the entity to the particular trade debtor.

(ii) At the end of the accounting period
Dr Profit and loss account
Cr Discounts allowed account
With the total amount of discounts allowed to customers during the particular accounting period.

4. Provisions for Discounts Allowable

An entity sometimes provides for discounts allowable. Such a provision should be based on the closing trade debtors AFTER deducting any specific bad debts and for any provision for bad and doubtful debts.

5. Provisions for Discounts Receivable

Some entities make a provision for discounts receivable. Such a procedure appears to be contravening the accounting rule of prudence, because it is anticipating income, although it may seem logical to do so if a provision is also made for discounts allowable.

Example 1. Your firm has recently obtained a quotation for some typewriters for resale. The price and terms quoted are as follows:

List price £110 each, less trade discount 25%, less a further 2.5% if invoice is settled within 14 days.

Assuming your firm buys four typewriters and pays within the 14 days, what is the total amount your firm will have to pay?

NOTE: Ignore Value Added Tax.

(RSA Elementary)

Solution

	£
List price: £110 each x 4 =	440.00
Less: trade discount of 25%	110.00
	330.00
Less: cash discount of 2.5%	8.25
Amount payable	£321.75

Example 2. J Gordon is one of your suppliers. His account in your ledger is set out below:

J Gordon

19X7		£	19X7		£
5 Dec.	Bank	96	1 Dec.	Balance b/d	98
5 Dec.	Discount	2	9 Dec.	Purchases	135
10 Dec.	Returns	25	23 Dec.	Purchases	56
28 Dec.	Bank	105			
28 Dec.	Discount	5			
31 Dec.	Balance c/d	56			
		289			289
			1 Jan.	Balance b/d	56

On 1 January 19X8 you receive the following statement of account from J Gordon.

		Dr. £	Cr. £	Bal. £
1 Dec.				98
6 Dec.	Bank		96	2
6 Dec.	Discount		2	-
11 Dec.	Sales	135		135
14 Dec.	Returns		25	110
24 Dec.	Sales	56		166
29 Dec.	Sales	80		246

Required:

(a) Prepare a statement reconciling the balance shown as due to J Gordon with the amount shown as owing in your ledger;

(b) explain why the entries debited in your ledger account appear as credit entries on the statement received from J Gordon; and

(c) explain how the differences between the final balances can arise.

(RSA Elementary)

Solution:

(a) **Ledger Account Reconciliation at 31 December 19X8**

J Gordon's Account   £

Balance as per ledger account	56
ADD: purchases on 29 12 X7	80
Amended ledger account balance at 31 December 19X7	**£136**

STATEMENT RECEIVED FROM J GORDON   £   £

Balance as per statement		246
Less: amount paid on 28 12 X7, not yet received	105	
discount thereon	5	110
Amount owing at 31 December 19X7		**£136**

(b) The debit entries in J Gordon's account in our ledger account represent what has been paid to Gordon and the cash discounts that we have received (i.e. been allowed) by him.

The credit entries in our account in his books represent what we have paid him, and any cash discounts that he has allowed us.

(c) The differences between the final balances arise because of time delays during the transfer of cash through the banking system from one entity to another. Such differences may also arise because of errors and omissions made in entering amounts in ledger accounts in either one or both entities.

EXERCISES

4.1   Hoyle allows a 5% cash discount if his trade debtors settle their respective accounts within 28 days of the receipt of an invoice. The following transactions took place during the early part of 19X1:

Customer Name	Balance at 1 January 19X1	January Credit Sales	Cash received	Date cash received
	£	£	£	
Ash	300 Dr	1,000	1,250	12 1 X1
Elm	100 Dr	200	290	20 2 X1
Oak	400 Dr	700	1,065	18 2 X1

Notes:

1. The amount outstanding at 1 January 19X1 reflected sales made in October 19X0.
2. Customers were invoiced for January 19X1 sales on 10 February 19X1.
3. There were no sales made during February 19X1.

Required:

(a) Taking into account the above information, write up the following ledger accounts:
   (i)   Sales ledger: Ash,
                           Elm,
                           Oak;
   (ii) Discounts allowed; and

(b) balance the accounts as at 28 February 19X1, and bring down the balances as at 1 March 19X1.

4.2   Board purchases goods on credit. He trades with a number of suppliers, all of whom allow him a cash discount of 2.5% if he settles his account within 14 days of the date of an invoice. The following details relate to three suppliers for the month of March 19X2:

Suppliers' Name	Balance at 1 March 19X2	Date goods purchased	Credit purchases during March 19X2	Cash Paid 10 April 19X2
	£		£	£
Bush	7,000 Cr	20.2.X2	6,000	12,850
Grass	10,000 Cr	24.2.X2	9,000	18,775
Plant	8,000 Cr	26.2.X2	12,000	19,700

Note: No goods were purchased during April 19X2

Required:

(a) Taking into account the above information, write up the following ledger accounts:
   (i)   Purchase ledger: Bush,
                              Grass,
                              Plant; and
   (ii) balance the accounts as at 30 April 19X2 and bring down the balances as at 1 May 19X2.

34

4.3   The following information relates to Debray:

Purchases Ledger

Suppliers' Name	Balance at 1 May 19X3 Cr	Credit purchases during May 19X3	Purchase Returns	Amount paid on 31 May 19X3	Cash discount claimed
	£	£	£	£	£
Arctic	13,000	10,000	2,000	12,610	390
Indian	18,000	15,000	1,000	17,100	900

Sales Ledger

Customer's Name	Balance at 1 May 19X3 Dr	Credit sales during May 19X3	Sales Returns	Amount received on 31 May 19X3	Cash discount claimed
	£	£	£	£	£
Dane	5,000	4,000	1,500	4,500	500
Finn	14,000	15,000	5,000	20,000	700

Required:

(a) Write up the following ledger accounts for May 19X3:
    (i) purchase ledger accounts;
    (ii) sales ledger accounts;
    (iii) purchases return;
    (iv) sales return;
    (v) discounts received;
    (vi) discounts allowed.

(b) balance the accounts at 31 May 19X3, and bring down the balance as at 1 June 19X3.

4.4   F Main is a sole trader whose financial year ends on 31 December. For the month of Jan 19X9 the cashier made the following entries in F Main's Cash Book.

CASH BOOK

19X9	Discount Allowed	Cash	Bank	19X9		Discount Received	Cash	Bank
	£	£	£			£	£	£
1 Jan. Balances b/d		329	5,919	1 Jan.	Rent			600
				3 Jan.	Telephone			115
10 Jan Sales			3,385	5 Jan	Electricity			107
18 Jan Sales			4,872	9 Jan	Purchases			3,160
29 Jan D. Evans	25		975	11 Jan.	Stationery		48	
				16 Jan.	Purchases			2,315
				21 Jan.	Cleaning		18	
				23 Jan.	Postage		45	
				24 Jan.	Stationery			142
				27 Jan.	Salaries			4,540
				30 Jan.	F Weare & Son	12		488
				31 Jan.	Balances c/d		218	3,684
	£25	£329	£15,151			£12	£329	£15,151
1 Feb. Balances b/d		218	3,684					

Besides the balances on the Cash Book, the following accounts had balances as stated at 1 January 19X9.

Telephone	£25 (Cr)	Stationery	£236 (Dr)
Electricity	£32 (Cr)	D Evans	£1,000 (Dr)
F Weare & Son	£500 (Cr)		

Required:

Open accounts for all items in the Cash Book and post the opening balances, where applicable. Complete the double entry postings from the Cash Book and balance the accounts where necessary, bringing down the balance at 1 February.

(LCCI 2nd Level, 1988)

COMMON ERRORS

The treatment of discounts allowable and discounts receivable often gives rise to two common errors. These are as follows:

1. Confusion over the Terms

It is easy to become confused over the terms discounts allowed and discounts received. Discounts allowed are an EXPENSE of the entity and they must be DEBITED to the discounts allowed account. Discounts received are a form of INCOME of the entity, and they must be CREDITED to the discounts received account.

2. Treatment in the Final Accounts

Some students transfer the respective balances on the discounts received and discounts allowed account to the trading account. This is incorrect, because the treatment of cash discounts is considered to be a matter of financial policy (rather than trading policy).

Remember that the balance on the discounts received account should be CREDITED to the profit and loss account, whilst the balance on the discounts allowed account should be DEBITED to the profit and loss account.

5 VALUE ADDED TAX

MAIN POINTS

1. Background

Value added tax (VAT) is a charge levied on goods and services supplied within the United Kingdom (although there are similar taxes in other countries). The current rate of VAT is 15%.

Apart from very small businesses, all businesses have to register with Customs and Excise. Subject to various exceptions they then have to add the current rate of VAT to any goods and services that they supply (known as OUTPUTS). Any VAT charged on goods and services supplied to them (known as INPUTS) may be deducted from the total amount of VAT that they have charged to their customers. Only the NET amount of VAT is payable to the Customs and Excise Department.

Some goods and services are ZERO-RATED, for example, food, fuel and power. This means that a zero rate of VAT is charged on such supplies: in effect, such goods are not subject to VAT. The supplier will, however, be able to claim back any VAT on any inputs which HAVE been subject to VAT.

There is also another category of goods and services which are not subject to VAT. These are known as EXEMPT supplies, for example, insurance and educational services. This category is not as favourable to the supplier as the zero rated category, because an exempt trader cannot claim back any VAT levied on his inputs. His supplies, therefore, cost him the extra amount of the value added tax.

2. Accounting Treatment

    (a) Purchases: if the VAT is recoverable, it should not be included in the cost of purchases.

        The book-keeping entries required to deal with VAT on purchases are as follows:

        (i)   On receipt of an invoice
            Dr.   Purchases
            Cr.   Creditor's account
            With the amount of the VAT levied on the purchase

        (ii) At the end of the VAT accounting period
            Dr.   Customs and Excise account
            Cr.   Purchases account
            With the total amount of VAT included in the purchases account.

(b) Sales: VAT levied on sales should not be included in sales. The book-keeping entries required to deal with VAT on sales are as follows:

(i) On issuing an invoice
Dr. Debtor's account
Cr. Sales account
With the amount of the VAT added to the customer's account.

(ii) At the end of the VAT accounting period
Dr. Sales account
Cr. Customs and Excise account
With the total amount of VAT included in the sales account.

(c) Customs and Excise account: a debit balance on this account means that the Customs and Excise should refund the amount to the trader. In the balance sheet it should be shown under CURRENT ASSETS. A credit balance on the account means that the trader is due to pay over the balance to Customs and Excise. In the balance sheet it should be shown under CURRENT LIABILITIES.

(d) Irrecoverable VAT: VAT that is irrecoverable should be included as part of the cost of purchasing the goods or services.

Example   Harold Peacock, a retailer, is registered for VAT purposes.

During September 19X6, the following transactions took place in Harold Peacock's business:

1.	18th September	Goods bought, on credit, from T King and Sons Limited, list price £640 subject to trade discount of 10% and also a cash discount of 2.5% for payment within 30 days.
2.	22 September	New car, for the use in the business, bought from XL Garages Limited at an agreed price of £8,000, payment to be effected on delivery.
3.	25 September	Goods sold on credit to G Siddle Limited, list price of £1,200 subject to trade discount of 15% and cash discount of 2% for payment within 30 days.

Note: All the above transactions are subject to VAT at 15%

Required:

Record the above transactions in the ledger accounts of Harold Peacock.

Note: Harold Peacock does not maintain total or control accounts for debtors or creditors.

(AAT Intermediate)

Solution

**Harold Peacock
Purchases Account**

	£		£
18 9 X6 T King & Sons (Wkg.1)	576.00		

T King and Sons account

	£		£
		18 9 X6 Purchases (Wkg.1)	576.00
		18 9 X6 HM Customs & Excise (Wkg.1)	84.24

HM Customs and Excise account

	£		£
18 9 X6 T King & Sons	84.24	25 9 X6 G Siddle Ltd	149.94

Motor car account

	£		£
22 9 X6 XL Garages Ltd. (Wkg.2)	9,200.00		

XL Garages Ltd account

	£		£
		22 9 X6 Motor car account (Wkg.2)	9,200.00

Sales account

	£		£
		25 9 X6 G Siddle Ltd (Wkg.3)	1,020.00

G Siddle Ltd account

	£		£
25 9 X6 Sales (Wkg.3)	1,020.00		
25 9 X6 HM Customs & Excise (Wkg.3)	149.94		

Workings

1. Purchases from T King and Sons Ltd.

	£
List price	640.00
Less: 10% trade discount	64.00
	576.00
Less: 2.5% cash discount	14.40
	561.60
VAT at 15%	£84.24

Therefore net amount of invoice = £576.00 + 84.24 = £660.24

2. Car purchased on 22 9 X6

	£
Agreed price	8,000
Add: 15% VAT	1,200
	£9,200

3. Sale to G Siddle Ltd   £
    List price   1,200.00
    Less: 15% trade discount

                                                              180.00
                                                           £1,020.00
        Less: 2% cash discount   20.40
                                                              999.60

        VAT at 15% =   £149.94

Therefore net amount of invoice = £1,020.00 + £149.94 = £1,169.94

EXERCISES

5.1   You are employed by Anderson and Littlewood, suppliers of office equipment and materials. On the 29 February 19X1 your firm had supplied the following goods to T Woodward of 44 Market Cross, Driffield, North Humberside YO16 4NL. The invoice number is 66161.

> 100 reams of A4 paper at $4 per ream;
> 200 bottles of correction fluid at 48p per bottle;
> 150 boxes of address labels at 80p per box;
> 1 four drawer metal filing cabinet at £120

VAT is charged at 10% on all items.

Required:

Prepare an invoice to be sent to T Woodward

(RSA Elementary, adapted)

5.2   Alexander's Sports Suppliers manufacture a range of sporting equipment. On 1 April 19X8 he received an order for the following items from J Gower and Sons, 9 Highwood Lane, Norton.

The goods were supplied on invoice number 927JX dated 5 April as follows:

Quantity	Item	Catalogue Ref.	Recommended Retail Price
20 pairs	Cricket Pads	Z92	£16.00 per pair
10	Track Suits	A102	£19.00 each
16	Table Tennis Bats	B174	£9.60 each

A trade discount of 25% is allowed on the normal retail price by Alexander's Sports Suppliers, and all prices are subject to 10% VAT.

Required:

(a) Design a credit note which could be issued by Alexander's Sports Suppliers when J Gower and Sons return two pairs of cricket pads, and one table tennis bat as faulty on 9 April 19X8; and

(b) calculate the gross profit which J Gower and Sons could expect to obtain if all saleable goods from the above order are sold at the recommended retail selling price. Show your workings for each item.

(RSA Elementary, amended)

5.3   A Wiseman owns a retail store, During the month of May 19X3, the following transactions took place:

May	1	Purchased stock on credit from A Sellors list price £250. He was allowed trade discount of 20%
	5	Purchased stock on credit from Nicholson list price £180. He was allowed trade discount of 33.3%.
	8	Sold goods on credit £280 to B Buyer.
	12	Purchased a new typewriter on credit from Office Supplies £220. This was for use in the firm's office.
	18	B Buyer returned goods having a list price of £30.
	22	Sent a cheque to A Sellors in full settlement of his account.
	27	Returned goods list price £30 to Nicholson as being unsuitable.
	29	Received a cheque from B Buyer in full settlement of his account

The above transactions are subject to VAT at 10%.

Required:

Write up the nominal accounts, the personal accounts, the bank account and the VAT account as they would appear in the ledger of Wiseman. The accounts are to be closed off as at the end of the month.

(RSA Elementary, amended)

5.4   On April 1 19X9 Spencer Chapman had £250 in the bank. His trading transactions during the month of April 19X8 were as follows:

April 1	Purchased goods on credit from I Pike for £300 on which he was allowed 20% trade discount. Transaction subject to 10% VAT.
April 3	Sold goods on credit to J Cooper to whom he allowed 10% discount on the catalogue price of £500. Transaction subject to 10% VAT.
April 10	J Cooper returned goods as unsuitable - catalogue price £80.
April 13	Sold goods on credit to J Cooper at a catalogue price of £300 on which 10% discount was allowed. Transaction subject to 10% VAT.
April 15	Purchased Motor Van on credit from RMF Vehicles Ltd for use in the business for £2,600. Transaction subject to 10% VAT.
April 18	Received £50 rent by cheque from subletting of property (not subject to VAT).
April 20	Received cheque from J Cooper as settlement of his account in full.
April 24	Sent cheque to I Pike in full settlement of his account.

Required:

Write up, and balance (where there is more than one entry in the account) the appropriate asset, nominal, personal, bank and VAT accounts as they would appear in the ledger of Spencer Chapman at the end of April 19X8.

(RSA Elementary)

COMMON ERRORS

1. Recoverable VAT

VAT on goods and services that is recoverable should NOT be included in either purchases or sales.

2. Irrecoverable VAT

VAT on goods and services that cannot be recovered should be included as part of their cost. Note the special case of motor cars. No deduction of input tax is allowed on motor cars purchased for use in the business.

3. Customs and Excise Account

The balance on this account should NOT be written off to the profit and loss account. A debit balance represents an amount owing BY the Customs and Excise. It should be disclosed in the balance sheet under CURRENT ASSETS. A credit balance represents what the trader owes TO the Customs and Excise. It should be disclosed in the balance sheet under CURRENT LIABILITIES.

6

THE CASH BOOK AND OTHER LEDGERS

MAIN POINTS

1. Background

Even in a small business there may be so many accounts that it would be inconvenient to keep them in one LEDGER. A number of ledgers may, therefore, be kept. Each ledger will contain a number of accounts that reflect similar transactions.

The ledgers may be bound books, loose-leaf folders or computerized sheets.

2. The Cash Book

The Cash book usually contains columns for both bank and cash transactions. It is customary to refer to it as the Cash Book, and not as the Cash Ledger.

The Cash Book sometimes contains MEMORANDUM columns for noting DISCOUNTS ALLOWED to customers and DISCOUNTS RECEIVED from suppliers.

At the end of each accounting period the total of the discount allowed column is debited to the discounts allowed account, and the total of the discounts received column is credited to the discounts received account.

The format of a cash book will vary depending upon the size and complexity of a particular entity. Some cash books, for example, contain multi-columns so that it is possible to analyse in detail both incomes and expenditures within the cash book itself.

3. The General (or Impersonal or Nominal) Ledger

A small entity will usually keep a General Ledger which will contain all the accounts in the system, apart from the bank and cash accounts. The bank and the cash accounts will usually be kept in a separate Cash Book.

In larger entities, separate ledgers may be maintained to disclose information about individual entities. These are known as personal ledgers.

The General Ledger will then contain only REAL and NOMINAL accounts, that is, accounts that are largely impersonal in nature, such as fixed assets and stocks.

4. The Purchase (or Bought or Creditors) Ledger

A separate Purchases Ledger may be kept to record all the accounts relating to trade and other creditors. This type of ledger is an example of a personal ledger.

5. The Sales (or Sold or Debtors) Ledger

Accounts relating to trade and other debtors may also be kept in a separate ledger. This again is an example of a personal ledger.

6. The Private Ledger

Some accounts may be kept separately in a PRIVATE ledger. A Private Ledger may contain the capital and drawings account of the proprietors, and any other account that is not intended for general inspection.

7. Other Ledgers

Separate ledgers may also be kept for other types of transactions, if there are a considerable number entries relating to them, for example, bills payable, bills receivable, petty cash transactions, branch accounts, and hire purchase accounts.

8. Memorandum Ledgers

The entity may also use a number of memorandum ledgers. They may be used to record details about certain types of transactions before they are entered in summary in the main ledgers.

Memorandum ledgers do NOT form part of the double-entry system. They have three main purposes:

(a) to record more detail than may be found in the main ledgers;
(b) to serve as a means of posting entries to the main ledger; and
(c) to provide periodic totals of certain transactions so that only the TOTAL need be posted to an account in one of the main ledgers.

The main memorandum ledgers are the Journal, the Purchases Day Book and the Sales Day Book.

Example. The following cash book transactions relate to Shah for the month of March 19X3.

March 19X3

1 Cash balance £20, bank balance £6,900 (overdrawn).
2 Paid by cheque further capital of £10,000 into the business.
3 Cash sales of £500.
4 Paid Smith £1,500 by cheque: cash discount of £100 claimed
10 Paid office expanses of £200 in cash.
15 Cheques received from trade debtors of £9,300: £700 of discounts claimed.
20 Transferred £150 of cash to the bank.
21 Bank charges of £50.
25 Bank paid standing order of £350 for rates.
30 Shah received notification from the bank of £800 direct debit transfer to his account from trade debtors.
31 Balance of cash paid into the bank to leave a float of £20.

Required:

(a) Enter the above transactions in three column cash book and balance the accounts as at 31 March 19X3; and
(b) prepare the discount allowed and discounts received accounts.

Solution

CASH BOOK

19X9		Discount £	Cash £	Bank £	19X9		Discount £	Cash £	Bank £
1 3 X3	Balance b/d		20		1 3 X3	Balance b/d			6,900
2 3 X3	Capital			10,000	4 3 X3	Smith	100		1,500
3 3 X3	Sales		500		10 3 X3	Office expenses		200	
15 3 X3	Sales ledger	700		9,300	20 3 X3	Bank		150	
20 3 X3	Cash			150	21 3 X3	Bank charges			50
30 3 X3	Sales ledger			800	25 3 X3	Rates			350
31 3 X3	Cash			150	31 3 X3	Bank		150	
					31 3 X3	Balance c/d		20	11,600
		£700	£520	£20,400			£100	£520	£20,400
1 4 X3	Balances b/d		20	11,600					

Discounts allowed account

		£			£
31 3 X3	Trade debtors	700			

Discounts received account

		£			£
			31 3 X3	Trade creditors	100

EXERCISES

6.1

(a) Why is it often necessary for a business to subdivide its ledger?

(b) Describe how the ledger might logically be subdivided. Name the various subsidiary ledgers and describe the account you would expect to be contained in each.

(AAT Preliminary)

6.2

(a) On 18 December 19X7, JM England's cheque book counterfoil shows that he has a balance of £198.00 in his bank account. On the same date he receives an account from A Brown for £50.00. Design and prepare a cheque and counterfoil slip to settle A Brown's account after deducting 2% cash discount.

(b) Suggest how the cheque would be used where the slip system of recording transactions is in operation.

(RSA Elementary, amended)

6.3 You are employed by White & Co. as a cashier at their Westminster Branch. Their Bank current account (no. 76543211) is maintained at the Lombard Street Branch of Entry Bank. On 15 May 19X7 you pay the following items into the local branch of Entry bank:

5	£50 notes
2	£20 notes
8	£10 notes
130	£1 coins
55	50p coins
24	20p coins
20	10p coins
100	2p coins

Cheques made payable to White & Co from:

R S Adams	£169.95
T Bromley	£261.14
A Kent	£61.24

Required:

Design and complete a bank paying-in slip.

(RSA, Elementary, adapted)

6.4 Henry York is a sole trader who keeps records of his cash and bank transactions in a three column cash book. His transactions for the month of March 19X6 were as follows:

MARCH

1	Cash in hand £100. Cash at bank £5,672.
4	York received from W Abbott a cheque for £246 which was paid directly into the bank.
6	Paid wages in cash £39.
8	Sold goods for cash £152.
10	Received cheque from G Smart for £315, in full settlement of a debt of £344; this was paid directly in the bank.
11	Paid sundry expenses in cash £73.
14	Purchased goods by cheque £406.
18	Paid J Sanders a cheque of £185 in full settlement of a debit of £201.
23	Withdrew £100 from the bank for office purposes.
24	Paid wages in cash £39
26	Sold goods for cash £94
28	Paid salaries by cheque £230.
31	Retained in office cash amounting to £150 and paid the remainder into the bank.

Required:

(a) Enter the above transactions in the three column Cash Book of Henry York; and

(b) balance the Cash Book at 31 March 19X6 and bring down the balances.

(LCCI Elementary)

6.5   Paul Barclay maintains a 3 column Cash Book.

ON 1 January 19X7 balances in hand were:

	£	
Cash	24.86	
Bank	2,310.38	(in Barclay's favour)

Transactions for January 19X7 were:

		£
3 January	Banked cheques from customers (Discounts allowed £3.10)	124.38
8 January	Paid rent by cheque	42.00
12 January	Cash sales	83.20
13 January	Barclay took cash for personal use	35.00
14 January	Banked cash with the exception of £20 retained as a cash float	
16 January	Paid employees' salaries by cheque	429.12
18 January	Banked cheques from customers (Discount allowed £17.19)	831.15
19 January	Purchased motor van	2,800.20
21 January	Paid suppliers' accounts by cheque (Discount received £9.36)	439.18
24 January	Cash sales	79.40
26 January	Paid sundry expenses in cash	4.24
28 January	Bank charges	8.10
29 January	Banked cash with the exception of £20 retained as a cash float.	

Required:

(a) Prepare Barclay's Cash Book to record the January transactions, balancing the amount at the end of the month; and

(b) indicate clearly the ledger postings in respect of each of the figures appearing in the discount column of the Cash Book.

(LCCI First Level)

6.6   Galaxy Traders Ltd had £57 cash on hand and a favourable balance of £216 in its business bank account as at the start of business on 2 May 19X8. The following is a list of cash and bank transactions for the week ending 7 May 19X8:

May 2	Paid an insurance premium of £130 by cheque.
May 3	Made cash sales of £276 including £36 Value Added Tax.
May 3	Paid travelling expenses in cash £17.
May 3	Paid an invoice for £110 from Goodies Ltd. in full after deducting 10% for prompt settlement.
May 4	Received a cheque for £114 from Freda Dexter, a credit customer. Ms Dexter was settling an invoice for £120 and had been entitled to £6 discount.
May 5	Made cash sales of £414 including £54 Value Added Tax.
May 6	Made cash purchases of £161 including £21 Value Added Tax.
May 6	Paid employees their week's wages of £182 by cheque.
May 6	Paid £500 from the safe into the business bank account.

Required:

Write up Galaxy Traders Ltd's Cash Book for the week commencing 2 May 19X8 with separate columns for the folio number, discount, VAT, cash and bank. Balance the cash Book as at 7 May 19X8.

(AAT Certificate, amended)

6.7 The following is a list of transactions:

(1) the purchase of goods on credit from suppliers
(2) the sales of goods on credit
(3) a cheque received from a credit customer
(4) a payment to a supplier by cheque for goods previously supplied
(5) an allowance to a credit customer upon the return of faulty goods
(6) daily cash takings paid into the bank
(7) monthly salaried paid to employees.

Required:

For each of the above types of transactions identify the way in which the data will be incorporated into the double entry system stating which ledger, and which account would normally be used (ignore the use of day books).

(AAT Preliminary, amended)

COMMON ERRORS

1. Book-Keeping Errors

The use of a number of ledgers means that it is even easier to make the more usual double-entry book-keeping mistakes: for example, the omission of a part or the whole of any entry, reversing an entry, and incorrect totalling and balancing.

In addition, it is particularly easy to choose the wrong ledger, and hence to make the entry in the wrong TYPE of account.

2. The Cash Book

A common error is to be found in dealing with the Cash Book. Remember to bring down a credit balance in the bank column (that is, an overdraft) at the end of an accounting period as a CREDIT balance at the beginning of the next accounting period.

3. Discounts

The discounts allowed and discounts received columns in the Cash Book are only for memorandum purposes. At this stage, they do NOT form part of the double entry.

Although the discounts allowed column is shown on the DEBIT side of the Cash Book, the total of discounts allowed must be debited to the discounts allowed account. The corresponding credit for EACH discount will have been credited to each customer's personal account.

Similarly, although discounts received will have been noted on the CREDIT side of the Cash Book, the total must be CREDITED to the discounts received account. The corresponding debit for EACH discount received will have been debited to each supplier's personal account.

7 BANK RECONCILIATION STATEMENTS

MAIN POINTS

1. Background

From time to time, the bank will supply an entity with a copy of its account as recorded in the bank's books. This is usually known as the bank statement.

The account should be a mirror image of the bank account in the entity's OWN books, that is, debit entries in the Cash Book will appear as credit entries in the bank statement, and credit entries in the Cash Book will appear as debit entries in the bank statement.

The balance shown in the bank statement will not always agree with the balance shown in the entity's cash book. The difference may arise because of delays in entering transactions in the Cash Book, or because of arithmetical, book-keeping and clerical errors made by the entity.

Similarly, there may be some transactions missing from the bank statement, or the bank could also have made some errors.

2. Benefits of Reconciliation

It is useful to reconcile the two balances for three main reasons:
  - (a) to make sure that all transactions are entered in the Cash Book;
  - (b) to act as a check on the entity's own book-keeping; and
  - (c) to make sure that the bank has not made any mistake in dealing with the customer's account;

3. Steps in the Preparation of a Bank Reconciliation Statement

  - (a) Enter those transactions in the Cash Book that have not yet been entered, for example, bank charges, bank interest, direct debit payments, dishonoured cheques, and standing orders payments.
  - (b) Correct the Cash Book for any arithmetical, clerical and double-entry book-keeping errors.
  - (c) Calculate an amended Cash Book balance.
  - (d) Correct the bank statement total for any errors made by the bank.
  - (e) Prepare a bank reconciliation statement beginning with the balance shown in the bank statement.
  - (f) ADD to the balance those items not yet credited by the bank, such as receipts paid into the bank.

(g) DEDUCT from the balance those items not yet debited by the bank, such as cheques drawn but not yet presented.

(h) Calculate the amended bank statement balance.

(i) Confirm that the amended Cash Book balance agrees with the amended bank statement balance.

(j) If the two balances still do not agree, check the corrections made in the attempted reconciliation, and all additions, subtractions and balances in the Cash Book. Compare EACH entry in the Cash Book with the corresponding entry in the bank statement. If the balances still cannot be reconciled, it is possible that there could be an arithmetical error in the bank statement, and this will have to be checked in detail.

Example. The Treasurer of the Camford School Fund is attempting to reconcile the balance shown in the cash book with that appearing on the bank pass sheets. According to the cash book, the balance at the bank as at 31 May 19X2 was £1,900, whilst the bank pass sheets disclosed an overdrawn amount of £470.

Upon investigation, the Treasurer discovers the following errors:

1   A cheque paid to Summer Limited for £340 had been entered in the Cash Book as £430.

2   Cash paid into the bank for £100 had been entered in the Cash Book as £90.

3   A transfer of £1,500 to the Midlands Savings Bank had not been entered in the Cash Book.

4   A receipt of £10 shown on the bank statement had not been entered in the Cash Book.

5   Cheques drawn amounting to £40 had not been paid into the bank.

6   The cash book balance had been incorrectly brought down at 1 June 19X1 as a debit balance of £1,200 instead of a debit balance of £1,100.

7   Bank charges of £20 do not appear in the cash book.

8   Receipts of £900 paid into the bank on 31 May 19X2 do not appear on the bank pass sheets until 1 June 19X2.

9   A standing order payment of £30 had not been entered in the cash book.

10 A cheque for £50 previously received and paid into the bank had been returned by the subscriber's bank marked "account closed".

11 The bank received a direct debit of £100 from an anonymous subscriber.

12 Cheques paid into the bank had been incorrectly totalled. The total amount should have been £170 instead of £150.

Required:

Draw up a bank reconciliation statement as at 31 May 19X2.   *(AAT Level 2)*

Solution

CAMFORD SCHOOL FUND
CASH BOOK AMENDMENTS AS AT 31 MAY 19X2

	£	£
Balance as per Cash Book as at 31 May 19X2		1,900
Add:		
Correction of the amount paid to Summer Limited	90	
Incorrect entry of receipt	10	
Receipt not entered	10	
Direct debit	100	210
		2,110

	£	£
Less:		
Transfer to the Midlands Savings Bank	1,500	
Incorrect balance brought down at 1 June 19X1	100	
Bank charges	20	
Standing order	30	
Cheque returned	50	1,700
AMENDED CASH BOOK BALANCE AS AT 31 MAY 19X2		£410

Bank reconciliation as at 31 May 19X2

	£
Balance as per the bank pass sheets	(470)
Add:	
Receipts not yet credited	20
Incorrect amount credited to the account	900
	450
Less:	
Cheques drawn, not presented	40
BALANCE AS PER THE CASH BOOK AS AT 31 MAY 19X2	£410

EXERCISES

7.1   At the start of business on 31 December 19X7 the cash and bank columns of J Darker's cash book showed debit balances of £370 and £1,790 respectively.

A bank statement written up to the same date disclosed that the following items had not been entered in the cash book.

(i)   A standing order of £125 for rates had been paid on 3 December;

(ii)   Bank charges of £65 had been charged directly to J Darker's account on 18 December;

(iii)   A standing order of £150 had been paid to the Kingsley Trust on 30 December;

(iv)   P Sills, a debtor had settled his debt of £70 in full by credit transfer on 30 December.

A further check revealed the following:

(i)   Cheques sent to creditors totalling £245 had been entered in the cash book but had not yet been presented.

(ii)   Cash and cheques totalling £390 had been deposited at the bank on 30 December and had been entered in the cash book but did not appear in the bank statement.

Also on 31 December J Darker paid all but £50 of the cash in hand into the bank account after taking £100 in cash for his own private expenses and reimbursing the petty cashier with £45.

Required:

   (a) Write up the cash book on 31 December after taking the above into account and to balance the cash book ready for the start of business on 1 January 19X8; and

   (b) prepare a bank reconciliation statement starting with the updated cash book figure and ending with the bank statement figure clearly shown.

(RSA Elementary)

7.2   At the close of business on 31 May 19X5, the Bank Statement of Amos Jones, a sole trader, showed that his balance with the bank amounted to £1,960. This does not agree with the bank balance according to his cash book, and the following transactions account for the difference:

   (1) On 31 May the bank allowed Jones interest amounting to £76, but this had not yet been entered in the cash book.

   (2) During May 19X5 the bank had paid on behalf of Jones, under a banker's standing order the rent of his business premises amounting to £110. This had not been entered in the cash book.

   (3) On 31 May William Smith, a debtor of Jones paid direct to Jones' account with his bankers the sum of £89, but this had not yet appeared in the cash book.

   (4) During May, Jones had drawn several cheques but, at the close of business on 31 May 19X5, the following three cheques had not yet been presented for payment, £21, £44 and £39.

Required:

Commencing with the bank statement balance of £1,960, prepare the Bank Reconciliation Statement of Amos Jones as at 31 May 19X5, ending with the correct bank balance as shown in his Cash Book.

(LCCI Elementary 1985)

7.3   T Smallpiece received the following bank statement from his bank for the month of June 19X6.

Date 19X6	Particulars	Dr	Cr	Balance
1 June	Balance			3,160 Cr.
4 June	007496	50		3,110 Cr.
5 June	Sundries		510	3,620 Cr.
7 June	007499	130		3,490 Cr.
10 June	15 (Standing Order)	100		3,390 Cr.
12 June	007495	78		3,312 Cr.
15 June	Sundries		460	3,772 Cr.
18 June	07502	165		3,607 Cr.
20 June	T Mann (Credit Transfer)		180	3,787 Cr.
24 June	007503	110		3,677 Cr.
26 June	007500	92		3,585 Cr.
29 June	007504	38		3,547 Cr.
30 June	Charges	50		3,497 Cr.

Smallpiece does not really understand his bank statements, and wonders why the £3,497 balance at the bank does not agree with his cash book figure.

Required:

Set out briefly your answers to T Smallpiece, explaining the following points:

(a) He asks you to explain briefly the following entries which appear in the bank statement, but do not appear in the Cash Book:

    (i)   10 June
    (ii) 20 June
    (iii) 30 June;

(b) he wonders why his cash book shows cheques, as listed below which do not appear on the statement:

007498   £62
007501   £107;

(c) on 30 June he paid £360 into his bank. Why did this not appear on the bank statement?

(LCCI Elementary 1987)

7.4   The cash book, bank columns, for January 19X4 of S Simpson, sole trader is as follows:

19X4		£	19X4		£
1 Jan	Balance	1,507.71	2 Jan	Electricity Board	43.10
9 Jan	Sales	1,370.00	2 Jan	John Jones Ltd	149.10
17 Jan	Sales	168.54	4 Jan	Printers' Printers Ltd.	29.30
23 Jan	T White Ltd	310.00	5 Jan	Kingsway Products	37.08
24 Jan	Sales	150.00	12 Jan	Harold Smith Ltd	138.32
30 Jan	Sales	44.70	17 Jan	Gray's Machines Ltd	645.10
31 Jan	Sales	210.00	24 Jan	Giant displays	70.56
			26 Jan	P Swann	124.64
			30 Jan	Deposit Account	2,000.00
			30 Jan	Wages	320.40
			31 Jan	Balance	203.35
		£3,760.95			**£3,760.95**

On 6 February 19X4, S Simpson received his bank statement for the previous month; the bank statement was as follows:

Mr S Simpson - Statement of account with North Bank Plc., Main Street Branch, Westford.

Date 19X4	Particulars	Payments £	Receipts £	Balance £
1 January	Balance			1,468.21
3 January	Bank Giro Credit		100.00	1,568.21
4 January	145688	149.10		1,419.11
5 January	145686	60.50		1,358.61
6 January	Charges	15.40		1,343.21
9 January	Standing order	12.00		1,331.21
10 January	Bank Giro Credit		1,370.00	2,701.21

Date 19X4	Particulars	Payments £	Receipts £	Balance £
11 January	145687	43.10		2,658.11
13 January	145690	37.08		2,621.03
17 January	Sundry Credit		168.54	2,789.57
18 January	145691	138.32		2,651.25
20 January	145689	29.30		2,621.95
23 January	Sundry Credit		310.00	2,931.95
26 January	Standing Order	44.00		2,887.95
27 January	Bank Giro Credit		150.00	3,037.95
30 January	Deposit account	2,000.00		1,037.95
30 January	Sundry Credit		44.70	1,082.65
31 January	145693	70.56		1,012.09

On 8 February 19X4, S Simpson discovers that the Sales debited in the cash book on 31 January 19X4 should read "£230.00" not "£210.00" and is advised by the bank that the standing order charge of £44.00 on 26 January was made in error and that the bank account has now been credited with £44.00.

Required:

Prepare a bank reconciliation statement as at 31 January 19X4

(AAT Intermediate)

COMMON ERRORS

1. Misunderstanding

The bank statement is a record of the entity's bank account in the BANK's own books. Make sure, therefore, that the entries in the Cash Book are on the opposite side of the account to the corresponding entries shown in the bank statement.

2. Overdrawn Balance

If the bank balance is overdrawn, remember to ADD unpresented cheques, and to DEDUCT receipts not yet credited by the bank.

3. Corrections to the Cash Book

The Cash Book balance should be adjusted for any entries not made in the Cash Book, or for any corrections to the Cash Book balance. If necessary, the bank reconciliation statement should have a separate section illustrating the various corrections to the Cash Book balance.

Note that the corrections will have to be entered into the Cash Book after the respective balances have been reconciled so that the correct balance may be carried down to begin the new accounting period.

4. Dishonoured Cheques

If a customer's cheque had been dishonoured, the amount should be written back into the Cash Book, the entries being as follows:

Dr.   The customer's account
Cr.   Cash book
With the amount of the dishonoured cheque.

8 THE PETTY CASH BOOK

MAIN POINTS

1. Background

For control purposes, it is recommended that creditors be paid by cheque, and that any receipts from debtors should be paid straight into the bank.

There are some transactions, however, that are too small to be paid by cheque, for example, bus and taxi fares, the purchase of the occasional newspaper and magazine and tips to waiters.

Such cash transactions should be kept to a minimum, and they should only relate to minor purchases. Nonetheless, even in small businesses, there may be a considerable number of them.

2. The Imprest System

In order to avoid having to enter hundreds of small transactions in the main Cash Book, many entities operate a subsidiary Cash Book. This is known as the PETTY CASH BOOK. The Petty Cash Book may be operated under the IMPREST SYSTEM.

The Imprest System involves transferring a fixed amount of the main cash account to the petty cash account. This amount is sometimes referred to as the FLOAT.

Small items of expenditure may then be paid out of petty cash, the details of which are entered in the petty cash book. At the end of (say) each week or each month, the total amount of expenditure is calculated. That amount is then reimbursed out of the main cash account. Thus the total amount of petty cash is reinstated to the level of the original float.

This method of keeping account of petty cash is considered to be a good way of maintaining control of small amounts of expenditure, since the person in charge of petty cash is required to account for the exact amount of petty cash expenditure before the float is reinstated.

It is not recommended that amounts received in cash (however small) should be put through the petty cash account, because they are then much more difficult to control.

Such receipts should be paid directly into the bank, and accounted for through the main cash account.

3. The Double-Entry Procedure

(a) In establishing the float

    Dr.   Petty cash account
    Cr.   Bank account
    With the amount of the petty cash float drawn in cash from the bank.

(b) In re-establishing the float

    Dr.   Petty cash account
    Cr.   Bank account.
    With the amount necessary to bring back the float to its original level.

(c) Dr.   Various expense accounts (for example, travel, postage, stationery)
    Cr.   Petty cash account
    With the petty cash expenditure incurred.

4. Analytical Petty Cash Book

The Petty Cash Account is usually divided into columns, each column representing a certain type of expenditure. This means that it is not necessary to debit the respective expenditure account EACH time that that type of expenditure is incurred.

At the end of each accounting period, each column is totalled, and only the TOTAL of each column need to be debited to the respective expenditure account in the General Ledger.

This procedure avoids having to include a great many entries in the respective expenditure accounts, each one reflecting only a small amount of expenditure.

Example. James Walton is a sole trader who keeps his petty cash on the imprest system, the imprest amount being £50. At the start of business on 1 October 19X5, the petty cash in hand was £3.75.

Walton's petty cash transactions for the month of October 19X5 were as follows:

1 October	Petty cash restored to Imprest amount
4 October	Wages paid - £11.60
5 October	Stamps purchased - £3.95
8 October	Stationery purchased - £4.09
11 October	Stamps purchased - £2.00
18 October	Wages paid - £12.93
21 October	Paid to F Smith, a creditor - £3.42
24 October	Stationery purchased - £4.66
28 October	Stamps purchased - £3.80

Required:

Draw up Walton's Petty Cash Book for the month of October 19X5, carry down the balance on 31 October 19X5, and restore the petty cash to the imprest amount on 1 November 19X5.

Note: Your analysis columns should be Wages, Postage, Stationery and Ledger.

(LCCI Elementary 1986)

Solution

JAMES WALTON
Petty Cash Book

Receipts	Date	Details	Voucher No.	Total Payments	Wages	Postage	Stationary	Ledgers
£				£	£	£	£	£
3.75	1 10 X5	Balance b/d						
46.25	1 10 X5	Bank						
	4 10 X5	Wages		11.60	11.60			
	5 10 X5	Stamps		3.94		3.94		
	8 10 X5	Stationery		4.09			4.09	
	11 10 X5	Stamps		2.00		2.00		
	18 10 X5	Wages		12.93	12.93			
	21 10 X5	F Smith		3.42				3.42
	24 10 X5	Stationery		4.66			4.66	
	31 10 X5	Balance c/d		7.36				
£50.00				£50.00	£24.53	£5.94	£8.75	£3.42
7.36	1 11 X5	Balance b/d						
42.64	1 11 X5	Bank						

EXERCISES

8.1 A trader keeps a petty cash book on the imprest system with a current imprest balance of £50. He balances the book monthly, making the balance up to the amount of the imprest on the last day of each month by means of a cheque drawn on his Bank Account. His records show the following entries in the petty cash book for the month of May 19X5:

Petty Cash Book

£			£
		April total expenditure	43.60
	30 April	Balance c/d	6.40
50.00			50.00
6.40	30 April	Balance b/d	
43.60	1 May	Bank	
	3 May	Stationery	5.20
	5 May	Carriage Inwards	4.10
	8 May	Postage stamps	4.50
	11 May	Settlement of creditor's A/c	8.50
	14 May	Stationery	2.80
	17 May	Cleaning expenses	7.00
	20 May	Donation to local charity	3.00
	24 May	Taxi fares	2.70
	28 May	Postage stamps	3.60
	30 May	Cleaning expenses	6.00

At the end of May, he decides to increase the imprest to £70.

Required:

(a) What is meant by the "petty cash imprest system"?

(b) Complete the petty cash book after balancing it for May 19X5, making whatever changes you consider appropriate to the entries made by the trader. You should include analysis columns based on the following classifications of petty cash outlay:

> stationery
> postages
> travelling expenses
> sundry expenses
> ledger accounts; and

(c) specify the ledger to which each of the expenditure column totals will be posted.

(LCCI First Level 1988)

8.2 A Mobbs runs a small business where all receipts are paid into the firm's bank account at the end of each day and all payments are made by cheque except those for less than £20 which are regarded as petty cash items.

The following information relates to November 19X7

November:	£
Balance at bank	2,104.55
Petty cash balance	25.75
Vouchers held by petty cashier	24.25

The following receipts and payments occurred during the first week of November 19X7:

November		Amount £	Cash Discount £
2	The petty cash imprest was restored from the bank		
	A cheque was paid to J Tearle	50.00	
4	Cheques were received from:		
	J Sanders	111.00	10.55
	M Marchand	54.00	6.00
	Payments were made to:		
	J Darker	90.00	5.50
	Sundry stationery items	4.25	
	P Sills	5.00	
5	Cheque were received from:		
	M Marchand	59.40	6.60
	C Ford	4.50	0.50
	P Woodbine	126.00	14.00
	Payments were made to:		
	The Office Cleaner	10.00	
	A Brown for Travel Expenses	5.45	

	£	£
7	Payments were made:	
	Rent	120.00
	A Mobbs' drawings	50.00
	Motor expenses	45.00
	Postage stamps and string	7.45
	S Connor	245.00	24.50

Required:

(a) Write up the petty cash book for the week ending 7 November 19X7. Balance the petty cash book but do not restore the imprest. Use suitable petty cash voucher numbers; and

(b) write up the bank cash book for the week ending 7 November 19X7 and balance the account at that date.

(RSA Elementary, adapted)

8.3 The following is a summary of the petty cash transaction of Jockfield Ltd for May 19X2.

May 1	Received from cashier £300 as petty cash float.	
		£
May 2	Postages	18
3	Travelling	12
4	Cleaning	15
7	Petrol for delivery van	22
8	Travelling	25
9	Stationery	17
11	Cleaning	18
14	Postage	5
15	Travelling	8
18	Stationery	9
	Cleaning	23
20	Postage	13
24	Delivery van 5,000 mile service	43
26	Petrol	18
27	Cleaning	21
29	Postage	5
30	Petrol	14

Required:

(a) Rule up a suitable petty cash book with analysis columns for expenditure on cleaning, motor expenses, postage, stationery, travelling;

(b) enter the month's transactions;

(c) enter the receipt of the amount necessary to restore the imprest and carry down the balance for the commencement of the following month; and

(d) state how the double entry for the expenditure is completed.

(AAT Level 1)

COMMON ERRORS

1. Omissions

When using an analytical petty cash account book, remember to carry across each payment to the respective expenditure column.

At the end of the accounting period, total ALL the columns, and make sure that they cross add.

2. Double-Entry Errors

The petty cash account forms part of the double-entry system. At the end of each accounting period do not forget to DEBIT the respective expenditure accounts in the General Ledger with the total amount of petty cash expenditure extracted from each analysis column in the petty cash book.

Make sure that you have completed double-entry throughout the system, and that you have not made any arithmetical or balancing mistakes.

3. Closing and Opening Balances

Make sure that the closing balance on the petty cash account is correct. Under the imprest system, this is the amount that will be reimbursed.

Once reimbursed, the balance should be equal to the float.

Make sure that the closing balance at the end of the previous period is brought down as a DEBIT balance at the beginning of the next accounting period. It is impossible to have a credit balance in a cash account.

9 DAY BOOKS

MAIN POINTS

1. Background

Buying and selling goods on credit may involve an entity in making hundreds of separate ledger account entries.

A separate entry will have to be made in the respective personal accounts for each transaction that takes place, because the entity will need to have an up-to-date record of the balance on each personal account.

By using DAY BOOKS it is possible to cut down the number of ledger account entries. Day Books are memorandum books of account. They do NOT form part of the double-entry system.

To complete double entry, the day book total must be credited or debited to the appropriate ledger account.

2. Benefits

(a) Day Books help to reduce the number of entries that it is necessary to make in ledger accounts.

(b) They can contain more detail than it is possible to include in a ledger account.

(c) They can help control the entries made in a ledger account system.

(d) They can assist in locating quickly and isolating speedily book-keeping errors.

3. Main Types of Day Book

(a) Purchases Day Books

Each purchase obtained on credit terms will be listed in a purchase day book and each separate purchase CREDITED to the supplier's account in the Purchase Ledger.

The purchases listed in the Day Book will be totalled periodically, and DEBITED to the purchases account in the General Ledger.

(b) Purchases Returns Day Book

Goods returned to suppliers will be listed separately in the Purchase Returns Day Book, and DEBITED to each supplier's account in the Purchases Ledger.

The Day Book will be totalled periodically, and the total CREDITED to the purchases returns account in the General Ledger.

(c) Sales Day Book

Sales made on credit terms to customers will be entered in the Sales Day Book. The total amount of each sale will be entered in the Day Book and DEBITED to the customer's account in the Sales Book.

The sales recorded in the Day Book will be totalled periodically and CREDITED to the sales account in the General Ledger.

(d) Sales Returns Day Book

Details of goods returned by customers will be entered in the Sales Returns Day Book. The value of the goods returned will be CREDITED to each customer's account in the Sales Ledger. Periodically, the Day Book will be totalled, and the total DEBITED to the sales returns account in the General Ledger.

Example 1. Photoplot Ltd received the following invoices from suppliers during the week commencing 20 October 19X6. All purchases made by Photoplot Ltd are subject to Value Added Tax at 15%.

The following list gives the gross value of each invoice.

Date Received	Invoice Number	Date of Invoice	Supplier	Gross Amount £
Oct 20	11450	Oct 15	Mendalins Ltd	375.13
Oct 20	S861017	Oct 10	T Muir and Sons	103.04
Oct 20	33455	Oct 17	Modrin Supplies	51.52
Oct 21	G7733	Oct 17	Picketts plc	1,526.05
Oct 21	S15551	Oct 16	Sugdens Electricals	747.96

On 23 October Photoplot Ltd returned all the goods purchased on 15 October from Mendalins Ltd (Invoice number 11450) along with a debit note (D103) for the full amount.

On 24 October Photoplot Ltd returned some of the goods purchased on 17 October from Picketts Plc (Invoice number G7733). Photoplot Ltd's debit note (D104) for a gross value of £100.51 was sent back with the goods.

Required:

(a) Write up Photoplot Ltd's Purchases Day Book and Purchases Returns Day Book for the week commencing 20 October 19X6 totalling the columns off as at 24 October 19X6; and

(b) describe how the above information would be incorporated into Photoplot Ltd's ledger (assuming that Control Accounts are not used).

(AAT Certificate, amended)

Solution
(a)

PURCHASES DAY BOOK

Date	Supplier	Invoice Number	Purchase Ledger Folio Number	Net £	VAT £	Gross £
20 10 X6	Mendalins Ltd	11450		326.20	48.93	375.13
20 10 X6	T Muir & Sons	S861017		89.60	13.44	103.04
20 10 X6	Modrin Supplies	33455		44.80	6.72	51.52
21 10 X6	Pickets plc	G7733		1,327.00	199.05	1,526.05
21 10 X6	Sugdens Electricals	SI15551		650.40	97.56	747.96
				£2,438.00	£365.70	£2,803.70

Purchases Returns Day Book

Date	Supplier	Debit Note Number	Purchase Ledger Folio Number	Net £	VAT £	Gross £
23 10 X6	Mendalins Ltd	D103		326.20	48.93	375.13
24 10 X6	Picketts plc	D104		87.40	13.11	100.51
				£413.60	£62.04	£475.64

(b) Purchases Day Book

Dr. Purchases account in the nominal ledger with £2,438.00.

Dr. HM Customs and Excise account in the nominal ledger with £365.70.

Cr. Each supplier's account in the purchases ledger with the gross amount purchased from each supplier as per the purchases day book.

Purchase Returns Day Book

Dr. Each supplier's account in the purchases ledger with the gross amount as listed in the purchases returns day book.

Cr. Purchases returns account in the nominal ledger with £413.60.

Cr. HM Customs and Excise account in the nominal ledger with £62.04.

Example 2. Mudgee Ltd issued the following invoices to customers in respect of credit sales made during the last week of May 19X7. The amounts stated (on the following page) are all net of Value Added Tax. All sales made by Mudgee Ltd are subject to VAT at 15%.

Invoice Number	Date	Customer	Amount £
3045	May 25	Laura Brand	1,060.00
3046	May 27	Brown Bros.	2,200.00
3047	May 28	Penfold's	170.00
3048	May 29	T Tyrrell	460.00
3049	May 30	Laura Brand	1,450.00
			£5,340,00

Required:

(a) Show how the above transactions would be recorded in Mudgee Ltd's sales day book for the week ended 30 May 19X7; and

(b) describe how the information in the sales day book would be incorporated in Mudgee Ltd's double entry system.

(AAT Preliminary, amended)

Solution
(a)

MUDGEE LIMITED
Sales Day Book

Date	Customer	Invoice Number	Sales Ledger Folio Number	Net £	VAT £	Gross £
25 5 X7	Laura Brand	3045		1,060.00	159.00	1,219.00
27 5 X7	Brown Bros	3046		2,200.00	330.00	2,530.00
28 5 X7	Penfold's	3047		170.00	25.50	195.50
29 5 X7	T Tyrrell	3048		460.00	69.00	529.00
30 5 X7	Laura Brand	3049		1,450.00	217.50	1,667.50
				£5,340.00	£801.00	£6,141.00

(b) Dr The personal account of each customer in the sales ledger with the gross amount sold as per (a) above.

Cr. Sales account in the nominal ledger with £5,340.00.

Cr. HM Customs and Excise account in the nominal ledger with £801.00.

EXERCISES

9.1 The following is a list of typical business transactions:

(1) the purchase of raw materials on credit from suppliers;
(2) allowances received from suppliers upon return of faulty raw materials;
(3) wages and salaries paid to employees;
(4) credit card sales.

Note: Assume that Total or Control accounts are not used

Required:

For each transaction identify:

    (i)   the originating document(s) for the data

    (ii) the book of original entry for the transaction, and

    (iii) the way in which the data will be incorporated into the double entry system.

(AAT Preliminary, adapted)

9.2   Modrix Ltd received the following invoices from suppliers during the week commencing 23 November 19X7. All purchases made by Modrix Ltd are subject to Value Added Tax at 15%.

Date Received	Invoice Number	Supplier	Net Amount £	VAT £	Gross Amount £
Nov 23	GL788	Glixit plc	440.00	66.00	506.00
Nov 24	899330	Moblin Ltd	100.00	15.00	115.00
Nov 25	G1101	S & G Gates	630.00	94.50	724.50

On 25 November Modrix Ltd rejected all the goods invoiced by Moblin Ltd (Invoice number 899330) because they were not what had been ordered. The goods were returned to Moblin Ltd along with Modrix Ltd's debit note (D56) for the full invoice amount.

On 26 November Modrix Ltd had to return some of the goods purchased from S & G Gates (Invoice number G1101) because they were sub-standard. A debit note (D57) for a *gross value* of £241.50 was returned with the goods.

Required:

  (a) Write up Modrix's Ltd's Purchases Day Book and Purchases Returns Day Book for the week commencing 23 November 19X7 totalling the columns off as at 28 November 19X7; and

  (b) describe how the information in the Purchases Day Book and Purchases Returns Day Book would be incorporated into Modrix Ltd's ledger.

(AAT Certificate, amended)

9.3   Patel issued the following invoices during March 19X3:

Date	Invoice Number	Customer	Amount £
2 2 X3	1234	Hatt	200
10 3 X3	1235	Coates	1,000
12 3 X3	1236	Gloves	100
20 3 X3	1237	Scarfe	300

All of these invoices are subject to VAT being added at a rate of 15%.

Two of the customers returned faulty goods on 25 March 19X3.

The details were as follows:

$$\left.\begin{array}{ll}\text{Coates} & \text{£200} \\ \text{Scarfe} & \text{£100}\end{array}\right\}\ \text{Net amount of goods returned}$$

Required:

Show how the above transactions would be recorded in Patel's sales day book and sales returns day book for the month of March 19X3.

9.4   C Berry, a retailer, divides his business into three departments: Kitchen Hardware, Electrical and Garden.

During the month of June 19X6, he bought the following goods on credit:

4 June	Grofast Seeds Ltd	1,200 packets of garden seeds costing £5 per 100.
6 June	E Gaze	Various kitchen utensils for £240 list price less 20% trade discount.
16 June	Light & Shade Ltd	70 electric light shades at £5 each.
20 June	E Gaze	50 Frying pans at £4 each. 200 peat flower pots for a total of £25.
26 June	Lighting Wire Co.	100 yards of electric wire at £120 list price less 10% trade discount.
29 June	The Rich Loam Co.	60 bags of garden compost at £6 per bag.

Required:

(a)   Write up the purchases day book of C Berry for the month of June 19X6, using the following columnar ruling:

Date   Name of Supplier   Ledger Folio   Total   Kitchen Hardware   Electrical   Garden

[**Note:** Details of invoices need not be entered]; and

(b)   post the totals of the columns to the appropriate ledger.

(LCCI First level 1988)

9.5   Rebecca Brown is in business selling soft furnishings. Her financial position on 1st February 19X8 was as follows:

Amounts owing to suppliers:
R Wren   £300
P Shaw   £242

Amounts owed by customers:
T Swallow   £1,019
L Soames   £539

Balance in bank   £5,000

Her bank paying-in book and cheque counterfoils show the following:
Details of Paying-in Slips:
5 February: T Swallow £1,019

Details of Cheque counterfoils:

1 February	No. 100001	Rent and rates of shop	£500
1 February	No. 100002	Insurance	£100
15 February	No. 100003	Wages	£125
22 February	No. 100004	P Shaw	£242

She recorded details of her credit purchases and sales in day books which are shown below:

PURCHASES DAY BOOK

			Net Price	VAT	Total
1 February	R Wren	200			
	Trade discount	40	160	16	176
16 February	P Shaw	850			
	Trade discount	170	680	68	748

SALES DAY BOOK

			Net Price	VAT	Total
3 February	T Swallow	400			
	Trade discount	100	300	30	330
18 February	T Swallow	600			
	Trade discount	90	510	51	561
29 February	L Soames	100			
	Trade discount	20	80	8	88

Required:

Prepare the ledger accounts and bank account of Rebecca Brown for the month of February. The accounts should be balanced at the end of the month. (Accounts with only one entry need not be balanced.)

(RSA Elementary)

COMMON ERRORS

1. Memorandum Only

Day books are only memorandum books of account. Double-entry has not been completed if a transaction has merely been entered in a day book. To complete double entry, it is necessary to credit or debit the appropriate account in one of the main ledgers.

2. Omission

The books of account will not balance if an entry has been omitted in one of the day books, but the corresponding entry HAS been made in one of the personal accounts. If an error occurs it may be necessary to check each entry in the day books against each entry in the personal ledgers.

3 . Arithmetic

It is easy to make mistakes in totalling the day books and in carrying a balance to the appropriate account in the General Ledger.

Make sure that your arithmetic is correct.

4 . Original Entry

An entry may be hidden if an entry has been omitted from a day book and from one of the personal accounts. The error may be discovered when the invoices are checked against the entries in the day books, or when a supplier or customer disputes the amount owed to or by him.

10 THE JOURNAL

MAIN POINTS

1. Background

The Journal is a memorandum book of account. It is used as a book of original (or prime) entry in which to record details of certain types of transactions prior to posting to the ledger accounts.

At one time, all entries were first made in the Journal. Hence it was possible to make ALL the ledger account postings directly from the Journal.

Nowadays, the Journal is only used to record those transactions for which a detailed narration is required (such as for bad debts written off, the correction of errors, and the purchase and sale of fixed assets).

2. Format

There is a rather precise and formal method that should be adopted in making journal entries. A simple journal contains a date, narration, folio and debit and credit columns. The format is shown below (Exhibit 10.1).

			Folio Number	Debit	Credit
				£	£
Date	Ledger account details	Dr	X	X	
	To: Ledger account details		X		X
	Being .... (i.e the explanation for the journal entry)				

Exhibit 10.1 Format of a Journal Entry

Once the details of the transaction have been entered in the Journal, the respective ledger accounts must be debited and credited.

69

3. Advantages of using a Journal

(a) There is less risk of omitting transactions from the ledger accounts.
(b) There is less risk of not completing double-entry
(c) More detailed explanations can be given about the respective entries.
(d) There is less risk of fraud and error if additional information is kept of particular transactions.

Example. On 1 July 19X3 A West had the following assets and liabilities:

	£
Freehold premises	80,000
Motor van	5,500
Furniture	12,000
Mortgage on premises	50,000
Stock	17,500
Creditors	27,600
Debtors	11,200
Cash at bank	4,300
Cash in hand	1,890
Rates paid in advance	210
Loan from Land Securities Ltd	25,000

On 2 July 19X3 A West received a cheque for £65 as the first and final dividend on a debt of £220 owed by T Barker, who had been adjudged bankrupt.

Required:

Prepare in the books of A West:
(a) the opening journal entries; and
(b) the journal entry necessary to record the transaction on 2 July 19X3

(LCCI First Level 1988)

Solution

A West, Journal

			Cr £	Dr £
1 7 X3	Freehold premises account	Dr	80,000	
	Motor van account	Dr	5,500	
	Furniture account	Dr	12,000	
	Stock account	Dr	17,500	
	Debtors account	Dr	11,200	
	Cash at bank account	Dr	4,300	
	Cash at bank account	Dr	1,890	
	Rates account	Dr	210	
	To: Mortgage on premises account			50,000
	Creditors account			27,600
	Loan from Land Securities Ltd account			25,000
	Capital account			30,000
			£132,600	£132,600

Being the ledger account balances

as at 1 July 19X3
A West, Journal (cont.)

			Cr £	Dr £
2 7 X3	Bank account	Dr		65
	To: T Barker account		65	

Being first and final dividend on a debt of £220 owed by T Barker

2 7 X3	Bad debt account	Dr		155
	To: T Barker account		155	

Being amount of debt owed by T Barker not likely to be recovered.

EXERCISES

10.1 Brenda Dean, a sole trader in fancy goods, had the following transactions during January 19X6:

(1) She purchased a new cash register for £180. In exchange for this she traded in her old cash register at an agreed figure of £30 and issued a cheque for £150. The book value of the old cash register was £50.

(2) She bought goods amounting to £136 from John Clements. The entries made in both the Purchases Day Book and the ledger gave the figure as £163.

(3) One of her assistants installed some fitments in her office outside normal working hours. The additional amount of £45 paid to him had been debited to Wages Account and credited to Cash Account.

(4) Brenda took from the store goods which had cost £52 to give to her friends as presents.

Required:

Draw up the journal entries in respect of items (1) and (4) and also to correct the errors in (2) and (3).

Note: Bank entries should be journalised.

(LCCI Elementary 1986)

10.2 During the month of August 19X5 D Evans, a sole trader, had the following business transactions:

(1) He purchased special Fixtures and Fittings on credit from Woodwork Ltd costing £2,100 and these were delivered on 3 August. He had arranged for a fitter named G Mason to install these Fixtures and Fittings for him. Mason duly installed the items and left an invoice for £150 to cover the installation cost. No payment was made at this time.

(2) As at 31 July, PG Cox owed Evans £172. Subsequently Cox was declared bankrupt and, on 7 August, Evans received £38 as a first and final dividend in respect of the debt. Evans wrote the remainder off as a Bad Debt on the same day.

(3) During July, Evans had used his own workers to extend a storage shed with materials costing £410 and wages of £160. On 14 August Evans noticed that his book-keeper had posted these amounts to Purchases and Wages, in error. He put through a journal entry for the book-keeper to

correct the situation.

(4)   At the end of July the book-keeper had posted details of Cash Discounts, Allowed and Received, amounting to £215 and £120 respectively from the Cash Book to the Discounts Accounts. Unfortunately, he had entered both amounts in the Discounts Allowed Account posting £215 to the debit side and £120 to the credit side in error. On 21 August this error was discovered.

(5)   On 30 August Evans purchased a new car costing £5,300. He traded in his old car in part exchange at the agreed price of £3,000. The old car appears in his ledger at the written down value of £3,250. He drew a cheque for the amount due to the supplier of his new car.

Required:

Draw up the journal entries necessary to record (1) (2) and (5) and to correct the errors in (3) and (4).

(LCCI Elementary 1987)

10.3 Tinker commenced business on 1 October 19X0. His first trial balance extracted at 30 September 19X1 proved arithmetically correct, although a number of errors and omissions were discovered. These were as follows:

1   A bank reconciliation undertaken at 30 September 19X1 showed that Tinker's drawings of £4,000 for the year had been debited to the Bank Account and credited to his Capital Account, and that bank charges amounting to £50 for the year had not been entered.

2   Credit sales of £250 made to Scott had been completely omitted from the books of account.

3   Purchases of £1,500 obtained on credit from Black had been posted to the credit of Buck's Account.

4   The Wages' Account and the Rent Received Account had both been undercast by £20.

5   Tinker owed Leigh £120 and a contra entry had been made in the respective Purchase and Sales Ledger Accounts; this had been entered as £210 in both accounts.

6   A motor car costing £3,500 had been debited to the Purchases' Account; during the year, the car had been used for delivering goods to customers.

Required:

Correct the above items by means of journal entries.

(AAT Level 2)

10.4 Although the Treasurer of the Lion Sports Club had balanced the books of the Club as at 31 March 19X2, he discovered sometime later a number of errors that were not disclosed in the trial balance. These were as follows:

1   Hill's subscription of £10 had been credited to High's Account.

2   The purchase of some bar equipment costing £250 had been included in bar purchases.

3   The debit entry in the Wages Account had been brought down as £530, instead of £350, and the credit balance on the Subscriptions Account had

been brought down as £10,976, instead of as £10,796.

4   An amount of £50 for rent received was debited to the Rent Account and credited to the Bank Account.

5   A cash donation received of £210 had been entered in the books as £110.

6   A creditor was demanding payment of £75 for bar purchases which he had supplied. No details could be found in the books of this transaction, although the barman accepts that the goods had been received.

Required:

Correct by means of Journal entries the above transactions, being careful to state in your explanation of each journal entry the type of book-keeping error that has occurred.

(AAT/IAS Part 1)

COMMON ERRORS

Examination candidates are often asked to answer questions which require journal entries to be made, since Journal entry questions do not take as much time to complete as do ledger account questions.

However, it is less easy to see the double-entry effect, so students often find such questions difficult to answer.

1. Presentation

Journal entries should be written out formally with a detailed LEGIBLE explanation following each entry.

2. Confusion

Entries made in the Journal do not form part of the double-entry procedure, but the rules of double-entry should still be applied in stating which account should be debited and which account should be credited.

3. Memorandum Only

If the question also requires ledger accounts to be prepared, do not forget to post the details to BOTH the respective ledger accounts.

11 BILLS OF EXCHANGE

MAIN POINTS

1. Definition

A bill of exchange is "an unconditional order in writing, addressed by one person to another, signed by the person giving it, requiring the person to whom it is addressed to pay on demand or at a fixed or determinable future time a sum certain in money to or to the order of a specified person or to bearer" (Bills of Exchange Act, 1882).

2. Purpose and Procedure

A bill of exchange is a convenient method of settling debts. It enables an entity to provide legal evidence of amounts owed to its creditors.

A DRAWER (that is, a creditor) makes out a bill to a DRAWEE (that is, the entity). If the drawee accepts the bill, the bill becomes negotiable. In effect, the creditor can be paid what is owing to him, because he can discount (or sell) the bill to the bank for cash. When the bill MATURES, the bill will be presented by the person holding it to the drawee. The drawee will then be expected to honour the bill, that is, pay the amount stated in the bill.

Note that a bill can also be made out to a PAYEE (that is, someone other than the drawer), instead of being made out to the drawer.

Bills may be either FOREIGN bills (that is, used in connection with exporting), or INLAND bills (that is, for use within a country).

3. Accounting Treatment

  (a) Bills payable
      (i)   When the bill is initiated
            Dr   Creditor's account
            Cr.   Bills payable account
            With the amount of the bill
      (ii)   When the bill is presented to the bank for payment
            Dr.   Bills payable account
            Cr.   Bank
            With the amount of the bill payable on maturity
  (b) Bills receivable
      (i)   When the bill is raised
             Dr.   Bills receivable account
             Cr.   Debtor's account
            With the amount of the bill

(ii) When the bill is discounted or when it matures

    1.   Dr.   Bank
          Cr   Bills receivable account
          With the amount received for the bill when it is discounted or when the bill matures

    2.   Dr.   Discount on bills account
          Cr.   Bank
          With the amount of any discount charged by the bank.

(iii) If the bill is negotiated

      Dr.   Creditor's account
      Cr.   Bills receivable account
      With the amount of the bill

(iv) If the bill is dishonoured

    1.   Dr.   Debtor's account
          Cr.   Bills receivable account
          With the amount of the dishonoured bill

    2.   Dr.   Debtor's account
          Cr.   Bank account
          With the amount of the noting charge

Example. On 31 July 19X5, James Giles, a sole trader, had debtors as follows:

Alfred Ames	£360
Bertram Brown	£287

He also had the following creditors:

Thomas Tilling	£190
Samuel Searl	£400

The following transactions took place:

1 August	Giles drew a Bill of Exchange, at 2 months after date, on Alfred Ames for £360 (Bill No. 1).
	This was accepted by Ames.
10 August	Thomas Tilling drew a Bill of Exchange, at 1 month after date, on Giles for £190 (Bill No. 2).
	This was accepted by Giles.
21 August	Giles discounted Bill No 1. with his Banker - bank interest charges £25.
31 August	Giles drew a Bill of Exchange, at 2 months after date, on Bertram Brown for £287 (Bill no 3)
	This was accepted by Brown.
4 September	Giles endorsed Bill No. 3 and transferred it to Samuel Searl. Giles also sent to Searl a cheque for the balance due to him.

All the bills of Exchange were paid on the due dates EXCEPT No. 1, which was dishonoured - bank charges £5

Required:

(a) Draw up the ledger accounts of the Debtors and Creditors of James Giles and enter therein the balances at 31 July 19X5; and

(b) record the above transactions in the accounts of the Debtors, Creditors, Bills Payable, Bills Receivable and Bank, in the books of James Giles.

(LCCI Elementary 1986)

Solution

JAMES GILES

Alfred Ames account

		£			£
31 7 X5	Balance b/d	360	1 8 X5	Bills receivable	360
1 10 X5	Bank	360			
1 10 X5	Bank (charges)	5	1 10 X5	Balance c/d	365
		£725			£725
2 10 X5	Balance b/d	365			

Bertram Brown account

		£			£
31 7 X5	Balance b/d	287	31 8 X5	Bills receivable	287

Thomas Tilling account

		£			£
10 8 X5	Bills payable	190	31 7 X5	Balance b/d	190

Samuel Searl Account

		£			£
4 9 X5	Bills receivable	287	31 7 X5	Balance b/d	400
4 9 X5	Bank	113			
		£400			£400

Bills receivable account

		£			£
1 8 X5	Alfred Ames (Bill No. 1)	360	21 8 X5	Bank (Bill No. 1)	360
31 8 X5	Bertram Brown (Bill No. 3)	287	4 9 X5	Samuel Searl (Bill No. 3)	287
		£647			£647

Bills payable account

		£			£
1 9 X5	Bank (Bill No.2)	190	10 8 X5	Thomas Tilling (Bill No.2)	190

Bank account

		£			£
21 8 X5	Bills receivable	360	21 8 X5	Discounting charges	25
			4 9 X5	Samuel Searl	113
			10 9 X5	Bills payable (Bill No.2)	190
			1 10 X5	Alfred Ames (Bill No.1)	360
1 10 X5	Balance c/d	333	1 10 X5	Alfred Ames (Bank charges)	5
		£693			£693
			2 10 X5	Balance b/d	333

EXERCISES

11.1 On 1 November 19X6, the following balances were included in the ledger of John Kenley, a sole trader:

			£
Debtors	-	L Stamper	360
	-	F Brandon	283
Creditors	-	K Timmins	164
	-	S Quick	357

The following transactions took place:

2 November	-	Timmins drew a Bill of Exchange (Bill No.1)for £164 on Kenley, due two months after date. This was accepted by Kenley.
5 November	-	Kenley drew a Bill of Exchange (Bill No.2) for £283 on Brandon, due two months after date. Brandon duly accepted the bill.
9 November	-	Kenley discounted Bill No.2 for £271.
16 November	-	Kenley accepted a Bill of Exchange (Bill No.3) drawn by Quick and payable one month after date. The amount of the bill, £340, was in full settlement of the debt.
23 November	-	Kenley drew a Bill of Exchange (Bill No.4) for £360 on Stamper, due three months after date. This was accepted by Stamper.

All the Bills of Exchange were paid on the due dates apart from Bill No. 4 which was dishonoured. Kenley paid the costs of dishonoured amounting to £10 and charged them to Stamper.

Required:

Prepare, on behalf of John Kenley, to the end of February 19X7:

(a) The ledger accounts of Stamper, Brandon, Timmins and Quick, to incorporate the above transactions;

(b) the Bank Account, to include the relevant entries; and

(c) the Bills Receivable Account and Bills payable account

Note: Your entries should indicate the Bill numbers, as appropriate.

(LCCI Elementary 1987)

11.2 On 1 February 19X5, A purchased goods from B for £1.600 and, on 10 February, 19X8, A accepted a Bill of Exchange from B at 3 months for that amount. On 20 February 19X5, A returned to B goods which had been damaged, invoice value £60. On 10 March 19X5, B discounted his Bill of Exchange at Town Bank, Fenton, the discount charges being £5. On maturity, this bill was dishonoured, noting charges being £5. On 12 May 19X5, B drew another Bill of Exchange on A at one month for the balance of A's account, including noting charges plus £12 for the extension of credit. The bill was accepted by A on 16 May 19X5 and paid on maturity.

Required:

Prepare the following accounts, paying particular attention to dates and narrations (i.e. the name of the other account).

(a) In A's ledger:

(i) Bills payable
(ii) B's account

(b) In B's ledger

(i) Bills Receivable
(ii) A's Account

(LCCI Intermediate 1986)

11.3 Ramsden Brothers import and export agricultural equipment. They also sell the equipment in the United Kingdom. On 31 December 19X6, their Balance sheet included the following items:

	£
Debtors (for UK sales)	83,264
Bills received (for export sales)	131,800
Bills payable	146,300
Bank (in Ramsden Brothers favour)	11,285

Bill details are as follows:

Supplier	£	Due Date
AM of Frankfurt	60,000	8 April 19X7
Lesch (Zurich)	58,600	6 February 19X7
Lesch (Zurich)	27,700	29 January 19X7
	146,300	

Customers	£	Due Date
A	30,000	26 January 19X7
B	49,200	28 February 19X7
C	38,800	8 March 19X7
D	13,800	31 January 19X7
	131,800	

Some of the transactions of Ramsden Brothers during January 19x7 are:

(1) Purchased equipment fro AM of Frankfurt and accepted bill for £38,000.
(2) Sales on credit to UK customers - £46,212.
(3) Cash received from UK customers - £61,310.
(4) Export sales, bills accepted by customers:

A	£11,300
E	£12,600
F	£18,100

(5) Bills receivable and bills payable falling due in January were honoured on the due date.
(6) Another bill for £24,000, accepted by customer C, had a due date of 15 January 19X7. However, this bill had been discounted on 12 November 19X6, the net proceeds having been £23,550. This bill was not honoured on the due date. Customer C then accepted a new bill for £24,690 with a due date of 15 March 19X7.
(7) Business expenses paid in cash - £31,260.

Required:

In the ledger of Ramsden Brothers, prepare accounts for the month of January 19X7 for:

(a) Debtors;
(b) Bills receivable;
(c) Bills payable;
(d) Bank.

(LCCI Intermediate 1987)

COMMON ERRORS

1. Terminology

Some students confuse the terms bills PAYABLE and bills RECEIVABLE. Bills payable should be CREDITED to the bills payable account; the corresponding entry is DEBITED to a creditor's account.

Bills receivable should be DEBITED to the bills receivable account; the corresponding entry is CREDITED to a debtor's account.

2. Discounting Charge

If a bill is discounted, the charge should be DEBITED to the discounting charges account, and CREDITED to the bank account. The bill receivable account is not affected.

3. Noting Charges

If a bill is dishonoured, the debtor's account should be DEBITED with the amount of the charge, and the bank account credited. Thus the debtor is charged with the cost of dishonouring the bill. This is only fair, as he is presumably responsible for the bill not being met.

The bills receivable account is not affected by the amount of the noting charge; the dishonoured bill is merely written back by debiting the debtor's account, and crediting the bills receivable account.

12

CONTROL AND TOTAL ACCOUNTS

MAIN POINTS

1. Definitions

(a) Control account: a balancing account included in a specific ledger in order to make that ledger self-balancing.

(b) Total account: a summary account of the details contained within a specific ledger.

Both control and total accounts are MEMORANDUM accounts: they do not form part of the overall double-entry system.

2. Purposes

Both control and total accounts have similar purposes:

(a) control: they provide a double-check on the entries made within a specific ledger;

(b) summary: they provide a useful summary of the respective debit and credit entries made within that ledger; and

(c) location of errors: they help to isolate errors that may have been made in the overall book-keeping system.

The most common types of control or total accounts are to be found in the purchases ledger and the sales ledger.

3. Purchases Ledger Control Account Entries

(a)	**Debit entry**	**Source**
	Purchases	Purchases day book
(b)	**Credit entries**	**Source**
	Purchases returns	Purchases returns day book
	Cash paid	Cash book
	Discounts received	Cash book

4. Sales Ledger Control Account Entries

(a)	**Debit entries**	**Source**
	Sales returns	Sales returns day book
	Cash received	Cash book
	Discounts allowed	Cash book
	Bad debts	Journal

(b) **Credit entries**   **Source**
Sales   Sales day book

5. Purchases Ledger Total Account Entries

(a) **Debit entries**   **Source**
Purchases returns   Purchases returns day book
Cash paid   Cash book
Discounts received   Cash book

(b) **Credit entry**   **Source**
Purchases   Purchases day book

6. Sales Ledger Total Account Entries

(a) **Debit entry**   **Source**
Sales   Sales day book

(b) **Credit entries**   **Source**
Sales returns   Sales returns day book
Cash received   Cash book
Discounts allowed   Cash book
Bad debts   Journal

7. Total Amounts Only

It is only necessary to enter the TOTAL amount for a particular period in a control or a total account. If the purchases and sales day books are written up on a daily basis, for example, only the day's purchases or the day's sales will be entered in the control or total account.

8. Control Accounts: Opposite Entries

Control account enable the ledger to become self-balancing. The entries made in each personal account will follow the normal double-entry book-keeping rule, that is, the receiving account is debited and the giving account is credited. However, in order to complete double-entry WITHIN the ledger, the daily totals in a CONTROL account are entered on the OPPOSITE side of those entries to be found in the individual personal accounts.

This is not the case with TOTAL accounts. With total accounts, the daily totals are entered in accordance with the customary debit and credit rules.

Example 1. The financial year of Handile plc ended on 31 March 19X6. A trial balance extracted as at that date reveals a difference of £100 in the books. It is decided to draw up a Sales Ledger Control Account and a Purchases Ledger Control Account to help locate any errors. The trial balance figures for debtors and creditors were £16,940 and £23,188 respectively. These represent the totals of the balances on the individual debtors and creditors accounts in the Sales and Purchases ledgers.

The following information is obtained from the books of original entry:

Cash Book	£
Discounts allowed	3,112
Cash and cheques from customers	125,050
Discounts received	2,097
Cash and cheques paid to suppliers	139,830
Refunds given to customers	231
Customers' cheques dishonoured	55

Journal

Balances in the Purchases Ledger set off against balances
in the Sales Ledger ... 460
Bad debts written off ... 661
Decrease in the Provision for Bad Debts ... 51
Sales Book ... 130,411
Purchases Book ... 155,603
Returns In Book ... 3,150
Returns Out Book ... 3,227

According to the audited accounts for the previous year debtors and creditors as at 1 April 19X5 were £18,776 and £13,199 respectively.

Required:

(a) Draw up the relevant Control Accounts.
(b) Suggest where an error might have been made.

(AAT Preliminary)

Solution

(a)

HANDILE PLC
Sales ledger control account

	£		£
Returns in	3,150	Balances b/d	18,776
Cash received	125,050	Sales	130,411
Discounts allowed	3,112	Cheque dishonoured	55
Bad debts	661	Refunds to customers	231
Set offs from creditors ledger	460		
Balances c/f	17,040		
	£149,473		£149,473
		Balance b/d	17,040

Purchases ledger control accounts

	£		£
Balances b/d	13,199	Returns outwards	3,227
Purchases	155,603	Cash payments	139,830
		Discounts received	2,097
		Set offs to Debtors Ledger	460
		Balance c/f	23,188
	£168,802		£168,802
Balances b/d	23,188		

RECONCILIATION
Trade Debtors

	£
- as per individual accounts	16,940
- as per Control Account	17,040
Difference	£100

		£
Trade Creditors:		
-	as per individual accounts	23,188
-	as per control account	23,188

(b) The error revealed by the Trial Balance suggests that it might be connected with Trade Debtors.

Example 2. The financial year of the OK Trading Company ended on 30 November 19X7. You have been asked to prepare a Total Debtors Account and a Total Creditors Account in order to produce end-of-year figures for Debtors and Creditors for the draft final accounts.

You are able to obtain the following information for the financial year from the books of original entry:

	£
Sales (all on credit)	268,187
Purchases (all on credit)	496,600
Receipts from customers	255,680
Payment to suppliers	489,530
Discounts allowed	5,520
Discounts received	3,510
Balance in the sales ledger set off against balance in the purchases ledger	70
Bad debts written off	780
Increase in the provision for bad debts	90
Credit notes issued to credit customers	4,140
Credit notes received from credit suppliers	1,480

According to the audited financial statement for the previous year debtors and creditors as at 1 November 19X6 were £26,555 and £43,450 respectively.

Required:

Draw up the relevant Total Accounts entering end-of-year totals for debtors and creditors.

(AAT Certificate)

Solution

OK TRADING COMPANY
Total debtors account

		£			£
1 11 X6	Balance b/d	26,555	31 10 X7	Returns in	4,140
31 10 X7	Sales	268,187	31 10 X7	Cash received	255,680
			31 10 X7	Discounts allowed	5,520
			31 10 X7	Bad debts	780
			31 10 X7	Set offs to creditors ledger	70
			31 10 X7	Balances c/d	28,552
		£294,742			£294,742
1 11 X7	Balances b/d	28,552			

83

Total creditors Account

		£			£
31 10 X7	Returns outwards	1,480	1 11 X6	Balances b/f	43,450
31 10 X7	Cash payments	489,530	31 10 X6	Purchases	496,600
31 10 X7	Discounts received	3,510			
31 10 X7	Set offs from debtors ledger	70			
31 10 X7	Balance b/d	45,460			
		£540,050			£540,050
			1 11 X7	Balance b/d	45,460

EXERCISES

12.1 On 1st October 19X7 the Purchase Ledger of J Almeida contained the following creditors:

	£
C Blade	175
J Duff	130
L Stone	75

Returns Outwards Book		£	**Purchases Day Book**		£
October 3	J Duff	40	October 14	L Stone	90
October 9	C Blade	25	October 22	J Duff	155
			October 26	L Stone	60
			October 30	C Blade	140

Cheques paid to creditors

		Discount £	Bank £
October 5	J Duff	9	81
October 15	C Blade	5	145
October 24	L Stone		75

Required:

(a) Write up J Almeida's Purchases Ledger for October and balance the accounts at the end of the month; and

(b) draft the Purchases Ledger Control Account for October 19X7 using the following totals:

Opening balance	380
Purchases during month	445
Returns during month	65
Payments received	301
Cash discount allowed	14

(RSA Elementary)

12.2 The A2Z Company presents you with the following balances for December 19X7:

			£
1 December 19X7	Sales ledger	Dr	202,100
		Cr	2,800
	Purchase ledger	Dr	330
		Cr	115,900

31 December 19X7
Transactions

	£
Credit sales	534,000
Cash sales	213,600
Credit purchases	282,700
Payments to creditors	238,600
Payments received from debtors	449,500
Bad debts written off	1,900
Provision for bad debts	9,700
Purchase returns	4,500
Sales returns	5,800
Discounts received	5,900
Discounts allowed	9,500
Balances in Debtors Ledger set off against balances in Creditors Ledger	3,400
Customer's cheque dishonoured	500

31 December 19X7	Sales ledger	Dr	?
		Cr	2,100
	Purchase ledger	Dr	420
		Cr	?

Note: Not all this data is needed

Required:

Draw up the Creditors and Debtors Control Accounts for December 1987, showing all the closing balances.

(RSA Intermediate, adapted)

12.3 J Mason keeps Control Accounts for the Purchases and Sales Ledgers. The following details were extracted from the books for the month of August 19X5:

		£
Balances - 1 August 19X5		
Purchases Ledger - Debit		212
Credit		5,185
Sales Ledger - Debit		9,364
Credit		510
Goods purchased on credit		19,283
Discounts allowed		356
Bad debts written off		237
Goods returned to suppliers		615
Discounts received		241

	£
Cash received from credit customers	24,607
Legal expenses charged to customers	112
Provision for Bad and Doubtful debts	300
Credit sales	27,440
Cash paid to suppliers	16,824
Sales ledger credit transferred to Purchases Ledger per contra	260
Cash sales	11,500
Returns by customers	292
Sales ledger credit balances at 31 august 19X5	376
Purchases ledger debit balances at 31 August 19X5	143

Required:

(a) Prepare Control Accounts for the month ended 31 August 19X5 for the Purchases Ledger and for the Sales Ledger, bringing down the balances at 1 September 19X5.

(b) Show the amounts which would appear in J Mason's Balance Sheet as at 31 August 19X5 for debtors and creditors.

(LCCI Internediate 1987)

12.4 The following information for the year ended 31 March 19X4 has been extracted from the accounting records of Loner Limited.

Sales ledger control account as at 1 April 19X3	£
Debit balance	25,684
Credit balance	748
Credit sales	194,710
Goods returned by trade debtors	1,420
Payments received from trade debtors	*188,176
Discounts allowed to trade debtors	6,710

*This figure includes cheque totalling £304 which were dishonoured before 31 March 19X4, the debts in respect of which remained outstanding at 31 March 19X4. The only sales ledger account with a credit balance at 31 March 19X4 was that of T Stones with a balance of £532.

After the preparation of the sales ledger control account for the year ended 31 March 19X4, from the information given above, the following accounting errors were discovered:

1. The sales day book for November 19X3 had been undercast by £1,400.

2. In July 19X3, a debt due of £160 from Peter Smith had been written off as bad. Whilst the correct entries have been made in Peter Smith's personal account, no reference to the debt being written off has been made in the sales ledger control account.

3. Cash sales of £5,000 in September 19X3 have been included in the "Payments received from trade debtors £188,176".

4. No entries have been made in the personal accounts for goods returned from trade debtors of £1,420.

5. The debit side of L Brown's personal account has been overcast by £140.

6   "Credit sales £194,710" includes goods costing £5,000 returned to suppliers by Loner Limited.

7   No entry has been made in the company's books of account for the set off of a debt due from G Kelly of £300 against an amount due to him of £1,200 in the purchases ledger.

Required:

(a) Prepare the sales ledger control account for the year ended 31 March 19X4 as it would have been before the various accounting errors outlined above were discovered; and

(b) prepare a computation of the amount arising from the sales ledger to be shown as trade debtors in the balance sheet as at 31 March 19X4 of Loner Limited.

(AAT Intermediate)

12.5   April Showers sells goods on credit to most of its customers. In order to control its debtor collection system, the company maintains a sales ledger control account. In preparing the accounts for the year to 31 October 19X3, the accountant discovers that the total of all the personal accounts in the sales ledger amounts to £12,802, whereas the sales ledger control account balance discloses a balance of £12,550.

Upon investigating the matter, the following errors were discovered:

1   Sales for the week ending 27 March 19X3 amounting to £850 had been omitted from the control account.

2   A debtor's account balance of £300 had not been included in the list of balances.

3   Cash received of £750 had been entered in a personal account as £570.

4   Discounts allowed totalling £100 had not been entered in the control account.

5   A personal account balance had been undercast by £200.

6   A contra item of £400 with the purchase ledger had not been entered in the control account.

7   A bad debt of £500 had not been entered in the control account.

8   Cash received of £250 had been debited to a personal account.

9   Discounts received of £50 had been debited to Bell's Sales Ledger Account.

10   Returns inwards valued at £200 had not been included in the control account.

11   Cash received of £80 had been credited to a personal account as £8.

12   A cheque for £300 received from a customer had been dishonoured by the bank, but no adjustment had been made in the control account.

Required:

(a) Prepare a corrected sales ledger control account, bringing down the amended balance as at 1 November 19X3; and

(b) prepare a statement showing the adjustments that are necessary to the list of personal account balances so that it reconciles with the amended sales ledger control account balance.

(AAT Level 2)

12.6 The following information relates to Roxy Limited for the year to 31 May 19X3;

Extract from the Purchases Ledger Control Account at 31 May 19X3:

	£
Trade Creditors as at 1 June 19X2	20,000
Credit purchases	240,000
Payments made to Trade Creditors	232,000
Discounts received	6,000

The accountant has extracted a list of credit balances which total £23,800. There were no debit balances.

In checking these credit balances the following errors were discovered:

1. Goods costing £1,500 had been omitted from Collin's Account.
2. Discounts Received for January 19X3 amounting to £500 had not been entered in any of the personal accounts.
3. The credit side of Brown's Account had been undercast by £1,000.
4. A cash payment of £200 to Almond had been credited to his account.
5. A bank payment to Martin of £750 had been omitted from his account.
6. Ashton's balance of £2,000 had not been included in the list of balances.
7. The entry for a motor car purchased from Gill, and costing £5,000 should not have appeared in the Purchases Ledger.
8. Discounts Allowed totalling £350 had been debited to Crosby's Account.

Required:

(a) Prepare the Purchase Ledger Control Account for the year to 31 May 19X3; and

(b) prepare a statement showing the necessary corrections to the list of Purchase Ledger balances as originally extracted at 31 May 19X3.

(AAT Level 2)

COMMON ERRORS

1. Confusion over Terms

There is great confusion in the accounting literature over the meaning of CONTROL and TOTAL accounts. They are often regarded as being inter-changeable terms.

If a question refers to one or other of these terms, you are recommended to adopt the definitions used in this chapter, but it might be advisable to make a brief note to your solution explaining the reasons for your choice.

2. Memorandum Account Only

Control and total accounts do NOT form part of the overall double-entry system. In compiling a trial balance, therefore, it is not necessary to include both a total account balance AND the total of all the individual personal account balances.

3. Balancing

It is often the case that the balance shown in the control or total account does not agree with the total of all the individual personal account balances.

If such an error arises, make sure that:

(a) you have not missed anything out of the control or total account;

(b) check the total of all the daily balances extracted;

(c) check that you have entered the correct daily balance in the control or total account;

(d) check that you have entered the balances on the appropriate side of the control or total account; and

(e) check your arithmetic.

If the control or total account still does not agree, then you may have to check all of the entries in the personal accounts.

13 STOCK

MAIN POINTS

1. Definition

Stocks include the following items:

  (a) goods or other assets purchased for resale;
  (b) consumable stores;
  (c) raw materials and components purchased for incorporation into products for sale;
  (d) products and services in intermediate stages of completion;
  (e) long-term contract balances; nd
  (f) finished goods.

2. The Accounting Problem

Not all the goods bought during a particular accounting period will be sold during that same period. Thus some of the goods not sold in that period will be available for sale in the next accounting period.

In order to match the cost of goods sold against the sales made during a particular accounting period, therefore, it is necessary to allow for OPENING and CLOSING STOCKS.

The basic equation is as follows:

$$\text{Cost of goods sold} = (\text{opening stocks} + \text{purchases}) - \text{closing stocks}$$

3. Accounting Treatment

  (a) Closing stock

      Dr.   Stock account
      Cr.   Trading account
      With the value of the closing stock at the end of the accounting period

  (b) Opening stock

      Dr.   Trading account
      Cr.   Stock account
      With the value of the stock at the end of the previous accounting period.

  (c) Balance sheet

      The balance on the stock account will be shown in the balance sheet as the first item in the CURRENT ASSETS section.

4. Trading Account Presentation

(a) Horizontal format

	£		£
Opening stock	X	Sales	X
Purchases	X		
	$\overline{X}$		
Less: Closing stock	X		
Gross profit c/d	X		
	£X		£X

(b) Vertical format

	£	£
Sales		X
Less: Cost of goods sold		
Opening stock	X	
Purchases	X	-
	X	
Less: closing stock	X	X
Gross profit		£X

5. Valuation of Stock

Stock should be stated in periodic financial statements at the total of the lower of cost and net realisable value of the separate items of stock or of groups of similar items.

COST means the expenditure incurred in the normal course of business in bringing the product or service to its present location and condition.

This expenditure should include the COST OF PURCHASE. This is the purchase price, import duties, transport, handling and other directly attributable costs, less trade discounts, rebates and subsidies, and such costs of conversion as are appropriate to that location and condition (for example, direct labour, direct expenses and sub-contracted work, production overheads and other overheads that have been incurred in bringing the product or service to its present location or condition).

NET REALISABLE VALUE means the actual or estimated selling price (net of trade but before settlement discounts) LESS all further costs to completion and all costs to be incurred in marketing, selling and distributing.

6. Stock Valuation Methods

Before stock can be built into the books of account it has to be both QUANTIFIED and VALUED. It is not usually too difficult to quantify stock, but stock is often difficult to value if it has been purchased in different quantities at different prices. The main methods of valuing stock are as follows:

(a) Specific identification: the price paid for the various units of stock is identified with the various groups of purchases (no stock valuation problem arises if it is possible to adopt this method).

(b) First-in, first out (FIFO): goods sold are charged out at the price paid for each group of purchases in date order of purchase, so the CLOSING stock tends to be valued at current prices.

(c) Last-in, first-out (LIFO): goods sold are charged out at the latest price paid for each group of purchases, so the CLOSING stock tends to be valued at more historic prices.

(d) Periodic simple average: the prices paid for each group of purchases during a particular accounting period are totalled and divided by the NUMBER of prices in the total; the sum obtained is then multiplied by the quantity of goods in stock at the end of the period.

(e) Continuous simple average: similar to the previous method, except that the price is changed each time some purchases are made at a new unit price; the latest price is then applied to the quantity of goods in stock at the end of the period.

(f) Periodic weighted average: the value of each group of purchases made during a particular period is totalled and divided by the total QUANTITY purchased during the same period; the amount obtained is then multiplied by the quantity of the closing stock.

(g) Continuous weighted average method: this method is similar to the periodic weighted average method, except a running total is kept for the whole financial year; thus the average price will change each time more goods are taken into stock.

(h) Standard price: the entity may determine the price that it expects to pay for purchases during a particular accounting period, and this price will be used to value its closing stock.

7. Goods On Sale Or Return

Goods on sale or return should be included in stocks. They should NOT be recorded as sales until the ownership of the goods has been transferred from the entity to the customer.

Example 1. Ham commenced business on 1 January 19X3. The following details relate to the first two years that he was in business:

	19X3	19X4
	£	£
Purchases	60,000	75,000
Sales	78,000	96,000
Value of stock on hand at 31 December	5,000	8,000

Required:

(a) Prepare the purchases, sales and stock accounts to record the above transactions for each of the two years to 31 December 19X3 and 31 December 19X4, being careful to bring down the balances as at the end of each year; and

(b) show how the above transactions would be shown in Ham's trading account for each of the two years to 31 December 19X3 and 31 December 19X4.

Solution:

HAM
Purchases Account

		£			£
31 12 X3	Bank/trade creditors	60,000	31 12 X3	Trading account	60,000
31 12 X4	Bank/trade creditors	75,000	31 12 X4	Trading account	75,000

Sales account

		£			£
31 12 X3	Trading account	78,000	31 12 X3	Bank/trade debtors	78,000
31 12 X4	Trading account	96,000	31 12 X4	Bank/trade debtors	96,000

Stock account

		£			£
31 12 X3	Trading account	5,000	31 12 X3	Balances c/d	5,000
1 1 X4	Balance b/d	5,000	31 12 X4	Trading account	5,000
31 12 X4	Trading account	8,000	31 12 X4	Balance c/d	8,000
		£13,000			£13,000
1 1 X5	Balance b/d	8,000			

(b)

Ham
Trading Account for the year to:
31 December 19X3

Format 1

	£		£
Purchases	60,000	Sales	78,000
Gross profit (to profit and Loss account)	23,000	Stock at 31 December 19X3	5,000
	£83,000		£83,000

31 December 19X4

	£		£
Stock at 1 December 19X3	5,000	Sales	96,000
Purchases	75,000	Stock at 31 December 19X4	8,000
Gross profit (to profit and loss account)	24,000		
	£104,000		£104,000

Format 2

31 December 19X3

	£		£
Purchases	60,000	Sales	78,000
Less: Stock at 31 December 19X3	5,000		
	55,000		
Gross profit (to profit and loss account)	23,000		
	£78,000		£78,000

31 December 19X4

	£		£
Stock at 1 January 19X4	5,000	Sales	96,000
Purchases	75,000		
	80,000		
Less: Stock at 31 December 19X4	8,000		
	72,000		
Gross profit (to profit and loss account)	24,000		
	£96,000		£96,000

Format 3

31 December 19X3

		£	£
Sales			78,000
Less:	Cost of goods sold - Purchases	60,000	
Less:	stock at 31 December 19X3	5,000	55,000
Gross profit (to profit and loss account)			£23,000

31 December 19X4

		£	£
Sales			96,000
Less:	Cost of goods sold - Stock at 1 January 19X4	5,000	
	Purchases	75,000	
		80,000	
Less: stock at 31 December 19X4		8,000	72,000
Gross profit (to profit and loss account)			£24,000

Note: For examination purposes, Format 3 is preferred.

Example 2. Megalot Ltd made the following purchases and sales of Stock item C4321 during May 19X6:

May 10	Purchased 3,000 units at £6.00 each;
May 15	Sold 2,500 units at £9.00 each;
May 16	Purchased 1,000 units at £6.60 each;
May 23	Sold 900 units at £9.70 each.

Assume there were no units of Stock Item C4321 in stock as at 1 May 19X6.

Required:

(a) Compute the values for sales and purchases of Stock Item C4321 for May;
(b) how many units should there be in stock at 31 May 19X6?;
(c) compute the value of closing stock on each of the following bases:
  (i) FIFO, and
  (ii) LIFO;
(d) calculate the Gross Profit earned on this item during May if closing stock were to be valued under each of the two bases in (c) above; and
(e) suppose that a physical check of the numbers of items of C4321 in stock as at the end of May 19X6 revealed a number of different to what you had calculated in (b) above. What factors might account for the difference?

(AAT Preliminary)

Solution

£

(a) Sales:
May 15 - 2,500 units at £9.00 = 22,500
May 23 - 900 units at £9.70 = 8,730

£31,230

Purchases:
May 10 - 3,000 units at £6.00 = 18,000
May 16 - 1,000 units at £6.60 = 6,600

£24,600

(b) Number of units purchased = 3,000 + 1,000 = 4,000
Number of units sold = 2,500 + 900 3,400

Units left in stock 600

(c) First In-First Out:
The 600 units left in stock will be part of those purchased on 16 May.
Value of closing stock is therefore:
600 units at £6.60 = £3,960

Last In-First Out:
The 600 units left in stock will be part of those purchased on 10 May and part of those units purchased on 16 May.

Value of closing stock is therefore:

£

500 (3,000 - 2,500) units at £6.00 = 3,000
100 (1,000 - 900) units at £6.60 = 660

£3,660

95

(d)

Megalot Ltd

Stock item C4321 - Calculation of Gross Profit for May 19X6

		FIFO		LIFO	
		£	£	£	£
Sales			31,230		31,230
Less:	Cost of Goods sold:				
	Purchases	24,600		24,600	
	Less: Stock at 31				
	May	3,960	20,640	3,660	20,940
Gross profit			£10,590		£10,290

(e) The difference might be attributed to:

  (1) pilferage or theft:
  (2) deterioration or wastage of stock units:
  (3) errors in recording receipts and issues of stock, and in counting the numbers in stock at the end of May.

EXERCISES

13.1 Jock had 100 litres of foam liquid in stock as at 1 October 19X2, purchased at £2 per litre. During the month to 31 October 19X2, the following changes occurred in the stock position:

PURCHASES

Date	Quantity	Cost per litre
	Litres	£
7 10 X2	200	2.50
14 10 X2	300	3.00
21 10 X2	50	4.00
28 10 X2	100	3.50

ISSUES

Date	Quantity
	Litres
4 10 X2	80
11 10 X2	70
18 10 X2	250
25 10 X2	200

Required:

Calculate the value of the closing stock of foam liquid as at 31 October 19X2 using each of the following three methods of pricing the issue of materials to production:

  (i)   first-in, first-out (FIFO):
  (ii)   last-in, first-out (LIFO); and
  (iii) continuous weighted average.

(AAT Level 2, adapted)

13.2 On 14 April 19X5, the warehouse of Joseph Shipley caught fire and the whole of his stock in trade was destroyed apart from goods with a cost price value of £285.

Fortunately Shipley's books and records were kept in a fire proof safe and the following information is available:

(1) Stock in trade at 31 December 19X4 was £1,344 at cost price.
(2) Purchases from 1 January 19X5 to the date of the fire amounted to £1,960. Of these, goods to the cost price of £70 were still in transit at the time of the fire.
(3) Sales from 1 January 19X5 to the date of the fire amounted to £2,775 and all these goods had been despatched BEFORE the fire took place.
(4) Shipley's Gross Profit is 20% of Sales.

Required:

Calculate the value - at cost price - of the goods destroyed in the fire.
NOTE: Calculations must be shown.

(LCCI Elementary 1985)

13.3 The following information relates to the acquisition and issue of Material 2XA by Roe Limited, a small manufacturing company, for the three months to 31 March 19X3:

MATERIAL 2XA

Date	Acquisitions Quantity kg	Price per kg £	Issues Quantity
1 1 X3	100	3.00	
15 1 X3	200	4.00	
29 1 X3			150
17 2 X3	400	4.50	
5 3 X3			450
16 3 X3	100	5.00	
31 3 X3			50

Note: There was no material in stock at 1 January 19X3.

Required:

(a) Calculate the closing stock value of MATERIAL 2XA using each of the following methods of pricing the issue of stock to production:
(i) First-in, first-out (FIFO);
(ii) Last-in, first-out (LIFO);
(iii) Periodic Simple Average;
(iv) Periodic Weighted Average;
(v) Continuous Weighted Average; and
(b) examine the effect on gross profit of using the first-in, first-out (FIFO) and last-in, first out (LIFO) methods of pricing the issue of stock to production assuming that price levels are rising.

(AAT Level 2, adapted)

13.4 Big and Small keep a detailed stock record of all material purchases and of all issues of materials to production. The following information relates to the purchase and issue to production of Material MF for the month of October 19X4:

Date	Quantity Kg	RECEIPTS Price £	Value £	Quantity Kg	ISSUES Price £	Value £	BALANCE Quantity Kg	Value £
1 10 X4							200	200
1 10 X4				100				
5 10 X4	700	3.00	2,100					
8 10 X4				300				
12 10 X4	400	5.00	2,000					
15 10 X4				300				
19 10 X4	800	2.00	1,600					
22 10 X4				600				
26 10 X4	1,100	4.00	4,400					
29 10 X4				1,500				

Required:

(a) Calculate the total charge to production of material MF during October 19X4 using the first-in, first out (FIPO) method of pricing the issue of goods to production;

(b) calculate the closing stock value of material MF as at 31 October 19X4 using the last-in, first-out (LIFO) method of pricing the issue of goods to production;

(c) calculate the issue price per kilogram of material MF on 29 October 19X4 using the continuous weighted average method of pricing the issue of goods to production;

(d) calculate the issue price per kilogram of material MF during the month of October 19X4 using the periodic weighted average method of pricing the issue of goods to production.

(AAT Level 2)

13.5 Hook, a wholesaler, started operations on 1 April 19X7. During his first year in business, the following transactions occurred in respect of Product A.

Date		Units	Cost per unit £	Selling Price per unit £
19X7				
April	purchased	100	60	
May	purchased	100	68	
July	sold	80		75
September	purchased	200	80	
December	sold	300		90
19X8				
February	purchased	100	88	

Hook uses a perpetual inventory system for stock recording, i.e. transfers are made from the stock account to the cost of goods sold account at the time of each sale. Cost of goods sold is measured on a weighted average cost basis.

On 31 March 19X8 a physical count showed there were 115 units of Product A in stock, no further sales having been made.

Required:

(a) Prepare for Hook the Stock Account of Product A for the year ended 31 March 19X8 in a form suited to your calculations;

(b) calculate the gross profit made by Hook on Sales of Product A for the year ended 31 March 19X8;

(c) calculate the gross profit made by Hook on Sales of Product A for the year ended 31 March 19X8 using a *periodic* inventory system for stock recording instead of the *perpetual* inventory system; and

(d) show how the difference between the gross profit calculated in parts (b) and (c) of your answer has arisen.

(LCCI 3rd Level 1988)

13.6 Following a physical count at the end of 19X6, the stock of Berry plc was valued at £243,700. An investigation of the stock sheets revealed the following matters:

(1) On one stock sheet a sub-total of £8,300 had been carried forward as £3,800 and on another 400 units costing £2.50 each had been valued at £25 each.

(2) Goods with a sales value of £18,000 (being cost plus 20%), sent to customers on a sale or return basis, have not yet been returned by them and have been excluded from the physical count. However, the customers have not indicated their acceptance of the goods.

(3) Cress plc has sent Berry plc some free (non-returnable) examples of its goods. These have been included in stock at £350.

(4) It has been discovered that goods included in stock at their cost of £6,500 have been damaged since delivery. It will cost £950 to repair them after which they have a resale value of £7,150.

(5) Included in the stock were goods purchased from Prune Ltd on credit, for £5,200. Berry plc had not yet paid for these by the end of 19X6.

(6) In the last quarter of 19X6, Berry plc purchased 36 units of Product X for £20 each. A trade discount of £80 was received and, as a further discount, 4 additional units were supplied free of charge. 15 units remained in stock at the end of 19X6 and these have been valued at £20 each.

(7) 600 units of Product Y have been included at their original cost of £12 each. These could currently be purchased for only £7 each as the manufacturer is selling them off as a discontinued line. Berry plc expects to be able to continue to resell these units for £18 each, after incurring further manufacturing and selling costs of £4 each.

(8) 150 units of Product Z in stock have been valued as follows:

	£
Labour and material costs	4,000
Manufacturing Overhead (all fixed)	6,000
Selling and Administration (all fixed)	2,000
	£12,000

£

Actual annual production 600 units

$$\text{Stock value} = 150 \times \frac{£12,000}{600}$$

3,000

Annual production is in fact normally 1,000 units.

Required:

(a) Calculate (showing all your workings) the closing stock figure for inclusion in Berry plc's accounting statements at the end of 19X6; and

(b) for each item (2) to (8) listed in the question, briefly state the reason(s) for your treatment of it in (a) above.

(LCCI Higher 1986)

COMMON ERRORS

1. Book-Keeping Errors

Make sure that the opening stock has been DEBITED, and the closing stock CREDITED to the TRADING account, especially when using the vertical format for the trading account, because the debit and credit entries are not so obvious.

2. The Balance Sheet

Make sure that in the balance sheet you include the CLOSING stock as the first item under the heading CURRENT ASSETS.

3. Stock Valuation Methods

You must know how to calculate the value of closing stock by using all of the main valuation methods. The arithmetic can be very cumbersome, especially when using the FIFO and LIFO methods, so take your time, and think clearly when making your calculations.

You might find it helpful to work through the calculations by drawing up a STOCK LEDGER ACCOUNT which has quantity and value columns for receipts and issues of stock, and for the closing stock.

4. The Weighted Average Method

The terminology used by different examiners is not always identical, especially when dealing with the average methods. If an examiner simply requires the WEIGHTED average method, you are recommended to adopt the CONTINUOUS weighted average method, but add a brief note to your solution stating that there is another weighted average method.

14 ACCRUALS AND PREPAYMENTS

MAIN POINTS

1. Background

There are many different methods of accounting. One method sometimes advocated is known as CASH FLOW accounting. Cash flow accounting matches cash received during an accounting period against cash paid during the same period.

In ACCRUALS' accounting, the REVENUE for an accounting period is matched against the COST of earning the revenue for that same period, irrespective of when the cash was received or paid. Accruals' accounting is the most common method of accounting.

2. Capital And Revenue Transactions

The first step in accrual's accounting is to distinguish between capital and revenue transactions.

Capital items are those transactions that affect more than one accounting period, that is, they have a long term effect.

Revenue transactions only relate to one accounting period, and they have, therefore, only a short term effect. As a result, they may be renewed in subsequent accounting periods.

It should be noted that the distinction between capital and revenue items is not always easy to make.

3. Definitions of Accruals and Prepayments

An accrual is an amount owed at the end of an accounting period for goods or services received during that accounting period. A prepayment is an amount paid in one accounting period in respect of goods or services expected to be delivered during a future accounting period.

4. Calculation of Expenditure

	£	£
Cash paid		X
Add: Opening prepayments		X
Closing accruals		X
		X
Less: Opening accruals	X	
Closing prepayments	X	X
Expenditure for the period		£X

5. Book-Keeping Entries for Expenditure

(a) An accrual
- Dr. Expenditure account at the END of the accounting period
- Cr. Expenditure account at the BEGINNING of the next accounting period.

  With the amount of the accrual

(b) A prepayment
- Dr. Expenditure account at the BEGINNING of the next accounting period.
- Cr. Expenditure account at the END of the accounting period.

  With the amount of the prepayment

By adopting this procedure, double-entry is completed within the SAME account.

6. Balance Sheet Disclosure: Expenditure

Opening accruals and prepayments will already have been written off to the profit and loss account, so only CLOSING accruals and prepayments will be shown in the balance sheet.

Accruals will be shown under CURRENT LIABILITIES, usually after trade creditors.

PREPAYMENTS will be shown under CURRENT ASSETS, usually as the third item.

7. Calculation of Income

In order to adjust cash received on to an accruals' basis, the following adjustments should be made:

	£	£
Cash received		X
Add: Incomes received in advance in the previous period		X
Incomes due but not yet paid at the end of the current period		X
		X
Less: Incomes due but not received during the current period	X	
Incomes received in the current period relating to future periods	X	X
Income for the period		£X

8. Book-Keeping Entries for Incomes

(a) An accrual
- Dr. Income account at the beginning of the next period
- Cr. Income account at the end of the current period

  With the amount of the income due to be received

(b) A prepayment
- Dr. Income account at the end of the current period
- Cr. Income account at the beginning of the next period

  With the amount of the income received in advance.

By adopting this procedure, double-entry is achieved within the SAME account.

9. Balance Sheet Disclosure: Incomes

Incomes receivable should be included in the balance sheet under CURRENT ASSETS and described as ACCRUED INCOME. It should be included after prepayments.

Incomes received in advance should be included in the balance sheet under CURRENT LIABILITIES and described as DEFERRED INCOME. It should be included after accruals.

Example 1. In each of the following sets of data which relate to the year ended 30 April 19X2, ascertain the amount of the missing item(s), showing full details of your workings:

		£
(a)	Opening balance of debtors	1,234
	Closing balance of debtors	1,950
	Cash received from debtors	7,200
	Sales	?
(b)	Opening balance of creditors	3,120
	Closing balance of creditors	4,960
	Purchases	19,750
	Cash paid to creditors	?
(c)	Opening creditor for stationery	150
	Closing creditor for stationery	190
	Opening stock of stationery	80
	Closing stock of stationery	100
	Cash paid to suppliers of stationery	1,250
	Cost of stationery consumed during year	?
(d)	Cash paid to creditors	19,880
	Opening balance of creditors	6,180
	Opening stock	6,500
	Closing balance of creditors	7,750
	Closing stock	7,200
	Cost of goods sold	?
	Purchases	?

(AAT Level 1)

Solution

(a)

Debtors Account

	£		£
Opening balance	1,234	Cash	7,200
Sales	7,916	Closing balance	1,950
	£9,150		£9,150

Missing figure: Sales £7,916

(b)

Creditors account

	£		£
Cash	17,910	Opening balance	3,120
Closing balance	4,960	Purchases	19,750
	£22,870		£22,870

Missing figure: Cash £17,910

(c)

Stationery account

	£		£
Opening stock	80	Opening creditor	150
Cash	1,250	Profit and loss	1,270
Closing creditor	190	Closing stock	100
	£1,520		£1,520

Missing figure: cost of stationery consumed during the year £1,270

(d)

Creditors Account

	£		£
Cash	19,880	Opening balance	6,180
Closing balance	7,750	Purchases	21,450
	£27,630		£27,630

Trading Account

	£		£
Opening stock	6,500	Closing stock	7,200
Purchases	21,450	Cost of goods sold	20,750
	£27,950		£27,950

Missing figures: Cost of goods sold £20,750; Purchases £21,450

Example 2. The following information relates to Eden, a sole trader, for the year to 30 September 19X5:

   (1)   At 30 September 19X4 and at 30 September 19X5, Eden owed £250 and £280 respectively to the gas board. During the year to 30 September 19X5 he had paid cheques totalling £620 to the same gas board.

   (2)   Eden paid his insurance company £1,710 during the year to 30 September 19X5. At 30 September 19X4, he had paid £70 in advance to the company, and at 30 September 19X5 the amount that he had paid in advance amounted to £45.

Required:

Compile the following accounts for the year to 30 September 19X5, and bring down the balances as at that date.

   (a)   gas account; and
   (b)   insurance account

(AAT Level 2, amended)

Solution

Gas Account

	£		£
30 9 X5 Bank	620	1 10 X4 Balance b/d	250
Balance c/d	280	30 9 X5 Profit and loss	650
	£900		£900
		1 10 X5 Balance b/d	280

Insurance account

	£		£
1 10 X4 Balance b/d	70	30 9 X5 Profit and loss	1735
30 9 X5 Bank	1,710	Balance c/d	45
	£1,780		£1,780
1 10 X5 Balance b/d	45		

EXERCISES

14.1 Senga has been in business for some years and you are provided with the following information:

£

(1) Electricity: amount outstanding at 31 December 19X2 — 500

(2) Rents received: amount received in advance at 31 December 19X2 (for three months to 31 March 19X3) — 750

(3) Insurance: amount paid in advance at 31 December 19X2 — 50

(4) Bank payment during the year to 31 December 19X3:

	Electricity £	Insurance £
21 1 X3	700	-
26 4 X3	1,000	300
15 7 X3	400	-
20 10 X3	600	400

(5) Bank receipts during the year to 31 December 19X3:

Rents Received
£
25 3 X3 — 800 (for three months to 30 June 19X3)
24 6 X3 — 900 (for three months to 30 September 19X3)
28 9 X3 — 950 (for three months to 31 December 19X3)
25 12 X3 — 700 (for three months to 31 March 19X4)

(6) It is estimated that Senga owes £800 for electricity consumed for the three months to 31 December 19X3.

(7) Insurance paid in advance at 31 December 19X3 amounted to £200.

Required:

Write up Senga's electricity, rents received and insurance ledger accounts for the year to 31 December 19X3 being careful to bring down the balances as at 1 January 19X4.

14.2   Michael Lennon starts in business as a sole trader on 1 January 19X6.

The rent of his business premises is £3,000 per annum, payable in quarterly instalments at the end of March, June, September and December. The rates on the premises, which are payable in advance, are at an annual rate of £900 until 31 March 19X6 and thence at an annual rate of £1,000. The actual payments are made as follows:

Rent	**19X6**	
	2 April	3 months to 31 March
	5 July	3 months to 30 June
	28 September	3 months to 30 September
	19X7	
	5 January	3 months to 31 December 19X6
Rates	**19X6**	
	3 January	3 months to 31 March
	12 April	6 months to 30 September
	7 October	6 months to 31 March

He takes out insurance cover for 6 months, and pays the premium of £130 on 1 January. In due course, he realises that the cover is inadequate and negotiates with the same insurance company for extended insurance protection as from 1 July 19X6. The new contract is at an annual rate of £340, payable in advance. He pays the first annual premium on 26 June.

Required:

(a) Show the following expense accounts in respect of the financial year ended 31 December 19X6, complete with year end adjustments and balances brought down:

    (i)   Rent account;
    (ii) Rates account;
    (iii) Insurance account; and

(b) show the relevant extracts covering these items from the balance sheet of Michael Lennon as at 31 December 19X6.

(LCCI Elementary 1987)

14.3 (i) The Spinola Restaurant commenced business on 1 June 19X4. Its financial year ends on 31 March, though the first trading period was shorter. The management pays fire insurance annually in advance on 1 June each year, as follows:

	£
1 June 19X4	600
1 June 19X5	660
1 June 19X6	720

Required:

(a) Show the Fire Insurance Account in Spinola Restaurant's books for the year ending 31 March 19X6 and 31 March 19X7 respectively; and

(b) show the relevant extract from Spinola Restaurant's Balance Sheet as at 31 March 19X6 and as at 31 March 19X7.

(ii) The Rent and Rates Account in the ledger of F Stannerton, a sole trader, showed that on 31 December 19X5 the rent for the 3 months to 31 December was outstanding and that the rates for the half-year ended 31 March 19X6, amounting to £256, had been paid. During the year to 31 December 19X6, the following payments relating to rent and rates were made by cheque.

19X6		Rent £	Rates £
12 January	3 months ended 31 12 X5	420	
21 March	3 months ended 31 3 X6	420	
27 May	6 months ended 30 9 X6		284
12 July	3 months ended 30 6 X6	420	
23 September	3 months ended 30 9 X6	480	
21 December	3 months ended 31 12 X6	480	
19X7			
18 January	6 months ended 31 3 19X6		284

Required:

(a) Prepare the Rent and Rates Account as it would appear after the books have been balanced on 31 December 19X6; and

(b) show how the balance sheet would appear in respect of Rent and Rates as at 31 December 19X5.

(LCCI Intermediate 1987)

COMMON ERRORS

1. Double-Entry

Many students find it difficult to cope with adjustments for accruals and prepayments. A common type of examination question is one where the candidate is presented with a trial balance, followed by a number of adjustments that had not been entered into the books of accounts at the time that the trial balance was prepared.

Such adjustments often include items relating to accruals and prepayments.

Remember to complete double-entry within your answer, otherwise your balance sheet will not balance.

An accrual should be ADDED to an expense account. Do not forget to include it as an accrual in the balance sheet under CURRENT LIABILITIES.

Similarly, you must deduct a closing prepayment from an expense account. It should be included as a prepayment in the balance sheet under CURRENT ASSETS.

2. Incomes

Remember that some incomes may require adjustment. Interest due to be received, for example, should be added to INTEREST RECEIVABLE. In the balance sheet, the amount due should be shown under CURRENT ASSETS as ACCRUED INCOME.

It may be relatively uncommon to find incomes received in advance, although it is possible. If so, deduct the income received in advance from the appropriate income account, and include it in the balance sheet under CURRENT LIABILITIES as DEFERRED INCOME.

3. Opening Accruals and Prepayments

Some questions may require you to deal with opening accruals and prepayments.

In the case of expenditure, an opening prepayment will be brought down as a DEBIT balance in the expenditure account, whilst an opening accrual will be brought down as a CREDIT balance.

In the case of incomes, income received in advance in the previous period will be brought down as a CREDIT balance in the income account whereas income due at the end of the previous period will be brought down as a DEBIT balance.

15 BAD AND DOUBTFUL DEBTS

MAIN POINTS

1. Background

The realisation rule allows credit to be taken for goods sold during a particular period, even if the debtor is only expected to pay for them in a subsequent period.

If the debtor defaults, the period in which the sales were made will have been overstated. It is impossible, however, to correct errors made in earlier accounting period, so the matter has to be dealt with in the period that the default comes to light.

In order to avoid distortions of profit in subsequent accounting periods caused by defaulting debtors, a PROVISION FOR BAD AND DOUBTFUL DEBTS may be set up.

2. Definitions

(a) Bad debt
A bad debt is an amount owed by a debtor that he cannot or will not be able to settle.

(b) Doubtful debt
A doubtful debt is an amount owed by a debtor that is unlikely to be received from the debtor.

(c) Provision for bad and doubtful debts
A provision for bad and doubtful debts is an amount set aside in order to allow for bad and doubtful debts.

3. Estimating the Provision for Bad and Doubtful Debts.

The provision for bad and doubtful debts should be based on an estimate of the bad debts that are likely to arise. An agreed percentage is usually applied to the total amount of trade debtors as at the end of the financial year. Such a percentage will be based on the company's experience of its bad debts, particular trade conditions and the general economic climate.

4. Accounting Treatment for Bad and Doubtful Debts

(a) Setting up a provision

Dr. Profit and loss account
Cr. Provision for bad and doubtful debts account
With the amount needed to set up the provision.

(b) Maintaining the provision

Increasing the provision		Reducing the provision	
Dr.	Profit and loss account	Dr.	Provision for bad and doubtful debts
Cr.	Provision for bad and doubtful debts accounts	Cr.	Profit and loss account
With the extra amount needed to INCREASE the provision		With the extra amount needed to DECREASE the provision	

5. Writing Off Bad Debts

(a) Dr. Bad debts account
    Cr   Trade debtor's personal account
    With the amount of the bad debt

(b) Dr. Profit and loss account
    Cr. Bad debts account
    With the total amount of bad debts recorded in the bad debts account.

Entry (b) will normally be made at the end of the financial year.

6. Writing Off Bad Debts against a Provision

(a) Dr. Provision for bad and doubtful debts account
    Cr. Trade debtor's personal account
    With the amount of the bad debt

(b) EITHER

EITHER		OR	
Dr.	Profit and loss account	Dr.	Provision for bad and doubtful debts account
Cr.	Provision for bad and doubtful debts account	Cr.	Profit and loss account
With the INCREASE needed to maintain the provision at the determined level		With the DECREASE needed to maintain the provision at the determined level.	

7. Recovery of Bad Debts: Accounting Treatment

(a) Dr. Bank account
    Cr. Bad debts recovered account
    With the amount of the bad debt recovered

(b) EITHER

EITHER		OR	
Dr.	Bad debts recovered account	Dr.	Bad debts recovered account
Cr.	Profit and loss account	Cr.	Bad debts account
With the total bad debts recovered during the financial year.		With the total bad debts recovered during the financial year.	

8. Balance Sheet Presentation

The provision for bad and doubtful debts should be shown in the balance sheet under CURRENT ASSETS as a DEDUCTION from trade debtors.

Example 1. At 31 December 19X1, Ace owed Pendle £1,000. It is unlikely that Pendle will ever receive the amount owing to him.

Required:
Write up Ace's personal account, the bad debts account, and an extract of the profit and loss account in Pendle's books of account for the year to 31 December 19X1.

Solution

Ace's (personal) account

	£			£
31 12 X1 Balance b/d	1,000	31 12 X1	Bad debts	1,000
	£1,000			£1,000

Bad debts account

	£			£
31 12 X1 Ace	1,000	31 12 X1	Profit and loss account	1,000
	£1,000			£1,000

Profit and loss account (extract) for the year to 31 December 19X1

	£		£
Expenses			
Bad debt written off	1,000		

Example 2. Young's total trade debtors at 31 December 19X1 and 31 December 19X2 were £24,000 and £26,000 respectively. Young keeps a provision for bad and doubtful debts, equivalent to 5% of his total trade debtors as at the end of year year.

Required:
Write up Young's provision for bad and doubtful debts account and an extract of the profit and loss account for the two years to 31 December 19X1 and 19X2 respectively.

Solution

Provision for bad and doubtful debts account

	£			£
		31 12 X1	Profit and loss account*	1,200
31 12 X1 Balance c/d	1,200			
	£1,200			£1,200
		1 1 X2	Balance b/d	1,200
31 12 X2 Balance c/d	1,300	31 12 X2	Profit and loss account +	100
	£1,300			£1,300
		1 1 X3	Balance b/d	1,300

* Setting up the provision: 5% x £24,000
\+ Increase in the provision: (5% x £26,000) - 1,200

Profit and loss account (extract for the year to 31 December 19X1)

	£	£
Expenses		
Amount required to set up a provision for bad and doubtful debts	1,200	

Profit and loss account (extract) for the year to 31 December 19X2)

	£	£
Expenses		
Increase in provision for bad and doubtful debts	100	

Example 3. Chan maintains a provision for bad and doubtful debts account equivalent to 5% of his total trade debtors as at the end of each financial year. The following information relates to the financial year ending 31 December 19X6:

1. Provision for bad and doubtful debts (as at 1 January 19X6): £2,500
2. Songs personal account £2,000 (Dr.)
3. Chan's total trade debtors at 31 December 19X6 amounted to £60,000 (excluding the amount owned by Song). It is unlikely that Song will ever to be able to pay the amount that he owes Chan.

Required:

Write up Song's personal account, the bad debts account, and the provision for bad and doubtful debts account, and an extract of the profit and loss account for the year to 31 December 19X6.

Solution

METHOD 1

Song's (personal) account

	£		£
31 12 X6 Balance B/d	2,000	31 12 X6 Bad debts	2,000

Bad debts account

	£		£
31 12 X6 Song	2,000	31 12 X6 Profit and loss	2,000

Provision for bad and doubtful debts account

	£		£
		1 1 X6 Balance b/d	2,500
31 12 X6 Balance c/d	3,000	31 12 X6 Profit and loss*	500
	£3,000		£3,000
		1 1 X7 Balance b/d	3,000

* Increase needed in the provision: (5% x £60,000) - 2,500)

112

Profit and loss account (extract for the year to 31 December 19X6

	£	£
Expenses		
Bad debt written off	2,000	
Increase in the provision for bad and doubtful debts	500	

METHOD 2

Provision for bad and doubtful debts

	£			£
		1 1 X6	Balance b/d	2,500
31 12 X6 Song	2,000	31 12 X6	Profit and loss*	2,500
31 12 X6 Balance c/d	3,000			
	£5,000			£5,000
		1 1 X7	Balance b/d	3,000

*Provision required: 5% x £60,000 = £3,000

Profit and loss account (extract) for the year to 31 December 19X6

	£	£
Expenses		
Increase in provision for bad and doubtful debts	2,500+	

+Balance in the provision account after deducting the bad debt = £500 (£2,500 - 2,000) therefore increase in the provision = £2,500 (£3,000 - 500).

Note:

Both methods 1 and 2 result in the same total charge of £2,500 being made to the profit and loss account, but Method 1 analyses the charge between the bad debt written off (£2,000) and the increase needed in the provision account (£500).

Example 4.   The following information relates to Chin as at 31 December 19X4:

	£
Trade debtors (including a specific bad debt of £1,000)	11,000
Provision for bad and doubtful debts (at 1 January 19X4)	400

On 1 July 19X4 a bad debt of £50 (written off two years earlier) was recovered from Blue.

Chin maintains a provision for bad and doubtful debts equivalent to 5% of his outstanding trade debtors as at the end of each financial year.

Required:

Write up the following accounts for the year to 31 December 19X4:
    (a)   bad debts account;
    (b)   bad debts recovered account;
    (c)   provision for bad and doubtful debts account; and
    (d)   profit and loss account (extract).

Solution
METHOD 1

Bad debts account

	£			£
31 12 X4 Trade debtors	1,000	31 12 X4 Profit and loss		1,000

Bad debts recovered account

	£			£
31 12 X4 Profit and loss	50	31 12 X4 Bank (from Blue)		50

Provision for bad and doubtful debts account

		£			£
			1 1 X4	Balance b/d	400
31 12 X4 Balance c/d		500	31 12 X4	Profit and loss (increase in the provision*)	100
		£500			£500
			1 1 X5	Balance b/d	500

* (5% x £11,000 - 1,000) - 400 = £100

Profit and loss account (extract) for the year to 31 December 19X4

	£	£
Incomes		
Bad debt recovered		50
Expenses		
Bad debt	1,000	
Increase in the provision for bad and doubtful debts	100	

METHOD 2

Bad debts account

	£			£
31 12 X4 Trade debtors	1,000	31 12 X4 Bank (bad debt recovered from Blue*)		50
		31 12 X4 Profit and loss		950
	£1,000			£1,000

* The bad debt recovered could be credited to a bad debts recovered account. At the end of the year, the balance on the bad debts recovered account would be transferred to the bad debts account.

Provision for bad and doubtful debts account as per method 1

Profit and loss account (extract) for the year to 31 December 19X4

	£	£
Expenses		
Bad debts	950	
Increase in the provision for bad and doubtful debts	100	

EXERCISES

15.1   The following is an ageing schedule of debtors of Ming plc as at 31 October 19X4, the end of its financial year:

Days outstanding	Debtors £
Under 30	25,000
30 to under 60	13,000
60 to under 100	5,000
100 and over	2,000
	£45,000

Ming plc calculates its provision for bad debts by providing for 25% on debts which have been outstanding for more than 100 days, 10% on debts outstanding for 60 to under 100 days and 2% on debts outstanding for 30 to under 60 days. No provision is made on debts outstanding for less than 30 days.

Required:

Calculate Ming plc's provision for bad debts.

At 1 November 19X3 Ming plc had a provision for bad debts brought forward from the previous year of £1,000.

Required:

Show the Provision for Bad Debts Account for the year ended 31 October 19X4.

(AAT Preliminary)

15.2   B Careful had a balance of £350 on his provision for bad debts account on 1 November 19X6. On 31 October 19X7 he finds that he had incurred bad debts of £750 during the past financial year and that his debtors amount to £8,750 before the debts have been written off. He decides to write off the bad debts and to maintain a provision for bad debts at the level of 5% of debtors.

Required:

(a)   show the bad debts account and the provision for bad debts account for the year ended 31 October 19X7; and

(b)   briefly state the effects, if any, that
(i)   bad debts and
(ii)   maintaining a bad debts provision will have upon the cash flow, and the profits of a business.

(RSA intermediate)

15.3   During the financial year ended 31 December 19X5, M Block, a sole trader, suffered the following Bad Debts:

T Mann	£48 written off on 1 February 19X5
B Cope	£110 written off on 20 April 19X5
G Wallace	£56 written off on 16 August 19X5
H Dalton	£77 written off on 10 November 19X5

At the end of the financial year M Block had decided to increase the Provision for Bad/Doubtful debts to become 5% of the debtors figure (£4,200). His Provision for Bad/Doubtful Debts Account had a balance of £105 at 1 January 19X5.

Required:

   (a) Draw up M Block's Bad Debts Account, and also his Provision for Bad/Doubtful Debts Account for the year ended 31 December 19X5.

       (NOTE: Your should clearly show the amounts to be transferred to the Profit and Loss Account); and

   (b) set out the Balance Sheet extract, covering the item for Sundry Debtors.

(LCCI Elementary 1986)

15.4 Wentworth Enterprises maintains a Provision for Bad and Doubtful Debts Account, the amount of which is related at the end of each year, on a percentage basis, to current business conditions. The following summarises the debts that have been written off and the basis of the Provision over recent years.

	Debts written off-year to 31 December	Debtors at 31 December	Per cent Provision for Bad and Doubtful Debts
	£	£	%
19X2	-	6,000	5
19X3	452	8,500	5
19X4	860	11,000	8
19X5	650	12,000	6

Required:

Draw up the Bad Debts Account and the Provision for Bad and Doubtful Debts Account to show, as appropriate, the summarised information over the four years, including the transfer to the Profit and Loss Account at the end of each year.

(LCCI Elementary 1986)

15.5 P Prince is a trader in electrical goods who sells goods on both cash and credit terms. Credit customers are expected to pay in full by the end of the month following the month in which the credit sale is made. For example, a customer who is sold goods on credit during September should pay for them in full by the end of October.

Prince's financial year end is 31 December.

At each financial year end Prince looks at a schedule of outstanding debtors, makes any necessary specific provisions, and then provides for doubtful debts. Doubtful debts are taken to be 12% of those debts which should have been settled by 31 December, excluding amounts in respect of which specific provision has been made.

On 1 January 19X7, he made a specific provision of £30 and a general provision of £424.

The information on the following page relates to the year ended 31 December 19X7.

116

	September £	October £	November £	December £
Cash sales	3,400	5,100	2,900	2,600
Credit Sales	2,800	3,200	4,800	3,600
Outstanding debtors at 31 December 19X7	100	900	2,200	3,600

There were no outstanding debtors in respect of sales prior to September.

Prince recognised that an amount of £300 that was unlikely to be recovered was included in the debtors related to the November sales. He decided to make a specific provision in full in respect of this item.

Required:

    (a) BRIEFLY explain the reason for making a provision for doubtful debts;

    (b) prepare the Provision for Doubtful Debts Account;
        (Note: All workings must be shown); and

    (c) show the figure that will appear as debtors in Prince's Balance sheet as at 31 December 19X7.

(LCCI Intermediate 1987)

15.6   The Balance Sheet as at 31 December 19X5 of William Spoke, a trader, included the following entry:

	£
Debtors	18,000
LESS: Provision for Bad and Doubtful Debts	720
	17,280

For the next two years, the figures for Debtors before deducting any Provision for Bad and Doubtful Debts were 19X6 £16,500, 19X7 £21,000. In compiling the Balance Sheets for these two years, the Provision was calculated on the same percentage basis as for 19X5.

The amounts for Bad Debts actually written off were: 19X6 £705, 19X7 £795.

For 19X7 Spoke decided in addition to make provision for discount receivable calculated at the rate of 2.5% on £15,000 (the amount of Trade Creditors at 31 December 19X7 before making such provision). Cash discounts received during 19X7 totalled £3,150.

Required:

    (a) Prepare the following accounts in William Spoke's ledger for 19X6 and 19X7:
        (i) Bad debts;
        (ii) Provision for Bad and Doubtful Debts;

    (b) prepare the following accounts for 19X7:
        (i) Discounts Receivable;
        (ii) Allowance for Discounts Receivable; and

    (c) show the final entry for debtors in the 19X7 Balance Sheet after allowing 2% on good debts for discount allowed.

(LCCI 2nd Level 1988, adapted)

15.7 George is a wholesale retailer, and the following information relates to the year ending 30 September 19X2:

1. Goods are sold on credit terms, but some cash sales are also transacted.

2. At 1 October 19X1, George's trade debtors amounted to £30,000 against which he had set aside a provision for doubtful debts of 5%.

3. On 15 January 19X2, George was informed that Fall limited had gone into liquidation, owing him £2,000. This debt was outstanding from the previous year.

4. Cash sales during the year totalled £46,800, whilst credit sales amounted to £187,800.

5. £182,500 was received from trade debtors.

6. Cash discounts allowed to credit customers were £5,300.

7. Apart from Fall Limited's bad debt, other certain bad debts amounted to £3,500.

8. George intends to retain the Provision for Doubtful Debts Account at 5% of outstanding trade debtors as at the end of the year, and the necessary entries are to be made.

Required:

Enter the above transactions in George's ledger accounts, and apart from the cash and bank and profit and loss accounts, balance off the accounts and bring down the balances as at 1 October 19X2.

(AAT Level 2)

COMMON ERRORS

1. Confirmation of Bad Debts

Only write off a debt when it is absolutely certain that it is bad, for example, when an individual is declared bankrupt, or when a company has gone into liquidation.

2. Writing Off of Bad Debts

The bad debt should be written off EITHER directly to the profit loss account, or DEBITED to the provision for bad and doubtful debts account.

3. Calculating the Provision

Examination questions should give you the details of how to calculate the provision for bad and doubtful debts. A common method is to apply a stated percentage to the level of trade debtors as at the end of the financial year.

Remember to reduce the trade debtors by the amount of any SPECIFIC bad debts that are to be written off, as there is no point in providing for debts that are being written off.

4. Completing Double-Entry

Many examination questions provide you with a trial balance at the end of an accounting period. You are then required to adjust the accounts for bad debts, and to make provisions for bad and doubtful debts. Make sure that you always complete double-entry:

(a) adjust the trade debtor's account AND the bad debts or provision account; and

(b) adjust the provision account AND make an entry in the profit and loss account.

5. Disclosure

(a) Profit and loss account

(i) An INCREASE in the provision will be shown as a DEBIT entry.

(ii) A DECREASE in the provision will be shown as a CREDIT entry.

(iii) A bad debt written off DIRECTLY to the profit and loss account should be shown separately from any increase or decrease in the provision.

(iv) A bad debt written off against the provision account will NOT be shown separately in the profit and loss account

(v) A bad debt recovered that is credited to the bad debts account will NOT be shown separately in the profit and loss account.

(vi) Bad debts recovered that are taken DIRECTLY to the profit and loss account will be shown as a CREDIT entry. There will be a separate DEBIT entry for any specific bad debts written off.

(b) Balance sheet

The balance on the provision for bad and doubtful debts account should be DEDUCTED from the trade debtors. Only the NET amount should be built into the total of CURRENT ASSETS.

Note, however, that in advanced accounting, you may be required to show the provision as a separate item in the liabilities section of the balance sheet under the heading PROVISION FOR LIABILITIES AND CHARGES.

16 DEPRECIATION

MAIN POINTS

1. Background

Entities often purchase assets intended for long-term use in the business that will provide a benefit or a service over a number of accounting periods. Such assets are known as FIXED ASSETS.

Under the matching concept, it is necessary to charge a proportion of the cost of a fixed asset to EACH accounting period that is expected to benefit from its use.

Such a charge is known as DEPRECIATION.

2. Definition

According to SSAP 12 (Accounting for depreciation). Depreciation is: "the measure of the wearing out, consumption or other reduction in the useful economic life of a fixed asset whether arising from use, effluxion of time or obsolescence through technological or market changes."

3. Accounting Treatment

SSAP 12 requires that a provision for depreciation should be made for those fixed assets having a finite useful economic life by 'allocating the cost (or revalued amount) less estimated residual value of the assets as fairly as possible to the periods expected to benefit from their use".

4. Depreciation Methods

  (a) Straight line

$$\text{Annual depreciation charge} = \frac{\text{Cost - Estimated residual value}}{\text{Number of years of expected use}}$$

  (b) Reducing balance

Annual depreciation charge = (Cost - Accumulated depreciation to date) $\times$ r%

$$\text{where } r\% = 1 - \sqrt[n]{\frac{R}{C}}$$

and   r = rate of depreciation to be applied
        n = life of the assets in number of years
        R = estimated residual value
        C = cost of the asset

(c) Revaluation

First year's depreciation = (Revalued amount at the end of the year - cost)

Subsequent year's depreciation = (Revalued amount at the end of the year - revalued amount at the beginning of the year)

(d) Machine hour

Annual depreciation =

$$\frac{(Cost - Residual\ value) \times Annual\ actual\ machine\ running\ hours}{Total\ machine\ running\ hours}$$

(e) Sum of the year's digit

Annual depreciation charge =

$$\frac{Life\ of\ asset\ in\ years \times (Cost - Estimated\ residual\ value)}{Total\ sum\ of\ number\ of\ years\ life\ of\ the\ asset\ *}$$

$$* = \frac{n(n+1)}{2} \quad \text{where n = number of years}$$

5. Book-Keeping Entries

(a) Purchase of an asset
   Dr.   Fixed asset account
   Cr.   Bank (or supplier's) account
   With the cost of the fixed asset

(b) Annual depreciation
   Dr.   Profit and loss account
   Cr.   Fixed asset accumulated depreciation account
   With the amount of the depreciation charge for the year

(c) Sale of a fixed asset
   (i)   Dr.   Fixed asset disposal account
         Cr.   Fixed asset account
         With the cost of the fixed asset

   (ii) Dr.   Fixed asset accumulated depreciation account
         Cr.   Fixed asset disposal account
         With the total mount of depreciation provided for on the fixed asset

   (iii) Dr.   Bank
         Cr.   Fixed asset disposal account
         With the amount received on disposal of the asset

   (iv) EITHER   OR
         Dr. Fixed asset disposal account   Dr. Profit and loss account
         Cr. Profit and loss account   Cr. Fixed asset disposal account
         With the balance on the   With the balance on the
         fixed asset disposal account   fixed asset disposal
         (=over-depreciation)   account (=under-depreciation)

6. Balance Sheet Disclosure

(a) The cost of each group of fixed assets should be shown in the balance sheet under FIXED ASSETS; and

(b) the accumulated depreciation for each group of fixed assets should be shown as a DEDUCTION from each respective group of fixed assets.

Example. J B Prince, a sole trader, bought a new van for his business on 1 January 19X6. He needs to depreciate the van but has not decided whether to use the straight line method or the reducing balance method. The cost of the new van was £5,600 and his financial year ends on 31 December each year.

If Price uses the straight line method, he allows for 5 years useful life of the van, and a scrap value of £400. For the reducing balance method, he wishes to write off 40% per annum of the balance of the van at the year end.

Required:

Draw up the Delivery Van Account as it would appear in the ledger of J B Prince for the three years from the date on which Price purchased the van, using:

(i) the straight line method;

(ii) the reducing balance method.

Notes:

1 It is essential to indicate clearly in your answer which method you are using in each case.

2 Calculations should be to the nearest £.

(LCCI Elementary 1987)

Solution

J B PRICE
Delivery van account

	£			£
1 1 X6 Bank	5,600			

Provision for depreciation account

(i) <u>Straight line method</u>

	£			£
		31 12 X6	Profit and loss (£5600-400x20%)	1,040
31 12 X7 Balance c/d	2,080	31 12 X7	Profit and Loss	1,040
	£2,080			£2,080
		1 1 X8	Balance b/d	2,080
31 12 X8 Balance c/d	3,120	31 12 X8	Profit and Loss	1,040
	£3,120			£3,120
		1 1 X9	Balance b/d	3,120

(ii) Reducing balance method

	£				£
		31 12 X6	Profit and loss (£5600-400x40%)	2,080
		31 12 X7	Profit and loss [(£5,600-400-2080) x40%]	1,248
31 12 X7 Balance c/d	3,328			
	£3,328			£3,328
		1 1 X8	Balance b/d	3,328
		31 12 X8	Profit and loss [(£5,600-400-3,328) x40%]	749
31 12 X8 Balance c/d	4,077			
	£4,077			£4,077
		1 1 X9	Balance b/d	4,077

EXERCISES

16.1 (a) What factors cause fixed assets to depreciate?

(b) The financial year of Mosgins and Sons ends on 30 June each year. On 1 August 19X4 it purchased two motor vehicles. The first cost £9,500. Its purchase was partly financed by a loan for £5,000 from Motor Finance plc. The balance was paid by cheque. The second cost £6,500 and was paid for by cheque. That second motor vehicle was sold for £4,500 on 1 March 19X6 and replaced by a new motor vehicle costing £7,000. The new vehicle was paid for by cheque.

Mosgins and Sons provide for depreciation on Motor Vehicles at 30% per annum using the reducing balance method with a full year's depreciation charged in the year of purchase and no depreciation being charged in the year of sale.

Required:

Show how the above transactions would be recorded in the following accounts in the ledger of Mosgins and Sons:

(i) the Motor Vehicles Account;
(ii) the Provision for Depreciation - Motor Vehicles Account; and
(iii) the Assets Disposals Account.

(AAT Certificate, amended)

16.2 On 1 January 19X3 Mr Reed commenced business as a printer and purchased a typesetting machine for £2,000. On 1 July 19X3 he purchased a printing press at a cost of £8,000 and on 1 April 19X4 he purchased a collating machine for £4,000.

He depreciates all his machinery at the rate of 10% per annum on the cost price. Mr Reed posted the depreciation to his Machinery Account and did not keep a special Provision Account.

Required:

Prepare the Machinery Account of Mr Reed to cover the THREE years from 1 January 19X3 to 1 January 19X6. The financial year of Mr Reed is from 1 January to 31 December.

(LCCI Elementary 1986)

16.3 An airline company purchased and put into operation a jet aircraft on 1 February 19X1 for £7,000,000. The expectation then was that the aircraft would be flown for a total of 10,000 hours over a period of 4 years and then traded in for a new model. The trade-in value was expected to be £1,500,000 at the end of January 19X5. The number of flying hours actually logged by the aircraft was as follows:

1 February 19X1 -	31 January 19X2	3,000
1 February 19X2 -	31 January 19X3	2,800
1 February 19X3 -	31 January 19X4	2,300
1 February 19X4 -	31 January 19X5	500

The aircraft had a serious accident in June 19X4 and was a total write-off - although an insurance company agreed to pay £1,200,000 in settlement.

Required:

(a) Calculate the depreciation charges for each of the four financial years to 31 January 19X5:

    (i) using the straight line method (applied on a full year basis), and
    (ii) on a basis of flying hours logged;

(b) state with reasons which of these two methods of depreciation you consider to be the more appropriate in the circumstances; and

(c) show the appropriate ledger accounts for the year ended 31 January 19X5 using

    (i) the straight line method and
    (ii) the flying hours logged method.

(AAT Preliminary, adapted)

16.4 Two companies - The Go Ahead Company Ltd and the Forceful Company Ltd have the same year end, 31 December.

The Go Ahead Company purchased a machine on 1 January 19X5 for £20,000. This was to be depreciated at 40% per annum using the Reducing Balance Method.

The Forceful Company purchased a similar machine also on 1 January 19X3 for £20,000. **But** this was to be depreciated at 20% per annum using the Straight Line Method.

Each company makes £50,000 profit each year before depreciation.

On 1 January 19X8, each company sold its machine for £7,000.

Required:

(a) Draw up a table using the headings indicated below showing the annual depreciation, Net Book Value, and Net Profit (after depreciation) for each of the first three years of life of each machine.

Date	Annual Depreciation £	Net Book Value £	Revised Net Profit £

(b) Calculate the Profit or Loss on each sale.

(c) Draw up the Disposal Account for the Go Ahead Company only.

(d) State one example when (i) the straight line and (ii) the reducing balance method are best suited.

(RSA Intermediate)

16.5 JPR Haulage Ltd specialises in long distance haulage of raw materials. On 1 January 19X5, the company had three lorries which had been purchased for cash as follows:

Lorry	Purchase date	Purchase cost £
A	1 January 19X3	16,500
B	1 October 19X3	18,100
C	1 January 19X4	19,400

The company depreciates its lorries on a straight line basis over five years with no residual value. The company's financial year ends on 31 December each year.

A full year's depreciation is charged in the year of acquisition, but no depreciation is charged in the year of disposal.

The following transactions took place in the year ended 31 December 19X5:

Lorry

D Purchased 5 April 19X5 for £20,200 cash.

B Sold on 30 June 19X5 for £4,720 cash.

E Purchased 8 August 19X5 on hire purchase terms. The cash price was £18,000. The hire purchase terms provided for a deposit of £7,200 and 24 monthly instalments of £560.

F Purchased 9 September 19X5 for £16,900 cash.

Required:

(a) Prepare a depreciation schedule in the following format:

Year ended 31 December Lorry	19X3	19X4	19X5	Total
A				
B				
C				
D				
E				
F				
Total				

(b) Prepare **total** accounts for the year ended 31 December 19X5 for
  (i) Motor lorries;
  (ii) Accumulated depreciation on motor lorries.

NOTE: Individual lorry details should not appear in these total accounts.

(LCCI Intermediate 1986)

16.6 The following is an extract from the balance sheet of United Marbles as at 31 May 19X4:

Fixed Assets	Cost £000	Depreciation £000	Net Book Value £000
Buildings	360	126	234
Equipment	200	100	100
	£560	£226	£334

During the year to 31 May 19X5, transactions affecting the fixed assets accounts took place as follows:

1. Some buildings which originally cost £20,000 were sold for £4,000. Their net book value at 31 May 19X4 was £10,000.

2. New premises were purchased on 1 October 19X4 at a cost of £40,000.

3. Equipment (with a book value of £15,000) was sold for £18,000. It had originally been purchased for £20,000 on 1 December 19X3.

4. New equipment was purchased on 1 April 19X4 for £15,000.

Additional information:

(a) Buildings are depreciated on a straight-line basis over an expected life of 20 years. It is not expected that they will have any residual value at the end of their life.

(b) Equipment is depreciated on a reducing balance basis at a rate of 25% per annum.

(c) For both buildings and equipment a full year's depreciation is charged in the year of acquisition, but no depreciation is charged in the year of disposal.

Required:

Write up the following accounts for the year to 31 May 19X5:

(i) buildings account;
(ii) buildings depreciation account
(iii) equipment account;
(iv) equipment depreciation account; and
(v) fixed assets (buildings and equipment) disposal account.

(AAT Level 2)

COMMON ERRORS

1. Miscalculation Of The Annual Depreciation Charge

(a) Note carefully the depreciation method to be adopted. Extract the correct figures from the question, and double-check your arithmetic.

(b) Note whether a FULL year's depreciation is to be charged in the year of acquisition of an asset.

(c) Note whether any depreciation is to be charged in the year of disposal of an asset.

2. Profit And Loss Account

(a) Make sure that you include only the total amount of depreciation for the YEAR in the profit and loss account (some students include the accumulated depreciation!).

(b) A debit balance transferred from the fixed assets disposal account to the profit and loss account should be described as UNDER-depreciation (in preference to describing it as a LOSS on sale).

(c) A credit balance transferred from the fixed assets disposal account to the profit and loss account should be described as OVER-depreciation (in preference to describing it as a PROFIT on sale).

3. Balance Sheet

(a) Do not forget to adjust the cost of fixed assets brought forward at the beginning of the year for any ADDITIONS or DISPOSALS of fixed assets during the year.

(b) Adjust the accumulated depreciation charge brought forward at the beginning of the year for the accumulated depreciation on any fixed asset disposed of during the year.

(c) Remember to add the current year's depreciation charge to the accumulated depreciation balance brought forward (after making adjustment (b) above).

17 FINAL ACCOUNTS

MAIN POINTS

1. Types of Entities

This book is mainly concerned with three main types of entities: sole traders, partnerships and limited liability companies.

2. Types of Final Accounts

The main types of final accounts usually consist of a trading account, a profit and loss account, a profit and loss appropriation account (usually only for partnerships and for limited liability companies), and a balance sheet.

3. Preparation of the Final Accounts

Stages:
(a) preliminary balancing of the accounts
(b) extraction of the balances
(c) preparation of the trial balance
(d) correction of any book-keeping errors
(e) balancing of the trial balance
(f) adjustments for other items not included in the trial balance
(g) preparation of the trading account
(h) preparation of the profit and loss account
(i) preparation of the profit and loss appropriation account
(j) preparation of the balance sheet
(k) entry of all year end adjustments in the ledger accounts
(l) formal balancing of the accounts
(m) bringing down of the balances in the respective ledger accounts

4. The Trading Account

The trading account is used to match sales revenue (sales less sales returns) with the cost of goods sold (opening stock + (purchases - purchases returns) + carriage inwards) - closing stock) to arrive at GROSS PROFIT.

Gross profit is then carried down to the profit and loss account.

5. The Profit And Loss Account

The profit and loss account is used to match the gross profit + other revenue incomes against revenue expenditure. The difference equals NET profit (or loss) for the period.

The net profit is then transferred either to the proprietor's capital (or current) account or the profit and loss appropriation account.

6. The Profit and Loss Appropriation Account

The profit and loss account is used to show how the net profit for the year is shared between the respective owners of the entity.

7. The Balance Sheet

The balance sheet does NOT form part of the double entry system (unlike the trading account, the profit and loss account and the profit and loss appropriation account). The balance sheet merely summarizes all the balances that remain in the ledger after compiling the final accounts.

The balance sheet is divided into a number of sections. The precise format may vary depending upon the nature of the entity. Irrespective of the format, the balance sheet can be expressed in the form of an equation:

Fixed assets + investments + current assets = Capital + loans + current liabilities

The balance sheet must always balance (like an equation). If it does not balance, then it is obvious that a mistake must have been made somewhere in the double-entry system.

Example. The following trial balance has been extracted from the ledger of Rita Rowe who trades as a general merchant:

Trial Balance as at 31 October 19X7

	Dr £	Cr £
Sales		530,887
Purchases	388,645	
Drawings	20,800	
Administration expenses	31,841	
Selling and distribution expenses	65,517	
Loan interest	1,650	
Debtors	26,550	
Creditors		36,887
Cash on hand	515	
Bank account		3,466
Stock at 1 November 19X6	12,306	
Equipment - at cost	141,450	
- accumulated depreciation		55,320
Loan		13,500
Capital		49,214
	£689,274	£689,274

The following additional information as at 31 October 19X7 is available:

1. Loan interest is accrued by £150
2. Equipment is to be depreciated at 10% per annum using the straight line method.
3. Stock at the close of business was valued at £14,521.

Required:

Prepare Rita Rowe's Trading and Profit and Loss Account for the year ended 31 October 19X7 and her Balance Sheet as at that date.

(AAT Certificate)

Solution :

RITA ROWE
Trading and Profit and Loss Account
for the year ended 31 October 19X7

			£	£
Sales				530,887
Less:	Cost of Goods sold			
	Stock at 1 November 19X6	12,306		
	Purchases	388,645		
		400,951		
	Less: Stock at 31 October 19X7	14,521		
				386,430
GROSS PROFIT				144,457
Less:	Operating Expenses			
	Selling and distribution expenses	65,517		
	Administration	31,841		
	Loan interest (£1,650+150)	1,800		
	Depreciation (10%x £141,450)	14,145		113,303
NET PROFIT				£31,154

RITA ROWE
Balance Sheet at 31 October 19X7

Fixed Assets	Cost	Accumulated Depreciation	Net Book Value
	£	£	£
Equipment	141,450	69,465	71,985
Current Assets			
Stock at cost		14,521	
Debtors		26,550	
Cash on hand		515	
		41,586	
Current Liabilities			
Creditors	36,887		
Accrued expenses	150		
Bank overdraft	3,466	40,503	
			1,083
Net assets			£73,068
Financed by:			
Capital			
At 1 November 19X6			49,214
Net Profit		31,154	

	Cost	Accumulated Depreciation	Net Book Value
	£	£	£
Less : Drawings		20,800	10,354
			59,568
Loan			13,500
			£73,068

EXERCISES

17.1 Melanie Rogers began business on 1 March 19X7. During the year she paid £3,100 for advertising, £2,150 for insurance and received commission of £18,200.

At the end of the year she had an outstanding bill for advertising of £100, commission due to her £2,500 and had pre-paid insurance of £300.

Required:

Prepare the ledger accounts for advertising, insurance and commission received showing clearly the amounts to be transferred to the final accounts.

After preparation of the Trading Account the following additional information (which does not constitute a Trial Balance) was extracted from the books on the 29 February 19X8:

	£
Capital	45,000
Drawings	8,700
Rent and Rates	9,000
Lighting and heating	5,400
Stationery	820
Commissions allowed	3,100
Discounts allowed	1,200
Discounts received	1,450
Machinery and equipment	24,300
Profit on Trading	27,350
Debtors	9,780
Creditors	12,120
Wagers and salaries (office)	9,500
Bad debts	125
Motor expenses	4,200
General expenses	5,600

Required:

Prepare the Profit and Loss Account of the business for the year ending 29 February 19X8 (A Balance Sheet is NOT required)

(RSA Elementary)

17.2 Cottle Stores is located in the suburbs of a large town, selling mainly stationery and confectionery. The owner of the business is anxious to know how profitable her first year of trading has been.

The Trial Balance was extracted from the books at 30 April 19X8:

	£	£
Capital (introduced 1 May 19X7)		8,200
Cash	200	
Bank	8,345	
Drawings	4,160	
Fittings	4,400	
Rent	2,100	
Loan		3,000
Miscellaneous Expenses	706	
Wages	3,900	
Discounts received for Stationery		25
Debtors and Creditors	2,000	4,630
Electricity	435	
Purchases	59,150	
Sales		70,600
Advertising	1,059	
	£86,455	£86,455

The following adjustments need to be made:
(i) Rent has been prepaid by £700. (ii) Electricity payments are £51 in arrears. (iii) Stock at 30 April 19X8 was valued at £4,550.

Required:

(a) Prepare a Trading and Profit and Loss Account for the year ended 30 April 19X8; and

(b) prepare a Balance Sheet for the business showing the accumulated capital, as at 30 April 19X8.

(RSA Elementary)

17.3 The financial year of E Long, a sole trader, ended on 31 October 19X7. The books were balanced on that date and the following Trial Balance was extracted:

Trial Balance as at 31 October 19X7

	£	£
Purchases and Sales	25,790	38,465
Sales Returns	300	
Stock at 1 November 19X6	2,750	
Rent received from sub-letting		1,500
Carriage inwards	650	
Wages	4,500	
Rent	1,000	
Rates	450	
General expenses	365	
Freehold buildings	15,000	
Fixtures and fittings	1,550	
Debtors and Creditors	760	1,260
Cash	55	
Bank (overdraft)		1,495
Capital, 1 November 19X6		10,450
	£53,170	£53,170

Additional information :

(i) There was a Stock on Hand of £2,150.

(ii) On 31 October 19X7 E Long took goods value at £150 from the business for her own private use.

(iii) There was £50 Rent received owing to the firm.

Required:

(a) Prepare a Trading and Profit and Loss Account for the year just ended clearly indicating the Cost of Goods Sold; and

(b) a Balance Sheet as at 31 October 19X7.

(RSA Elementary)

17.4 Mr Chai has been trading for some years as a wine merchant. The following list of balances has been extracted from his ledger as at 30 April 19X7, the end of his most recent financial year:

	£
Capital	83,887
Sales	259,870
Trade creditors	19,840
Returns out	13,407
Provision for bad debts	512
Discounts allowed	2,306
Discounts received	1,750
Purchases	135,680
Returns inwards	5,624
Carriage outwards	4,562
Drawings	18,440
Carriage inwards	11,830
Rent, rates and insurance	25,973
Heating and lighting	11,010
Postage, stationery and telephone	2,410
Advertising	5,980
Salaries and wages	38,521
Bad debts	2,008
Cash on hand	534
Cash at bank	4,440
Stock as at 1 May 19X6	15,654
Trade debtors	24,500
Fixtures and fittings - at cost	120,740
Provision for depreciation on fixtures and fittings - as at 30 April 19X7	63,020
Depreciation	12,074

The following additional information as at 30 April 19X7 is available:

(a) Stock at the close of business was valued at £17,750.

(b) Insurances have been prepaid by £1,120.

(c) Heating and lighting is accrued by £1,360.

(d) Rates have been prepaid by £5,435.

(e) The provision for bad debts is to be adjusted so that it is 3% of trade debtors.

133

Required:

Prepare Mr Chai's Trading and Profit and Loss Account for the year ended 30 April 19X7 and a Balance Sheet as at that date. *(AAT Preliminary)*

17.5 B Norris is in business as a wholesale supplier of motor equipment. The following is his trial balance as at 31 March 19X3:

	Dr £	Cr £
Accumulated Van Depreciation (at 1 April 19X2)		15,000
Capital (at 1 April 19X2)		8,400
Creditors		10,000
Cash at bank	200	
Debtors	16,700	
Drawings	11,000	
Office expenses	12,600	
Opening stock	5,000	
Provision for Doubtful Debts (as 1 April 19X2)		600
Purchases	62,000	
Rates	1,500	
Sales		100,000
Vans, at cost	25,000	
	£134,000	£134,000

You are provided with the following additional information:

1. The value of closing stock at 31 March 19X3 was £6,000.
2. Debtors include a certain bad debt of £500.
3. The provision for doubtful debts is to be made equal to 5% of outstanding debtors as at 31 March 19X3.
4. At 31 March 19X3, Norris owed £300 for rates.
5. Insurance prepaid at 31 March 19X3 amounted to £100.
6. Norris uses the reducing balance method of depreciation at a rate of 60% per annum. There were no purchases or sales of vans during the year.
7. Stock withdrawn for personal use during the year was estimated to be worth £1,000.
8. No entry had been made in the books of account for a cheque received from a debtor on 15 March 19X3 made payable to Norris for £200.

Required:

Prepare B Norris Trading and Profit and Loss Account for the year to 31 March 19X3 and a Balance Sheet as at that date. *(AAT Level 2)*

17.6 Paul Peters commenced retail trading on 1 January 19X3 with his capital consisting of stock in trade valued at £1,200 and a balance at the bank of £4,800.

During his first year's trading, whilst all receipts and payments were passed through the business bank account, Paul Peters did not keep a full set of accounting records. However, the following information has been obtained relating to the year ended 31 December 19X3:

1. Bank account - summarised transactions   £

    RECEIPTS

	£
Loan from Paul Peter's father	4,000
Cash sales	17,000
Received from trade debtors	43,400

    PAYMENTS

	£
Purchase of motor vehicle	5,000
Suppliers of goods	47,200
Rent and Rates	3,400
Electricity	600
Motor Vehicle running expenses	5,800
Sundry trading expenses	2,700
Drawings	4,100

2. Current assets, other than the balance at the bank, as at 31 December 19X3

	£
Stock in trade, at cost	5,100
Trade debtors	4,600
Amounts prepaid: Rent and rates	200

3. Current liabilities as at 31 December 19X3

	£
Trade creditors	3,200
Accrued charges: Electricity	100
Motor vehicle running expenses	250

4. Paul Peters obtains a gross profit of 30% on all sales.

5. During the year, Paul Peters has taken a quantity of goods out of the business's stock for his own use. Unfortunately a record has not been kept of these goods.

The loan from Paul Peter's father is interest free until 1 January 19X6.

It has been decided to provide for depreciation annually at the rate of 20% of the original cost of motor vehicles held at each accounting year end.

Required:

Prepare a trading and profit and loss account for the year ended 31 December 19X3 and a balance sheet as at that date.

(AAT Intermediate)

17.7   At 31 December 19X4, H Seymour's assets and liabilities were:

	£
Fixtures and fittings at cost	2,760
Fixtures and fittings - accumulated depreciation	1,818
Stocks	5,832
Debtors	2,192
Prepaid rent	80
Creditors	1,347
Bank balance in hand	1,380
Accrued electricity	78

His summarised cash book for 19X5 was as follows.

	£	£
Opening balance	1,380	
Receipts	113,079	
Payments to suppliers		87,057
Rent		480
Electricity		840
Wages		15,411
Other expenses		8,617
New fixtures and fittings		2,835
Bank balance 31 December 19X5	781	
	£115,240	£115,240

The item "receipts" includes £320 from the sale of some fixtures and fittings which originally cost £1,425 and had a book value of £285. Otherwise it consists of the net amount of receipts from customers after Seymour had taken drawings of £3,800 and had paid cash expenses of £185.

Provision for depreciation of fixtures and fittings is at a rate of 20% on cost per annum, charging a full year's depreciation in the year of acquisition.

At 31 December 19X5:

1. Debtors were £2,248.
2. Trade creditors were £1,210
3. £40 was owed for rent.
4. Seymour valued his stocks at £5,408 (cost price).

Required:

(a) Prepare Seymour's Trading and Profit and Loss Account for 19X5; and

(b) repair Seymour's Balance Sheet as at 31 December 19X5

(LCCI Higher 1986, amended)

17.8   Given below is the Trial Balance of Derwent at 31 March 19X5:

	Dr £000	Cr £000
Purchases and Sales	284	354
Drawings and Capital	12	152
Freehold Shop at cost and accumulated depreciation thereon	78	30
Fixtures, fittings at cost and accumulated depreciation thereon	30	11
Debtors and creditors	54	34
Stock at cost (1 April 19X4)	64	
Wages	37	
Insurance	3	
Other expenses	28	
Bank		9
	£590	£590

The following additional information is available:

1. Depreciation is to be provided at the rate of 10% on both the cost of fixtures and fittings and the cost of the freehold shop, at 31 March 19X5.

2. Insurance includes £2,000 paid in respect of the year to 30 September 19X5.
3. Stock as at 31 March 19X5 comprised three categories (I, II and III) valued as follows:

	I £000	II £000	III £000
Cost	32	35	30
Net realisable value	44	30	40

4. Wages owing at 31 March 19X5 amounted to £2,000.
5. Debtors include £4,000 regarded by the year end as irrecoverable and it has been decided to provide for further bad debts at the rate of 2% on the balance.
6. Derwent has employed an advertising agency to carry out a campaign during the three months to 31 March 19X5. He has not yet either paid (or recorded) the £10,000 estimated cost of this campaign and expects to benefit from it during the middle part of his next financial year.
7. Other expenses include £12,000 spent on adapting his shop to satisfy new government fire regulations.

Required:

(a) Prepare Derwent's Trading and Profit and Loss Account for the year ended 31 March 19X5 and his Balance Sheet at that date; and

(b) briefly explain your treatment in (a) above of additional information (3). (6) and (7), justifying the treatment, in each case, by reference to relevant accounting concepts and conventions.

(LCCI Higher 1985)

COMMON ERRORS

1. Capital and Revenue Transactions

Normally, only revenue income and revenue expenditure balances should be included in the trading account or the profit and loss account. Sometimes, however, by adopting the prudence concept, capital items may be included in the profit and loss account, although usually they will be included in the balance sheet.

Make sure that you are aware of the difference between capital and revenue transactions.

2. Year End Adjustments

Make sure that you have entered all the year end adjustments in your final accounts. In an examination question, these are usually given as ADDITIONAL INFORMATION. Check that you have made any adjustment TWICE, otherwise you will not have completed double-entry.

3. Cash and Trade Discounts

Cash discounts should be included in the profit and loss account. Trade discounts should not be entered in the books of account, so make sure that they are not included in your purchases and sales.

4. Purchases and Sales Returns

Purchases returns should be deducted from purchases in the trading account. Sales returns should be deducted from sales in the trading account.

5. Carriage Inwards and Outwards

Carriage INWARDS should be added to the cost of purchases in the trading account. Carriage OUTWARDS should be included in the profit and loss account.

6. Depreciation

Make sure that you only include the depreciation for the year in the profit and loss account, and that you make the calculations correctly. Check that the depreciation is not based on the reducing balance method.

7. Bad Debts and Provisions for Bad Debts

These often cause problems. Make sure that you have calculated the provision correctly, and that you have only included the INCREASE (or DECREASE) in the provision for the year in the profit and loss account.

8. Net Profit (Or Loss) for the Year

Unless an appropriation account is used, the net profit for the year should be ADDED to the proprietor's capital account in the balance sheet (net loss, DEDUCTED).

9. Proprietor's Drawings

In the case of a sole trader, the proprietor's cash drawings should be deducted from the proprietor's capital account shown in the balance sheet.

If he had drawn goods from the business, deduct the COST of them from purchases in the trading account, and deduct the same amount from his capital account in the balance sheet.

Note that in partnership and company accounts, the appropriation of profit is dealt with by using an appropriation account.

10. Fixed Assets And Accumulated Depreciation

Fixed assets should be shown at cost in the balance sheet. The accumulated depreciation up to the date of the balance sheet (including the current year's depreciation) should be shown as a deduction from the cost of the fixed assets.

11. Presentation

Presentation is most important in preparing the final accounts, as they are often used as a means of assessing the entity's performance.

Make sure that you have laid out your accounts in a neat and acceptable format, and that you have scheduled your entries in a logical order.

18 ERROR CORRECTION

MAIN POINTS

1. Background

It is very easy to make a mistake in double-entry book-keeping, so the trial balance may not always balance at the first attempt.

Sometimes errors can be located very quickly. On other occasions, the preparation of the final accounts may be delayed if a lot of time is spent searching for an error. As the error may come to light during the preparation of the final accounts, it may be convenient to start preparing them before the trial balance has been balanced.

As a temporary measure, therefore, an error may be posted to a SUSPENSE account.

2. Cause of Errors

Errors may be caused by:
- (a) incorrect opening balances;
- (b) single entries;
- (c) entering a different credit and debit amount for the same transaction;
- (d) incorrect additions, subtractions and balancing;
- (e) incorrect extraction of the balances into the trial balance; and
- (f) omission of balances and arithmetical errors in the trial balance.

3. The Suspense Account; Book-Keeping Entries

(a) If an error comes to light, DEBIT (or CREDIT) the suspense account.

(b) When the cause of the error has been found:

EITHER Dr. Suspense Account   OR   Dr. Offending account
        Cr. Offending account   Cr. Suspense account.
        With the amount of the error

4. Final Accounts

A suspense account should NOT be entered in the final accounts. The error must be found by checking all the opening balances, each debit entry against each credit entry, all additions and subtractions, and the extraction and insertion of the closing balances into the final accounts.

Example. The totals of the draft Trial Balance of Boris Cord as at 30 November 19X7 did not agree. The difference was posted to a Suspense Account pending investigation of the accounts. This revealed the following errors:

1. The total of the Sales Book had been undercast by £1,000.

2. The total of the Purchases Book had been undercast by £585.

3. Discount received of £27 from Penn Supplies Ltd., a supplier, had been entered correctly in the Cash Book but had not been posted to Penn Supplies Ltd's personal account.

4. The total of the Discount Allowed column in the Cash Book had been undercast by £90.

5. Value Added Tax (at 15%) amounting to £45 collected on Cash Sales of £300 had not been entered in the VAT column in the Cash Book. Instead the sales had been recorded in the cash column as £345.

6. Some goods returned to Penny Pace, a supplier, have been recorded at a value of £59 in the Returns Outwards Book. The value of the goods returned was, in fact, £95.

Required:

Prepare Journal Entries (which should include dates and narratives) to show how the above errors would be corrected.

(AAT Certificate)

Solution

BORIS CORD
Journal

				Dr. £	Cr. £
30 11 X7	(1)	Suspense account	Dr	1,000	
		To:- Sales			1,000
		Being correction of undercasting of the Sales Book total			
30 11 X7	(2)	Purchases	Dr	585	
		To:- Suspense account			585
		Being correction of undercasting of the Purchase Book total			
30 11 X7	(3)	Penn Supplies Ltd	Dr	27	
		To:- Discount received			27
		Being discount not posted from Cash Book to supplier's account. Error now corrected.			
30 11 X7	(4)	Discount allowed	Dr	90	
		To:- Suspense account			90
		Being correction of undercasting of the Discount Allowed column in the Cash Book			

				Dr. £	Cr. £
30 11 X7	(5)	Sales	Dr	45	
		To:- Value Added Tax			45

Value Added Tax of £45 on Sales
of £300 omitted from VAT Column
of the Cash Book and included in
Sales. Error now corrected.

30 11 X7	(6)	Penny Pace	Dr	36	
		To:- Returns Outwards			36

Being Goods returned to supplier
Penny Pace recorded erroneously
in the Returns Outwards book as £59
instead of £95. Error now corrected.

EXERCISES

18.1 The following Trial Balance was extracted from the books of Andrew Scott, a retailer selling newspapers and confectionery, on the 29 February 19X8:

	£ Dr	£ Cr
Capital		40,100
Drawings	5,000	
Rent and rates	2,500	
Lighting and heating	2,400	
Advertising	220	
Motor expenses	1,200	
Wages and Salaries	8,500	
Insurance	500	
Purchases	26,100	
Sales		55,320
Creditors		2,500
Motor vehicles	15,000	
Equipment	20,000	
Stock of Goods 1 March 19X7	12,000	
Cash in hand	100	
Cash at bank	4,400	
	£97,920	£97,920

After preparation of the Trial Balance, the following errors were found:

(a) 15 June 19X7   A payment of £200 by cheque to D Smith, a creditor, had been debited to the account of D Smithson.

(b) 13 August 19X7:   An invoice for the purchase of sweets and confectionery for £340 from R Wallis and Co. had not been entered in the books.

(c) 24 September 19X7:   A payment for repairs to the Motor Vehicles of £500 had been entered in the Motor vehicles account.

(d) 30 October 19X7: Andrew Scott had bought petrol for his own use costing £200. This had been entered in the motor expenses account.

Required:

(a) Show the Journal entries necessary to correct these errors; and

(b) Rewrite the Trial Balance after the errors have been corrected.

(RSA Elementary)

18.2 John Barrington, a sole trader who keeps a double entry set of books, calculated that his Net Profit for the year ended 31 August 19X6 was £11,200. Subsequently he found that the following errors had been made during the year:

1. An invoice for £183 entered correctly in the Sales Day Book had been posted to the customer's account as £83.

2. One month's total of £34 Discount Allowed in the Cash Book had been posted to the credit of the Discount Received Account.

3. Barrington had omitted to record a withdrawal of £60 cash for personal use during the last two weeks of the accounting year.

4. The year-end stock list had been overcast by £100.

5. Barrington sent a cheque for £300 to Longer Loans Corporation in part repayment of a loan and inadvertently posted the amount to the debit of Interest on Loans Account.

Required:

Prepare a statement as illustrated below to show the effect of each of these errors on the Net Profit. If there is no effect on the Net Profit in any instances, state "No effect".

	N.P. Over-stated	N.P. Under-stated
1.		
2.		
3.		
4.		
5.		

At the end of your answer state the CORRECT figure for Net Profit.

(LCCI Elementary 1987)

18.3 (a) The draft Trial Balance of James McLippie and Son as at 30 April 19X8 did not agree and the difference was posted to a Suspense Account. Subsequent investigation of the accounts revealed the following errors:

1. The Discount Received column in the Cash Book had been overcast by £100.

2. J Stanley, a customer, had not been credited with £8 discount although this had been correctly entered in the Cash Book.

3. The Sales Book had been overcast by £900.

4. An invoice made out (correctly) for £45 in respect of sales made to H Purcell had been recorded in the Sales Book as £54. (This is quite apart from the error in the Sales Book referred to above).

5. The Purchases Book had been undercast by £360.

6. Goods returned from J Blow, a customer, had been recorded in the Returns Inward Book as £108. In fact, the value of the goods returned had been subsequently agreed with the customer at £88 but no adjustment had been made in accounting records.

7. Value Added Tax (at 15%) amounting to £15 collected on Cash Sales of £100 had not been entered in the VAT column in the cash book. Instead the sales had been entered in the cash book. Instead the sales had been recorded in the cash column as £115.

Required:

Prepare Journal entries to show how the above errors would be corrected.
(*Note*: Dates and narratives are not required).

(b) Before discovering the above errors, James McLippie and Son had proceeded with the preparation of draft final accounts for the financial year ended 30 April 19X6. These showed a profit for the year of £512,030.

Required:

What is the profit for the year after correcting the above errors?

(AAT Preliminary)

18.4 A Trader's trial balance at 31 March 19X8 did not agree. He transferred the difference to a suspense account, prepared his trading and profit and loss account and drew up the following balance sheet:

A Trader
Balance sheet as at 31 March 19X8

	£	£
Fixed Assets		
Furniture and Fittings	2,800	
Motor vehicles	4,500	7,300
Current Assets		
Stock	4,250	
Debtors	1,400	
Bank and Cash	752	
	6,402	
Current Liabilities	1,600	4,802
		£12,102
Financed by:		
Capital	11,075	
Add: Net profit	7,180	
	18,255	
Less: Drawings	6,400	11,855
Suspense account		247
		£12,102

143

The following errors were subsequently discovered:

1. A debit balance of £100 on rent and rates account had been omitted from the trial balance.

2. The purchase of a new fitment for the stockroom at a cost of £150 had been debited to purchases.

3. A cash receipt of £170 by L Stevens a debtor had been correctly entered in the cash book but no entry had been made in the debtors account.

4. A purchase of goods from A Chubb £95 was entered in the purchases and Chubb's account as £59.

5. A purchase of goods £90 from T Smith has been correctly entered in purchases but debited to Smith's account.

6. A sum of £13 petty cash had not been included in the bank and cash figures.

7. The sales day book had been undercast by £10.

Required:

(a) Prepare the suspense account making the appropriate entries therein to eliminate the balance;

(b) prepare a statement showing the correct net profit for the year; and

(c) draw up a corrected balance sheet as at 31 March 19X8.

(RSA Intermediate)

18.5 Farley Moore, a sole trader, extracted a Trial Balance from the books at the close of business on 31 May 19X6. This did not agree, so Moore posted the difference to a Suspense Account, and proceeded to prepare his Trading and Profit and Loss Accounts. These final accounts produced a net profit of £5,680 for the year ended 31 May 19X6.

During the following week, Moore checked the entries in his books, and discovered that the Trial Balance difference was due to the errors listed below:

1. A telephone bill of £125 had been paid by cheque, but had been posted to the Telephone Account as £152.

2. A Bad Debt of £96 had been cleared from M Hamm's account to close that account but the double entry had not been completed.

3. Discounts Allowed of £148 had been posted in error to the credit of Discounts Received.

4. The Sales Day Book total for the month of January, £3,820, had been posted to Sales Account as £5,820.

5. The Purchases Day book had been overcast by £300.

6. An Advertising bill of £560 had been paid in April but no entry had been made in the Advertising Account.

Required:

(a) Indicate how, and the extent to which, each of the above errors affected the Trial Balance. Your answers should take the form of the table on the following page.

Error	Debit Understated	Overstated	Credit Understated	Overstated
(1)				
(2)				
(3)				
(4)				
(5)				
(6)				

(b) Calculate the correct Net Profit, showing your workings.

(LCCI First Level 1988)

18.6 The trial balance as at 30 April 19X7 of Timber Products Limited was balanced by the inclusion of the following debit balance:

Difference on trial balance suspense account £2,513

Subsequent investigations revealed the following errors:

1. Discounts received of £324 in January 19X7 have been posted to the debit of the discounts allowed account.

2. Wages of £2,963 paid in February 19X7 have not been posted from the cash book.

3. A remittance of £940 received from K Mitcham in November 19X6 has been posted to the credit of B Mansell Limited.

4. In December 19X6, the company took advantage of an opportunity to purchase a large quantity of stationery at a bargain price of £2,000. No adjustments have been made in the accounts for the fact that three quarters, in value, of this stationery was in stock on 30 April 19X7.

5. A payment of £341 to J Winters in January 19X7 has been posted in the personal account as £143.

6. A remittance of £3,000 received from D North, a credit customer, in April 19X7 has been credit to Sales.

The draft accounts for the year ended 30 April 19X7 of Timber Products Limited show a net profit of £24,760.

Timber Products Limited has very few personal accounts and therefore does not maintain either a purchases ledger control account or a sales ledger control account.

Required:

(a) Prepare the difference on trial balance suspense account showing, where appropriate, the entries necessary to correct the accounting errors;

(b) prepare a computation of the corrected net profit for the year ended 30 April 19X7 following corrections for the above accounting errors; and

(c) outline the principal uses of trial balances.

(AAT Intermediate)

18.7 The firm of Hill and Son extracted a Trial Balance from its books on 30 June 19X6 and found that the credit side exceeded the debit side by £920. This difference was entered into a Suspense Account and the final accounts prepared.

The following mistakes were subsequently discovered:

1. Machinery repairs of £400 had been entered on the debit side of the Machinery Account.
2. Cash discount of £20 allowed by Elemes Ltd., a creditor, had not been entered in Elemes Ltd. Account.
3. The purchase of a computer for £3,200 had been entered in the Office Equipment Account as £2,300.
4. The Sales Day Book had been undercast by £100.
5. Loan interest charged by the bank, £600, had been entered in the Bank Account but not posted to the interest on Loan Account.
6. £250 received for the sale of an old office desk had been debited in the Cash Book and also debited to the Office Equipment Account.

Required:

(a) Draft the Journal entries required to correct these errors (ignore depreciation);
(b) write up the Suspense Account; and
(c) prepare a table similar to the one shown below indicating the effect of the correction of the above errors on Assets and Profit:

	ASSETS	PROFIT
1.		
2.		
3.		
4.		
5.		
6.		

(LCCI 2nd Level 1988)

18.8 Pender has presented you with his profit and loss account for the year to 30 June 19X5. The account shows a net profit of £45,700. Upon investigating his books of account, however, you discover the following apparent errors and omissions:

1. Pender's personal drawings for the year amounting £10,000 have been charged against profit.
2. A motor car costing £5,000 had been included in purchases.
3. £400 paid in advance for insurance at 30 June 19X5 had not been deducted from the insurance charge for the year to 30 June 19X5.
4. At 30 June 19X5 it had become known that a customer had gone into liquidation owing Pender £3,000. This debt was totally irrecoverable.
5. Pender had forgotten that he owed £600 for various motoring expenses for the year to 340 June 19X5.
6. The closing stock at 30 June 19X5 had been underestimated by £3,000.
7. Additional capital of £7,000 introduced by Pender during the year had been included in sales.

8. The depreciation charge for furniture and fittings for the year to 30 June 19X5 amounting to £1,600 had been omitted from the profit and loss account.

9. The accumulated depreciation on buildings at 30 June 19X4 amounted to £6,000 and to £8,000 as at 30 June 19X5. Pender had incorrectly charged the total accumulated depreciation on buildings as at 30 June 19X5 to the profit and loss account for that year instead of just the year's depreciation charge.

10. Discounts allowed for £1,000 had been credited to the profit and loss account and discounts received of £700 had been debited to it.

11. Outstanding trade debtors at 30 June 19X5 amounting to £50,000 (including the bad debt detailed in 4. above). Pender had forgotten to amend the provision for bad debts account which stood at £2,050 as at 30 June 19X4. His policy is to set aside a provision for bad debts amounting to 5% of outstanding trade debtors as at the end of each year.

12. Pender had had some unquoted investments revalued. These investments had been revalued at £4,000 in excess of their original cost. The £4,000 had not been credited to his profit and loss account for the year to 30 June 19X5.

Required:

Prepare a schedule with supporting narrative correcting Pender's net profit for the year to 30 June 19X5.

{AAT Level 2, amended)

18.9 Jepsal Ltd. reports the last three years net profits as:

19X8 £36,000: 19X9 £15,000: 19X0 £25,000

On January 19X1 whilst reviewing the books for 19X1, but after the previous years accounts have been published, you ascertain that the following errors had been made in earlier years.

	19X8	19X9	19X0
Overstatement of stock valuation	£3,200	£6,800	£3,600
Overstatement of accrued interest income	500	-	300
Understatement of accrued advertising	500	1,200	600
Omission of depreciation on certain items still in use	1,800	1,200	1,200

Required:

Tabulate the various corrections and state the corrected net profits for each of the three years.

(AAT/IAS Part 2)

COMMON ERRORS

1. Knowledge of Double-Entry Book-Keeping

Examiners frequently set ERROR CORRECTION questions, as they are a good test of a candidate's understanding of double-entry book-keeping. Such questions require the candidate to find and correct the errors made in a set of accounts.

You will have difficulty doing this type of question if you are unsure of the rules of double-entry book-keeping. Make sure that you have a thorough grasp of them.

2. Approach

In order to tackle error correction questions, examine the following points most carefully:

(a) check that the opening balances have been brought down correctly (especially if the bank account balance is a credit)

(b) check that the correct balances have been extracted.

(c) check that the entries (or balances) have been entered on the correct side of each account, and that this has been followed through to the trial balance or the final accounts.

(d) check your arithmetic most carefully.

19 INCOMPLETE RECORDS

MAIN POINTS

1. Background

Not all entities keep a full set of double-entry books. Indeed, some entities keep few, if any, detailed accounting records. In such situations, accountants have to construct a profit and loss account and a balance sheet from some extremely inadequate information.

2. Construction of the Accounts

It is possible to construct a set of final accounts by taking details of cash and bank transactions, and converting them on to an accruals' basis.

This may be quite a difficult exercise, especially if the entity does not operate a bank account. There may be a few records of cash transactions. and it would be unusual to find a proprietor who could remember details of all cash transactions for an entire financial year.

3. Statement of Affairs

A statement of affairs is simply a listing of all the entity's assets and liabilities at a certain point in time, the net amount being the equivalent of the proprietor's capital.

The accounting profit for a particular accounting period may be calculated by preparing a statement of affairs at the beginning of the period, and one at the end of the period.

The difference between the two net amounts will be the estimated profit for the year (although an allowance has to be made for any new capital introduced, or for any drawings made during the period).

4. Major Adjustments

		£	£
(a)	Sales		
	Cash received during the period		X
	Add: Closing debtors		X
			X
	Less: Opening debtors		X
	Sales revenue for the period		£X

149

		£	£
(b)	Purchases		
	Cash paid during the period		X
	Add: Closing creditors		X
			X
	Less: Opening creditors		X
	Purchases for the period		£X
(c)	Incomes		
	Cash received during the period		X
	Add: Opening amounts received in advance		X
	Closing amounts due to be received		X
			X
	Less: Opening amounts due to be received	X	
	Closing amounts received in advance	X	X
	Income for period		£X
(d)	Expenditure		
	Cash paid during the period		X
	Add: Opening prepayments		X
	Closing accruals		X
			X
	Less: Opening accruals	X	
	Closing prepayments	X	X
	Expenditure for the period		£X

Example 1. Frank Emery is a sole trader who does not operate the double entry system of book-keeping. His records are accurate, however, and from them the following information has been obtained.

	31 May 19X4 £	31 May 19X5 £
Stock	1,970	2,140
Debtors	2,330	2,790
Delivery van (Estimated value)	900	800
Creditors	1,660	1,720
Cash at Bank		740
Bank overdraft	390	

During the year ended 31 May 19X5 his drawings have been: Cash £1,250, Goods at cost price £110.

Required:

   (a) Showing your calculations in each case:

      (i) Calculate Emery's Capital at 31 May 19X4 and 31 May 19X5;

      (ii) Calculate Emery's Net Profit for the year ended 31 May 19X5; and

   (b) draw up Emery's Capital Account for the year ended 31 May 19X5 as it would appear under the double entry system.

(LCCI Elementary 1985)

Solution :

FRANK EMERY

(a) (i) Calculation of capital at 31 May 19X4 :

		£	£
Stock			1,970
Debtors			2,330
Delivery Van			900
			5,200
Less:	Creditors	1,660	
	Bank overdraft	390	2,050
Capital at 31 May 19X4			£3,150

(ii) Calculation of net profit for the year to 31 May 19X5 :

Capital at 31 May 19X5 :

	£	£
Stock		2,140
Debtors		2,790
Delivery van		800
Cash at bank		740
		6,470
Less: Creditors		1,720
		£4, 750
Capital at 1 June 19X4		3,150
Add : Net profit (by deduction)	2,960	
Less : Drawings (£1,250+110)	1,360	1,600
Capital at 31 May 19X5		£4,750

(b)

Capital Account

		£			£
31 5 X6	Drawings (cash)	1,250	1 6 X4	Balance b/d	3,150
31 5 X6	Drawings (goods)	110	31 5 X5	Net Profit	2,960
31 5 X6	Balance c/d	4,750			
		£6,110			£6,110
			1 6 X5	Balance b/d	4,750

Example 2.   D Alexander has operated his small business for a number of years without keeping full and complete records. He now decides that it would be beneficial to keep a double entry system, therefore on 1 April 19X8 he establishes the following balances from the records which he had kept.

Premises (freehold) £16,000; Vehicles £3,700; Stock £2,900; Fixtures £900; Cash £2,700; Bank overdraft £1,300;
Debtors: C Andrew £250, M Cox £50, C Woods £180;
20% of next year's insurance premium of £200 has been prepaid.
Creditors: P Bailey £750, J Fagan £1,200
25% of last year's £800 rates bill is still outstanding.

Unfortunately D Alexander has not taken particular care with his records and a number of corrections are required. These are as follows:

April 3   £90 of fixtures have been incorrectly included in the stock valuation

April 6   M Cox has been declared bankrupt and 60% of the account should be written off as a bad debt immediately.

April 8   The purchase of a machine on credit at 20% below its usual price of £600 from J Fagan has been completely omitted.

April 9   C Andrews' account has been shown in full, and should be adjusted to provide for the 10% trade discount which is normally allowed on all sales.

Required:

(a) Draft the journal entry necessary to open the books of account, and to calculate the owner's capital on 1 April 19X8; and

(b) prepare the journal entries in respect of the above errors which were discovered on the dates shown.

NB Ignore VAT in all instances.

(RSA Elementary, adapted)

Solution :

(a)

D ALEXANDER
Journal

				Dr £	Cr £
1 4 X8	Freehold premises		Dr	16,000	
	Vehicles		Dr	3,700	
	Fixtures		Dr	900	
	Stock		Dr	2,900	
	Debtors:	C Andrew	Dr	250	
		M Cox	Dr	50	
		C Woods	Dr	180	
	Insurance:	Prepayment	Dr	40	
	Cash/Bank overdraft		Dr	2,700	1,300
	To creditors:	P Bailey			750
		J Fagan			1,200
	To Rates:	accrual			200
	To Capital (balances)				23,270
				£26,720	£26,720

Being the entries necessary to open a double entry system of accounting

(b)

3 4 X8	Fixtures	Dr	90	
	To: Stock			90

Being incorrect entry of fixtures in stock

6 4 X8	Bad debts	Dr	30	
	To: M Cox			30

Being write-off of 60% of Cox's debt on being declared bankrupt

8 4 X8	Machine	Dr	480	
	To: J Fagan			480

Being the correction of item omitted from the original balances, machine purchased on credit from Fagan

9 4 X8	Capital	Dr	25	
	To: C Andrews			25

Being correction of amount owing from Andrews, 10% trade discount having not previously been deducted

TUTORIAL NOTE

	£	£
Capital at 1 April 19X8 as calculated in (a) above		23,270
Less: the following adjustments		
Reduction in closing stock	90	
Bad debt	30	
Trade discount	25	145
		£23,125

EXERCISES

19.1 Frank Bridgeman commenced in business as a painter and decorator on 1 April 19X6. He failed to keep a proper double entry record of his activities. You are however able to ascertain the following information at the conclusion of his first year's trading.

Summarised Bank Transactions

Bankings:	£	Cheques Drawn:	£
Capital introduced	500	Materials	2,940
Cheques from customers	12,310	Equipment	411
Cash from customers	915	Advertising	180
		Drawings	8,420
		Motor Van	1,500
		Balance	274
	£13,725		£13,725

Valuations are:

	1 April 19X6	31 March 19X7
	£	£
Equipment	150	380
Motor Van	-	1,350
Stock of materials	-	80

Required:

    (a) Prepare a statement of affairs for Bridgman:

        (i)   as at 1 April 19X6

        (ii) as at 31 March 19X7

        From a comparison of his capital at each date, adjusted as necessary, determine his NET profit for the year ended 31 March 19X7; and

    (b) prepare a Trading and Profit and Loss Account for Bridgman for the year ended 31 March 19X7.

(LCCI Elementary 1987)

19.2   P Green had been in business for several years and had not kept proper records. His new financial year began on 1 May 19X7 and he decides to convert his account to a full double entry system and ascertains the following balances from his personal records:

    Freehold Premises £32,000; Motor Van £2,600; Fixtures £1,800; Stock £6,400; Bank and Cash £2,965; Debtors - T Ross £90; A Baker £64; T Bone £128; Long Term Loan at 10% per annum £10,000; Trade Creditors - T Black £271; D Bacon £194; Rates Prepaid £42; Interest on loan outstanding £1,000.

Required:

    (a) Draft the journal entry necessary to open the books showing therein the proprietor's capital; and

    (b) prepare journal entries in respect of the following: (NB. Suitable narrations must be given in all cases).

			£
May 6	Purchased on credit fixtures from Micawber and Sons		950
8	Returned some of the fittings as unsuitable to Micawber & Sons		60
12	Green was notified that Baker had been declared bankrupt. The account was written off as a bad debt		64
22	Some of the fixtures which had been purchased from Micawber cost price £90 were found to be surplus to requirements and were sold to Gatt & Co. on credit		90
29	Correct an error in posting. T Davis had been debited in error instead of T Davies		130

(RSA Elementary)

19.3   On 1 January 19X4, John Walters of Hanley commenced business, as an electrical contractor. He borrowed £1,000 from Lloyds Bank, Stoke-on-Trent, and used his car (value £1,500) and garage (value £500) for business purposes. He did most of his work for cash and purchased most of his materials on credit. Initially he drew £50 a week from his cash receipts but, as business improved, he increased this to £70 after twenty-six weeks. At the end of the year he prepared a list of assets and liabilities as at 31 December 19X4 as follows:

	£
Stock in trade at cost	5,200
Trade debtors	420
Garage at valuation	400
Bank overdraft	1,520
Prepaid expenses	80
Trade creditors	2,150
Motor car at valuation	1,000
Cash in hand	105
Creditors for general expenses	145

In December 19X4, he paid £400 as a deposit on the hire purchase under a one year agreement of a delivery van (list price £2,000). He ascertained that he had used £500 worth of the materials purchased for work done on his home.

Required:

   (a) Prepare a Statement of Affairs as at 31 December 19X4;

   (b) from a comparison of the capital arrived at in (a) and the opening capital at 1 January 19X4, state the 'profit' for the year ended 31 December 19X4; and

   (c) calculate Walter's working Capital as at 31 December 19X4.

(LCCI Intermediate)

19.4 A Day runs a retail food store but does not keep proper accounts. A summary of his bank account for the year ended 31 October 19X7 was as follows:

Receipts	£
Balance in hand 1 November 19X6	2,085
Cash Sales	31,630
Legacy paid into business	400
Payments	
Trade creditors (goods for resale)	29,600
Purchase of fittings and fixtures	250
Rates	600
Light and Heat	290
Sundry expenses	120

The following information is also available:

   1. All takings have been paid into the bank with the exception of £100 per week which Day has withdrawn for private purposes and £50 per week which he pays a part-time assistant.

   2. Day's assets and liabilities (other than his bank balance) on the 1 November 19X6 were as follows:
       Premises £35,000, Fixtures and Fittings £2,750, Vehicle £6,000, Sundry expenses accrued £25, Stock £1,500, Creditors £900.

   3. On 31 October 19X7 Day's stock in hand was valued at £1,800 and his creditors were £750. There is an electricity bill of £90 outstanding, and rates have been prepaid by £50.

   4. Fixed assets have been purchased as per bank account and depreciation is to be written off as follows:
       Fittings and fixtures 10% of the book value at 31 October 19X7;
       Motor vehicles 25% of the book value at 31 October 19X7.

   5. During the year Day has taken goods costing £750 for his own use. No payment has been made for these goods.

Required:

Prepare Day's trading and profit and loss account for the year ended 31 October 19X7 and a balance sheet as at that date. *(RSA Intermediate)*

19.5 Jean Smith, who retails wooden ornaments, has been so busy since she commenced business on 1 April 19X5 that she has neglected to keep adequate accounting records. Jean's opening capital consisted of her life savings of £15,000 which she used to open a business bank account. The transactions in this bank account during the year ended 31 March 19X6 have been summarised from the bank account as follows:

	£
Receipts	
Loan from John Peacock, uncle	10,000
Takings	42,000
Payments	
Purchases of goods for resale	26,400
Electricity for period to 31 December 19X5	760
Rent of premises for 15 months to 30 June 19X6	3,500
Rates of premises for the year ended 31 March 19X6	1,200
Wages of assistants	14,700
Purchase of van, 1 October 19X5	7,600
Purchase of holiday caravan for Jean Smith's private use	8,500
Van licence and insurance, payments covering a year	250

According to the bank account, the balance in hand on 31 March 19X6 was £4,090 in Jean Smith's favour.

Whilst the intention was to bank all takings intact, it now transpires that, in addition to cash drawings, the following payments were made out of takings before bankings:

	£
Van running expenses	890
Postages, stationery and other sundry expenses	355

On 31 March 19X6, takings of £640 awaited banking: this was done on 1 April 19X6. It has been discovered that amounts paid into the bank of £340 on 29 March 19X6 were not credited to Jean's bank account until 2 April 19X6 and a cheque of £120, drawn on 28 March 19X6 for purchases was not paid until 10 April 19X6. The normal rate of gross profit on the goods sold by Jean Smith is 50% on sales. However, during the year a purchase of ornamental gold fish costing £600 proved to be unpopular with customers and therefore the entire stock bought had to be sold at cost price.

Interest at the rate of 5% per annum is payable on each anniversary of the loan from John Peacock on 1 January 19X6.

Depreciation is to be provided on the van on the straight line basis; it is estimated that the van will be disposed of after five year's use for £100.

The stock of goods for resale at 31 March 19X6 has been valued at cost of £1,900.

Creditors for purchases at 31 March 19X6 amounted to £880 and electricity charges accrued due at that date were £180.

Trade debtors at 31 March 19X6 totalled £2,300.

Required:

Prepare a trading and profit and loss account for the year ended 31 March 19X6 and a balance sheet as at that date.

(AAT Intermediate)

19.6 On 31 December 19X5, the Balance Sheet of Mark Tapster, a sole trader, was as follows:

	£	£
Capital		107,340
Current Liabilities		
Trade creditors	16,900	
Bank overdraft	7,800	24,700
		£132,040

Fixed Assets:	Cost	Accumulated Depreciation	Net
	£	£	£
Freehold premises	65,000	-	65,000
Fixtures and fittings	4,500	1,500	3,000
Motor vehicle	7,500	2,000	5,500
	77,000	3,500	73,500

Current Assets:		
Stock		34,100
Trade debtors		24,160
Cash in hand		280	58,540
		£132,040

A year later, with a view to preparing accounting statements, Mark noted the following information:

1. During the year, he had withdrawn from the business for private use goods and cash amounting to £8,300.

2. On 3 May he had acquired some additional fittings for the business at a cost of £500.

3. The following valuations applied as at 31 December 19X6:

	£
Stock	32,300
Trade debtors	21,260
Trade creditors	15,400
Cash in hand	170

In addition, he had managed to eliminate the bank overdraft and now had a debit balance in his Bank Account of £4,340.

4. Depreciation was to be calculated as follows:

Fixtures and fittings - 20% per annum on cost price.
Motor vehicle - 33 1/3% per annum on cost price

Depreciation is allowed for each complete six months of the accounting year that any asset is owned.

5. The amount of the overhead expenses for the year, exclusive of depreciation, was £19,200.

It was his practice to add 331/3% to the cost price of goods to arrive at the selling price.

Required:

(a) Prepare the Balance Sheet as at 31 December 19X6 and then derive the Net Profit for 19X6;

(b) show in a brief statement the change in Working Capital between the two years; and

(c) draft the Trading and Profit and Loss Account for 19X6.

(LCCI 2nd Level 1988)

COMMON ERRORS

1. Adjustments for Opening and Closing Balances

An incomplete record's question is a severe test of your understanding of the accruals' concept (that is why the Examiner sets such questions).

Make sure that you take the cash received and cash paid during the accounting period and that you have made the correct additions and subtractions for opening and closing creditors, debtors, accruals and prepayments.

2. Opening Capital

Opening capital (if not given) = opening assets - opening liabilities

3. Cash Account

Not all of the cash will necessarily be accounted for, and you may have to insert a balancing figure. If this is the case, maker absolutely certain that you have taken ALL of the cash receipts and ALL of the cash payments into account before inserting a balancing figure.

An incorrect balancing figure can cause great problems in trying to get the balance sheet to balance.

4. Double Entry Problems

If you have difficulty preparing incomplete records' questions, it is probably because your understanding of double-entry book-keeping is weak.

Check once again the adjustments that you have made for accruals and prepayments.

PART 2

SPECIAL TYPES OF ACCOUNT

20 DEPARTMENTAL ACCOUNTS

MAIN POINTS

1. Background

Those entities that have separate identifiable departments may require to have information about the financial results of each department.

This can be achieved by analysing the trading, and profit and loss accounts on a departmental basis. The balance sheet would normally be prepared for the business as a whole.

2. Purpose

(a) To control each section of the business more efficiently. One method of achieving close control is to issue goods to each department at SELLING price

(b) To identify, either:

   (i) the contribution to profit which each section of the business makes; or

   (ii) to calculate departmental profit or loss.

3. Format

Departmental accounts may be prepared on a columnar basis, each column representing an identifiable department within the business. It would also be usual to have a total column for the business as a whole.

4. Apportionment of Expenditure

It will usually be relatively easy to identify some expenses with respective departments. This is known as DIRECT expenditure.

If the entity wishes to calculate departmental profit or loss, an apportionment of expenditure will be needed. Such expenditure is known as INDIRECT expenditure.

Rent and rates, for example, may be apportioned on the basis of floor space occupied, and supervisory wages on the basis of number of staff working in different department.

It should be noted that if some expenses have to be apportioned, individual departmental managers have little control over such expenses, and therefore they can hardly be held responsible for OVERALL departmental profit or loss.

5. Apportionment of Incomes

If individual departmental profitability is to be measured, it may also be necessary to apportion some incomes. Incomes, however, do not usually relate very closely to any particular department, and so such an exercise is not particularly meaningful.

6. Contribution

Since the apportionment of income and expenses is an arbitrary exercise, and as departmental managers are not able to control such apportionments, some entities prepare departmental accounts on the basis of the CONTRIBUTION that each department makes to the overall profit or loss of the entity.

Contribution is the difference between sales revenue and the VARIABLE cost of such sales. Variable cost is the cost that would have been avoided if the sales had not been made. Most direct costs are also variable costs.

Example. Sing operates a retail shop in a rural village. The shop has two main departments: bakery (B) and general (G). The following details relate to the financial year ending 31 December 19X2:

		£
Delivery Van expenses		1,500
Insurance, rates, rent and telephone expenses		8,500
Lighting and heating		2,000
Office expenses		800
Purchases:	Department B	72,000
	Department G	78,000
Salaries		9,000
Sales:	Department B	150,000
	Department G	100,000
Stock at 1 January 19X2:	Department B	15,000
	Department G	6,000
Stock at 31 December 19X2	Department B	12,000
	Department G	4,000
Wages:	Department B	15,000
	Department G	16,000

Additional information:

1. Sing owed a delivery van which had cost £12,000. This is to be depreciated on a straight line basis assuming no residual value at a rate of 25% on cost.

2. Indirect costs are to be apportioned as follows:

	Bakery	General
	%	%
Delivery van expenses and depreciation	90	10
Insurance, rates, rent and telephone expenses	25	75
Lighting and heating	45	55
Office expenses	50	50
Salaries	60	40

Required:

Prepare Sing's trading and profit and loss account in columnar format (for each department and for the business as a whole) for the year to 31 December 19X2.

Solution :

Sing
Trading, profit and loss account
for the year to 31 December 19X2

Department	B £	G £	Total £
Sales	150,000	100,000	250,000
Less: Cost of goods sold			
Opening stock	15,000	6,000	21,000
Purchases	72,000	78,000	150,000
	87,000	84,000	171,000
Less: Closing stock	12,000	4,000	16,000
	75,000	80,000	155,000
GROSS PROFIT	75,000	20,000	95,000
Wages	15,000	16,000	31,000
CONTRIBUTION	60,000	4,000	64,000
Less: Indirect expenses			
Delivery van expenses (90:10)	1,350	150	1,500
Delivery van depreciation (25% x £12,000 x 90:10)	2,700	300	3,000
Insurance, rates, rent and telephone (25:75)	2,125	6,375	8,500
Lighting and heating (45:55)	900	1,100	2,000
Office expenses (50:50)	400	400	800
Salaries (60:40)	5,400	3,600	9,000
	12,875	11,925	24,800
NET PROFIT FOR THE YEAR	£47,125	£(7,925)	£39,200

EXERCISES

20.1 Landsdown Brothers is a family owned store. On the ground floor (Floor A), general household goods are sold, including linens, tableware, glassware etc., whilst on the second floor (Floor B) all the space is allocated to the sale of furniture.

Except for one week in the year when prices are reduced for the annual sale, prices are always determined by adding 25% to the purchase cost.

You are able to determine the following information:

	Floor	£000
Stocks 1 April 19X5	A	32
	B	54
For the year ended 31 March 19X6:		
Sales	A	294
	B	327

	Floor	£000
Purchases	A	253
	B	274
Wagers of sales assistants	A	29
	B	15

A physical stocktaking of goods in hand, taken on 31 March 19X6 and valued at purchase cost, showed:

	Floor	£000
	A	42
	B	60

The following costs were also incurred in the year ended 31 March 19X6:

	£000
Rates and insurance	10
Delivery costs	10
Administration costs	16
Heating and lighting	6

These costs should be apportioned as follows:

	Floor A	Floor B
Delivery costs	10%	90%
Rates and insurance	40%	60%
Other items	50%	50%

Required:

(a) Prepare a departmental Trading and Profit and Loss Account in columnar form for Landsdown Brothers for the year ended 31 March 19X6; and

(b) calculate the gross profit as a percentage (%) on cost of sales for each department

(LCCI Intermediate 1986)

20.2 Food and Clothing Supplies Ltd., Goldenhill, carried on business in two departments, Food (F) and Clothing (C). Separate accounts were kept for each department. The company had an Authorised Capital of £200,000 of which 50,000 Ordinary Shares of £1 each (out of 100,000) and 100,000 8 per cent Cumulative Preference Shares of £1 each had been issued and fully paid. The financial year ended on 31 December 19X4, when the following balances appeared on the accounts stated:

	£
Advertising	8,500
Discount received	500
Salaries and wages (C)	20,400
Salaries and wages (F)	19,000
Director's Fees	14,500
Motor vans at cost	20,000
Provision for depreciation on motor vans	8,000
Trade creditors	29,400
Motor vehicle expenses	4,800
Cash in hand	19,300
Goodwill	30,000
Rent and Rates	13,800

	£
Heating and Lighting (F)	7,300
Heating and Lighting (C)	8,900
Furniture and Fittings at Cost	30,000
Provision for deprecation on Furniture and Fittings	9,000
Trade debtors	54,000
Profit and Loss Cr balance 1 1 X4	6,600

Additionally:

1. The gross profit for 19X4 was Clothing Department (C) £64,000. Food Department (F) £57,000.

2. All expenses not designated (C) or (F) except Rent and Rates should be divided 40% Clothing (C) and 60% Food (F). Rent and Rates should be divided one-third Clothing (C) and two-thirds Food (F).

3. Provide £1,200 for one quarter's rent accrued due and unpaid.

4. Provide for one year's depreciation on motor vans (20% per annum on cost) and Furniture and Fittings (10% per annum on cost).

Required:

Prepare:

(a) A Profit and Loss Account for the year 19X4 in columnar form to show separately the profit or loss of each department.

Note: An Appropriation Account is NOT required.

(b) The 'Liabilities' side only of the Balance Sheet as at 31 December 19X4.

(LCCI Intermediate 1985)

20.3 Rose owns a retail outlet which is divided into two separate departments: Department B and Department S.

The following trial balance has been extracted from the books of account as at 31 March 19X3:

	Dr £	Cr £
Capital (at 1 April 19X2)		6,500
Cash at bank and in hand	4,000	
Creditors: Department B		10,000
Department S		7,000
Debtors: Department B	3,750	
Department S	11,250	
Drawings	12,000	
Furniture and Fixtures: at cost	15,000	
: accumulated depreciation (at 1 April 19X2)		7,500
General shop expenses	10,500	
Purchases: Department B	61,000	
Department S	86,000	
Rent and rates	12,500	
Sales: Department B		90,000
Department S		135,000

		Dr £	Cr £
Stock at 1 April 19X2:	Department B	7,000	
	Department S	8,000	
Wages:	Department B	11,000	
	Department S	14,000	
		£256,000	£256,000

Additional Information:

1. Rent owing at 31 March 19X3 amounted to £2,500.
2. Insurance paid in advance at 31 March 19X3 amounted to £500.
3. Stock at 31 March 19X3 was valued at £8,000 for Department B and £4,000 for Department S.
4. Depreciation is to be charged on furniture and fittings at a rate of 10% on cost.
5. Indirect expenses are to be apportioned as follows:

	Department B %	Department S %
Depreciation on furniture and fittings	20	80
General shop expenses	60	40
Rent and rates	75	25

Required:

Prepare Rose's departmental trading, profit and loss accounts (for each department and for the business as a whole) in columnar format for the year to 31 March 19X3, and a balance sheet as at that date (for the business as a whole).

COMMON ERRORS

1. Apportionment of Income and Expenditure

The examiner should provide you with the information necessary to apportion income and expenditure between departments. Make sure that you calculate the apportionment correctly.

If no detail is given, then you will only be expected to prepare departmental accounts on a CONTRIBUTION basis.

Indirect expenditure and other incomes will be dealt with in the overall profit and loss account

2. Inter-Departmental Transfers

Be on the look-out for any transfers between departments. If goods are issued from a central purchasing department at selling price, make sure that the inter-departmental transfers are also at selling price.

The trading, and profit and loss accounts for the business as a whole should not, of course, include any INTERNAL PROFIT.

21

MANUFACTURING ACCOUNTS

MAIN POINTS

1. Background

Instead of buying finished goods, many entities manufacture their own. This may involve purchasing raw materials and components, and incurring labour and other costs in converting the raw materials into a finished goods state.

In order to establish the cost of manufacturing its own goods, the entity will need to prepare a MANUFACTURING account.

2. Procedure

A manufacturing account will normally be prepared at the end of a financial accounting period. At that stage, both the DIRECT and INDIRECT expenditure associated with the manufacturing process will be transferred out of the individual expenditure accounts and DEBITED to the manufacturing account. Note that it is rare to find any incomes appearing in a manufacturing account.

When the manufacturing account has been prepared, the balance on the account is then transferred to the TRADING ACCOUNT.

The order of presentation of the final account is as follows:

> Manufacturing account
> Trading account
> Profit and loss account
> Profit and loss appropriation account (if a partnership or a company)
> Balance sheet.

3. Format

A VERTICAL manufacturing account may be presented in the following format:

	£	£
DIRECT MATERIALS		
Opening stock		X
Purchases		X
		X
Less: Closing stock		X
Direct Material consumed		X
DIRECT LABOUR		X
DIRECT EXPENSES		

167

	£	£
X	X	
X	X	
	—	X
Prime cost		X
Manufacturing overhead		
X	X	
X	X	
	—	X
Total manufacturing overhead incurred		X
Add: Opening work in progress		X
		X
Less: Closing work in progress		X
Manufacturing cost of goods produced		X
Manufacturing profit		X
MARKET VALUE OF GOODS PRODUCED		£X

4. Definitions

(a) Direct expenses: those expenses that are easily identified with a particular process, product, department or service.

(b) Indirect expenses: those expenses that are not easily and readily identifiable with a particular process, product, department or service.

(Note that indirect expenses may need to be APPORTIONED so that the manufacturing account receives a fair share of the total cost of such expenses).

(c) Overheads: the total of indirect costs. Overheads may be classified into administration, manufacturing, selling and distribution, and research and development overhead.

(d) Work in progress: goods in process of manufacture requiring further work to be done on them.

5. Manufacturing Profit

Instead of transferring the manufacturing COST of finished goods to the trading account, some entities add an amount for profit. This enables the entity to compare more fairly the internal manufacturing cost with the cost of purchasing the goods from an outside supplier.

The double-entry procedure is as follows:

    Dr   Manufacturing account
    Cr   Profit and loss account
    With the profit.

Note that the profit is purely a book entry: the credit in the profit and loss account contras with the debit entry in the manufacturing account.

Example.   Alan Jones owns and manages a small manufacturing business. Shown as follows are the balances that have been extracted from his books of account as at 31 March 19X2:

	£ Dr	£ Cr
Administration expenses	18,795	
Advertising	1,500	
Bank and Cash in Hand	675	
Capital (as at 1 April 19X1)		6,390
Creditors		10,750
Debtors	11,500	
Drawings	7,500	
Factory Direct Wages	8,500	
Factory Indirect Wages	2,000	
Factory Power	4,500	
Furniture and Fittings (all office)	2,300	
Heat and Light	2,000	
Plant and Equipment	34,600	
Plant Hire	500	
Provision for Bad Debts		400
Provision for Depreciation (at 1 April 19X1):		
Furniture and Fittings		1,150
Plant and Equipment		17,300
Raw Material Purchases	28,500	
Rent and Rates	2,500	
Sales		103,680
Selling and Distribution Expenses	8,300	
Stocks at cost (at 1 April 19X1):		
Raw materials	1,000	
Work in Progress	2,000	
Finished Goods	3,000	
	£139,670	£139,670

The following additional information has also been obtained:

1. Expenditure on Heat and Light, and Rent and Rates is to be apportioned between the factory and the office in the ratio of 9 to 1, and 3 to 2 respectively.

2. Accruals at 31 March 19X2 were:

	£
Factory Power	200
Rent and Rates	500

There was also a prepayment of £100 for salesmen's car insurance. None of these items had been included in the list of balances shown above.

3. Stocks at 31 March 19X2 were valued at cost as follows:

	£
Raw Materials	1,900
Work in progress	3,800
Finished Goods	5,700

4. Depreciation is to be charged on Plant and Equipment at a rate of 50% per annum using the reducing balance method, and at a rate of 10% per annum on Furniture and Fittings using the straight-line method of depreciation.

5. The provision for Bad Debts is to be made equal to 5% of Debtors outstanding at 31 March 19X2.

Required:
Prepare Jones' Manufacturing, Trading and Profit and Loss Account for the year to 31 March 19X2, and a Balance Sheet as at that date.   *(AAT/IAS Part 1)*

Solution :

ALAN JONES
Manufacturing, Trading and Profit and Loss Account for the year
to 31 March 19X2

	£	£
Direct Materials		
Raw Materials at 1 April 19X1	1,000	
Purchases	28,500	
	29,500	
Less: Raw Materials at 31 March 19X2	1,900	
Direct Materials consumed	27,600	
Direct Factory Wages	8,500	
Prime Cost		36,100
Overhead:		
Depreciation: Plant and Equipment	8,650	
Heat and Light (£2,000 x 90%)	1,800	
Indirect Wages	2,000	
Plant Hire	500	
Power (£4,500+200)	4,700	
Rent and Rates ((£2,500+500)x60%)	1,800	19,450
Total Factory overhead		55,550
Add: Opening Stock of Work in Progress		2,000
		57,550
Less: Closing Stock of Work in Progress		3,800
MANUFACTURING COST OF GOODS PRODUCED		£53,750
Sales		103,680
Less: Cost of goods sold		
Finished goods at 1 April 19X1	3,000	
Manufacturing cost of goods produced	53,750	
	56,750	
Less: Finished goods at 31 March 19X2	5,700	51,050
GROSS PROFIT		52,630
Less: Other Expenses		
Administration	18,795	
Advertising	1,500	
Depreciation: Furniture and Fittings	230	
Heat and Light (£2,000 x 10%)	200	
Increase in Provision for Bad Debts [(£11,500x5%)-400]	175	
Rent and Rates [(£2,500+500x40%]	1,200	
Selling and Distribution (£8,300-100)	8,200	30,300
NET PROFIT		£22,330

ALAN JONES
Balance Sheet at 31 March 19X2

Fixed Assets	£ Cost	£ Accumulated Depreciation	£ Net Book Value
Plant and Equipment	34,600	25,950	8,650
Furniture and Fittings	2,300	1,380	920
	£36,900	£27,330	9,570
Current Assets			
Stocks at cost:			
Raw Materials	1,900		
Work in Progress	3,800		
Finished Goods	5,700	11,400	
Debtors	11,500		
Less: Provision for Bad Debts	575	10,925	
Prepayment		100	
Bank and Cash in Hand		675	
		23,100	
Less: Current Liabilities			
Creditors	10,750		
Accruals	700	11,450	11,650
			£21,220
Capital			6,390
Net profit for the year		22,330	
Less: Drawings		7,500	14,830
			£21,220

EXERCISES

21.1 The following were some of the ledger balances in the books of Oven to Oven Ware Ltd., Stoke-on-Trent, on 31 December 19X7.

	£
Work in Progress 1 January 19X7	34,000
Stock of Finished Goods 1 January 19X7	31,600
Raw Materials Stocks 1 January 19X7	23,000
Bank Overdraft	15,000
Provisions for Depreciation :	
Leasehold Buildings	12,000
Plant and Machinery	28,700
Fixtures and Fittings	2,800
Repairs to Buildings	4,800
Carriage Outwards	7,300
Materials Purchases	125,300
Factory Rates	7,900
Direct Wages	110,000

	£
Sales	478,000
Leasehold Buildings at Cost	60,000
Factory Power	9,900
Plant and Machinery at Cost	75,200
Indirect Wages	97,300
Directors' Fees	3,500
Returns Inwards	2,000
Carriage Inwards	6,800
Reserved for Increased Replacement Costs of Fixed Assets	15,000

Notes:

(i) The factory buildings are held on a 30 years lease.

(ii) Stocks at 31 December 19X7 were:

Raw Materials £26,000; Work in Progress £36,000; Finished Goods £29,000.

(iii) Depreciate Plant and Machinery at 12-1/2% using the straight line method and Fixtures and Fittings at 10% using the reducing balance method.

(iv) The factory production was charged to the finished goods warehouse at a standard cost of £380,000.

Required:

Prepare a Manufacturing Account for Oven to Oven Ware Ltd for the year ended 31 December 19X7, selecting from the list of balances only those you will require for this purpose.

(LCCI Intermediate 1987)

21.2 The following balances as at 31 December 19X5 have been extracted from the books of William Speed, a small manufacturer:

		£
Stocks at 1 January 19X5:	Raw materials	7,000
	Work in progress	5,000
	Finished goods	6,900
Purchases of raw materials		38,000
Direct labour		28,000
Factory overheads:	Variable	16,000
	Fixed	9,000
Administrative expenses:	Rent and rates	19,000
	Heat and Light	6,000
	Stationery and postages	2,000
	Staff salaries	19,380
Sales		192,000
Plant and machinery:	At cost	30,000
	Provision for depreciation	12,000
Motor vehicles (for sales deliveries)		
	At cost	16,000
	Provision for depreciation	4,000
Creditors		5,500

	£
Debtors	28,000
Drawings	11,500
Balance at Bank	16,600
Capital at 1 January 19X5	48,000
Provision for unrealised profit at 1 January 19X5	1,380
Motor vehicle running costs	4,500

Additional information:

(1) Stocks at 31 December 19X5 were as follows:

	£
Raw materials	9,000
Work in progress	8,000
Finished goods	10,350

(2) The factory output is transferred to the trading account at factory cost plus 25% for factory profit. The finished goods stock is valued on the basis of amounts transferred to the debit of the trading account.

(3) Depreciation is provided annually at the following percentages of the original cost of fixed assets held at the end of each financial year:

Plant and machinery	10%
Motor vehicles	25%

(4) Amounts accrued due at 31 December 19X5 for direct labour amounted to £3,000 and rent and rates prepaid at 31 December 19X5 amounted to £2,000.

Required:

Prepare a manufacturing, trading and profit and loss account for the year ended 31 December 19X5 and a balance sheet as at that date.

Note: The prime cost and total factory cost should be clearly shown.

(AAT Intermediate)

21.3 The following information was extracted from the accounts of T Rasburn, a manufacturer, as at 30 June 19X7.

	£ Dr	£ Cr
Sales of Finished goods		200,000
Bank Loan		40,000
Premises	100,000	
Machinery and Plant at Cost	40,000	
Furniture and Fittings at Cost	8,000	
Debtors and Creditors	16,000	12,000
Balance at Bank and Cash in Hand	6,000	
Factory Wages (direct)	40,000	
(indirect)	8,000	
Office expenses	4,000	
Rates	8,000	
Office Salaries	6,000	
Machinery and Plant Maintenance	4,000	
Cleaning Costs	8,000	
Provision for Depreciation:		
Machinery and Plant		20,000

	£ Dr	£ Cr
Furniture and Fittings		6,000
Purchases of Raw Materials	88,000	
Stocks as at 1 July 19X6:		
Raw Materials	10,000	
Work-in-Progress	NIL	
Finished Goods	12,000	
Capital		100,000
Drawings	20,000	
	£378,000	£378,000

You are also given the following details:

(a) Stocks as at 30 June 19X7 :
   - Raw Materials   £8,000
   - Work-in-Progress   £2,000
   - Finished Goods   £14,000

(b) Interest on the Bank Loan to be 10% per annum.

(c) Cleaning and Rates are to be charged in the proportion of 3/4 to the factory, 1/4 to the office.

(d) Depreciate Furniture and Fittings by 25% on cost and Machinery and Plant by 10% on cost.

Required:

Prepare a Manufacturing and Trading and Profit and Loss Account for the year ended 30 June 19X7; and the Balance Sheet in vertical format as at that date highlighting in both cases:

(i) Prime Cost of Production
(ii) Cost of Finished Goods
(iii) Gross Profit
(iv) Net Profit
(v) Net Working Capital
(vi) Capital Employed (Net Assets)   *(RSA Intermediate)*

21.4 Blick began business as a manufacturer of office equipment on 1 January 19X7, but maintained rather inadequate accounting records. On 1 January 19X7, he transferred £100,000 to a new business bank account from his private bank account and purchased by cheque:

   - Business premises - £50,000
   - Manufacturing equipment - £48,000
   - Delivery vehicles - £22,000
   - Office equipment - £3,000

During the year to 31 December 19X7, he paid by cheque:

   - Raw materials - £70,000
   - Factory rates, water, electricity - £5,600
   - Office rates, water, electricity - £2,400
   - Personal (non-business) expenses - £3,000
   - Sundry office expenses (including salaries) - £12,000

He paid in cash (out of his sales receipts):

Manufacturing wages - £102,000
Sundry office expenses - £7,900
Minor raw material - £4,100
Delivery vehicle expenses - £13,000
Personal drawings - £12,000

Cash paid into the bank, after deducting these payments, amounted to £120,000.

On December 19X7:

Cash in hand was £800
Raw materials stocks (at cost) were £6,000
Finished goods stocks (at cost) were £7,000
There was no work in progress
Debtors for sales were £13,000
Creditors or materials were £24,000
Owing for factory electricity - £400
Factory rates were prepaid - £500
Owing for factory wages - £1,400
Owing for office salaries - £200
Owing for sundry office expenses - £2,000

Depreciation is to be provided on cost at the following annual rates:

Manufacturing equipment - 12-1/2%
Office equipment - 10%
Delivery vehicles - 20%

Also on 31 December 19X7, Blick had taken from his stock of finished goods (prior to the year end stock valuation which established the £7,000 stock value given above) equipment for his business office which he would otherwise have sold for £2,200. This price includes the same percentage gross profit to sales margin as all his other sales during the year.

Required:

(i) Prepare Blick's Manufacturing Trading and Profit & Loss account for 19X7.
(ii) Prepare Blick's Balance Sheet at 31 December 19X7.

(LCCI Higher 1985)

COMMON ERRORS

1. Identification Of Manufacturing Costs

It is sometimes difficult to identify clearly manufacturing costs. In general terms, any costs that appear to relate to a factory or a works should be charged to the manufacturing account.

The question should make it clear what proportion of other expenses (for example, administration, finance and selling and distribution expenses) should be charged to the manufacturing account. Make sure that you make these arithmetical apportionments correctly.

2. Direct and Indirect Expenditure

Check that you understand the distinction between direct and indirect expenditure, and that you are familiar with the type of expenditure that you might expect to find included in these categories.

3. Format

Make sure that you schedule the manufacturing expenses in the following order:

> Direct material
> Direct labour
> Direct expenses
> Manufacturing overhead
> Work in progress
> Manufacturing profit

List the various expenses under the appropriate headings, and do not hesitate to use a number of sub-totals. It is also helpful to label each sub-total, for example, PRIME COST or TOTAL MANUFACTURING OVERHEAD INCURRED.

4. Manufacturing Profit

Make sure that you ADD the manufacturing profit to the total manufacturing cost (that is, DEBIT it to the manufacturing account).

Similarly, when you prepare the profit and loss account, remember to ADD the manufacturing profit to the profit for the year (that is, CREDIT it to the profit and loss account).

5. The Trading, and Profit and Loss Account

As well as preparing the manufacturing account, you will probably be also required to prepare the trading, and the profit and loss account.

Remember that if you have charged a proportion of some expenses to the manufacturing and trading accounts, the balance should be charged to the profit and loss account.

In preparing the profit and loss account, it is also helpful to schedule the expenses under appropriate headings, for example, SELLING AND DISTRIBUTION, ADMINISTRATION and FINANCE

In some questions it may not always be clear where you should charge a particular expense. If this is the case, include it where it seems most appropriate, and make a BRIEF note stating that an alternative treatment is possible.

6. The Balance Sheet

Closing stocks should be shown under the following headings:
STOCKS
1. Raw materials and consumables
2. Work in progress
3. Finished goods and goods for resale
4. Payments on account

22 CONTAINER ACCOUNTS

MAIN POINTS

1. Background

Goods are often supplied to customers in some sort of container, such as a barrel or a cask. The container may form part of the overall selling price of the goods, and the customer will not be charged separately for it.

Sometimes, however, the customer will be expected to pay an extra amount for the container, although either part of or the whole of the extra charge may be refunded if it is returned within a certain time.

2. Book-Keeping Procedure: Containers Not Charged to Customers

(i)   Dr.   Containers account
      Cr.   Bank
      With the cost of purchasing the containers

(ii) Dr.   Containers account at the beginning of the next accounting period.
      Cr.   Containers account at the end of the current accounting period
      With the cost of the containers in hand at the end of the accounting period

(iii) Dr.   Profit and loss account
      Cr.   Containers account
      With the balance on the containers account at the end of the accounting period

3. Book-Keeping Procedure: Containers Charged to Customers

The respective ledger accounts will usually contain separate columns for recording the NUMBER of containers.

(i)   Dr.   Containers stock account
      Cr.   Bank
      With the containers purchased

(ii) Dr.   Containers stock account
      Cr.   Bank account
      With the cost of repairs, insurance and other costs of putting the containers into a saleable condition

(iii) Dr.   Debtor's account
      Cr.   Containers suspense account
      With the invoice price of the container

177

    (iv) Dr.   Containers suspense account
            Cr.   Containers stock account
          With any hire charge included in the invoice price.

    (v)   Dr.   Containers suspense account
            Cr.   Debtor's account
          With the credit value of the container allowedto the debtor on its return

    (vi) Dr.   Container suspense account
            Cr.   Containers stock account
          With the credit value of the container allowed to the debtor (assuming that it had been returned on time).

    (vii) Dr.   Containers stock account (at the beginning of the next accounting period)
            Cr.   Containers stock account (at the end of the current accounting period)
          With the cost of the containers in stock (both in hand and with customers)

    (viii) Dr.   Bank account
            Cr.   Containers stock account
          With the sales proceeds of any containers scrapped

    (ix) EITHER   OR
            Dr.   Containers stock account   Profit and loss account)
            Cr.   Profit and loss account   Containers stock account
          With the balance on the containers stock account at the end of the accounting period.

    (x)   Dr.   Containers suspense account (at the beginning of the next accounting period)
            Cr.   Containers suspense account (at the end of the current accounting period)
          With the balance on the account at the end of the current accounting period

4. Balance Sheet Presentation

    (a) The DEBIT balance on the containers stock account (consisting of containers in hand and container still with customers) will be included under CURRENT ASSETS.

    (b) The CREDIT balance on the containers suspense account will be DEDUCTED from the total of all the debtor's accounts. The containers suspense account does not require separate disclosure in the balance sheet.

Example.   Strong Ltd supplies goods in returnable kegs. The kegs are purchased at £10 each and they charged out to customers at £15 each. If the kegs are returned within three months the customer is credited with £5 for each keg returned.

    On 1 January 19X6 there were 500 kegs in the company's warehouse and 2,000 kegs in the hands of customer (all of which had been supplied during the time limited). Kegs in the warehouse and in customers' hands at the year end are valued at £3 each. During the year to 31 December 19X6, the following transactions took place:

(1) The company purchased 5,000 kegs.
(2) 25,000 kegs were supplied to customers
(3) 20,000 kegs were returned by customer within the time limit, and another 3,000 kegs were retained after the time limit.

Required:

Prepare the following ledger accounts:

   (i) the kegs stock account; and

  (ii) the kegs suspense account.

Solution

STRONG LTD
KEGS STOCK ACCOUNT

		No.	£			No.	£
1 1 X6	Balances b/d			31 12 X6	Profit on hire		
	in warehouse (at £3 ea)	500	1,500		(25,000x£10)	-	250,000
	With customers (at £3 ea)	2,000	6,000	31 12 X6	Retained by customers	3,000	15,000
31 12 X6	Purchases	5,000	50,000	31 12 X6	Balances c/d		
31 12 X6	Profit for year		221,000		In warehouse (£3 ea)	500	1,500
					With custmrs (£3 ea)	4,000	12,000
		7,500	£278,500			7,500	£278,500
1 1 X7	Balances b/d						
	In warehouse	500	1,500				
	With customers	4,000	12,000				

KEGS SUSPENSE ACCOUNT

		No.	£			No.	£
31 12 X6	Returns during year (£5 ea)	20,000	100,000	1 1 X6	Balance b/d With custmrs (£5 ea)	2,000	10,000
31 12 X6	Retained during year (£5 ea)	3,000	15,000	31 12 X6	Sales during year (£15 ea)	25,000	375,000
31 12 X6	Profit to Kegs Stock (25,000x£10)	-	250,000				
31 12 X6	Balance c/d with custmrs (£5 ea)	4,000	20,000				
		27,000	£385,000			27,000	£385,000
				1 1 X7	Balance b/d with custmrs	4,000	20,000

CHECK

Profit on hire (25,000x£10)	250,000
Profit on kegs retained [3,000-£(5-3)]	6,000
	256,000
Less Deprecn on year's purchase [5,000-£(10-3)]	35,000
Profit for year	**£221,000**

EXERCISES

22.1 Oswald supplied its goods in crates. The following details relate to the year ending 31 December 19X2:

  (1) Stock of crates at 1 January 19X2 :
      In hand   :   100
      With customers   :   200
  (2) Number of crates purchased during the year: 8,000
  (3) Number supplied to customers   :   30,000
  (4) Number returned by customers   :   27,000
  (5) Number retained by customers   :   2,000

  Additional information :

  (1) Stocks of crates in hand and with customers at the end of the year are valued at £5 per crate.
  (2) Crates are purchased at £9 each.
  (3) Customers are invoiced at £12 per crate, and credited with £7 per crate if returned within the agreed period.

Required:

Write up the crates stock account and the crates suspense account for the year to 31 December 19X2.

22.2 Crieff dispatches its goods in returnable bins. The following cost structure applies

	Per bin £
Purchase price	40
Invoiced to customer	50
Amount credited to customer if returned within two months	30
Amount credited to customer if returned after two months	12
Stock valuation (in hand and with customers)	10

The following details apply to the year to 31 March 19X8.

	Bins
(1) Number at 1 April 19X7 :	
In hand	400
With customers (all supplied since 1 February 19X7)	800
(2) Supplied to customers	6,000
(3) Returned by customers within the time period	5,000
(4) Returned late by customers	200
(5) Number purchased	1,000
(6) Number scrapped	50
(7) Cost of repairs to bins	£7,500

Required:

Write up the bins stock account and the bins suspense account for the year to 31 March 19X8.

22.3 Lagg Ltd sells its goods in cases. These cases are purchased by the company at £6 per case, but each case is written down to a standard book value (SBV) of £5 per case immediately it is purchased. For stocktaking purposes, all cases are valued at £5 per case irrespective of whether they are still in stock or in the hands of the customers. Cases are charged out to the customers at £10 per case, but the customer is credited with £8 per case if the case is returned in good condition within three months of receipt.

The following information relates to the year to 31 March 19X7:

		Cases
(1)	Stock of cases at 1 April 19X6:	
	In stock	1,000
	In hands of customers 1 January 19X6	3,000

(2) During the year, 2,000 cases were purchased.

(3) 25,000 cases were issued to customers.

(4) 23,000 cases were returned by customers within the time limit.

(5) 1,500 cases were not returned within the time limit and were duly paid for by the customers. Cases still in the hands of customers at 31 March 19X7 had all been invoiced since 1 January 19X7.

(6) 100 cases kept in stock by Lagg had been damaged and were beyond repair.

(7) £1,400 had been spent on repairing some slightly damaged cases.

(8) 50 other damaged cases had been sold for £2 per case.

In order to keep an accurate record of its transactions in cases, Lagg maintains (inter alia) the following accounts:

(a) a cases stock account in which cases are recorded at their standard book value;

(b) a cases suspense account in which cases in the hands of customers are recorded at their return price;

(c) a cases sent to customers account in which cases sent to customers are recorded at their issue price; and

(d) a cases profit and loss account.

Required:

Write up the following accounts in the books of Lagg Ltd for the year to 31 March 19X7;

(i) cases stock account;

(ii) cases suspense account;

(iii) cases sent to customers account; and

(iv) cases profit and loss account.

(AAT Final)

COMMON ERRORS

1. Memorandum Quantity Columns

You are recommended to use memorandum quantity columns in both the containers stock account and the containers suspense account. The use of such columns will help you to keep a check on the number of containers in stock, the number purchased, the number returned by debtors, and the number still in the hands of customers.

You need to keep a careful check of the number of containers, because many examination questions involve writing off some containers that have been lost.

Do NOT make any entry in the memorandum columns for HIRE CHARGES.

2. Containers Stock Account

Remember to insert the opening balance as a DEBIT in the containers stock account. The opening balance will consist of containers in the hands of the entity, AND in the hands of customers at the beginning of the period. You are recommended to enter these opening balances separately.

Both closing and opening stock balances of containers in hand and with customers will normally be valued at the containers' COST price.

3. Containers Suspense Account

The containers suspense account is written up at the price INVOICED to the customer.

Any profit earned on the containers issued to customer (that is, the hire charge) is DEBITED to the account and CREDITED to the containers stock account

4. The Double-Entry Effect

In dealing with container accounts, always make a point of thinking through extremely carefully the double-entry effect of each transaction.

If you think constantly in double-entry terms, you are not likely to miss out or reverse an entry.

23 CONTRACT ACCOUNTS

MAIN POINTS

1. Background

Entities that engage in construction work (for example, constructing roads or building hospitals) usually have to TENDER for the contract. In effect, this means that the selling price is agreed in advance. The contract price is usually for a fixed amount, although unforeseen extra costs may result in an additional amount being negotiated.

Some construction work may take only a short while to complete (such as building a small house), whilst other work may take years (for example, building a power station).

Both short and long term contract work expenditure requires to be carefully controlled in order to keep it below the tender price.

If a contract is going to take some time to complete, the entity may receive payments on account based on work certified to date. The work certified will usually be done by an architect.

Profit may also be taken on account if the contact extends beyond one accounting period.

2. Accounting Procedure

A separate account will be opened for each contract.

(i)   Dr.   Contract account
       Cr.   Bank account (or suppliers' accounts)
       With expenditure related to the contract

(ii)   Dr.   Contract account
       Cr.   Plant and equipment account
       With the plant and equipment sent to the site

(iii) Dr.   Contract account
       Cr.   Other expense accounts within the ledger
       With a share of the entity's general overhead expenditure

(iv)   Dr.   Bank account
       Cr.   Contractee account
       With the amounts received on account

(v) Dr. Contractee account
     Cr. Trading account
     With the turnover for the period

(vi) Dr. Trading account
      Cr. Contract account
      With the costs for the period related to the turnover for the period

3. Attributable Profit

The revised version of SSAP 9 (Stocks and long-term contracts) defines attributable profit as "that part of the total profit currently estimated to arise over the duration of the contract, after allowing for estimated remedial and maintenance costs and increases in costs so far as not recoverable under the terms of the contract, that fairly reflects the profit attributable to that part of the work performed at the accounting date".

It also makes the point that "there can be no attributable profit until the profitable outcome of the contract can be assessed with reasonable certainty".

4. Losses

Any loss likely to be incurred on a particular contract should be written off to the trading account as soon as it is recognised.

5. Balance Sheet Presentation

Details regarding long-term contracts should be disclosed in the balance sheet as follows:

	£
STOCKS	
.	
.	
Long -term contract balances	X
DEBTORS	
.	
.	
Amounts recoverable on contracts	X
CREDITORS	
.	
.	
Payments received on account	X
EITHER :	
CREDITORS	
Accrual for foreseeable losses	X
OR :	
PROVISIONS FOR LIABILITIES AND CHARGES	
Provision for foreseeable losses	X

Example.   Corin Plc was awarded a contract to build a local store for Good Buy at a contract price of £1,500,000.

The expenditure on the contract was as follows.

	£'000
Direct materials	640
Direct wages	400
Other direct expenses	40
Plant and machinery at cost	400
Other equipment at cost	60
Administrative expenses	20

Additional information:

(1) The value of the plant and machinery at the end of the contract was £320,000, and the value of the other equipment was £40,000.

(2) The contract was completed in time, by which time Conn plc had received £1,000 from Good Buy on account of work done.

Required:

Prepare Good Buy's Contract Account and Good Buy's Customer Account in the books of Corrin plc.

Solution :

CORIN plc

Good Buy's Contract Account

	£'000		£'000
Direct materials	640		
Direct wages	400	Plant (at written down value)	320
Other direct expenses	40	Other equipment (at written down value)	40
Plant and machinery at cost	400	Trading Account	1,200
Other equipment at cost	60		
Administrative expenses	20		
	£1,560		£1,560

Good Buy's Customer Account

	£		£
Trading account	1,500	Bank (on account)	1,000
		Balance c/d	*500
	£1,500		£1,500
Balance b/d	500		

* Amount recoverable on contract

EXERCISES

23.1 The following information relates to a contract undertaken by Perth Ltd.

	£'000
Contract Price	2,000
Costs up to 31 December 19X2:	
Direct materials	125
Direct wages	50
Other costs	10
Plant and equipment cost	500
at 1 June 19X2	

	£'000
Plant and equipment written down value at 31 December 19X2	460
Stock of materials on site at 31 December 19X2	15

Expected additional costs to complete contract £915,000.
Work on the contract began on 1 June 19X2.
The estimated completion date is 31 December 19X5.

Required:

Prepare the contract account in the books of Perth Ltd.

23.2 Mull Ltd is awarded a contract to build some community facilities. The contract price is £1.5 million, and it is estimated that the contract will take two years to complete.

The following information relates to the first year of the contract

	£'000
Direct materials	250
Direct labour	300
Plant and machinery at cost	400
Administrative expenses	50

The value of the plant and machinery at the end of the first year of the contract was £325,000.

The total cost of the contract to completion was estimated to be £1,050,000.

Required:

Write up the contract account in the books of Mull Ltd, and prepare the contract trading account for the year.

23.3 During the year to 31 March 19X3. Linton Plc has undertaken the following contract:

Commencement date:	1 May 19X2
Estimated completion date:	31 July 19X3
Contract price:	£1,000,000
Equipment at cost	£400,000

	Costs to 31 March 19X3	Estimated further completion costs
	£'000	£'000
Direct materials	288	50
Direct wages	240	100
Other site costs	60	40

Balances at 31 March 19X3 :	£'000
Materials	18
Equipment at written down value	300

The written down value of the equipment at 31 July 19X3 was estimated to be £230,000.

The amount received from contractee up to 31 March 19X3 was £450,000

Required:

Prepare Linton Plc's contract account, the contractee's account, and the trading account for the year to 31 March 19X3.

COMMON ERRORS

1. Double-Entry

Make sure that if you are debiting or crediting the contract account, you complete double-entry elsewhere within the ledger system.

2. Turnover, Related Costs and Attributable Profit.

The question should make it clear how you are to calculate turnover for the period, and the related costs attached to that turnover. Remember that there can be no attributable profit unless the profitable outcome of the contract can be assessed with reasonable certainty.

3. Turnover and Payments on Account.

The difference between the recorded turnover (that is, the value of the work done) and the cumulative payments on account should be disclosed in the balance sheet either in DEBTORS as AMOUNTS RECOVERABLE ON CONTRACTS, or in CREDITORS as PAYMENTS ON ACCOUNT.

4. Stocks

In the balance sheet, disclose as STOCKS the difference between:

(a) total costs incurred to date LESS cumulative amounts recorded as the cost of sales; and

(b) cumulative payments on account LESS cumulative turnover.

5. Provision (Or Accrual) for Foreseeable Losses

In the balance sheet include any provision (or accrual) for foreseeable losses either in PROVISIONS FOR LIABILITIES AND CHARGES, or in CREDITORS.

24

INVESTMENT ACCOUNTS

MAIN POINTS

1. Background

As well as manufacturing or trading goods, some entities buy and sell investments, such as debentures, government stock, and stocks and shares. If done on some scale, such dealings may become very complicated, especially when the purchase or selling price of the investment includes some accrued dividend or interest.

2. Accounting Procedure

(a) An account should be kept for each separate investment.

(b) The account should contain debit and credit columns for:
(i)   the nominal value of the investment;
(ii)   the dividend or interest; and
(iii) the capital amount.

(c) Purchases of investments should be DEBITED to the account, and CREDITED to the bank account.

(d) Sales of investment should be DEBITED to the bank account, and CREDITED to the investment account.

(e) Any income included in either the purchase or selling price of an investment should be extracted and entered in the INCOME column of the account (although this adjustment is not always made when dealing in ordinary shares).

(f) The entry in the CAPITAL column will be the purchase (or selling price) of the investment LESS any in-built income.

(g) Brokerage, stamp duty and other costs of purchasing an investment should be treated as part of the capital cost.

(h) Similarly, costs associated with selling an investment should be deducted from the sale proceeds.

3. Definitions

(a) CUM DIV/INT. If an investment is purchased cum div/int, the next dividend/interest payment will belong to the PURCHASER.

(b) EX DIV/INT. If an investment is sold ex div/int, the next dividend/interest payment, will belong to the SELLER.

4. Balance Sheet Presentation

(a) Long-term investments should be shown at cost under FIXED ASSETS after tangible fixed assets.

(b) Short-term investments should be shown at cost under CURRENT ASSETS after debtors.

(c) The market cost of both long and short-term investments should be shown as a note in the balance sheet.

(d) If the market value is less the historic cost and it is likely to remain so, the difference should be written off to the profit and loss account.

(e) If the market price is more than the historic cost and it is likely to remain so, the increase should be transferred to an INVESTMENT REVALUATION RESERVE ACCOUNT. This account will be included in the capital section of the balance sheet.

Example. Funam Ltd, a manufacturing company, has for some years invested surplus funds in Government 6% Stock, on which interest is paid gross in equal instalments every 1 February and 1 August.

At 1 January 19X5, the company held £8,000 nominal of this stock, with a total book value of £7,080, including interest thereon accrued since the last payment.

The company's sales and purchases of this stock over the next two years have been as follows:

31 March 19X5	Purchased £5,000 nominal for £4,500.
1 December 19X5	Sold £4,000 nominal for £3,860.
1 March 19X6	Sold all stock remaining for £6,345.

There is no intention of investing further funds in this way. When calculating the profit or loss at the time of a sale of stock, the company applied the "first in, first out" principle.

Required:

(a) Show the Investment Account "Government 6% Stock" in the books of Funam Ltd for the financial years ended 31 December 19X5 and 31 December 19X6; the account should be balanced off at both 31 December 19X5 and 31 December 19X6. Ignore brokerage and taxation; and

(b) assuming that the amount is material, state how the profit or loss arising from the sale of stock in 19X6 should appear in the Profit and Loss Account for that year. *(LCCI Higher 1987)*

Solution:

(a)

FUNAM LTD
INVESTMENT ACCOUNT
Government 6% stock

		Nominal £	Income £	Capital £			Nominal £	Income £	Capital £
1 1 X5	Balance b/d	8,000	200	6,880	1 2 X5	Bank	-	240	-
31 3 X5	Bank	5,000	50	4,450	1 8 X5	Bank	-	390	-
1 12 X5	Profit on sale	-	-	340	1 12 X5	Bank	4,000	80	3,780
31 12 X5	Profit and loss	-	685		31 12 X5	Accrued interest c/d	-	225	-
					31 12 X5	Balances c/d	9,000	-	7,890
		£13,000	£935	£11,670			£13,000	£935	£11,670

		Nominal £	Income £	Capital £			Nominal £	Income £	Capital £
1 1 X6	Accrued Interest b/d	-	225	-					
1 1 X6	Balances b/d	9,000	-	7,890	1 2 X6	Bank	-	270	-
31 12 X6	Profit & Loss	-	90	-	1 3 X6	Bank	9,000	45	6,300
					31 12 X6	Loss in sale	-	-	1,590
		£9,000	£315	£7,890			£9,000	£315	£7,890

(b) As the company has, for some years invested surplus funds in government 6% stock, changes in such stock can be regarded as part of the ordinary activities of the company. The loss on sale, therefore, of £1,590 should be shown separately in the profit and loss account as part of ordinary activities before taxation.

EXERCISES

24.1 Dolphin Ltd, which is not an investment company, invests temporarily surplus funds in 9% Atlantis Government Stock, on which interest is paid half yearly on 1 February and 1 August.

At 1 January 19X1 it owned £20,000 nominal value of 9% stock with a weighted average cost of £18,000. During 19X1 there were the following purchases and sales:

1 April	- Purchased	£12,000 nominal value for £11,220	(cum div)
1 July	- Sold	£8,000 nominal value for £7,620	(ex div)
30 November	- Purchased	£6,000 nominal value for £6,290	(cum div)

Dolphin Ltd calculates profits (and losses) on disposal on the basis of the weighted average cost of the opening balance and purchases made during the year. The closing balance is also valued on the basis of this cost.

Required:

(a) Show the 9% Atlantis Stock Account in Dolphin Ltd's books for 19X1. Show clearly your calculations of the closing balance in the "capital" column and of the profit (or loss) on sale of 9% Stock (neither should be treated as a residual); and

(b) a brief explanation of how, and why, your treatment of the income from the investment would have differed, had Dolphin Ltd purchased Ordinary Shares instead of Government Stock.

(LCCI Higher 1985)

24.2 Mondale Ltd carries out a number of investment transactions during each financial year, but at 1 January 19X2, the only investment it held was £20,000 10% debentures in Forfar plc purchased at a cost of £18,002.

Transactions during the year were as follows:

1 April	Purchased £50,000 10% debentures in Forfar plc for £45,000. Interest is paid half yearly on the 30 June and 31 December.
1 June	Purchased 1,000 £1 ordinary shares in Greengrass plc for £2,250 cum div.
30 September	Sold £10,000 10% debentures in Forfar plc for £9,600.
31 December	Received a dividend of 10p per share from Greengrass plc.

Profits and losses on disposal are calculated on the basis of the weighted cost of the opening balance and purchases made during the year. Income tax and charges may be ignored.

Required:

Record the above transactions in Mondale's investment ledger accounts for the year to 31 December 19X2.

24.3 The following investment transactions relate to Daffyd Ltd for the year to 31 March 19X3:

1 4 X2	£50,000 of 15% Government stock was purchased at 60. Interest is payable on 30 June and 31 December.
1 4 X2	£100,000 of 5% Eurostock was purchased at 55 ex div. Interest is payable on 31 March and 30 September.
1 4 X2	10,000 ordinary shares of £1 each in Kippen plc were purchased at £5 per share cum div.
1 10 X2	£50,000 of 5% Eurostock was sold at 60 ex div.
31 12 X2	An interim dividend of 10p per share was received from Kippen plc.
31 12 X3	A final dividend of 20p per share was received from Kippen plc.

Note: Income tax and costs may be ignored.

Required:

Write up the above transactions in Daffyd's Ltd's investment ledger account for the year to 31 March 19X3.

COMMON ERRORS

1. Apportionment Of Income

If an investment is sold CUM DIV, the purchaser will be entitled to any accrued income inherent in the purchase price. Remember to calculate the accrued income from the date of the last income payment up to the date of purchase, and to include it in the INCOME column of the investment account (a similar procedure applies if the entity is buying an investment).

Make sure that you calculate the apportionment correctly, and that you do so from the date of the LAST income payment up to the time of the purchase or sale.

If the income on an investment, for example, is received half-yearly, and it is sold three months after the LAST payment, only HALF of the next income payment should be treated as income as at the date of the sale (that is, one quarter of the YEAR'S total income).

This procedure is not necessary if the investment is sold EX DIV, because the seller is entitled to retain all of the accrued income, and the market price will have been adjusted for an investment being sold without the right to receive the next income payment.

2. Dividends Cum Div

When ordinary shares are purchased or sold cum div, the accrued dividend inherent in the purchase or selling price at the time of the sale should also be extracted and included in income. However, the amount of the next dividend may not be known for some time, and so an adjustment cannot always be made at the time the shares are bought or sold.

Furthermore, there is no guarantee that a dividend will be paid; consequently, an adjustment for accrued dividends on ORDINARY shares is not always made, especially when the entity's main business is not that of an investment company.

3. Costs

Remember to include the costs of purchases or sales in the CAPITAL column of the investment account.

25

CONSIGNMENT ACCOUNTS

MAIN POINTS

1. Background

It is sometimes customary for an entity to appoint an agent to sell goods on the entity's behalf. The entity is known as the CONSIGNOR, and the agent as the CONSIGNEE. This type of arrangement is particularly common in selling goods abroad.

The consignor will purchase the goods, and then send them to the consignee. The goods will continue to be owned by the consignor until they are sold by the consignee.

The consignee will be responsible for selling the goods, and for collecting the cash from customers. He will then transfer the cash to the consignor after deducting his commission.

2. Consignor's Books: Accounting Treatment

    (i)   Dr. Consignment account
            Cr.   Goods sent on consignment account
          With the cost of the goods dispatched to the consignee

    (ii)   Dr. Consignment account
            Cr.   Bank account
          With any costs associated with the consignment

    (iii) Dr. Consignee's account
            Cr.   Consignment account
          With the sales made by the consignee

    (iv) Dr. Consignment account
            Cr.   Consignee's account
          With any expenses incurred by the consignee, and with the consignee's commission

    (v)   Dr. Goods sent on consignment account
            Cr.   Trading account
          With the cost of all goods sent on consignment during the year

(vi) EITHER

Dr. Consignment account
Cr. Profit and loss account
With any PROFIT made on the
consignment for the year

OR

Dr. Profit and loss account
Cr. Consignment account
With any LOSS incurred on the
consignment for the year

(vii) Dr. Bank account
Cr. Consignee's account
With the amount of cash received from the consignee.

3. Consignee's Books: Accounting Treatment

(i) Dr. Bank account
Cr. Consignor's account
With cash sales

(ii) Dr. Customer's accounts
Cr. Consignor's account
With credit sales

(iii) Dr. Bank account
Cr. Customers' accounts
With the cash received from customers

(iv) Dr. Consignor's accounts
Cr. Bank account
With expenses incurred on behalf of the consignor

(v) Dr. Consignor's account
Cr. Commission receivable account
With the commissions earned on sales

(vi) Dr. Consignor's account
Cr. Bank account
With remittances made to the consignor.

Example.   John Black, a merchant in Stoke-on-Trent, obtained the franchise from Wicklore Pottery Ltd, Eire, to sell as agent the well known Wicklore ware pottery throughout North Staffordshire. The terms of the agency were that Black was entitled to commission of 15% on the proceeds of all sales plus 2 1/2% del credere commission on credit (invoice) sales. The first consignment (sales value £20,000) was received by Black on 10 June 19X5, on which date he accepted a Bill of Exchange at 4 months for £20,000. Black sent this back to Wicklore Pottery who discounted it with the bank on 15 June 19X5. On 30 June 19X5 Black paid £100 to British Road Lorries for transporting the pottery from Liverpool to Stoke-on-Trent. Subsequently the following transactions took place:-

Month of 19X5	Cash Sales	Invoice Sales	Total Sales	Cash received from Sales Debtors	Cash paid for Distribution Expenses
	£	£	£	£	£
June	3,000	1,500	4,500	50	40
July	2,500	2,300	4,800	1,400	40
August	4,500	5,200	9,700	2,300	60

On 30 July 19X5 Black wrote off a bad debt of £120, due in respect of a sale to a debtor on 13 June 19X5. (Black's financial year ended on 31 July 19X5 and he sent an Interim Account Sales to Wicklore Pottery up to this date).

Required:

Prepare, in the ledger of John Black:

(a) The Account for Wicklore Pottery Ltd, including the balance at the end of the financial year; and

(b) the Bad Debts Account.

(LCCI Intermediate 1986)

Solution:

(a)

JOHN BLACK
Wicklore Pottery Ltd Account

		£			£
10 6 X5	Bills payable	20,000	30 6 X5	Cash	3,000
30 6 X5	B R Lorries	100	30 6 X5	Debtors	1,500
30 6 X5	Distribution Expenses	40	31 7 X5	Cash	2,500
30 7 X5	Bad debts	120	31 7 X5	Debtors	2,300
31 7 X5	Distribution Expenses	40	31 7 X5	Balance c/d	12,490
31 7 X5	Commission (15%)	1,395			
31 7 X5	Del credere commission	95			
		£21,790			£21,790
1 8 X5	Balance b/d	12,490	31 8 X5	Cash	4,500
31 8 X5	Distribution Expenses	60	31 8 X5	Debtors	5,200
31 8 X5	Commission (15%)	1,455	31 8 X5	Balance c/d	4,435
31 8 X5	Del Credere commission	130			
		£14,135			£14,135
1 9 X5	Balance b/d	4,435			

(b)

Bad debts account

		£			£
30 7 X5	Debtors	120	31 7 X5	Wicklore Pottery Ltd	120

EXERCISES

25.1 Oddsox Ltd despatched a consignment of merchandise to a selling agent on 1 January 19X2. The goods in the consignment cost £18,000, and it was expected that the agent would sell them with a mark up of 24%.

Oddsox Ltd have paid transport costs and insurance amounting to £714 and £630 respectively.

At the end of January 19X2 the agent had sold half of the goods, achieving the intended mark up, and he remitted the cash due to Oddsox Ltd, after deducting his agreed commission of 2 1/2% on sales, storage charges of £280, and delivery expenses for goods sold in the sum of £87.

Required:

Account for this consignment in the books of Oddsox Ltd.

(AAT/IAS Part 2)

25.2 Dan Ltd has an agent in Chita. The following information relates to the six months to 30 June 19X5.

(1) Goods costing £50,000 were consigned on 1 January. The air freight was £3,500 and the insurance cost £1,500.
(2) On 31 May the agent forwarded a sales account showing sales of £46,875, commission of £4,600, and selling expenses of £875. The balance due was received by Dan on 30 June.
(3) One quarter of the goods remained unsold as at 30 June 19X5.

Required:

Prepare the ledger accounts relating to the above transactions in:

(1) Dan Ltd's books; and
(2) the agent's books.

25.3 Fleet is a London merchant. During the financial year to 31 March 19X8, he sent a consignment of goods to Sing, his agent in Balli. The details of the transaction were as follows:

(1) On April 19X7, 1,000 boxes were sent to Sing. These boxes had originally cost Fleet £20 each.
(2) Fleet's carriage, freight and insurance costs of the consignment paid on 30 April 19X7 amounted to £2,000.
(3) During the voyage to Balli, ten boxes were lost. On 30 September 19X7, Fleet received a cheque for £220 as compensation from his insurance company for the loss of the boxes.
(4) On 1 March 19X8, Fleet received £20,000 from Sing.
(5) Both Fleet and Sing's accounting year end is 31 March.
(6) On 15 April 19X8, Fleet received the following Interim Account Sales from Sing:

Interim Account

The Water Front
Gama
Balli

31 March 19X8
Consignment of goods sold on behalf of fleet, London: 950 boxes of merchandise.

	£	£
950 boxes at £30 each		28,500
Charges:		
Distribution expenses (at £2 per box)	1,900	
Landing charges and import duty (at £1 per box)	990	
Commission (5% x £28,500)	1,425	4,315
NET PROCEEDS PER DRAFT ENCLOSED		£24,185

31 March 19X8
Sing (signed)
Balli

Required:

Prepare the following ledger accounts for the year to 31 March 19X8:

- (a) in Fleet's books of account:
    - (i) Goods sent on consignment account;
    - (ii) Consignment to Sing's account;
    - (iii) Sing (consignee) account; and
- (b) in Sing's books of account;
    - (i) Fleet (London) account;
    - (ii) Commission account

(AAT Final)

COMMON ERRORS

1. Lack of Knowledge

Consignment accounting is not a common examination topic, and so students do not usually spend a lot of time studying it.

You can still earn reasonable number of marks, however, if you can remember the basic accounts to use, and you follow the principles of double-entry book-keeping.

2. Accounts to Use

- (a) Remember the CONSIGNOR uses one basic account: the CONSIGNMENT account. This account is a combined trading, and profit and loss account.

    All expenses (including those incurred by the consignee) are DEBITED to the consignment account, and all incomes relating to the consignment are CREDITED to it.

    The difference on the account represents profit or loss on the consignment.

- (b) The consignee also uses one basic account: the CONSIGNOR's account.

    Expenses incurred by the consignee on the consignor's behalf are DEBITED to the consignor's account, and sales revenue is CREDITED to it.

    The balance on the account represents the amount of cash the consignee is required to remit to the consignor.

3. Incomplete Assignments

If a consignment is incomplete at the end of an accounting period, the consignee will submit an interim ACCOUNTS SALES.

Remember to value closing stock at COST (unless the net realisable value is lower than cost). Cost includes the cost of carriage, freight, insurance, and import duties.

4. Del Credere Commission

If the consignee guarantees the debts incurred on the sales that he makes, he may be paid an extra commission. This is known as DEL CREDERE COMMISSION. The accounting treatment is similar to that for ordinary commission.

5. Writing up the Accounts

Marks are often lost in this type of question for poor presentation. Make sure you write up the respective accounts presented in formal double-entry format.

Each entry should include the date, a brief narration (usually the name of the account where the corresponding entry may be found), and the amount.

6 . Calculation of Closing Stock

In your calculation of closing stock, remember to include ALL costs associated with putting the goods into saleable condition. This also includes those costs incurred by the agent.

Remember to allow for any units of stock that have been lost in transit.

26 ROYALTY ACCOUNTS

MAIN POINTS

1. Background

A royalty is a payment for the right to copy work of an author, extract minerals, or use a patent. The royalty will depend upon the use made of it.

The agreement may require a MINIMUM payment to be made per annum. There may also be a right to recover in later periods the difference between the minimum payment and the royalties actually payable. The recovery will be made out of future royalties that are in excess of the minimum payment. Such an option will usually be only exercisable over a relatively short period of time.

The agreement may also permit the sub-contracting of work. The total royalties payable however, will have to be paid by the main contractor based on the total amount extracted or manufactured, or the overall use made of it.

2. Royalties Payable : Accounting Treatment

(i)   Dr.   Royalties payable account
      Cr.   Creditor's account
With the amount of royalties payable based on usage for a particular accounting period

(ii)   Dr.   Creditor's account
      Cr.   Bank
With the amount payable to the creditor for the period (which will be either the MINIMUM payment, or the royalties payable based on usage for the period)

(iii)   Dr.   Shortworkings recoverable account
      Cr.   Creditor's account
With any shortworkings arising during the period

(iv)   Dr.   Creditor's account
      Cr.   Shortworkings recoverable account
With any shortworkings recoverable during the period

(v)   Dr.   Manufacturing account
      Cr.   Royalties payable account
With the amount of royalties incurred during the period

(vi)   Dr.   Profit and loss account
      Cr.   Shortworking account
With any shortworkings not recoverable within the period laid down in the agreement.

3. Royalties Receivable : Accounting Treatment

(i)   Dr. Licensee'a account
       Cr. Royalties receivable account
      With the royalties earned during the year

(ii)   Dr. Bank
       Cr. Licensee's account
      With the amounts received during the accounting period

(iii)   Dr. Licensee's account
       Cr. Shortworkings allowable account
      With any shortworkings arising during the period

(iv)   Dr. Shortworkings allowable account
       Cr. Licensee's account
      With any shortworkings allowable during the period

(v)   Dr. Royalties receivable account
       Cr. Profit and loss account
      With the total royalties receivable for the period

(vi)   Dr. Shortworkings allowable account
       Cr. Profit and loss account
      With any shortworkings not allowable within the period laid down in the agreement.

Example.   Mustard Ltd obtained the right to extract gravel from the land of Vinegar Ltd. Under their agreement a royalty of £0.20 per ton extracted was payable with a minimum payment each year as follows:

19X1 £2,000; 19X2 £1,600; 19X3 £1,200; 19X4 £800

The actual tonnage extracted was:

19X1 - 5,000 tons; 19X2 - 6,000 tons; 19X3 - 8,000 tons; 19X4 - 8,000 tons; 19X5 -10,000 tons.

Shortworkings are recoverable up to the end of 19X4 only.

Required:

(a) Prepare the necessary Ledger Accounts in the books of Mustard Ltd in order to record the above transactions; and

(b) suggest why minimum payments are stipulated in such agreements and also why "shortworkings' are usually "recoverable", but only for a limited period.

(LCCI Higher 1986)

Solution:

(a)

MUSTARD LTD
Royalties Account

	£			£
19X1 Vinegar Ltd (5,000x£0.20)	1,000	19X1	Operating account	1,000
19X2 Vinegar Ltd (6,000x£0.20)	1,200	19X2	Operating account	1,200
19X3 Vinegar Ltd (8,000x£0.20)	1,600	19X3	Operating account	1,600
19X4 Vinegar Ltd (8,000x£0.20)	1,600	19X4	Operating account	1,600
19X5 Vinegar Ltd (10,000x£0.20)	2,000	19X5	Operating account	2,000

Vinegar Ltd's Account

	£			£
19X1 Bank	2,000	19X1	Royalties	1,000
		19X1	Short workings	1,000
	£2,000			£2,000
19X2 Bank	1,600	19X2	Royalties	1,200
		19X2	Short workings	400
	£1,600			£1,600
19X3 Bank	1,200	19X3	Royalties	1,600
19X3 Short workings	400			
	£1,600			£1,600
19X5 Bank	£2,000	19X5	Royalties	£2,000

Short workings account

	£			£
19X1 Vinegar	1,000			
19X2 Vinegar	400	19X2	Balance c/d	1,400
	£1,400			£1,400
19X3 Balance b/d	1,400	19X3	Vinegar Ltd	400
		19X3	Balance c/d	1,000
	£1,400			£1,400
19X4 Balance b/d	1,000	19X4	Vinegar Ltd	800
		19X4	Profit and Loss (amount now irrecoverable)	200
	£1,000			£1,000

(b) **Minimum payments**

(1) To provide the owner with a minimum income

(2) To allocate the royalties more evenly in the earlier years when they are more likely to fluctuate than in later years.

Short-workings: recoverable in the short-term only

(1) To give the user a chance to establish his business without being unduly penalised during the earlier years.

(2) Once established, the user has a better chance of ensuring that he meets any minimum royalty laid down.

EXERCISES

26.1 Raylow manufactures an electrical pump. He has agreed to pay a royalty to Paz of £5 for each pump manufactured.

The following details relate to the first years of the agreement:

Year	Pumps manufactured
1	1,000
2	1,500
3	2,000
4	4,000

The agreement provides for a minimum royalty payment of £8,000 per annum.

Any short-workings may only be recouped during the first three years of the agreement.

Required:

Prepare the following ledger accounts.

    (i) royalties;
    (ii) Paz; and
    (iii) short-workings.

26.2   Some years ago, Dunbar Ltd had been granted a licence to extract a mineral deposit from some land owned by Berwick plc. The terms of the licence were as follows:

    (1) Dunbar Ltd was to pay Berwick plc a royalty of £2 for each ton of mineral deposit extracted, subject to a minimum payment of £10,000 per annum.
    (2) If in any year, the total amount of mineral extracted was less than 5,000 tons. Dunbar was to be allowed to recoup any deficiency against royalties payable in excess of that amount during the following two years.
    (3) Both Dunbar's and Berwick's financial year end is 31 December, and Dunbar agreed to settle the amount due to Berwick on the next 31 January following the financial year end.

During the first five years of the agreement, the following tons of mineral deposit were extracted by Dunbar:

Year to 31 December	Quantity in tons
19X1	6,000
19X2	4,000
19X3	3,000
19X4	5,500
19X5	8,000

Required

Write up the following ledger accounts in the books of Dunbar for each of the five years to 31 December 19X1, 19X2, 19X3, 19X4 and 19X5 respectively:

    (i) royalties;
    (ii) short-workings; and
    (iii) Berwick plc.

Note: The above accounts must be balanced at the end of each financial year, and any balance on the respective accounts brought down at the beginning of the next financial year.

(AAT Final)

26.3   Bass plc is a mining and exploration company. It has recently discovered an estimated 10,000,000 tonnes of workable ore in Karogea. The government of Karogea is prepared to sell the ore to Bass plc and has offered two alternative contractual arrangements:

(1) Bass plc can purchase all the workable ore by making a single royalty payment of £100,000 on 1 January 19X3, immediately after which mining will begin.

(2) Bass plc can pay a royalty of £0.011 per tonne. This will be payable on 31 December of each year in which the ore is mined. It is subject to a minimum royalty of £35,000 payable for each of the three years 19X3, 19X4, 19X5; shortworkings are not recoverable.

Tonnage to be mined has been budgeted as follows:

19X3 1,600,000 tonnes
19X4 1,800,000 tonnes
19X5 2,000,000 tonnes
19X6 2,200,000 tonnes
19X7 2,400,000 tonnes

The payments to the government of Karogea (under either alternative) would be financed entirely by borrowing. The terms of the loan arrangement include that repayment, together with all the accumulated interest, will take place at the end of 19X7. Interest is currently charged at an annual rate of 20% compounded yearly.

Required:

(a) Show for alternative (1) the budgeted Royalties Account and the budgeted Loan and Loan Interest Account in respect of each of the five years 19X3 to 19X7 inclusive. The initial royalty payment is to be written off in the Royalties Account in proportion to the number of tonnes mined each year; and

(b) show for alternative (2) the budgeted Royalties Account and the budgeted Loan and Loan Interest in respect of each of the five years 19X3 to 19X7 inclusive.

(LCCI Higher 1987, amended)

COMMON ERRORS

1. Lack of Knowledge

Royalty accounts are not a particularly common examination topic, so students tend to have little experience in dealing with them.

2. Royalties Payable: Main Accounts

Remember that usually there are THREE main accounts:

(a) royalties account;
(b) creditor's (for example, landlord's account); and
(c) a shortworkings account.

The royalties account is DEBITED with the royalties payable for the period (based on usage for the period x rate per unit), and the creditor's account is CREDITED with the same amount.

All the other entries follow the usual double-entry principles (debit the account which receives, credit the account which gives), so make sure that you enter the transactions on the correct side of each account.

BE VERY CAREFUL THAT YOU DO NOT REVERSE THE ENTRIES.

3. Royalties Receivable

These are treated similarily to royalties payable, except that the entries are on the OPPOSITE side of the respective accounts.

Note that unlike royalties payable, the balance on the royalties receiveable account is written off to the PROFIT AND LOSS account, and not to the operating or manufacturing account.

27

CLUB AND SOCIETY ACCOUNTS

MAIN POINTS

1. Background

Besides preparing accounts for manufacturing and trading entities, accounts are also prepared for non-profit making (sometimes called not-for-profit) entities.

The main objective of such entities is usually to provide a service: they are not primarily in business to earn a profit. Even so, some non-profit making entities (such as a rugby or a social club), may have SOME profit-making activities. They may, for example, try to run the bar at a profit, or aim for a profit when they hold dances.

2. Accounting Treatment

The book-keeping and accounting requirements for non-profit making entities are very similar to those relating to profit-making entities.

  (a) Prepare separate profit and loss accounts for the main profit making activities of the entity.
  (b) (i) Prepare an INCOME AND EXPENDITURE account for the entity as a whole.
  (ii) Transfer the profits of losses on each profit making activities to the income and expenditure account. Describe the income and expenditure account balance as EXCESS OF INCOME OVER EXPENDITURE (or expenditure over income) FOR THE YEAR.
  (c) In the balance sheet, add (or deduct) the income and expenditure account balance to the ACCUMULATED FUND balance brought forward at the beginning of the period.

Example. The following is a summary of the receipts and payments of the Gaslite Club during the year ended 30 September 19X7.

Gaslite Club
Receipts and Payments Account
for the year ended 30 September 19X7

	£		£
Cash and Bank		Secretary's expenses	224
balances b/f	1,247	Rent	1,300
Member's subscriptions	4,388	Donations to charities	87

	£		£
Donations	150	Meeting expenses	559
		Heating and lighting	446
		Stationery and printing	320
		Purchase of office equipment	870
		Cash and Bank balances c/f	1,979
	£5,785		£5,785

The following valuations are also available:

As at 30 September	19X6	19X7
	£	£
Subscriptions in arrears	150	90
Heating and lighting accrued	110	83
Stocks of stationery	67	83

On 1 October 19X6 the Gaslite club owned office equipment costing £2,500 which had been depreciated by £500. The policy of the club is to depreciate office equipment at 10% per annum using the straight line method applied on a full year's basis. The club did not sell any office equipment during the year ended 30 September 19X7.

Required:

(a) Calculate the value of the Accumulated Fund of the Gaslite Club as at 1 October 19X6; and

(b) prepare an Income and Expenditure Account for the Gaslite Club for the year ended 30 September 19X7 and a Balance Sheet as at that date.

(AAT Certificate)

Solution:

(a)

Gaslite Club
Calculation of Accumulated Fund as at 1 October 19X6

	£
ASSETS:	
Equipment	2,000
Subscriptions in arrears	150
Stocks of stationery	67
Cash and Bank balances	1,247
	3,464
Less: LIABILITIES:	
Heating and lighting accrued	110
Accumulated fund	£3,354

(b)

Gaslite club
Income and Expenditure Account
for the year ended 30 September 19X7

	£	£
Subscriptions (Wkg 1)		4,328
Donations		150
		4,478

206

	£	£
Less: Expenses		
Secretary's expenses	224	
Rent	1,300	
Donations to charities	87	
Meeting expenses	559	
Heating and lighting (wkg 2)	419	
Stationery and printing (wkg 3)	304	
Depreciation [(£2,500+870)x10%]	337	3,230
Excess of income over expenditure for the year		£1,248

Gaslite Club
Balance sheet as at 30 September 19X7

	£	£
Fixed Assets :		
Office Equipment:		
At cost (£2,500+870)		3,370
Less: Accumulated depreciation (£500+337)		837
Net book value		2,533
Current Assets		
Stocks of stationery	83	
Subscriptions in arrears	90	
Bank and cash	1,979	
	2,152	
Less: Current liabilities		
Accrued expenses	83	2,069
		£4,602
Represented by:		
Accumulated fund as at 1 October 19X6		3,354
Add: Excess of income over expenditure for the year		1,248
		£4,602

Workings

Subscriptions

		£			£
1 10 X6	In arrears b/f	150	30 9 X7	Cash and Bank	4,388
30 9 X7	Income and Expenditure	4,328	30 9 X7	In arrears c/d	90
		£4,478			£4,478
1 10 X7	In arrears b/d	90			

Heating and lighting

		£			£
30 9 X7	Receipts and payments	446	1 10 X6	Balance b/f	110
30 9 X7	Balance c/d	83	30 9 X7	Income and expenditure	419
		£529			£529
			1 10 X7	Balance b/d	83

Stationery

		£			£
1 10 X6	Balance b/f	67	30 9 X7	Income and expenditure	304
30 9 X7	Receipts and payments	320	30 9 X7	Balance c/d	83
		£387			£387
1 10 X7	Balance b/d	83			

EXERCISES

27.1   The following is a summary of the receipts and payments of the Technicians Club during the year ended 31 December 19X6.

Technicians Club
Receipts and Payments Account
for the year ended 31 December 19X6

	£		£
Cash and Bank balances b/f	358	Secretary's expenses	150
Sales of disco tickets	632	Rent	800
Members' subscriptions	2,108	Meeting expenses	722
Donations	250	Heating and lighting	269
		Disco expenses	515
		Purchase of equipment	400
		Stationery and printing	287
		Cash and balances c/f	205
	£3,348		£3,348

The following valuations are also available:

As at 31 December	19X5	19X6
	£	£
Equipment, written down value (cost as at 31 December 19X5 - £1,800)	1,300	1,460
Subscriptions in arrears	80	110
Heating and lighting accrued	37	41
Stocks of stationery	54	46
Rent prepaid	200	240

Required:

Prepare an Income and Expenditure Account for the Technicians Club for the year ended 31 December 19X6 and a Balance Sheet as at that date.

(AAT Certificate)

27.2 The assets and liabilities of the Seashore Swimming Club as at 1st June 19X7 were:

Balance at bank £580. Equipment £290. Sundry expenses owing £15.
Stock of Refreshments £20. Rent prepaid £40. Accumulated fund £915.

The following is a summary of the receipts and payments of the club for the year ended 31st May 19X8.

Receipts	£	Payments	£
Opening balance 1 6 X7	580	Expenses of Dance	529
Annual Dance	917	Rent of Clubroom	540
Subscriptions	624	Purchase of Equipment	250
Locker Rents	248	Prizes for Competitions	95
Sales of Refreshments	268	Sundry Expenses	110
Competition Fees	142	Purchases of refreshments	160
Sale of Swimming Permits	60	Licence Fees to Council	90

The following information is also available:
(a) Stock of Refreshment at 31st May 19X8 was £10.
(b) Rent of Clubroom prepaid 31st May 19X8 £50.
(c) Sundry Expenses owing 31st May 19X8 £10.

Required:

(a) Calculate the club's bank balance as at 31st May 19X8; and
(b) prepare an income and expenditure account for the year ended 31st May 19X8 showing clearly the profit/loss on the dance and the sale of refreshments and a balance sheet as at that date.

(RSA Elementary)

27.3 The following Trial Balance was extracted by the Treasurer of the Pennine Kite Flying Association on 31 October 19X7.

	Dr £	Cr £
Accumulated Fund 1 November 19X6		685
Subscriptions received		2,040
Purchase of kite materials	460	
Rent of room	1,500	
Postages, printing and stationery	185	
Stock of kite materials, 1 November 19X6	170	
Income form refreshments		360
Purchases of refreshment supplies	340	
Cost of display by Chilean kite flyers	215	
Net income from social events		220
Sales of kite materials		620
Creditors for purchases of kite materials		110
Cash at bank	830	
Cash in hand	15	
Video equipment, at cost less depreciation	320	
	£4,035	£4,035

209

The following are to be taken into account:
(1) Subscriptions due but not received 31 October 19X7 - £140.
    Subscriptions received in advance of year ended 31 October 19X8 - £60.
(2) One quarter's rent room is outstanding - £500.
(3) Stock of kite materials 31 October 19X7 - £155.
(4) The video equipment is to be written down by £80.

Required:

Prepare the Income and Expenditure Account for the Pennine Kite Flying Association for the year ended 31 October 19X7, together with a Balance as at that date.   *(LCCI First Level, 1988)*

27.4 The following Trial Balance was obtained from the books of the Henton Cricket club on 31 March 19X6:

	Dr £	Cr £
Accumulated fund at 1 April 19X5		10,000
Cash at bank	3,600	
Cash in hand	700	
Investments at current value	4,500	
Sports equipment	4,000	
Furniture and fittings	2,000	
Restaurant stock of food at 1 April 19X5	200	
Members' subscriptions received		2,700
Income from cricket tournament		1,400
Income from social functions		2,600
Restaurant takings		9,200
Restaurant purchases of food	4,100	
Restaurant wages	3,700	
Administration expenses	1,100	
Expenses of social functions	800	
Rent and Rates	3,200	
Income from investments		400
Creditors		2,800
Purchase of lawn-mower on 31 March 19X6	1,000	
Insurance	200	
	£29,100	£29,100

Notes:
(1) Subscriptions due at 31 March 19X6 but not paid £400
(2) Restaurant stock of food at 31 March 19X6 £300
(3) Rates prepaid amounted to £300
(4) Provide for depreciation:
    Sports Equipment £1,200
    Furniture & Fittings £400

Required:

Prepare the Restaurant Trading Account, and the General Income and Expenditure Account for the year ended 31 March 19X6, together with a Balance Sheet as at that date.   *(LCCI Elementary 1986)*

27.5   The treasurer of the Newton Tennis Club has prepared the following summary of his cash book for the year ended 31 December 19X6.

Receipts	£	Payments	£
Balances at 1 January 19X6		Steward's wages	4,500
At bank	1,263	Purchase of new	
In hand	45	tennis equipment	530
Bar takings	17,448	Rent and Rates	1,900
Match Fees	274	Lighting & Heating	326
Subscriptions	1,520	Telephone	285
Sales of raffle tickets	571	Bar purchases	12,982
Gaming machine takings	1,285	Gaming machine rent	500
		Prizes for raffles	130
		Balances at	
		31 December 19X6:	
		At bank	1,170
		In hand	83
	£22,406		**£22,406**

The treasurer also provides the following information :

	At 31 December 19X6 £	At 31 December 19X6 £
Accumulated Fund	3,711	
Members' subscriptions:		
Due but unpaid	64	80
Paid in advance	40	48
Rates paid in advance	200	250
Bar stocks	1,326	1,543
Creditors for bar purchases	747	802
Clubhouse furnishings		
(at cost less depreciation)	680	
Tennis equipment		
(at cost less depreciation)	920	

You ascertain that :

(i)   The steward's wages are to be apportioned as:
    Bar three-fifths
    General maintenance two-fifths.

(ii) Part-time bar staff had been paid £810 during the year with cash takings not recorded in the till.

(iii) Depreciation is to be written off tennis equipment at 20% per annum and off clubhouse furnishings at 5% per annum, calculated on the book values at 1 January plus additions during the year.

(iv) New curtains and chairs costing £400 have been included in the figure for Bar purchases.

Required:

Prepare a Bar Trading Account (showing clearly the bar profit or loss) and Income and Expenditure Account for the year ended 31 December 19X6 (showing profit or loss on the raffle and the gaming machine), together with a Balance Sheet as at that date.   *(RSA Intermediate)*

27.6 The Balance Sheet of the Risley Gardening and Botanical Society as at 31 December 19X5 is as follows:

	£		£
Accumulated fund	6,675	Gardening implements at cost	6,400
		Less : accumulated depreciation	1,600
			4,800
Subscriptions received		Stock of plants and seeds	120
in advance	80	Subscriptions due from members	60
Amounts due to suppliers of		Cash at bank and in hand	1,840
plants and seeds	65		
	£6,820		£6,820

During the year ended 31 December 19X6, the society's Treasurer recorded transactions as follows:

1. The hiring out to members of gardening implements against cash fees amounting to £1,950.
2. The sale to members of plants and seeds for cash £830.
3. The payment in cash of rent for hire of hall and store, £2,500
4. The payment by cheque of lecturers' fees, £370.
5. The receipt in cash of members' subscriptions amounting to £2,600.
6. The purchase by cheque of a set of plant encyclopedias - £280 - to be written off over 4 years.
7. The purchase on credit of plants and seeds amounting to £670.
8. There is a net cash outlay over the year of £140 arising from organised visits to botanical gardens.
9. The purchase of new gardening equipment on 15 July for £600 by cheque.
10. £650 is paid by cheque to plant and seed suppliers.

At 31 December 19X6 it is noted that:

(A) The stock of plants and seeds is valued at £145.
(B) Subscription amounting to £70 have been received in advance for the year ended 31 December 19X7. No subscriptions are outstanding.
(C) Depreciation on gardening implements is calculated at 20% per annum on cost. Any new equipment acquired during any half-year is treated for this purpose as having been owned for the full half-year.

Required:

Prepare:
(a) A Plant and Seeds Account;
(b) a Members' Subscriptions Account;
(c) an Income and Expenditure Account in respect of the Society for the year ended 31 December 19X6, incorporating the closing balances obtained in (a) and (b) above; and
(d) a Balance Sheet for the Society as at 31 December 19X6.

Note : You should show your workings for obtaining the closing Cash/Bank balance.

(LCCI 2nd Level, 1988)

27.7 The following list of balances has been extracted from the accounting records of the Handle Social Club for the year to 31 March 19X5:

Summary of the Cash Book :

	Receipts £	Payments £
Opening balance brought forward	500	
Accountant's fee		200
Bar purchases		24,000
Bar sales	55,000	
Dances: expenses		900
sales	1,600	
Foods: purchases		4,500
sales	8,000	
Insurance		500
Electricity		1,500
Members' subscriptions	35,000	
Office expenses		22,000
Purchase of furniture and equipment (at 2 4 X4)		4,000
Rates		2,000
Salaries and wages: barmen		10,000
other staff		14,000
Telephone		3,000
Travelling expenses		13,000
Closing balance carried forward		500
	£100,100	£100,100

Other information :

(1) Fixed assets

	£	£
At 1 April 19X4		
Club premises at cost		18,000
Furniture and equipment at cost	35,000	
Less accumulated depreciation	14,000	
		21,000
		£39,000

(2) Accruals and Sundry Creditors

	At 1 4 X4 £	At 31 3 X5 £
Accountant's fee	200	250
Bar purchases	1,500	2,000
Electricity	400	300
Members' subscriptions (paid in advance)	1,000	800
Telephone	600	700

(3) Sundry prepayments

	At 1 4 X4 £	At 31 3 X5 £
Insurance	300	200
Members' subscriptions (in arrears)	6,000	7,000

(4) The Club did not keep a bank account, although it did have a building society account which had a balance of £2,500 on 1 April 19X4. It was not used during the year to 31 March 19X5 and the only entry in it was for interest of £200 which was credited to the account on 31 March 19X5.

(5) Furniture and equipment is depreciated at a rate of 10% per annum on cost with no allowance being made for any scrap value.

(6) Bar stock was valued at cost of £7,000 on 1 April 19X4 and at cost of £1,500 on 31 March 19X5.

(7) No apportionment of costs is made between bar activities and other club events.

Required:

    (a) Prepare the following account for the year to 31 March 19X5:
        (i)   the bar account; and
        (ii) the income and expenditure account.
    (b) A balance sheet as at this date.

(AAT Level 2)

COMMON ERRORS

1. Format

The income and expenditure account is very similar to a profit and loss account. However, if separate profit and loss accounts are not prepared for the specific profit making activities of the entity, net the income against the expenditure in the main income and expenditure account, for example:

	£	£
Income from dances	X	
Less: Expenses	X	X

2. Accruals and Prepayments

Club and society account questions usually require many adjustments for opening and closing accruals and prepayments. Make sure that you add and subtract these adjustments correctly: it may be helpful to draw up rough "T" accounts in your workings in order to make sure that you make the adjustments correctly.

Do not forget to enter the CLOSING accruals and prepayments in the balance sheet.

3. Subscriptions Due

It may not be prudent to accrue for subscriptions due from members of a voluntary organisation, since it can be very difficult to recover outstanding debts from members who have left the organisation.

Some questions, therefore, may not require you to accrue outstanding subscriptions.

4. Life Membership Subscriptions

Life membership subscriptions should be credited to a special account, and a proportion of them transferred annually to the income and expenditure account over the average life membership of such subscribers. A similar treatment may also be required for ENTRANCE FEES.

5. Depreciation Adjustments

It is very easy to make errors in calculating the depreciation for the year. The depreciation charged to the income and expenditure account is the depreciation FOR THE YEAR. In the balance sheet, ADD this amount to the accumulated depreciation brought forward at the beginning of the year.

28 PARTNERSHIP ACCOUNTS: INTRODUCTION

MAIN POINTS

1. Background

A partnership is defined in the 1890 Partnership Act as "the relation which subsists between persons carrying on a business in common with a view of profit".

The division of profit between the partners will usually be a matter for agreement between them. It will probably include arrangements for paying interest on capital and current account balances, drawings, interest charged on drawings, salaries, and the overall division of profit.

2. Accounting Treatment

(a) Capital accounts. An account will be kept for each partner recording the amount of capital contributed to the partnership.

(b) Current accounts. An account will normally be kept for each partner detailing the partner's drawings and his appropriation of profit. (Note that some partnerships do not keep separate capital and current accounts).

(c) Partners' loan accounts. If a partner has made a SPECIFIC loan to the partnership (irrespective of the capital that he has agreed to contribute), the loan should be CREDITED to a partners' loan account,

(d) Final accounts. The manufacturing, trading and profit and loss accounts are identical to those prepared for single entities.

(e) Profit and loss appropriation account. With a partnership entity, it is customary to prepare a profit and loss appropriation account; the appropriation account should come after the profit and loss account.

The profit and loss appropriation account shows in detail how the profit (or loss) for the year is shared between the partners, for example, it will include details about interest allowed or payable on capital, current and drawings account balances, bonuses, commissions, salaries paid to the partners, and how the remaining balance of profit is divided between the partners.

Note that interest on a specific loan made by a partner should be DEBITED to the PROFIT AND LOSS account, and NOT to the profit and loss appropriation account.

215

(f) Balance sheet. The preparation of the fixed assets, current assets, and current liabilities sections of the balance sheet is identical to that of single entities.

The financing section is shown in two sections:

(i) CAPITAL ACCOUNTS (listing the balance in each partner's capital account at the balance sheet date); and

(ii) CURRENT ACCOUNTS (listing the balance in each partner's current account at the balance sheet date).

Example 1. Beaver and Burroughes are two sole traders who decide to enter into partnership as from 1 March 19X6. Their respective Balance Sheets as at the close of business on 28 February 19X6 were as follows:

BEAVER

	£		£
Capital account	2,990	Office furniture	500
Creditors	850	Delivery van	660
Bank overdraft	320	Stock	1,440
		Debtors	1,530
		Cash in hand	30
	£4,160		£4,160

BURROUGHES

	£		£
Capital account	5,200	Office furniture	550
Creditors	920	Delivery van	750
		Stock	1,970
		Debtors	1,730
		Bank	1,120
	£6,120		£6,120

The partnership acquired ALL the assets and took over ALL the liabilities at the figures shown in the above Balance Sheets except that:

		Beaver	Burroughes
		£	£
(1)	Office Furniture is to be revalued	400	480
(2)	Stock is to be revalued	1,300	1,900
(3)	Goodwill is valued at	-	400
(4)	Bad debts are to be written off	120	80
(5)	The bank accounts are to be closed and a new partnership bank account opened:		

Required:

(a) Calculate the opening capital of each of the two partners. (Calculations must be shown); and

(b) draw up the opening Balance Sheet of the partnership.

(LCCI Elementary 1986)

216

Solution

(a) Calculation of opening capital

	Beaver £	Burroughes £
Goodwill	-	400
Office furniture	400	480
Delivery van	660	750
Stock	1,300	1,900
Debtors: (£1530-120; £1,730-80)	1,410	1,650
Cash at bank	-	1,120
Cash in hand	30	-
	3,800	6,300
Less: Creditors	850	920
Bank overdraft	320	-
	1,170	920
Opening capital at 1 March 19X6	£2,630	£5,380

(b)

BEAVER AND BURROUGHES

Balance sheet at 1 March 19X6

	£	£
Intangible assets		
Goodwill		400
Fixed assets		
Office furniture	880	
Delivery vans	1,410	2,290
Current assets		
Stock	3,200	
Debtors	3,060	
Cash at bank (£1,120-320)	800	
Cash in hand	30	
	7,090	
Less: **Current Liabilities**		
Creditors	1,770	5,320
		£8,010
Capital		
Beaver		2,630
Burroughes		5,380
		£8,010

Example 2. Robert, Susan and Thomas are in partnership. The capitals they have invested in the partnership are £50,000, £40,000 and £20,000 respectively. During the financial year ended 30 September 19X6 the partnership earned a net profit of £42,000. The partners have agreed the following appropriation scheme:

(i) Interest is to be allowed on capital at 12% per annum.

(ii) Susan and Thomas are to receive salaries of £4,000 and £5,000 respectively.

(iii) Profits are to be shared in the ratio 4:3:1 respectively.

The partners had the following balances on their Current Accounts as at 1 October 19X5:

	£	
Robert	121	(credit)
Susan	105	(debit)
Thomas	197	(credit)
	£213	

During the year ended 30 September 19X6 the partners withdrew the following amounts from the partnership:

	£
Robert	15,940
Susan	16,020
Thomas	10,400
	£42,360

Required:

(a) Show the Appropriation Account for the partnership for the year ended 30 September 1987 under the scheme; and

(b) prepare the partners' Current Accounts for the year ended 30 September 19X6.

(AAT Certificate)

Solution

(a)

ROBERT, SUSAN AND THOMAS

Appropriation Account for the year ended 30 September 19X6

				£
Net profit for the year				42,000

Appropriation:

	Robert	Susan	Thomas	Total
	£	£	£	£
Interest on capital	6,000	4,800	2,400	13,200
Salary	-	4,000	5,000	9,000
Share of balance	9,900	7,425	2,475	19,800
	£15,900	£16,225	£9,875	£42,000

(b)

Current accounts

		Robert £	Susan £	Thomas £			Robert £	Susan £	Thomas £
1 10 X5	Balance b/f	-	105	-	1 10 X5	Balances b/f	121	-	197
30 9 X6	Drawings	15,940	16,020	10,400	30 9 X6	Int. on Cap.	6,000	4,800	2,400
30 9 X6	Balance c/d	81	100	-	30 9 X6	Salary	-	4,000	5,000
					30 9 X6	Share of profits	9,900	7,425	2,475
					30 9 X6	Balances c/d	-	-	328
		£16,021	£16,225	£10,400			£16,021	£16,225	£10,400
1 10 X6	Balance b/d	-	-	328	1 10 X6	Balances b/d	81	100	-

EXERCISES

28.1 Graham, Harvey, Rutherford and Miles are in partnership. The capital they have invested in the partnership are £75,000, £70,000, £60,000 and £60,000 respectively.

The partners have agreed the following appropriation scheme:

(a) Interest is to be allowed on capital at 10% per annum.

(b) Graham, Harvey, Rutherford and Miles are to receive salaries of £10,000, £10,000, £8,000 and £8,000 respectively.

(c) Profits are to be shared as follows:

Graham	35%
Harvey	35%
Rutherford	20%
Miles	10%

(d) Interest to be charged on drawings at 10% per annum.

Additional information:

(1) During the year ended 31 December 19X6 the partners withdrew the following amounts from the partnership:

	£
Graham	23,050
Harvey	21,980
Rutherford	16,640
Miles	17,300
	£78,970

(2) The amounts chargeable to each partner for drawings for the year ended 31 December 19X6 are:

	£
Graham	1,729
Harvey	1,100
Rutherford	832
Miles	789
	£4,450

(3) The partners had the following balances on their Current Accounts as at the 1 January 19X6:

	£	
Graham	2,100	(credit)
Harvey	3,370	(credit)
Rutherford	1,240	(debit)
Miles	980	(credit)
	£5,210	

(4) During the financial year ended 31 December 19X6 the partnership earned a net profit of £85,550.

Required:

(a) Draw up the Appropriation Account for the partnership for the year ended 31 December 19X6; and

(b) prepare the partners' Current Accounts for the years ended 31 December 19X6.

(AAT Preliminary, adapted)

28.2 Grahame, Margo and Raj set up in partnership together some years ago with capitals of £50,000, £30,000 and £15,000 respectively. The following are summaries of the partners' Current Account for the year ended 31 December 19X5. Study these carefully and then answer the questions which follow:

Grahame - Current Account

19X5		£	19X5		£
Dec 31	Drawings	13,031	Jan 1	Balance b/f	366
Dec 31	Share of balance	200	Dec 31	Interest on Capital	6,000
Dec 31	Balance b/d	135	Dec 31	Salary	7,000
		£13,366			£13,366

Margo - Current Account

19X5		£	19X5		£
Dec 31	Drawings	10,640	Jan 1	Balance b/d	264
Dec 31	Share of Balance	120	Dec 31	Interest on capital	3,600
			Dec 31	Salary	6,500
			Dec 31	Balance c/f	396
		£10,760			£10,760

Raj - Current Account

19X5		£	19X5		£
Jan 1	Balance b/f	133	Dec 31	Interest on Capital	1,800
Dec 31	Drawings	7,598	Dec 31	Salary	5,500
Dec 31	Share of Balance	80	Dec 31	Balance c/f	511
		£7,811			£7,811

Required:

(a) Reconstruct the appropriation scheme Grahame, Margo and Raj have agreed for the division of profits and losses;

(b) calculate the net profit of the partnership for the year ended 31 December 19X5;

(c) how would the partners have shared this profit had they made no formal agreement as to the division of profits?; and

(d) what would the partners' shares in profit have been had the net profit for the year ended 31 December 19X5 been £60,000?

(AAT Preliminary)

28.3 Barbara Fielding and Philip Spence practice in partnership as accountants. Interest on fixed capital balances is allowed at 8% per annum and the remaining profits are shared equally. The following Trial Balance was extracted from the ledger at the year ended 31 December 19X6:

		£	£
Bank			2,940
Fixed Capital:	Fielding		15,000
	Spence		8,000
Current Accounts:	Fielding		680
	Spence		740
Fees invoiced to clients			104,900
Rent of Office Premises		12,100	
Motor Vehicles at cost		18,400	
Accumulated Depreciation on Motor Vehicles			4,600
Clients Accounts unpaid		16,900	
Creditors			912
Salaries of Employees		45,217	
Stationery		2,094	
Insurances		2,620	
Telephone		1,020	
Heat and light		2,938	
Motor Vehicles Running Costs (excluding depreciation)		5,134	
Interest on Bank Overdraft		224	
Computer Equipment at cost		8,400	
Drawings:	Fielding	10,620	
	Spence	10,111	
Staff Training costs		1,994	
		£137,772	£137,772

The following additional matters are to be taken into account:

(1) Rent due, but unpaid, amounts to £1,100.
(2) Insurances are prepaid by £390.
(3) Motor vehicles are to be depreciated at 25% on cost per annum.
(4) Computer equipment is to be depreciated on a straight line basis over 2 years. No scrap value is foreseen,
(5) Stationery stocks amount to £211.

Required:

Prepare the Profit and Loss Account of the partnership (including the appropriation section) for the year ended 31 December 19X6 and a partnership Balance Sheet in vertical format as at that date.

(LCCI Elementary 1987)

28.4 John Dobbinson and William Spencer are in partnership sharing profits and losses equally. The following Trial Balance was extracted from their books at the close of business on 31 October 19X6:

	Dr £	Cr £
Purchases and sales	18,250	36,360
Wages and salaries	7,320	
Office furniture	820	
Debtors and creditors	6,800	7,900
Motor vehicle	7,000	
Rent, rates and insurance	2,100	
Bank balance	3,950	
Cash in hand	260	
Discounts	580	370
Fixtures and fittings	1,200	
Sundry expenses	175	
Stock 1 November 19X5	3,840	
Motor Vehicle Expenses	815	
Capital Accounts 1 November 19X5:		
Dobbinson		7,000
Spencer		5,000
Current Accounts 1 November 19X5:		
Dobbinson		1,230
Spencer		1,160
Drawings: Dobbinson	3,100	
Spencer	2,600	
Purchases and Sales Returns	480	270
	£59,290	£59,290

The following factors need to be taken into account at the year end.

(1) The stock at 31 October 19X6 is valued at £5,160.

(2) The partners' Capital Accounts are to remain FIXED at the figures shown in the Trial Balance.

(3) Interest is to be allowed on the Capital Accounts at the rate of 5% per annum.

(4) Depreciation at the rate of 20% is to be allowed on the book value of the Motor Vehicle. No depreciation is to be allowed on Office Furniture or Fixtures and Fittings.

(5) Salaries of £100 are to be accrued at 31 October 19X6.

Required:

(a) The Trading and Profit and Loss Account for the year ended 31 October 19X6; and

(b) the Balance Sheet of the partnership as at 31 October 19X6.

(LCCI Elementary 1987)

28.5 See and Breeze are in partnership as accountants and the following balances were extracted from their books on 31 October 19X7:

	£	£
Freehold premises (at cost)	45,000	
Office machinery (at cost)	18,000	
Motor vehicles (at cost)	24,000	
Fees from clients		110,000
Commissions from insurance companies		2,750
Building society agency commissions		6,200
Stationery	1,850	
Insurance	1,400	
Staff salaries	52,000	
Light and heat	2,800	
Rates	1,400	
Telephone	1,600	
Vehicle expenses	4,800	
Capital:		
Sea		30,000
Breeze		20,000
Current accounts:		
Sea	1,000	
Breeze		3,000
Drawings:		
Sea	9,750	
Breeze	8,250	
Debtors and Creditors	14,000	8,000
Office expenses	2,800	
Provisions for depreciation:		
Office machinery		3,600
Vehicles		6,000
Cash and Bank	900	
	£189,550	£189,550

Notes:

1. There is a stock of stationery valued at £190 on October 31 19X7.

2. Office machinery is to be depreciated by 10% of its cost price and 25% of the book value of the vehicles is to be written off as depreciation.

3. One client who is at present on the books as a debtor for £100 has been declared bankrupt. It is decided to write this amount off as a bad debt.

4. Rates have been pre-paid by £200 and there is a telephone bill outstanding of £60.

5. The terms of the partnership agreement provide for Breeze to be paid a salary of £4,000 per annum and interest to be allowed on capital at 10% per annum. The balance of the profit is to be divided in the ratios in which partners have provided capital.

6. The partners maintain fixed capital accounts, all adjustments being made through the current accounts.

Required:

Prepare the profit and loss account and appropriation accounts together with the partners' current accounts for the year ended 31 October 19X7. [*Note*: A BALANCE SHEET IS NOT REQUIRED]. *(RSA Intermediate)*

28.6 Jean and Peter Phillips trade in partnership as "New Castle Antiques". The following Trial Balance was extracted from the firm's books at 31 March 19X7:

	Dr £	Cr £
Capital accounts: Jean Phillips		15,000
Peter Phillips		10,000
Current accounts: Jean Phillips		2,450
Peter Phillips		750
Freehold Property at cost	30,000	
Fixtures and Fittings (cost £3,300)	2,640	
Motor vehicle (cost £4,000)	3,200	
Drawings: Jean Phillips	3,500	
Peter Phillips	2,000	
Sales		20,000
Stock at 1 April 19X6	1,100	
Purchases	7,900	
Rates	1,100	
Insurance	220	
Electricity	310	
Telephone	260	
Motor expenses	640	
General expenses	170	
Loan account: Jean Phillips		5,000
Trade debtors and creditors	140	250
Bank	210	
Cash in had	60	
	£53,450	£53,450

The partnership agreement provides that:

(a) Partners are entitled to interest on their fixed capitals at 8% per annum.
(b) Interest on any loans made by a partner is allowed at 10% per annum.
(c) Jean Phillips is to receive an annual salary of £2,500.
(d) Profits and losses are to be shared, Jean two-thirds, Peter one-third.

The following information should also be taken into consideration:

(i) Depreciation is to be charged at 10% per annum on Fixtures and Fittings using the straight line method, and at 20% per annum on the motor vehicle using the reducing balance method.

(ii) On 31 March 19X7, insurance premium prepaid was £54, an electricity bill of £80 was due but unpaid and stock was valued at £1,000.

(iii) Motor expenses (excluding depreciation) chargeable to the partners for their private use of the firm's vehicle are:

Jean £100   Peter £150

(iv) The loan from Jean was made in one single payment on 1 October 19X6.

Required:

(a) Prepare the Trading and Profit and Loss Account (including the appropriation section) for New Castle Antiques for the year ended 31 March 19X7, together with a Balance Sheet as at that date; and

(b) the partners' Current Accounts, in columnar form, showing the balances to be carried down at 31 March 19X7.

(RSA Intermediate)

28.7 John Degg and William Sant were general merchants sharing profits and losses, Degg 3 parts, Sant 1 part. By a partnership deed, dated 1 December 19X4, their capital were fixed at Degg £12,000 and Sant £15,000. The following Trial Balance shows the positions at 31 December 19X7:

		£	£
Wages and salaries		8,416	
Discounts		336	284
Bank interest			205
Stock 1 1 X4		5,316	
Purchases and sales		21,135	35,366
Premises at cost		12,000	
Insurance		184	
General expenses		1,480	
Returns		687	351
Carriage outwards		483	
Carriage inwards		192	
Furniture and Fittings		1,880	
Bank Deposit Account		8,400	
Bank Current Account			214
Capital:	Degg		12,000
	Sant		15,000
Debtors and Creditors		2,217	4,148
Cash in hand		42	
Drawings:	Degg	1,800	
Drawings:	Sant	3,000	
		£67,568	£67,568

Other relevant information is:

1. Interest at the rate of 6% per annum should be allowed on the capital but no interest is to be charged on the drawings.

2. William Sant is entitled to a salary of £4,000 per year.

3. Furniture and Fittings were revalued at £1,600.

4. Prepayments of insurance totalled £42 and accruals of carriage outwards £51.

5. Three quarters of the wages and salaries are to be allocated to the Trading Account and one quarter to the Profit and Loss Account. (This does not apply to PARTNER'S salary).

6. Stock in trade at 31 December 19X4 was valued at cost £7,860.

Required:

Prepare a Profit and Loss Account and an Appropriation Account for the year ended 31 December 19X4 and a balance sheet as at that date.

(LCCI Intermediate 1985, amended)

28.8 Bottle and Glass are in partnership sharing profits and losses in the ratio 3:2. The following trial balance has been extracted from their books of account for the year to 31 May 19X5 after the calculation of the net profit for the year:

	£	£
Bank	2,000	
Capital at 1 June 19X4:		
Bottle		40,000
Glass		10,000
Creditors		130,000
Debtors	116,000	
Drawings:		
Bottle	20,000	
Glass	5,000	
Furniture and fittings at cost	12,000	
Furniture and fittings:		
Accumulated depreciation at 31 May 19X5		3,000
Loan (from Bottle)		25,000
Net profit for the year to 31 May 19X5		82,000
Stock at 31 May 19X5	80,000	
Vehicles at cost	65,000	
Vehicles: Accumulated depreciation at 31 May 19X5		10,000
	£300,000	£300,000

Additional information:

1. The partners do not keep current accounts and all the partnership adjustments are made within the capital accounts.

2. The partners have agreed to the following arrangements between themselves:
   (a) Interest is to be charged on drawings at a rate of 5% per annum.
   (b) The partners are to be credited with interest at a rate of interest of 10% per annum on their capital account balances as at 1 June in each year.
   (c) Glass is to be allowed a salary of £10,000 per annum.

3. Bottle's loan is to be repaid by 31 May 19X9.

4. The partners' drawings were made on 1 December 19X4.

Required:

(a) Prepare Bottle and Glass' appropriation account for the year to 31 May 19X5;

(b) compile their capital accounts for the year to 31 May 19X5 in columnar form; and

(c) prepare the partnership balance sheet as at 31 May 19X5.

(AAT Level 2)

28.9 The following list of balances as at 30 September 19X6 has been extracted from the books of Peter James and Angus Victor who are trading in partnership:

		£
Freehold property at cost at 30 September 19X5:		30,000
Provision for depreciation at 30 September 19X5		6,000
Fixtures and fittings at cost at 30 September 19X5:		18,000
Provision for depreciation at 30 September 19X5:		9,600
Stock at 30 September 19X6		11,000
Debtors		4,600
Creditors		5,800
Balance at bank		2,700
Gross profit		39,000
Establishment and administrative expenses		9,100
Sales and distribution expenses		13,000
Capital accounts at 30 September 19X5:	Peter James	25,000
	Angus Victor	15,000
Current accounts at 30 September 19X5:	Peter James	6,000 credit
	Angus Victor	2,300 debit
Loan from Peter James		10,000
Drawings:	Peter James	15,700
	Angus Victor	10,000

Additional information for the year ended 30 September 19X6:

1. Interest at the rate of 10% per annum is payable annually in arrears on the loan from Peter James, the loan was received on 1 April 19X6.

2. All sales produce a uniform rate of gross profit.

3. Provision is to be made for depreciation as follows:
    Freehold property 5% per annum on cost
    Fixtures and fittings   10% per annum on cost

4. Electricity charges accrued due at 30 September 19X6 amounted to £360.
    Note: The electricity charges are included in establishment and administrative expenses.

5. 2/3rds of sales took place in the second half of the year.

6. No provision has been made in the accounts for a sales commission of 2% of gross profit payable to sales staff as from 1 April 19X6.

7. Provision is to be made for a salary of £10,000 per annum to be credited to Angus Victor as from 1 April 19X6.

8. Partners are to be credited with interest on the balances of their capital accounts at the rate of 5% per annum.

Required:

(a) Prepare the profit and loss account and profit and loss appropriation partnership account for the year ended 30 September 19X6;

(b) prepare the partnership balance as at 30 September 19X6; and

(c) indicate one significant matter revealed in the accounting statements prepared which should be brought to the attention of the partners.

(AAT Intermediate)

28.10 D Eddy and P Dale were sole traders who decided that they would merge their businesses into a partnership on 1 January 19X8. Their agreement stated that capitals were to be fixed, that they were to be entitled to interest on capitals at 7% per annum, and that profits should be shared in the ratio of 2 (Eddy) to 1 (Dale). At 31 December 19X7, their Balance Sheets were as follows:

D Eddy
Balance Sheet
as at 31 December 19X7

	£		£	£
Capital Account	75,550	Fixed Assets		
		Freehold Premises		50,000
		Motor vehicles		8,500
		Fixtures and Fittings		6,500
				65,000
Current Liabilities		Current Assets		
Sundry Creditors	3,450	Stock	4,800	
		Debtors	5,600	
		Balance at Bank	3,600	
				14,000
	£79,000			£79,000

P Dale
Balance Sheet
as at 31 December 19X7

	£		£	£
Capital Account	31,000	Fixed Assets		
		Motor Vehicles		7,800
		Fixtures and fittings		9,400
				17,200
Current Liabilities		Current Assets		
Sundry Creditors	3,200	Stock	6,950	
		Debtors	7,250	
		Balance at Bank	2,800	
				17,000
	£34,200			£34,200

It was agreed that the partnership should take over all assets except the Bank Accounts at the following values:

	D Eddy	P Dale
	£	£
Freehold premises	60,000	-
Motor vehicles	6,000	7,000
Fixtures and fittings	5,000	8,000
Stock	3,500	6,000
Debtors	5,500	7,000

It was agreed that the creditors would be taken over at their book values.

Goodwill was valued at £6,000 for D Eddy's business and £5,700 for P Dale's business. The partners agreed that, although Goodwill was brought in to ascertain each partner's capital, they did not wish this Goodwill value to remain on the partnership accounts. They therefore agreed to write the Goodwill out of the Capital Accounts in the partnership profit and loss ratio.

To ensure the partnership had a bank balance, they brought in cash as follows:

D Eddy	£5,250
P Dale	£3,400

Required:

  (a) Show journal entries in the partnership books to record the acquisition of assets and liabilities from each sole trader, the writing off of the Goodwill, and to ascertain each partner's Capital.
     (*Note*: Narrations are NOT required); and

  (b) prepare the opening balance sheet of the partnership as at 1 January 19X8.
(LCCI 2nd Level 1988)

28.11 Elsie and Ciah were in partnership sharing profits (and losses) in the ratio 3:2 respectively. On January 19X8 the credit balance on their capital accounts were Elsie £17,000, Ciah £13,000. During the year to 31 December 19X8 the partnership made a profit of £19,480 before taking into consideration the implications of ANY of the following transactions, etc:

1. On 1 July 19X8 land was purchased for £10,000 and plant and machinery (depreciable at 14% per year on cost) for £4,000.

2. In order to provide the necessary funds, and to bring their capital accounts into line with their profit sharing ratio, the partners agreed to contribute between them an additional £10,000 in cash. Elsie paid in the necessary sum on 1 September 19X8 and Ciah paid in the necessary sum on 1 November 19X8.

3. The partners agreed to calculate interest on their capitals at the rate of 12% per year, calculated on a monthly basis form 1 January 19X8. Current Accounts were to be opened to record partnership profits (including interest on capital) and drawings.

4. Interest on a temporary bank loan required during July and August 19X8 amounted to £260 and partnership drawings for the year (all in cash) were Elsie £8,000 and Ciah £5,000.

Required:

  (a) A statement showing the calculation of the final profit figure for 19X8 and its division between the partners;

  (b) partners' Capital and Current Accounts (preferably in columnar form) for 19X8; and

  (c) calculation of the net effect on the firm's overall cash position of the transactions, etc., listed above.
(LCCI Higher 1987)

COMMON ERRORS

1. Appropriation of Profit

The appropriation of profit by the partners (no matter how described) should ALL be dealt with through the profit and loss APPROPRIATION ACCOUNT. The only exception to this rule is the interest paid on a specific loan made to the partnership by a partner. Such interest should be charged to the profit and loss account.

After you have made the entries in the appropriation account, remember to complete double-entry by making equal but OPPOSITE entries in the partners' current accounts

2. Interest

Interest allowed on capital and current accounts, or charged on current accounts and drawings, may only be for part of the accounting period. Make sure that you calculate the interest allowable or chargeable to the partners in accordance with the STRICT requirements of the question.

3. Profit Sharing Ratio

Double check that you have shared out the profits amongst the partners in their PROFIT sharing ratio. The profit sharing ratio may be different from the capital sharing ratio.

4. Drawings

Partners's drawings should be DEBITED to their CURRENT accounts and NOT to the appropriation account.

5. Arithmetic

It is very easy to make arithmetical errors in dealing with the appropriation of profit amongst the partners.

If you make a mistake in the appropriation account, all the other accounts that follow will also be incorrect. This can make the completion of more advanced partnership questions extremely difficult:

DOUBLE CHECK YOUR ARITHMETIC AT EACH STAGE.

6. Presentation

In a partnership balance sheet, it is preferable to include a separate section for the balances on the partners' capital accounts, and a separate section for the balances on their current accounts. Unless the question requires detailed capital and current accounts, the movements on these accounts should be shown as workings.

29

PARTNERSHIP ACCOUNTS: JOINT VENTURES

MAIN POINTS

1. Background

A joint venture is a temporary form of partnership. It is usually limited to one venture.

The partners in the venture will probably operate separate books of account, but in order to calculate the profit and loss on the joint venture a MEMORANDUM joint venture account has to be prepared.

2. Accounting Treatment

In each partner's books of account:

(i) Dr. Joint venture account
Cr. Bank or creditor's account
With the cost of purchases incurred in the joint venture

(ii) Dr. Joint venture account
Cr. Bank
With expenses incurred on behalf of the joint venture

(iii) Dr. Bank or debtor's account
Cr. With the joint venture sales

(iv) EITHER	OR
Dr. Joint venture account	Profit and loss account
Cr. Profit and loss account	Joint venture account
With the partner's share of the PROFIT made on the joint venture	With the partner's share of the LOSS incurred on the joint venture
(v) EITHER	OR
Dr. Bank account	Joint venture account
Cr. Joint venture account	Bank account
With the amount received from the other partners.	With the amount paid to the other partners

3 Memorandum Joint Venture Account

This account is not part of the double-entry system. In effect, it is a profit and loss account for the entire venture.

It matches all the incomes received against all of the expenditure incurred in operating the joint venture.

The balance on the account is shared out amongst the partners in their agreed profit sharing ratio.

231

Example.   In 19X2 North and South entered into a joint venture to buy and sell second hand books. Details of the joint venture were as follows:

2 1 X2   North rented some premises for £500.

4 1 X2   North purchased some books for £2,000.

6 1 X2   North purchased some more books for £9,000 in cash.

10 1 X2   South purchased some books for £3,000.

15 1 X2   South purchased a van for £4,000.

31 1 X2   Sales of books for the month received:

          North   £15,000
          South   £1,000

15 2 X2   South purchased books costing £6,000.

28 2 X2   Sales of remaining books:

          North   £12,000
          South   £2,000

28 2 X2   South sold the van for £2,500.

28 2 X2   Office expenses incurred:

          North   £3,000
          South   £1,500

Notes:

1   The joint venture was ended on 28 February 19X2.
2   It was agreed that profits and losses should be shared in the ratio of North 4/5ths and South 1/5th.
3   Any outstanding balances between the two parties were settled on 31 March 19X2.
4   All transactions were conducted on cash terms.

Required:

(a) Show the joint venture accounts in the books of each of the parties; and
(b) draw up a memorandum joint venture account at 31 March 19X2.

Solution

(a)   **North and South**

NORTH'S BOOKS
Joint Venture with South Account

		£			£
2 1 X2	Rent	500	31 1 X2	Sales	15,000
4 1 X2	Purchases	2,000	31 2 X2	Sales	12,000
6 1 X2	Purchases	9,000			
28 2 X2	Office expenses	3,000			
28 2 X2	Profit on joint venture	2,800			
31 3 X2	Cash to South	9,700			
		£27,000			£27,000

SOUTH'S BOOKS
Joint Venture with North Account

		£			£
10 1 X2	Purchases	3,000	31 1 X2	Sales	1,000
15 1 X2	Van	4,000	28 2 X2	Sales	2,000
15 2 X2	Purchases	6,000	28 2 X2	Sales of van	2,500
28 2 X2	Office expenses	1,500			
28 2 X2	Profit on joint venture	700	28 2 X2	Cash from North	9,700
		£15,200			£15,200

NORTH AND SOUTH
Memorandum joint venture account
for the period 1 January 19X2 to 28 February 19X2

	£	£
Sales (£15,000 + 12,000 + 1,000 + 2,000)		30,000
Less: Purchases (£2,000 + 9,000 + 3,000 + 6,000)		20,000
GROSS PROFIT		10,000
Less: Expenses		
Rent	500	
Office expenses (£3,000 + 1,500)	4,500	
Loss on sale of van (£4,000 - 2,500)	1,500	6,500
Net profit		3,500
Appropriation:		
North (4/5ths)	2,800	
South (1/5th)	700	3,500

EXERCISES

29.1 Frank and Louis entered into a joint venture to buy and sell crockery. The joint venture only lasted for three months, and the following are the transactions that took place during the time.

Date	Frank	Louis
1 1 X1	Delivery van purchased on credit for £7,000 from Dobson	Purchased £15,000 of crockery in cash.
5 1 X1	Cash purchased of £65,000.	Cash purchases of £20,000.
7 1 X1	Cash sales of £1,000.	Storage rooms rent for £2,000 paid by cheque to Salt.
10 1 X1	Dobson's account was settled by cheque.	-
31 1 X1	Credit sales of £20,000.	Credit sales £40,000.
31 1 X1	Office expenses incurred in cash of £1,000	Office expenses incurred in cash of £2,500.
4 2 X1	Credit purchases of £16,000	Credit purchases of £30,000.

Date	Frank	Louis
15 2 X1	Van expenses of £1,800 paid in cash	
28 2 X1	Credit sales of £45,000.	Credit sales of £50,000.
31 3 X1	Credit sales of £10,000.	Cash sales of £19,000.
31 3 X1	Frank paid all his outstanding creditors by cheque.	Louis settled all his outstanding creditors by cheque.
31 3 X1	Office expenses of £3,000 paid in cash.	Office expense paid in cash of £6,000.
31 3 X1	Van sold for £5,000 received in cash.	All debtors settled their accounts by cheque.
31 3 X1	All debtors (apart from one bad debt of £4,000) settled their accounts by cheque.	Travelling expenses of £700 incurred in cash.

Notes:

1 Frank and Louis agreed to share profits and losses equally.
2 The settlement between the partners took place on 31 May 19X1, any payment/receipt being made in cash.

Required:

(a) Draw up the joint venture account in the books of both Frank and Louis; and
(b) prepare the memorandum joint venture account for the period 1 January 19X1 to 28 February 19X1.

29.2 Thunder and Lightning Ltd have been trading together in a joint venture for several years, manufacturing goods in the United Kingdom and exporting them to the Far East. Profits on the joint venture have been shared in proportion to the sales value of the goods produced, and sold by each company, each year, in the venture.

Profits (losses) of the last three years on the venture were shared as follows:

Year	Thunder Ltd £	Lightning Ltd £	Total £
19X3	72,000	24,000	96,000
19X4	(15,000)	(21,000)	(36,000)
19X5	40,000	60,000	100,000

On January 19X6 Hipo Ltd joined the venture on the following terms:

(a) Hipo Ltd would be the sole importer for the joint venture in the Far East.

(b) In order to "buy into" the venture, Hipo would pay a premium equal to 20% of the weighted average of the profits less losses earned by the joint venture in the previous three years, 19X3 to have weight 1; 19X4 to have weight 2; and 19X5 to have weight 3. This premium was to be divided between Thunder Ltd and Lightning Ltd in proportion to their average individual profits less losses from the venture weighted in exactly the same way.

(c) Hipo Ltd would be entitled to a commission of 0.5% of the sales value of all goods sold and to an 8% share in the profits. This profit share was to be calculated after deducting the commission and AFTER DEDUCTING THE PROFIT SHARE ITSELF.

In 19X6, the total profits on the venture (before charging Hipo Ltd's commission) increased by 20% on 19X5. The goods supplied by Lightning Ltd for the venture had exactly the same sales value as 19X6, but the sales value of the goods supplied by Thunder increased sharply. The total joint venture sales for 19X6 were, therefore, £2,400,000 showing an increase of 100% on 19X5. It is joint venture policy that all goods produced for the joint venture are sold within the financial year in which they are produced.

Required:

(a) Calculate the premium payable by Hipo Ltd and its division between Thunder Ltd and Lightning Ltd; and

(b) show the division of the joint venture profit for 19X6 between the three participating companies. *(LCCI Higher 1986)*

29.3 Hew Johnson, an Edinburgh wine merchant agreed to join Margaret Beaton, the proprietrix of a hotel, in the purchase and sale of 600 cases of Beaujolais Nouveau, the profits to be shared equally. The shipment was received at Leith on 17 November 19X3 and on that day Johnson made payment of £6,000 for the wine and £4,200 for the duty thereon. Beaton paid Johnson her half share by bank giro.

Johnson settled the following accounts:

	£
Landing and deck charges	402
Carriage	326
Insurance	155
Warehousing	217

Both parties agreed that the wine would be marketed at £28 per case, less 5% discount per case if more than 10 cases were purchased. Johnson and Beaton initially agreed to purchase 50 cases and 20 cases respectively at £26 per case, settlement to be made at the end of the venture.

By 2 February 19X4 the following sales had been made by Beaton through her trade contracts, the income being received and banked by her:

		Delivery
Hawk Hotels	35 cases	10 December 19X3
Silver Inn Group	85 cases	12 December 19X3
Tornish Hotels	65 cases	17 December 19X3
Glen Allan Lodge	8 cases	14 January 19X4
Northern Globe Hotels	280 cases	21 January 19X4
Ancorn Guest House	7 cases	1 February 19X4

Johnson agreed to take over all remaining stock on the same terms as he had made on his previous purchase.

All accounts were settled by cheque on the delivery date with the exception of the Northern Globe Hotels account which was settled by a bill of exchange at three months. Beaton discounted this at her bank at a rate of 5%.

Accounts settled by Beaton were:

	£
Telephone	110
Printing and Stationery	78
Delivery and insurance	892

Required:

Prepare

(a) The joint venture account in each party's ledger reflecting the above transactions; and

(b) a statement bringing out the profit on the joint venture.

NOTES:

1 Make all calculations to the nearest £.

2 Ignore VAT and excise duties, except where indicated.

(ICAS Part 1)

COMMON ERRORS

1. Main Account

In dealing with joint venture accounts, there is only one extra account to open in EACH of the partner's books of account: a JOINT VENTURE WITH ..... ACCOUNT.

Remember to DEBIT this account with all the expenses incurred by the partner of behalf of the joint venture. Similarly, CREDIT the account with all incomes received in respect of the joint venture.

2 Memorandum Joint Venture Account

This account does not form part of any partner's double entry system. It is simply a working document that enables the overall profit or loss on the joint venture to be calculated, and to be apportioned between the partners in their agreed profit sharing ratio.

Make sure that it includes ALL incomes and all expenses connected with the joint venture, from ALL of the joint venture accounts in the books of ALL partners.

Once the profit or loss on the joint venture has been calculated, DEBIT the joint venture account in a partner's own books with his share of the profit (or CREDIT the account if it is a loss).

If the account is now in DEBIT, the partner will be entitled to receive the balance in cash from the other partners. If it is a CREDIT balance, he will have to pay the difference to the other partners.

30 PARTNERSHIP ACCOUNTS: CHANGES IN PARTNERS

MAIN POINTS

1. Background

When one partner dies or retires from a partnership, that partnership ceases to exist. Even if the remaining partners carry on in business, they are considered to be involved in a new partnership. In such circumstances, it is unusual, however, to close the books of account in an old partnership, and open a completely different set of books for a new one.

Changes in partnerships may take place for the following reasons:

(a) a partner dies or retires;
(b) a new partner joins the partnership;
(c) a partnership is completely disbanded;
(d) two or more partnerships are amalgamated; and
(e) a partnership is converted into a limited liability company. The accounting treatment necessary to deal with all these changes is very similar. (Note that (e) is dealt with in the next chapter).

2. Accounting Treatment

(i) EITHER
Dr. Revaluation account
Cr. Asset account
With any DECREASE in the value of an asset on the change in the partnership

OR
Dr. Asset account
Cr. Revaluation account
With any INCREASE in the value of an asset on the change in the partnership

(ii) EITHER
Dr. Revaluation account
Cr. Liability account
With any INCREASE in the amount owed on revaluation

OR
Dr. Liability account
Cr. Revaluation account
With any DECREASE in the amount owed on revaluation

(iii) Dr. Revaluation account
Cr. Bank account
With any costs arising form the change in partners

(iv) EITHER
Dr. Goodwill account
Cr. Revaluation account

OR
Dr. Goodwill account
Cr. Partners' capital accounts

With the amount of goodwill agreed to arise on the change of partnership

237

   (v)   EITHER   OR

Dr. Revaluation account	Dr. Partners' capital account
Cr. Partners' capital accounts	Cr. Revaluation account
With the SURPLUS on revaluation in profit sharing ratios	With the DEFICIT on revaluation in profit sharing ratios

   (vi)   EITHER   OR

Dr. Partners' current accounts	Partners capital accounts
Cr. Partners' capital accounts	Partners current accounts
With the CREDIT balance on the partners' current accounts	With the DEBIT balance on the partners' current accounts

  (vii)   EITHER

        Dr. Partners' capital accounts
        Cr. Bank or loan accounts (or partners capital accounts at the beginning of the new partnership)
        With the CREDIT balance on the capital accounts at the end of the old partnership

        OR

        Dr. Bank account
        Cr. Partners' capital accounts with the DEBIT balance on the capital accounts at the end of the old partnership.

3. Goodwill

Goodwill may be defined as "the difference between the value of a business as a whole and the aggregate of the fair values of its separable net assets" (SSAP 22: Accounting for goodwill).

If the new partners do not wish to retain goodwill in the books of the partnership it may be eliminated as follows:

     Dr. New partners' capital accounts in the new PROFIT sharing ratio
     Cr. Goodwill account
     With the balance in the goodwill account.

4. Garner v Murray

If a partner has a DEBIT balance on his capital account, and he is insolvent, write off the balance on his account to the remaining partners' capital accounts in the ratio of their last agreed CAPITAL balances.

5. Piecemeal Realisation

Note that on a partnership dissolution, it is unlikely that all of the assets and all of the liabilities will be realised on the same day.

Consequently the cash available for distribution should be shared in such a way that no partner takes more than his fare share.

The distribution of cash on a piecemeal basis is considered to be an ADVANCED accounting technique, and it is not covered in this book.

6. Realisation Account

If a partnership is to be dissolved, or it is to be amalgamated with another partnership, a realisation account will be used instead of a revaluation account.

The book-keeping entries are identical to those for a revaluation account.

7. Profit and Loss Account

If a change takes place in a partnership part way through a financial year, and a profit and loss account is not prepared at that time, the profit (or loss) for the year will have to be apportioned between the old and the new partnerships.

Example. Root and Branch are in partnership sharing profits and losses in the ratio 3:2. The following trial balance has been extracted from the books of account as at 31 October 19X2:

	£	£
Partners' Capital Accounts:		
Root		22,000
Branch		9,000
Net profit for the year to 31 October 19X2		35,000
Creditors		3,000
Office equipment, at cost	50,000	
Debtors	10,000	
Cash	9,000	
	£69,000	£69,000

Notes:

1 No appropriations of profit for the year have yet been made.

2 Branch is entitled to a salary of £5,000 per annum.

3 Root decides to retire on 31 October 19X2, and Twig will join Branch in partnership as from 1 November 19X2. Profits and losses will be shared equally.

4 The goodwill of the old partnership is estimated to be worth £10,000. Twig is to introduce £20,000 in cash immediately as his capital, but no goodwill account is to be opened.

5 The amount owing to Root on his retirement is to be retained as a loan to the new partnership, except for £16,000 which will be drawn in cash. At the same time, Branch will also withdraw £10,000 in cash.

6 Current Accounts are not kept.

Required:

(a) Prepare the Capital Accounts of the old and new partnership necessary to record the above transactions; and

(b) compile the balance sheet of Branch and Twig as at 1 November 19X2.

(AAT/IAS Part 1)

Solution

ROOT AND BRANCH
Partners Capital Accounts

	Root £	Branch £		Root £	Branch £
Cash	16,000	10,000	Balance b/d	22,000	9,000
Loan	30,000		Salary	-	5,000
Balance b/d		20,000	Net profit		
			(£35,000-5,000x3:2)	18,000	12,000
			Goodwill (3:2)	6,000	4,000
	£46,000	£30,000		£46,000	£30,000

	Branch	Twig		Branch	Twig
Goodwill (2:2)	5,000	5,000	Balance b/d	20,000	-
Balances b/d	15,000	15,000	Cash	-	20,000
	£20,000	£20,000		£20,000	£20,000
			Balance b/d	15,000	15,000

(b)

Branch and Twig
Balance Sheet at 1 November 19X2

	£	£
Fixed Asset		
Office Equipment, at cost		50,000
Current Assets		
Debtors	10,000	
Cash (£9,000+20,000-16,000-10,000)	3,000	
	13,000	
Less: Current liability		
Creditors	3,000	10,000
		£60,000
Capital:		
Branch		15,000
Twig		15,000
		30,000
Loan:		
Root		30,000
		£60,000

EXERCISES

30.1 Alan and Brian are in partnership sharing profits as:

Alan	Salary of £4,000 per annum
Balance	Alan: 5/8 : Brian: 3/8.

Their balance sheet as 30 April 19X5 showed the following:

	£000		£000
Capital: Alan	80	Goodwill	2
Brian	116	Fixed tangible assets	148
Current liabilities	34	Cash at bank	6
		Other current assets	74
	£230		£230

On 1 May 19X5, Colin was admitted to the partnership with the following agreement:

(i) Goodwill is to be valued at one year's purchase of the weighted average profits of the preceding three years which were 19X2/3: £25,000; 19X3/4 £34,000; 19X4/5: £37,000.

(ii) Colin is to bring £50,000 cash and his car valued at £10,000 into the partnership.

(iii) The profit sharing ratio from 1 May 19X5 is to be:

Alan:	Salary of £6,000 a year
Colin:	Salary of £10,000 a year
Balance:	Alan 5/17: Brian 6/17: Colin 6/17.

Required:

Record the changes resulting from the change in the partnership by showing:

(a) The goodwill account - the balance of this account is to be written off immediately after the admission of Colin;

(b) the partners' capital accounts in columnar form; and

(c) the balance sheet after the admission of Colin.

(RSA Advanced)

30.2 Chair and Table were in partnership as surveyors sharing profits (and losses) in the ratio of 2:1 respectively. Their business was conducted from offices in Leeds and Manchester. It was agreed that the partnership should be dissolved as from 31 March 19X5 with Chair taking over the Leeds office and Table taking over the Manchester office. Their Balance Sheet at that date was as follows:

Balance Sheet

	£000			£000
Capital Accounts:		Goodwill		10
Chair	50	Furniture		9
Table	13	Debtors:	Leeds	10
	63		Manchester	5
Creditors	11	Bank		40
	£74			£74

Goodwill was revalued at Leeds £7,000; Manchester £5,000.
Furniture was revalued at Leeds £5,000; Manchester £3,000.

Besides the above, each partner agreed to take over the debtors associated with his office at their book value less 8% provision for bad debts. Chair agreed to pay off all the partnership creditors on which cash discounts received amounted to £300.

It was also agreed (1) that amounts of £2,500 and £700 should be allowed to Chair and Table respectively towards redecorating the premises previously occupied by the partnership and (2) that the dissolution costs of £1,100 should be paid by the partnership.

Required:

Assuming that all the transactions relating to the partnership dissolution were carried out as agreed, show:

  (a) The Realisation Account;
  (b) the Bank Account; and
  (c) the Capital Accounts (in columnar form)

(LCCI 3rd Level 1988)

30.3 Adams, Bartram and Charlton were retailers in Stoke on Trent who were partners sharing profits and losses in the ratio 3:2:1 respectively. Their Balance Sheet dated 31 December 19X7 showed:

Capital Accounts	£	Fixed Assets	£	£
Adams	10,000	Premises	7,300	
Bartram	8,000	Motor vehicles at		
Charlton	4,000	Net book value	11,100	
	22,000			18,400

Current Accounts			Current Assets		
	£			£	
Adams	2,000		Stock in trade	2,960	
Bartram	(1,000)		Debtors	10,976	
Charlton	1,000	2,000			13,936
		24,000			

Current Liabilities				
Creditors	3,700			
Bank Overdraft	4,636	8,336		
		£32,336		£32,336

Bartram retired on 1 January 19X8 on which date Dixon was admitted as a partner and introduced £7,000 cash as capital, taking the same share of the profits (or losses) as Bartram.

Adjustments:

  1   Bartram retained a motor vehicle - book value £2,800.
  2   Bartram took £2,500 in cash and the balance due to him was transferred to a Loan Account.
  3   A Goodwill Account was opened to record Goodwill valued at £6,000.
  4   The premises were revalued at £9,700.

Required:

(a) Prepare Capital Accounts in columnar form for Adams, Bartram, Charlton and Dixon incorporating the necessary adjustments, and bring down any balances at 1 January 19X8; and

(b) prepare the opening Balance Sheet of the new partnership as at 1 January 19X8.   *(LCCI 2nd Level 1988)*

30.4 Rachel, Andrew and William are partners in a firm which shared profits in the ratio 3:2:1 respectively with Andrew being entitled to a 4% commission on sales. On 1 July 19X5 George was admitted to the partnership and the profit-sharing arrangements were as follows:

Salaries:	Andrew	£16,000 per annum
	William	£8000 per annum
Commission on	William:	8%
total sales:	George:	4%
Balance:	Rachel and Andrew	3/10 each
	George and William	2/10 each

On the admission of George it was decided:

(a) to revalue the goodwill to £26,000 and then to write it out of the books;

(b) that George should introduce £15,000 cash into the business.

The trial balance at 31 December 19X5 was as follows:

	£000	£000
Capital accounts as at 31 12 X4:		
Rachel		36
Andrew		30
William		17
Cash introduced by George		15
Drawings:		
Rachel	5	
Andrew	7	
William	10	
George	2	
Sales		350
Purchases	185	
Stock 31 12 X4	31	
Fixed assets at cost	200	
Depreciation provision at 31 12 X4		58
Debtors	39	
Bank balance	7	
Goodwill at 31 12 X4	20	
General overheads	32	
Creditors		32
	£538	£538

Notes:

(i) Sales, gross profit and general overheads can be assumed to accrue on a time basis.

(ii) Depreciation of all fixed assets is 25% on cost.

(iii) Stock at 31 12 X5 was valued at £34,000.

Required:

(a) Trading and Profit and Loss Account for the year ended 31 December 19X5, showing the division of the profit between the two half years and the appropriation of the profit amongst the partners;

(b) the partners' capital accounts for the years ending 31 December 19X5 (there are no separate accounts); and

(c) balance sheet as at 31 December 19X5.

(RSA Advanced)

30.5 Mark and Luke have been in partnership as builders' merchants for many years, sharing profits equally. Their balance sheet at 31 December 19X7 showed:

	£		£
Mark	46,000	Fixed Assets	25,000
Luke	34,100	Goodwill	5,000
Creditors	41,200	Stock	64,000
Overdraft	15,700	Debtors	43,000
	£137,000		£137,000

The business has ceased to be profitable and on 1 January, they agreed to close the business and dissolve the partnership.

The events of the dissolution were:

1 The fixed assets were sold for £21,000;
2 The stock was sold at auction for £41,000;
3 The debtors were collected but only after bad debts of £6,500;
4 The creditors were paid in full with the addition of £3,500 redundancy pay to the workforce;
5 The expenses (£650) of the dissolution were paid.

Required:

(a) Draw up the realisation account;
(b) draw up the cash book; and
(c) draw up the capital accounts of the two partners.

NOTE: All accounts should be in double-entry form.

(RSA Advanced)

30.6 Tess, Max and Henrietta have dissolved their partnership on 30 November 19X4 when the balance sheet was:

BALANCE SHEET AS AT 30 NOVEMBER 19X4

Fixed Assets (at book value)	£000	£000
Freehold Property		100
Equipment		35
		135
Current assets		
Stocks	40	
Debtors	32	
Cash at bank	20	
	92	

Current Liabilities	£000	£000
Creditors	41	51
		£186

Financed by:

Capital Accounts

Tess	46	
Max	75	
Henrietta	1	122

Current Accounts

Tess	36	
Max	2	
Henrietta	(5.5)	32.5

Long term liability

Loan: Max		31.5
		£186

The partners failed to find a buyer for the business and had to sell the assets separately for the following amounts:

	£000
Freehold Property	110
Equipment	24
Stock	27

The partnership granted £4,000 discount to debtors and a £1,500 discount was received from creditors. Dissolution expenses were £2,000.

The partners share profits and losses in the ratio 3:6:1.

Required:

Prepare the

(a) Cash book;
(b) Realisation account;
(c) Capital Account

To record the effects of the above transactions.

(RSA Advanced)

30.7 Apple and Orange are in partnership, as are Pear and Plum. It was decided that they should amalgamate on 1 January 19X9 to form a new partnership to be called Fruit and Co. The balance sheets of the two respective partnerships as at 31 December 19X8 were as follows:

	Apple and Orange £	Pear and Plum £		Apple and Orange £	Pear and Plum £
Capital A/cs:			Property	30,000	50,000
Apple	20,000		- Fixtures & fittings	8,000	14,000
Orange	20,000		- Vehicles	7,000	10,000

	£	£		£	£
Pear	-	50,000	Stocks	2,000	5,000
Plum	-	25,000	Debtors	1,000	1,000
Creditors	8,500	6,500	Bank and cash	500	1,500
	£48,500	£81,500		£48,500	£81,500

Further Information:

1   Apple and Orange share profits and losses equally, and Pear and Plum in the ratio 2:1. In the new partnership, profits and losses will be shared equally between all four partners.

2   The old partnership assets will be taken over by Fruit and Co. at the following values:

	Apple & Orange £	Pear & Plum £
Property	25,000	85,000
Fixtures and fittings	5,000	10,000
Motor vehicles	-	6,000
Goodwill	8,000	25,000
Stocks	2,000	5,000
Debtors	600	-
Bank and cash	500	1,500

3   Orange agrees to take over the Apple and Orange's vehicles at an agreed value of £2,000.

4   The liabilities will be taken over at their book value.

5   Goodwill will not be retained in the books of the new partnership.

6   The total capital of the new partnership is to be £160,000 shared equally between the partners.

Required:

(a)   Prepare in columnar format Apple and Orange's and Pear and Plum's Realisation Account and Capital Account (assuming that all transactions take place on 1 January 19X9), and

(b)   prepare Fruit and Co's balance sheet at 1 January 19X9.

30.8   Swale and Aire are in partnership sharing profits and losses in the ratio of 2 to 1. The partnership balance sheet as at 30 September 19X5 is shown below:

Fixed Assets	£ Cost	£ Deprec- iation	£ Net Book Value
Property	35,000	10,500	24,500
Plant and equipment	27,000	17,000	10,000
	£62,000	£27,500	34,500

Current Assets

Stocks at cost		10,000	
Debtors and prepayments		12,000	
Cash at bank		1,000	
		23,000	

Less: Current liabilities

Creditors and accruals	7,000	
		16,000
		£50,500

Capital Accounts

Swale	30,000	
Aire	5,000	35,000

Current Accounts

Swale	2,000	
Aire	3,500	
		5,500

Loan Account

Swale		10,000
		£50,500

Additional Information:

1. Swale decided to retire on 30 September 19X5, and Aire then came to an agreement with Wharfe to form a new partnership as from 1 October 19X5.

2. Upon Swale's retirement, all of the assets and liabilities of the partnership were revalued. The following new valuations were agreed:

	£
Property	40,000
Plant and equipment	8,000
Stocks	13,000
Debtors and prepayments	11,000
Creditors and accruals	10,500

3. The partnership had been a successful one and goodwill based on five years' super profits was agreed at a value of £42,000.

4. Aire allowed Swale to retain a motor car (revalued at £3,000 and included in the plant and equipment revaluation as disclosed in note 2 above) as part payment of the amount owing to him on his retirement.

5. It was agreed that Swale's old loan of £10,000 should be repaid on 1 October 19X5.

6. Swale agreed to leave half of the final amount owing to him on the dissolution of the partnership as a long term loan in the new partnership, the other half being paid to him in cash on 1 October 19X5.

7. Wharfe agreed to transfer £45,000 to the partnership bank account on 1 October 19X5 as his capital account contribution.

8. Swale and Aire's respective current account are to be closed off by transferring the balances to their capital accounts.

9. Aire and Wharfe are to share profits and losses equally.

10. Goodwill is not to be retained in the books of Aire and Wharfe.

Required:

(a) Prepare Swale and Aire's revaluation account as at 30 September 19X5;

(b) prepare Swale, Aire and Wharfe's respective capital accounts in columnar format in order to reflect the changes in the old partnership and the formation of the new one; and

(c) compile Aire and Wharfe's balance sheet as at 1 October 19X5 after all of the above changes have taken place.   *(AAT Level 2)*

30.9   Proudie, Slope and Thorne were in partnership sharing profits and losses in the ratio 3:1:1. The draft balance sheet of the partnership as at 31 May is shown below:

Fixed Assets	£000 Cost	£000 Depreciation	£000 Net Book Value
Land and buildings	200	40	160
Furniture	30	18	12
Motor vehicles	60	40	20
	£290	£98	£192
Current Assets			
Stocks		23	
Trade debtors	42		
Less: Provision for doubtful debts	1		
		41	
Prepayments		2	
Cash		10	
		76	
Less: **Current Liabilities**			
Trade creditors	15		
Accruals	3		
		18	
			58
			£250
Capital Accounts:			
Proudie		100	
Slope		60	
Thorne		40	
			200
Current Accounts			
Proudie		24	
Slope		10	
Thorne		8	
			42
			242
Loan: Proudie			8
			£250

Additional Information:

1   Proudie decided to retire on 31 May 19X6. However, Slope and Thorne agreed to form a new partnership out of the old one as from 1 June 19X6. They agreed to share profits and losses in the same ratio as in the old partnership.

2   Upon the dissolution of the old partnership, it was agreed that the following adjustments were to be made to the partnership balance sheet as at 31 May 19X6:

   (a)   Land and buildings were to be revalued at £200,000.
   (b)   Furniture was to be revalued at £5,000.
   (c)   Proudie agreed to take over one of the motor vehicles at a value of £4,000, the remaining motor vehicles being revalued at £10,000.
   (d)   Stocks were to be written down by £5,000.
   (e)   A bad debt of £2,000 was to be written off, and the provision for doubtful debts was then to be adjusted so that it represented 5% of the then outstanding trade debtors as at 31 May 19X6.
   (f)   A further accrual of £3,000 for office expenses was to be made.
   (g)   Professional charges relating to the dissolution were estimated to be £1,000.

3   It has not been the practice of the partners to carry goodwill in the books of the partnership, but on the retirement of a partner it had been agreed that goodwill should be taken into account. Goodwill was to be valued at an amount equal to the average annual profits of the three years expiring on the retirement. For the purpose of including goodwill in the distribution arrangement when Proudie retired, the net profits for the last three years were as follows:

	£000
Year to 31 May 19X4	130
Year to 31 May 19X5	150
Year to 31 May 19X6	181

The net profit for the year to 31 May 19X6 had been calculated before any of the items listed in 2 above were taken into account. The net profit was only adjusted for items listed in 2 (d), 2 (e) and 2 (f) above.

4   Goodwill is not to be carried in the books of the new partnership.

5   It was agreed that Proudie's old loan of £8,000 should be repaid to him on 31 May 19X6, but any further amount owing to him as a result of the dissolution of the partnership should be left as a long-term loan in the books of the new partnership.

6   The partners' current accounts were to be closed and any balances on them as at 31 May 19X6 were to be transferred to their respective capital accounts.

Required:

   (a)   prepare the revaluation account as at 31 May 19X6;
   (b)   prepare the partners' capital accounts as at the date of dissolution of the partnership and bring down any balances on them in the books of the new partnership; and
   (c)   prepare Slope and Thorne's balance sheet as at 1 June 19X6.

(AAT Final)

COMMON ERRORS

1. Net Profit for the Year

If a partner leaves the partnership part way through the financial year, remember to credit him with only his share of profits for the time that he was a partner.

2. Drawings

Do NOT debit drawings to the profit and loss appropriation account: they should be debited to the partners' current accounts.

3. Interest Charged to the Partners

Remember that if a partner is charged interest, CREDIT it to the profit and loss appropriation account.

4. Balance on Revaluation or Realisation

The balance on the revaluation or realisation account should be written off to the partners' CAPITAL accounts in their PROFIT sharing ratio.

5. Goodwill

Adjustments for goodwill may be dealt with through the revaluation or realisation account, OR through the partners' capital accounts.

Goodwill introduced into the books should be credited to the partners' capital accounts in their PROFIT sharing ratio.

In a new partnership, goodwill may be eliminated from the books by writing it back to the partners' capital accounts in their NEW profit sharing ratio.

6. Insolvent Partner

A debit balance on an insolvent partner's account should be written off to the remaining solvent partners' capital accounts in the ratio of their last agreed CAPITAL account balances.

7. Double-Entry and Arithmetical Errors

Students in examinations frequently do badly in this type of question because they do not always complete the double-entry effect of any changes that they make. They also complicate matters further by making numerous arithmetical mistakes.

MAKE SURE THAT YOU COMPLETE DOUBLE-ENTRY, and that you DOUBLE-CHECK YOUR ARITHMETIC.

31

PARTNERSHIP ACCOUNTS: CONVERSIONS

MAIN POINTS

1. Background

As a partnership grows in size, the partners may need further capital, or they may wish to seek the protection of limited liability. They may, therefore, convert the partnership into a limited liability company.

Similarly, they may sell the partnership to a company, the purchase consideration perhaps being a combination of cash and shares in the company.

2. Accounting Treatment

(a) Realisation account

    (i) The changes in the asset and liability account balances should be transferred to the realisation account in exactly the same way as if the partnership was being dissolved.

    (ii) Dr. Limited liability company account
        Cr. Realisation account
    With the purchase price paid by the company.

    (iii) The balance on the realisation account can now be written off to the partners' capital accounts in their PROFIT sharing ratio.

(b) Goodwill. Goodwill may be dealt with either through the realisation account, or through the partners' capital accounts.

(c) Current accounts. Transfer the partners' current account balances to their capital accounts.

(d) Purchase consideration.

    (i) Dr. Bank account
        Cr. Limited liabilitiy company account
    With any cash received (assuming that it forms part of the consideration).

    (ii) Dr. Partner's capital accounts
        Cr. Limited liability company account
    With the VALUE of the shares that each partners is to receive

    (iii) Dr. Partners' capital account
        Cr. Bank account
    With any cash that each partner is to withdraw from the partnership.

Example. The following trial balance has been extracted from the books of Gain and Main as at 31 March 19X2; Gain and Main are in partnership sharing profits and losses in the ratio 3 to 2.

	£	£
Capital Accounts:		
Gain		10,000
Main		5,000
Cash at Bank	1,550	
Creditors		500
Current Accounts:		
Gain		1,000
Main	2,000	
Debtors	2,000	
Depreciation: Fixtures and fittings		1,000
Motor vehicles		1,300
Fixtures and fittings	2,000	
Land and buildings	30,000	
Motor vehicles	4,500	
Net profit (for the year to 31 March 19X2)		26,250
Stock, at cost	3,000	
	£45,050	£45,050

In appropriating the net profit for the year, it has been agreed that Main should be entitled to a salary of £9,750. Each partner is also entitled to interest on his opening capital account balance at the rate of 10% per annum.

Gain and Main have decided to convert the partnership into a limited company, Plain Limited, as from 1 April 19X2. The company is to take over all the assets and liabilities of the partnership, except that Gain is to retain for his personal use one of the motor vehicles at an agreed transfer price of £1,000.

The purchase consideration will consist of 40,000 ordinary shares of £1 each in Plain Limited, to be divided between the partners in profit sharing ratio. Any balance of the partners' capital accounts is to be settled in cash.

Required:

Prepare the main ledger accounts of the partnership in order to close off the books as at 31 March 19X2. *(AAT Level 2)*

Solution

GAIN AND MAIN
Profit and loss appropriation account for year ended 31 March 19X2

	£	£	£
Net profit b/d			26,250
Salary: Main		9,750	
Interest on Capital:			
Gain	1,000		
Main	500	1,500	
Balance of profit:			
Gain	9,000		
Main	6,000	15,000	
			26,250

Current Accounts

	Gain £	Main £			Gain £	Main £
31 3 X2 Balance b/d	-	2,000	31 3 X2	Balance b/d	1,000	-
			31 3 X2	Profit and Loss		
				Salary	-	9,750
				Interest on Capital	1,000	500
31 3 X2 Capital	11,000	14,250		Balance of profit	9,000	6,000
	£11,000	£16,250			£11,000	£16,250

Capital Accounts

	Gain £	Main £			Gain £	Main £
31 3 X2 Motor vehicle	1,000	-	31 3 X2	Balances b/d	10,000	5,000
31 3 X2 Plain Ltd	24,000	16,000	31 3 X2	Current	11,000	14,250
31 3 X2 Cash	-	4,170	31 3 X2	Realisation	1,380	920
			31 3 X2	Cash	2,620	-
	£25,000	£20,170			£25,000	£20,170

Realisation Account

	£		£
Debtors	2,000	Creditors	500
Fixtures and fittings	2,000	Provision for depreciation:	
Land and buildings	30,000	Fixtures and fittings	1,000
Motor vehicles	4,500	Motor vehicles	1,300
Stock	3,000	Current (Gain - Motor vehicle)	1,000
Current (balance written off): Gain (3/5)	1,380	Plain Ltd (purchase consideration)	40,000
Main (2/5)	920		
	£43,800		£43,800

Cash at Bank Account

	£		£
Balance b/d	1,550	Current (Main)	4,170
Current (Gain)	2,620		
	£4,170		£4,170

Plain Ltd Account

	£		£
Realisation (Purchase Consideration)	40,000	Current: Gain	24,000
		Main	16,000
	£40,000		£40,000

EXERCISES

31.1 Grain and Salt are in partnership selling herbs and spices, and sharing profits in the ratio 3:2 respectively. Their draft Balance Sheet at 31 December 19X6 is:

	Cost £	Depreciation £	Net £
Fixed Assets			
Freehold premises	40,000	-	40,000
Furniture and fittings	5,000	3,000	2,000
Motor vehicles	4,000	1,000	3,000
	£49,000	£4,000	45,000
Current Assets			
Stock-in-trade		8,000	
Sundry debtors		12,000	
Cash at bank		800	
		20,800	
Less: **Current Liabilities**			
Sundry creditors		13,600	
Net Current Assets			7,200
			£52,200
Capital Accounts			
Grain	24,000		
Salt	5,000		29,000
Current Accounts			
Grain	4,200		
Salt	1,000		5,200
			34,200
Loan: Grain			18,000
			£52,200

Herbsbest Limited is incorporated in order to take over the partnership business as at 1 January 19X7. The company is to acquire the Freehold Premises at a valuation of £50,000 and the other assets (with the exception of Cash and Motor Vehicles) at book value. The Current Liabilities are also taken over by the new company.

The purchase consideration of £75,000 is to be settled by 40,000 Ordinary £1 Shares issued at a premium of 25% in Herbsbest Limited and cash of £25,000. Salt is to take over the Motor Vehicle at a valuation of £2,300 and the partners have agreed to divide the shares in the company in their profit-sharing ratios. Grain's loan is to be repaid by the partnership.

Required:

In the books of the partnership, show:

   (a) The Capital Accounts of the partners - in columnar form;

   (b) the Realisation Account;

   (c) the Bank Account; and

   (d) the account for Herbsbest Limited.

(LCCI Intermediate 1987, adapted)

31.2 Oak Ltd was formed in December 19X1 to take over the partnership of Birch and Larch. Oak Ltd's Authorised Share Capital was £250,000, all issued for cash at par. Preliminary expenses were £880. At 31 December 19X1 the Balance Sheet of Birch and Larch was:

		£		£
Capital:	Birch	27,000	Premises	22,000
	Larch	12,000	Plant and machinery	8,120
			Vehicles	6,800
Trade creditors		3,860	Stock	3,600
Bank overdraft		2,400	Debtors	4,740
		£45,260		£45,260

It was agreed that Oak Ltd would take over all of the assets of Birch and Larch, and responsibility for their trade creditors, subject to the following matters:

1   On 1 January 19X2 one of the vehicles, with a book value of £900, was sold to an employee of Birch and Larch for £750. The take-over value of the remaining vehicles was agreed at £5,250.

2   The premises were re-valued at £26,000, and the plant and machinery at £6,600.

3   The stock consisted of items of three types, whose values were as follows:

	Cost	Net Realisable Value
Type A	£720	£935
Type B	£1,070	£1,040
Type C	£1,810	£2,648

It was decided that the "category" method should be used for their valuation, instead of the "aggregate" method previously used.

4   It was agreed that a provision for bad debts of £230 should be made.

The purchase consideration consisted of £5,000 cash and 74,000 Ordinary Shares in Oak Ltd issued at par. Birch and Larch divided the shares between themselves in their normal profit/loss sharing ratio, 3:2 respectively. Birch and Larch paid the cash proceeds of sales of assets into the partnership bank account, before final dissolution of the firm.

Required:

   (a) The Realisation Account and the Capital Accounts in the books of Birch and Larch (include appropriate entries on dissolution of the partnership);

   (b) the Balance Sheet of Oak Ltd immediately after the conclusion of the business purchase (assume that the company had no other transactions); and

   (c) briefly suggest how the company should deal prudently with the intangible and/or fictitious assets appearing in Oak Ltd's Balance Sheet at the end of the first year's trading.

(LCCI Higher 1985)

31.3 Crow and Nest were in partnership sharing profits and losses in the ratio 2:1. On 31 October 19X4 they formed a company in order to take over the partnership. The new company was called Crownest Limited and it had an authorised share capital of 200,000 ordinary shares of £1 each.

The following trial balance was extracted from the books of account of the partnership as at 31 October 19X4:

	£ Dr	£ Cr
Bank	1,000	
Capital Accounts (at 1 November 19X3):		
Crow		50,000
Nest		20,000
Drawings:		
Crow	8,000	
Nest	6,000	
General expenses	170,000	
Purchases	260,000	
Rates	20,000	
Sales		500,000
Stock (at 1 November 19X3)	30,000	
Trade creditors		35,000
Trade debtors	80,000	
Vehicles at cost	40,000	
Vehicle depreciation at (1 November 19X3)		10,000
	£615,000	£615,000

The following additional information is to be taken into account:

1   The closing stock at 31 October 19X4 was valued at £40,000.

2   At 31 October 19X4, the partnership owed an additional amount for general expenses of £10,000.

3   At 31 October 19X4, the rates included £5,000 paid in advance.

4   Vehicles were depreciated on a straight line basis at a rate of 25% per annum at an assumed nil residual value. During the year to 31 October 19X4 there were no purchases or sales of vehicles.

5   Nest was entitled to a salary of £8,000 per annum. No entry had been made in the books of account for the year to 31 October 19X4 in respect of this amount.

6   The partnership agreement allowed for interest at a rate of 10% per annum on the partners' capital account balance as at the beginning of each year. Interest had not been taken into account in compiling the above trial balance.

7   In converting the partnership into a limited liability company, it was agreed that the following adjustments should be made:
    (a)   the vehicles were to be revalued at £14,000.
    (b)   goodwill was estimated to be worth £24,000.
    (c)   other assets and liabilities were to be transferred at their respective book values as at 31 October 19X4.

8   The partners' capital account balances as at 31 October 19X4 were to be closed by the issue of ordinary shares in Crownest Limited at their par value.

9   The partners did not keep separate capital and current accounts and all the partnership adjustments are to be made in the partners' capital accounts.

Required:

(a) Prepare Crow and Nest's Trading, Profit and Loss and Profit and Loss Appropriation Accounts for the year to 31 October 19X4;

(b) compile Crow and Nest's Capital Accounts for the year to 31 October 19X4; and

(c) prepare a balance sheet for Crownest Limited as at 1 November 19X4.

(AAT Level 2)

31.4   Amis, Lodge and Pym were in partnership sharing profits and losses in the ratio 5:3:2. The following trial balance has been extracted from their books of account as at 31 March 19X8:

	£	£
Bank interest received		750
Capital accounts (as at 1 April 19X7):		
Amis		80,000
Lodge		15,000
Pym		5,000
Carriage inwards	4,000	
Carriage outwards	12,000	
Cash at bank	4,900	
Current accounts		
Amis	1,000	
Lodge	500	
Pym	400	
Discounts allowed	10,000	
Discounts received		4,530
Drawings:		
Amis	25,000	
Lodge	22,000	
Pym	15,000	
Motor vehicles		
at cost	80,000	
accumulated depreciation (at 1 April 19X7)		20,000
Office expenses	30,400	
Plant and machinery:		
at cost	100,000	
accumulated depreciation (at 1 April 19X7)		36,600

257

	£	£
Provision for bad and doubtful debts (at 1 April 19X7)		420
Purchases	225,000	
Rent, rates, heat and light	8,800	
Sales		404,500
Stock (at 1 April 19X7)	30,000	
Trade creditors		16,500
Trade debtors	14,300	
	£583,300	£583,300

Additional Information:

1 Stock at 31 March 19X8 was valued at £35,000.

2 Depreciation on the fixed assets is to be charged as follows:

Motor vehicles — 25% on the reduced balance.
Plant and machinery — 20% on the original cost.

There were no purchases or sales of fixed assets during the year to 31 March 19X8.

3 The provision for bad and doubtful debts is to be maintained at a level equivalent to 5% of the total trade debtors as at 31 March 19X8.

4 An office expense of £405 was owing to 31 March 19X8 and some rent amounting to £1,500 had been paid in advance as at that date. These items had not been included in the list of balances shown in the trial balance.

5 Interest on drawings and on the debit balance on each partner's current account is to be charged as follows:

	£
Amis	1,000
Lodge	900
Pym	720

6 According to the partnership agreement, Pym is allowed a salary of £13,000 per annum. This amount was owing to Pym for the year to 31 March 19X8, and needs to be accounted for.

7 The partnership agreement also allows each partner interest on his capital account at a rate of 10% per annum. There were no movements on the respective partners' capital accounts during the year to 31 March 19X8, and the interest had not been credited to them as at that date.

8 On April 19X8, Fowles Limited agreed to purchase the business on the following terms:

(a) Amis to purchase one of the partnerships motor vehicles at an agreed value of £5,000, the remaining vehicles being taken over by the company at an agreed value of £30,000.

(b) the company agreed to purchase the plant and machinery at a value of £35,000 and the stock at a value of £38,500.

(c) the partners to settle the trade creditors, the total amount agreed with the creditors being £16,000.

(d) the trade debtors were not to be taken over by the company, the partners receiving cheques on 1 April 19X8 amounting to £12,985 in total from the trade debtors in settlement of the outstanding debts.

(e) the partners paid the outstanding office expense on 1 April 19X8, and the landlord returned the rent paid in advance by cheque on the same day.

(f) as consideration for the sale of the partnership, the partners were to paid £63,500 in cash by Fowles Limited and to receive 75,000 in £1 ordinary shares in the company, the shares to be apportioned equally amongst the partners.

9 Assume that all the matters relating to the dissolution of the partnership and its sale to the company took place on 1 April 19X8.

Required:

(a) Prepare:
   (i) Amis', Lodge's and Pym's trading, profit and loss, and profit and loss appropriation account for the year to 31 March 19X8; and
   (ii) Amis', Lodge's and Pym's current accounts (in columnar format) for the year to 31 March 19X8 (the final balance on each account is to be then transferred to each partner's respective capital account); and

(b) compile the following accounts:
   (i) the partnership realisation account for the period up to and including 1 April 19X8;
   (ii) the partners' bank account for the period up to and including 1 April 19X8; and
   (iii) the partners' capital accounts (in columnar format) for the period up to and including 1 April 19X8.

(AAT Final)

COMMON ERRORS

1. Realisation Account

Make sure that you enter the correct change in value for all assets and liabilities in the realisation account.

Remember to CREDIT the total purchase consideration to the realisation account.

2. Purchasing Company's Account

Open an account for the purchasing company, and DEBIT the total purchase consideration to it.

The share of the consideration should be CREDITED to the account and DEBITED to the partners' capital accounts in the agreed proportions.

3. Share Value

The agreed purchase consideration may include shares valued at more than their nominal value, that is, at a premium. The nominal value of the shares PLUS the premium must be debited to the partners' capital accounts and credited to the company's account in the agreed proportions.

In the COMPANY'S balance sheet, the shares will be included at their NOMINAL value, whilst the premium will be included in a share premium account.

4. Share Denomination

The shares issued in the company may not always have a nominal value of £1. Be careful that they are not 25p, 50p or some other denomination of shares, as the partners may be entitled to a certain NUMBER of shares.

5. Double-Entry and Arithmetical Errors

Finally, check that you have completed double-entry, and that you have not made any arithmetical errors.

32 COMPANY ACCOUNTS: INTRODUCTION

MAIN POINTS

1. Background

A limited liability company may be formed as an entirely new entity, or an existing sole trader or partnership entity may be converted into a company.

Limited liability gives protection to the owners. Limited liability means that shareholders can only be called upon to contribute an agreed amount of capital. The owners are known as SHAREHOLDERS, each owner usually holding a number of shares in the company.

As the business grows, it may become a PUBLIC company (although a company may be formed as a public company). Public limited companies have their SHARES listed on a recognised stock exchange. This means that the general public can buy and sell shares in the company.

The distribution of profit to shareholders is in the form of a DIVIDEND, that is, the shareholders will be entitled to receive a return on their investment of Xp per share.

Companies have to prepare detailed accounts for their shareholders in accordance with the Companies Act 1985. These accounts are often referred to as PUBLISHED accounts. The published accounts have also to be sent to the Registrar of Companies in order to make them available for public inspection, although smaller companies may file MODIFIED accounts (that is, simpler accounts).

Published accounts form part of an advanced accounting syllabus.

2. Financing

Companies may be financed from three main sources:

(a) Shares
   (i) Ordinary shares.
       Ordinary shareholders are not automatically entitled entitled to a dividend. In the event of LIQUIDATION of the company (that is, when the business is closed down), they are the last group to receive any cash distribution.
   (ii) Preference shares.
        Preference shareholders are usually entitled to a fixed level of dividend. They receive preference over the shareholders when the company is liquidated.

261

(b) Debentures

Debentures are usually long-term loans made to the company at a fixed rate of interest, and an agreed redemption date. Debenture loans may be secured on some or all of the company's assets. Debenture holders are not shareholders.

(c) Retained profits

The company may decide not to pay out all of its profits in dividends, the retained profits thereby helping to finance the future expansion of the company.

3. Taxation

Sole trader and partnership entities are not charged any taxation. Instead, the proprietors of such entities pay income tax on what profits they receive from the business. By contrast, companies are charged CORPORATION TAX based on their profits for the year.

4. Accounting Treatment: Internal Accounts

Company accounts prepared for internal purposes are very similar to those prepared for sole trader and partnership entities. The final accounts of a trading company will include a trading account, a profit and loss account, a profit and loss appropriation account, and a balance sheet.

The main differences are as follows:

(a) Profit and loss appropriation account. This account shows the corporation tax payable on the profits for the year, and the dividends paid or proposed to be paid to the shareholders.

(b) Balance sheet: capital and reserves section. This section lists the different types of shares that make up the SHARE CAPITAL of the company, PLUS any capital of revenue account balances.

Note that as debenture holders are not shareholders in the company, debentures should not be included in the share capital section of the balance sheet. They should be included in a separate section of the balance sheet under the heading of LONG-TERM LOANS.

Example   The following trial balance as at 31 December 19X3 has been extracted from the books of XYZ Limited:

	£	£
Ordinary shares - 20,000 of £1 each		20,000
Profit and loss account		3,800
Sales		210,000
Purchases	160,000	
Rent and rates	9,000	
Light and heat	7,600	
Administrative expenses	11,300	
Motor vehicles: at cost	16,000	
provision for depreciation		3,000
Stock at 1 January 19X3	15,500	
Debtors	24,400	
Creditors		10,000
Balance at bank	3,000	
	£246,800	£246,800

Additional information relating to the year ended 31 December 19X3:

1. Since the above trial balance, a bill has been received for rates of £2,000 for the half year ending 31 March 19X4.
2. The company has decided that a provision for doubtful debts be created of 2% of the debtors as at 31 December 19X3.
3. Stock as at 31 December 19X3 has been valued at £13,500.
4. Depreciation is provided annually on motor vehicles at the rate of 25% of the cost of vehicles held at each accounting year end.
5. No entries have been made in the company's books for the sale on credit to Barry Dale of goods for £7,800 on 1 December 19X3; payment for the goods was received on 20 January 19X4.
6. It has been decided to transfer £5,000 to general reserve and to recommend that there be no dividends paid on the ordinary share capital for the year under review.

Required:

Prepare a trading and profit and loss account for the year ended 31 December 19X3 and a balance sheet as at that date.

(AAT Intermediate)

Solution

XYZ Limited
Trading and Profit and Loss Account
for the year ended 31 December 19X3

		£	£
Sales (£210,000 + 7,800)			217,800
less:	Cost of sales		
	Opening stock	15,500	
	Purchases	160,000	
		175,500	
less:	Closing stock	13,500	
			162,000
Gross Profit			55,800
less:	Rent and rates (£9,000+1,000)	10,000	
	Light and heat	7,600	
	Administrative expenses	11,300	
	Motor vehicle depreciation	4,000	
	Provision for doubtful debts (2%x£32,200)	664	
			33,544
Net profit			22,256
Appropriation: General reserve			5,000
			17,256
Undistributed profit at 1 January 19X3			3,800
Undistributed profit at 31 December 19X3			£21,056

Balance sheet as at 31 December 19X3

	£	£
Fixed Assets:		
Motor vehicles - at cost	16,000	
Provision for depreciation	7,000	
		9,000
Current Assets		
Stock	13,500	
Debtors (£24,400+7,800-664)	31,556	
Balance at bank	3,000	
	48,056	
Less: Current liabilities		
Creditors and accruals (£10,000+1,000)	11,000	
		37,056
		£46,056
CAPITAL		
20,000 Ordinary shares of £1 each		20,000
Reserves: General reserve	5,000	
Undistributed profit	21,056	
		26,056
		£46,056

EXERCISES

32.1 The following balances appeared in the ledger of the Potteries Manufacturing Company Ltd after the preparation of the trading and Profit and Loss Accounts for the year ended 31 December 19X4:

	£
Ordinary share capital	100,000
8% Preference share capital	40,000
Finished goods stock	29,000
FIxed assets at cost	141,000
Provision for depreciation - fixed assets	55,200
Reserve for increased replacement costs of fixed assets	15,000
Interim ordinary dividend paid	7,500
Debtors	59,200
Trade creditors	40,400
Work in progress	36,000
Raw materials stock	26,000
Bank overdraft	10,000
Profit and loss account credit balance 1 January 19X4	4,000
Preference dividend paid 30 June 19X4	1,600
Net profit for 19X4	35,700

The following additional information is given:

(1) The Authorised Capital of the company is 300,000 Ordinary Shares of 50p each and 75,000 8% Preference shares of £1 each.

(2) A final dividend of 6.25p per Ordinary share is proposed.

(3) The Reserve for increased replacement costs of Fixed Assets is to be increased to £20,000.

Required:

(a) A Profit and Loss Appropriation Account for the year to 31 December 19X4; and

(b) a Balance Sheet, preferably in vertical form, as at 31 December 19X4.

(LCCI Intermediate 1987, amended)

32.2 The following balances remained on the books of Mainstream plc at 31 March 19X8 after the preparation of the Trading Account:

	Dr £	Cr £
Authorised and Issued share capital		
100,000 ordinary shares at £1 each		100,000
40,000 10% preference shares at £1 each		40,000
10% Debentures		60,000
Fixed assets at cost	195,000	
Provision for depreciation		15,000
Gross profit		69,000
Stock at 31 March 19X8	37,800	
Rent and Rates and Insurances	2,600	
General expenses	4,800	
Administrative expenses	10,000	
Bad debt written off	147	
Directors' fees	2,150	
Interim dividends paid £		
Preference 2,000		
Ordinary 4,000	6,000	
Debenture Interest to 30 September 19X7	3,000	
Debtors and Creditors	18,800	6,600
Retained profits at 1 April 19X7		5,829
Bank	16,132	
	£296,429	£296,429

The following information is also available:

(i)   A provision for bad debts equivalent to 2% of debtors is to be created.

(ii) Rates have been prepaid by £500 whilst there is an amount of £300 owing from administrative expenses.

(iii) Fixed assets are to be depreciated by 10% of cost.

(iv) The directors propose to pay a final dividend of 6p per share on the Ordinary Shares making 10p in all and to pay the remainder of the preference dividend.

Required:

Prepare the profit and loss and appropriation accounts of Mainstream plc for the year ended 31 March 19X8 and a balance sheet as at that date.

NOTE: Your accounts should be in vertical form and are for internal use. Notes to the accounts are not required.

(RSA Intermediate)

32.3 The following draft balance sheet as at 30 September 19X6 of Prime Products limited has been prepared by the company's assistant accountant:

	Cost £	Aggregate Depreciation £	Net book value £
Fixed assets			
Plant and machinery	31,000	19,375	11,625
Motor vehicles	17,000	10,200	6,800
	£48,000	£29,575	18,425
Current assets			
Stock		12,400	
Trade debtors and prepayments		9,600	
Balance at bank		3,900	
		25,900	
Less: Current liabilities			
Creditors and accrued charges		5,100	20,800
			£39,225
Financed by:			
Share capital - ordinary shares of £1 each, fully paid			20,000
Share premium account			5,000
Reserves - General			10,000
Retained earnings			4,225
			£39,225

The following discoveries were made after the preparation of the above balance sheet.

1. No entry has been made in the company's accounts for bank charges of £15.00 debited in the company's bank statements on 25 September 19X6.

2. The draft accounts prepayments figure of £400 does not include insurance premiums of £300 prepaid at 30 September 19X6.

3. A significant costing error has now been found in the stock valuation sheets of 30 September 19X5. As a result the stock valuation at 30 September 19X5 should have been £16,000 not £10,000 as included in the company's published accounts for the year ended 30 September 19X5.

4. On 1 September 19X6, the company forwarded goods costing £1,200 to John Peters of Aberdeen on a sale or return basis. None of these goods were sold to John Peters until late in October 19X6. However, in preparing the draft accounts for the year ended 30 September 19X6 of Prime Products Limited it was assumed that all the goods sent to John Peters had been sold.

    Note: Prime Products Limited obtains a gross profit of 25% on all sales.

5. No entries have been made in the company's accounts for a bonus (scrip) issue of ordinary shares on 10 September 19X6 involving the issue of one ordinary share of £1 for every four ordinary shares previously held.

    Note: It is the company's policy to maintain the maximum flexibility so far as the availability of reserves for the payments of dividends are concerned.

6. It has now been decided to introduce a provision for doubtful debts of 2.5% of trade creditors at 30 September 19X6.

7. A bonus of 1% gross profit is payable to the sales manager for all sales of the company on or after 1 October 19X5; the bonus is payable annually on 30 November for the immediately preceding accounting year. Provision was made for this bonus in the preparation of the draft accounts for the year ended 30 September 19X6.

Required:

Prepare a corrected balance sheet as at 30 September 19X6 of Prime Products Limited.

(AAT Intermediate)

32.4   The following balances were taken from the books of R Higson Ltd on 31 July 19X7:

		£
Profit and loss account 1 August 19X6	Cr	21,760
Creditors		38,555
Bank overdraft		31,900
General reserve		14,600

Additional information:

(i)   The company was formed and commenced business on 1 August 19X5 with an authorised share capital of 260,000 £1 ordinary shares and 80,000 10% preference shares.

(ii)   200,000 Ordinary shares and 60,000 preference shares have been issued fully paid.

(iii) £50,000 12.5% debenture stock had been issued on 1 August 19X6. The interest on this stock has been paid for the year ending 31 July 19X7.

(iv) In the year ended 31 July 19X7, the company made a profit of £68,800 before appropriation of share dividends, and before £1,730 was transferred to the existing General Reserve Account.

(v)   On 1 August 19X7, the company resolved to pay the dividend on the preference shares and declared a dividend of 11p per share on the Ordinary Share Capital for the for the year ended 31 July 19X7.

Required:

Show how the relevant items including current liabilities would appear in the LIABILITIES section of the balance sheet as at 31 July 19X7.

Note: (a) It is NOT necessary for your balance sheet to be prepared in a form suitable for publication.

(b) Ignore Taxation.

(RSA Intermediate, adapted)

32.5 The balance sheets of William Penn, a sole trader and Bilston Ltd at 31 March 19X5 are:

WILLIAM PENN
Balance sheet as at 31 March 19X5

	£000			£000
Capital	161	Fixed assets		
Current liabilities		Premises		50
Creditors	63	Equipment		28
		Vehicles		31
				109
		Current assets		
		Stock	62	
		Debtors	47	
		Bank	6	115
	£224			£224

BILSTON LTD
Balance sheet as at 31 March 19X5

	£000			£000
Ordinary Share		Fixed assets		
Capital £1	100	Premises		150
Reserves	298	Equipment		60
	398	Vehicles		93
				303
Current liabilities				
Creditors	77			
Accruals	30	107	Current assets	
			Stock	104
			Debtors	90
			Bank	8	202
	£505			£505

On 1 April 19X5 Bilston Ltd took over the business assets and liabilities of Penn at an agreed price of £200,000. The only assets not taken over were the premises, a car with a book value of £4,000 and the bank balance.

The assets taken over were revalued for the takeover purposes at

Equipment £20,000; Vehicles £15,000; Stock £68,000; Debtors £44,000

The purchase consideration was to be satisfied by a cash payment of £20,000, and 50,000 shares in Bilston Limited.

Required:

(a) The ledger accounts (sale of business, bank and capital only) in the books of Penn to close his books.

(b) The ledger account "acquisition of business" in Bilston Ltd's books to record the acquisition.

(c) The balance sheet of Bilston Ltd immediately after the takeover.

(RSA Advanced)

32.6 A new company, Merged plc, has been formed to enable the amalgamation of the business of C V Badge and the company, Rupert plc, to take place with effect from 1 July 19X5.

Merged plc has issued 200,000 ordinary shares of £1 each at par and £100,000 10% debentures at par, in each case for cash.

Balance sheets as at 30 June 19X5

	CV Badge £000	CV Badge £000		Rupert plc £000	Rupert plc £000
			Fixed assets (at book value)		
	120		Freehold property	240	
	100		Plant and machinery	125	
	16		Vehicles	20	
	31		Equipment	10	
		267			395
			Current assets		
	66		Stocks	45	
	30		Debtors	25	
	14		Cash at bank	21	
	110			91	
			Current liabilities		
	41		Creditors	39	
	-		Proposed dividends	17	
	41			56	
		69	NET CURRENT ASSETS		35
		£336			£430
			Financed by:		
			Capital account		
		336	CV Badge		
		£336			
			Share Capital		£000
			Ordinary shares of £1 each fully paid		300
			Reserves - Retained profits		130
					£430

Merged plc have agreed to acquire all the assets of C V Badge except for the Bank balance. This was retained by C V Badge to repay part of the creditors. The other assets were taken over at the following values:

	£000
Freehold property	150
Plant and machinery	80
Vehicles	10
Equipment	25
Stocks	60
Debtors	25

The agreed purchase price consisted of £35,000 in cash and 300,000 Ordinary shares of £1 each fully paid at a premium of £0.10 per share.

C V Badge then repaid the remaining creditors.

Merged plc acquired all the assets of Rupert plc, agreeing to repay the creditors, at the following values:

	£000
Freehold property	250
Plant and machinery	100
Vehicles	16
Equipment	10
Stocks	40
Debtors	24
Creditors	37

Goodwill was valued at £97,000.

Merged plc is to make a purchase consideration of £500,000 to Rupert plc consisting of 300,000 Ordinary Shares of £1 each fully paid in Merged plc and £50,000 in cash, enabling Rupert plc to pay the proposed dividend and liquidation expenses of £10,000

Required:

(a) Make the necessary entries in the realisation and capital accounts of C V Badge, and Rupert plc showing the winding up of these concerns; and

(b) the balance sheet of Merged plc after the transactions have been completed.

(RSA Advanced)

COMMON ERRORS

1. Format of Accounts

You are recommended to adopt the vertical format, and to present the final accounts (preceded by the appropriate title and date) in the following order:

(a) Manufacturing account
(b) Trading account
(c) Profit and loss account
(d) Profit and loss appropriation account
(e) Balance sheet.

2. Debenture Interest

Remember to charge the GROSS amount of interest to the PROFIT AND LOSS ACCOUNT. Any income tax deducted before payment to the debenture holders should be CREDITED to an income tax account.

3. Appropriation Account

The taxation charge for the year should be deducted from the net profit for the year. This gives NET PROFIT FOR THE YEAR AFTER TAXATION. Then deduct the dividends both PAID and PROPOSED for the year. This gives the RETAINED PROFIT FOR THE YEAR.

4. Dividends

Remember to calculate the dividends payable on the ISSUED share capital of the company, and not on the authorised amount. The dividends should be declared at Xp per share, so make sure that you multiply X by the NUMBER of shares, and not just the total value of the share capital. No taxation adjustment needs to be made to the paid or proposed dividends included in the profit and loss appropriation account.

5. Balance Sheet

The retained profit for the year should be added to the retained profits brought forward at the beginning of the year, and included in the CAPITAL AND RESERVES section in the balance sheet.

6. Debenture Holders

Remember that debenture holders are NOT shareholders. In the balance sheet, include any debenture stock in the 'LONG-TERM LOANS' section of the balance sheet.

7. Corporation Tax

Note that corporation tax is due to be paid NINE months after the year end. Corporation tax due to be paid is, therefore, a CURRENT LIABILITY.

If a company pays a dividend, some corporation tax has to be paid in advance of this date. This is known as ADVANCE corporation tax (ACT), and it is based on the amount of dividend paid. At the basic or intermediate level, you should not have to deal with ACT.

33 COMPANY ACCOUNTS: SHARES AND DEBENTURES

MAIN POINTS

1. Background

A company may issue shares at their NOMINAL (or face) value, or at their nominal value plus a PREMIUM. Those share applicants who are allotted shares may be required to pay the entire amount for the shares (including any premium) on a given date, or they may be allowed to pay for them in instalments. When an instalment is required the company will make what is known as a CALL on the shareholders. The procedure for issuing debentures is similar to that of issuing shares.

Companies may also REDEEM shares, that is, buy them back from the shareholders. Debentures may also be redeemed.

In order to comply with the Companies Act 1985, and to ensure good practice, some strict accounting procedures are necessary to deal with the issue and redemption of shares and debentures.

2. Issue and Forfeiture of Shares: Accounting Treatment

(a) Dr.　Bank account
Cr.　Application and allotment account
With the cash received on application

(b) Dr.　Application and allotment account
Cr.　Bank account
With any cash returned to applicants

(c) Dr.　Application and allotment account
Cr.　Share capital account
With the total amount due for the shares on application and allotment.

(d) Dr.　Application and allotment account
Cr.　Share premium account
With the share premium due on application and allotment

(e) Dr.　Bank account
Cr.　Application and allotment account
With the cash received on allotment

(f) Dr.　Call account (or first call account, second call account etc.)
Cr.　Share capital account
With the cash due on call (or first call, second call etc.)

(g) Dr.　Bank account
Cr.　Call account
With the cash received on call (or first call, second call etc.)

272

(h) Dr. Investments - own shares account
　　Cr. Application and allotment account
　　With any cash in arrears on application and allotment

(i) Dr. Investments - own shares account
　　Cr. Call account (or first call, second call etc.)
　　With any cash in arrears on call (or first call, second call etc.)

(j) Dr. Bank
　　Cr. Investments - own shares account
　　With the cash received on the reissue of the forfeited shares

(k) Dr. Investments - own shares
　　Cr. Share premium account
　　With the balance in the investments - own shares account after the reissue of shares

3. Issue and Forfeiture of Shares: Balance Sheet Disclosure

	£
CAPITAL AND RESERVES	
Called up share capital	X
Share premium	X
CURRENT ASSETS	
(a) After a call but before forfeiture	
Debtors - called up share capital not paid	X
(b) After forfeiture but before reissue	
Investments - own shares	X

4. Issue Of Debentures: Accounting Treatment

Dr. Bank account
Dr. Share premium account (or profit and loss account)
Cr. Debenture loan stock account
With the proceeds of the debenture issue (including any discount on the issue)

5. Debentures: Balance Sheet Disclosure

Redeemable within twelve months: show in CURRENT LIABILITIES as the first item.

Redeemable after twelve months: show under LONG-TERM LOANS

6. Redemption of Shares: Accounting Treatment

(a) Dr. Bank account
　　Cr. Share capital account
　　Cr. Share premium account
　　With the cash received on the issue of new shares (plus any premium) in order to support the redemption of old shares

(b) Dr. Redeemable shares account
　　Dr. Profit and loss account (with the premium) (or share premium account, if permitted by the 1985 Companies Act)
　　Cr. Bank
　　With the total amount paid on the redemption of the shares

(c) Dr. Profit and loss account
   Cr. Capital redemption reserve account
   With the difference between the nominal value of the shares redeemed, and the nominal value of the shares issued (but ONLY if the nominal value of the shares issued is LESS than the nominal value of the shares redeemed).

7. Redemption of Debentures: Accounting Treatment

Dr. Debenture loan stock account
Dr. Share premium account (or profit and loss account) with the premium
Cr. Bank account
With the amount payable on redemption (including any premium)

8. Debenture Redemption Funds: Accounting Treatment

(a) Dr. Profit and loss appropriation account
   Cr. Debenture redemption fund account
   With the annual contribution to the debenture redemption fund

(b) Dr. Bank account
   Cr. Debenture redemption fund account
   With any interest received on the debenture redemption fund investments

(c) Dr. Debenture redemption fund investment account
   Cr. Bank account
   With the annual contribution PLUS the interest received on investments during the year

(d) Dr. Bank account
   Cr. Debenture redemption fund investments account
   With the cash received for the sale of any investments

(e) EITHER   OR
   Dr. Debenture redemption   Debenture redemption fund
       fund investments   account
       account
   Cr. Debenture investment   Debenture redemption fund
       fund account   investments account
       With the PROFIT made   With the LOSS incurred on
       on the sale of   the sale of an investments
       investments

(f) Dr. Debenture redemption fund account
   Cr. Capital reserve
   With the balance on the debenture redemption fund account (when the debenture redemption fund is closed)

Example 1.   ISSUE OF SHARES

The following information relates to Fair plc:

(1) The directors invited applications for 100,000 ordinary shares of £1 each at a premium of 50p per share payable as follows:

On application	30p	
On allotment	80p	(including premium)
On call	40p	

(2) Applications for the 100,000 shares were duly applied for and allotted accordingly. The allotment was met in full.

(3) The call resulted in 10,000 shares not being met and those shares were forfeited.

(4) The forfeited shares were reissued and sold for 50p per share, credited as fully paid.

Required:

Prepare the following ledger accounts:

   (i)   application and allotment;
   (ii) ordinary share capital;
   (iii) share premium;
   (iv) call; and
   (v) investments - own shares.

Solution

(i)

FAIR PLC
Applications and allotment account

	£		£
Ordinary share capital (2)	60,000	Bank (100,000 x 30p) (1)	30,000
Share premium (3)	50,000	Bank (100,000x80p)	80,000
	£110,000		£110,000

(ii)   **Ordinary share capital account**

	£		£
		Applications and allotment (2)	60,000
Balance c/d (5)	100,000	Call (4)	40,000
	£100,000		£100,000
		Balance b/d (5)	100,000

Share premium account

	£		£
		Applications and allotment (3)	50,000
Balance c/d (10)	51,000	Investments - own shares (9)	1,000
	£51,000		£51,000
		Balance b/d (10)	51,000

Call account

	£		£
Ordinary share capital (4)	40,000	Bank (90,000x40p) (6)	36,000
		Investments - own share (7)	4,000
	£40,000		£40,000

Investments - own shares' account

	£		£
Call (7)	4,000	Bank (10,000x50p) (8)	5,000
Share premium (9)	1,000		
	£5,000		£5,000

Note: The number shown after each entry indicates the sequence of entries.

Notes:

(1) The number shown after each entry illustrates the sequence of entries.

(2) (a) As the redeemable preference shares are being redeemed only partly out of a new issue of shares of £50,000, £50,000 must be transferred from the profit and loss appropriation account to a capital redemption reserve account. (b) The £10,000 premium on redemption of the redeemable preference shares may be charged against the share premium account, because it is less than either the original share premium (£25,000) obtained when the shares were first issued, or the new balance after receiving the premium on the issue of the ordinary shares (i.e.£20,000+£25,000).

Example 2.   REDEMPTION OF SHARES

Far plc decided to redeem 100,000 of its redeemable preference shares. These shares had originally been issued at a premium of 20p. The details of the redemption were as follows:

(1) It issued 50,000 ordinary shares of £1 each at a premium of 50p payable on application. The total amount required was duly received, and allotted accordingly.

(2) The preference shares were redeemed at a premium of 10p per share.

(3) The only balance on the share premium account, before the issue and redemption of the shares, related to the premium originally received on the issue of the redeemable preference shares.

Required:

Prepare the following ledger accounts:

(i)   ordinary share applicants;
(ii) ordinary share capital;
(iii) share premium;
(iv) redeemable preference share purchase;
(v)   redeemable preference share capital; and
(vi) capital redemption reserve.

Solution
(i)

FAR PLC
Ordinary share applicants account

	£			£
Ordinary share capital (3) (50,000x£1)	50,000	Bank	(50,000x£1.50) (2)	75,000
Share premium (50,000x50p) (4)	25,000			
	£75,000			£75,000

(ii)

Ordinary share capital

	£		£
		Ordinary share applicants (3)	50,000

276

(iii)

Share premium account

	£		£
Redeemable share preference purchase (7)	10,000	Balance b/d (1)	20,000
Balance c/d (8)	35,000	Ordinary share applicants (4)	25,000
	£45,000		£45,000
		Balance b/d (3)	35,000

(iv)

Redeemable share preference purchase account

	£		£
Bank (£100,000+10,000) (9)	110,000	Redeemable share preference (5)	100,000
		Share premium (6)	10,000
	£110,000		£110,000

(v)

Redeemable preference share capital account

	£		£
Redeemable share preference purchase (5)	100,000	Balance b/d (1)	100,000

(vi)

Capital redemption reserve

	£		£
		Profit and loss appropriation (6)	50,000

NOTE: The number shown after each entry indicates the sequence of entries.

Example 3. DEBENTURE REDEMPTION FUNDS

Some years ago, Webber plc issued £100,000 of 10% redeemable debentures at par repayable on 31 December 19X4. In order to provide sufficient cash for the eventual redemption of the debentures, the company set up a debenture redemption fund (DRF).

The following relevant balances were brought down in the books of account at 1 January 19X3:

	Dr. £	Cr. £
10% redeemable debentures		100,000
Debenture redemption fund		75,000
Debenture redemption fund investments	75,000	

An annual contribution of £5,000 is made towards the redemption of the debentures. The annual contribution is then invested, along with the re-investment of the interest earned on the debenture redemption fund investments. The interest received in the year to 31 December 19X3 amounted to £8,000, and to £10,000 for the year to 31 December 19X4.

The debentures were redeemed at par on 31 December 19X4, and the debenture redemption fund investments sold for £80,000. The interest for the year to 31 December 19X4 and the appropriation were not invested.

Required:

Write up the following ledger accounts for the year to 31 December 19X3 and 31 December 19X4 respectively:

   (i)   10% redeemable debentures;
  (ii) debenture redemption fund (DRF); and
 (iii) debenture redemption fund (DRF) investments.

Solution

WEBBER PLC
10% redeemable debentures account

		£			£
31 12 X4	(10)	100,000	1 1 X3	Balance b/d (1)	100,000

Debenture redemption fund account

		£			£
			1 1 X3	Balance b/d (1)	75,000
			31 12 X3	Bank (interest received) (2)	8,000
31 12 X3	Balance c/d (5)	88,000	31 12 X3	Profit and loss (annual appropriation) (3)	5,000
		£88,000			£88,000
31 12 X4	DRF investments (loss on sale of investments) (9)	8,000	1 1 X4	Balance b/d (5)	88,000
			31 12 X4	Bank (interest received) (6)	10,000
31 12 X4	Capital reserve (11)	95,000	31 12 X4	Profit and loss (annual appropriation) (7)	5,000
		£103,000			£103,000

Debenture fund investments account

		£			£
1 1 X3	Balance b/d (1)	75,000			
31 12 X3	Bank (amount invested: £8,000 + £5,000) (4)	13,000	31 12 X3	Balance c/d (5)	88,000
		£88,000			£88,000
1 1 X4	Balance b/d (5)	88,000	31 12 X4	Bank (investments sold) (8)	80,000
			31 12 X4	DRF (loss transferred) (9)	8,000
		£88,000			£88,000

NOTE: The number shown after each narration relates to the sequence of entries.

EXERCISES

33.1   The following balance sheet of Bell Foods Ltd as at 31 May 19X0 included the following items:

Share capital - ordinary shares of £1 each	£
Authorised	300,000
Issued and fully paid	175,000
9% Redeemable Debenture Stock 19X1	50,000
Interest payable on 28 May and 28 November	

During the year ended 31 May 19X1 the following transactions occured:

1.   On 31 October 19X0 the directors allotted 85,000 ordinary shares of £1 each at a premium of 20p payable as follows:

On application	25p
On allotment	35p (including premium)
First call	30p
Second call	30p

Applications for the shares were received on 27 October 19X0 and amounts payable on allotment were received on 4 November 19X0. The first and second calls were made on 28 November and 31 December 19X0 respectively.

The first call was met in full on 3 December 19X0 but the second call was not met on 2,000 shares and these were forfeited on 31 March 19X1. The second call on 83,000 shares was met on 5 January 19X1.

2.   On 14 November 19X0 £20,000 of the 9% Redeemable Debenture stock was redeemed at 98 ex interest due on 28 November. These debentures were cancelled on redemption.

Required:

Prepare the journal entries necessary to record the following transactions in the books of Bell Foods Ltd. for the year ended 31 May 19X1.

(ICAS Part 1)

33.2   On 31 December 19X3 the Balance Sheet of Porter Industries plc included the following items:

	£
80,000 £1 7% Redeemable preference Shares	800,000
8,000,000 50p Ordinary shares	4,000,000
8% Debentures (Repayable 19X9)	2,000,000
7% Debentures (Repayable 19X4)	3,000,000
The profit and loss Account balance	1,890,200
Proposed Ordinary Dividend	320,000

The Profit and Loss Account balance at the end of 19X2 had been £1,700,000 and, during 19X3, an interim Ordinary Dividend of amounting to £80,000 had been paid.

Preference dividends and Loan Interest are paid half yearly as follows:

Preference Capital	30 June - 31 December
8% Debentures	31 March - 30 September
7% Debentures	31 May - 30 November.

On 31 March 19X4 the Preference Shares are to be redeemed at par, and the 7% Debentures will be repaid, also at par. Dividends and interest will both be paid up to the repayment date.

To fund the repayments the company will, on 15 March 19X4, issue 4,000,000 50p Ordinary Shares at £1.10 each, payable in full upon application. Any surplus cash will be invested in new buildings.

Required:

(a) Show the Profit and Loss Appropriation Account (including the Net Profit brought down) of Porter Industries plc for the year ended 31 December 19X3; and

(b) journalise the transactions of 15 March and 31 March 19X4, including the purchase of new fixed assets. Cash entries should be journalised.

(LCCI 2nd Level 1988)

33.3   Reylap Ltd was incorporated on 2 February 19X9 with an authorised share capital of 1,000,000 ordinary 25p shares. The directors offered for sale 800,000 shares at 35p each with 5p payable on application and 20p payable on allotment.

The offer for sale proceeded as follows:

1   On 1 March 19X9 applications were received for 1,600,000 shares.
2   On 16 March 19X9 allotments were issued on the basis of each applicant receiving 1 share for every 2 shares applied for.
3   On 22 March 19X9 the sums payable on allotment were received.
4   The final call was made on 30 March 19X9 for payment on 9 April 19X9.

Required:

(a) Prepare journal entries to record the above transactions in the books of Reylap Ltd; and

(b) prepare a draft balance sheet as at 31 March 19X9 on the assumption that no trading has taken place.

(ICAS Part 1)

33.4   The Newstead Trading Estate Co. Ltd. had an Authorised Capital of 400,000 shares of £1 each, divided equally between Ordinary Shares and 8% Redeemable Cumulative Preference Shares. The issued Capital was 150,000 Ordinary Shares and 100,000 Preference Shares.

It was decided to:

(1) Issue the remainder of the Ordinary Shares at a premium of 25%.
(2) Issue 50,000 8% debentures of £1 each at a discount of 5%, redeemed at par in 19XX.
(3) Use the proceeds of the above two isssues to redeem all the Preference Shares.

The Ordinary Shares were applied for with full cash on 25 February 19X5 and allotted on 1 March 19X5, as were the debentures, the dates being 25 March and 1 April 19X5, respectively. The Preference shares were redeemed in cash at par on 1 May 19X5. On 1 September 19X5 the company paid an interim dividend of two pence per share on the whole of its ordinary share capital. On 1 October 19X5 the company paid the first half yearly instalment of its debenture interest.

Required:

(a) Show by means of Journal Entries (including cash items) how you would record the above in the books of the Newstead Trading Estate Co Ltd; and

(b) indicate whether the debenture interest should be a charge against profits or an appropriation of profits

(LCCI Intermediate 1986)

33.5 During the year to 30 September 19X7, Kammer plc made a new offer of shares. The details of the offer were as follows:

(1) 100,000 ordinary shares of £1 each were issued payable in instalments as follows:

	Per share £
On application at 1 November 19X6	0.65
On allotment (including the share premium of (£0.50 per share) on 1 December 19X6	0.55
On first and final call on 1 June 19X7	0.30
	£1.50

(2) Applications for 200,000 shares were received and it was decided to deal with them as follows:

(a) to return cheques for 75,000 shares;

(b) to accept in full applications for 25,000 shares; and

(c) to allot the remaining shares on the basis of three shares for every four shares applied for.

(3) On the first and final call, one applicant who had been allotted 5,000 shares, failed to pay the due amount, and his shares were duly declared forfeited. They were then re-issued on 1 September 19X7 at a price of £0.80 per share fully paid.

Note: Kammer's share capital on 1 October 19X6 consisted of 500,000 ordinary shares of £1 each.

Required:

Record the above transactions in the following ledger accounts:

(i) ordinary share capital;

(ii) share premium;

(iii) application and allotment;

(iv) first and final call; and

(v) investments - own shares.

(AAT Final, amended)

33.6 On 30 March 19X4 the directors of Rudolph Ltd. allotted 150,000 ordinary shares of £1 each at a premium of 30p payable as follows:

On application	20p	
On allotment	40p	(including premium)
First call	35p	
Second call	35p	

Amounts due on application were received on 23 March and amounts due on allotment were received on 5 April. The calls were made on 30 April and 25 June.

The first and second calls were not met on 10,000 shares and these were forfeited on 31 July, but all other amounts due were received on 4 May and 29 June for the first and second calls respectively.

On 31 July, the company redeemed £40,000 of 7% redeemable debenture stock at 96% ex interest, these debentures being immediately cancelled. The company has had £80,000 of this debenture stock in issue for a number of years, interest being payable half-yearly on 15 February and 15th August.

Required:

Prepare journal entries to record the foregoing transactions in the books of Rudolph Ltd fot the year ended 31 August 19X4.

(ICAS Part 1)

33.7 Jones PLC issued a prospectus inviting applications for 200,000 ordinary shares of 25p each at a premium of 7p payable in 19X4 as follows:

Due Date	Event	Amount	
31 March	Application	5p	
29 April	Allotment	12p	(including premium)
30 June	First call	10p	
31 August	Second call	5p	

Applications were received for 300,000 shares and allotments were made **pro rata.** Money overpaid on application was applied on account of sums due on allotment.

400 shares were allotted to Mr John Smith who paid only the application money and 600 shares were allotted to Mr James Brown, who failed to pay the two calls. All 1,000 shares were forfeited after the second call and subsequently sold to Mr William Black, credited as fully paid, for 22p per share which was received on 30 September.

Required:

Show in journal entry form the foregoing transactions in the books of Jones PLC for the year ended 31 October 19X4

(ICAS Part 1)

33.8 John Potter Ltd., a light engineering company of Stoke-on-Trent, borrowed £3,000 cash on 1 January 19X2 from the Ceramic Finance Co. Ltd on the security of £3,000 8% debentures redeemable on 1 January 19X5. The borrower established a Sinking Fund Investment Account with annual instalments of £915 on 31 December each year. The instalments were immediately invested at 9% per annum interest, yielding £82 in 19X3 and £173 in 19X4. John Potter Ltd paid debenture interest annually to the finance company on 31 December.

The Sinking Fund Investment was sold on 31 December 19X4 for £1,912. The final instalment and interest were added to the proceeds, and the total of £3,000 redeemed the debenture on 1 January 19X5.

Required:

Prepare a record of the above transactions in so far as they affect the following accounts in Potter's ledger:

(i) Cash
(ii) 8% Debentures
(iii) Debenture Sinking Fund
(iv) Appropriation
(v) Profit and Loss

Note: Dates and narrations must be included.

(LCCI Intermediate 1985)

TUTORIAL NOTE: The term SINKING FUND is sometimes used to refer to the debenture redemption fund.

COMMON ERRORS

1. Double-Entry

The issue and redemption of shares and debentures requires a good knowledge of which accounts to use, and a high degree of accuracy in making the correct debit and credit entries in each account.

If you are in doubt about which account to use, open another one and give it an appropriate title.

2. Forfeiture

If shares are forfeited , do NOT debit the share capital account. Transfer the amount forfeited to an INVESTMENT - OWN SHARES account.

3. Redemption of Shares

Under the 1985 Companies Act, companies now have greater power to redeem their own shares. The procedures are extremely complex, and you are not likely to meet them until you take an advanced accounting course.

The basic points are as follows:

either

(a) the share capital has to be replaced by another issue of shares;

or

(b) the amount NOT covered by the nominal value of a new issue of shares has to be transferred from the profit and loss account to a CAPITAL REDEMPTION RESERVE account.

4. Issue of Debentures

Note that it is not normal practice to issue debentures at a premium.

5. Debenture Redemption Fund

Remember that the debit balance on the debenture redemption fund investments account should always equal the credit balance on the debenture redemption fund account.

6 . Sinking Funds

Note that instead of using the term DEBENTURE REDEMPTION FUND, some accountants use the term SINKING FUND.

34 BRANCH ACCOUNTS: HEAD OFFICE BOOKS

MAIN POINTS

1. Background

Some entities, particularly trading entities, may operate with their main operations located in one area (the HEAD OFFICE) and a number of subsidiary operations located elsewhere (the BRANCHES).

The head office may be responsible for keeping all the detailed accounting records for both itself and all of the branches. Alternatively, each branch may keep its own full set of double-entry books of account (this form of branch accounting is dealt with in the next chapter).

2. Stock Adjustment Method: Accounting Treatment

(a) Dr. Branch stock account (at selling price)
    Cr. Goods sent to branch account (at cost)
    Cr. Branch stock adjustment account (mark-up)
    With the SELLING price of the goods sent to the branch

(b) Dr. Goods sent to branch account (at cost)
    Dr. Branch stock adjustment account (at mark-up)
    Cr. Branch stock account
    With the goods returned to head office at SELLING price

(c) Dr. Bank
    Cr. Branch stock account
    With the cash sales banked by the branch

(d) Dr. Debtor's account
    Cr. Branch account
    With sales made by the branch on credit terms to customers

(e) Dr. Branch stock adjustment account
    Cr. Branch stock account
    With any reductions in the normal selling price that the branch is permitted to make

(f) Dr. Branch stock adjustment account
    Cr. Branch stock account
    With the cost of any normal wastage

(g) Dr. Branch stock account at the beginning of the NEXT accounting period
    Cr. Branch stock account at the end of the CURRENT accounting period
    With the selling price of the closing stock held by the branch at the end of the current accounting period.

(h) Dr. Branch stock losses account (cost only)
     Dr. Branch stock adjustment account (mark-up only)
     Cr. Branch stock (at selling price)
     With the stock loss as disclosed by the branch stock account

(i) Dr. Goods sent to branch account
    Cr. Trading account
    With the cost of goods sent to the branch during the accounting period

(j) Dr. Branch profit and loss account
    Cr. Branch stock losses account
    With the balance on the branch stock losses account

(k) Dr. Branch stock adjustment account (at the end of the current accounting period)
    Cr. Branch stock adjustment account (at the beginning of the next accounting period)
    With the provision for unrealised profit on stock held by the branch at the end of the accounting period

(l) Dr. Branch stock account
    Cr. Branch profit and loss account
    With the balance on the branch stock account

3. Stock Adjustment Method: Balance Sheet Treatment

The value of the stock to be shown in the balance sheet should be disclosed as follows:

	£	£
Stock at selling price (as per the branch stock account)	X	
Less: Provision for unrealised profit (as per the branch stock adjustment account)	X	X

4. Memorandum Column Method: Accounting Treatment

(a) Dr. Branch stock account
    Cr. Goods sent to branch account
    With the COST of goods sent to the branch by the head office

(b) Dr. Goods sent to branch account
    Cr. Branch stock account
    With the COST of goods returned by the branch to the head office

(c) Dr. Bank account
    Cr. Branch stock account
    With cash sales made by the branch

(d) Dr. Debtors' accounts
    Cr. Branch stock account
    With the credit sales made by the branch

(e) Dr. Branch stock losses account
    Cr. Branch stock account
    With any stock losses

(f) Dr. Branch stock account (at the beginning of the next accounting period)
    Cr. Branch stock account (at the begining of the current accounting period)
    With the COST of the stock held by the branch at the end of the current accounting period)

(g) Dr.   Goods sent to branch account
     Cr.   Trading account
     With the cost of the goods sent to the branch during the period

(h) Dr.   Branch stock account
     Cr.   Branch profit and loss account
     With the balance on the branch stock account at the end of the accounting period

(i) Dr.   Branch profit and loss account
     Cr.   Branch stock losses account
     With the balance on the branches stock losses account at the end of the accounting period

(j) Branch stock account MEMORANDUM columns at SELLING PRICE

DEBIT	CREDIT
Balance brought down	Goods returned by branch
Goods sent to branch	Cash sales
	Credit sales
	Reductions in selling price
	Stock Losses
	Balance carried down

5. Memorandum Column Method: Balance Sheet Treatment

The balance sheet amount for closing stock will be extracted from the cost column in the branch stock account. No adjustment is required.

Example Treece and Co. sells general merchandise from a main store in Winchester and from a branch store in Watford. Sales are mainly on credit. Most branch customers settle their accounts through the office which is situated at the main store. All accounting records are maintained at this office which also operates a centralised buying system. Merchandise is supplied by the main store to the branch at selling price i.e. cost plus 20%.

The following figures relating to the Watford Branch for the month of October 19X1 are at selling prices:

	£
Balances at 1 October 19X1	
Branch stock	5,088
Branch Debtors	3,360
Transactions during October 19X1	
Goods transferred to Watford from Main Store	27,282
Goods returned to Main Store by Watford	252
Cash sales	1,236
Credit sales	28,380
Damaged stock written off by Watford	72
Credit sales returned by customers to Watford	180
Receipts from Watford credit customer	
by Main Store	26,640
by Watford Branch	1,200

A physical stock check on 31 October 19X1 produced a closing stock figure of £2,100 at selling price.

Required:

Post and balance the appropriate accounts for the Watford Branch in the Winchester ledger for the month of October 19X1.

(AAT Level 3)

Solution

TREECE AND CO.

(a) <u>Stock Adjustment method</u>

Branch stock account

	£		£
Balance b/d	5,088	Goods sent to Branch-Returns	252
Goods sent to branch	27,282	Branch debtors-credit sales	28,380
Branch debtors (returns)	180	Branch cash-cash sales	1,236
		Branch expenses-damaged stock	72
		Balance c/f - closing stock	2,100
		Branch stock adjustment	
		stock loss	510
	£32,550		£32,550

Goods sent to Branch account

	£		£
Branch stock adjustment		Branch stock	27,282
(1/6x£27,282)	4,547	Branch stock adjustment -	
Branch stock - returns	252	returns (1/6x£252)	42
Head Office trading A/c	22,525		
	£27,324		£27,324

Branch stock adjustment account

	£		£
Goods sent to Branch	42	Balance b/d (1/6x£5,088)	848
Branch stock (1/6x£72)	12	Goods sent to branch	4,547
Branch stock -stock loss	510		
Balance c/f (1/6x2,100)	350		
Branch profit and loss	4,481		
	£5,395		£5,395

The branch debtors account is the same as that shown below under the memorandum column method.

(b) <u>Memorandum column method</u>

Branch Stock Account

	Memo £	Cost £		Memo £	Cost £
Opening stock	5,088	4,240	Goods sent to Branch		
Goods sent to Branch	27,282	22,735	(returns to Main Store)	252	210

	£	£		£	£
Branch debtors - returns	180	180	Branch debtors - credit sales	28,380	28,380

Branch Stock Account (continued)

	Memo £	Cost £		Memo £	Cost £
Branch profit and loss	-	4,481	Branch cash - cash sales	1,236	1,236
			Branch expenses - damaged stock	72	60
			Closing stock c/f	2,100	1,750
			Stock loss	510	-
	£32,550	£31,636		£32,550	£31,636

Goods sent to Branch account

	£		£
Branch stock A/c (5/6x£252)	210	Branch stock A/c (5/6x£27,282)	22,735
Head Office Trading A/c	22,525		
	£22,735		£22,735

Branch debtors account

	£		£
Balance b/d	3,360	Branch stock a/c - returns	180
Branch stock a/c	28,380	Winchester Bank	26,640
		Watford Bank	1,200
		Balance c/f	3,720
	£31,740		£31,740

WORKINGS

(1) If selling price is cost plus 20% (1/5). the profit margin on sales will be 1/6.

(2) Branch profit calculation

	£	£
Opening stock		4,240
Goods sent to Branch		22,735
		26,975
Closing stock	1,750	
Returns	210	
Damaged (written off)	60	2,020
		£24,955

	£
Branch profit (£24,955x20%) expected	4,991
Less: Stock loss	510
Branch Profit Achieved	£4,481

EXERCISES

34.1 Thomas Minton, a trader whose Head Office is in Hanley, has two branches, one in Tunstall and one in Longton. Goods are purchased by Head Office and sent to branches for sale, the selling price being the cost price plus 50%. The following information relates to the month of September 19X5:

	Tunstall £	Longton £
Stock at cost 1 September 19X5	4,800	9,600
Goods sent to Branches during September 19X5 at cost	24,000	76,800
Goods returned by Branches to Head Office at cost	2,400	3,840
Stock at cost 30 September 19X5	4,400	8,600
Sales during September 19X5 at selling price;		
for cash	29,880	100,000
on credit	3,000	10,000

Required:

Prepare ONE Branch Stock account for the two branches showing for each Branch, in vertical columns headed Cost Price and Memorandum Selling Price respectively, the transaction of Thomas Minton for the month of September 19X5.

Note: No total column is required.

(LCCI Intermediate 1986)

34.2 Britten, Holst and Bax commence in partnership on 1 January 19X1 sharing profits and losses 2:1:1 respectively. The partnership agreement provides for 8% interest on capital before the sharing of profits or losses.

The accounting records are maintained at Head Office and the business operates through two retail branches, managed by Britten and Holst respectively. Bax, who is located at Head Office, deals with purchasing and administration.

All purchased goods are delivered direct to branch by suppliers.

In the accounting records, goods are charged to branch at their normal selling price (cost plus $33\frac{1}{3}$%), the profit margin being dealt with through an Adjustment Account.

On 31 December 19X1, Bax extracts the following Trial Balance from the ledger.

		£	£
Capital:	Britten		44,000
	Holst		31,000
	Bax		12,000
Leasehold premises:	Head Office	42,000	
Rent:	Branch A	5,400	
	Branch B	6,800	
Purchases at cost:	Branch A	138,000	
	Branch B	144,000	

Sales:	Branch A		146,400
	Branch B		168,220
		£	£
Expenses:	Head Office	24,350	
	Branch A	17,475	
	Branch B	26,785	
Creditors:			23,200
Returns from branch customers (cash refunds given):	Branch A	960	
	Branch B	820	
Branch debtors:	Branch A	740	
	Branch B	870	
Bank overdraft:			5,380
Motor vehicle at cost:	Head Office	15,000	
Drawings:	Britten	4,000	
	Holst	1,000	
	Bax	2,000	
		£430,200	£430,200

The following additional information is made available:

(1) On 31 December 19X1 Branch Stocks, valued at normal selling price:
£

Branch A	38,560
Branch B	24,600

(2) The motor vehicle is to be depreciated at 20% per annum on cost and charged:

Branch A	40%
Branch B	60%

(3) The leasehold is to be amortised (depreciated) over a 10 year period.

(4) All Head Office expenses (except motor vehicle depreciation) to be charged:

Branch A	50%
Branch B	50%

Required:

(a) Prepare for 19X1, in columnar form (one column for Branch A and one column for Branch B):

(i) Branch Account
(ii) Branch Stock Adjustment Account
(iii) Branch Profit and Loss Account

Note: Total columns are NOT required; and

(b) prepare an Appropriation Account for the partnership for the year.

(LCCI Intermediate 1987)

34.3 Delity plc has several branches and due to local conditions, the branches charge different selling prices for the same goods. All purchases are made by head office but goods are sometimes transferred directly between branches. As goods are invoiced from head office to branches at selling prices, the branch adjustment accounts of the branches concerned have to be amended when such transfers are made. Branches pay local expenses and remit all the remaining cash received from

291

debtors to head office.

The following information relates to two branches for 19X4:

		Aville £	Betown £
Stocks:	1 January at selling prices	60,000	90,000
Debtors:	1 January	49,100	72,000
	31 December	53,400	94,000
Discounts allowed to debtors		32,400	41,500
Bad debts written off		-	3,000
Local expenses paid by branch		24,000	28,500
Other expenses paid by head office		43,740	120,125
Goods sent to branches at selling price		810,000	1,222,000
Cash remitted to head office		690,000	1,083,500
Goods returned to head office		20,000	30,000
Stock destroyed at branch		-	2,000
Gross profit on selling price included in invoices from head office		20%	25%

During 19X4, goods invoiced to Aville branch for £36,000 were transferred to the Betown branch. All sales were on credit and there were no stock losses other than the stock destroyed at Betown branch.

Required:

Prepare, in columnar form for EACH branch, the following accounts in the books of Delity plc for 19X4:

(i)   Stock
(ii) Stock adjustment
(iii) Debtors
(iv) Cash
(v)   Profit and loss

(LCCI 3rd Level 1988)

34.4 Paper Products has a head office in London and a branch in Bristol. The following information has been extracted from the head office books of account as at 31 March 19X6:

(1) Information relating to the branch

Balances	Opening £000	Closing £000
Branch bank account (positive balance)	3	12
Branch debtors	66	81
Branch stock (at transfer price)	75	90

Transactions during the year	£000
Bad debts written off	15
Branch general expenses (paid from bank branch account)	42
Cash received from credit customers and banked	390
Cash sales banked	120

	£000
Cash transferred from branch to head office bank account	459
Credit sales	437
Discounts allowed to credit customers	9
Goods returned by credit customers	8
Goods returned from branch (at transfer price from head office)	30
Goods sent to branch (at transfer price from head office)	600

(2) **Information relating to head office**

Balances	Opening £000	Closing £000
Stock	180	220

Transactions during the year	£000
Bad debts written off	24
Cash sales	1,500
Credit sales	2,000
Discounts allowed to credit customers	29
General expenses	410
Goods returned by credit customers	40
Purchases	2,780

Additional Information:

(1) Most of the accounting records relating to the branch are kept by the head office in its own books of account.

(2) All purchases are made by the head office and goods are invoiced to the branch at selling price, that is, at cost price plus 50%.

Required:

(a) Write up the following ledger accounts for the year to 31 March 19X6, being careful to bring down any balances as at that date:

(i) Branch stock account;
(ii) goods sent to branch account;
(iii) branch stock adjustment account;
(iv) branch debtors account; and
(v) branch bank account;

and

(b) compile Paper Products' trading and profit and loss account for the year to 31 March 19X6.

(AAT Final)

COMMON ERRORS

1. Double Entry Problems

Branch accounting is a difficult subject. Unless informed otherwise, you are recommended to use the stock adjustment method.

This method involves using two main accounts:

(a) a branch stock account: remember to DEBIT it with goods sent to the branch at SELLING price, and CREDIT it with cash and credit sales; and

(b) a branch stock adjustment account: remember to CREDIT this account with the difference between the selling price of goods sent to the branch and the cost price of those goods.

2. Arithmetic

Double-check all your arithmetic, especially that relating to mark-up; for example, a 25% mark-up on goods costing £100 = 20% on the selling price (25/(100+25) x100).

3. Provision for Unrealised Profit

If you are using the stock adjustment method, remember to deduct the unrealised profit on the branch closing stock from the branch stock account balance (as shown in the branch stock account).

35 BRANCH ACCOUNTS: BRANCH BOOKS

MAIN POINTS

1. Background

Some entities allow their branches to keep a full set of double-entry books.

The branch capital will be supplied by the head office.

The head office will keep a branch CURRENT account in its books. Each branch will keep a head office current account in its books. The respective current accounts are used to record inter-company transactions.

Otherwise, the branches keep their books as though they were independent entities.

2. Head Office Books: Branch Current Account

MAIN TYPES OF DEBIT ENTRIES
- Balance brought down at the beginning of the year
- Fixed assets supplied by head office
- Goods purchased by head office, and sent to the branch
- Head office expenses paid by head office
- Net profit for the year of the branch

MAIN TYPES OF CREDIT ENTRIES
- Cash sent by branch to head office
- Cash drawings by a partner at the branch
- Goods in transit at the year end between the head office and the branch
- Cash in transit at the year end between the branch and the head office
- Net loss for the year of the branch
- Balance carried down at the end of the year

3. Branch Books: Head Office Current Account

MAIN TYPES OF DEBIT ENTRIES
- Cash sent to head office
- Cash drawings made by a partner at the branch
- Net loss for the year of the branch
- Balance carried down at the end of the year

MAIN TYPES OF CREDIT ENTRIES
- Balance brought down at the beginning of the year
- Fixed assets supplied by the head office
- Goods sent to the branch from the head office
- Expenses paid by the head office on behalf of the branch
- Net profit for the year of the branch

Example. Goal has a head office in London and a branch in York. The branch maintains a full set of accounts. The following information is a summary of the branch transactions recorded in the books of the head office for the year to 31 December 19X5:

	£
Balance due from the branch at 1 January 19X5	130,000
Goods supplied to the branch	500,000
Goods returned by the branch	25,000
Cash received from the branch	455,000
Expenses paid on behalf of the branch	15,000

Additional information:

1. The branch profit for the year to 31 December 19X5 was £35,000.
2. Goods costing £20,000 supplied to the branch had not been recorded until 10 January 19X6.
3. Cash remitted by the branch of £30,000 had not been received by the head office until 5 January 19X6.

Required:

Prepare

(a) the branch current account in the books of the head office; and
(b) the head office current account in the books of the branch.

Solution

GOAL
Head Office books
Branch Current Account

	£		£
Balance b/d	130,000	Goods returned	25,000
Goods supplied	500,000	Cash from branch	455,000
Bank: expenses paid	15,000	Goods in transit c/d	20,000
Branch net profit	35,000	Cash in transit c/d	30,000
		Balance c/d	150,000
	£680,000		**£680,000**
Goods in transit b/d	20,000		
Cash in transit b/d	30,000		
Balance b/d	150,000		

Branch books
Head office current account

	£		£
Goods returned to head office	25,000	Balance b/d	130,000
Remittances to head office (£455+30)	485,000	Goods from head office (£500-20)	480,000
Balance c/d	150,000	Expenses paid by head office	15,000
		Net profit	35,000
	£660,000		**£660,000**
		Balance b/d	150,000

EXERCISES

35.1 Irene has a head office in Ayr and a branch in Perth. The branch keeps its own accounts, although all purchases are made by head office and are invoiced to the branch at cost. The following trial balances were extracted from the respective books of account at 31 March 19X1:

	Ayr Dr £000	Ayr Cr £000	Perth Dr £000	Perth Cr £000
Administrative expenses	130		40	
Bank	5		1	
Capital		111		
Creditors		32		5
Debtors	65		8	
Fixed assets: at cost	90		20	
: accumulated depreciation at 1 April 19X0		36		6
Goods transferred		70	70	
Head office/branch current account	34			34
Purchases	415			
Sales		510		100
Stock at 1 April 19X0	20		6	
	£759	£759	£145	£145

Additional information:
  (1) Stocks at 31 March 19X1: Ayr £25,000, Perth £8,000.
  (2) The fixed assets are to be depreciated by 10% on cost.

Required:
  (a) Prepare the trading, and profit and loss account in columnar format for the head office and the branch for the year to 31 March 19X1, and a combined balance sheet as at that date; and

  (b) compile the branch current account in the books of the head office, and the head office current account in the branch books after the trading, and the profit and loss accounts have been prepared.

35.2 Song has a head office in Dava and a branch in Mana. All goods are purchased by the head office; they are invoiced to the branch cost plus 25%.

The following trial balances were extracted from the books of account at 31 December 19X2:

	Dava £000	Mana £000	Dava £000	Mana £000
Administrative expenses	50		20	
Capital at 1 January 19X1		132		
Cash	16		5	
Creditors		35		2
Debtors	60		65	
Drawings	12			

	£000	£000	£000	£000
Plant and Equipment				
: at cost	80		20	
: accumulated depreciation (at 1.1.X1)		40		5
Goods transferred at invoice price		125	125	
Head office/branch current accounts	38			38
Provision for unrealised profit on stock		4		
Purchases	400			
Sales		350		210
Stocks (at 1 January 19X1)	30		20	
	£686	£686	£255	£255

Additional information:
(1) Stocks at 31 December 19X1: Dava £40,000, Mana £30,000.
(2) The plant and equipment is to be depreciated at a rate of 25% on cost.

Required:

(a) Prepare the trading, and profit and loss accounts in columnar format for the year to 31 December 19X1 for the head office and the branch, and a combined balance sheet as at that date; and
(b) compile the branch current account in the books of the head office, and the head office current account in the branch books after the trading, and profit and loss account has been prepared.

35.3 Scott operates a retail business with a head office in Arbroath and a branch office in Montrose. The branch keeps a full set of books of account. The head office makes all the purchases for the business and invoices them to the branch at cost plus 10%. The following trial balances have been extracted from the books of account as at 30 June 19X3:

	Arbroath Dr £000	Cr £000	Montrose Dr £000	Cr £000
Bank	6		4	
Capital (at 1 July 19X2)		17		
Creditors		20		2
Debtors	5		3	
Furniture and fittings: at cost	30		15	
: accumulated depreciation (at 1 July 19X2)		20		5
Current accounts	54			34
Delivery expenses	18		6	
Drawings	14			
Goods transferred at invoice price		99	88	
Provision for unrealised stock profit		3		
Purchases	280			
Sales		300		120
Shop expenses	17		12	
Stock (at July 19X2)	35		33	
	£459	£459	£161	£161

Additional information
1. Stock at 30 June 19X3: Arbroath £40,000, Montrose £55,000
2. The furniture is to be depreciated at a rate of 10% per annum on the reduced balance.
3. On 30 June 19X3 goods in transit worth £11,000 at invoice price to the branch from head office had not been recorded in the branch books.
4. On 30 June 19X3, cash in transit of £9,000 from the branch to head office had not been recorded in the head office books.

Required:
(a) Prepare the trading, and profit and loss account in columnar format for both the head office and the branch for the year to 30 June 19X3 and a combined balance sheet at that date; and
(b) show the closing entries in (i) the branch current account in the head office books; and (ii) the head office current account in the branch books.

35.4 Devon operates a head office in Exeter and a branch in Torquay. Torquay keeps a complete set of books of account. Exeter purchases goods on behalf of the branch and invoices them at cost price plus 50%, but Torquay also purchases goods on its own behalf.

The following trial balances have been extracted from the books of account as at 30 April 19X4:

	Exeter Dr £000	Exeter Cr £000	Torquay Dr £000	Torquay Cr £000
Capital (at 1 May 19X3)		283		
Cash at bank and in hand	8		6	
Creditors		110		14
Current accounts	80			62
Debtors	250		35	
Drawings	24			
Equipment: at cost	175		60	
: accumulated depreciation 1 May 19X3		105		24
General expenses	65		16	
Goods transferred		75	60	
Provision for unrealised stock profit		9		
Purchases	710		173	
Sales		750		300
Stocks (at 1 May 19X3)	20		50	
	£1,332	£1,332	£400	£400

Additional information
1. The branch stock at 1 May 19X3 included £27,000 of goods invoiced from Exeter.
2. Stocks at 30 April 19X4: Exeter £40,000, Torquay £25,000 (including £15,000 of goods transferred from Exeter).
3. The equipment is to be depreciated at 20% on cost
4. At 30 April 19X4 goods invoiced at £15,000 were in transit to the branch, and £3,000 cash was in transit from the branch to head office.

Required:

Prepare, in columnar format, a trading account and profit and loss account for the head office, the branch and the combined head office and branch for the year to 30 April 19X4, and balance sheets for the head office, the branch and combined head office and branch balance sheets as at that date.

35.5 Mapp Ltd's head office is in London and it has a branch in Brighton. The following trial balances have been extracted from the respective books of account of both the head office and the branch as at 30 June 19X8:

	Head Office		Branch	
	Dr	Cr	Dr	Cr
	£	£	£	£
Administrative expenses	135,000		9,000	
Branch current account	46,000			
Called-up share capital				
(ordinary shares of £1 each)		300,000		
Cash at bank and in hand	19,000		2,000	
Creditors		22,500		5,000
Debtors	15,000		20,000	
Distribution costs	30,000		12,000	
Goods sent to branch		166,000		
Head office current account				24,000
Plant and machinery (net				
book value)	383,000		38,000	
Profit and loss account (at				
1 July 19X7)		28,000		
Provision for unrealised				
profit on stock held by the				
branch		1,500		
Purchases	225,000		154,000	
Sales		350,000		215,000
Stock at cost or cost to				
branch at 1 July 19X7	15,000		9,000	
	£868,000	£868,000	£244,000	£244,000

Additional information:

1. Stock at 30 June 19X8 was valued as follows:

	£
Head office at cost	20,000
Branch at cost to branch	24,000
Goods in transmit to branch at cost to branch	12,000

2. Goods purchased by the head office and sold to the branch are transferred at cost plus 20%.

3. At 30 June 19X8 the branch had transferred £10,000 to the head office's bank account, but as at that date no record had been made in the head office's books of account.

Required:

Prepare in adjacent columns the following:

(a) the head office, the branch, and the combined trading, and profit and loss accounts for the year to 30 June 19X8; and

(b) the head office, the branch, and the combined balance sheets as at that date.

(AAT Final)

COMMON ERRORS

1. Unrealised Profit

If stocks have been supplied by the head office at cost with the addition of a mark-up for internal profit, make sure you deduct any inter-company profit from the branch's closing stocks.

2. Current Account Balances

Make any adjustments for goods and cash in transit between the head office and the branches (or the branches and head office) at the end of the accounting period in the HEAD OFFICE books of account.

Check that the DEBIT balance in the head office books for each branch at the end of the accounting period is equal to the CREDIT balance in the branches books (it is unlikely to be the other way round).

3. Final Accounts' Format

Many examinations questions require you to produce a trading and a profit and loss account for each branch, and for the business as a whole. Use the vertical columnar format, but remember that as a result of inter-company profit, the total amount for each transaction for all of the branches will not necessarily cross-add to the total for the business.

Some questions also require you to produce a balance sheet for each branch, as well as an overall balance sheet, so again, use the columnar vertical account format.

The branch's capital is effectively represented by the head office' current account balance. This balance should equal the branch current account's DEBIT balance in the head office books. When preparing the COMPANY'S balance sheet, therefore, make sure that the two balances cancel each other out.

36 HIRE PURCHASE ACCOUNTS: THE PURCHASER

MAIN POINTS

1. Background

It is quite common for an entity to purchase some fixed asserts, and to arrange for the payment of them over a number of years. This type of purchasing arrangement is known as HIRE PURCHASE.

The total amount eventually paid may be well in excess of the normal selling price, the difference between the two amounts being a FINANCE CHARGE.

The purchaser does not normally become the OWNER of the asset until certain conditions in the agreement have been fulfilled (often not until the last instalment has beern paid).

2. Finance Charge

The finance charge may be apportioned between respective accounting period by using one of two methods:

(a) Actuarial method

This method involves multiplying the rate of interest implicit in the hire purchase agreement by the amount outstanding at the end of each accounting period.

(b) Sum of digits

Formula:

$$\text{Sum of digits} = \frac{X(X+1)}{2}, \text{ where } X = \text{the number of instalments}$$

$$\text{The annual charge} = \frac{Y \times \text{total finance charge}}{\text{Sum of digits}}$$

where Y = instalment number (starting with the last instalment number, and working backwards)

<u>Example:</u>   Three instalments

$$\text{Sum of digits} = \frac{3(3+1)}{2} = 6$$

Annual charge:

$$\text{Period } 1 = \frac{1}{6} \times \text{total finance charge}$$

$$\text{Period } 2 = \frac{2}{6} \times \text{total finance charge}$$

$$\text{Period } 3 = \frac{3}{6} \times \text{total finance charge}$$

3. Instalment method: Accounting Treatment

(a) Dr. Fixed asset account
    Cr. Hire purchase company account
    With the CASH price of the asset

(b) Dr. Hire purchase company account
    Cr. Bank account
    With each instalment

(c) Dr. Hire purchase interest account
    Cr. Hire purchase company account
    With the interest paid during the accounting period

(d) Dr. Profit and loss account
    Cr. Hire purchase interest account
    With the interest paid on the agreement during the accounting period.

(e) Dr. Profit and loss account
    Cr. Fixed asset accumulated depreciation account
    With the depreciation for the year based on the COST price of the asset.

4. Interest Suspense Method: Accounting Treatment

(a) Dr. Fixed asset account (cash price only)
    Dr. Hire pruchase interest account (total interest payable as per the agreement)
    Cr. Hire purchase loan account
    With the hire purchase price of the fixed asset

(b) Dr. Hire purchase loan account
    Cr. Bank account
    With each instalment

(c) Dr. Profit and loss account
    Cr. Hire purchase interest account
    With the amount of interest paid on the agreement during the year

(d) Dr. Fixed asset account
    Cr. Fixed asset accumulated depreciation account
    With the depreciation for the year based on the COST price of the asset.

5. Balance Sheet Presentation

		£
(a)	Fixed asset at cost	X
	Less: Accumulated depreciation	X
	Net book value	X
(b)	Long-term liabilities	
	Obligations under hire purcahse contracts	X
(c)	Current liabilities	
	(that is, within the next twelve months)	
	Obligations under hire purchase contracts	X

Example   Ryan bought a machine on hire purchase. The cost price was £10,000. Ryan paid a deposit of £2,000 on 1 January 19X6, and he agreed to pay two instalments of £3,798 and a final instalment of £3,797 on 31 December at a rate of 25% per annum on cost.

Notes:

(1) The implicit rate of int4erest in the agreement is 20%.

(2) Differences caused by arithmetical roundings are to be adjusted in the final year of the agreement.

Required:

Account for the above in the books of Ryan for each of the three years to 31 December 19X6, 19X7 and 19X8 respectively.

Solution

RYAN
Machine Account

	£			£
1 1 X6 H P Loan	10,000			

Machine accumulated depreciation account

		£			£
			31 12 X6 Profit and loss		
			(25% x £10,000)		2,500
31 12 X7	Balance c/d	5,000	31 12 X7 Profit and loss		
			(25% x £10,000)		2,500
		£5,000			£5,000
			1 1 X8 Balance b/d		5,000
31 12 X8	Balance c?d	7,500	31 12 X8 Profit and loss		
			(25% x £10,000)		2,500
		£7,500			£7,500
			1 1 X9 Balance b/d		7,500

INSTALMENT METHOD

Hire Purchase loan account

		£			£
1 1 X6	Bank	2,000	1 1 X6	Machine	10,000
			31 12 X6	HP Interest	
31 12 X6	Bank	3,798		(20% x £10,000-2,000)	1,600
31 12 X6	Balance c/d	5,802			
		£11,600			£11,600
31 12 X7	Bank	3,798	1 1 X7	Balance b/d	5,802
31 12 X7	Balance c/d	3,164	31 12 X7	HP interest	
				(20% x £5,802)	1,160
		£6,962			£6,962
31 12 X7	Bank	3,797	1 1 X8	Balance b/d	3.164
			31 12 X8	HP Interest	
				(20% x £3,164)	633
		£3,797			£3,797

Hire purchase loan interest account

		£			£
31 12 X6	HP Loan	1,600	31 12 X6	Profit and loss	1,600
31 12 X7	HP Loan	1,160	31 12 X7	Profit and loss	1,160
31 12 X8	HP Loan	633	31 12 X8	Profit and loss	633

INTEREST SUSPENSE METHOD

Hire Purchase loan account

		£			£
1 1 X6	Bank	2,000	1 1 X6	Machine	10,000
31 12 X6	Bank	3,798	1 1 X6	HP Interest Suspense	
31 12 X6	Balance c/d	7,595		(£8,000-(2x£3,798	
				+3,797))	3,393
		£13,393			£13,393
31 12 X7	Bank	3,798	1 1 X7	Balance b/d	7,595
31 12 X7	Balance c/d	3,797			
		£7,595			£7,595
31 12 X8	Bank	£3,797	1 1 X8	Balance b/d	£3,797

Hire purchase interest suspense acount

		£			£
1 1 X6	HP Loan	3,393	31 12 X6	Profit and loss	
				(20%x£10,000-2,000)	1,600
			31 12 X6	Balance c/d	1,793
		£3,393			£3,393

		£			£
1 1 X7	Balance b/d	1,793	31 12 X7	Profit and loss [20%x(£8,000 +1,600-3,798)]	1,160
			31 12 X7	Balance c/d	633
		£1,793			£1,793
1 1 X8	Balance b/d	£633	31 12 X8	Profit and loss	£633

Note: The above solutions apportion the total interest charge of £3,393 using the acturial method. With short-term hire purchase arrangements, an acceptable alternative would be to use the sum of digits method. The interest would then be apportioned as follows:

Year to 31 December	Sum of digits*	Comparison: Actuarial method
	£	£
19X6	£3393x3/6 = 1,697	1,600
19X7	£3393x2/6 = 1,131	1,160
19X8	£3393x1/6 = 565	633
	£3,393	£3,393

$$*\text{Sum of digits} = \frac{n(n+1)}{2} = \frac{3(3+1)}{2} = 6$$

Therefore, year to 31 12 X6   apportioned 1/6
31 12 X7   apportioned 2/6
31 12 X8   apportioned 3/6

EXERCISES

36.1 Troy bought a van costing £16,000 under a hire purchase agreement on 1 January 19X1. He paid a deposit of £4,000 on that date, following by 6 half yearly instalments of £3,200 payable on 30 June and 31 December in each year of the agreement.

Interest charges are to be apportioned using the sum of the digits method.

Required:

Write up thje following ledger accounts for each of the three years to 31 December 19X1 and 19X3 respectively:

(i) van;
(ii) hire purchase loan; and
(iii) hire purchase loan interest

36.2 Robin bought some machinery costing £50,000 on hire purchase. He paid an initial depost of £12,500, followed by five annual instalments of £11,454 payable at the end of each year of the agreement.

Required:

Using annuity tables, calculate the rate of interest implicity in the above agreement.

36.3 On April 19X4, Jennie bought a car costing £9,000 on hire purchase. She paid an initial depost of £3,000, followed by 36 monthly instalments of £222 payable at the end of each month. The implicit rate of interest in the agreement is 20%. Jennie depreciates the car at a rate of 25% on cost.

Required

Prepare the following ledger accounts for the year to 31 March 19X5:

    (i)   car;
    (ii) car depreciation;
    (iii) hire purchase loan; and
    (iv) hire purchase interest.

36.4 Bulwell Aggregates Ltd. wish to expand their transpoort fleet and have purchased three heavy lorries with a list price of £18,000 each. Robert Bulwell has negotiated hire purchase finance to fund this expansion, and the company has entered into a hire purchase agreement with Granby Garages plc on 1 January 19X1. The agreeement states that Bulwell Aggregates will pay a depost of £9,000 on 1 January 19X1, and two annual instalments of £24,000 on 31 December 19X1, 19X2 and a final instalment of £20,391 on 31 December 19X3.

Interest is to be calculated at 25% on the balance outstanding on 1 January each year and paid on 31 December each year.

The depreciation policy of Bulwell Aggregates Ltd. is to write off the vehicles over a four year period using the straight line method and assuming a scrap value of £1,333 for each vehicle at the end of its useful life.

Required:

Account for he above transactions in the books of Bulwell Aggregates Ltd showing the entries in the Profit and Loss Account and Balance Sheet for the years 19X1, 19X2, 19X3 and 19X4.

Calculations to the nearest £

(AAT/IAS Part 2, amended)

36.5 Midge bought a car costing £20,000 on hire purchase om 1 May 19X5. He paid a depost of £5,000 followed by three annual instalments of £6,460 payable on 30 April 19X6, 19X7 and 19X8 respectively.

The rate of interest implicit in the agreement is 14%

On 31 October 19X7, the car was involved in an accident, and it was an immediate write-off. The insurance company paid Midge £6,000 under the terms of Midge's comprehensive insurance cover. The hire purchase company accepted £14,000 for the termination of the agreement. Midge depreciates the car on a straight line basis of 25% based on cost.

Required:

(a) Write up the following ledger accounts:

   (i)   car;
   (ii) car accumulated depreciation:
   (iii) hire purchase loan;
   (iv) hire purchase loan intertest; and
   (v)   car disposal account;
   and

(b) prepare the balance sheet extracts for the above transactions as at 30 April 19X6.

COMMON ERRORS

1. Reversal of Entries

The amount borrowed from a hire purchase company is a LOAN, so make sure that you CREDIT the hire purchase company's account with the amount borrowed. Each instalment should be DEBITED to the account (irrespective of whether you use the instalment or the interest suspense method).

2. Hire Purchase Interest

You will need to calculate the total amount of hire purchase interest included in each instalment in order to calculate the hire purchase charge for the year.

You can do this by using either the actuarial or the sum of digits' method. Both methods are suitable for agreements of less than about seven years. For longer periods, use the annuity method.

If the queston states the rate of interest implicit in the agreement, the examiner is effectively telling you to use the acturial method.

3. The Balance Sheet

Remember to include a fixed asset bought on hire purchase in the balance sheet. Although the entity does not legally own the asset until the agreement has been completed, it is considered that it is the right to use the asset that is being capitalised, and not the strict legal ownership of it.

4. Depreciation

Remembert to base the depreciation charge for the year on the COST price of the asset, and NOT on the total hire purchase price.

37

HIRE PURCHASE ACCOUNTS: THE SELLER

MAIN POINTS

1. Background

An entity selling goods on hire purchase has to decide what proportion of the total hire purchase selling price (that is, ordinary gross profit plus the finance charge)should be credited to each year's profit and loss account during the life of the agreement.

2. Sales System Method: Accounting Treatment:

(a) Using this method the seller claims the ordinary gross profit, and credits it to the trading account for the financial year in which the hire purchase agreement was signed.

(b) The total finance charge would be apportioned by using either the actuarial method or the sum of digit's methods.

Book-keeping entries:

(i) Dr. Hire purchase debtor's account (with the total hire purchase price)
Cr. Sales accounts (with the cash price)
Cr. Hire purchase interest account (with the total finance charge)

(ii) Dr. Bank account
Cr. Hire purchase debtor's account
With the instalments received.

(iii) Dr. Hire purchase interest account
Cr. Profit and loss account
With the finance charge earned during the financial year (using either the actuarial or the sum of digit's method)

(c) Balance sheet presentation

	£	£
Debtors: hire purchase customers	X	
Less: Finance charges on instalments not yet due	X	X

3. Stock Method: Accounting Treatment

(a) This method involves apportioning the TOTAL profit earned on the hire purchase sale (ordinary gross profit + the total finance charge).

The apportionment may be made as follows:

$$\frac{\text{Instalments not yet due} \times \text{Total hire purchase profit}}{\text{Total hire purchase selling price}}$$

Book-keeping entries:

(i) Dr. Hire purchases debtor's account
    Cr. Sales account
    With the hire purchase selling price

(ii) Dr. Sales account
    Cr. Trading account
    With the total hire purchase sales for the financial year

(iii) Dr. Profit and loss account
    Cr. Provision for unrealised profit on hire purchase sales
    With the provision required

(b) Balance sheet presentation

	£	£
Debtors: hire purchase customers	X	
Less: Provision for unrealised profit on hire purchase sales	X	X

4. Repossessions

(a) Dr. Repossessed good account
    Cr. Hire purchase debtor's account
    With the outstanding instalments

(b) Dr. Hire purchase interest suspense account
    Cr. Repossesed goods account
    With the finance charge not yet earned

(c) Dr. Repossessed goods account
    Cr. Bank account
    With the cost of repossession

(d) Dr. Debtor's account
    Cr. Repossessed goods account
    With the selling price obtained for the sale of the repossessed goods

(e) EITHER
Dr. Repossessed goods account   OR Dr. Profit and loss account
Cr. Profit and loss account   Cr. Repossessed goods account
With the profit made on selling the repossessed goods / With the loss incurred on selling the repossessed goods

Example. On 1 July 19X6, Burn sold a machine costing £5,000 on hire purchase terms to Dale for £8,000. Dale agreed to pay an immediate deposit of £2,000 followed by two annual instalments of £2,760 and a final instalment of £2,759 payable on 30 June 19X7, 19X8 and 19X9 respectively.

The rate of interest implicit in the agreement is 18%.

Required:

Account for the above transactions in the books of Burn for each of the three years to 30 June 19X7, 19X8, 19X9.

Solution

BURN

Sales System Method

(i)

Dale's Account

		£			£
1 7 X6	Hire purchase sales	8,000	1 7 X6	Bank(deposit)	2,000
30 6 X7	Hire purchase interest		30 6 X7	Bank(instalment)	2,760
	(18%x£8,000-2,000)	1,080	30 6 X7	Balance c/d	4,320
		£9,080			£9,080
1 7 X7	Balance b/d	4,320	30 6 X8	Bank (instalment)	2,760
30 6 X8	Hire purchase interest				
	(10%x£4,320)	778	30 6 X8	Balance c/d	2,338
		£5,098			£5,098
1 7 X8	Balance b/d	2,338			
30 6 X9	Hire purchase interest				
	(18%x£2,338	421	30 6 X9	Bank (instalment)	2,579
		£2,759			£2,759

(ii)

Hire purchase interest account

		£			£
30 6 X7	Hire purchase trading	1,080	30 6 X7	Date	1,080
30 6 X8	Hire purchase trading	778	30 6 X8	Date	778
30 6 X9	Hire purchase trading	421	30 6 X9	Date	421

(iii)

Hire purchase trading account

		£			£
1 7 X6	General trading	5,000	1 7 X6	Hire purchase sales	8,000
30 6 X7	Trading account	3,000	30 6 X7	Hire purchase	
	(gross profit)			interest	1,080
30 6 X7	Profit and loss account	1,080			
		£9,080			£9,080
30 6 X8	Profit and loss	778	30 6 X8	Hire purchase interest	778
30 6 X9	Profit and loss	£421	30 6 X9	Hire purchase interest	£421

Stock Method:

(i)

Dale's account

		£			£
17 X6	Hire purchase sales	10,279	1 7 X6	Bank (deposit)	2,000
			30 6 X7	Bank (instalment)	2,760
			30 6 X7	Balance c/d	5,519
		£10,279			£10,279
1 7 X7	Balance b/d	5,519	30 6 X8	Bank (instalment)	2,760
			30 6 X8	Balance c/d	2,759
		£5,519			£5,519
1 7 X8	Balance b/d	£2,759	30 6 X8	Bank (instalment)	£2,759

(iii)

Hire purchase trading account

		£			£
1 7 X6	General trading	5,000	1 7 X6	Hire purchase sales	10,279
30 6X7	Provision for unrealised profit c/d	2,834			
30 6 X7	Trading account (gross profit)	2,445			
		£10,279			£10,279
30 6X8	Provision for unrealised profit c/d	1,417	1 7 X7	Balance b/d	2,834
30 6 X7	Trading account (gross profit)	1,417			
		£2,834			£2,834
30 6 X9	Trading account (gross profit)	£1,417	1 7 X9	Balance b/d	£1,417

WORKING:

Total hire purchase profit = £10,279 - 5,000 = £5,279

Provision calculated on the basis of balance not due divided by total hire purchase sale:

$$\text{Year to 30 6 X6} = \frac{£5,519}{£10,279} \times £5,279 = £2,834$$

$$\text{Year to 30 6 X7} = \frac{£2,759}{£10,279} \times £5,279 = £1,417$$

Note: In the balance sheet the provision for unrealised profit will be deducted from the instalments due from Dale.

EXERCISES

37.1 Granby Garages PLC has entered into a hire purchases agreement to sell three heavy lorries with a list price of £18,000 each to Bulwell Aggregates Ltd. The agreement states that Bulwell Aggregates wil pay a deposit of £9,000 on 1 January 19X1, and two annual instalments of £24,000 on 31 December 19X1, 19X2, and a final instalment of £20,391 on 31 December 19X3. Interest is to be calculated at 25% on the balance outstanding 31 December each year. The cost of the vehicles to Granby Garages is £14,400 each.

Required:

Account for the above transactions in the books of Granby Garages PLC, showing the entries in the Hire Purchase Trading Account for the years 19X1, 19X2and 19X3. This is the only hire purchase transaction undertaken by the company.

(AAT/IAS Part 2, adapted)

37.2 Bromford Ltd sells office equipment and a number of its transactions are on hire purchase terms. The following information relates to a photocopier sold on hire purchase terms to Till and Co. a firm of accountants.

1. Date of hire purchase sale - 30 June 19X6.

2. Terms of hire purchase sale
   Depost of £480
   Instalments : 24 of £95 each.

3. Instalments are payable at the end of each month, the first being due on 31 July 19X6.

4. Cash selling price £2,400 which gives Bromford Ltd a $33\frac{1}{3}$% profit on the purchase cost of the photocopier.

Till and Co decide to depreciate the photocopier over 3 years on a straight line basis with no residual value, with monthly apportionments as necessary.

The respective financial year ends of the two businesses are:

Bromford Ltd	-31 December
Til and Co.	-31 March

Required:

On the assumption that all instalments are paid as due:

(a) Prepare the Hire Purchase Trading Account for the photocopier in the books of Bromford Ltd for the year ended 31 December 19X6; and

(b) (i) show the entries in the Profit and Loss Account in respect of the photocopier for the year ended 31 March 19X7;

   (ii) show the entries in the Balance Sheet in respect of the photocopier as at 31 March 19X7.

(LCCI Intermediate 1987)

37.3 John Murray, a dealer, advertised the sale of a new model of a saloon car in a statement set out in the following form:-

SALOON XY

List Price	Depost	Monthly Payments	Number of Payments	Total instal- ments	Total Hire Purchase Price
£3,850	20%	£96	36	£3,456	£4226

During the year 19X4 on the dates set out below, he sold 5 cars (A, B, C, D and E) for which the deposit and number of instalments stated had been paid.

A	-2 January	(11 instalments)
B	-2 March	(9 instalments)
C	-4 April	(5 instalments) *
D	-5 August	(4 instalments)
E	-6 October	(2 instalments)

*No payment had been made for Car C after September and the dealer repossessed the car in December 19X4. Car C was in stock at the end of the year valued at £2,000 which was two thirds of the cost of the car when new (£3,000).

In all cases the deposit was paid at the time of sale and the first instalment of the 36 instalments paid in the following month.

Profit on sales was credited in full immediately, but Hire Purchase interest earned was credited to Trading Account at the rate of £10 per instalment paid over the life of the agreement.

Required:

(a) Complete a tabulation of the sales for the year under the headings set out above and with the car identification letter and date sold inserted vertically on the left hand side; and

(b) prepare a Trading Account for the year to 31 December 19X4 showing the gross profit.

(LCCI Intermediate 1985)

37.4 Tain sells some of his goods on hire purchase. The terms of the hire purchase agreements are such that an initial deposit of 25% is required, followed by six equal monthly instalments. The first instalment is payable one month after the agreement has been signed.

The following information relates to the year to 31 March 19X6.

1.

Hire Purchase sales	Cost price	Hire purchases Selling price
	£	£
1 May 19X5	450	600
1 July 19X5	750	1,000
1 December 19X5	200	300
1 January 19X6	1,000	1,200

2. The goods sold on 1 December 19X5 were returned on 15 February 19X6, the deposit and the instalments due having been paid up to 1 February 19X6. Other instalments were received as and when due.

3. Tain credits gross profit and interest to the profit and loss account in the proportion that deposits and instalments received bear to the hire purchase price.

Required:

Prepare the hire purchase trading account for the year to 31 March 19X6.

37.5 Rock commenced business on 1 September 19X3 selling televisions and videos on cash and hire purchase terms. The following summarised trial balance was extracted from his books of account as at 31 August 19X4.

	£ Dr	£ Cr
Bank overdraft		8,475
Capital (cash introduced on 1 September 19X3)		50,000
Cash sales: televisions (600 at £300 each)		180,000
Creditors		121,000
Debtors	1,000	
Drawings	16,000	
Fixed assets at cost	45,000	
Hire purchase debtors: televisions	105,000	
videos	342,000	
Hire purchase sales: televisions (350 at £400 each)		140,000
Hire purchase sales: videos (380 at £1,260 each)		478,800
Purchases: televisions (1,000 at £150 each)	150,000	
videos (400 at £350 each)	140,000	
Retailing expenses	179,275	
	£978,275	£978,275

Additional information

1. During the year, Rock purchased 1,000 televisions at a cost of £150 each. HGe sold them either on cash terms for £300 each or on hire purchase. The hire purchase terms were an initial deposit of £100, followed by two annual instalments of £150 each, payable by the customer on the first and second anniversary resptively of the date of purchase of the television.

2. Rock had also purchased 400 videos for £350 each. Although he was prepared to sell them on cash terms (for £1,000 each) all the video sales had been on hire purchase. An initial deposit of £360 was required, followed by two annual instalments of £450 each, payable by the customer on the first and second anniversay respectively of the date of purchase video.

315

3. In the annual accounts, Rock decided to take credit for gross profit on hire purchase sales in accordance with the following policy.

   (a) Televisions: to allow for both the ordinary gross profit and hire purchase interest in proportion to the total cash collected from customers sold televisions on hire purchase terms: and

   (b) Videos: to take the ordinary gross profit on videos sold on hire purchase in the year of sale, and to apportion the interest on hire purchase equally over the two years of the agreement.

4. Depreciation is to be provided on fixed assets at 20% per annum on cost

Required:

(a) Prepare columnar trading, profit and loss account for the year to 31 August 19X4, and a balance sheet as at that date for:

   (i) televisions,
   (ii) videos, and
   (iii) the business as a whole, and a combined profit and loss account for the year to 31 August 19X4;

(b) Prepare a balance sheet as at 31 August 19X4.

(AAT Final)

COMMON ERRORS

1. Complex questions

Hire purchase questions dealing with the seller's book are extremely complex, especially when the examiner does not always make it clear what method you should use in dealing with the hire purchase profit.

2. Finance Charge

Unless given instructions to the contrary, claim the ordinary gross profit in the year of sale. If the rate of interest is given, apportion the finance charge using the actuarial method. If the rate of interest is not given, use the sum of digits' method.

3. Total Profit

If the total profit is to be apportioned between respective financial years, do not forget to provide for unrealised profit on hire purchase sales.

If a provision already exisits, the profit and loss account should only be charged with the change necessary to bring the provision to the level reequired as at the end of the financial year.

4. Balance Sheet

Do NOT include assets that have been sold on hire purchase terms in the balance sheet. Although the seller may still retain the legal title to them, he had lost his right to the USE of them.

It follows that sets sold on hire purchase terms should not be depreciated by the SELLER.

Amounts owed by hire purchase customers should be included in debtors.

PART 3

APPRAISAL OF ACCOUNTS

38

CASH FLOW STATEMENTS

MAIN POINTS

1. Background

In traditional accounting statements, the sales revenue earned during a particular accounting period is matched against the expenditure incurred in earning that revenue during the same period. This is not the same as matching cash received against cash paid. Hence accounting profit (or loss) is not necessarily the same as the difference between cash received and cash paid.

Nonetheless, an entity cannot ignore the effect of CASH FLOW on its operations. Irrespective of the level of accounting profit over a period of time, if an entity has insufficient cash to settle its debts as they fall due, it is technically INSOLVENT. It is unlawful for an insolvent entity to continue operating, and so it must cease trading.

Besides preparing a profit statement, therefore, it is also helpful to prepare a LIQUIDITY statement, that is, a statement showing its cash position. Whilst it is useful to prepare such a statement on an historical basis, it is even more useful to prepare a forecasted or budgeted cash flow statement. By doing so, likely future cash flow problems can be tackled before they become serious.

2. Types

(a) Historical. Historical cash flow summaries relate to a previous accounting period. As such, they do not provide any control over future cash flows, and they are only of interest as a historical record of what did happen.

(b) Forecasted. A forecast is technically a PREDICTION of what is likely to happen, on the assumption that no attempt will be made to control it. It follows that a forecasted cash flow statement is a prediction of what is likely to happen to the cash position, assuming that no action is taken to change that position. Note that in financial accounting, a forecast is often taken to be the same as a BUDGET.

(c) Budgeted. A budgeted cash flow statement is a carefully drawn up PLAN of future cash flow. It charts what the entity intends to happen, assuming that certain policies and actions are adopted.

319

3. Format

A cash flow statement may be comprised of three main sections:

CASH RECEIPTS

Main items:
Sales
Receipts from debtors
Dividends, interest and rent received
Issue of shares and debentures
Sales of fixed assets

CASH PAYMENTS

Main items:
Purchases
Payments to creditors
Expenses
Purchases of fixed assets
Drawings
Taxation paid
Dividends paid

NET CASH

Main items:
Net cash flow for the period (receipts - payments)
Opening cash
Closing cash

4. Definition of Cash

(Cash in hand at the bank) - bank overdrafts

Cash equivalents (for example, investments held as current assets, and borrowings payable within one year) may also be included in the definition of cash.

Example. You are presented with the following forecasted information relating to Blackley Limited for the three months to 31 March 19X7:

Forecasted profit and loss accounts (abridged) for the three months to 31 March 19X7

	January 19X7 £'000	February 19X7 £'000	March 19X7 £'000
Sales	250	300	350
Cost of goods sold	(200)	(240)	(280)
Gross profit	50	60	70
Depreciation	(3)	(20)	(4)
Administration, selling and distribution expenses	(37)	(40)	(42)
Forecasted net profit	£10	-	£24

320

Forecasted balances	31 December 19X6 £'000	31 January 19X7 £'000	28 February 19X7 £'000	31 March 19X7 £'000
Debit Balances				
Tangible fixed assets at cost	360	240	480	480
Investments at cost	15	5	5	10
Stocks at cost	40	30	40	55
Trade debtors	50	65	75	80
Cash at bank and in hand	80			
Credit Balances				
Debentures (10%)	-	-	-	50
Trade creditors	80	120	140	150
Taxation	8	-	-	-
Proposed dividend	15	-	-	-

Additional information:

1 Sales of tangible fixed assets in January 19X7 were expected to realise £12,000 in cash.

2 Administration, selling and distribution expenses were expected to be settled in cash during the months in which they were incurred.

Required:

Prepare in columnar format Blackley Limited's forecasted net cash position at 31 January, 28 February and 31 March 19X7 respectively.

(AAT Final, adapted)

Solution

BLACKLEY LIMITED

Forecasted net cash position for the three months to March 19X7

	Month to		
	31 January 19X7 £'000	28 February 19X7 £'000	31 March 19X7 £'000
Receipts			
Trade debtors (Wkg 1)	235	290	345
Tangible fixed assets	12	-	-
Investments	10	-	-
Debentures	-	-	50
	257	290	395

321

	£'000	£'000	£'000
Payments			
Trade creditors (Wkg 2)	150	230	285
Administration, selling and distribution expenses	37	40	42
Tangible fixed assets	-	240	-
Investments	-	-	5
Taxation	8	-	-
Dividend	15	-	-
	210	510	332
Forecasted net cash flow	47	(220)	63
Add: Opening cash	80	127	(93)
Forecasted closing cash	£127	£(93)	£(30)

WORKINGS

1   Trade debtors: forecasted cash receivable

	31 January 19X7 £,000	28 February 19X7 £,000	31 March 19X7 £,000
Sales	250	300	350
Less: Closing trade debtors	65	75	80
	185	225	270
Add: Opening trade debtors	50	65	75
Forecasted cash receipts	£235	£290	£345

2.   Trade creditors: forecasted cash payable

	31 January 19X7 £'000	28 February 19X7 £'000	31 March 19X7 £'000
Opening stock	40	30	40
Purchases (by deduction)	190	250	295
	230	280	335
Less: Closing stock	30	40	55
Cost of sales	£200	£240	£280
Purchases (as above)	190	250	295
Less: Closing trade creditors	120	140	150
	70	110	145
Add: Opening trade creditors	80	120	140
Forecasted cash payment	£150	£230	£285

EXERCISES

38.1 You are presented with the following information for Penny:

**Trading and Profit and Loss Account
for the year ended 31st May 19X5**

	£		£
Cost of sales	150,000	Sales	200,000
Gross Profit c/d	50,000		
	200,000		200,000
Fixed Overhead	20,000	Gross Profit b/d	50,000
Wages	24,000		
Administration			
Expenses	12,000	Net Loss	6,000
	£56,000		£56,000

In order to retrieve the business, it is decided to:

(i)   Reduce selling prices by 3% in anticipation of a 5% increase in volume of sales.
(ii) Negotiate a 2.5% reduction in purchase prices.
(iii) Reduce staff saving £5,000 in wages.
(iv) Make administrative economies of £1,500.

Rates and other fixed overheads are expected to rise by 1%.

All elements of cost of sales are variable.

Required:

Prepare a forecast trading and profit and loss account for the year ended 31st May 19X6.

(RSA Advanced, adapted)

38.2 Because of a miners' strike, fuel supplies for Trent PLC will run out exactly in two weeks time, production will then cease and the labour force will be laid off. The following data are available:

1   Current assets at the beginning of Week 1 are - finished goods £70,000 (1,000 units), materials (at cost) £36,000, debtors £96,000 (two-thirds receivable during Week 1, remainder week 2), bank £15,000.
2   Current liabilities at the beginning of Week 1 are - creditors for materials £21,000 and wages owing £9,000 (all payable during Week 1).
3   Budgeted production: Week 1 - 900 units, Week 2 - 1,100 units.
4   Budgeted sales - 800 units per week at £100 per unit until stocks run out.
5   Manufacturing costs per unit - wages £10, materials £35, overheads (all fixed) £25. Overheads have been allocated to units on the basis of the normal output level of 800 units per week and include depreciation of £4,000 per week.
6   Manufacturing overheads now consist entirely of fixed cash outlays amounting to £18,000 per week.
7   From Week 3 (when there will be no production) outlays on overheads will be reduced by £8,000 per week and wages expense will no longer be incurred.

8   Stocks of materials will be increased at the end of Week 1 to £40,000 and reduced to £25,000 at the end of Week 2.

9   All sales are on credit, 50% being received in cash in the week following the week of sale and 50% in the week after that.

10   Creditors for materials are paid in the week following purchase, and wages are paid one week in arrears. All outlays on overheads are paid in the week they are incurred.

Required:

(a) Calculate:-
  (i)   How long it will be before finished goods stocks will be exhausted (assume sales are made evenly over each week);
  (ii) the purchases of materials for Week 1 and Week 2; and

(b) prepare a cash budget in columnar form showing the balances of cash at the end of each of the weeks 1 to 6.

(LCCI Higher 1985, adapted)

38.3   The directors of Brain plc are considering the dividend the company will be in a position to pay in respect of the year ending 31 December 19X7. The following information is available:

**Trading and Profit and Loss Account
for the year ended 31 December 19X6**

	£000	£000
Sales		30,000
Less Cost of goods sold		20,000
Gross profit		10,000
Less: Sales Commissions (1% of sales)	300	
Loan interest for one year	150	
Administration Expenses	3,500	
Directors' Fees	300	
Bank Overdraft Interest	300	
Depreciation - calculated on the reducing balance basis	2,000	
Uninsured fire loss (April 19X6)	950	7,500
Net Profit		£2,500

Balance Sheet as at 31 December 19X6

	£000	£000		£000	£000
Ordinary Share Capital		25,000	Fixed Assets		18,000
Reserves		1,000			
		26,000			
Loan (Repayable 30 June 19X7)		1,500	Current Assets		
Current Liabilities			Stock	5,000	
Creditors	500		Debtors	7,500	12,500
Bank	2,500	3,000			
		£30,500			£30,500

The directors budget that in 19X7:

1. Though selling prices will remain the same, the volume of sales will increase by 10%, with sales commission increasing proportionally. By the end of 19X7, it is expected that the credit period allowed to debtors will be half that allowed at 31 December 19X6.

2. Due to improved purchasing arrangements, the proportion of gross profit to sales will increase by 5%.

3. Both administration expenses and directors' fees will increase by 5%.

4. Bank overdraft interest will fall by 50%.

5. Loan interest will be at the same rate as in 19X6.

6. Stock and creditors at 31 December will be the same amounts as they were at the end of the year 19X6.

Required:

Prepare, in respect of Brian plc, a budgeted:

(i) Trading and Profit and Loss Account for the year to 31 December 19X7;
(ii) summarised Bank Account for the year to 31 December 19X7; and
(iii) Balance Sheet as at 31 December 19X7.

(LCCI Higher 1987)

38.4 Ron Belt has worked for many years in the clothing industry as a marketing consultant. On 1 January 19X8 he intends to start up in business as a clothing retailer. He is currently preparing a budget based on the following averaged data, obtained from the clothing retailers association:

Current	3:1
Net profit to sales	10%
Stock turnover per year (based on average stock)	7 times
Creditors payment period (based on closing creditors)	54.75 days
Gross profit to sales	30%
Sales to total assets (based on closing assets)	2:1
Debtors collection period	73.00 days

He will be paying £55,000 into a business bank account on 1 January 19X8 which will include a loan of £5,000 from his sister repayable in four years' time and on which he has promised to pay interest of 12% per year. He will then buy for cash sundry fixed assets all with a five year life and zero residual value and spend £12,000 on his opening stock of goods for resale. Otherwise all purchases and sales will be on credit.

At 31 December 19X8 his second accrued expenses (other than interest) are budgeted at £2,000 and prepaid expenses at £1,000. His closing stock is to be such that the average of his opening and closing stocks amounts to £16,000.

Required:

Assuming that sundry expenses, bank and drawings are to be found as residual items, prepare Ron Belt's budgeted Trading and Profit and Loss Account for the year ended 31 December 19X8 and his budgeted Balance Sheet at that date in good style.

(LCCI Higher 1987)

325

COMMON ERRORS

1. Types of Questions

Questions requiring the preparation of a cash flow statement usually involve converting a traditional profit and loss account and balance sheet into a cash flow statement.

This is a good test of your knowledge of the matching rule, so if you have difficulty with this type of question, do some more questions involving adjustments for accruals and prepayments.

Check that you have not made a mistake in converting the cost of goods sold and the sales from an accruals basis on to a cash basis:

PAYMENTS TO CREDITORS:

Cash paid = opening creditors PLUS credit purchases LESS closing creditors.

CASH RECEIVED FROM DEBTORS:

Cash received = opening debtors PLUS credit sales LESS closing debtors.

2. Correct Period

You may be asked to prepare a cash flow statement for a number of accounting periods, such as weeks, months or years. Make sure that you assess correctly the exact period in which cash will be paid or received. Not all debtors, for example, will settle their debts a month after being invoiced; similarly, the entity may delay payment of some of its creditors.

3. Cumulative Errors

Make sure that you do not make any arithmetical errors, especially in the earlier period. Your closing cash becomes the opening cash of the next period, and consequently, mistakes become cumulative.

If you have been given the balance sheet for the last period, your CLOSING cash should be equal to the balance as shown in the closing balance sheet. In order to isolate the period in which you have made a mistake, check the closing cash for each accounting period against the closing balance sheet for that period.

39

SOURCE AND APPLICATION OF FUNDS' STATEMENTS

MAIN POINTS

1. Background

Whilst it is possible to disclose details about liquidity in a cash flow statement, it is more common to do so in a STATEMENT OF SOURCE AND APPLICATION OF FUNDS (or flow of funds' statement).

2. Format

SSAP 10 (Statements of source and application of funds) requires an entity with a turnover of £25,000 or more to include a source and application of funds' statement as part of its financial accounts.

The standard does not lay down a mandatory format, but a recommended one is provided in the appendix.

There are three main sections:

(a) SOURCE OF FUNDS

Main items:

Profit before tax
Adjustments for items not involving the movement of funds:
Depreciation
Increase in provision for bad and doubtful debts
Funds from other sources:
Issue of shares and debentures for cash
Cash received from the sale of fixed assets

(b) APPLICATION OF FUNDS:

Main items:

Dividend paid
Tax paid
Purchase of fixed assets

(c) INCREASE/DECREASE IN WORKING CAPITAL

Main items:

Increase/(decrease) in stocks
Increase/(decrease) in debtors
(Increase)/decrease in creditors (BUT excluding taxation and proposed dividends)
Increase/(decrease) in cash balances and short-term investments.

Example 1. A summary of Thomas's balance sheet as at 31 August 19X1 and 19X2 respectively is as follows:

	£	£	£	£
Fixed assets				
Equipment at cost	15,000		21,000	
Less: Depreciation	10,000	5,000	14,200	6,800
Current assets				
Stocks	10,000		15,000	
Debtors	30,000		35,000	
Cash at bank	5,000		-	
	45,000		50,000	
Less: Current liabilities				
Creditors	15,000		10,000	
Bank overdraft	-		11,800	
	15,000	30,000	21,800	28,200
		£35,000		£35,000
Financed by:				
Capital		10,000		15,000
Net profit for the year	7,000		15,000	
Less: Drawings	2,000	5,000	5,000	10,000
Loan		20,000		10,000
		£35,000		£35,000

Note: There were no disposals of fixed assets during the year.

Required:

Prepare a statement of source and application of funds for the year to 31 August 19X2.

(AAT Part 1)

Solution

Thomas
Statement of source and application of funds
for the year to 31 August 19X2

	£	£
Source of funds		
Profit for the year		15,000
Adjustment for item not involving the movement of funds:		
Depreciation (£14,200-10,000)		4,200
Total generated from operations		19,200
Application of funds		
Purchase of equipment (£21,000-15,000)	(6,000)	
Drawings	(5,000)	
Loan (£20,000-10,000)	(10,000)	(21,000)
		(1,800)

	£	£
Decrease in working capital		
Increase in stock	5,000	
Increase in debtors	5,000	
Decrease in creditors	5,000	
Movement in net liquid funds:		
(Decrease) in cash balances	(16,800)	(1,800)

Example 2. The following information had been extracted from the books of Scarfe Ltd:

Profit and loss account for the year to 31 March 19X3

	£'000
Net profit before tax	95
Taxation	(18)
	77
Dividends (interim paid: £15,000; proposed £30,000)	(45)
Retained profit for the year	£32

Balance sheet at 31 March 19X3

	19X2 £'000	19X3 £'000
Fixed assets	571	530
Current assets		
Stocks	78	82
Debtors	143	136
Cash at bank	-	5
	221	223
Current liabilities		
Bank overdraft	(93)	-
Creditors	(110)	(83)
Taxation	(24)	(18)
Proposed dividend	(25)	(30)
	(252)	(131)
Net current assets	(31)	92
	£540	£622
Capital and reserves		
Called up share capital	500	500
Profit and loss account	40	72
	540	572
Long-term loan	-	50
	£540	£622

Additional information:

1 During the year to 31 March 19X3, Scarfe sold a fixed asset for £60,000 in cash. The net book value of this asset at 1 April 19X2 was £71,000.
2 Purchases of fixed assets during the year to 31 March 19X3 amounted to £75,000.

Required:

Prepare Scarfe Ltd's statement of source and application of funds for the year to 31 March 19x3.

Solution

Scarf Ltd
Statement of source and application of funds
for the year to 31 March 19X3

	£'000	£'000
Source of funds		
Profit before tax		95
Adjustments for items not involving the movement of funds:		
Depreciation (Wkg)	45	
Loss on disposal of fixed asset (£71 - 60)	11	56
Total generated from operations		151
Funds from other sources		
Long-term loan	50	
Cash from sale of fixed asset	60	110
		261
Application of funds		
Dividends paid (£25+15)	(40)	
Tax paid	(24)	
Purchase of fixed assets	(75)	(139)
		122
Increase in working capital		
Increase in stocks	4	
Decrease in debtors	(7)	
Decrease in creditors	27	
Movement in net liquid funds:		
Increase in cash balances (£93+5)	98	122

WORKING

Fixed assets

	£'000
Balance at 1 4 X2	571
Purchases	75
Disposal	(71)
	575
Balance at 31 3 X3	530
therefore Depreciation for the year =	£45

EXERCISES

39.1   The following summarised information relates to Cliff Ltd.

Profit and Loss Account for Year ended 31 December 19X5

	£000	£000
Turnover		456
Less: Depreciation of machinery	18	
Other costs	450	468
Loss on trading		(12)
Profit on sale of machinery		4
Net loss		£8

Balance Sheets as at 31 December

	19X4	19X5
	£000	£000
Issued Ordinary £1 Shares	300	420
Share Premium	146	86
Property revaluation reserve	-	35
Profit and Loss Account	47	39
Trade creditors	23	37
Bank overdraft	3	-
	£519	£617
Freehold property at cost	130	12
Freehold property at revaluation	-	165
Machinery	37	42
Stocks	233	243
Debtors	119	117
Bank	-	38
	£519	£617

During 19X5 machinery with a book value of £12,000 was sold and replaced by new machinery. No property was sold. No dividends were paid or proposed but shareholders all accepted a capitalisation issue of "one for five" and then subscribed in full for a rights issue of "one for six" at par.

Required:

Prepare a Statement of Source and Application of Funds for 19X5 in good style, based on the accounts as originally given.

(LCCI Higher 1985, adapted)

39.2 A Green carries on business in the retail trade and has prepared the following balance sheets for both the current and previous years:

A Green
Balance sheets at 30 June

	19X1		19X0	
	£	£	£	£
Fixed assets				
Freehold property at cost		100,000		100,000
Furniture and fittings				
at cost	16,000		15,000	
Less: depreciation	11,600	4,400	10,000	5,000
		104,400		105,000
Current assets				
Stocks	18,000		17,000	
Debtors and prepayments	25,000		17,000	
Cash at bank and in hand	2,000		1,000	
	45,000		35,000	
Less: current liabilities				
Trade and accrued expenses	12,000	33,000	10,000	25,000
		£137,400		£130,000
Financed by				
Capital account				
A Green		127,400		130,000
Loan account				
M Green		10,000		-
		£137,400		£130,000

Note: The net profit for 19X1 was £20,000, and A. Green's drawings amounted to £22,600.

Required:

Prepare a source and application of funds statement for the year to 30 June 19X1.

(AAT Level 2)

39.3 The following information has been extracted from the books of account of W. Stone as at 30 April 19X5:

	19X5 £'000	19X4 £'000
Fixed assets		
Buildings at cost	320	320
Plant, vehicles and equipment at net book value	90	80
	410	400

	19X5 £'000	19X4 £'000
Current assets		
Stocks	75	58
Trade debtors	90	85
Cash	5	7
	170	150
	£580	£550
Financed by:		
Capital		
As at 1 May	520	480
Net profit for the year	35	80
Proprietor's drawings	(55)	(40)
	500	520
Current liabilities		
Trade creditors	40	20
Bank overdraft	40	10
	80	30
	£580	£550

Other information:

1 There were no purchases or sales of buildings during the year to 30 April 19X5, and depreciation is not charged on the buildings.

2 During the year to 30 April 19X5, there were the following changes to the plant, vehicles and equipment account:

(a) on 1 May 19X4, some plant was sold for £5,000. It had been purchased on 1 May 19X1 at a cost of £30,000. Depreciation had been charged on it using the straight-line method at a rate of 25% per annum on cost after allowing for an estimated scrap value of £6,000.

(b) plant, vehicles and equipment depreciation charged to the profit and loss account for the year to 30 April 19X5 amounted to £30,000.

Required:

Prepare a statement of source and application of funds for the year to 30 April 19X5.

(AAT Level 2)

39.4 Pool's summarised balance sheets at 31 May 19X1 and 19X2 are as follows:

	19X1 £	£	19X2 £	£
Fixed assets				
Motor vehicles at cost	10,500		18,500	
Less: depreciation	3,900	6,600	6,300	12,200
Furniture at cost	1,500		1,500	
Less: depreciation	900	600	1,050	450
		7,200		12,650

	19X1		19X2	
	£	£	£	£
Current assets				
Stocks	12,100		14,600	
Debtors	800		2,000	
Cash at bank	9,000		-	
	21,900		16,600	
Less: current liabilities				
Creditors	3,600		4,000	
Bank overdraft	-		7,600	
	3,600	18,300	11,600	5,000
		£25,500		£17,650
Financed by:				
Capital		15,000		15,500
Net profit for the year	9,000		12,150	
Less: drawings	8,500	500	10,000	2,150
		15,500		17,650
Loan		10,000		-
		£25,500		£17,650

Note: During the year to 31 May 19X2, Pool received £600 in cash for the sale of a motor vehicle. The motor vehicle had originally cost £2,000, and at 1 June it had been depreciated by £1,500.

Required:

Prepare a source and application of funds' statement for the year to 31 May 19X2.

(AAT/IAS Part 1)

39.5 The following summarised profit and loss account shows the result of Winter plc's operations for the year ended 31st October 19X7.

	£	£
Sales		250,000
Less Cost of Goods sold		180,000
Gross profit		70,000
Profit on sale of fixed assets		600
		70,600
Operating expenses		28,400
Net profit		42,200
Balance brought forward		28,000
		70,200
Dividends		
paid	10,000	
proposed	15,000	25,000
Balance carried forward		£45,200

The balance sheets of the company as at 31st October 19X6 and 19X7 are as follows:

	19X6			19X7		
	£	£	£	£	£	£
Assets employed						
Fixed assets at cost	280,000			282,000		
Less Depreciation		48,000	232,000		52,000	230,000
Current assets						
Stock		16,000			22,000	
Debtors		12,500			16,000	
Cash at bank		17,000			7,000	
		45,500			45,000	
Less Current Liabilities						
Creditors	12,000			15,000		
Dividends Proposed	7,500	19,500	26,000	15,000	30,000	15,000
			£258,000			£245,000
Financed by						
Share Capital		150,000			190,000	
Reserves						
Share Premium Account		-			9,800	
Profit & Loss Account		28,000			45,200	
		178,000			245,000	
8% Debentures		80,000			-	
			£258,000			£245,000

During the year a fixed asset which had originally cost £4,000 and on which depreciation of £3,000 had been written off to date had been sold for £1,600.

Required:

(a) Prepare a Source and Application of Funds Statement for the year ended 31st October 19X7 showing the changes in working capital.

(b) Prepare a "cash flow" statement for the year ended 31st October 19X7 to show the movements of cash during the year and as a reconciliation with the amount of cash shown in the balance sheet.

(RSA Intermediate)

39.6 The following are the balance sheets of Allevo Ltd as at 31 December 19X9 and 31 December 19X0, together with a profit and loss account for the year ended 31 December 19X0.

Allevo Ltd
Balance sheets

	31 December 19X9		31 December 19X9	
	£	£	£	£
Fixed assets				
Plant and equipment	73,500		83,320	
Accumulated depreciation	(16,800)		(20,160)	
	56,700		62,160	
Goodwill	9,240		8,400	
Investments at cost	8,400		5,040	
Current assets				
Stock	50,400		73,500	
Debtors	25,200		39,984	
Cash at bank	9,660		2,400	
	85,260		115,884	
Current liabilities				
Bank overdraft	-		(1,684)	
Creditors	(41,370)		(57,500)	
Taxation	(1,260)		(2,100)	
	(42,630)	42,630	(61,284)	54.600
		£116,970		£130,200
Ordinary share capital in £1 shares	45,600		52,400	
Undistributed profits	35,070		42,000	
	80,670		94,400	
Deferred Taxation	9,000		8,500	
12% Debenture stock (2XX0 - 2XX5)	27,300		27,300	
		£116,970		£130,200

Abridged profit and loss account
for the year ending 31 December 19X0

	£	£
Sales		210,000
Cost of goods sold		(126,000)
		84,000
Depreciation	(4,620)	
Administrative expenses	(18,480)	
Selling expenses	(31,500)	(54,600)
Net profit before taxation		29,400
Taxation		(12,600)
Net profit after taxation		16,800

	£	£
Profit on sale of equipment		380
Profit on sale of investments		340
Undistributed profits brought forward		35,070
		52,590
Less: dividends		(10,590)
Undistributed profits		£42,000

The following additional information is also available:

    (a) During 19X0 plant and equipment was acquired at a cost of £10,500.

    (b) Goodwill has been written off as part of the administrative expenses.

    (c) The sale of investments realised a profit of £340.

    (d) Equipment which had originally cost £1,680 was sold during the year. The accumulated depreciation on the equipment at that date amounted to £1,260 and the sale realised a profit of £380.

    (e) A further 6,800 £1 ordinary shares were issued during the year.

Required:

Prepare a source and application of funds statement for the year to 31 December 19X0.

(AAT/IAS Part 2)

COMMON ERRORS

1. Profit Before Tax

Make sure that you take the profit BEFORE tax. If you take the profit AFTER tax, your statement of source and application of funds will not balance: remember that creditors for taxation are EXCLUDED from the working capital section.

2. Adjustments for Items not Involving the Movement of Funds

Examine the profit and loss account carefully. All those entries that have NOT changed the cash position for the period (apart from accruals and prepayments) should be included in this section; for example, depreciation, increases or decreases in provision for doubtful debts, and increases or decreases in provisions for discounts. Remember to DEDUCT decreases (insert them in brackets).

3. Funds from other Sources

Include in this section, CASH received from the sale of fixed assets, and the cash raised in issuing shares or debentures. Do not include an increase in the share capital if it results from a bonus issue. A bonus issue does not effect the cash position.

4. Dividends Paid

This is one of the most common errors. Only include dividends PAID during the year. The amount paid will often be a combination of last uear's PROPOSED dividend plus the current year's INTERIM dividend. Do not include this year's PROPOSED dividend.

5. Tax Paid

This is also another common error. Only include the amount for taxation that has actually been PAID during the year. This may be a combination of last year's accrued tax plus some of the current year's tax paid on account (that is, advance corporation tax or ACT).

6. Purchase of Fixed Assets

Examination questions frequently require you to calculate the amount paid for fixed assets during the year. To obtain this figure, you may have to work from the opening and closing balances for fixed assets.

You may also have to allow for both the cost and the accumulated depreciation of assets sold during the year.

7. Working Capital Movements

Make sure that you calculate the movement in stocks, debtors, and creditors correctly. The movement is simply the difference between the opening and closing balances.

8. Debtors

Debtors may also include movements in prepayments.

If you have allowed for increases or decreases in provisions for bad and doubtful debts as part of the sources' section, the movement for debtors will be the difference between the opening and closing debtors BEFORE any deduction is made for the opening and closing balance on the provision account.

9. Creditors

Creditors also include movements in accruals.

Do NOT include creditors for taxation and for proposed dividends.

10. Short-Term Investments

If some investments are only held for the short-term (that is, for less than one year), include the MOVEMENT on them in the working capital section.

If the investments are intended for long-term investment, any cash proceeds from sales of investments should be included in the sources' section, whilst cash paid for the purchase of such investments should be included in the applications' section.

11. Balancing

Make sure that the net source (or net application) of funds balances with the net movement in working capital. If it does not balance, check your arithmetic. If it still does not balance, you will have to go back and check each item in the statement. Make sure that you have not missed any item out of the statement.

40

VALUE ADDED STATEMENTS |

MAIN POINTS

1. Background

Some accountants believe that the traditional statements do not clearly reflect the collective efforts of everyone concerned with the success of a particular entity. They argue that this can best be done by preparing a VALUE ADDED STATEMENT.

2. Definition

The Corporate Report (1975) defined value added as "the wealth the reporting entity has been able to create by its own and its employees' efforts".

3. Format

There are no statutory or professional accounting requirements for the presentation and publication of value added statements. The Corporate Report suggested the following format:

	£
Turnover	X
Bought-in materials and services	(X)
VALUE ADDED	£X
Applied the following ways:	
To pay employees	X
To pay providers of capital	X
To pay government	X
To provide for maintenance and expansion of assets	X
VALUE ADDED	£X

Example. You are presented with the following information relating to Marsh Ltd.

Trading, Profit and Loss Account for the year to 31 March 19X4

	£'000	£'000
Sales		400
Less: Cost of goods sold		280
GROSS PROFIT		120
Less: Expenses		
Wages and related costs	40	
Office expenses	30	
Depreciation	20	
Loan interest	1	91

339

	£'000	£'000
Net profit for the year before taxation		29
Corporation tax		9
Net profit for the year after taxation		20
Dividends		15
Retained profit for the year		£5

Required:

Prepare a statement of value added for the year to 31 March 19X4.

Solution

MARCH LTD
Statement of value added for the year to 31 March 19X4

	£'000	£'000
Turnover		400
Bought-in materials and services (£280+30)		310
		£90
VALUE ADDED		
Applied the following way:		
TO PAY EMPLOYEES		
Wages and related costs		40
TO PAY PROVIDERS OF CAPITAL		
Interest on loan	1	
Dividents to shareholders	15	16
TO PAY GOVERNMENT		
Corporation tax payable		9
TO PROVIDE FOR MAINTENANCE AND		
EXPANSION OF ASSETS		
Depreciation	20	
Retained profits	5	25
		£90

EXERCISES

40.1 You are presented with the following information relating to Current Ltd for the year to 31 December 19X1:-

	NOTES	£'000
Turnover		760
Cost of sales	1	(415)
GROSS PROFIT		345
Distribution and administration expenses	2	(247)
Loan interest payable		(50)
Profit before taxation		48
Corporation tax		(15)
Profit after taxation		33
Dividends		19
Retained profit for the year		£14

NOTES

1. Includes wages and related employment costs of £88,000, and depreciation of £32,000.

2. Includes wages and related employment costs of £40,000 and depreciation of £26,000.

Required:

Prepare a statement of value added for the year to 31 December 19X1.

40.2   You are presented with the following information relating to Tay Ltd for the year to 31 January 19X2:-

	£'000
Sales	2,820
Materials consumed	1,407
Salaries and related employment costs	270
Wages and related employment costs	450
Local authority rates	75
Heat and light	55
Office expenses	110
Hire of plant and machinery	18
Depreciation	95
Corporation tax payable	120
10% preference shares	150
15% debenture loan stock	200
Proposed ordinary dividend	45

Required:

Prepare a statement of value added for the year to 31 January 19X2.

40.3   The following information has been extracted from the account of Don Ltd for the year to 28 February 19X3.

	£'000
Sales	750
Cost of sales	(500)
GROSS PROFIT	250
Overhead expenses (see note)	(205)
Bank interest	
interest receivable	20
Loan interest	
interest payable	(15)
Profit before taxation	50
Corporation tax	(10)
Profit after taxation	40
Dividends	(30)
Retained profit for the year	£10

NOTES:

Overhead expenses include the following items:

	£'000
Depreciation	21
Audit fees and expenses	17
Wages, salaries and pension costs	110
Directors' emoluments	40
Local authority rates	12
Hire of plant and machinery	5

Required:

Prepare a statement of value added for the year to 28 February 19X3.

COMMON ERRORS

1. Format

There is no generally agreed format for value added statements. You are recommended, therefore, to follow the broad format given in The Corporate Report.

2. Non-Trading Credits

It is suggested that non-trading credits (such as dividends and interest received) should be included in a value added statement as follows:

	£
Turnover	X
Bought-in materials and services	X
Value added	X
Non-trading credits (list what they are)	X
TOTAL VALUED ADDED	£X

The total of the applications's section should also be labelled TOTAL VALUE ADDED.

3. Payments to Employees

Some accountants may include the remuneration paid to employees as part of bought-in materials and services. However, it is probably clearer to include them separately in the applications' section, since employees' efforts are a major part of the wealth created by the entity.

4. Depreciation

Include depreciation in the maintenance and expansion of assets' section.

5. Transfers to Reserves and Retained Profit

Include transfers to reserves and the retained profit for the year in the maintenance and expansion of assets' section.

6. Balancing

The preparation of a value added statement merely involves the re-arrangement of the items disclosed in the profit and loss account.

Make sure that the two sections of your value added statement balance. If they do not, check your arithmetic, and double check that you have not omitted any balance that should have been extracted from the profit and loss account.

41 ACCOUNTING FOR CHANGING PRICES

MAIN POINTS

1. Background

In preparing accounting statements, it is usually assumed that the monetary unit is stable, that is, it is assumed that (say) goods purchased in one period would cost exactly the same in a later period.

INFLATION is used to describe the situation when prices are rising, that is, when it costs MORE to buy the same QUANTITY of goods than it did in an earlier period.

DEFLATION describes a situation when prices are falling, that is, the same quantity of goods cost LESS than they did in an earlier period. Generally, however, the price of most goods and services tends to rise over a period of time.

All goods and services may be affected by changes in prices, or it is possible that only specific prices may be affected.

It is very difficult to prepare meaningful accounts when prices are rising. During a period of inflation, for example, £1,000 of sales in period 2 may not be the same as £1,000 of sales in period 1, since £1,000 in period may not purchase the same QUANTITY of goods as it did in period 1.

In the United Kingdom, the most common measure of changing prices is the RETAIL PRICE INDEX (RPI). This index measures the change in prices that an average middle income family pays for its purchases, Thus the index may not be suitable for a specific family, for poorer or richer households, or for business entities. Nonetheless, it is a generally accepted guide to the way that prices are changing.

2. Problems of Historical Cost Accounting

When prices are rising, historical cost accounting gives rise to the following major problems (the reverse is true when prices are falling):

(a) <u>Overstatement of profit</u>
As current revenues are matched against historic costs, profit tends to be overstated. This may result in larger payments of dividends. Stocks and fixed assets, however, will cost more to replace, but the entity may not have sufficient to cash to do so, especially if it has paid out large dividends.

(b) <u>Unrealistic balance sheet values</u>
The value of assets recorded in a balance sheet is out-of-date, thereby giving a misleading impression of the entity's worth.

343

(c) <u>Holding gains and losses ignored</u>
Holding gains and losses are not recorded in the accounts. During a period of inflation, for example, an entity gains on amounts that it borrows (because it pays back an amount that buys less than when it borrowed it), but loses on amounts it lends (because it receives back an amount that will purchase less goods than when the loan was first made).

(d) <u>Misleading impression</u>
A misleading impression is given of the entity's performance. It reports, for example, an apparent high level of profit on a relatively low level of fixed assets.

3. Solutions

The accountancy profession has not yet found an acceptable solution to the problem of preparing accounts during periods of changing prices. Two main methods are sometimes suggested:

(a) Current purchasing power accounting (CPP). This method involves preparing the historic cost accounts and then indexing them using a general index, such as the RPI.

(b) Current cost accounting (CCA). This method basically involves including stocks and fixed assets in the accounts at their REPLACEMENT cost, instead of at their historic cost. By using this method, in a period of inflation,the cost of goods sold and the depreciation charge will be higher (thus making the profit lower). Sometimes an adjustment may also be made for holding gains and losses, for example, on borrowings.

4. Recommendations

Until clearer guidance is given by the accountancy profession, you are recommended to adopt the following proposals:

(a) <u>Periodic summaries.</u>
Index the amounts in periodic summaries (such as for turnover and profits) using the retail price index.

(b) <u>Cost of goods sold.</u>
Match the sales revenue against the cost of sales using REPLACEMENT COST (that is, at the price that would have to be paid for those goods if they were replaced) instead of the cost of the goods purchased.

(c) <u>Fixed assets.</u>
Include the fixed assets in the balance sheet (or in a note) at their replacement cost. This means charging an extra amount for depreciation to the profit and loss account. The fixed assets would then be shown at their GROSS replacement cost less accumulated depreciation (based on gross replacement cost) to give the NET replacement cost.

5. Format

Prepare the historic accounts, and then include additional notes to take account of the changes recommended above to show (a) the effect on profit; and (b) the effect on the balance sheet.

Example 1. You are presented with the following information relating to Carr plc for the five years to 31 December 19X1 to 19X5 respectively.

	Historical Cost Turnover £'000	Inflation index (average for the year)
19X1	29,000	28
19X2	40,000	34
19X3	56,000	40
19X4	68,000	46
19X5	79,000	50

Required

Restate the turnover figures in current purchasing power terms as at 31 December 19X5.

Solution

CARR PLC
Turnovers in current purchasing power terms as at 31 December 19X5

	Historical cost turnover £'000	Factor	Turnover 31 12 X5 £'000
19X1	29,000	50/28	51,786
19X2	40,000	50/34	58,824
19X3	56,000	50/40	70,000
19X4	68,000	50/46	73,913
19X5	79,000	50/50	79,000

Example 2. An office machine cost £10,000 on 1 January 19X2. It was decided to depreciate it on a straight line basis over a ten year period, assuming no residual at the end of its life.

At 31 December 19X4, the machine's gross replacement cost was £18,000.

Required:

(a) Calculate the depreciation charge for the year to 31 December 19X4 on a historical cost basis;

(b) calculate the ADDITIONAL depreciation charge for the year to 31 December 19X4 on a replacement cost basis; and

(c) show how the replacement cost relating to the fixed asset would be shown in the current cost balance sheet at 31 December 19X4.

Solution

(a) Historical cost depreciation charge

$$\frac{£10,000}{10} = \underline{£1,000}$$

(b) Additional depreciation charge on a current cost basis

$$\frac{£18,000}{10} = £[1,800 - 1,000] = \underline{£800}$$

(c) Current cost balance sheet at 31 December 19X4

	£
Fixed asset	
Office machine at gross replacement cost	18,000
Less: Accumulated depreciation	
(3x£1,800)	5,400
NET REPLACEMENT COST	12,600

Example 3. You are presented with the following information relating to Todd for the year to 31 March 19X3:

	£
Sales	1,000
Cost of sales	(400)
GROSS PROFIT	600
Expenses	(100)
Profit for the year	£500

Notes:

1. There were no opening or closing stocks. Todd purchased 400 units at £1 per unit.

2. Units are expected to cost £2 per unit in 19X3.

Required:

Calculate how much of the retained profit Todd may safely withdraw from the business if he is to maintain at least the same level of operating capability in 19X4 as he experienced in 19X3.

Solution

TODD
Current cost profit and loss account for the year to 31 March 19X3

	£
Sales	1,000
Current cost of sales (400 x £2)	(800)
	200
Expenses	(100)
Current cost profit for the year	£100

Maximum drawings therefore = £100

EXERCISES

41.1   Bill purchases a machine for £100. The cost of the machine rises by 5% per annum.

Required:

Assuming that an identical machine is available, calculate how many years it will take before Bill has to pay £200 for a similar machine.

41.2   Context plc has earned the following profits before tax:

Year to 31 December	Profit before tax £000	Index
19X1	97	83
19X2	169	87
19X3	142	91
19X4	141	96
19X5	158	100

Required:

Using the index shown above, calculate Context's profits before tax in £' 31 12 X5.

41.3   Dee plc's stock on 1 January 19X3 was valued at cost at £80,000 and at 31 December 19X3 at £100,000.

The following stock index is relevant for the period in question:

31 10 X2	110
31 12 X2	115
30 6 X3	120
31 10 X3	125
31 12 X3	130

The index at 30 June 19X3 also represents the average for the year. Stock in hand represents the purchases made two months earlier.

Required:

(a)   Using current cost accounting, calculate what additional amount for stock should be charged to the profit and loss account if Dee is to maintain its operating capability; and

(b)   calculate what value Dee would show in its current cost balance sheet for stock at 31 December 19X3.

41.4   Weaver plc, bought a machine costing £50,000 on 1 January 19X2. Its replacement cost on 31 December 19X3 was £80,000.

Weaver depreciates the machine at a rate of 20% on cost, assuming no residual value.

Required:

(a)   Using current cost accounting, calculate the additional depreciation charge to the profit and loss account for the year to 31 December 19X3; and

(b)   show how the machine would be shown on a current cost balance sheet at 31 December 19X3.

COMMON ERRORS

1. Method

Accounting for changing price is an extremely complex subject, especially when the accountancy profession has not yet come to any firm conclusion. It is unlikely, therefore, that at the basic or intermediate level you will have to deal with very difficult questions.

Read the question carefully, and comply EXACTLY with what is required.

2. Definitions

Make sure that you understand the meaning of the terms INFLATION and DEFLATION. Note that these terms are not easy to define.

3. Limitations

You need to know the reasons why historical cost accounts are considered to be unsatisfactory during periods of changing prices, and also to be able to explain the effect of INFLATION on such accounts.

4. Indexing

You need to become familiar with indexing sets of data. Many students go wrong in choosing the incorrect index point. Read the question very carefully in order to make sure that you have chosen the correct one.

42 INTERPRETATION OF ACCOUNTS

MAIN POINTS

1. Background

The amount of information disclosed in a profit and loss account and in a balance sheet (especially when the comparative figures for the previous financial year are also given) is quite considerable.

Nonetheless, it is difficult to put the information into context, it does not measure performance, and there is no comparison with other entities. To be useful, therefore, traditional accounting information needs to be adapted so that it become much more meaningful and comparable.

2. Methods of Analysing Information

(a) Vertical Analysis.

The respective profit and loss account and balance sheet items are expressed as a percentage of the total.

(b) Horizontal Analysis.

A line-by-line comparison is made of the accounts over (say) a five year period.

(c) Trend Analysis.

A value of (say) 100 is given to the first period's accounts, and then subsequent periods' results are related to the base period of 100.

(d) Ratio Analysis.

This form of analysis involves relating (say) factor (a) to factor (b), and expressing it in the form of a percentage. The real key to ratio analysis is in making sure that (a) and (b) do relate closely to each other.

3. Types of Ratio

(a) <u>Profitability ratios</u>

(i) Return on capital employed

Either: $\dfrac{\text{Net profit before tax}}{\text{Shareholders funds}} \times 100$

or: $\dfrac{\text{Net profit after tax and preference dividend}}{\text{Shareholder's funds - preference shares}} \times 100$

or: $\dfrac{\text{Net profit before tax and interest}}{\text{Shareholder's funds + long-term loans}} \times 100$

(ii) Gross profit

$$\frac{\text{Gross profit}}{\text{Sales}} \times 100$$

(iii) Mark-up

$$\frac{\text{Gross profit}}{\text{Cost of goods sold}} \times 100$$

(iv) Net profit

$$\frac{\text{Net profit}}{\text{Sales}} \times 100$$

(b) <u>Liquidity ratios</u>

(i) Current assets

$$\frac{\text{Current assets}}{\text{Current liabilities}}$$

(ii) Acid test

$$\frac{\text{Current assets - stocks}}{\text{Current liabilities}}$$

(c) <u>Efficiency ratios</u>

(i) Stock turnover

$$\frac{\text{Cost of goods sold}}{\text{Stock}}$$

(ii) Fixed assets turnover

$$\frac{\text{Sales}}{\text{Fixed assets (at net book value)}}$$

(iii) Trade debtor collection period

$$\frac{\text{Trade debtors}}{\text{Credit sales}} \times 365 \text{ days}$$

(iv) Trade creditor payment period

$$\frac{\text{Trade creditors}}{\text{Credit purchases}} \times 365 \text{ days}$$

(d) <u>Investment ratios</u>

(i) Dividend yield

$$\frac{\text{Nominal value of the share}}{\text{Market price of the share}} \times \text{declared dividend}$$

(ii)   Ordinary dividend cover

$$\frac{\text{Net profit after tax - preference dividend}}{\text{Paid and proposed ordinary dividends}}$$

(iii)   Interest cover

$$\frac{\text{Net profit before interest and tax}}{\text{Interest}}$$

(iv)   Earnings per share

$$\frac{\text{Net profit after tax - preference dividend}}{\text{Number of shares in issue during the year}}$$

(v)   Price/earnings ratio

$$\frac{\text{Market price per share}}{\text{Earnings per share}}$$

(vi)   Capital gearing

$$\frac{\text{Preference shares + long-term loans}}{\text{Shareholder's funds + long-term loans}} \times 100$$

4. Interpretation

The analysis of accounting data simply results in even more data. The next stage is to establish some common pattern from all the available date, and then to derive some logical conclusions. It is from these conclusions that the accountant may then be in a position to make some recommendations.

Example.   You are presented with the following summarised information concerning J. Free:

J FREE
Trading, Profit and Loss Account (Extracts) for the year
to 30 April 19X2 and 30 April 19X3

	19X3	19X2
	£	£
Sales (all on credit)	200,00	120,000
Cost of Sales	150,000	80,000
Gross profit	50,000	40,000
Expenses	15,000	10,000
Net profit	£35,000	£30,000

J FREE
Balance sheet (Extracts) at 30 April 19X2 and 30 April 19X3

	19X3 £	19X3 £	19X2 £	19X2 £
Fixed assets (net book value)		12,000		15,000
Current Assets				
Stocks	18,000		7,000	
Trade Debtors	36,000		12,000	
Cash at bank	-		1,000	
		54,000		20,000
		£66,000		£35,000
Capital Account				
Balance at 1 April	29,000		12,000	
Net profit for the year	35,000		30,000	
	64,000		42,000	
Less: Drawings	23,000		13,000	
		41,000		29,000
Current Liabilities:				
Trade creditors	15,000		6,000	
Bank overdraft	10,000		-	
		25,000		6,000
		£66,000		£35,000

Notes:

1 There were no purchases or disposals of fixed assets during the year.
2 During 19X2/X3 Free reduced his selling price in order to stimulate sales.
3 It may be assumed that price levels were stable.

Required:

(a) Calculate the following ratios for both 19X2 and 19X3:

  (i)   percentage mark-up on cost of sales;
  (ii) gross profit on sales;
  (iii) return on capital employed;
  (iv) debtor collection period;
  (v)   current ratio;
  (vi) acid test (or quick) ratio; and

(b) comment upon the apparent effect that the increase in sales has had on profit and cash flow.

(AAT: Level 2, adapted)

Solution

J FREE

(a) Ratio Calculations

		19X3	19X2

(i) Mark-up on Sales

$$\frac{50{,}000 \times 100}{150{,}000} \qquad \frac{40{,}000 \times 100}{80{,}000}$$
$$= 33.3\% \qquad\qquad = 50.0\%$$

(ii) Gross profit on Sales

$$\frac{50{,}000 \times 100}{200{,}000} \qquad \frac{40{,}000 \times 100}{120{,}000}$$
$$= 25.0\% \qquad\qquad = 33.3\%$$

(iii) Return on Capital Employed

$$\frac{35{,}000 \times 100}{41{,}000} \qquad \frac{30{,}000 \times 100}{29{,}000}$$
$$= 85.4\% \qquad\qquad = 103.4\%$$

(iv) Debtor Collection Period

$$\frac{36{,}000 \times 365}{200{,}000} \qquad \frac{12{,}000 \times 365}{120{,}000}$$
$$= 66 \text{ days} \qquad\qquad = 37 \text{ days}$$

(v) Current ratio

$$\frac{54{,}000}{25{,}000} \qquad\qquad \frac{20{,}000}{6{,}000}$$
$$= 2.2{:}1 \qquad\qquad = 3.3{:}1$$

(vi) Acid Test (or Quick Ratio)

$$\frac{54{,}000 - 18{,}000}{25{,}000} \qquad \frac{20{,}000 - 7{,}000}{6{,}000}$$
$$= 1.4{:}1 \qquad\qquad = 1.1{:}1$$

(b) Profit and cash flow: points to be examined and commented upon.

1. Note the increase in sales and compare with the increase in gross and net profit. Are the various charges proportionate? If not, why not?

2. Why has the debtor collection period increased so substantially? Apart from reducing his selling prices to stimulate sales, did Free give more generous credit terms? Or was he so busy dealing with the increased volume that he did not have to insist on his debtors settling their accounts more promptly?

3. Note the effect of an increase in the net profit on capital employed. Is Free still getting an adequate return? Note also the various methods of calculating the return on capital employed. Would the average return on capital employed for the year be more appropriate?

4. Bearing in mind the fairly healthy current and acid ratios, is Free's liquidity position as satisfactory as it might first appear?
5. Would a Statement of Source and Application of Funds make the position clearer when comparing Free's profit and the liquidity for the year to 30 April 19X2?

EXERCISES

42.1 P Witt Ltd, a retail store, presents you with three years' accounts for the year ending 31 December 19X7:

	19X5 £000	19X6 £000	19X7 £000
Fixed Assets			
Book value			
Land and buildings	1,960	2,565	4,180
Fixtures and Fittings	785	1,030	1,240
	2,745	3,595	5,430
Current Assets			
Stock	700	800	1,100
Debtors	400	500	750
Bank	240	160	-
Current Liabilities			
Creditors	200	400	700
Bank overdraft	-	-	450
Dividend	140	150	190
Tax	100	120	180
Capital Employed			
Share Capital	3,000	3,800	4,500
Reserves	40	60	80
Loan	605	525	1,180
Sales (80% credit sales)	3,400	3,800	4,800
Gross profit	1,200	1,250	1,300
Net profit	300	340	380

Required:

(a) Write down the formulae used to calculate each of the following ratios:

Current or Working Capital Ratio, Rate of Stock Turnover, Time taken by debtors to pay bills (in weeks), Gross Profit as % Sales, Net Profit as % Sales;

(b) Calculate each of these ratios for 19X6 and 19X7;

(c) comment on the results and changes over the two years; and

(d) indicate three courses of action that would improve the Company's performance next year:

Note:

(i) Work to 2 decimal places.

(ii) Show all your workings.

(RSA Intermediate)

42.2 The summarised accounting statements of Shirt plc were as follows:

Profit and Loss Account for the year ended 30 April 19X7

	£000		£000
Cost of goods sold	415	Sales	530
Selling and administration	58		
Debenture interest	12		
Depreciation	25		
Dividend for the year	13		
Retained profit	7		
	£530		£530

Balance Sheet at 30 April 19X7

	£000		£000
Share capital	260	Fixed assets	410
Reserves	359	Stock	220
Debentures	150	Trade debtors	105
Trade creditors	50	Bank	117
Accrued expenses	20		
Proposed dividend	13		
	£852		£852

The trade association to which Shirt plc belongs has recently produced the following, based on averages calculated from the data submitted by the members:

1	Gross profit margin	15%
2	Net profit margin	11%
3	Return of shareholders' funds	12% *
4	Profit before interest to total assets	10% *
5	Current assets to current liabilities	3.6:1
6	Stock turnover	9 weeks*
7	Debtors turnover	8 weeks*
8	Creditors turnover	7 weeks*

* based on closing balances.

Required:

(a) Calculate the same data in respect of Shirt plc, numbered 1 to 8, as in the question;

(b) suggest what the most significant differences are between the data of Shirt and that of the trade association; and

(c) briefly identify the problems associated with making such comparisons.

(LCCI Higher July 1987)

42.3 Cone is in business as a motor factor. His condensed financial accounts for the last three years are summarised on the following page.

Profit and loss accounts for the year to 31 March

	19X0		19X1		19X2	
	£000	£000	£000	£000	£000	£000
Sales (all on credit)		400		630		870
Less: cost of Goods sold:						
Opening Stock	20		25		50	
Purchases	325		550		790	
	345		575		840	
Less: Closing Stock	25	320	50	525	100	740
GROSS PROFIT		80		105		130
Less: Expenses	40		50		60	
Loan interest	-	40	-	50	10	70
NET PROFIT		£40		£55		£60

Balance Sheets as at 31 March

	19X0		19X1		19X2	
	£000	£000	£000	£000	£000	£000
Fixed assets		89		93		101
Current Assets						
Stocks	25		50		100	
Trade Debtors	50		105		240	
Cash at Bank	10	85	5	160	-	340
		£174		£253		£441
Financed by:						
Capital		100		118		141
Add: Net profit						
for the year	40		55		60	
Less: Drawings						
(all on 31 March)	22	18	32	23	36	24
		118		141		165
Loan		-		-		100
Current Liabilities						
Creditors	56		112		166	
Bank overdraft	-	56	-	112	10	176
		£174		£253		£441

Required:

(a) Compute the following ratios for 19X0, 19X1 and 19X2:
- (i) gross profit on sales;
- (ii) gross profit on cost of goods sold;
- (iii) stock turnover;
- (iv) return on capital employed;
- (v) current ratio;
- (vi) liquidity (or quick) ratio;
- (vii) debtor collection period; and

(b) comment briefly on the results of the business over the last three years using the ratios you have computed in answer to part (a) of the question.

(AAT Level 2)

42.4 The following is the balance sheet at 31 March 19X5, of Claregate Ltd., a manufacturing company which sells entirely on credit to wholesalers:

	£000		£000	£000
Share Capital	200	Fixed Assets		500
Reserves	175	Current Assets:		
Debentures at 10%	400	Stock	490	
Current Liabilities	465	Debtors	250	740
	£1,240			£1,240

The Profit and Loss Account for 19X4/5 included:

	£000
Sales	1,000
Net profit before interest	124
Interest	40
Net profit after Interest	84

The following ratios were calculated for the year ended 31 March 19X4:

(i)	Debtors average credit time	- 70 days
(ii)	Profit to all long term capital employed	- 24%
(iii)	Return on shareholders equity	- 26%
(iv)	Net profit after interest to turnover	- 7%
(v)	Turnover to fixed assets	- 220%

Required:

(a) calculate the ratios for the year ending 31 March 19X5;

(b) state whether the 19X4/5 ratios are BETTER or worse than the 19X3/4 ratio's; and

(c) give TWO possible causes for the ratios having changed.

Assume that there are 360 days only in a year. Ignore tax and dividends.

(RSA Advanced)

42.5 The following information has been extracted from the accounts of Witton Way Ltd;

Profit and loss account for the year to 30 April 19X6

	19X5 £000	19X6 £000
Turnover (all credit sales)	7,650	11,500
Less: Cost of sales	(5,800)	(9,430)
GROSS PROFIT	1,850	2,070
Other expenses	(150)	(170)
Loan interest	(50)	(350)
PROFIT BEFORE TAXATION	1,650	1,550
TAXATION	(600)	(550)
PROFIT AFTER TAXATION	1,050	1,000
Dividends (all ordinary shares)	(300)	(300)
RETAINED PROFITS	£750	£700

Balance sheet as 30 April 19X6

	19X5 £000	19X6 £000
Fixed Assets		
Tangible assets	10,050	11,350
Current Assets		
Stock	1,500	2,450
Trade debtors	1,200	3,800
Cash	900	50
	3,600	6,300
Creditors: amounts falling due within one year	2,400	2,700
Net Current Assets	1,200	3,600
Total Assets less current Liabilities	11,250	14,950
Creditors: amounts falling due after more than one year		
Loans and other borrowings	350	3,350
	£10,900	£11,600
Capital and Reserves:		
Called up share capital	5,900	5,900
Profit and loss account	5,000	5,700
	£10,900	£11,600

Additional Information:

During the year to 30 April 19X6, the company tried to stimulate sales by reducing the selling price of its products and by offering more generous credit terms to it customers.

Required:

(a) Calculate SIX accounting ratios specifying the basis of your calculations for each of the two years to 30 April 19X5 and 19X6 respectively which will enable you to examine the company's progress during 19X6;

(b) from the information available to you, including the ratios calculated in part (a) of the questions, comment upon the company's results for the year to 30 April 19X6 under the heads of "liquidity", "profitability", "efficiency" and "shareholders' interests"; and

(c) state what additional information you would require in order to assess the company's attempts to stimulate sales during the year to 30 April 19X6.

(AAT Final)

42.6   You are presented with the following information for three quite separate and independent companies:

Summarised balance sheets at 31 March 19X7

	Chan plc £000	Ling plc £000	Wong plc £000
Total assets less current liabilities	600	600	700
Creditors, amounts falling due after more than one year			
10% Debenture stock	-	-	(100)
	£600	£600	£600
Capital and reserves:			
Called up share capital			
Ordinary shares of £1 each	500	300	200
10% Cumulative preference shares of £1 each	-	200	300
Profit and loss account	100	100	100
	£600	£600	£600

Additional information:

1. The operating profit before interest and tax for the year to 31 March 19X8 earned by each of the three companies was £300,000.
2. The corporation tax based on the profits for the year for the three companies is as follows:

	£
Chan plc	90,000
Ling plc	90,000
Wong plc	87,000

3. An ordinary dividend of 20p for the year to 31 March 19X8 is proposed by all three companies, and any preference dividends are to be provided for.
4. The market prices for ordinary shares at 31 March 19X8 were as follows:

	£
Chan plc	8.40
Ling plc	9.50
Wong plc	10.38

5. There were no changes in the share capital structure or in long-term loans of any of the companies during the year to 31 March 19X8.

Required:

(a) Insofar as the information permits, prepare the profit and loss account for each of the three companies (in columnar format) for the year to 31 March 19X8 (formal notes to the accounts are NOT required);

(b) calculate the following accounting ratios for each company:
   (i) earnings per share;
   (ii) price earnings;
   (iii) gearing {taken as total borrowings (preference share capital and long term loans) to ordinary shareholders' funds]; and

(c) using the gearing ratios calculated in answering part (b) of the question, briefly examine the importance of gearing if you were thinking of investing in some ordinary shares in one of the three companies assuming that the profits of the three companies were fluctuating.

(AAT Final, adapted)

COMMON ERRORS

1. Calculation of Ratios

You must know the formulae for the common basic accounting ratios. Remember that it is possible to calculate them in various ways, but provided that you are consistent, it does not really matter which method you adopt.

It is important to achieve some logic between the numerator and the denominator. If you are wanting to know the return on capital employed from the point of view of the ORDINARY shareholders, for example, you need to relate what profit ordinary shareholders are entitled to, compared with the amount that they have invested in the company.

Where there are preference shareholders, it would not be logical to relate the ordinary shareholders' return to TOTAL shareholders' funds, because the ordinary shareholders have not provided all of the funds. Thus net profit (either before or after tax) less preference dividend must be related to the total of shareholders' funds LESS the preference share capital.

2. Insufficient Data

In examination questions you are not always supplied with sufficient data to calculate ratios that are entirely representative. You my need, for example, to calculate ratios using year-end data, even though an AVERAGE for the year may be more appropriate.

3. Interpretation

This is often the hardest part of an examination question. If you do not know how to calculate some basic accounting ratios, or you cannot calculate them accurately, it obviously becomes even more difficult.

Examine the changes in each ratio over a period of time. Compare the movement with the changes in other ratios in cases where you think that there may be a close correlation. An expansion in sales, for example, will often lead to an increase in the trade debtor collection period (because new customers may be less credit worthy, or because the entity has not had the time to make sure that its debts are settled promptly).

Similarly, the build-up in stocks may lead to a decrease in the bank balance, or the issue of shares for cash may be connected with the purchase of new premises.

4. Choice of Ratios

Unless you are told to calculate a select number of ratios, do not calculate too many, especially if yo have to do so for a number of accounting periods or for a number of entities. The calculations will take too long, and you will not have the time to discuss them properly.

PART 4

CASE STUDIES

43

CASE STUDY 1: STARTING A BUSINESS

BOB, KATE AND WAYNE

Content

The advantages and disadvantages of starting a new business
The problems of starting a new business
Types of business entities
The legal background to forming a new business
The accounting requirements of new businesses
The sources of finances open to a new business

Background Information

Bob Barker is 35 years old. He has been married to Kate for 10 years, and she is two years his junior. They have three children: Dan aged 9, Jill aged 6, and Wendy who has just had her fourth birthday.

Bob works for a local manufacturing company. He has received fairly rapid promotion, and he is currently earning about £25,000 per year. He has every prospect of further promotion, although he is realistic enough to appreciate that he is unlikely ever to become an extremely senior manager of the company. His working conditions are good, and he will retire when he is 60 on a very good pension.

Until the children arrived, Kate was a typist in the same company as Bob. She has no great desire to return to work, although she recognises that once all the children are at school, she may want to do so.

Bob and Kate have moved house twice since they married. They now live in a detached house, currently valued at £100,000 on which they have a mortgage of £20,000.

Bob enjoys his work, although he becomes a little irritable when he has to refer even minor decisions to senior management. In recent years, Bob has become a little more unsettled. He now feels that he would like to go into business on his own. Kate is sympathetic, particularly as she realises that she may be able to help him in any business that he sets up.

They would like to move to a rural area, perhaps to run a general shop in an attractive village. Bob has calculated that he could sell their house and invest the proceeds in a general store that also included living accommodation. He has discussed his ideas with a maiden aunt, and she is willing to loan him up to £30,000 at a favourable rate of interest. It is likely, however, he would still need additional finance from other sources.

The more that the project has been discussed with Kate, the more that Bob has become excited about it.

In his spare time, Bob plays squash. One of his playing partners is 25 years' old Wayne young, and Bob has told him of his ambition to run his own business.

Wayne is single, and lives in a rented flat. He works as a double-glazing salesman, and he is paid almost entirely on commission. Wayne is an extremely good salesman, and for the last three years he has earned a very high salary. He lives for each day, and so all of his earnings are spent on alcohol, attractive young women, cars, and clothes.

Wayne is not a fool, and he is aware that his fast life will not last for ever. When he heard about Bob's project, he offered to join him in business. This rather disconcerted Bob, because he had not meant to confide in Wayne, still less go into business with him. In so far as he had thought about it, Bob's intention had been to work on his own, with the possibility that when the children were all at school, Kate would join him.

Bob does not want to hurt Wayne's feelings, but he is uncertain whether he could work with him. Wayne leads a highly active social life, and he spends a lot of money. On the other hand, Bob recognises that Wayne is an extremely good salesman, and that he could be useful in any business venture.

Neither Bob nor Wayne know much about accounting, finance or the law relating to starting up and operating a business. Kate knows something about office work, but it is a long time since she worked.

Tasks

1. Examine the arguments for and against Bob starting his own business.

2. Consult some of the books in your library that give advice on starting your own business, and then summarise the advantages and disadvantages of the following types of business entity:

    (a) sole trader;
    (b) partnership; and
    (c) limited liability company.

    In preparing your answer, concentrate on the accounting and financial considerations.

3. Assuming that Bob decides to start a business, advise him on the type of business entity that he should adopt, and on the problems that he might encounter if Wayne joins him.

    Note: These tasks are suitable for presentation in a written or in a verbal form, and they are also suitable for group activity.

44

CASE STUDY 2: THE DETERMINATION OF PROFIT

ROSS PUMPS

Content

Incomplete records

Receipts and payments accounts

Depreciation

Historical cost manufacturing, trading, profit and loss accounts

Historical cost balance sheets

The concept of net realisable value

Background Information

As a young man, Ross had trained as an engineer in a local factory. He continued to work for the company after he had served his apprenticeship, but he had become more frustrated at just playing a small part in a large multi-national organisation.

In his spare time, Ross liked to work on modelling railway engines. After developing one of his engines, he realised that a larger scale pump could have commercial possibilities. He sought some specialist advice which confirmed his views, and after much consideration he decided to set up in business on his own.

Ross' wife was a teacher. They lived in a large detached house on which they had a small mortgage. The area had benefitted considerably from the rise in property values. His wife liked the idea of Ross being a business man, and so she encouraged him to start out on his own.

They had sold their house, and they had moved into his wife's parents' house. Along with some savings, Ross had invested the proceeds from the sale of his house in a company he decided to call ROSS PUMPS. Ross' Uncle Ben admired his enterprise, and he had agreed to loan him £100,000. The exact terms were not discussed, but it was understand that Ross would pay back the loan, along with some interest as soon as the business could afford it.

Ross was an extremely good engineer, and he had a highly personable character, but he had had no experience of sales, marketing or finance.

He began in business on 1 April 19X3. For the first few months there was little activity but once he had sold some pumps, he was overwhelmed with orders. Ross took on some staff to help him in the factory and to deal with the unavoidable office work.

Ross worked long hours, and he had little time for paper work. As the business expanded, he was vaguely aware that he ought to keep some detailed accounting records, and to do something about value added tax.

By the end of his first year in business, Ross thought that he had created a reasonably healthy business: his pump worked, he made a good product, it was in demand, and he had more orders than he could really cope with.

He was not sure just how financially successful the business had been, so one weekend he prepared his accounts (Appendix 44.1). He was quite pleased with the results, as it would appear that he had made a profit of £42,000 for the year.

Ross showed these accounts to Norrie. Norrie was one of his nephews. He was reading accounting at university, and he had come to do some labouring work for Ross during the Easter vacation.

Norrie pointed out that the £42,000 could hardly be called profit, as it included such items as the cash Ross had put into the business and the loan from Uncle Ben.

Ross was a little chastened as he felt that he had made himself look very foolish, but he swallowed his pride and asked Norrie to calculate his profit for the year.

Unfortunately, Norrie was full of his new found learning. He asked his uncle what sort of profit he wanted: cash flow, current cost, economic income, historical cost, net replacement cost, or net realisable value? Norrie became even more carried away. "Perhaps Uncle Ross," he queried. "you would prefer a mixed value system of income determination?".

By now Ross was thoroughly confused. He was beginning to wish that he was back working in the local factory, or at least Norrie was back at University.

"Look Norrie," he said diplomatically, "I don't want to put you to so much trouble. Perhaps you might select just one or two of those methods". Norrie was rather relieved, as he had not the faintest idea how to go about implementing most of these methods of determining profit.

He readily agreed, but he said that he would want more information from his uncle. Ross gave him some more details about the business (Appendix 44.2). Even so, Norrie still found it necessary to obtain additional information from outside the business so that he could compile a set of conventional historical cost accounts.

Tasks

1. Prepare Ross Pump's receipts and payments account for the year to 31 March 19X4, and a balance sheet as at that date.

2. By referring to the annual reports of a number of companies, newspapers, journals and magazines, and any other information that you can obtain:
   (i) recommend to Ross suitable depreciation methods for his fixed assets; and
   (ii) advise him how he should deal with the interest on Uncle Ben's loan.

3. Using the information obtained in Task 2, prepare Ross Pump's manufacturing, trading, and profit and loss account for the year to 31 March 19X4 and a balance sheet as at that date.

4. Prepare a balance sheet for Ross Products as at 31 March 19X4 using net realisable values.

5. By referring to a number of accounting text books in the library, list the advantage and disadvantages of adopting the following methods of profit determination:
   (a) cash flow;
   (b) historical cost; and
   (c) net realisable value.

Appendix

<u>Exhibit 44.1</u>

ROSS

Bank and cash receipts for the year to 31 March 19X4

PAYMENTS	£'000	RECEIPTS	£'000
Cash paid for raw materials	100	Paid in to start the business	230
Cash paid to suppliers for raw materials purchased on credit	250	Loan received from Uncle Ben	100
Rent of premises	30	Cash sales	220
Rates	10	Cash received from	
Insurances	4	customers sold goods	
Heat, light and power	15	on credit	100
Factory staff wages	51		
Office staff salaries	25		
Office expenses	12		
Van expenses	6		
Purchase of delivery vans	30		
Purchase of office furniture	10		
Purchase of factory equipment	45		
Withdrawn by proprietor	20		
BALANCE = PROFIT	42		
	£650		£650

<u>Exhibit 44.2</u>

ADDITIONAL INFORMATION

(1) Amounts due to be received from trade debtors at the end of the year were estimated to be worth £100,000.

(2) Ross estimated that he owed £50,000 to trade creditors at the end of the year.

(3) One fifth of the raw materials purchased during the year was estimated to be in stock at the year end.

(4) The office takes up 10% of the total area of the business premises.

(5) Ross estimates that the offices uses 5% of the heat, light and power.

(6) The cost of insurance should be split equally between the factory and the office.

(7) Outstanding expenses at 31 March 19X4 were as follows:

	£'000
Wages	1
Heat, light and power	5

(8) Insurances paid in advance at 31 March 19X4 amounted to £2,000.

(9) Work-in-progress at 31 March 19X4 was estimated to be equivalent to 10% of the total factory cost for the year.

(10) Finished goods in stock at 31 March 19X4 amounted to 15% of the total cost of goods produced during the year.

Exhibit 44.3

ESTIMATED NET REALIZABLE VALUES AT 31 MARCH 19X4

	£'000
Delivery vans	15
Factory equipment	15
Finished goods	40
Office furniture	1
Prepayments	1
Raw materials	60
Work-in-progress	NIL
Trade debtors	90
Trade creditors	50
Accruals	6
Loan interest	?

45

CASE STUDY 3: PARTNERSHIP PROBLEMS

CLYDE, FORTH AND TAY

Content

Incomplete records

Accruals and prepayments

Hire purchase accounting

Partnership accounts

Partnerships: appropriation of profit

Valuation of partnership goodwill

Introduction of a new partner

Background Information

Clyde and Forth went into partnership on 1 January 19X7 buying and selling high quality second hand goods.

They were both good business men, and the business soon established itself. Both the partners had to work a minimum 16 hour day in order to keep up with demand for their goods.

The amount of trade that they were soon doing left little time for paper work, and in any case, neither Clyde nor Forth had much interest or experience of accounting. They did not keep any formal accounting records, and they both thought that second hand goods were not subject to value added tax.

Their first year in business passed quickly. During the year, both Clyde and Forth withdrew from cash takings any money that they wanted for their personal needs. However, they were anxious to know just how much profit they had made, as their personal overdrafts had resulted in the bank manager calling them in for an interview.

They had also agreed that the growth of the business was such that they needed another partner, and so they had approached Tay with a view to him joining the partnership.

Tay had asked a lot of questions which neither Clyde nor Forth could answer. They then realized that they had no clear agreement between them how they should manage the existing business, and how they should share profits. Tay pointed out that there would probably be little disagreement when the business was doing well, but they were quite likely to fall out if trade began to fall.

"If I was in your shoes," said Tay, "I would decide how you are going to share profits and losses, and then draw up a profit and loss account for the year." "When you have done that." he went on. "we can decide how much capital you would want me to contribute to the business, how we should share the management of the business, and how we would share profits and losses."

Tay also let it be known that if he joined the partnership, he would want a guaranteed minimum salary of £15,000 per annum in order to compensate him for giving up a secure job.

After a great deal of effort, Clyde and Forth managed to extract some information about the year's results from their rather inadequate records. The details are contained in Appendix 45.1

Tay had also said, "Oh, by the way, if I join the partnership, you would have to agree to keep a set of double-entry books." Neither Clyde nor Forth knew what he meant, but they both felt that they had better agree. Apparently such a step was necessary if they were to avoid the extreme anger and vengeance of the Customs and Excise Department.

Tasks

1. Consult the 1890 Partnership Act in your library. In the absence of a partnership agreement, state how according to the Act, profits and losses are to be shared amongst partners.

2. Work out a suitable partnership agreement for Clyde and Forth.

3. Devise a suitable accounting policy for dealing with the estate cars bought on hire purchase.

4. Based on the above tasks, prepare Clyde and Forth's trading, profit and loss, and profit and loss appropriation account for the year to 31 December 19X7, and a balance sheet as at that date.

5. Prepare a report for Tay advising him on the various matters that he will need to take into consideration before joining Clyde and forth in partnership, including the amount of capital that he should contribute to the new partnership, and the accounting treatment of goodwill.

Appendix

Exhibit 45.1

ADDITIONAL INFORMATION

		£'000
(1)	Cash receipts during the year	
	Sales	500
(2)	Bank receipts during the year	
	Capital introduced	
	Clyde	60
	Forth	20
	Received from trade creditors	220
	Transfers from cash	370

(3) Cash payments during the year

Goods for resale	80
Office expenses	13
Car expenses:	2
Drawings:	
Clyde	10
Forth	15

(4) Cheque payments during the year

Land and building (land £10,000)	40
Shop furniture and equipment	20
Rent of warehouse (eight months to 31 August 19X7)	28
Hire purchase deposits	4
Hire purchase instalments	12
Goods for resale	400
Electricity:	
quarter to 31 March 19X7	16
quarter to 30 June 19X7	2
quarter to 30 September 19X7	3
Rates:	
three months to 31 March 19X7	4
twelve months to 31 March 19X8	20
Insurances:	
twelve months to 31 December 19X7	10
twelve months to 31 December 19X8	12
Shop expenses (ten months to 31 October 19X7)	60
Car expenses (nine months to 30 September 19X7)	3

(5) Hire purchase

Two cars were purchased on hire purchase from the Gofar Finance Company on 1 January 19X7. The terms of each agreement were: an initial deposit of £2,000 followed by 36 monthly installments of £500 payable in advance. The ordinary cash price of each car was £14,000.

(6) Depreciation should be provided for on the cost of the fixed assets as follows:

	%
Buildings	5
Shop furniture and equipment	20
Cars	15

(7) Trade creditors owing at 31 December 19X7: £70,000.

(8) Trade debtors outstanding at 31 December 19X7: £30,000.

(9) All goods are sold at cost plus 50%.

46

CASE STUDY 4: INTERPRETATION OF ACOUNTS

NOVELTIES LIMITED

Content

Preparation of statements of source and application of funds

Calculation of accounting ratios

Preparation of data using trend and vertical analysis

Account for inflation

Analysis of accounts

Background Information

Novelties Limited is a small private company located in the north west of England. It was formed some ten years ago.

The company is a wholesale company. Its main object is to buy and sell novelty products for supply to various holiday resorts located in the north west of England, although some years ago it began to sell its products more widely.

The company has four directors, and there are about 40 shareholders, including all of the directors.

Since its formation, the company has always been reasonably profitable, and until recently there have been few liquidity problems.

The business began to grow rapidly from 19X1 onwards. Since its formation, the company had a policy of financing its growth from internal investment, but in 19X2 and 19X4 more shares were issued to its existing shareholders in order to support the projected growth in the company.

During the period of rapid growth, the accounting and reporting procedures had been rather neglected. The 19X4 results showed a sharp decline in profitability, and for the first time in the company's history, special overdraft facilities had to be arranged with the bank.

The position was even worse in 19X5. The company made a loss, and the overdraft increased to an alarming level.

As a result of the loss, the company reviewed its business strategy, its future operations and its funding requirements. It was then able to negotiate special overdraft facilities with the bank based on some very strict operational and trading requirements.

The directors realised that it would not be very easy to arrest the decline in the business's profitability and liquidity. The rate of inflation had begun to rise rapidly during the period 19X1 to 19X5, and the holiday trade in the North West of England had begun to be affected by the popularity of continental holidays.

Tasks

1. Prepare a statement of source and application of funds for each of the four years to 31 December 19X2 to 19X5 inclusive.

2. Calculate profitability, liquidity and efficiency ratios for each of the five years to 31 December 19X1 to 19X5 inclusive.

3. Prepare for each of the five years 19X1 to 19X5 inclusive:

   (a) a trend analysis: and
   (b) a vertical analysis.

   Note: you may find it is necessary to be selective in preparing the trend analysis.

4. From the information provided and the tasks undertaken above, extract the key statistics which you think help to explain Novelties Limited's performance during the period 19X1 to 19X5.

5. Adjust the main data to allow for changing prices during the five year period.

6. Prepare a brief report for the directors explaining how the company's profitability and liquidity became so critical in 19X4 and in 19X5.

Exhibit 46.1

YEAR ENDED 31 DECEMBER

	19X1 £'000	19X2 £'000	19X3 £'000	19X4 £'000	19X5 £'000
TRADING RESULTS					
Sales (all credit)	8,200	12,800	18,700	25,600	46,400
Cost of goods sold					
Opening stock	1,200	1,600	1,800	1,900	7,500
Purchases (all credit)	5,800	8,800	13,800	25,700	40,900
	7,000	10,400	15,600	27,600	48,400
Less: Closing stock	1,600	1,800	1,900	7,500	8,000
	5,400	8,600	13,700	20,100	40,400
GROSS PROFIT	2,800	4,200	5,000	5,500	6,000
Distribution costs	2,100	3,140	3,400	4,100	5,900
Administrative expenses	290	350	600	700	890
NET PROFIT/(LOSS) BEFORE TAXATION	410	710	1,000	700	(790)
Taxation	(10)	(10)	(50)	(100)	(10)
NET PROFIT/(LOSS) AFTER TAXATION	400	700	950	600	(800)
Dividends	100	200	400	800	-
RETAINED PROFIT/(LOSS) FOR THE YEAR	£300	£500	£550	£(200)	£(800)

BALANCE SHEETS

FIXED ASSETS (net book value)

Land and buildings	1,020	1,010	1,000	1,040	1,030
Motor vehicles	950	1,710	2,890	3,880	5,465
Equipment	100	150	200	185	170
	2,070	2,870	4,090	5,105	6,665

CURRENT ASSETS

Stocks	1,600	1,800	1,900	7,500	8,000
Trade debtors	700	1,300	2,200	4,300	9,000
Prepayments	100	110	100	200	200
Cash at bank and in hand	30	20	20	-	-
	2,430	3,230	4,220	12,000	17,200

CURRENT LIABLITIES

Bank overdraft	-	-	-	950	3,800
Trade creditors	1,800	2,550	3,950	10,400	16,000
Accruals	40	40	60	80	80
Taxation	10	10	50	100	10
Proposed dividend	100	200	400	800	-
	1,950	2,800	4,460	12,330	19,890
NET CURRENT ASSETS	480	430	(240)	(330)	(2,690)
	£2,550	£3,300	£3,850	£4,775	£3,975

CAPITAL AND RESERVES

Called up share capital £1 ordinary shares	500	750	750	1,500	1,500
Share premium account	-	-	-	375	375
Reserves	2,050	2,550	3,100	2,900	2,100
	£2,550	£3,300	£3,850	£4,775	£3,975

Exhibit 46.2

DIRECTORS' EMOLUMENTS

	£'000
19X1	140
19X2	170
19X3	400
19X4	450
19X5	600

<u>Exhibit 46.3</u>

CHANGING PRICE INDEX FOR ALL ITEMS

	Annual average
19X0	21
19X1	22
19X2	24
19X3	28
19X4	35
19X5	40
19X6	45

SOLUTIONS TO EXERCISES

SOLUTIONS TO CHAPTER 1 EXERCISES

EXERCISE 1.1   PAGE 8

Accounting is concerned with the supply of information for those user groups who have a need for it. There is no limit to the amount of information that could be supplied, so accountants restrict the information collected to that information which can be quantified and valued in monetary terms. Good industrial relations, for example, is not normally included in accounting statements because it is not easy to quantify and to value.

Quantifiable information is hence collected and recorded in monetary terms into books of account, usually in such a way that the giving and receiving effect of each transaction is captured within the system. This is known as the dual aspect rule.

Periodically, the information is summarised in the form of a profit and loss account and a balance sheet. These statements enable the proprietor of an entity to assess his profit for a specific period of time and to note the state of indebtedness of the business. Such information enables him to take decisions about the future operational activities of the entity. This point applies whether he is operating in either the profit making sector of the economy or the not-for-profit making sector.

Nowadays, accounting plays a much wider role than simply supplying information about profitability and states of indebtedness. The information obtained is frequently used and extended in order to help management take decisions on a day-to-day basis.

EXERCISE 1.2   PAGE 8

(i) **Entity**. Only those matters that relate to the affairs of the entity should be included in its financial accounts (except insofar as there is a state of indebtedness between the entity and outside parties). Items that relate to the private affairs of the proprietors such as, for example, the cost of a holiday for the proprietor's wife, should not be included in the entity's profit and loss account.

(ii) **Going concern**. Financial statements should be prepared on the basis that the entity will continue its operations into the forseeable future. Fixed assets, for example, are normally included at their historical cost less an allowance for accumulated depreciation based on their historical cost. If the entity was likely to be liquidated in the near future, then such assets would be valued at their realisable value.

(iii) **Accruals (or matching)**. Incomes and expenses are normally included in financial statements at the amount that relates to the period in question, and not just to the cash received or paid during that period. Thus goods sold to customers during Period 1 will be treated as sales during that period even though some customers may not pay for them until Period 2. Similarly, the entity may have consumed a certain quantity of gas during Period 1 but it may not have paid the Gas Board for the gas that it has consumed. It will, therefore, estimate the cost of gas consumed for which it has not paid and include that cost in Period 1's accounts even though it will not pay for the gas until Period 2.

(iv) Conservatism (or prudence). A considerable number of estimates have usually to be made in preparing financial statements, for example, gas consumed to be paid for in the next period, and for insurances paid, some of which relate to the next accounting period. It is not always possible to be absolutely accurate about such estimates, and where it is unavoidable it is usually prudent to overstate estimates of expenditure and understate estimates of income, or to treat items as revenue rather than as capital. By being cautious, the profit is not thereby overstated, and there is not then the danger of paying out too much of the profit in cash. If subsequently the estimates are proved to have been over cautious, then an increased profit can be reported in a later period when there is not the danger of depleting the entity of the operational cash resources that it needs.

(v) Consistency. Entities are free to adopt a wide range of accounting rules and to interpret them to suit the business and operational requirements of particular entities. Once adopted and interpreted, however, an entity's accounting policies should be consistently applied. Accounting policies should not be abandoned to suit short-term considerations or because of individual whims. If business or operational considerations make such a change desirable, then it is permissible to make changes provided that the users of financial statements are alerted to such changes.

EXERCISE 1.3   PAGE 8

Part (a)

(1) **Entity Rule**. The partners' income tax affairs are a private matter. Any income tax paid on behalf of the partners should be charged to their respective Drawings Account.

(2) **Quantification/Money Measurement rules**. It is difficult both to quantify and to place a monetary value on the worth of an employee. Consequently, apart from his salary being included in the profit and loss account, no attempt will be made to include this type of asset on the balance sheet.

(3) **Historic cost/Going concern rules**. The equipment would normally be reflected in the books of account at its historic cost and depreciated on that basis. Only if the business was likely to be liquidated in the near future would it be included at its net realisable value.

(4) **Consistency/Objectivity rules**. The stock should continue to be valued on a FIFO basis unless there are sound business or operational reasons for adopting another valuation method. This does not normally include a natural desire to pay less tax.

(5) **Materiality rule**. Two gallons of petrol is not a material amount. There is no need to value the closing stock of such an insignificant amount, and it can be written off to the profit and loss account as part of the overall petrol charge.

(6) **Accruals (or matching) rule**. The £2,000 should be added to the overall rates charge for the year as it is an expense of the period.

(7) **Prudence rule**. Enquiries should be made of the customer's affairs. If there is no doubt that he has gone into liquidation and there is no possibility that any of the debt will be recovered, the £500 should be written off to the current year's profit and loss account. Otherwise the amount should be taken into account in calculating the current year's provision for bad and doubtful debts.

(8) **Realisation rule**. If the goods have been sold to the customer during the year to 31 March 19X5 and he is required to pay for them, the sales may be included in the 19X5 Trading Account.

Part (b)

Statements of standard accounting practice (SSAP's) help accountants prepare accounting statements in two main ways :

(1) They are authoritative statements on accounting practice; and

(2) they narrow the areas of difference and variety in the accounting treatment of the matters with which they deal.

EXERCISE 1.4   PAGE 9

(1) **Quantification/Money Measurement rules**. It is difficult both to quantify and to place a monetary value on good industrial relations, so it would be difficult to include it in the company's accounts.

(2) **Going concern rule**. If the company is not likely to continue operating in the very near future, then different accounting rules would be adopted, for example, fixed assets would be valued at their net realisable value instead of at their historic cost.

(3) **Realisation rule**. Until the customers have actually accepted the legal responsibility for the goods they should not be included in the current year's accounts.

(4) **Entity rule**. This is a private matter relating to one of the owners, and it will not be reflected in the company's accounts.

(5) **Accruals (or matching) rule**. The outstanding amount should be added to the year's electricity charge because it is a cost of that period, even though it has not yet been settled in cash.

(6) **Historic cost rule**. It is usual to include fixed assets on the balance sheet at their historic cost and to depreciate them on that basis. However, fixed assets are sometimes revalued if there has been a material change in their value; the annual depreciation charge would then be based on the revalued amount.

(7) **Materiality rule**. The cost of the pencils would be written off to the profit and loss account for the period in which they were purchased, as it is not normally worth accounting for insignificant amounts.

(8) **Consistency rule**. Stock should continue to be valued on a consistent basis irrespective of the year's results. If the FIFO method is no longer a suitable method to adopt, perhaps because of a change in the company's operational activities, then it would be permissible to use a different valuation method.

(9) **Prudence**. It would be prudent to include an extra provision for bad and doubtful debts for the amount owed by the debtor if there is some evidence of the rumour.

(10) **Objectivity/Prudence rules**. The accountant would have to present some evidence for believing that the shares are worthless, otherwise he is being prejudiced in putting forward such a view. If he is correct in his view then it would be prudent to provide for a reduction in the value of the shares.

Solutions to CHAPTER 1 Exercises

EXERCISE 1.5 PAGE 9

In responding to your client the following main points could be made :

(1) Income and expenditure is analysed between capital and revenue income and expenditure. Revenue income and expenditure is transferred to the profit and loss account for a particular period, whilst capital income and expenditure is entered in the balance sheet.

(2) Accounts are normally prepared using a number of accounting rules. In this case two rules are particularly pertinent :

(a) the realisation rule which requires sales to be included in the period when the sales are made and not when the cash is received; and

(b) the accruals (or matching) rule which requires incomes and expenses to be dealt with in the period to which they relate, instead of the period when cash is received or paid.

(3) A proportion of some capital expenditure, for example, for fixed assets, is usually transferred to each period's profit and loss account.

(4) An assessment has to be made of the quantity and value of stock and work-in-progress at the end of each accounting period.

(5) Provisions are often built into the profit and loss account, for example, for bad and doubtful debts.

All of the above points mean that the amount of accounting profit for a particular period does not necessarily equal the increase or decrease in the company's bank balance. At its simplest, for example, the company may have purchased a considerable quantity of fixed assets, only part of which may be reflected as depreciation in the profit and loss account for the period during which the purchases were made. Hence whilst the company may be reporting a profit for the period, its bank balance may well have been significantly reduced.

SOLUTIONS TO CHAPTER 2 EXERCISES

EXERCISE 2.1 PAGE 13

Transaction	Account	
	Debit	**Credit**
(a)	Cash	Capital
(b)	Bank	Cash
(c)	Purchases	Cash
(d)	Cash	Sales
(e)	Office expenses	Cash

EXERCISE 2.2 PAGE 14

Transaction	Account	
	Debit	**Credit**
(a)	Cash	Capital
(b)	Bank	Cash
(c)	Purchases	Cash
(d)	Purchases	Pope
(e)	Lynn	Sales
(f)	Pope	Purchases returns
(g)	Sales returns	Lynn
(h)	Petty cash	Bank
(i)	Rent payable	Bank
(j)	Electricity	Cash

EXERCISE 2.3 PAGE 14

Transaction	Account	
	Debit	**Credit**
(a)	Cash	Minor's loan
(b)	Bank	Capital
(c)	Petty cash	Bank
(d)	Purchases	Law
(e)	Gas	Cash
(f)	Loan interest	Cash
(g)	Cash	Sales
(h)	Drawings	Cash
(i)	Wages	Bank
(j)	Moor	Sales
(k)	Car	Bank
(l)	Travelling expenses	Petty cash
(m)	Law	Purchases returns
(n)	Drawings	Cash
(o)	Sales returns	Moor
(p)	Car expenses	Bank
(q)	Office stationery	Cash
(r)	Office expenses	Bank
(s)	Drawings	Purchases
(t)	Purchases	Cash

EXERCISE 2.4   PAGE 14

Transaction	Account	
	Debit	**Credit**
(1)	Bank	Capital
(2)	Equipment	Bank
(3)	Purchases	Lapp Supplies Ltd
(4)	Petty cash	Bank
(5)	C Trewar	Sales
(6)	Rent payable	Bank
(7)	Motor expenses	Petty cash
(8)	Drawings	Petty cash
(9)	Sales returns	C Trewar
(10)	Lapp Supplies Ltd	Bank

EXERCISE 2.5   PAGE 15

Transaction		Account	
		Debit	**Credit**
(1)	5 August	Rent payable £150	Bank £150
(2)	10 August	Bank £165	J Chisholm £165
		Discounts allowed £5	J Chisholm £5
(3)	15 August	Bad debts £112	Kohn £112
(4)	13 August	Electricity £78	Bank £78
	20 August	Telephone £78	Electricity £78
(5)	31 August	Suspense £90	Purchases £90
			(£1,430-£1,340)

EXERCISE 2.6   PAGE 16

(A) Goods of £27,000 have been purchased from a supplier on credit terms (stocks have increased by £27,000 and trade creditors have increased by the same amount).

(B) Land and buildings worth £35,000 have been purchased through a loan for the same amount (both items have increased by £35,000).

(C) Sales of £30,000 have been made to trade debtors (trade debtors have increased by £30,000, stocks have decreased by £20,000, the balance of £10,000 being transferred to capital which has increased from £730,000 to £740,000).

(D) £13,000 has been received from trade debtors (trade debtors have decreased by £13,000 and the cash at the bank has increased by the same amount).

(E) Bad debts of £2,000 have been written off to profit (both trade debtors and capital have decreased by £2,000).

(F) Drawings of £5,000 have been made to the proprietors, and £3,000 of accrued expenses have been paid (cash has decreased by £8,000, capital by £5,000 and accrued expenses by £3,000).

(G) £30,000 of equipment has been sold, the amount received being paid into the bank, and the proprietor has made drawings of £9,000 (equipment has been decreased by £30,000, capital by £9,000, but the cash at the bank has increased by £21,000 [£42,000 + £30,000 - £9,000 = £63,000]).

(H) The proprietor has withdrawn £1,000 of goods for his own use (stocks and capital have both decreased by £1,000).

(I) The proprietor has withdrawn £6,000 in cash (cash and capital have both decreased by £6,000).

Explanation

(1) The proprietor has withdrawn £6,000 for his own personal use.
(2) The business settled an amount owing that related to a private matter of the proprietor.

SOLUTIONS TO CHAPTER 3 EXERCISES

EXERCISE 3.1 PAGE 25

Part (a)

W FLOWER
Bank Account

		£			£
1 3 X8	Capital	200	1 3 X8	Rent payable	100
24 4 X8	Cash	800	4 3 X8	Purchases	500
			18 3 X8	Vehicle expenses	50
			28 3 X8	Heating expenses	40
			30 3 X8	Drawings	100
			31 3 X8	Balance c/d	210
		£1,000			£1,000
1 4 X8	Balance b/d	210	1 4 X8	Rent payable	100
27 4 X8	Cash	950	4 4 X8	Purchases	800
			7 4 X8	Vehicle expenses	60
			28 4 X8	Heating expenses	50
			29 4 X8	Drawings	100
			30 4 X8	Balance c/d	50
		£1,160			£1,160
1 5 X8	Balance b/d	50			

Rent Payable Account

		£			£
1 3 X8	Bank	100			
1 4 X8	Bank	100	30 4 X8	Balance c/d	200
		£200			£200
1 5 X8	Balance b/d	200			

Purchases Account

		£			£
4 3 X8	Bank	500			
4 4 X8	Bank	800	30 4 X8	Balance c/d	1,300
		£1,300			£1,300
1 5 X8	Balance b/d	1,300			

Vehicle Expenses Account

		£			£
18 3 X8	Bank	50			
7 4 X8	Bank	60	30 4 X8	Balance c/d	110
		£110			£110
1 5 X8	Balance b/d	110			

Capital Account

		£			£
			1 3 X8	Bank	200

Heating Expenses Account

		£			£
28 3 X8	Bank	40			
28 4 X8	Bank	50	30 4 X8	Balance c/d	90
		£90			£90
1 5 X8	Balance b/d	90			

Drawings Account

		£			£
30 3 X8	Bank	100			
29 4 X8	Bank	100	30 4 X8	Balance c/d	200
		£200			£200
1 5 X8	Balance b/d	200			

Cash Account

		£			£
24 3 X8	Sales	800	24 4 X8	Bank	800
27 4 X8	Sales	950	27 4 X8	Bank	950
		£1,750			£1,750

Sales Account

		£			£
30 4 X8	Balance c/d	1,750	24 3 X8	Cash	800
			27 4 X8	Cash	950
		£1,750			£1,750
			1 5 X8	Balance b/d	1,750

Part (b)

W FLOWER
Trial Balance as at 30 April 19X8

	Dr	Cr
	£	£
Bank	50	
Capital		200
Rent payable	200	
Purchases	1,300	
Vehicle expenses	110	
Heating expenses	90	
Drawings	200	
Sales		1,750
	£1,950	£1,950

EXERCISE 3.2   PAGE 25

Part (a)

PETER HOUSE
Bank Account

		£			£
2 11 X7	Capital	10,000	2 11 X7	Petty cash	200
13 11 X7	Commissions account	600	3 11 X7	Office rent	750
			4 11 X7	Grunwicks plc	600
			25 11 X7	Jacob Podmore	410
			28 11 X7	Drawings	604
			30 11 X7	Balance c/d	8,036
		£10,600			£10,600
1 12 X7	Balance b/d	8,036			

Capital Account

		£			£
			2 11 X7	Bank	10,000

Petty Cash Account

		£		£
2 11 X7	Bank	200		

Office Rent Account

		£		£
3 11 X7	Bank	750		

Office Furniture Account

		£		£
4 11 X7	Grunwicks plc	2,400		

Grunwick plc's Account

		£			£
4 11 X7	Bank	600	4 11 X7	Office furniture	2,400
30 11 X7	Balance c/d	1,800			
		£2,400			£2,400
			1 12 X7	Balance b/d	1,800

Commissions Received Account

		£			£
			13 11 X7	Bank	600
30 11 X7	Balance c/d	1,475	19 11 X7	Jacob Podmore	875
		£1,475			£1,475
			1 12 X7	Balance b/d	1,475

Jacob Podmore's Account

	£		£
19 11 X7 Commissions received	875		
25 11 X7 Advertising	110	30 11 X7 Balance c/d	985
	£985		£985
1 12 X7 Balance b/d	985		

Advertising Account

	£		£
25 11 X7 Bank	410	25 11 X7 Jacob Podmore	110
		30 11 X7 Balance c/d	300
	£410		£410
1 12 X7 Balance b/d	300		

Drawings Account

	£		£
28 11 X7 Bank	604	28 11 X7 Motor expenses	84
		30 11 X7 Balance c/d	520
	£604		£604
1 12 X7 Balance b/d	520		

Motor Expenses Account

	£		£
28 11 X7 Drawings	84		

Part (b)

PETER HOUSE
Trial Balance as at 30 November 19X7

	Dr	Cr
	£	£
Bank	8,036	
Capital		10,000
Petty cash	200	
Office rent	750	
Office furniture	2,400	
Grunwick plc		1,800
Commissions received		1,475
Jacob Podmore	985	
Advertising	300	
Drawings	520	
Motor expenses	84	
	£13,275	£13,275

EXERCISE 3.3 PAGE 26

Part (a)

CHARLES

Capital Account

		£			£
			1 7 X2	Cash	20,000

Cash Account

		£			£
1 7 X2	Capital	20,000	2 7 X2	Bank	18,000
23 7 X2	Sales	1,500	5 7 X2	Rent	500
			9 7 X2	Purchases	1,000
			31 7 X2	Cash	150
				Balance c/d	1,850
		£21,500			£21,500
1 8 X2	Balance b/d	1,850			

Bank Account

		£			£
2 7 X2	Cash	18,000	6 7 X2	Shop equipment	300
31 7 X2	Frodsham	250	31 7 X2	Balance c/d	17,950
		£18,250			£18,250
1 8 X2	Balance b/d	17,950			

Rent Payable Account

		£		£
5 7 X2	Cash	500		

Shop Equipment Account

		£		£
6 7 X2	Bank	300		

Purchases Account

		£			£
9 7 X2	Cash	1,000			
15 7 X2	Seddon	2,000	31 7 X2	Balance c/d	3,000
		£3,000			£3,000
1 8 X2	Balance b/d	3,000			

Seddon's Account

		£			£
20 7 X2	Purchases Returns	200	15 7 X2	Purchases	2,000
31 7 X2	Balance c/d	1,800			
		£2,000			£2,000
			1 8 X2	Balance b/d	1,800

Purchases Returns Account

	£			£
		20 7 X2 Seddon		200

Sales Account

		£			£
			23 7 X2	Cash	1,500
31 7 X2	Balance c/d	2,500	26 7 X2	Frodsham	1,000
		£2,500			£2,500
			1 8 X2	Balance b/d	2,500

Frodsham's Account

		£			£
26 7 X2	Sales	1,000	28 7 X2	Sales Returns	500
			31 7 X2	Bank	250
			31 7 X2	Balance c/d	250
		£1,000			£1,000
1 8 X2	Balance b/d	250			

Sales Returns Account

		£	£
28 7 X2	Frodsham	500	

Drawings Account

		£	£
31 7 X2	Cash	150	

Part (b)

CHARLES
Trial Balance as at 31 July 19X2

	Dr £	Cr £
Capital		20,000
Cash	1,850	
Bank	17,950	
Rent payable	500	
Furniture	300	
Purchases	3,000	
Seddon		1,800
Purchases returns		200
Sales		2,500
Frodsham	250	
Sales returns	500	
Drawings	150	
	£24,500	£24,500

EXERCISE 3.4   PAGE 26

Part (a)

CONNIE'S LEDGER ACCOUNTS
Bank Account

		£000			£000
1 4 X4	Balance b/d	12	30 4 X4	Winnie	6
30 4 X4	Abe	19	30 4 X4	Yule	15
30 4 X4	Burke	9	30 4 X4	Zara	60
30 4 X4	Crane	4	30 4 X4	Office expenses	11
30 4 X4	Cash	170	31 5 X4	Winnie	5
31 5 X4	Abe	16	31 5 X4	Yule	14
31 5 X4	Burke	3	31 5 X4	Zara	64
31 5 X4	Crane	2	31 5 X4	Office expenses	14
31 5 X4	Cash	80	30 6 X4	Winnie	7
30 6 X4	Abe	18	30 6 X4	Yule	16
30 6 X4	Burke	7	30 6 X4	Zara	56
30 6 X4	Crane	3	30 6 X4	Office expenses	32
30 6 X4	Cash	140	30 6 X4	Capital	8
			30 6 X4	Balance c/d	175
		£483			£483
1 7 X4	Balance b/d	175			

Capital Account

		£000			£000
			1 4 X4	Balance b/d	49

Cash Account

		£000			£000
1 4 X4	Balance b/d	2	30 4 X4	Purchases	90
30 4 X4	Sales	300	30 4 X4	Drawings	12
30 4 X4	Rents received	5	30 4 X4	Office expenses	22
31 5 X4	Sales	272	30 4 X4	Bank	170
31 5 X4	Rents received	5	31 5 X4	Purchases	150
31 5 X4	Plant and equipment	5	31 5 X4	Drawings	15
30 6 X4	Sales	250	31 5 X4	Office expenses	27
30 6 X4	Rent received	5	31 5 X4	Bank	80
			30 6 X4	Purchases	68
			30 6 X4	Drawings	20
			30 6 X4	Office expenses	16
			30 6 X4	Bank	140
			30 6 X4	Balance c/d	34
		£844			£844
1 7 X4	Balance b/d	34			

Drawings Account

		£000			£000
30 4 X4	Cash	12			
30 4 X4	Purchases	2			
31 5 X4	Cash	15			
31 5 X4	Purchases	3			
30 6 X4	Cash	20			
30 6 X4	Purchases	4			
30 6 X4	Bank	8	30 6 X4	Balance c/d	64
		£64			£64
1 7 X4	Balance b/d	64			

Office Expenses Account

		£000			£000
30 4 X4	Cash	22			
30 4 X4	Bank	11			
31 5 X4	Cash	27			
31 5 X4	Bank	14			
30 6 X4	Cash	16			
30 6 X4	Bank	32	30 6 X4	Balance c/d	122
		£122			£122
1 7 X4	Balance b/d	122			

Plant and Machinery Account

		£000			£000
1 4 X4	Balance b/d	75	31 5 X4	Cash	5
			30 6 X4	Balance c/d	70
		£75			£75
1 7 X4	Balance b/d	70			

Purchases Account

		£000			£000
30 4 X4	Cash	90	30 4 X4	Drawings	2
30 4 X4	Winnie	5	31 5 X4	Drawings	3
30 4 X4	Yule	17	30 6 X4	Drawings	4
30 4 X4	Zara	64			
31 5 X4	Cash	150			
31 5 X4	Winnie	7			
31 5 X4	Yule	18			
31 5 X4	Zara	56			
30 6 X4	Cash	68			
30 6 X4	Winnie	10			
30 6 X4	Yule	19			
30 6 X4	Zara	61	30 6 X4	Balance c/d	556
		£565			£565
1 7 X4	Balance b/d	556			

Purchases Returns Account

		£000				£000
			30 4 X4	Yule		2
			31 5 X4	Yule		3
			30 6 X4	Yule		1
30 6 X4	Balance c/d	10	30 6 X4	Zara		4
		£10				£10
			1 7 X4	Balance b/d		10

Rents Received Account

		£000				£000
			30 4 X4	Cash		5
			31 5 X4	Cash		5
30 6 X4	Balance c/d	15	30 6 X4	Cash		5
		£15				£15
			1 7 X4	Balance b/d		15

Sales Account

		£000				£000
			30 4 X4	Cash		300
			30 4 X4	Abe		20
			30 4 X4	Burke		4
			30 4 X4	Crane		3
			30 4 X4	Cash		272
			31 5 X4	Abe		22
			31 5 X4	Burke		8
			31 5 X4	Crane		4
			30 6 X4	Cash		250
			30 6 X4	Abe		16
			30 6 X4	Burke		6
30 6 X4	Balance c/d	906	30 6 X4	Crane		1
		£906				£906
			1 7 X4	Balance b/d		906

Sales Returns Account

		£000				£000
30 4 X4	Abe	8				
30 4 X4	Crane	1				
31 5 X4	Crane	2	30 6 X4	Balance c/d		11
		£11				£11
1 7 X4	Balance b/d	11				

Winnie's Account

		£000			£000
30 4 X4	Bank	6	1 4 X4	Balance b/d	6
31 5 X4	Bank	5	30 4 X4	Purchases	5
30 6 X4	Bank	7	31 5 X4	Purchases	7
30 6 X4	Balance c/d	10	30 6 X4	Purchases	10
		£28			£28
			1 7 X4	Balance b/d	10

Yule's Account

		£000			£000
30 4 X4	Bank	15	1 4 X4	Balance b/d	15
30 4 X4	Purchases returns	2	30 4 X4	Purchases	17
31 5 X4	Bank	14	31 5 X4	Purchases	18
31 5 X4	Purchases returns	3	30 6 X4	Purchases	19
30 6 X4	Bank	16			
30 6 X4	Purchases returns	1			
30 6 X4	Balance c/d	18			
		£69			£69
			1 7 X4	Balance b/d	18

Zara's Account

		£000			£000
30 4 X4	Bank	60	1 4 X4	Balance b/d	60
31 5 X4	Bank	64	30 4 X4	Purchases	64
30 6 X4	Bank	56	31 5 X4	Purchases	56
30 6 X4	Purchases returns	4	30 6 X4	Purchases	61
30 6 X4	Balance c/d	57			
		£241			£241
			1 7 X4	Balance b/d	57

Abe's Account

		£000			£000
1 4 X4	Balance b/d	26	30 4 X4	Bank	19
30 4 X4	Sales	20	30 4 X4	Sales returns	8
31 5 X4	Sales	22	31 5 X4	Bank	16
30 6 X4	Sales	16	30 6 X4	Bank	18
			30 6 X4	Balance c/d	23
		£84			£84
1 7 X4	Balance b/d	23			

Burke's Account

		£000			£000
1 4 X4	Balance b/d	10	30 4 X4	Bank	9
30 4 X4	Sales	4	31 5 X4	Bank	3
31 5 X4	Sales	8	30 6 X4	Bank	7
30 6 X4	Sales	6	30 6 X4	Balance c/d	9
		£28			£28
1 7 X4	Balance b/d	9			

Crane's Account

		£000			£000
1 4 X4	Balance b/d	5	30 4 X4	Bank	4
30 4 X4	Sales	3	30 4 X4	Sales returns	1
31 5 X4	Sales	4	31 5 X4	Bank	2
30 6 X4	Sales	1	31 5 X4	Sales returns	2
			30 6 X4	Bank	3
			30 6 X4	Balance c/d	1
		£13			£13
1 7 X4	Balance b/d	1			

Part (b)

CONNIE
Trial Balance as at 30 June 19X4

		Dr £000	Cr £000
Bank		175	
Capital			49
Cash		34	
Drawings		64	
Office expenses		122	
Plant and machinery		70	
Purchases		556	
Purchases returns			10
Rent received			15
Sales			906
Sales returns		11	
Trade creditors :			
	Winnie		10
	Yule		18
	Zara		57
Trade debtors :			
	Abe	23	
	Burke	9	
	Crane	1	
		£1,065	£1,065

EXERCISE 3.5   PAGE 28

ANDREW FLINT
Trial Balance as at 31 January 19X7

	Dr £	Cr £
Rent and rates	560	
Discount received		170
Purchases	8,340	
Sales		16,530
Drawings	840	

	Dr £	Cr £
Stocks (at 1 February 19X6)	3,610	
Provision for doubtful debts		200
Office furniture at cost	900	
Discount allowed	460	
Sundry debtors	3,820	
Sundry creditors		3,540
Sales returns	210	
Cash in hand	130	
Wages and salaries	7,620	
Bad debts written off	490	
Bank overdraft		1,320
General expenses	280	
Capital account		5,500
	£27,260	£27,260

EXERCISE 3.6 PAGE 28

D MALT
Trial Balance as at 31 December 19X5

	Dr £	Cr £
Freehold premises	50,000	
Sundry creditors		2,980
Drawings	4,160	
Purchases	28,200	
Sundry debtors	3,600	
Provision for depreciation of office furniture		1,040
Stock at 1 January 19X5	2,280	
Bad debts	240	
Rent receivable		1,600
Sales		42,300
Office furniture	5,200	
Provision for bad/doubtful debts		150
General expenses	310	
Returns inwards	370	
Discounts received		210
Wages and salaries	8,150	
Bank overdraft		3,130
Capital account		51,100
	£102,510	£102,510

SOLUTIONS TO CHAPTER 4 EXERCISES

EXERCISE 4.1   PAGE 34

Ash's Account

		£			£
1 1 X1	Balance b/d	300	12 2 X1	Cash	1,250
31 1 X1	Sales	1,000	12 2 X1	Discounts allowed	50
		£1,300			£1,300

Elm's Account

		£			£
1 1 X1	Balance b/d	100	20 2 X1	Cash	290
31 1 X1	Sales	200	20 2 X1	Discounts allowed	10
		£300			£300

Oak's Account

		£			£
1 1 X1	Balance b/d	400	18 2 X1	Cash	1,065
31 1 X1	Sales	700	18 2 X1	Discounts allowed	35
		£1,100			£1,100

Discounts Allowed Account

		£			£
12 2 X1	Ash	50			
18 2 X1	Oak	35			
20 2 X1	Elm	10	28 2 X1	Balance c/d	95
		£95			£95
1 3 X1	Balance b/d	95			

EXERCISE 4.2   PAGE 34

Bush's Account

		£			£
10 4 X2	Bank	12,850	1 3 X2	Balance b/d	7,000
10 4 X2	Discounts received	150	31 3 X2	Purchases	6,000
		£13,000			£13,000

Grass's Account

		£			£
10 4 X2	Bank	18,775	1 3 X2	Balance b/d	10,000
10 4 X2	Discounts received	225	31 3 X2	Purchases	9,000
		£19,000			£19,000

Plant's Account

		£			£
10 4 X2	Bank	19,700	1 3 X2	Balance b/d	8,000
10 4 X2	Discounts received	300	31 3 X2	Purchases	12,000
		£20,000			£20,000

Discounts Received Account

		£			£
			10 4 X2	Bush	150
			10 4 X2	Grass	225
30 4 X2	Balance c/d	675	10 4 X2	Plant	300
		£675			£675
			1 5 X2	Balance b/d	675

EXERCISE 4.3   PAGE 35

Arctic's Account

		£			£
31 5 X3	Purchases returns	2,000	1 5 X3	Balance b/d	13,000
31 5 X3	Bank	12,610	31 5 X3	Purchases	10,000
31 5 X3	Discounts received	390			
31 5 X3	Balance c/d	18,000			
		£23,000			£23,000
			1 6 X3	Balance b/d	18,000

Indian's Account

		£			£
31 5 X3	Purchases returns	1,000	1 5 X3	Balance b/d	18,000
31 5 X3	Bank	17,100	31 5 X3	Purchases	15,000
31 5 X3	Discounts received	900			
31 5 X3	Balance c/d	14,000			
		£33,000			£33,000
			1 6 X3	Balance b/d	14,000

Dane's Account

		£			£
1 5 X3	Balance b/d	5,000	31 5 X3	Sales returns	1,500
31 5 X3	Sales	4,000	31 5 X3	Bank	4,500
			31 5 X3	Discounts allowed	500
			31 5 X3	Balance c/d	2,500
		£9,000			£9,000
1 6 X3	Balance b/d	2,500			

Finn's Account

		£				£
1 5 X3	Balance b/d	14,000	31 5 X3	Sales returns		5,000
31 5 X3	Sales	15,000	31 5 X3	Bank		20,000
			31 5 X3	Discounts allowed		700
			31 5 X3	Balance c/d		3,300
		£29,000				£29,000
1 6 X3	Balance b/d	3,300				

Purchases Returns Account

		£			£
			31 5 X3	Arctic	2,000
31 5 X3	Balance c/d	3,000	31 5 X3	Indian	1,000
		£3,000			£3,000
			1 6 X3	Balance b/d	3,000

Sales Returns Account

		£			£
31 5 X3	Dane	1,500			
31 5 X3	Finn	5,000	31 5 X3	Balance c/d	6,500
		£6,500			£6,500
1 6 X3	Balance b/d	6,500			

EXERCISE 4.4   PAGE 35

Discounts Allowed Account

		£		£
31 1 X9	Cash book	25		

Discounts Received Account

		£			£
			31 1 X9	Cash book	12

Sales Account

		£			£
			10 1 X9	Bank	3,385
31 1 X9	Balance c/d	8,257	18 1 X9	Bank	4,872
		£8,257			£8,257
			1 2 X9	Balance b/d	8,257

D Evan's Account

		£			£
1 1 X9	Balance b/d	1,000	29 1 X9	Discounts allowed	25
			29 1 X9	Bank	975
		£1,000			£1,000

Rent Payable Account

		£			£
1 1 X9	Bank	600			

Telephone Account

		£			£
3 1 X9	Bank	115	1 1 X9	Balance b/d	25
			31 1 X9	Balance c/d	90
		£115			£115
1 2 X9	Balance b/d	90			

Electricity Account

		£			£
5 1 X9	Bank	107	1 1 X9	Balance b/d	32
			31 1 X9	Balance c/d	75
		£107			£107
1 2 X9	Balance b/d	75			

Purchases Account

		£			£
9 1 X9	Bank	3,160			
16 1 X9	Bank	2,315	31 1 X9	Balance c/d	5,475
		£5,475			£5,475
1 2 X9	Balance b/d	5,475			

Stationery Account

		£			£
1 1 X9	Balance b/d	236			
11 1 X9	Cash	48			
24 1 X9	Bank	142	31 1 X9	Balance c/d	426
		£426			£426
1 2 X9	Balance b/d	426			

Cleaning Account

		£			£
21 1 X9	Cash	18			

Postage Account

		£			£
23 1 X9	Cash	45			

Salaries Account

		£			£
27 1 X9	Bank	4,540			

F Weare and Son Account

		£			£
30 1 X9	Discounts received	12	1 1 X9	Balance b/d	500
30 1 X9	Bank	488			
		£500			£500

SOLUTIONS TO CHAPTER 5 EXERCISES

EXERCISE 5.1   PAGE 40

INVOICE

ANDERSON AND LITTLEWOOD
22 CASTLE STREET
EDINBURGH EH1 7DU

To   T Woodward Esq
44 Market Cross
DRIFFIELD
North Humberside
YO16 4NL

Invoice No. 66161

Date :

Vat Reg. No. 12345678

Qty	Description	Unit Price £	Total Net £	VAT Rate %	VAT amount £	Total £
100 Reams	A4 Paper	4.00	400.00	10	40.00	440.00
200 Bottles	Correction fluid	0.48	96.00	10	9.60	105.60
150 Boxes	Address labels	0.80	120.00	10	12.00	132.00
1	Four drawer metal Filing cabinet	120.00	120.00	10	12.00	132.00
				TOTAL	73.60	809.60
				Amount due		£883.20

TERMS: Net within 21 days

EXERCISE 5.2   PAGE 40

Part (a)

CREDIT NOTE
ALEXANDER'S SPORTS SUPPLIERS

To :   No. 1234
J Gower and Sons
7 Highwoods Lane   Date :
Norton
                                        Vat Reg. No. 987654321

Qty	Description	Ref.	Unit Price £	Discount per unit %	Total Value £	VAT Rate %	Total amount £
2	Cricket pads	Z92	16.00	25	24.00	10	26.40
1	Table tennis bat	B174	9.60	25	7.20	10	7.92

		Total Value	£34.32

Reasons for Credit :   Faulty goods
Original Invoice No : 927JX   Dated : 9 April 19X8

Part (b)

J GOWER AND SONS
Calculation of expected gross profit

	£	£
Cricket pads (18 pairs) at £16.00 per pair	288.00	
Less : cost of goods (18 x £12.00)	216.00	72.00
Track suits : 10 at £19 each	190.00	
Less : cost of goods (10 x £14.25)	142.50	47.50
Table tennis bats (15 x £9.60)	144.00	
Less : cost of goods (15 x £7.20)	108.00	36.00
Expected gross profit		**£155.50**

EXERCISE 5.3   PAGE 41

A WISEMAN
Purchases Account

		£			£
1 5 X3	A Sellars	200			
5 5 X3	Nicholson	120	31 5 X3	Balance c/d	320
		£320			£320
1 6 X3	Balance b/d	320			

A Sellar's Account

		£			£
22 5 X3	Bank	220	1 5 X3	Purchases	200
			1 5 X3	HM Customs & Excise	20
		£220			£220

Nicholson's Account

		£			£
27 5 X3	Purchases returns	30	5 5 X3	Purchases	120
27 5 X3	HM Customs & Excise	3	5 5 X3	HM Customs & Excise	12
31 5 X3	Balance c/d	99			
		£132			£132
			1 6 X3	Balance b/d	99

Sales Account

		£
	8 5 X3 B Buyers	280

B Buyer's Account

		£			£
8 5 X3	Sales	280	18 5 X3	Sales returns	30
8 5 X3	HM Customs & Excise	28	18 5 X3	HM Customs & Excise	3
			29 5 X3	Bank	275
		£308			£308

HM Customs and Excise Account

		£			£
1 5 X3	A Sellars	20	8 5 X3	B Buyers	28
5 5 X3	Nicholson	12	27 5 X3	Nicholson	3
12 5 X3	Office supplies	22	31 5 X3	Balance c/d	26
18 5 X3	B Buyers	3			
		£57			£57
1 6 X3	Balance b/d	26			

Office Equipment Account

		£		£
12 5 X3	Office supplies	220		

Office Supplies Account

		£			£
			12 5 X3	Office equipment	220
31 5 X3	Balance c/d	242	12 5 X3	HM Customs & Excise	22
		£242			£242
			1 6 X3	Balance b/d	242

Sales Returns Account

		£		£
18 5 X3	B Buyers	30		

Bank Account

		£			£
29 5 X3	B Buyers	275	27 5 X3	A Sellars	220
			31 5 X3	Balance c/d	55
		£275			£275
1 6 X3	Balance b/d	55			

Purchases Returns Account

		£		£
			27 5 X3	Nicholson	30

EXERCISE 5.4   PAGE 41

SPENCER CHAPMAN
Bank Account

		£			£
1 4 X8	Balance b/d	250.00	24 4 X8	I Pike	264.00
18 4 X8	Rents receivable	50.00	30 4 X8	Balance c/d	685.80
20 4 X8	J Cooper	649.80			
		£949.80			£949.80
1 5 X8	Balance b/d	685.80			

Purchases Account

		£		£
1 4 X8	I Pike	240.00		

I Pike Account

		£			£
30 4 X8	Bank	264.00	1 4 X8	Purchases	240.00
			1 4 X8	HM Customs & Excise	24.00
		£264.00			£264.00

HM Customs and Excise Account

		£			£
1 4 X8	I Pike	24.00	3 4 X8	J Cooper	45.00
10 4 X8	J Cooper	7.20	13 4 X8	J Cooper	27.00
15 4 X8	RMF Vehicles Ltd	260.00	30 4 X8	Balance c/d	219.20
		£291.20			£291.20
1 5 X8	Balance b/d	219.20			

Sales Account

		£			£
			3 4 X8	J Cooper	450.00
30 4 X8	Balance c/d	720.00	13 4 X8	J Cooper	270.00
		£720.00			£720.00
			1 5 X8	Balance b/d	720.00

J Cooper's Account

		£			£
3 4 X8	Sales	450.00	10 4 X8	Sales returns	72.00
3 4 X8	HM Customs & Excise	45.00	10 4 X8	HM Customs & Excise	7.20
13 4 X8	Sales	270.00	20 4 X8	Bank	649.80
13 4 X8	HM Customs & Excise	27.00			
		£792.00			£729.00

Sales Returns Account

		£		£
10 4 X8	J Cooper	72.00		

Motor Van Account

		£		£
15 4 X8	RMF Vehicles Ltd	2,600.00		

RMF Vehicles Ltd Account

		£			£
			15 4 X8	Motor van	2,600.00
30 4 X8	Balance c/d	2,860.00	15 4 X8	HM Customs & Excise	260.00
		£2,860.00			£2,860.00
			1 5 X8	Balance b/d	2,860.00

Rents Receivable Account

	£			£
		1 4 X8	Bank	50.00

Capital Account

	£			£
		1 4 X8	Bank	250.00

SOLUTIONS TO CHAPTER 6 EXERCISES

EXERCISE 6.1   PAGE 45

(a)   Reasons for subdividing a ledger.

(1) **Size :**
There may be too many accounts and too many entries within them to include within one ledger.

(2) **Specialisation :**
Subdivision enables different employees to work on and specialise in different types of ledger work.

(3) **Accuracy :**
Greater accuracy can be achieved if the ledger work is subdivided and each section is separately checked and balanced.

(4) **Control :**
It is more difficult for fraud and misappropriation to take place if the whole of the ledger is not readily available.

(5) **Computerisation :**
It is frequently necessary to subdivide the ledger if the detailed work is done using a computer package.

(b)   The ledger may logically be divided into the following sections :

(1) The **Cash Book** (incorporating the cash and bank accounts).

(2) The **Petty Cash Book** (incorporating the petty cash account).

(3) The **Sales Ledger** (incorporating the personal accounts of customers).

(4) The **Purchases Ledger** (incorporating the accounts of individual suppliers).

(5) The **Private Ledger** (incorporating those accounts of the proprietors that are required to be left confidential such as the capital and drawings accounts).

(6) The **General Ledger** (incorporating all of the other accounts not included in other ledgers).

EXERCISE 6.2   PAGE 45

(a)

18 Dec 19X7	ENTRY BANK PLC	18 Dec 19X7
To : A. Brown	QUEEN STREET, EDINBURGH, EH1 1XX 00-00-00	

```
18 Dec 19X7              ENTRY BANK PLC            18 Dec 19X7
To :                     QUEEN STREET, EDINBURGH, EH1 1XX    00-00-00
A. Brown
                         PAY  A. Brown
                         Forty-nine pounds                    £49  00
b/f 198.00               only
This
Cheque 49.00                                              J M England
c/f 149.00                                                J.M.ENGLAND

                         CHEQUE  NO. BRANCH  NO. ACCOUNT  NO.
 00000000                   000000      00 00 00      00000000
```

(b)   The cheque counterfoil would be used to post the £49.00 to the credit of the bank account, and to the debit of A Brown's account.

EXERCISE 6.3   PAGE 46

See the table on the following page.

EXERCISE 6.4   PAGE 46

HENRY YORK
Cash Book

		Discount £	Cash £	Bank £			Discount £	Cash £	Bank £
1 3 X6	Balances b/d		100	5,672	6 3 X6	Wages		39	
4 3 X6	W Abbott			246	11 3 X6	Sundry expenses		73	
8 3 X6	Sales		152		14 3 X6	Purchases			406
10 3 X6	G Smart	29		315	18 3 X6	J Sanders	16		185
26 3 X6	Sales		94		23 3 X6	Office expenses			100
31 3 X6	Cash			45	24 3 X6	Wages		39	
					28 3 X6	Salaries			230
					31 3 X6	Bank		45	
					31 3 X6	Balances c/d		150	5,357
		£29	£346	£6,278			£16	£346	£6,278
1 4 X6	Balances b/d		150	5,357					

Answer to Exercise 6.3

ENTRY BANK PLC   CREDIT

DATE 15 May 19X7
LOMBARD STREET BRANCH
ACCOUNT White and Co.
ACCOUNT NUMBER 765432 1
PAID IN BY X.Y. Zed
00 0000

	£	
NOTES £50	250	00
NOTES £20	40	00
NOTES £10	30	00
NOTES £5		
NOTES/COIN £1	130	00
50P	27	50
20P	4	80
SILVER	2	00
BRONZE	2	00
TOTAL CASH	536	30
CHEQUES	492	33
TOTAL CREDIT £	1028	63

Counterfoil

DATE 15 May X7
ACCOUNT White + Co
A/c NUMBER 765432 1

	£	
NOTES £50	250	00
NOTES £20	40	00
NOTES £10	30	00
NOTES £5		
NOTES/COIN £1	130	00
50P	27	50
20P	4	80
SILVER	2	00
BRONZE	2	00
TOTAL CASH	536	30
CHEQUES	492	33
TOTAL CREDIT £	1028	63

CHEQUES

	£	
R.S. Adams	169	95
T. Bromley	261	14
A. Kent	61	24
TOTAL CARRIED OVERLEAF £	492	33

EXERCISE 6.5   PAGE 47

(a)

PAUL BARCLAY
Cash Book

		Disc. £	Cash £	Bank £			Disc. £	Cash £	Bank £
1 1 X7	Balances b/d		24.86	2,310.38	6 1 X7	Rent payable			42.00
3 1 X7	Sales				13 1 X7	Drawings		35.00	
	Ledger	3.10		124.38	14 1 X7	Bank		53.06	
12 1 X7	Sales		83.20		16 1 X7	Salaries			429.12
14 1 X7	Cash			53.06	19 1 X7	Motor van			2,800.20
18 1 X7	Sales				21 1 X7	Purchases			
	Ledger	17.19		831.15		Ledger	9.36		439.18
24 1 X7	Sales		79.40		26 1 X7	Sundry			
29 1 X7	Cash			75.16		expenses		4.24	
31 1 X7	Balance c/d			324.47	28 1 X7	Bank charges			8.10
					29 1 X7	Bank		75.16	
					31 1 X7	Balance c/d		20.00	
		£20.29	£187.46	£3,718.60			£9.36	£187.46	£3,718.60
1 2 X7	Balance b/d		20.00		1 2 X7	Balance b/d			324.47

(b)

Discounts Allowed Account

		£		£
31 1 X7	Trade creditors	20.29		

Discounts Received Account

		£		£
			31 1 X7 Trade debtors	9.36

EXERCISE 6.6   PAGE 47

GALAXY TRADERS LIMITED
Cash Book

Receipts

		Folio	Discounts £	VAT £	Cash £	Bank £
2 5 X8	Balances b/d				57	216
3 5 X8	Sales	NL		36	276	
4 5 X8	Freda Dexter	SL	6			114
5 5 X8	Sales	NL		54	414	
6 5 X8	Cash	¢				500
			£6	£90	£747	£830
8 7 X8	Balances b/d				69	419

Payments

		Folio	Discounts £	VAT £	Cash £	Bank £
2 5 X8	Insurance	NL				130
3 5 X8	Travelling expenses	NL			17	
3 5 X8	Goodies Ltd	PL	11			99
6 5 X8	Purchases	NL		21	161	
6 5 X8	Wages	NL				182
6 5 X8	Bank	¢			500	
7 5 X8	Balances c/d				69	419
			£11	£21	£747	£830

Notes : NL = Nominal Ledger
SL = Sales Ledger
PL = Purchases Ledger
¢ = Contra

EXERCISE 6.7   PAGE 48

(1)   The purchase of goods on credit from suppliers.

Dr   Purchases account in the Nominal Ledger.
Cr   Creditor's account in the Purchases Ledger.

(2)   The sale of goods on credit.

Dr   Debtor's account in the Sales Ledger.
Cr   Sales account in the Nominal Ledger.

(3)   A cheque received from a credit customer.

Dr   Bank column in the Cash Book.
Cr   Debtor's account in the Sales Ledger.

(4)   A payment to a supplier by cheque for goods previously supplied.

Dr   Creditor's account in the Purchases Ledger.
Cr   Bank column in the Cash Book.

(5)   An allowance to a credit customer upon the return of faulty goods.

Dr   Sales Returns account in the Nominal Ledger.
Cr   Debtor's account in the Sales Ledger.

(6)   Daily cash takings paid into the bank.

Dr   Bank column in the Cash Book.
Cr   Cash column in the Cash Book.

(7)   Monthly salaries paid to employees.

Dr   Salaries account in the Nominal Ledger.
Cr   Bank column in the Cash Book.

SOLUTION TO CHAPTER 7 EXERCISES

EXERCISE 7.1   PAGE 51

(a)

J DARKER
Cash Book

	Cash £	Bank £			Cash £	Bank £
1 12 X7 Balances b/d	370	1,790	3 12 X7 Rates			125
30 12 X7 P Sills		70	18 12 X7 Bank charges			65
31 12 X7 Cash		175	30 12 X7 Kingsley Trust			150
			31 12 X7 Drawings		100	
			31 12 X7 Petty cash		45	
			31 12 X7 Bank		175	
			31 12 X7 Balances c/d		50	1,695
	£370	£2,035			£370	£2,035
1 1 X8 Balances b/d	50	1,695				

(b)   **Bank reconciliation statement at 31 December 19X7**

	£
Balance as per Cash Book at 31 December 19X7	1,695
Add : Cheques drawn, not yet presented	245
	1,940
Less : Cash and cheques not yet credited	390
Balance as per bank pass sheets at 31 December 19X7	£1,550

EXERCISE 7.2   PAGE 52

AMOS JONES

Bank reconciliation statement as at 31 May 19X5

	£	£
Balance as per bank statement at 31 May 19X5		1,960
Less : Cheques drawn, not presented	21	
	44	
	39	104
Correct Cash Book balance at 31 May 19X5		£1,856
Uncorrected Cash Book balance at 31 May 19X5		*1,801
Add : Items not yet debited in the Cash Book :		
Bank interest	76	
Direct debit (from William Smith)	89	
	165	
Less : Standing order - rent	110	55
Correct Cash Book balance at 31 May 19X5		£1,856

*obtained by deduction

EXERCISE 7.3 PAGE 52
T SMALLPIECE

(a) (i) 1 June 19X6

T Smallpiece has arranged with his bank for £100 to be paid to a creditor. This saves Smallpiece from having to remember to write out a cheque and send it directly to the creditor. However he must remember to credit the payment in his Cash Book.

(ii) 20 June 19X6

T Main has arranged to pay an amount to Smallpiece (on 20 June 19X6 the amount was £180) through the banking system without him having to send a cheque directly to Smallpiece. Smallpiece must remember to enter the amount received as a debit in his Cash Book.

(iii) 30 June 19X6

The bank has charged Smallpiece £30 for services rendered. It has claimed this amount by taking it directly out of his bank account. Smallpiece must remember to credit his Cash Book with this amount.

(b) These are cheques drawn and not presented, that is, the bank has not had time (or the cheques have not yet been paid into the bank) to put them through the bank's books of account.

(c) The bank has probably not had time to put this through its books of account as at 30 June 19X6.

EXERCISE 7.4 PAGE 53
S SIMPSON
Bank reconciliation statement at 31 January 19X4

	£	£
Balance as per Cash Book		203.35
Add: Adjustment for Cash Book error -		
31 January sales debited in Cash Book as £210.00		
instead of £230.00		20.00
		223.35
Less: Bank charges	15.40	
Standing order	12.00	27.40
Amended Cash Book balance at 31 January 19X4		**£195.95**
Balance as per bank statement		1,012.09
Add: Bank lodgement not yet entered	230.00	
Standing order debited in error, now cancelled	44.00	274.00
		1,286.09
Less: Cheques drawn, not presented		
Gray's machines Ltd	645.10	
P Swann	124.64	
Wages	320.40	1,090.14
Balance as per amended Cash Book balance at 31 January 19X4		**£195.95**

Bank reconciliation statement at 1 January 19X4

	£
Balance as per bank statement	1,468.21
Add : Receipt not yet entered	100.00
	1,568.21
Less : Cheque drawn not presented (145686)	60.50
Balance as per the Cash Book at 1 January 19X4	£1,507.71

SOLUTIONS TO CHAPTER 8 EXERCISES

EXERCISE 8.1   PAGE 57

A TRADER

(a)   The Petty Cash Imprest System is an attempt to control the total amount of expenditure paid out of cash. A relatively small and fixed amount of cash (often known as the float) is transferred to the petty cash account from the main bank/cash account. Small items of expenditure may be paid for out of petty cash. Periodically, the total amount of petty cash expenditure is assessed, and an amount equal to that expenditure will be transferred from the main bank/cash account. Thus the float is restored to its original level.

By limiting the total amount of expenditure to a fixed and small amount, some control is exercised over goods and services paid for out of cash, large items being paid out of the bank account, where more control can be exercised.

(b) and (c)

The solution to these two parts is on the following page.

EXERCISE 8.2   PAGE 58

(a) and (b)

The solution to these two parts is on the following pages.

EXERCISE 8.3   PAGE 59

(a) (b) (c)

The solution to these three parts is on the following pages.

(d)   The totals of each analysis column will be debited to the respective accounts in the Nominal Ledger.

EXERCISE 8.1

(b)

Receipts	Date	Details	Voucher No.	Total Payment	Stat'y	Postage	Travelling expenses	Sundry expenses	Ledger accounts
£				£	£	£	£	£	£
6.40	1 5 X5	Balance b/d							
43.60	1 5 X5	Bank							
	3 5 X5	Stationery		5.20	5.20				
	5 5 X5	Carriage in		4.10					4.10
	8 5 X5	Stamps		4.50		4.50			
	11 5 X5	Creditors		8.50					8.50
	14 5 X5	Stationery		2.80	2.80				
	17 5 X5	Cleaning		7.00				7.00	
	20 5 X5	Charity donation		3.00				3.00	
	24 5 X5	Taxi		2.70			2.70		
	28 5 X5	Stamps		3.60		3.60			
	30 5 X5	Cleaning		6.00				6.00	
67.40	31 5 X5	Bank							
	31 5 X5	Balance c/d		70.00					
£117.40				£117.40	£8.00	£8.10	£2.70	£16.00	£12.60
70.00	1 6 X5	Balance b/d							

(c) Stationery, postage, travelling and sundry expenses and carriage inwards will be posted to accounts in the Nominal Ledger. The £8.50 will be debited to the creditor's account in the Creditor's Ledger.

EXERCISE 8.2

(a)

A MOBBS
Petty Cash Book

Receipts	Date	Details	Voucher No.	Total Payment	Travelling expenses	Cleaning	Postages & stationery	Ledger accounts
£				£	£	£	£	£
25.75	1 11 X7	Balance b/d						
24.25	2 11 X7	Bank						
	4 11 X7	Stationery	687	4.25			4.25	
	4 11 X7	P Sills	688	5.00				5.00
	5 11 X7	Office cleaner	689	10.00		10.00		
	5 11 X7	A Brown	690	5.45	5.45			
	7 11 X7	Stamps & string	691	7.45			7.45	
	7 11 X7	Balance c/d		17.85				
£50.00				£50.00	£5.45	£10.00	£11.70	£5.00
17.85	8 11 X7	Balance b/d						

(b)

Bank Cash Book

Date	Details	Discount Allowed	Bank	Date	Details	Discount Received	Bank
		£	£			£	£
1 11 X7	Balance b/d		2104.55	2 11 X7	Petty cash		24.25
4 11 X7	J Sanders	10.55	111.00	2 11 X7	J Tearle		50.00
4 11 X7	M Marchand	6.00	54.00	4 11 X7	J Darker	5.50	90.00
5 11 X7	M Marchand	6.60	59.40	7 11 X7	Rent		120.00
5 11 X7	C Ford	0.50	4.50	7 11 X7	Drawings		50.00
5 11 X7	P Woodbine	14.00	126.00	7 11 X7	Motor expenses	24.50	45.00
				7 11 X7	S Connor		245.00
				7 11 X7	Balance c/d		1835.20
		£37.65	£2459.45			£30.00	£2459.45
8 11 X7	Balance b/d		1835.20				

EXERCISE 8.3

(a), (b) and (c).

JOCKFIELD LTD
Petty Cash Book

Receipts £	Date	Voucher No.	Details	Total Payment £	Cleaning £	Motor expenses £	Postage £	Stat'y £	Travelling expenses £
300	1 5 X2								
	2 5 X2		Postage	18			18		
	3 5 X2		Travelling	12					12
	4 5 X2		Cleaning	15	15				
	7 5 X2		Petrol	22		22			
	8 5 X2		Travelling	25					25
	9 5 X2		Stationery	17				17	
	11 5 X2		Cleaning	18	18				
	14 5 X2		Postage	5			5		
	15 5 X2		Travelling	8					8
	18 5 X2		Stationery	9				9	
	18 5 X2		Cleaning	23	23				
	20 5 X2		Postage	13			13		
	24 5 X2		Van service	43		43			
	26 5 X2		Petrol	18		18			
	27 5 X2		Cleaning	21	21				
	29 5 X2		Postage	5			5		
	30 5 X2		Petrol	14		14			
286	31 5 X2		Cash						
	31 5 X2		Balance c/d	300					
£586				£586	£77	£97	£41	£26	£45
300	1 6 X2		Balance b/d						

SOLUTIONS TO CHAPTER 9 EXERCISES

EXERCISE 9.1   PAGE 64

A TRADER

(1) The purchase of raw materials on credit from suppliers.

Originating documents :   Purchase Invoices received
Book of original entry :   Purchases Day Book
Double-entry system :
Dr   Purchases account in the Nominal Ledger with the Purchases Day Book total.
Cr   Each individual creditor's account in the Purchase Ledger.

(2) Allowances received from suppliers upon return of faulty raw materials.

Originating documents :   Credit notes supplied
Book of original entry :   Purchases Returns Day Book
Double-entry system :
Dr   Each individual creditor's account in the Purchase Ledger.
Cr   Purchases returns account in the Nominal Ledger with the Purchases Returns Day Book total.

(3) Wages and salaries paid to employees.

Originating documents :   Wage slips in the Wages Book
Book of original entry :   Cash Book
Double-entry system :
Dr   Wages and Salaries account in the Nominal Ledger.
Cr   Bank column in the Cash Book.

(4) Credit cash sales.

Originating documents :   Copy vouchers of credit card sales
Book of original entry :   Cash Book
Double-entry system :
Dr   Credit card company's account in the Sales Ledger, or the Cash column in the Cash Book.
Cr   Sales account in the Nominal Ledger.

EXERCISE 9.2   PAGE 65

(a)

MODRIX LTD
Purchases Day Book

Date	Supplier	Invoice No.	Purchases Ledger Folio No.	Net £	VAT £	Gross £
23 11 X7	Glixit plc	GL 788		440.00	66.00	506.00
24 11 X7	Moblin Ltd	899339		100.00	15.00	115.00
25 11 X7	S & G Gates	G1101		630.00	94.50	724.50
				£1,170.00	£175.50	£1,345.50

Purchases Returns Day Book

Date	Supplier	Debit Note No.	Purchases Ledger Folio No.	Net £	VAT £	Gross £
25 11 X7	Moblin Ltd	D56		100.00	15.00	115.00
26 11 X7	S & G Gates	D57		210.00	31.50	241.50
				£310.00	£46.50	£356.50

(b) **Purchases Day Book**

Dr Purchases account in the Nominal Ledger with £1,170.00.
Dr HM Customs and Excise account in the Nominal Ledger with £175.50.
Cr Each supplier's account in the Purchases Ledger with the GROSS amount purchased from each supplier as listed in the Purchases Day Book.

Purchases Returns Day Book

Dr Each supplier's account in the Purchases Ledger with the GROSS amount purchased from each supplier as listed in the Purchases Returns Day Book.
Cr Purchases returns account in the Nominal Ledger with £310.00.
Cr HM Customs and Excise account in the Nominal Ledger with £46.50.

EXERCISE 9.3   **PAGE 65**

PATEL
Sales Day Book

Date	Customer	Invoice No.	Sales Ledger Folio No.	Net £	VAT £	Gross £
2 3 X3	Hatt	1234		200	30	230
10 3 X3	Coates	1235		1,000	150	1,150
12 3 X3	Gloves	1236		100	15	115
20 3 X3	Scarfe	1237		300	45	345
				£1,600	£240	£1,840

Sales Returns Day Book

Date	Customer	Credit Note No.	Sales Ledger Folio No.	Net £	VAT £	Gross £
25 3 X3	Coates			200	30	230
25 3 X3	Scarfe			100	15	115
				£300	£45	£345

EXERCISE 9.4   PAGE 66

(a)

C BERRY
Purchases Day Book

Date	Supplier	Purchases Ledger Folio No.	Total £	Kitchen Hardware £	Elec. £	Garden £
4 6 X6	Grofast Seeds Ltd		60			60
6 6 X6	E Gaze		192	192		
16 6 X6	Light & Shade Ltd		350		350	
20 6 X6	E Gaze		225	200		25
26 6 X6	Lighting Wire Co.		108		108	
29 6 X6	The Rich Loam Co.		360			360
			£1,295	£392	£458	£445

(b)

Purchases Account : Kitchen Hardware

		FO	£			FO	£
30 6 X6	Purchases Day Book	PD?	392				

Purchases Account : Electrical

		FO	£			FO	£
30 6 X6	Purchases Day Book	PD?	458				

Purchases Account : Garden

		FO	£			FO	£
30 6 X6	Purchases Day Book	PD?	445				

Grofast Seeds Ltd Account

	FO	£			FO	£
			4 6 X6	Purchases : Garden	PD?	60

E Gaze Account

	FO	£			FO	£
			6 6 X6	Purchases : Kitchen H'ware	PD?	192
			20 6 X6	Purchases : Kitchen H'ware and Garden	PD?	225

Light and Shade Ltd Account

	FO	£			FO	£
			16 6 X6	Purchases : Electrical	PD?	350

Lightning Wire Company Account

	FO	£			FO	£
			26 6 X6	Purchases : Electrical	PD?	108

The Rich Loam Company Account

	FO	£			FO	£
			29 6 X6	Purchases : Garden	PD?	360

EXERCISE 9.5 PAGE 66

REBECCA BROWN
Bank Account

		£			£
1 2 X8	Balance b/d	5,000	1 2 X8 Rent and Rates		500
5 2 X8	T Swallow	1,019	1 2 X8 Insurance		100
			15 2 X8 Wages		125
			22 2 X8 P Shaw		242
			29 2 X8 Balance c/d		5,052
		£6,019			£6,019
1 3 X8	Balance b/d	5,052			

R Wren Account

		£			£
			1 2 X8 Balance b/d		300
29 2 X8	Balance c/d	476	1 2 X8 Purchases Day Book		176
		£476			£476
			1 3 X8 Balance b/d		476

P Shaw Account

		£			£
22 2 X8	Bank	242	1 2 X8 Balance b/d		242
29 2 X8	Balance c/d	748	16 2 X8 Purchases Day Book		748
		£990			£990
			1 3 X8 Balance b/d		748

T Swallow Account

		£			£
1 2 X8	Balance b/d	1,019	5 2 X8 Bank		1,019
3 2 X8	Sales Day Book	330			
18 2 X8	Sales Day Book	561	29 2 X8 Balance c/d		891
		£1,910			£1,910
1 3 X8	Balance b/d	891			

L Soames Account

		£			£
1 2 X8	Balance b/d	539			
29 2 X8	Sales Day Book	88	29 2 X8	Balance c/d	627
		£627			£627
1 3 X8	Balance b/d	627			

Rent and Rates Account

		£			£
1 2 X8	Bank	500			

Insurance Account

		£			£
1 2 X8	Bank	100			

Wages Account

		£			£
15 2 X8	Bank	125			

Purchases Account

		£			£
29 2 X8	Purchases Day Book	924	29 2 X8	HM Customs & Excise	84
			29 2 X8	Balance c/d	840
		£924			£924
1 3 X8	Balance b/d	840			

Sales Account

		£			£
29 2 X8	HM Customs & Excise	89	29 2 X8	Sales Day Book	979
29 2 X8	Balance c/d	890			
		£979			£979
			1 3 X8	Balance b/d	890

HM Customs and Excise Account

		£			£
29 2 X8	Purchases	84	29 2 X8	Sales	89
29 2 X8	Balance c/d	5			
		£89			£89
			1 3 X8	Balance b/d	5

SOLUTION TO CHAPTER 10 EXERCISES

EXERCISE 10.1   PAGE 71

BRENDA DEAN
Journal

			Dr £	Cr £
31 1 X6	Shop Equipment Account	Dr	180	
	To : Bank Account			150
	Shop Equipment Disposal Account			30

Being purchase of new cash register and the exchange of an old one at an agreed amount of £30.

			Dr £	Cr £
31 1 X6	Profit and Loss Account	Dr	20	
	To : Shop Equipment Disposal Account			20

Being the loss on the disposal of old shop equipment now written off to the profit and loss account.

			Dr £	Cr £
31 1 X6	John Clements Account	Dr	27	
	To : Purchases Account			27

Being correction of posting caused by a transpositional error (£163-£136).

			Dr £	Cr £
31 1 X6	Office Fitments Account	Dr	45	
	To : Wages Account			45

Being transfer of entry debited in error to the wages account.

			Dr £	Cr £
31 1 X6	Drawings Account	Dr	52	
	To : Purchases Account			52

Being amount of goods withdrawn by Brenda Dean for personal use.

EXERCISE 10.2   PAGE 71

D EVANS
Journal

			Dr £	Cr £
3 8 X5	Fixtures and Fittings Account	Dr	2,100	
	To : Woodwork Ltd Account			2,100

Being special fixtures and fittings bought on credit.

3 8 X5	Fixtures and Fittings Account	Dr	150	
	To : Mason's Account			150
	Being cost of installing fixtures and fittings owed to Mason.			

7 8 X5	Bank Account	Dr	38	
	Bad Debts Account	Dr	134	
	To : P G Cox's Account			172
	Being amount received from P G Cox as a first and final dividend, the balance being written off as a bad debt as unlikely to be recovered.			

14 8 X5	Storage Shed Account	Dr	570	
	To : Purchases Account			410
	Wages Account			160
	Being amounts incorrectly charged to the wrong accounts, now corrected (part of the cost of extending a storage shed).			

21 8 X5	Discounts Allowed Account	Dr	120	
	To : Discounts Received Account			120
	Being transfer of amount credited to the wrong account.			

30 8 X5	Car Account	Dr	5,300	
	To : Bank Account			2,300
	Car Disposal Account			3,000
	Being purchase of a new car and the trade-in in part exchange for an old car.			

30 8 X5	Car Disposal Account	Dr	3,250	
	To : Car Account			3,250
	Being transfer of the balance on the old car account in part exchange for the new one.			

30 8 X5	Profit and Loss Account	Dr	250	
	To : Car Disposal Account			250
	Being loss on disposal of car in part exchange for a new one now written off to the profit and loss account.			

EXERCISE 10.3   PAGE 72

TINKER
Journal

		Dr £	Cr £
3 8 X1	Capital Account Dr	8,000	
	To: Bank Account		8,000
	Being reversal and subsequent correction of original entry (£4,000) regarding Tinker's personal drawings for the year.		
	Bank Charges Account Dr	50	
	To: Bank Account		50
	Being omission of bank charges for the year.		
	Scott's Account Dr	250	
	To: Sales Account		250
	Being credit sales omitted.		
	Buck's Account Dr	1,500	
	To: Black's Account		1,500
	Being credit purchases incorrectly posted to the wrong account.		
	Wages Account Dr	20	
	To: Rent Received Account		20
	Being correction of compensating undercasts in both accounts.		
	Leigh's Sales Ledger Account Dr	90	
	To: Leigh's Purchase Ledger Account		90
	Being incorrect contra entry in both accounts.		

EXERCISE 10.4   PAGE 72

LION SPORTS CLUB
Journal

		Dr £	Cr £
31 1 X2	High's Account Dr	10	
	To: Hill's Account		10
	Being error of **commission**, subscription credited in error to the wrong personal account.		
	Bar Equipment Account Dr	250	
	To: Bar Purchases Account		250
	Being error of **principle**, bar purchases debited to a fixed asset account.		

Subscription Account	Dr	180	
To: Wages Account			180

Being **compensating** error, now corrected in both accounts.

Bank Account	Dr	100	
To: Rent Received Account			100

Being complete **reversal of entry**, now corrected in both accounts, £50 being the original entry now entered.

Cash Account	Dr	100	
To: Donations Account			100

Being error of **original entry**, now entered.

Bar Purchases	Dr	75	
To: Creditors Account			75

Being error of **omission**, now agreed as being correct.

SOLUTIONS TO CHAPTER 11 EXERCISES

EXERCISE 11.1   PAGE 77

JOHN KENLEY
L Stamper Account

		£			£
1 11 X6	Balance b/d	360	23 11 X6	Bills receivable (Bill No. 4)	360
23 2 X7	Bills receivable (Bill No. 4)	360			
23 2 X7	Bank : costs thereon	10	23 2 X7	Balance c/d	370
		£730			£730
24 2 X7	Balance b/d	370			

F Brandon Account

		£			£
1 11 X6	Balance b/d	283	5 11 X6	Bills receivable (Bill No. 2)	283
		£283			£283

K Timmins Account

		£			£
2 11 X6	Bills payable (Bill No. 1)	164	1 11 X6	Balance b/d	164
		£164			£164

S Quick Account

		£			£
16 11 X6	Bills payable (Bill No. 3)	340	1 11 X6	Balance b/d	357
16 11 X6	Discounts received	17			
		£357			£357

Bills Receivable Account

		£			£
5 11 X6	F Brandon (Bill No. 2)	283	9 11 X6	Bank (Bill No. 2)	271
23 11 X6	L Stamper (Bill No. 4)	360	9 11 X6	Discounting charges	12
			23 2 X7	L Stamper (Bill No. 4)	360
		£643			£643

Bills Payable Account

		£			£
16 12 X6	Bank (Bill No. 3)	340	2 11 X6	K Timmins (Bill No. 1)	164
2 1 X7	Bank (Bill No. 1)	164	16 11 X6	S Quick (Bill No. 3)	340
		£504			£504

Bank Account

		£			£
9 11 X6	Bills receivable (Bill No. 2)	271	16 12 X6	Bills payable (Bill No. 3)	340
			12 1 X7	Bills payable (Bill No. 1)	164
			23 2 X7	L Stamper (Bill No. 4 - costs of discounting)	10
23 2 X7	Balance c/d	243			
		£514			£514
			24 2 X7	Balance b/d	243

EXERCISE 11.2   PAGE 78

A AND B

(a)

A's LEDGER
Bills Payable Account

		£			£
10 5 X5	B's account (bill dishonoured)	1,600	10 2 X5	B's account	1,600
12 5 X5	Balance c/d	1,557	12 5 X5	B's account	1,557
		£3,157			£3,157
			13 5 X5	Balance b/d	1,557

B's Account

		£			£
10 2 X5	Bills payable	1,600	1 2 X5	Purchases	1,600
20 2 X5	Purchases returns	60	1 5 X5	Bills payable (dishonoured)	1,600
2 5 X5	Bills payable	1,557	12 5 X5	Noting charge	5
			12 5 X5	Interest payable	12
		£3,217			£3,217

(b)

B's LEDGER
Bills Receivable Account

		£			£
10 2 X5	A's account	1,600	10 3 X5	Bank	1,600
12 2 X5	A's account	1,557	12 5 X5	Balance c/d	1,557
		£3,157			£3,157
13 5 X5	Balance b/d	1,557			

Solutions to CHAPTER 11 Exercises

A's Account

		£			£
1 2 X5	Sales	1,600	10 2 X5	Bills receivable	1,600
10 5 X5	Bank (bill dishonoured)	1,600	20 2 X5	Sales returns	60
10 5 X5	Bank (noting charge)	5	12 5 X5	Bills receivable	1,557
12 5 X5	Interest receivable	12			
		£3,217			£3,217

EXERCISE 11.3   PAGE 78

RAMSDEN BROTHERS
UK Debtors Account

		£			£
1 1 X7	Balance b/d	83,264	31 1 X7	Bank	61,310
31 1 X7	Sales	46,212	31 1 X7	Balance c/d	68,166
		£129,476			£129,476
1 2 X7	Balance b/d	68,166			

Bills Receivable Account

		£			£
1 1 X7	Balance b/d	131,800	26 1 X7	Bank (A)	30,000
15 1 X7	Export sales : C	24,690	31 1 X7	Bank (D)	13,800
31 1 X7	Export sales : A	11,300			
	: E	12,600			
	: F	18,100	31 1 X7	Balance c/d	154,690
		£198,490			£198,490
1 2 X7	Balance b/d	154,690			

Bills Payable Account

		£			£
29 1 X7	Bank	27,700	1 1 X7	Balance b/d	146,300
31 1 X7	Balance c/d	156,600	31 1 X7	A M Frankfurt	38,000
		£184,300			£184,300
			1 2 X7	Balance b/d	156,600

Bank Account

		£			£
1 1 X7	Balance b/d	11,285	15 1 X7	Bills dishonoured (C)	24,000
26 1 X7	Bills receivable (A)	30,000	29 1 X7	Bills payable	
31 1 X7	Debtors	61,310		(Lesch - Zurich)	27,700
31 1 X7	Bills receivable (D)	13,800	31 1 X7	Business expenses	31,260
			31 1 X7	Balance c/d	33,435
		£116,395			£116,395
1 2 X7	Balance b/d	33,435			

SOLUTIONS TO CHAPTER 12 EXERCISES

EXERCISE 12.1   PAGE 84

J ALMEIDA
C Blade's Account

		£			£
9 10 X7	Purchases returns	25	1 10 X7	Balance b/d	175
15 10 X7	Bank	145	20 10 X7	Purchases	140
15 10 X7	Discounts received	5			
31 10 X7	Balance c/d	140			
		£315			£315
			1 11 X7	Balance b/d	140

J Duff's Account

		£			£
3 10 X7	Purchases returns	40	1 10 X7	Balance b/d	130
5 10 X7	Bank	81	22 10 X7	Purchases	155
5 10 X7	Discounts received	9			
31 10 X7	Balance c/d	155			
		£285			£285
			1 11 X7	Balance b/d	155

L Stone's Account

		£			£
24 10 X7	Bank	75	1 10 X7	Balance b/d	75
31 10 X7	Balance c/d	150	14 10 X7	Purchases	90
			26 10 X7	Purchases	60
		£225			£225
			1 11 X7	Balance b/d	150

Purchases Ledger Control Account

		£			£
1 10 X7	Balances b/d (£175+£130+£75)	380	31 10 X7	Purchases returns (£40+£25)	65
31 10 X7	Purchases (£90+£155+£60+£140)	445	31 10 X7	Bank (£81+£145+£75)	301
			31 10 X7	Discounts received (£9+£5)	14
			31 10 X7	Balances c/d	445
		£825			£825
1 11 X7	Balances b/d (£140+£155+£150)	445			

EXERCISE 12.2 PAGE 85

A2Z COMPANY
Creditors Control Account

		£			£
1 12 X7	Balances b/d	115,900	1 12 X7	Balances b/d	330
31 12 X7	Purchases	282,700	31 12 X7	Bank	238,600
			31 12 X7	Purchases returns	4,500
			31 12 X7	Discounts received	5,900
			31 12 X7	Set off to Debtors Ledger	3,400
31 12 X7	Balances c/d	420	31 12 X7	Balances c/d	146,290
		£399,020			£399,020
1 1 X8	Balances b/d	146,290	1 1 X8	Balances b/d	420

Debtors Control Account

		£			£
1 12 X7	Balances b/d	2,800	1 12 X7	Balances b/d	202,100
31 12 X7	Bank	449,500	31 12 X7	Sales	534,000
31 12 X7	Bad debts	1,900	31 12 X7	Bank (dishonoured cheque)	500
31 12 X7	Sales returns	5,800	31 12 X7	Balances c/d	2,100
31 12 X7	Discounts allowed	9,500			
31 12 X7	Set off from Creditors Ledger	3,400			
31 12 X7	Balances c/d	265,800			
		£738,700			£738,700
1 1 X8	Balances b/d	2,100	1 1 X8	Balances b/d	265,800

EXERCISE 12.3 PAGE 85

(a)

J MASON
Purchases Ledger Control Account

		£			£
1 8 X5	Balances b/d	5,185	1 8 X5	Balances b/d	212
31 8 X5	Purchases	19,283	31 8 X5	Purchases returns	615
31 8 X5	Balances c/d	143	31 8 X5	Discounts received	241
			31 8 X5	Bank	16,824
			31 8 X5	Set off to Debtors Ledger	260
			31 8 X5	Balances c/d	6,459
		£24,611			£24,611
1 9 X5	Balances b/d	6,459	1 9 X5	Balances b/d	143

Sales Ledger Control Account

		£			£
1 8 X5	Balances b/d	510	1 8 X5	Balances b/d	9,364
31 8 X5	Discounts allowed	356	31 8 X5	Legal expenses	112
31 8 X5	Bad debts	237	31 8 X5	Sales	27,440
31 8 X5	Bank	24,607	31 8 X5	Balances c/d	376
31 8 X5	Set off from Purchases Ledger	260			
31 8 X5	Sales returns	292			
31 8 X5	Balances c/d	11,030			
		£37,292			£37,292
1 9 X5	Balances b/d	376	1 9 X5	Balances b/d	11,030

(b) **Balance sheet (extracts) at 31 August 19X5**

	£
Current assets	
Trade debtors	11,030
Other debtors	143
Current liabilities	
Trade creditors	6,459
Other creditors	376

EXERCISE 12.4   PAGE 86

(a)

LONER LIMITED
Sales Ledger Control Account

		£			£
1 4 X3	Balances b/d	748	1 4 X3	Balances b/d	25,684
31 3 X4	Sales returns	1,420	31 3 X4	Sales	194,710
31 3 X4	Discounts allowed	6,710	31 3 X4	Bank (cheques dishonoured)	304
31 3 X4	Bank	188,176			
31 3 X4	Balances c/d	24,176	31 3 X4	Balances c/d	532
		£221,230			£221,230
1 4 X4	Balances b/d	532	1 4 X4	Balances b/d	24,176

(b) Computation of the amount arising from the sales ledger to be shown as trade debtors in the balance sheet as at 31 March 19X4.

31 3 X4	£	£
Sales ledger control account debit balance (before correction of errors)		24,176
Add : Correction of sales day book undercast November 19X3		1,400
Cash sales September 19X3 included in payments received from trade debtors		5,600
		31,176

		£	£
Less :	Bad debt written off - Peter Smith	160	
	Goods returned to suppliers included in credit sales	5,000	
	Set off of debt due from G Kelly against amount due to him in the purchases ledger	300	5,460
	Trade debtors as at 31 March 19X4 (ex sales ledger)		£25,716

EXERCISE 12.5   PAGE 87

(a)

APRIL SHOWERS
Sales Ledger Control Account

	£			£
31 10 X3 Omission of discounts allowed	100	31 10 X3	Balances as originally extracted	12,550
31 10 X3 Contra item with Purchase Ledger	400	31 10 X3	Omission of sales	850
31 10 X3 Bad debt	500	31 10 X3	Cheque dishonoured	300
31 10 X3 Returns Inwards omitted	200			
31 10 X3 Balances c/d	12,500			
	£13,700			£13,700

(b) **Sales Ledger Account : List of Balances as at 31 October 19X3**

	£	£
Total as originally extracted		12,802
Add : **the following adjustments** -		
Balance omitted	300	
Undercasting of balance	200	500
		13,302
Less : **the following adjustments** -		
Cash received : correction of transposition error	180	
Cash received incorrectly debited (x2)	500	
Discounts received entered in Bell's Account	50	
Error in crediting cash received (£80-£8)	72	802
Amended Sales Ledger Account balances as at 31 October 19X3		£12,500

EXERCISE 12.6   PAGE 88

(a)

ROXY LIMITED
Purchases Ledger Control Account

		£			£
31 5 X3	Balance b/d	20,000	31 5 X3	Bank	232,000
31 5 X3	Purchases	240,000	31 5 X3	Discounts received	6,000
			31 5 X3	Balances c/d	22,000
		£260,000			£260,000
1 6 X3	Balances b/d	22,000			

435

(b)   **Purchase Ledger Balances : Amendment to the list of Balances as at 31 May 19X3**

		£	£
Total balances as originally extracted			23,800
Add : **the following adjustments -**			
Purchases omitted from Collin's Account		1,500	
Undercast of Brown's Account		1,000	
Ashton's balance omitted		2,000	
Discounts Allowed debited to Crosby's Account		350	4,850
			28,650
Less : **the following adjustments -**			
Discounts Received for January 19X3 not entered		500	
Cash payment of £200 credited to Almond's			
Account instead of being debited (x2)		400	
Omission of bank payment to Martin		750	
Motor car incorrectly entered in Gill's Account		5,000	6,650
Corrected Total Balances as at 31 May 19X3			**£22,000**

SOLUTIONS TO CHAPTER 13 EXERCISES

EXERCISE 13.1   PAGE 96
JOCK

(i)   First-in, first-out (FIFO)

Calculation of Closing Stock Quantity :

	Litres
Opening stock	100
Total purchases for the month (200+300+50+100)	650
	750
Less : total issues for the month (80+70+250+200)	600
Closing stock quantity	150

	£
Valued at the latest prices :	
100 @ £3.50 per litre	350
50 @ £4.00 per litre	200
Closing Stock Value	**£550**

(ii)   Last-in, first-out (LIFO)

Date 19X2	PURCHASES			ISSUES			BALANCE	
	Quantity Litres	Price £	Value £	Quantity Litres	Price £	Value £	Quantity Litres	Value £
1 10							100	200
4 10				80	2.00	160	20	40
7 10	200	2.50	500				220	540
11 10				70	2.50	175	150	365
14 10	300	3.00	900				450	1,265
18 10				250	3.00	750	200	515
21 10	50	4.00	200				250	715
25 10				200	50 @ 4.00] 50 @ 3.00] 100 @ 2.50]	600	50	115
28 10	100	3.50	350				150	465

Closing Stock Value £465

(iii)   Weighted Average

Date 19X2	PURCHASES			ISSUES			BALANCE	
	Quantity Litres	Price £	Value £	Quantity Litres	Price £	Value £	Quantity Litres	Value £
1 10							100	200
4 10				80	2.00	160	20	40
7 10	200	2.50	500				220	540
11 10				70	2.45	172	150	368
14 10	300	3.00	900				450	1,268
18 10				250	2.82	705	200	563
21 10	50	4.00	200				250	763
25 10				200	3.05	610	50	153
28 10	100	3.50	350				150	503

Closing Stock Value £503

EXERCISE 13.2   PAGE 97

JOSEPH SHIPLEY
Calculation of the cost of goods destroyed in a fire

	£	£
Opening stock		1,344
Purchases	1,960	
Less : goods in transit	70	1,890
		3,234
Less : sales	2,775	
Deduct : gross profit on sales (20% of sales)	555	2,220
		1,014
Less : goods not destroyed		285
Cost price of goods destroyed		£729

EXERCISE 13.3   PAGE 97

(a)   **Closing Stock Valuation**

(i)   **FIFO** 100 kg x £5.00   500
            50 kg x £4.50   225

                                £725

(ii)   **LIFO** 50 kg x £5.00   250
            100 kg x £3.00   300

                                550

(iii)   **Simple Average**

Receipts	Price per kg
	£
1 1 X3	3.00
15 1 X3	4.00
17 2 X3	4.50
16 3 X3	5.00

                4) 16.50 = 4.125 x 150 kg   £619

(iv)   **Periodic Weighted Average**

Receipts	Quantity	Value
	kg	£
1 1 X3	100	300
15 1 X3	200	800
17 2 X3	400	1,800
16 3 X3	100	500
	800	) 3,400

                800) 3,400 = 4.25 x 150 kg   £638

(v) **Weighted Average**

Stock at	Quantity kg	Value £	Average Price £
15 1 X3	300	1,100	3.67
29 1 X3	150	550	3.67
17 2 X3	550	2,350	4.27
5 3 X3	100	428	4.27
16 3 X3	200	928	4.64
31 3 X3	150	696	4.64

Therefore closing stock value is £696

(b) By adopting FIFO during an inflationary period (i.e. using the oldest prices first), the closing stock will have a higher value than by using LIFO (a method whereby the latest prices are used to charge issues of material to production).

The higher the value placed on closing stock, the greater the gross profit (and vice versa).

During the next accounting period, the effect should correct itself, however, because the opening stock under FIFO will be higher than under LIFO. As a result, the cost of goods sold will be correspondingly higher.

LIFO is not an acceptable method of valuing stock in the United Kingdom for taxation purposes, probably because it results in a smaller amount of tax revenue. As tax is computed on the basis of annual profit, long-term corrections of profit are not considered relevant for LIFO to be acceptable. LIFO is not a popular method, therefore, for pricing the issue of stores to production and for valuing closing stock.

EXERCISE 13.4   PAGE 97

(a) Total charge to production
See Wkg. 1 (Issues column £100+700+600+2,400+4,500)   £8,300

(b) Closing stock value using LIFO at 31 October 19X4 (Wkg. 2)   £1,300

(c) Issue price per kilogram on 28 October 19X4 using the continuous weighted average method (Wkg. 3)   £3.47 per kilogram

(d) Issue price per kilogram during October 19X4 using the periodic weighted average method :

$$\frac{\text{Total value of receipts during October}}{\text{Total quantity purchased during October}}$$

$$= \frac{2,100 + 2,000 + 1,600 + 4,400}{700 + 400 + 800 + 1,100}$$

$$= \frac{10,100}{3,000}$$

$$= \text{£3.37 per kilogram}$$

439

Workings

DATE	RECEIPTS			ISSUES			BALANCE	
19X4	Quantity kg.	Price £	Value £	Quantity kg.	Price £	Value £	Quantity kg.	Value £
1. FIFO								
1.10							200	200
1.10				100	1.00	100	100	100
5.10	700	3.00	2,100				800	2,200
8.10				300	100@£1			
					200@£3	700	500	1,500
12.10	400	5.00	2,000				900	3,500
15.10				200	3.00	600	700	2,900
19.10	800	2.00	1,600				1,500	4,500
22.10				600	300@£3			
					300@£5	2,400	900	2,100
26.10	1,100	4.00	4,400				2,000	6,500
29.10				1,500	100@£5			
					800@£2			
					600@£4	4,500	500	2,000
2. LIFO								
1.10							200	200
1.10				100	1.00	100	100	100
5.10	700	3.00	2,100				800	2,200
8.10				300	3.00	900	500	1,300
12.10	400	5.00	2,000				900	3,300
15.10				200	5.00	1,000	700	2,300
19.10	800	2.00	1,600				1,500	3,900
22.10				600	2.00	1,200	900	2,700
26.10	1,100	4.00	4,400				2,000	7,100
29.10				1,500	1,100@£4			
					200@£2			
					200@£5	5,800	500	1,300
3. CONTINUOUS WEIGHTED AVERAGE								
1.10							200	200
1.10				100	1.00	100	100	100
5.10	700	3.00	2,100				800	2,200
8.10				300	2.75	825	500	1,375
12.10	400	5.00	2,000				900	3,375
15.10				200	3.75	750	700	2,625
19.10	800	2.00	1,600				1,500	4,225
22.10				600	2.82	1,692	900	2,533
26.10	1,100	4.00	4,400				2,000	6,933
29.10				1,500	3.47	5,205	500	1,728

EXERCISE 13.5   PAGE 98

(a)

HOOK
Stock Account

Date	RECEIPTS			ISSUES			BALANCE	
	Units	Price £	Value £	Units	Price £	Value £	Units	Value £
19X7								
April	100	60	6,000				100	6,000
May	100	68	6,800				200	12,800
July				80	64	5,120	120	7,680
Sept.	200	80	16,000				320	23,680
Dec.				300	74	22,200	20	1,480
19X8								
Feb.	100	86	8,600				120	£10,080
	500		£37,400	380		£27,320		

(b)   **Calculation of gross profit for year to 31 March 19X8**

	£
Sales (80 x £75) + (300 x £90)	33,000
Less : cost of goods sold	27,320
Gross profit	£5,680

(c)   **Calculation of gross profit for year to 31 March 19X8 using the periodic inventory system of stock control**

	£	£
Sales		33,000
Less : cost of goods sold		
purchases	37,400	
Less : closing stock		
(£37,400/500 = £74.80 x 120)	8,976	28,424
Gross profit		£4,576

(d)   The periodic inventory system uses an average purchase price per unit. In this example, one price (£74.80) is used for the whole year. By using the perpetual (or continuous) inventory method the average price of goods in stock is changed every time that there is a new receipt into stock at a different price from the price previously paid on the previous occasion goods were purchased.

Hence the difference arises because of a difference in the method of valuing stock. One method uses an average price for the year, whereas the other method uses a price that may be changing continuously.

EXERCISE 13.6 PAGE 99

(a)

BERRY PLC
Calculation of closing stock at the end of 19X6

	£	£
Original valuation		243,700
Add : the following adjustments -		
(1) Stock sheet error (£8,300 - £3,800)	4,500	
(2) Goods on sale or return(£18,000 x $\frac{100}{120}$)	15,000	19,500
		263,200
Deduct : the following adjustments -		
(1) Stock sheet error		
[(400 x £2.50) = 1,000 - (400 x £25)]	9,000	
(3) Goods supplied at NIL cost	350	
(6) Revaluation of Product X at £16 per unit		
[(36 x £20 = 720) - 80 = 640) (640/40 = £16)		
(£16 - £20 = £4) x 15]	60	
(7) Revaluation of Product Y [(£12 - £7) x 600]	3,000	
(8) Revaluation of Product Z [(£10,000/1,000 = £10)		
(£10 x 150 = 1,500) - 3,000]	1,500	13,910
Adjusted stock value		**£249,290**

(b) **Reasons for the above adjustments**

(2) The goods are still owned by Berry plc and they must be included in stock at their cost price.

(3) Goods should be valued at the lower of cost or net realisable value.

(4) The cost of these goods is £6,500 (excluding any future work on them), and this is lower than their expected resale value. No adjustment, therefore, is necessary

(5) No adjustment is necessary as the date of payment for goods accepted by Berry plc is irrelevant.

(6) The cost of these goods is £16 each, as Berry effectively purchased 40 units at a cost of £640, so 15 units of closing stock amounts to £240 and not £300.

(7) The net realisable value of these units is £7, which is lower than the original cost of £12. Future costs are irrelevant.

(8) Selling and administration overhead should be excluded, and the production cost should be divided by the normal activity of 1,000 units.

SOLUTIONS TO CHAPTER 14 EXERCISES

EXERCISE 14.1   PAGE 105

SENGA
Electricity Account

		£			£
21 1 X3	Bank	700	1 1 X3	Balance b/d	500
26 4 X3	Bank	1,000			
5 7 X3	Bank	400			
20 10 X3	Bank	600	31 12 X3	Profit and Loss	
31 12 X3	Balance c/d	800		Account	3,000
		£3,500			£3,500
			1 1 X4	Balance b/d	800

Rents Received Account

		£			£
			1 1 X3	Balance b/d	750
			25 3 X3	Bank	800
			24 6 X3	Bank	900
31 12 X3	Profit and Loss		29 9 X3	Bank	950
	Account	3,400	25 12 X3	Bank	700
31 12 X3	Balance c/d	700			
		£4,100			£4,100
			1 1 X4	Balance b/d	700

Insurance Account

		£			£
1 1 X3	Balance b/d	50			
26 4 X3	Bank	300	31 12 X3	Profit and Loss Account	550
20 10 X3	Bank	400	31 12 X3	Balance c/d	200
		£750			£750
1 1 X4	Balance b/d	200			

EXERCISE 14.2   PAGE 106

(a)

MICHAEL LENNON
Rent Account

		£			£
2 4 X6	Bank	750			
5 7 X6	Bank	750			
28 9 X6	Bank	750	31 12 X6	Profit and Loss	
31 12 X6	Balance c/d	750		Account	3,000
		£3,000			£3,000
			1 1 X7	Balance b/d	750

Rates Account

		£			£
3 1 X6	Bank	225			
12 4 X6	Bank	500	31 12 X6	Profit and Loss Account	975
7 10 X6	Bank	500	31 12 X6	Balance c/d	250
		£1,225			£1,225
1 1 X7	Balance b/d	250			

Insurance Account

		£			£
1 1 X6	Bank	130	31 12 X6	Profit and Loss Account	300
26 6 X6	Bank	340	31 12 X6	Balance c/d	170
		£470			£470
1 1 X7	Balance b/d	170			

(b) **Balance sheet (extracts) at 31 December 19X6**

	£
Current assets	
Prepayments (£250 + 170)	420
Current liabilities	
Accrual	750

EXERCISE 14.3   PAGE 106

(a)

SPINOLA RESTAURANT
Fire Insurance Account

		£			£
1 6 X4	Bank	600	31 3 X5	Profit and Loss Account	500
			31 3 X5	Balance c/d	100
		£600			£600
1 4 X5	Balance b/d	100	31 3 X6	Profit and Loss Account	650
1 6 X5	Bank	660	31 3 X6	Balance c/d	110
		£760			£760
1 4 X6	Balance b/d	110	31 3 X7	Profit and Loss Account	710
1 6 X6	Bank	720	31 3 X7	Balance c/d	120
		£830			£830
1 4 X7	Balance b/d	120			

Balance sheet (extracts) at 31 March

	19X6	19X7
	£	£
Current assets		
Prepayments	110	120

(b)

F STANNERTON
Rent and Rates Account

		Rent £	Rates £			Rent £	Rates £
1 1 X6	Balance b/d	-	128	1 1 X6	Balance b/d	420	-
12 1 X6	Bank	420	-				
21 3 X6	Bank	420	-				
27 5 X6	Bank	-	284				
12 7 X6	Bank	420	-				
23 9 X6	Bank	480					
21 12 X6	Bank	480					
31 12 X6	Balance c/d	-	142	31 12 X6	Profit and Loss Account	1,800	554
		£2,220	£554			£2,220	£554
				1 1 X7	Balance b/d	-	142

Balance sheet (extracts) at 31 December 19X5

	£
Current liabilities	
Accrual	128

SOLUTIONS TO CHAPTER 15 EXERCISES

EXERCISE 15.1 PAGE 115

Debts outstanding £	%	Provision £
25,000	0	0
13,000	2	260
5,000	10	500
2,000	25	500
£45,000		£1,260

Provision for Bad Debts Account

	£		£
31 10 X4 Balance c/d	1,260	1 11 X3 Balance b/d	1,000
		31 10 X4 Profit and Loss Account	260
	£1,260		£1,260
		1 11 X4 Balance b/d	1,260

EXERCISE 15.2 PAGE 115

(a)

B CAREFUL
Bad Debts Account

	£		£
1 10 X7 Debtors	750	31 10 X7 Profit and Loss Account	750

Provision for Bad Debts Account

	£		£
		1 11 X6 Balance b/d	350
		31 10 X7 Profit and Loss Account	
31 10 X7 Balance c/d	400	[(5%x(£8,750-750))-350]	50
	£400		£400
		1 11 X7 Balance b/d	400

(b)   (i)   The writing off of a bad debt will not affect cash flow, but it will reduce the profit for the period in which the bad debt is written off.

      (ii)   The maintenance of a bad debts provision will also reduce the profit for a particular period (unless the provision is reduced). It will not affect cash flow.

EXERCISE 15.3 PAGE 115

M BLOCK
Bad Debts Account

	£		£
1 2 X5 T Mann	48		
20 4 X5 B Cope	110		
16 8 X5 G Wallace	56		

		£			£
10 11 X5 H Dalton		77	31 12 X5 Profit and Loss Account		291
		£291			£291

Provision for Bad/Doubtful Debts Account

	£			£
		1 1 X5 Balance b/d	105
		31 12 X5 Profit and Loss Account	
31 12 X5 Balance c/d	210	[(5% x £4,200) - 105]	105
	£210		£210
		1 1 X6 Balance b/d	210

EXERCISE 15.4   PAGE 116

WENTWORTH ENTERPRISES
Bad Debts Account

	£		£
31 12 X3 Debtors	452	31 12 X3 Profit and Loss Account	452
31 12 X4 Debtors	860	31 12 X3 Profit and Loss Account	860
31 12 X5 Debtors	650	31 12 X3 Profit and Loss Account	650

Provision for Bad Debts Account

	£		£
		31 12 X2 Profit and Loss Account	
		(5% x £6,000)	300
		31 12 X3 Profit and Loss Account	
31 12 X3 Balance c/d	425	[(5% x £8,500) - 300]	125
	£425		£425
		1 1 X4 Balance b/d	425
		31 12 X4 Profit and Loss Account	
31 12 X4 Balance c/d	880	[(8% x £11,000) - 425]	455
	£880		£880
31 12 X5 Profit and Loss Account		1 1 X5 Balance b/d	880
[(6% x £12,000) - 880]	160		
31 12 X5 Balance c/d	720		
	£880		£880
		1 1 X6 Balance b/d	720

Note : It is assumed that the debtors at 31 December are shown AFTER deducting any specific bad debts for the year.

EXERCISE 15.5 PAGE 116

(a) In order to reduce the profit on those credit sales which may not be settled by debtors whose financial position appears highly unsatisfactory.

(b)

P PRINCE
Provision for Doubtful Debts Account

	£			£
		1 1 X7	Specific provision b/d	30
		1 1 X7	General provision b/d	424
31 12 X7 Specific provision c/d	300	31 12 X7	Profit and Loss Account	194
31 12 X7 General provision c/d	348			
	£648			£648
		1 1 X8	Specific provision b/d	300
		1 1 X8	General provision b/d	348

Workings

	£	£
Debtors		
September		100
October		900
November	2,200	
Less : specific debt	300	1,900
		2,900 x 12%
General provision required at 31 12 X7		348
General provision at 1 1 X7		(424)
Specific provision at 1 1 X7		(30)
		(106)
Specific provision required		300
Profit and Loss Account		£194

(c) **Balance sheet (extracts) at 31 December 19X7**

	£
Current assets	
Debtors (£100 + 900 + 2,200 +3,600)	6,800
Less : provision for bad and doubtful debts (£300 + 348)	648
	£6,152

EXERCISE 15.6 PAGE 117

(a) (i)

WILLIAM SPORE
Bad Debts Account

	£		£
31 12 X6 Debtors	705	31 12 X6 Profit and Loss Account	705
31 12 X7 Debtors	795	31 12 X7 Profit and Loss Account	795

(ii)

Provision for Bad and Doubtful Debts Account

	£			£
31 12 X6 Profit and Loss Account [£720 - (4% x 16,500)]	60	1 1 X6	Balance b/d	720
31 12 X6 Balance c/d (4% x £16,500)	660			
	£720			£720
31 12 X7 Balance c/d	823	1 1 X7	Balance b/d	660
		31 12 X7	Profit and Loss Account [(£21,000 - 420) x 4% - 660]	163
	£823			£823
		1 1 X8	Balance b/d	823

(b) (i)

Discounts Receivable Account

	£		£
31 12 X7 Profit and Loss Account	3,150	31 12 X7 Creditors	3,150

(ii)

Allowance for Discounts Receivable Account

	£		£
		31 12 X7 Profit and Loss Account (2.5% x £15,000)	375

(c)

WILLIAM SPORE

Balance Sheet (extracts) at 31 December 19X7

	£	£
Current Assets		
Debtors		21,000
Less : provision for discounts allowed (2%)	420	
provision for bad and doubtful debts [(£21,000 - 420) x 4%]	823	1,243
		£19,757

Note : It is assumed that the debtors figures given in the question were AFTER deducting the specific bad debts.

EXERCISE 15.7   PAGE 118

GEORGE
Trade Debtors Account

		£			£
1 10 X1	Balance b/d	30,000	15 1 X2	Bad debt (Fall Ltd)	2,000
30 9 X2	Sales	187,800	30 9 X2	Bank	182,500
			30 9 X2	Discounts allowed	5,300
			30 9 X2	Bad debts	3,500
			30 9 X2	Balance c/d	24,500
		£217,800			£217,800
1 10 X2	Balance b/d	24,500			

Provision for Doubtful Debts Account

		£			£
30 9 X2	Profit and Loss Account - reduction in provision [(5% x £24,500) - 1,500]	275	1 10 X1	Balance b/d	1,500
30 9 X2	Balance c/d	1,225			
		£1,500			£1,500
			1 10 X2	Balance b/d	1,225

Discounts Allowed Account

		£			£
30 9 X2	Trade debtors	5,300	30 9 X2	Profit and Loss Account	5,300

Bad Debts Account

		£			£
15 1 X2	Trade debtors (Fall Ltd)	2,000	30 9 X2	Profit and Loss Account	5,500
30 9 X2	Trade debtors	3,500			
		£5,500			£5,500

Sales Account

		£			£
			30 9 X2	Trade debtors	187,800
30 9 X2	Profit and Loss Account	234,600	30 9 X2	Cash	46,800
		£234,600			£234,600

Profit and Loss Account (extract)

		£			£
30 9 X2	Bad debts	5,500	30 9 X2	Sales	234,600
30 9 X2	Discounts allowed	5,300	30 9 X2	Provision for doubtful debts - reduction	275

Cash and Bank Account (extract)

		£		£
30 9 X2	Trade debtors	182,500		
30 9 X2	Sales	46,800		

SOLUTIONS TO CHAPTER 16 EXERCISES

EXERCISE 16.1   PAGE 123

(a)   Physical deterioration, mainly from wear and tear
      Economic factors, mainly from obsolescence
      Passage of time, such as a period of copyright
      Depletion, for example, mines and quarries

(b)   (i)

Motor Vehicles

		£			£
1 8 X4	Bank	4,500	30 6 X5	Balance c/d	16,000
1 8 X4	Motor Finance plc	5,000			
1 8 X4	Bank	6,500			
		£16,000			£16,000
1 7 X5	Balance b/d	16,000	1 3 X6	Assets Disposals	6,500
1 3 X6	Bank	7,000	30 6 X6	Balance c/d	16,500
		£23,000			£23,000
1 7 X6	Balance b/d	16,500			

(ii)

Provision for Depreciation - Motor Vehicles

		£			£
30 6 X5	Balance c/d	4,800	30 6 X5	Profit and Loss	4,800
1 3 X6	Assets Disposals	1,950	1 7 X5	Balance b/d	4,800
30 6 X6	Balance c/d	6,945	30 6 X6	Profit and Loss (£16,500-4,800+1,950) x 30%	4,095
		£8,895			£8,895
			1 7 X6	Balance b/d	6,945

Assets Disposal

		£			£
1 3 X6	Motor Vehicle	6,500	1 3 X6	Provision for Depreciation	1,950
			1 3 X6	Bank	4,500
			30 6 X6	Profit and Loss	50
		£6,500			£6,500

EXERCISE 16.2   PAGE 123

MR REED
Machinery Account

Date		£	Date		£
1 1 X3	Bank	2,000	31 12 X3 Profit and Loss		
1 7 X3	Bank	8,000	(£2,000x10%) +		
			(£8,000x10%)/2		600
			31 12 X3 Balance c/d		9,400
		£10,000			£10,000
1 1 X4	Balance b/d	9,400	31 12 X4 Profit and Loss		
1 4 X4	Bank	4,000	(£10,000x10%) +		
			(£4,000x10%) x 3/4		1,300
			31 12 X4 Balance c/d		12,100
		£13,400			£13,400
1 1 X5	Balance b/d	12,100	31 12 X5 Profit and Loss		
			(£14,000x10%)		1,400
			31 12 X5 Balance c/d		10,700
		£12,100			£12,100
1 1 X6	Balance b/d	10,700			

EXERCISE 16.3   PAGE 124

(a) (i) **Straight Line Method**

	£
Cost	7,000,000
Less : expected residual value	1,500,000
Expected depreciation	£5,500,000
Depreciation per annum	£1,375,000

Annual charge	
Year to 31 January 19X2	1,375,000
Year to 31 January 19X3	1,375,000
Year to 31 January 19X4	1,375,000
Year to 31 January 19X5 (balance)	1,675,000
Actual depreciation (£7,000,000 - £1,200,000)	£5,800,000

(ii) **Flying Hours Logged Method**

	£
Cost	7,000,000
Less : expected residual value	1,500,000
Expected depreciation	£5,500,000
Expected flying hours	10,000
Depreciation per flying hour	£550

Annual charge	£
Year to 31 January 19X2 (3,000 x £550)	1,650,000
Year to 31 January 19X3 (2,800 x £550)	1,540,000
Year to 31 January 19X4 (2,300 x £550)	1,265,000
Year to 31 January 19X5 (balance)	1,345,000
Actual depreciation (£7,000,000 - £1,200,000)	£5,800,000

(b) Depreciation should be allocated so as to charge a fair proportion of the cost (or valuation), less estimated residual value, of the asset as fairly as possible to the periods expected to benefit from its use. Provided that the number of flying hours logged in each period can be estimated accurately, depreciation should be calculated on that basis as it is more likely to reflect the benefit provided in each period than is the straight line method of depreciation.

(c) (i) **Straight Line Method**

Aircraft Account

		£			£
1 2 X4	Balance b/d	7,000,000	30 6 X4	Assets Disposals	7,000,000

Provision for Depreciation - Aircraft

		£			£
30 6 X4	Assets Disposals	4,125,000	1 2 X4	Balance b/d	4,125,000

Assets Disposals Account

		£			£
30 6 X4	Aircraft	7,000,000	30 6 X4	Provision for depreciation	4,125,000
			30 6 X4	Bank	1,200,000
			31 1 X5	Profit and Loss	1,675,000
		£7,000,000			£7,000,000

(c) (ii) **Flying Hours Logged Method**

Aircraft Account

		£			£
1 2 X4	Balance b/d	7,000,000	30 6 X4	Assets Disposals	7,000,000

Provision for Depreciation - Aircraft

		£			£
30 6 X4	Assets Disposals	4,455,000	1 2 X4	Balance b/d	4,455,000

Assets Disposals Account

	£			£
30 6 X4 Aircraft	7,000,000	30 6 X4	Provision for depreciation	4,455,000
		30 6 X4	Bank	1,200,000
		31 1 X5	Profit and Loss	1,345,000
	£7,000,000			£7,000,000

EXERCISE 16.4   PAGE 124

(a)

THE GO AHEAD COMPANY AND THE FORCEFUL COMPANY LTD

Date	Annual Depreciation £	Net Book Value £	Revised Net Profit £
Go Ahead Company			
31 12 X5	8,000	12,000	42,000
31 12 X6	4,800	7,200	45,200
31 12 X7	2,880	4,320	47,120
Forceful Company Ltd			
31 12 X5	4,000	16,000	46,000
31 12 X6	4,000	12,000	46,000
31 12 X7	4,000	8,000	46,000

(b)   **Loss on Sale**

Go Ahead Company	£7,000 - 4,320 = £2,680 (gain)
Forceful Company Ltd	£7,000 - 8,000 = £1,000 (loss)

(c)

GO AHEAD COMPANY
Disposal Account

	£			£
1 1 X8 Machine	20,000	1 1 X8	Bank	7,000
31 12 X8 Profit and Loss	2,680	1 1 X8	Provision for depreciation	15,680
	£22,680			£22,680

(d)   (i)   Straight line method for furniture and fittings.

(ii)   Reducing balance method for motor vehicles.

EXERCISE 16.5   PAGE 125

(a)

JFR HAULAGE LTD
Depreciation schedule

	Year ended 31 December			
Lorry	19X3 £	19X4 £	19X5 £	TOTAL £
A	3,300	3,300	3,300	9,900
B	3,620	3,620	-	7,240
C	-	3,880	3,880	7,760
D	-	-	4,040	4,040
E	-	-	3,600	3,600
F	-	-	3,380	3,380
TOTAL	£6,920	£10,800	£18,200	

(b)

Motor Lorries Account

		£			£
1 1 X3	Bank	16,500			
1 10 X3	Bank	18,100	31 12 X3 Balance c/d		34,600
		£34,600			£34,600
1 1 X4	Balance b/d	34,600			
1 1 X4	Bank	19,400	31 12 X4 Balance c/d		54,000
		£54,000			£54,000
1 1 X5	Balance b/d	54,000	30 6 X5 Disposals		18,100
5 4 X5	Bank	20,200			
8 8 X5	Hire purchase company	18,000			
9 9 X5	Bank	16,900	31 12 X5 Balance c/d		91,000
		£109,100			£109,100
1 1 X6	Balance b/d	91,000			

Motor Vehicles Accumulated Depreciation Account

		£			£
30 6 X5	Disposals	7,240	1 1 X5	Balance b/d (£6,920+10,800)	17,720
31 12 X5	Balance c/d	28,680	31 12 X5	Profit and Loss	18,200
		£35,920			£35,920
			1 1 X6	Balance b/d	28,680

EXERCISE 16.6   PAGE 126

UNITED MARBLES
Buildings Account

		£000			£000
1 6 X3	Balance b/d	360	31 5 X4	Fixed assets disposals	20
31 5 X4	Bank	40	31 5 X4	Balance c/d	380
		£400			£400
1 6 X4	Balance b/d	380			

Buildings Depreciation Account

		£000			£000
31 5 X4	Fixed assets disposals	10	1 6 X3	Balance b/d	126
			31 5 X4	Profit and Loss : depreciation for the year	
31 5 X4	Balance c/d	135		(£380 /20)	19
		£145			£145
			1 6 X4	Balance b/d	135

Equipment Account

		£000			£000
1 6 X3	Balance b/d	200	31 5 X4	Fixed assets disposals	20
31 5 X4	Bank	15	31 5 X4	Balance c/d	195
		£215			£215
1 6 X4	Balance b/d	195			

Equipment Depreciation Account

		£000			£000
31 5 X4	Fixed assets disposals	5	1 6 X3	Balance b/d	100
			31 5 X4	Profit and Loss : depreciation for the year	
31 5 X4	Balance c/d	120		[£195 - (100-5)] x25%	25
		£125			£125
			1 6 X4	Balance b/d	120

Fixed Assets Disposal Account

		£000			£000
31 5 X4	Buildings	20	31 5 X4	Buildings depreciation	10
31 5 X4	Equipment	20	31 5 X4	Bank	4
			31 5 X4	Equipment depreciation	5
			31 5 X4	Bank	18
			31 5 X4	Profit and Loss : loss on disposal of fixed assets	3
		£40			£40

SOLUTIONS TO CHAPTER 17 EXERCISES

EXERCISE 17.1 PAGE 131

MELANIE ROGERS
Advertising Account

		£			£
29 2 X8	Bank	3,100	29 2 X8	Profit and Loss	
29 2 X8	Balance c/d	100		Account	3,200
		£3,200			£3,200
			1 3 X8	Balance b/d	100

Insurance Account

		£			£
29 2 X8	Bank	2,150	29 2 X8	Profit and Loss	
				Account	1,850
			29 2 X8	Balance c/d	300
		£2,150			£2,150
1 3 X8	Balance b/d	300			

Commissions Received Account

		£			£
29 2 X8	Profit and Loss		29 2 X8	Bank	18,200
	Account	20,700	29 2 X8	Balance c/d	2,500
		£20,700			£20,700
1 3 X8	Balance b/d	2,500			

MELANIE ROGERS
Profit and Loss Account for the year ending 29 February 19X8

	£	£
Profit on trading		27,350
Add :		
Commissions received	20,700	
Discounts received	1,450	22,150
		49,500
Less : Expenses -		
Advertising	3,200	
Insurance	1,850	
Rent and rates	9,000	
Lighting and heating	5,400	
Stationery	820	
Commissions allowed	3,100	
Discounts allowed	1,200	
Office wages and salaries	9,500	
Bad debts	125	
Motor expenses	4,200	
General expenses	5,600	43,995
Net profit for the year		£5,505

EXERCISE 17.2   PAGE 131

COTTLES STORES

Trading, Profit and Loss Account for the year to 30 April 19X8

	£	£
Sales		70,600
Less : Cost of goods sold -		
Purchases	59,150	
Less : Closing stock	4,550	54,600
Gross profit		16,000
Less : Expenses -		
Rent (£2,100 - 700)	1,400	
Miscellaneous expenses (£706 - 25)	681	
Wages	3,900	
Electricity (£435 + 51)	486	
Advertising	1,059	7,526
Net profit for the year		£8,474

Balance Sheet at 30 April 19X8

	£	£	£
Fixed assets			
Fittings			4,400
Current assets			
Stocks		4,550	
Debtors		2,000	
Prepayment		700	
Bank		8,345	
Cash		200	
		15,795	
Less : **Current liabilities**			
Creditors	4,630		
Accrual	51	4,681	11,114
			£15,514
Capital			
At 1 May 19X7			8,200
Net profit for the year		8,474	
Less : Drawings		4,160	4,314
			12,514
Loan			3,000
			£15,514

EXERCISE 17.3   PAGE 132

E LONG

Trading, Profit and Loss Account for the year to 31 October 19X7

	£	£	£
Sales			38,465
Less : Sales returns			300
			38,165
Less : Cost of goods sold -			
Opening stock		2,750	
Purchases		25,790	
Carriage inwards		650	
		29,190	
Less : Goods withdrawn for private use	150		
Closing stock	2,150	2,300	26,890
Gross profit			11,275
Add : Income -			
Rents received (£1,500 + 50)			1,550
			12,825
Less : Expenses -			
Wages		4,500	
Rent		1,000	
Rates		450	
General expenses		365	6,315
Net profit for the year			£6,510

Balance Sheet at 31 October 19X7

	£	£	£
Fixed assets			
Freehold buildings			15,000
Fixtures and fittings			1,550
			16,550
Current assets			
Stocks		2,150	
Debtors (£760 + 50)		810	
Cash		55	
		3,015	
Less : **Current liabilities**			
Creditors	1,260		
Bank overdraft	1,495	2,755	260
			£16,810

Capital	£	£	£
Balance at 1 November 19X6			10,450
Net profit for the year		6,510	
Less : Drawings		150	6,360
			£16,810

EXERCISE 17.4   PAGE 133

MR CHAL
Trading, Profit and Loss Account for the year to 30 April 19X7

	£	£
Sales (£259,870 - 5,624)		254,246
Less : Cost of goods sold		
Stock at 1 May 19X6	15,654	
Purchases (£135,680 - 13,407)	122,273	
Carriage in	11,830	
	149,757	
Less : Stock at 30 April 19X7	17,750	132,007
Gross profit		122,239
Add : Income -		
Discounts received		1,750
		123,989
Less : Expenses -		
Salaries and wages	38,521	
Rent, rates and insurances (£25,973 - 1,120 - 5,435)	19,418	
Heating and lighting (£11,010 + 1,360)	12,370	
Postage, stationery and telephone	2,410	
Carriage	4,562	
Advertising	5,980	
Discounts allowed	2,306	
Bad debts [£2,008 + (3% x £24,500) - 512]	2,231	
Depreciation	12,074	99,872
Net profit		£24,117

MR CHAL
Balance Sheet at 30 April 19X7

	£	£	£
Fixed assets			
Fixtures and fittings at cost			120,740
Less : Accumulated depreciation			63,020
			57,720
Current assets			
Stock at cost		17,750	
Debtors (£24,500 - 735)		23,765	
Prepaid expenses (£1,120 + 5,435)		6,555	
Cash at bank		4,440	
Cash on hand		534	
		53,044	

	£	£	£
Less : **Current liabilities**			
Creditors	19,840		
Accrued expenses	1,360	21,200	31,844
Net Assets			£89,564

	£	£	£
Financed by :			
Capital			
As at 1 May 19X6			83,887
Net profit for the year		24,117	
Less : Drawings		18,440	5,677
			£89,564

EXERCISE 17.5   PAGE 134

B NORRIS
Trading, Profit and Loss Account for the year to 31 March 19X3

	£	£
Sales		100,000
Less : Cost of goods sold		
Opening stock	5,000	
Purchases (£62,000 - 1,000)	61,000	
	66,000	
Less : Closing stock	6,000	60,000
Gross profit		40,000
Less : Expenses -		
Bad debt	500	
Depreciation on van	6,000	
Increase in provision for doubtful debts	200	
Office expenses (£12,600 - 100)	12,500	
Rates (£1,500 + 300)	1,800	21,000
Net profit		£19,000

Balance Sheet at 31 March 19X3

	£	£	£
Fixed assets			
Vans at cost		25,000	
Less : Accumulated depreciation (£15,000 + 6,000)		21,000	4,000
Current assets			
Stock		6,000	
Debtors (£16,700 - 200 - 500)	16,000		
Less : provision for doubtful debts	800	15,200	
Prepayment		100	
Cash at bank and in hand (£200 + 200)		400	
		21,700	

	£	£	£
Less : **Current liabilities**			
Creditors	10,000		
Accrual	300	10,300	11,400
			£15,400

Financed by :			
Capital			
Balance at 1 April 19X2			8,400
Net profit for the year		19,000	
Less : Drawings (£11,000 + 1,000)		12,000	7,000
			£15,400

EXERCISE 17.6   PAGE 134
PAUL PETERS
Trading, Profit and Loss Account for the year to 31 December 19X3

	£	£
Sales (Wkg 1)		65,000
Less : Cost of sales		
Opening stock	1,200	
Purchases (balancing)	49,400	
	50,600	
Less : Closing stock	5,100	45,500
Gross profit (30% of sales)		19,500
Less : Expenses -		
Rent and rates (£3,400 - 200)	3,200	
Electricity (£600 + 100)	700	
Motor vehicle running expenses (£5,800 + 250)	6,050	
Motor vehicle depreciation	1,000	
Sundry trading expenses	2,700	13,650
Net profit for the year		£5,850

Balance Sheet as at 31 December 19X3

	£	£
Fixed assets		
Motor vehicle at cost	5,000	
Less : Provision for depreciation	1,000	4,000
Current assets		
Stock	5,100	
Debtors and prepayments (£4,600 + 200)	4,800	
Balance at bank (Wkg 2)	400	
	10,300	
Less : **Current liabilities**		
Creditors and accruals	3,550	6,750
		£10,750

	£	£
Capital		
At 1 January 19X3 (£1,200 + 4,800)	6,000	
Add : Net profit for the year	5,850	
	11,850	
Less : Drawings [£4,100 + 1,000 (Wkg 4)]	5,100	6,750
Loan (interest free until 1 January 19X6)		4,000
		£10,750

Workings

	£
1. Sales :	
Credit sales - Cash received from trade debtors	43,400
Add : Trade debtors at 31 December 19X3	4,600
	48,000
Cash sales	17,000
	£65,000
2. Balance at bank as at 31 December 19X3 :	
Opening balance	4,800
Add : Total receipts 19X3	64,400
	69,200
Less : Total payments 19X3	68,800
	£400
3. Creditors and accruals as at 31 December 19X3 :	
Trade creditors as at 31 December 19X3	3,200
Accrued charges as at 31 December 19X3	350
	£3,550
4. Goods for own use :	
Cash paid suppliers of goods	47,200
Trade creditors as at 31 December 19X3	3,200
	50,400
Less : Purchases	49,400
	£1,000

EXERCISE 17.7   PAGE 135
H SEYMOUR
Trading, Profit and Loss Account for the year to 31 December 19X5

	£	£	£
Sales (£113,079 - 320 +3,800 +185 - 2,192 +2,248)			116,800
Less : Cost of goods sold -			
Opening stocks		5,832	
Purchases (£87,057 - 1,347 +1,210)		86,920	
		92,752	
Less :Closing stock		5,408	87,344
Gross profit			29,456
Less : Expenses -			
Rent (£480 + 80 +40)		600	
Electricity (£840 - 78)		762	
Wages		15,411	
Other expenses (£8,617 + 185)		8,802	
Fixtures and fittings depreciation [20% x (£2,760 - 1,425 + 2,835)]	834		
Over-depreciation on sale of fixtures and fittings (£320 - 285)	35	799	26,374
Retained profit for the year			£3,082

Balance Sheet at 31 December 19X5

	£	£	£
Fixed assets			
Fixtures and fittings at cost (£2,760 - 1,425 + 2,835)			4,170
Less : Accumulated depreciation (£1,818 - 1,140 + 834)			1,512
			2,658
Current assets			
Stocks		5,408	
Debtors		2,248	
		7,656	
Less : **Current liabilities**			
Trade creditors	1,210		
Accrual	40		
Bank overdraft	781	2,031	5,625
			£8,283
Capital			
Balance at 1 January 19X5 [(£2,760-1,818+5,832+2,192+80+1,380) - (£1,347+78)]			9,001
Net profit for the year		3,082	
Less : Drawings		3,800	(718)
			£8,283

EXERCISE 17.8 PAGE 136

(a)

DERWENT
Trading, Profit and Loss Account for the year to 31 March 19X5

	£000	£000
Sales		354
Less : Cost of goods sold -		
Opening stock	64	
Purchases	284	
	348	
Less : Closing stock	92	256
Gross profit		98
Less : Expenses -		
Advertising	10	
Wages (£37 + 2)	39	
Insurance (£3 - 1)	2	
Other expenses (£28 - 12)	16	
Depreciation : Freehold shop [10% x (£78 + 12)]	9	
Fixtures and fittings (10% x £30)	3	
Bad debts	4	
Provision for bad and doubtful debts [(£54 - 4) x 2%]	1	84
Retained profit for the year		£14

Balance Sheet at 31 March 19X5

	£000 Cost	£000 Accumulated Depreciation	£000 Net Book Value
Fixed assets			
Freehold shop (£78 + 12)	90	39	51
Fixtures and fittings	30	14	16
	£120	£53	67
Current assets			
Stocks		92	
Debtors (£54 - 4)	50		
Less :			
Provision for bad and doubtful debts	1	49	
Prepayment		1	
		142	
Less : **Current liabilities**			
Creditors	34		
Accruals (£2 + 10)	12		
Bank overdraft	9	55	87
			£154

	£000 Cost	£000 Accumulated Depreciation	£000 Net Book Value
Capital			
At 1 April 19X4			152
Add : Net profit for the year		14	
Less : Drawings		12	2
			£154

(b) Item (3) Stock should be valued at the lower of cost or net realisable value.

Item (6) The benefit is expected to arise in the next financial year but there is no certainty that any benefit will be forthcoming. It is prudent, therefore, to write off the cost of the campaign as it arises.

Item (7) This is an item of capital expenditure. It should be added to the cost of the freehold shop and depreciated accordingly.

SOLUTIONS TO CHAPTER 18 EXERCISES

EXERCISE 18.1 PAGE 141

(a)

ANDREW SCOTT
Journal

			Dr £	Cr £
15 6 X7	D Smith	Dr	200	
	To : D Smithson			200
	Being correction of item debited to the incorrect personal account			
13 8 X7	Purchases	Dr	340	
	To : R Wallis & Co.			340
	Being recording of transaction omitted from the books of account			
24 9 X7	Motor expenses	Dr	500	
	To : Motor vehicles			500
	Being correction of item for repairs being entered in the wrong account			
30 10 X7	Drawings	Dr	200	
	To : Motor expenses			200
	Being correction of item for petrol expenses entered in the wrong account			

(b)

Trial Balance at 29 February 19X8

	Dr £	Cr £
Capital		40,100
Drawings (£5,000 + 200)	5,200	
Rent and rates	2,500	
Lighting and heating	2,400	
Advertising	220	
Motor expenses (£1,200 + 500 - 200)	1,500	
Wages and salaries	8,500	
Insurance	500	
Purchases (£26,100 + 340)	26,440	
Sales		55,320
Creditors (£2,500 + 340)		2,840
Motor vehicles (£15,000 - 500)	14,500	
Equipment	20,000	
Stock of goods at 1 March 19X7	12,000	
Cash in hand	100	
Cash at bank	4,400	
	£98,260	£98,260

EXERCISE 18.2   PAGE 142

JOHN BARRINGTON

	Net profit overstated	Net profit understated
(1)		No effect
(2)	By £68	
(3)		No effect
(4)	By £100	
(5)		By £300

Correction of net profit

	£	£
Net profit as originally calculated		11,200
Add : Reduction of loan interest (5)		300
		11,500
Less : Correction of item credited to discount		
received account (2)	34	
Correction of over-casting of stock list	100	134
Corrected net profit		£11,366

EXERCISE 18.3   PAGE 142

(a)

JAMES McLIPPIE AND SON
Journal

			Dr £	Cr £
(1)	Discount received	Dr	100	
	To : Suspense			100
(2)	Suspense	Dr	8	
	To : J Stanley			8
(3)	Sales	Dr	900	
	To : Suspense			900
(4)	Sales	Dr	9	
	To : H Purcell			9
(5)	Purchases	Dr	360	
	To : Suspense			360
(6)	J Blow	Dr	20	
	To : Returns inward			20
(7)	Sales	Dr	15	
	To : Value added tax			15

	£	£
(b) Profit for the year per draft accounts		512,030
Add : Reduction in returns inwards		20
		512,050

		£	£
Less :	Reduction in discounts received	100	
	Reduction in sales	900	
	Reduction in invoice value	9	
	Increase in purchases	360	
	VAT excluded from sales	15	1,384
Adjusted profit for the year			£510,666

EXERCISE 18.4   PAGE 143

(a)

A TRADER
Suspense Account

	£		£
K Stevens	170	Balance as entered	247
T Smith (£90 x 2)	180	Rent and rates	100
Sales	10	Petty cash	13
	£360		£360

(b)

Calculation of the corrected net profit for the year

		£	£
Net profit originally calculated			7,180
Add :	Stock room cost debited to purchases	150	
	Undercasting of the sales day book	10	160
			7,340
Less :	Rent and rates omitted	100	
	Purchases - correction of transposition	36	136
Corrected net profit for the year			£7,204

(c)

Corrected Balance Sheet as at 31 March 19X8

		£	£
Fixed assets			
	Furniture and fittings (£2,800 + 150)	2,950	
	Motor vehicles	4,500	7,450
Current assets			
	Stock	4,250	
	Debtors (£1,400 - 170)	1,230	
	Bank and cash (£752 + 13)	765	
		6,245	
Less : **Current liabilities**			
	Sundry Creditors (£1,600 + 36 +180)	1,816	4,429
			£11,879

	£	£
Capital		
At 1 April 19X7		11,075
Add : Net profit	7,204	
Less : Drawings	6,400	804
		£11,879

EXERCISE 18.5   PAGE 144

(a)

FARLEY MOORE

Error	Debit		Credit	
	Understated £	Overstated £	Understated £	Overstated £
(1)		27		
(2)	96			
(3)	148			148
(4)				2,000
(5)		300		
(6)	560			

(b)

Calculation of the corrected net profit for the year to 31 May 19X6

	£	£
Net profit as originally calculated		5,680
Add : Telephone bill - overstated	27	
Overcasting of the purchases daybook	300	327
		6,007
Less : Bad debt	96	
Discounts allowed treated as discounts received	296	
Overstatement of the sales daybook	2,000	
Advertising bill	560	2,952
Corrected net profit for the year		£3,055

EXERCISE 18.6   PAGE 145

(a)

TIMBER PRODUCTS LTD
Suspense Account

	£		£
Balance as per trial balance	2,513	Wages	2,963
Discounts allowed	324	J Winters	198
Discounts received	324		
	£3,161		£3,161

471

(b)

Computation of corrected net profit for the year ended 30 April 19X7

		£	£
Net profit as originally calculated			24,760
Add :	Discounts	648	
	Stationery stock	1,500	2,148
			26,908
Less :	Wages	2,963	
	N North - remittance	3,000	5,963
Corrected net profit for the year			£20,945

(c)   Principal uses of trial balances :

    (1) Evidence of arithmetical accuracy of accounting records.
    (2) Useful for preparation of annual accounts.
    (3) Can act as a means of control.

EXERCISE 18.7   PAGE 145
HILL AND SON
Journal

			Dr £	Cr £
30 6 X6	Machinery repairs	Dr	400	
	To : Machinery account			400
	Being machinery repairs incorrectly debited to the machine account			
30 6 X6	Elemes Ltd	Dr	20	
	To : Suspense			20
	Being discount received omitted from the creditor's account			
30 6 X6	Office equipment	Dr	900	
	To : Suspense			900
	Being correction of transposition error			
30 6 X6	Suspense	Dr	100	
	To : Sales			100
	Being correction of the undercasting of the sales daybook			
30 6 X6	Loan interest	Dr	600	
	To : Suspense			600
	Being bank loan interest omitted from the loan interest account			
30 6 X6	Office equipment	Dr	500	
	To : Suspense			500
	Being correction of entry made on the wrong side of the account			

(b)

Suspense Account

	£		£
Balance as per trial balance	920	Elemes Ltd	20
Sales	100	Office equipment	900
Office equipment	500	Loan interest	600
	£1,520		£1,520

(c)

	Assets £	Profit £
(1)	- £400	- £400
(2)	No effect (reduction in liability)	No effect
(3)	+ £900	No effect
(4)	No effect	+ £100
(5)	No effect	- £600
(6)	- £500	No effect

EXERCISE 18.8   PAGE 146

PENDER

Correction to the profit and loss account for the year to 30 June 19X5

		£	£
Net profit for the year as originally calculated			45,700
Add : the following adjustments -			
(1)	Drawings incorrectly charged against profits	10,000	
(2)	Motor van incorrectly included in purchases	5,000	
(3)	Insurance prepaid at 30 June 19X5	400	
(6)	Stock at 30 June 19X5 underestimated	3,000	
(9)	Excess depreciation on buildings incorrectly charged (£8,000 - 2,000)	6,000	
(10)	Discounts received wrongly credited (x2)	1,400	25,800
			71,500
Deduct : the following adjustments -			
(4)	Provision for specific bad debt	3,000	
(5)	Motor expenses omitted	600	
(7)	New capital introduced by Pender included in sales	7,000	
(8)	Omission of depreciation on furniture and fittings	1,600	
(10)	Discounts allowed wrongly debited (x2)	2,000	
(11)	Increase in the bad debts provision [(£50,000 - 3,000) x 5% - £2,050]	300	14,500
Corrected net profit for the year to 30 June 19X5			£57,000

Note :

Pender was correct in not including the increase in the value of his investments in his profit and loss account (Question note 12). The increase in value should be credited to a capital reserve account.

EXERCISE 18.9   PAGE 147

Net profit adjustments for the three years to 31 December 19X8, 19X9 and 19X0

	19X8	19X9	19X0
	£	£	£
Net profit	36,000	15,000	25,000
Overstatement of stock	(3,200)	3,200	-
" "	-	(6,800)	6,800
" "	-	-	(3,600)
Overstatement of accrued interest income	(500)	500	(300)
Understatement of accrued advertising	(500)	500	-
" "	-	(1,200)	1,200
" "	-	-	(600)
Omission of depreciation	(1,800)	(1,200)	(1,500)
Corrected net profit	£30,000	£10,000	£27,000

SOLUTIONS TO CHAPTER 19 EXERCISES

EXERCISE 19.1   PAGE 153

(a)   (i)   (ii)

FRANK BRIDGEMAN
Statement of Affairs

	At 1 April 19X6	At 31 March 19X7
	£	£
Equipment	150	380
Motor van	-	1,350
Stock of materials	-	80
Bank	500	274
CAPITAL	£650	£2,084

Calculation of net profit for the year to 31 March 19X7

	£	£
Capital at 1 April 19X6		650
Net profit for the year (by deduction)	9,854	
Less : Drawings	8,420	1,434
		£2,084

(b)

Trading, Profit and Loss Account for the year to 31 March 19X7

	£	£
Turnover (£12,310 + 915)		13,225
Less : Direct expenses		
Materials	2,940	
Less : Closing stock	80	2,860
Gross profit		10,365
Less : Other expenses		
Advertising	180	
Depreciation : Motor van (£1,500 - 1,350)	150	
: Equipment (£150 + 411 - 380)	181	511
Net profit for the year		£9,854

EXERCISE 19.2   PAGE 154

(a)

P GREEN
Journal

			Dr	Cr
			£	£
1 5 X7	Freehold premises	Dr	32,000	
	Motor van	Dr	2,600	
	Fixtures	Dr	1,800	
	Stock	Dr	6,400	
	Debtors : T Ross	Dr	90	
	A Baker	Dr	64	
	T Bone	Dr	128	
	Rates : prepayment	Dr	42	
	Bank and cash	Dr	2,965	
	To : Trade creditors : T Black			271
	D Bacon			194
	To : Loan interest accrual			1,000
	To : Long term loan			10,000
	To : Capital (balance)			34,624
			£46,089	£46,089

Being opening balances in ledger accounts
upon the introduction of a double entry system

(b)

6 5 X7	Fixtures and fittings	Dr	950	
	To : Micawber and Sons			950

Being purchase of fixtures on credit

8 5 X7	Micawber and Sons	Dr	60	
	To : Fixtures and fittings			60

Being return of unsuitable fittings

12 5 X7	Bad debts	Dr	64	
	To : Baker			64

Being a bad debt written off on the
declaration of bankruptcy of Baker

22 5 X7	Gatt & Co.	Dr	90	
	To : Fixtures and fittings			90

Being the sale on credit of surplus fittings

29 5 X7	T Davies	Dr	130	
	To : T Davis			130

Being the transfer of an entry made to
the wrong account

EXERCISE 19.3   PAGE 154

(a)

JOHN WALTERS OF HANLEY
Statement of Affairs at 31 December 19X4

	£	£	£
Fixed assets			
Garage			400
Delivery van			2,000
Car			1,000
			3,400
Current assets			
Stock in trade		5,200	
Trade debtors		420	
Prepaid expenses		80	
Cash in hand		105	
		5,805	
Less : **Current liabilities**			
Trade creditors	2,150		
Hire purchase company (£2,000 - 400)	1,600		
Creditors for general expenses	145		
Bank overdraft	1,520	5,415	390
Apparent capital at 31 December 19X4			£3,790

(b)

	£	£
Apparent capital at 31 December 19X4		3,790
Less : Capital at 1 January 19X4		
(£1,500 + 500 +1,000 - 1,000)		2,000
		1,790
Add : Drawings [(£26 x 50) + (£26 x 70)]		3,120
Net profit for the year		£4,910

(c)   Working capital at 31 December 19X4 = £390 (£5,805 - 5,415)

EXERCISE 19.4   PAGE 155

A DAY
Trading, Profit and Loss Account for the year ended 31 October 19X7

	£	£	£
Sales (£31,630 + 5,200 +2,600)			39,430
Less : Cost of goods sold -			
Opening stock		1,500	
Purchases (£29,600 - 900 +750 -750)		28,700	
		30,200	
Less : Closing stock		1,800	28,400
Gross profit			11,030

		£	£
Less : Expenses -			
Rates (£600 - 50)		550	
Light and heat (£290 + 90)		380	
Wages (52 x £50)		2,600	
Sundry expenses (£120 -25)		95	
Depreciation : Fixtures and fittings	300		
Motor vehicles	1,500	1,800	5,425
Net profit for the year			£5,605

Balance Sheet at 31 October 19X7

1986		£	£	£
£		Cost	Accumulated Depreciation	NetBook Value
	Fixed assets			
35,000	Premises	35,000	-	35,000
2,750	Fixtures and fittings	3,000	300	2,700
6,000	Motor vehicles	6,000	1,500	4,500
43,750		£44,000	£1,800	42,200
	Current assets			
1,500	Stock in hand		1,800	
-	Prepayment		50	
2,085	Bank		3,255	
3,585			5,105	
	Less : **Current liabilities**			
900	Creditors	750		
25	Accrual	90	840	4,265
925				
£46,410				£46,465
	Capital			
	At 1 November 19X6			46,410
	Introduced during the year			400
	Net profit for the year		5,605	46,810
	Less : Drawings (£5,200 + 750)		5,950	(345)
				£46,465

EXERCISE 19.5   PAGE 156

JEAN SMITH
Trading, Profit and Loss Account for the year ended 31 March 19X6

	£	£	£
Sales			50,400
Less : Cost of goods sold -			
Purchases (Wkg 1)		27,400	
Less : Closing stock		1,900	25,500
Gross profit (£25,500 - 600)			24,900

478

	£	£	£
Less : Expenses -			
Rent (£3,500 - 700)	2,800		
Rates	1,200		
Electricity (£760 + 180)	940	4,940	
Postages, stationery and other sundry expenses		355	
Wages		14,700	
Van	890		
Van licence and insurance (£250 -125)	125		
Van depreciation	750	1,765	
Loan interest		125	21,885
Net profit for the year			£3,015

Balance Sheet at 31 March 19X6

	£	£	£
Fixed assets			
Motor van, at cost		7,600	
Less : Provision for depreciation		750	6,850
Current assets			
Stock	1,900		
Debtors	2,300		
Prepayments (£700 + 125)	825		
Bank (Wkg 2)	4,310		
Cash in hand (Wkg 3)	640	9,975	
Less : **Current liabilities**			
Creditors	880		
Accrued charges (£125 + 180)	305	1,185	8,790
			15,640
Loan			10,000
			£5,640
Capital			
At 1 April 19X5			15,000
Add : Net profit for the year		3,015	
Less : Drawings (£3,875 + 8,500)		12,375	(9,360)
			£5,640

Workings :

Purchases Account

	£		£
Bank (£26,400 +120)	26,520	Trading Account	27,400
Closing creditors c/d	880		
	£27,400		£27,400

Bank Account

	£		£
Opening capital	15,000	Purchases (£26,400 + 120)	26,520
Loan from John Peacock	10,000	Electricity	760
Cash banked (£42,000 + 340)	42,340	Rent	3,500
		Rates	1,200
		Wages	14,700
		Van	7,600
		Holiday caravan	8,500
		Van licence and insurance	250
		Balance c/d (£4,090 + 340 - 120)	4,310
	£67,340		£67,340

Cash Account

	£		£
Cash sales (£50,400 - 2,300)	48,100	Van running expenses	890
		Postages, stationery and sundry expenses	355
		Banked	42,340
		Drawings (balancing figure)	3,875
		Balance c/d	640
	£48,100		£48,100

EXERCISE 19.6   PAGE 157

(a)

MARK TAPSTER
Balance Sheet at 31 December 19X6

	£ Cost	£ Accumulated Depreciation	£ Net Book Value
Fixed assets			
Freehold premises	65,000	-	65,000
Fixtures and fittings	5,000	2,450	2,550
Motor vehicles	7,500	4,500	3,000
	£77,500	£6,950	70,550
Current assets			
Stock		32,300	
Trade debtors		21,260	
Bank		4,340	
Cash in hand		170	
		58,070	
Less : **Current liabilities**			
Trade Creditors		15,400	42,670
			£113,220

Capital

At 1 January 19X5		107,340
Add : Net profit for the year	14,180	
Less : Drawings	8,300	5,880
		£113,220

(b)

Changes in working capital	31 12 X5 £	31 12 X6 £	Movement £
Stock	34,100	32,300	(1,800)
Trade debtors	24,160	21,260	(2,900)
Trade creditors	(16,900)	(15,400)	1,500
	41,360	38,160	(3,200)
Bank	(7,800)	4,340	12,140
Cash in hand	280	170	(110)
Working capital	£33,840	£42,670	£8,830

(c)

Trading, Profit and Loss Account for the year to 31 December 19X6

	£	£	£
Sales			147,320
Less : Cost of goods sold -			
Opening stock		34,100	
Purchases		108,690	
		142,790	
Less : Closing stock		32,300	110,490
Gross profit (25% of sales)			36,830
Less : Expenses -			
Overhead expenses		19,200	
Depreciation : Fixtures and fittings	950		
Motor vehicle	2,500	3,450	22,650
Net profit for the year (derived)			£14,180

SOLUTIONS TO CHAPTER 20 EXERCISES

EXERCISE 20.1   PAGE 163

(a)

LANDSDOWNE BROTHERS
Departmental Trading Profit and Loss Account
for the year ended 31 March 19X6

Department	A £000	B £000	Total £000
Sales	294	327	621
Less : Cost of goods sold			
Opening stock	32	54	86
Purchases	253	274	527
	285	328	613
Less : Closing stock	42	60	102
	243	268	511
Gross profit	51	59	110
Wages	29	15	44
Contribution	22	44	66
Less : Indirect expenses			
Rates and insurance (40 : 60)	4	6	10
Delivery costs (10 : 90)	1	9	10
Administration costs (50 : 50)	8	8	16
Heating and lighting (50 : 50)	3	3	6
	16	26	42
Net profit	£6	£18	£24

(b)   Calculation of gross profit :

Department A $\dfrac{51}{294}$ x 100 = 17.3%

Department B $\dfrac{59}{327}$ x 100 = 18.0%

EXERCISE 20.2 PAGE 164

(a)

FOOD AND CLOTHING SUPPLIES LTD
Profit and Loss Account for the year to 31 December 19X4

Department	C £	F £	Total £
Gross profit	64,000	57,000	121,000
Add : Other income			
Discount received (assumed 40 : 60)	200	300	500
	64,200	57,300	121,500
Less : Expenses			
Advertising (40 : 60)	3,400	5,100	8,500
Salaries and wages	20,400	19,000	39,400
Directors' fees (40 : 60)	5,800	8,700	14,500
Motor vehicle expenses (40 : 60)	1,920	2,880	4,800
Rent and rates (£13,800 + 1,200) (1 : 2)	5,000	10,000	15,000
Heating and lighting	8,900	7,300	16,200
Depreciation : Motor vans (20% x £20,000) (40 : 60)	1,600	2,400	4,000
Furniture and fittings (10% x £30,000) (40 : 60)	1,200	1,800	3,000
	48,220	57,180	105,400
Net profit	£15,980	£120	£16,100

(b)

Balance Sheet (extract) at 31 December 19X4

Capital	£ Authorised	£ Issued and fully paid
Ordinary shares of £1 each	100,000	50,000
8% Cumulative preference shares	100,000	100,000
	200,000	150,000
Profit and loss account (£6,600 + 16,100)		22,700
		£172,700

<u>Note</u> : This answer assumes that no taxation or dividends were paid during the year.

EXERCISE 20.3   PAGE 165

ROSE
Trading Profit and Loss Account for the year to 31 March 19X3

Department	B £	S £	Total £
Sales	90,000	135,000	225,000
Less : Cost of goods sold			
Opening stock	7,000	8,000	15,000
Purchases	61,000	86,000	147,000
	68,000	94,000	162,000
Less : Closing stock	8,000	4,000	12,000
	60,000	90,000	150,000
Gross profit	30,000	45,000	75,000
Wages	11,000	14,000	25,000
Contribution	19,000	31,000	50,000
Less : Indirect expenses			
Depreciation : Furniture and fittings (10% x £18,000)	300	1,200	1,500
General shop expenses (£10,500 - 500)	6,000	4,000	10,000
Rent and rates (£12,500 + 2,500)	11,250	3,750	15,000
	17,550	8,950	26,500
Net profit	£1,450	£22,050	£23,500

Balance Sheet at 31 March 19X3

Fixed assets	£	£	£
Furniture and fittings (at cost)			15,000
Less : Accumulated depreciation			9,000
			6,000
Current assets			
Stocks (£8,000 + 4,000)		12,000	
Debtors (£3,750 + 11,250)		15,000	
Prepayments		500	
Cash at bank and in hand		4,000	
		31,500	
Less : **Current liabilities**			
Creditors (£10,000 + 7,000)	17,000		
Accrual	2,500	19,500	12,000
			£18,000
Capital			
Balance at 1 April 19X2			6,500
Add : Net profit for the year		23,500	
Less : Drawings		12,000	11,500
			£18,000

SOLUTIONS TO CHAPTER 21 EXERCISES

EXERCISE 21.1   PAGE 171

OVEN TO OVEN WARE LTD
Manufacturing Account for the year ended 31 December 19X7

	£	£
Direct materials		
Stock at 1 January 19X7		23,000
Purchases	125,300	
Carriage inwards	6,800	132,100
		155,100
Less : Stock at 31 December 19X7		26,000
Direct materials consumed		129,100
Direct wages		110,000
PRIME COST		239,100
Manufacturing overheads		
Building repairs	4,800	
Factory rates	7,900	
Factory power	9,900	
Indirect wages	97,300	
Depreciation : Factory building (£60,000/30)	2,000	
Plant and machinery (£75,200 x 12.5%)	9,400	131,300
		370,400
Add : Work in progress 1 January 19X7		34,000
		404,400
Less : Work in progress 31 December 19X7		36,000
WORKS COST OF GOODS PRODUCED		368,400
Profit on manufacture		11,600
Transfer to finished goods stock		£380,000

Note :   It is assumed that fixtures and fittings do not relate to the manufacturing operations.

EXERCISE 21.2   PAGE 172

WILLIAM SPEED
Manufacturing, Trading and Profit and Loss Account
for the year ended 31 December 19X5

	£	£	£
Direct materials			
Stock at 1 January 19X5			7,000
Purchases			38,000
			45,000
Less : Stock at 31 December 19X5			9,000
			36,000
Direct labour (£28,000 + 3,000)			31,000
PRIME COST			67,000
Manufacturing overheads			
Variable		16,000	
Fixed		9,000	
Depreciation : Plant and machinery		3,000	28,000
			95,000
Add : Work in progress 1 January 19X5			5,000
			100,000
Less : Work in progress 31 December 19X5			8,000
Total factory cost			92,000
Factory profit (25% of factory cost)			23,000
WORKS COST OF GOODS PRODUCED			£115,000
Sales			192,000
Less : Cost of sales			
Stock at 1 January 19X5		6,900	
Cost of goods produced		115,000	
		121,900	
Less : Stock at 31 December 19X5		10,350	111,550
Gross profit			80,450
Factory profit			23,000
			103,450
Administrative expenses :			
Rent and rates (£19,000 - 2,000)		17,000	
Heat and light		6,000	
Stationery and postages		2,000	
Staff salaries		19,380	
		44,380	

	£	£	£
Motor vehicle expenses :			
Running costs	4,500		
Depreciation	4,000	8,500	
Increase in provision for unrealised profit (Wkg)		690	53,570
Net profit for the year			£49,880

Balance Sheet at 31 December 19X5

	£ Cost	£ Aggregate Depreciation	£ Net Book Value
Fixed assets			
Plant and machinery	30,000	15,000	15,000
Motor vehicles	16,000	8,000	8,000
	£46,000	£23,000	23,000
Current assets			
Stocks : Raw materials		9,000	
Work in progress		8,000	
Finished goods	10,350		
Less : provision for unrealised profit	2,070	8,280	
		25,280	
Debtors		28,000	
Prepayments		2,000	
Balance at bank		16,600	
		71,880	
Less : **Current liabilities**			
Creditors	5,500		
Accruals	3,000	8,500	63,380
			£86,380
Capital account			
At 1 January 19X5			48,000
Add : Net profit for the year		49,880	
Less : Drawings		11,500	38,380
			£86,380

WORKINGS

Provision for unrealised profit at 31 December 19X5 $= \frac{25}{125} \times £10,350 = £2,070$

Charge in profit and loss account $= £1,070 - £1,380 = £690$

EXERCISE 21.3   PAGE 173

T RASBURN
Manufacturing, Trading and Profit and Loss Account
for the year ended 30 June 19X7

	£	£
Direct materials		
Stock at 1 July 19X6		10,000
Purchases		88,000
		98,000
Less : Stock at 30 June 19X7		8,000
Direct materials consumed		90,000
Direct labour		40,000
PRIME COST		130,000
Manufacturing overhead		
Indirect wages	8,000	
Rates (3/4 x £8,000)	6,000	
Cleaning costs (3/4 x £8,000)	6,000	
Machinery and plant maintenance	4,000	
Depreciation : Machinery and plant (10% x £40,000)	4,000	28,000
		158,000
Less : Work in progress 30 June 19X7		2,000
WORKS COST OF GOODS PRODUCED		£156,000
Sales		200,000
Less : Cost of goods sold		
Finished goods stock at 1 July 19X6	12,000	
Cost of goods produced	156,000	
	168,000	
Less : Finished goods stock at 30 June 19X7	14,000	154,000
Gross profit		46,000
Less : Expenses -		
Bank loan interest (10% x £40,000)	4,000	
Office expenses	4,000	
Rates (1/4 x £8,000)	2,000	
Office salaries	6,000	
Cleaning costs (1/4 x £8,000)	2,000	
Depreciation : Furniture and fittings (25% x £8,000) (assumed all office expenses)	2,000	20,000
Net profit for the year		£26,000

Balance Sheet at 30 June 19X7

	£ Cost	£ Accumulated Depreciation	£ Net Book Value
Fixed assets			
Premises	100,000	-	100,000
Machinery and plant	40,000	24,000	16,000
Furniture and fittings	8,000	8,000	-
	£148,000	£32,000	£116,000
Current assets			
Stocks : Raw materials	8,000		
Work in progress	2,000		
Finished goods	14,000	24,000	
Debtors		16,000	
Cash at bank and in hand		6,000	
		46,000	
Less : Current liabilities			
Creditors (£12,000 + 4,000)		16,000	
Net working capital			30,000
			146,000
Less : Bank loan			40,000
Capital employed			£106,000
Capital			
At 1 July 19X6			100,000
Add : Net profit for the year		26,000	
Less : Drawings		20,000	6,000
			£106,000

EXERCISE 21.4   PAGE 174

BLICK
Manufacturing, Trading and Profit and Loss Account
for the year to 31 December 19X7

	£	£	£
Direct materials			
Purchases (£70,000 + 4,100 + 24,000)			98.100
Less : Stock at 31 December 19X7			6,000
Direct materials consumed			92,100
Direct labour (£102,000 + 1,400)			103,400
PRIME COST			195,500
Manufacturing overheads			
Factory rates, water and electricity (£5,600 + 400 - 500)		5,500	
Depreciation : Manufacturing equipment (12.5% x £48,000)		6,000	11,500
WORKS COST OF GOODS PRODUCED			£207,000

	£	£	£
Sales (£102,000 + 7,900 +4,100 +13,000 +12,000 +120,000 +13,000 + 800)			272,800
Less : Cost of goods sold			
Cost of goods produced	207,000		
Less : Transfer to office equipment (Wkg1)	1,600	205,400	
Less : Stock at 31 December 19X7		7,000	198,400
Gross profit			74,400
Administration expenses :			
Office rates, water and electricity	2,400		
Sundry office expenses, including salaries (£12,000 + 7,900 + 200 +2,000)	22,100		
Depreciation : Office equipment [10% x (£3,000 + 1,600)]	460	24,960	
Selling and distribution expenses :			
Delivery vehicle expenses	13,000		
Depreciation : delivery vehicles (20% x £22,000)	4,400	17,400	42,360
Net profit for the year			£32,040

Balance Sheet at 31 December 19X7

	£ Cost	£ Accumulated Depreciation	£ Net Book Value
Fixed assets			
Business premises	50,000	-	50,000
Manufacturing equipment	48,000	6,000	42,000
Office equipment	4,600	460	4,140
Delivery vehicles	22,000	4,400	17,600
	£124,600	£10,860	113,740
Current assets			
Stocks : Raw materials	6,000		
Finished goods	7,000	13,000	
Trade debtors		13,000	
Prepayment		500	
Bank balance (Wkg2)		4,000	
Cash in hand		800	
		31,300	
Less : Current liabilities			
Trade creditors	24,000		
Accruals (£400 + 1,400 + 200 + 2,000)	4,000	28,000	3,300
			£117,040

490

	£	£
	Accumulated Depreciation	**Net Book Value**
Capital		
At 1 January 19X7		100,000
Add : Net profit for the year	32,040	
Less : Drawings (£12,000 + 3,000)	15,000	17,040
		£117,040

Workings

(1) **Calculation of profit on goods transferred to office equipment**

	£	£
Sales		272,800
Add : Transfer at selling price		2,200
		275,000
Less : Cost of goods sold :		
Cost of goods purchased	207,000	
Less : Stock at 31 December 19X7	7,000	200,000
GROSS PROFIT		£75,000

Cost of transfer therefore :

$$x + \frac{75x}{200} = 2,200$$

$$= £1,600$$

(2) **Bank balance at 31 December 19X7**

Capital introduced	100,000
Cash paid in	120,000
	220,000
Less : Payments (£50,000 + 48,000 + 22,000 + 3,000 + 70,000 + 5,600 + 2,400 + 3,000 + 12,000)	216,000
	£4,000

SOLUTIONS TO CHAPTER 22 EXERCISES

EXERCISE 22.1   PAGE 180

OSWALD
Crates Stock Account

	No	£		No	£
1 1 X2 Balances b/d :			31 12 X2 Profit on hire		
In hand (at £5)	100	500	(30,000 x £5)	-	150,000
With customers			31 12 X2 Retained by		
(at £5)	200	1,000	customers		
31 12 X2 Purchases			(at £7)	2,000	14,000
(at £9)	8,000	72,000	31 12 X2 Balances c/d :		
31 12 X2 Profit for year	-	122,000	In hand		
			(at £5)	5,100	25,500
			With customers		
			(at £5)	1,200	6,000
	8,300	£195,500		8,300	£195,500
1 1 X3 Balance b/d :					
In hand	5,100	25,500			
With customers					
	1,200	6,000			

Crates Suspense Account

	No	£		No	£
1 1 X2 Returns			1 1 X2 Balance b/d		
(at £7)	27,000	189,000	(at £7)	200	1,400
31 12 X2 Retained			31 12 X2 Sales		
(at £7)	2,000	14,000	(at £12)	30,000	360,000
31 12 X2 Profit on hire					
(30,000 x £5)	-	150,000			
31 12 X2 Balance c/d					
(at £7)	1,200	8,400			
	30,200	£361,400		30,200	£361,400
			1 1 X3 Balance b/d	1,200	8,400

Check :

	£
Profit on hire (30,000 x £5)	150,000
Profit on crates retained [2,000 x (£7 - £5)]	4,000
	154,000
Less : Depreciation on crates purchased	
[8,000 x (£9 - £5)]	32,000
Profit for the year	£122,000

EXERCISE 22.2   PAGE 180

CRIEFF
Bins Stock Account

		No	£			No	£
1 4 X7	Balances b/d :			31 3 X8	Profit on hire		
	In hand (£10)	400	4,000		(£20)	-	120,000
	With customers			31 3 X8	Profit on late		
	(£10)	800	8,000		returns (£18)	-	3,600
31 3 X8	Purchases			31 3 X8	Scrapped	50	-
	(£40)	1,000	40,000	31 3 X8	Balances c/d :		
31 3 X8	Repairs	-	7,500		In hand (£10)	550	5,500
31 3 X8	Profit for year	-	85,600		With customers		
					(£10)	1,600	16,000
		2,200	£145,100			2,200	£145,100
1 4 X8	Balance b/d :						
	In hand	550	5,500				
	With customers						
		1,600	16,000				

Bins Suspense Account

		No	£			No	£
31 3 X8	Returns			1 4 X7	Balance b/d		
	(£30)	5,000	150,000		(£30)	800	24,000
31 3 X8	Profit on hire			31 3 X8	Sales (£50)	6,000	300,000
	(£20)	-	120,000				
31 3 X8	Late returns						
	(£12)	200	2,400				
31 3 X8	Profit on late						
	returns						
	(£30 - £12)	-	3,600				
31 3 X8	Stock with						
	customers c/d						
	(£30)	1,600	48,000				
		6,800	£324,000			6,800	£324,000
				1 4 X8	Balance b/d	1,600	48,000

Check :

		£	£
Profit on hire (6,000 x £20)			120,000
Profit on late returns (200 x £18)			3,600
			123,600
Less :	Loss on scrapped cases (50 x £10)	500	
	Depreciation on year's purchases		
	(1,000 x £30)	30,000	
	Repairs	7,500	38,000
Profit for the year			£85,600

EXERCISE 22.3   PAGE 181

LAGG LIMITED
Cases Stock Account (SBV of £5 per case)

		No	£			No	£
1 4 X6	Balances b/d :			31 3 X7	Cases P & L		
	On premises	1,000	5,000		(2000 purchased		
	Customers	3,000	15,000		w/d to SBV £5)	-	2,000
31 3 X7	Purchases	2,000	12,000	31 3 X7	Sales	1,500	7,500
				31 3 X7	Cases P & L		
					- damaged	100	500
					- sold	50	250
				31 3 X7	Balances c/d :		
					On premises	850	4,250
					Customers	3,500	17,500
		6,000	£32,000			6,000	£32,000
1 4 X7	Balances b/d :						
	On premises	850	4,250				
	Customers	3,500	17,500				

Cases Suspense Account (at return price of £8 per case)

		No	£			No	£
31 3 X7	Returns	23,000	184,000	1 4 X6	Balance b/d	3,000	24,000
31 3 X7	Cases stock			31 3 X7	Charged to		
	(purchases)	1,500	12,000		customers	25,000	200,000
31 3 X7	Balance c/d	3,500	28,000				
		28,000	£224,000			28,000	£224,000
				1 4 X7	Balance b/d	3,000	28,000

Cases Sent to Customers Account (at issue price of £10 per case)

		No	£			No	£
1 4 X6	Balance b/d	3,000	30,000	31 3 X7	Cases		
31 3 X7	Issues :	25,000			returned	23,000	184,000
	Cases suspense	-	200,000	31 3 X7	Bank - cases		
	Cases P & L	-	50,000		retained	1,500	15,000
				31 3 X7	Cash from		
					customers		
					(23,000x£2)	-	46,000
				31 3 X7	Balance c/d	3,500	35,000
		28,000	£280,000			28,000	£280,000
1 4 X7	Balance b/d	3,500	35,000				

Cases Profit and Loss Account

		£			£
31 3 X7	Cases Stock A/C		31 3 X7	Cases sent to customers	
	- purchases w/d	2,000		(25,000 x £2)	50,000
	- cases damaged	500	31 3 X7	Profit on sales to	
	- cases sold	250		customers (cases	
31 3 X7	Cash - repairs	1,400		retained)	4,500
31 3 X7	General P & L A/C	50,450	31 3 X7	Cash - sale proceeds	100
		£54,600			£54,600

SOLUTIONS TO CHAPTER 23 EXERCISES

EXERCISE 23.1   PAGE 185

FORTH LTD
Contract Account

	£		£
31 12 X2 Direct wages	125	31 12 X2 Stock of materials c/d	15
Direct materials	50	Plant and equipment (at	
Other costs	10	WDV) c/d	460
Plant and equipment		Work in progress	
at cost	500	(balance) c/d	210
	£685		£685
1 1 X3 Stock of materials b/d	15		
Plant and equipment b/d	460		
Work in progress b/d	210		

Note :   As the contract is in its early stages, it would not be prudent to claim any attributable profit for the year to 31 December 19X2.

EXERCISE 23.2   PAGE 186

MULL LTD
Contract Account

	£000		£000
Direct materials	250	Plant and machinery	
Direct labour	300	at WDV c/d	325
Plant and machinery,		Trading Account	675
at cost	400		
Administrative expenses	50		
	£1,000		£1,000
Plant and machinery			
at WDV, b/d	325		

Note :   Estimated profit represents 30% of the contract price. The turnover equivalent to the attributable profit is, therefore, £964,000 (approx.).

Trading Account

	£000		£000
Contract account		Turnover (being value of work	
(attributable costs)	675	done)	964
Gross profit (attributable			
profit) c/d	289		
	£964		£964
		Gross profit b/d	289

Workings
Attributable profit

$$\text{Total profit} \times \frac{\text{Costs to date}}{\text{Total estimated costs}}$$

$$= (£1,500\text{-}1,050) \times \frac{(£250+300+400+50\text{-}325)}{1,050}$$

$$= 450 \times \frac{675}{1,050}$$

$$= £289,000$$

EXERCISE 23.3   PAGE 186

LINTON PLC
Contract Account

		£000			£000
31 3 X3	Direct materials	288	31 3 X3	Materials c/d	18
	Direct labour	240		Equipment c/d	300
	Other site costs	60		Work in progress c/d	6
	Equipment at cost	400		Trading Account	664
		£988			£988
1 4 X3	Materials b/d	18			
	Equipment b/d	300			
	Work in progress b/d	6			

Contractee Account

		£000			£000
31 3 X3	Trading Account	714	31 3 X3	Bank	450
				Balance c/d	264
		£714			£714
1 4 X3	Balance b/d	264			

Trading Account

	£000		£000
Cost of sales (attributable costs - Wkg)	664	Turnover	714
Gross profit (attributable profit) c/d	50		
	£714		£714
		Gross profit b/d	50

Working

Calculation of attributable profit

	£000	£000	£000
Contract price			1,000
Costs to date :			
Materials (£288 - 18)		270	
Wages		240	
Other site costs		60	
Equipment (£400 - 300)		100	
		670	
Expected future costs :			
Materials	50		
Wages	100		
Other site costs	40		
Equipment (£300 - 230)	70	260	930
Estimated total profit			£70

Proportion recognised in the year to 31 March 19X3 :

$$\text{Total profit} \times \frac{\text{Costs to date}}{\text{Total estimated costs}} = £70 \times \frac{670}{930} = \underline{£50,000} \text{ (say)}$$

Estimated total profit = 7% of the contract price. The turnover on an attributable profit of £50,000 is, therefore, £714,000 (approx.).

SOLUTIONS TO CHAPTER 24 EXERCISES

EXERCISE 24.1   PAGE 190

(a)

DOLPHIN LTD
9% Atlantis Government Stock Account

		Nominal £	Income £	Cost £			Nominal £	Income £	Cost £
1 1 X1	Balance b/d	20,000	-	18,000	1 2 X1	Bank	-	900	-
1 1 X1	Balance b/d (accrued interest)	-	750	-	1 7 X1	Bank (ex div.)	8,000	-	7,620
1 4 X1	Bank	12,000	180	11,040	1 8 X1	Bank	-	1,440	-
1 7 X1	Profit on disposal	-	-	360	31 12 X1	Accrued interest c/d	-	1,125	-
30 11 X1	Bank	6,000	180	6,110	31 12 X1	Balance c/d	30,000	-	27,890
31 12 X1	Profit and Loss	-	2,355	-					
		£38,000	£3,465	£35,510			£38,000	£3,465	£35,510
1 1 X2	Accrued interest b/d	-	1,125	-					
1 1 X2	Balance b/d	30,000	-	27,890					

(b) With ordinary shares at the end of the financial year, it is not customary to allow for dividends which may be paid on the shares held.

EXERCISE 24.2   PAGE 190

MONDALE LTD
10% Debenture in Forfar plc Account

		Nominal £	Income £	Cost £			Nominal £	Income £	Cost £
1 1 X2	Balance b/d	20,000	-	18,002	30 6 X2	Bank	-	3,500	-
1 4 X2	Bank	50,000	1,250	48,750	30 9 X2	Bank	10,000	250	9,350
31 12 X2	Profit and Loss	-	5,500	-	30 9 X2	Loss on disposal (1/7)	-	-	186
					31 12 X2	Bank	-	3,000	-
					31 12 X2	Balance c/d	60,000	-	57,216
		£70,000	£6,750	£66,752			£70,000	£6,750	£66,752
1 1 X3	Balance b/d	60,000	-	57,216					

Greengrass plc Ordinary Shares of £1 Account

		Nominal £	Income £	Cost £			Nominal £	Income £	Cost £
1 6 X2	Bank	1,000	-	2,250	31 12 X2	Bank	-	100	-
31 12 X2	Profit and Loss	-	100	-	31 12 X2	Balance c/d	1,000	-	2,250
		£1,000	£100	£2,250			£1,000	£100	£2,250
1 1 X3	Balance b/d	1,000	-	2,250					

EXERCISE 24.3 PAGE 191

DAFFYD LTD
15% Government Stock Account

		Nominal £	Income £	Capital £			Nominal £	Income £	Capital £
1 4 X2	Bank	50,000	1,875	28,125	30 6 X2	Bank	-	3,750	-
31 3 X3	Profit and				31 12 X2	Bank	-	3,750	-
	Loss	-	7,500	-	31 3 X3	Accrued interest c/d	-	1,875	-
					31 3 X3	Balance c/d	50,000	-	28,125
		£50,000	£9,375	£28,125			£50,000	£9,375	£28,125
1 4 X3	Accrued interest b/d	-	1,875	-					
1 4 X3	Balance b/d	50,000	-	28,125					

5% Eurostock Account

		Nominal £	Income £	Capital £			Nominal £	Income £	Capital £
1 4 X2	Bank	100,000	-	55,000	30 9 X2	Bank	-	2,500	-
1 10 X2	Profit on disposal	-	-	2,500	1 10 X2	Bank	50,000	-	30,000
31 3 X3	Profit and				31 3 X3	Bank	-	1,250	-
	Loss	-	3,750	-	31 3 X3	Balance c/d	50,000	-	27,500
		£100,000	£3,750	£57,500			£100,000	£3,750	£57,500
1 4 X3	Balance b/d	50,000	-	27,500					

Kippen plc Ordinary £1 Shares Account

		Nominal £	Income £	Capital £			Nominal £	Income £	Capital £
1 4 X2	Bank	10,000	-	50,000	31 12 X2	Bank	-	1,000	-
31 3 X3	Profit and				31 3 X3	Bank	-	2,000	-
	Loss	-	3,000	-	31 3 X3	Balance c/d	10,000	-	50,000
		£10,000	£3,000	£50,000			£10,000	£3,000	£50,000
1 4 X3	Balance b/d	10,000	-	50,000					

SOLUTIONS TO CHAPTER 25 EXERCISES

EXERCISE 25.1   PAGE 195

ODDSOX LTD
Goods Sent on Consignment Account

		£			£
1 1 X2	Trading	18,000	1 1 X2	Consignment	18,000

Consignment (to Agent) Account

		£			£
1 1 X2	Goods sent on consignment	18,000	31 1 X2	Consignee - sales	11,160
31 1 X2	Transport costs	714	31 1 X2	Consignee - stock c/d (Wkg)	9,812
31 1 X2	Insurance	630			
31 1 X2	Consignee - commission	280			
31 1 X2	Consignee - storage charges	280			
31 1 X2	Consignee - delivery expenses	87			
31 1 X2	Profit and Loss	981			
		£20,972			£20,972
1 2 X2	Balance b/d	9,812			

Consignee Account

		£			£
31 1 X2	Consignment - sales	11,160	31 1 X2	Consignment - commission	280
			31 1 X2	Consignment - storage charges	280
			31 1 X2	Consignment - delivery expenses	87
			31 1 X2	Balance c/d	10,513
		£11,160			£11,160
1 2 X3	Balance b/d	10,513			

Working - Stock at 31 January 19X2

	£
Goods	18,000
Insurance	630
Transport	714
Storage	280
	£19,624
One half	£9,812

EXERCISE 25.2   PAGE 196

DAN LTD

(i)   **Dan Ltd's books**

Goods Sent on Consignment Account

		£			£
1 1 X5	Trading	50,000	1 1 X5	Consignment	50,000

Consignment Account

		£			£
1 1 X5	Goods sent on consignment	50,000	31 5 X5	Consignee - sales	46,875
1 1 X5	Air freight	3,500	31 5 X5	Stock c/d (£50,000 + 3,500 + 1,500) x 1/4	13,750
1 1 X5	Insurance	1,500			
31 5 X5	Commission	4,600			
31 5 X5	Selling expenses	875			
30 6 X5	Profit and Loss	150			
		£60,625			£60,625
1 6 X5	Stock b/d	13,750			

Consignee Account

		£			£
31 5 X5	Consignee - sales	46,875	31 5 X5	Consignee - Commission	4,600
			31 5 X5	Consignee - Selling expenses	875
			30 6 X5	Bank	41,400
		£46,875			£46,875

(ii)   **Agent's books**

Dan Ltd (Consignor) Account

		£			£
31 5 X5	Bank - Selling expenses	875	31 5 X5	Debtors/Cash	46,875
31 5 X5	Commission	4,600			
30 6 X5	Bank	41,400			
		£46,875			£46,875

EXERCISE 25.3   PAGE 196

FLEET

(i)   **Fleet's books**

Goods Sent on Consignment Account

		£			£
31 3 X8	Trading Account	20,000	1 4 X7	Consignment	20,000

Consignment to Sing Account

			£				£
1 4 X7	Goods sent on consignment		20,000	30 9 X7	Bank (insurance claim)		220
30 4 X7	Bank (carriage, freight and insurance)		2,000	31 3 X8	Sing (consignee) - Sales		28,500
31 3 X8	Sing (consignee)			31 3 X8	Stock c/d (Wkg)		920
	- Distribution expenses	1,900					
	- Landing charges and import duty	990					
	- Commission	1,425					
31 3 X8	Profit and Loss		3,325				
			£29,640				£29,640
1 4 X8	Stock b/d		920				

Sing (consignee) Account

		£			£
31 3 X8	Consignment to Sing	28,500	1 3 X8	Bank	20,000
			31 3 X8	Consignment to Sing :	
				- Distribution expenses	1,900
				- Landing charges and import duty	990
				- Commission	1,425
			31 3 X8	Balance c/d	4,185
		£28,500			£28,500
1 4 X8	Balance b/d	4,185			

(ii)   **Sing's books**

Fleet (London) Account

		£			£
1 3 X8	Bank	20,000	31 3 X8	Debtors	28,500
31 3 X8	Bank :				
	- Distribution expenses	1,900			
	- Landing charges and import duty	990			
31 3 X8	Commission	1,425			
31 3 X8	Balance c/d	4,185			
		£28,500			£28,500
			1 4 X8	Balance b/d	4,185

Commission Account

	£			£
31 3 X8 Profit and Loss	1,425	31 3 X8 Fleet (London)		1,425

Working - Stock on hand at 31 March 19X8

	£
Fleet : Purchase price per box	20
Add : Attributable expenses :	
Fleet - carriage, freight and insurance (2,000/1,000)	2
Sing - landing charges and import duty	1
COST PER BOX LANDED	£23
Closing stock = £23 x (990 - 950)	£920

SOLUTIONS TO CHAPTER 26 EXERCISES

EXERCISE 26.1   PAGE 201

RAYLOW
Royalties Account

		£			£
19X1	Paz (1,000 x £5)	5,000	19X1	Operating	5,000
19X2	Paz (1,500 x £5)	7,500	19X2	Operating	7,500
19X3	Paz (2,000 x £5)	10,000	19X3	Operating	10,000
19X4	Paz (4,000 x £5)	20,000	19X4	Operating	20,000

Paz Account

		£			£
19X1	Bank	8,000	19X1	Royalties	5,000
			19X1	Short Workings	3,000
		£8,000			£8,000
19X2	Bank	8,000	19X2	Royalties	7,500
			19X2	Short Workings	500
		£8,000			£8,000
19X3	Bank	8,000	19X3	Royalties	10,000
19X3	Short Workings	2,000			
		£10,000			£10,000
19X4	Bank	£20,000	19X4	Royalties	£20,000

Short Workings Account

		£			£
19X1	Paz	3,000			
19X2	Paz	500	19X2	Balance c/d	3,500
		£3,500			£3,500
19X3	Balance b/d	3,500	19X3	Paz	2,000
			19X3	Profit and Loss (amount now irrecoverable)	1,500
		£3,500			£3,500

EXERCISE 26.2 PAGE 202

DUNBAR LTD
Royalties Account

	£		£
31 12 X1 Berwick (6,000 x £2)	12,000	31 12 X1 Operating Account	12,000
31 12 X2 Berwick (4,000 x £2)	8,000	31 12 X2 Operating Account	8,000
31 12 X3 Berwick (3,000 x £2)	6,000	31 12 X3 Operating Account	6,000
31 12 X4 Berwick (5,500 x £2)	11,000	31 12 X4 Operating Account	11,000
31 12 X5 Berwick (8,000 x £2)	16,000	31 12 X5 Operating Account	16,000

Berwick plc Account

	£		£
31 1 X2 Bank	12,000	31 12 X1 Royalties	12,000
		31 12 X2 Royalties	8,000
31 12 X2 Balance c/d	10,000	31 12 X2 Short Workings	2,000
	£10,000		£10,000
31 1 X3 Bank	10,000	1 1 X3 Balance b/d	10,000
31 12 X3 Balance c/d	10,000	31 12 X3 Royalties	6,000
		31 12 X3 Short Workings	4,000
	£20,000		£20,000
31 1 X4 Bank	10,000	1 1 X4 Balance b/d	10,000
31 12 X4 Short Workings		31 12 X4 Royalties	11,000
(recouped)	1,000		
31 12 X4 Balance c/d	10,000		
	£21,000		£21,000
31 1 X5 Bank	10,000	1 1 X5 Balance b/d	10,000
31 12 X5 Short Workings		31 12 X5 Royalties	16,000
(recouped)	4,000		
31 12 X5 Balance c/d	12,000		
	£26,000		£26,000
		1 1 X6 Balance b/d	12,000

Short Workings Account

	£		£
31 12 X2 Berwick	2,000	31 12 X3 Balance c/d	6,000
31 12 X3 Berwick	4,000		
	£6,000		£6,000

		£			£
1 1 X4	Balance b/d	6,000	31 12 X4 Berwick (recouped)		1,000
			31 12 X4 Profit and Loss		
			(now irrecoverable)		1,000
			31 12 X4 Balance c/d		4,000
		£6,000			£6,000
1 1 X5	Balance b/d	4,000	31 12 X5 Berwick (recouped)		4,000

EXERCISE 26.3   PAGE 202

BASS plc

Alternative (i)

Budgeted Royalties Account

		£			£
19X3	Karogen	100,000	19X3	Operating (£100 x 16/100)	16,000
			19X3	Balance c/d	84,000
		£100,000			£100,000
19X4	Balance b/d	84,000	19X4	Operating (£100 x 18/100)	18,000
			19X4	Balance c/d	66,000
		£84,000			£84,000
19X5	Balance b/d	66,000	19X5	Operating (£100 x 20/100)	20,000
			19X5	Balance c/d	46,000
		£66,000			£66,000
19X6	Balance b/d	46,000	19X6	Operating (£100 x 22/100)	22,000
			19X6	Balance c/d	24,000
		£46,000			£46,000
19X7	Balance b/d	24,000	19X7	Operating	24,000

Budgeted Loan and Loan Interest Account

		£			£
			19X3	Bank	100,000
			19X3	Profit and Loss	
19X3	Balance c/d	120,000		- interest (20%x£100)	20,000
		£120,000			£120,000

		£			£
			19X4	Balance b/d	120,000
			19X4	Profit and Loss	
19X4	Balance c/d	144,000		- interest (20%x£120)	24,000
		£144,000			£144,000
			19X5	Balance b/d	144,000
			19X5	Profit and Loss	
19X5	Balance c/d	172,800		- interest (20%x£144)	28,800
		£172,800			£172,800
			19X6	Balance b/d	172,800
			19X6	Profit & Loss - interest	
19X6	Balance c/d	207,360		(20%x£172,800)	34,560
		£207,360			£207,360
			19X7	Balance b/d	207,360
			19X7	Profit & Loss - interest	
19X7	Bank	248,832		(20%x£207,360)	41,472
		£248,832			£248,832

Alternative (ii)

Budgeted Royalties Account

		£			£
19X3	Karogen (1,600 x £0.011)	17,600	19X3	Operating Account	17,600
19X4	Karogen (1,800 x £0.011)	19,800	19X4	Operating Account	19,800
19X5	Karogen (2,000 x £0.011)	22,000	19X5	Operating Account	22,000
19X6	Karogen (2,200 x £0.011)	24,200	19X6	Operating Account	24,200
19X7	Karogen (2,400 x £0.011)	26,400	19X7	Operating Account	26,400

Budgeted Loan and Loan Interest Account

		£			£
			19X3	Bank (min. payment)	35,000
			19X4	Profit and Loss - interest	
				(20% x £35,000)	7,000
19X4	Balance c/d	77,000	19X4	Bank	35,000
		£77,000			£77,000
			19X5	Balance b/d	77,000

508

		£			£
			19X5	Profit and Loss - interest (20% x £77,000)	15,400
19X5	Balance c/d	127,400	19X5	Bank	35,000
		£127,400			£127,400
			19X6	Balance b/d	127,400
			19X6	Profit and Loss - interest (20% x £127,400)	25,480
19X6	Balance c/d	177,080	19X6	Bank	24,200
		£177,080			£177,080
			19X7	Balance b/d	177,080
			19X7	Profit and Loss - interest	
19X7	Bank	212,496		(20% x £177,080)	35,416
		£212,496			£212,496

Note: The royalty payable for 19X7 of £26,400 will not be borrowed as settlement takes place at the end of 19X7.

SOLUTIONS TO CHAPTER 27 EXERCISES

EXERCISE 27.1   PAGE 208

TECHNICIANS CLUB
Income and Expenditure Account
for the year ended 31 December 19X6

	£	£
Subscriptions		2,138
Donations		250
Surplus on Discos :		
Sales of tickets	632	
Less : Expenses	515	117
		2,505
Less : Expenses -		
Secretary's expenses	150	
Rent (Wkg1)	760	
Meeting expenses	722	
Heating and lighting (Wkg2)	273	
Stationery and printing (Wkg3)	295	
Depreciation of equipment (Wkg4)	240	2,440
Excess of income over expenditure for the year		£65

Balance Sheet as at 31 December 19X6

	£	£
Fixed assets		
Equipment at cost (£1,800 + 400)	2,200	
Less : Accumulated depreciation (£500 + 240)	740	1,460
Current assets		
Stocks of stationery	46	
Subscriptions in arrears	110	
Prepaid expenses	240	
Bank and cash	205	
	601	
Less : **Current liabilities**		
Accrued expenses	41	560
		£2,020
Accumulated Fund		
At 1 January 19X6 (Wkg5)		1,955
Add : Excess of income over expenditure for the year		65
		£2,020

510

Workings

Rent

	£		£
1 1 X6 Balance b/d	200	31 12 X6 Income & Expenditure	760
31 12 X6 Receipts and payments	800	31 12 X6 Balance c/d	240
	£1,000		£1,000
1 1 X7 Balance b/d	240		

Heating and Lighting

	£		£
31 12 X6 Receipts and payments	269	1 1 X6 Balance b/d	37
31 12 X6 Balance c/d	41	31 12 X6 Income & Expenditure	273
	£310		£310
		1 1 X7 Balance b/d	41

Stationery

	£		£
1 1 X6 Balance b/d	54	31 12 X6 Income & Expenditure	295
31 12 X6 Receipts and payments	287	31 12 X6 Balance c/d	46
	£341		£341
1 1 X7 Balance b/d	46		

Equipment

	£		£
1 1 X6 Balance b/d	1,300	31 12 X6 Depreciation	240
31 12 X6 Purchases	400	31 12 X6 Balance c/d	1,460
	£1,700		£1,700
1 1 X7 Balance b/d	1,460		

Calculation of Opening Accumulated Fund

	£
Equipment	1,300
Subscriptions in arrears	80
Stocks of stationery	54
Rent prepaid	200
Cash and bank balances	358
	1,992
Heating and lighting accrued	37
Accumulated fund as at 1 January 19X6	£1,955

EXERCISE 27.2   PAGE 209

SEASHORE SWIMMING CLUB

Calculation of the bank balance at 31 May 19X8

	£	£
Balance at 1 June 19X7		580
Add: **Receipts**		
Annual dance	917	
Subscriptions	624	
Locker rents	248	
Sale of refreshments	268	
Competition fees	142	
Sale of swimming permits	60	2,259
		2,839
Less: **Payments**		
Expenses of dance	529	
Rent of clubroom	540	
Purchase of equipment	250	
Prizes for competitions	95	
Sundry expenses	110	
Purchase of refreshments	160	
Licence fees to Council	90	1,774
Bank balance at 31 May 19X8		£1,065

SEASHORE SWIMMING CLUB

Income and Expenditure Account for the year ended 31 May 19X8

	£	£	£
Income			
Subscriptions			624
Locker rents			248
Competition fees			142
Sale of swimming permits			60
Annual dance : receipts		917	
Less : Expenses		529	388
Sale of refreshments : receipts		268	
Less : Cost of sales :			
Opening stock	20		
Purchases	160		
	180		
Less : Closing stock	10	170	98
			1,560

Expenditure

Rent of clubroom (£540 + 40 - 50)	530	
Prizes for competitions	95	
Sundry expenses (£110 - 15 + 10)	105	
Licence fees to Council	90	820
Excess of income over expenditure for the year		£740

Balance Sheet at 31 May 19X8

	£	£
Fixed assets		
Equipment (£290 + 250)		540
Current assets		
Stock of refreshments	10	
Prepayment	50	
Bank	1,065	
	1,125	
Less : **Current liabilities**		
Accrual	10	1,115
		£1,655
Accumulated Fund		
Balance at 1 June 19X7		915
Add : Excess of income over expenditure for the year		740
		£1,655

EXERCISE 27.3 PAGE 209
PENINE KITE FLYING ASSOCIATION
Income and Expenditure Account for the year to 31 October 19X7

	£	£	£
Income			
Subscriptions (£2,040 + 140 - 60)			2,120
Income from refreshments		360	
Less : Cost of refreshment supplies		340	20
Net income from social events			220
Sales of kite materials		620	
Less : Cost of purchase of kite material :			
Opening stock	170		
Purchases	460		
	630		
Less : Closing stock	155	475	145
			2,505
Expenditure			
Rent of room (£1,500 + 500)		2,000	
Postages, printing and stationery		185	
Cost of display by Chilean kite flyers		215	
Depreciation : Video equipment		80	2,480
Excess of income over expenditure for the year			£25

Balance Sheet at 31 October 19X7

	£	£	£
Fixed assets			
Video equipment at net book value (£320 - 80)			240
Current assets			
Stock of kite materials		155	
Subscriptions due		140	
Cash at bank		830	
Cash in hand		15	
		1,140	
***Less* : Current liabilities**			
Creditors for kite materials	110		
Subscription renewed in advance	60		
Accrual	500	670	470
			£710
Accumulated Fund			
Balance at 1 November 19X6			685
Add : Excess of income over expenditure for the year			25
			£710

EXERCISE 27.4   PAGE 210

HENTON CRICKET CLUB
Restaurant Trading Account for the year ended 31 March 19X6

	£	£
Takings		9,200
Less : Cost of meals supplied		
Opening stock of food	200	
Purchases	4,100	
	4,300	
Less : Closing stock of food	300	4,000
		5,200
Less : Restaurant wages		3,700
Profit on restaurant takings to general income and expenditure account		£1,500

General Income and Expenditure Account
for the year ended 31 March 19X6

	£	£	£
Income			
Profit from restaurant			1,500
Members' subscriptions (£2,700 +400)			3,100
Cricket tournament income			1,400
Social functions : income		2,600	
Less : Expenses		800	1,800
Investment income			400
			8,200

Expenditure

Administration expenses		1,100	
Rent and rates (£3,200 - 300)		2,900	
Insurance		200	
Depreciation : Sports equipment	1,200		
Furniture and fittings	400	1,600	5,800
Excess of income over expenditure for the year			£2,400

Balance Sheet at 31 March 19X6

	£ Cost	£ Accumulated Depreciation	£ Net Book Value
Fixed assets			
Sports equipment	4,000	1,200	2,800
Furniture and fittings	2,000	400	1,600
Lawn mower	1,000	-	1,000
	£7,000	£1,600	5,400
Current assets			
Stock of food		300	
Subscriptions due		400	
Prepayment		300	
Cash in bank		3,600	
Cash in hand		700	
		5,300	
Less : Current liabilities			
Creditors		2,800	2,500
			£12,400
Accumulated Fund			
Balance at 1 April 19X5			10,000
Add : Excess of income over expenditure for the year			2,400
			£12,400

EXERCISE 27.5 PAGE 211
NEWTOWN TENNIS CLUB
Bar Trading Account for the year ended 31 December 19X6

	£	£
Takings (£17,448 + 810)		18,258
Less : Cost of sales		
Opening stock	1,326	
Purchases (£12,982 - 400 - 747 + 802)	12,637	
	13,963	
Less : Closing stock	1,543	12,420
Gross Profit		5,838
Less : Steward's wages (3/5)	2,700	
Wages	810	3,510
Net Profit		£2,328

Income and Expenditure Account
for the year ended 31 December 19X6

	£	£
Income		
Bar net profit		2,328
Subscriptions (£1,520 - 64 + 40 + 80 - 48)		1,528
Match fees		274
Sales of raffle tickets	571	
Less : Prizes	130	441
Gaming machine takings	1,285	
Less : Rent	500	785
		5,356
Expenditure		
Steward's wages (2/5)	1,800	
Rent and rates (£1,900 + 200 - 250)	1,850	
Lighting and heating	326	
Telephone	285	
Depreciation : Tennis equipment [20% x (920 + 530)]	290	
Furnishings [5% x (680 + 400)]	54	4,605
Excess of income over expenditure for the year		£751

Balance Sheet at 31 December 19X6

	£	£	£
Fixed assets			
Clubhouse furnishings (£680 + 400 - 54)			1,026
Tennis equipment (£920 + 530 -290)			1,160
			2,186
Current assets			
Bar stock		1,543	
Subscriptions due		80	
Prepayment		250	
Bank		1,170	
Cash		83	
		3,126	
Less : **Current liabilities**			
Creditors for bar purchases	802		
Subscriptions in advance	48	850	2,276
			£4,462
Accumulated Fund			
Balance at 1 January 19X6			3,711
Add : Excess of income over expenditure for the year			751
			£4,462

EXERCISE 27.6 PAGE 212

RISLEY GARDENING AND BOTANICAL SOCIETY
Plant and Seeds Account for the year to 31 December 19X6

	£	£
Sales of plants and seeds		830
Less : Cost of sales		
Opening stock	120	
Purchases	670	
	790	
Less : Closing stock	145	645
Gross Profit transferred to the Income and Expenditure Account		£185

Members Subscriptions Account for the year to 31 December 19X6

	£	£
Received in cash		2,600
Add : Received in advance during 19X5		80
		2,680
Less : Due from members in 19X5	60	
Received in advance for 19X7	70	130
Transferred to the Income and Expenditure Account		£2,550

Income and Expenditure Account for the year to 31 December 19X6

	£	£	£
Income			
Gross profit on sales of plants and seeds			185
Subscriptions			2,550
Hire of gardening implements			1,950
			4,685
Expenditure			
Rent of hall and store		2,500	
Lecturers' fees		370	
Organised visits to botanical gardens		140	
Depreciation : Plant encyclopaedias (25% x £280)	70		
Gardening equipment			
[(20% x £6,400)+(10% x £600)]	1,340	1,410	4,420
Excess of income over expenditure for the year			£265

Balance Sheet at 31 December 19X6

	£ Cost	£ Accumulated Depreciation	£ Net Book Value
Fixed assets			
Gardening implements [(£6,400 + 600), (£1,600 + 1,340)]	7,000	2,940	4,060
Plant encyclopaedias	280	70	210
	£7,280	£3,010	4,270

517

Current assets

Stock of plants and seeds		145	
Cash at bank and in hand (Wkg1)		2,680	
		2,825	

***Less* : Current liabilities**

Creditors (Wkg2)	85		
Subscriptions received in advance	70	155	2,670
			£6,940

Accumulated Fund

Balance at 1 January 19X6	6,675
Add : Excess of income over expenditure for the year	265
	£6,940

WORKINGS

1. Bank and Cash Account

		£			£
1 1 X6	Balance b/d	1,840	31 12 X6	Rent	2,500
31 12 X6	Hire fees	1,950		Lecturers' fees	370
	Sale of plants and seeds	830		Encyclopaedias	280
	Subscriptions	2,600		Visits	140
				Gardening equipment	600
				Creditors - plants and seeds	650
				Balance c/d	2,680
		£7,220			£7,220
1 1 X7	Balance b/d	2,680			

2. Creditors (Suppliers of Plants and Seeds) Account

		£			£
31 12 X6	Bank	650	1 1 X6	Balance b/d	65
	Balance c/d	85	31 12 X6	Plants and seeds	670
		£735			£735
			1 1 X7	Balance b/d	85

EXERCISE 27.7 PAGE 212

HANDLE SOCIAL CLUB
Bar Account for the year to 31 March 19X5

	£	£
Bar sales		55,000
Less : Cost of goods sold		
Opening stock	7,000	
Purchases (£24,000 - 1,500 +2,000)	24,500	

	£	£
	31,500	
Less : Closing stock	1,500	30,000
		25,000
Salaries and wages of barmen		10,000
Bar Net Profit		£15,000

Income and Expenditure Account for the year to 31 March 19X5

	£	£
Income		
Bar net profit		15,000
Building society interest		200
Dances	1,600	
Less : Expenses	900	700
Food sales	8,000	
Less : Purchases	4,500	3,500
Members' subscriptions (Wkg1)		36,200
		55,600
Expenditure		
Accountant's fee (£200 - 200 + 250)	250	
Depreciation : Furniture and equipment (Wkg2)	3,900	
Insurance (£500 + 300 - 200)	600	
Electricity (£1,500 - 400 + 300)	1,400	
Office expenses	22,000	
Rates	2,000	
Salaries and wages	14,000	
Telephone (£3,000 - 600 + 700)	3,100	
Travelling expenses	13,000	60,250
Excess of expenditure over income for the year		£(4,650)

Balance Sheet at 31 March 19X5

	£ Cost	£ Accumulated Depreciation	£ Net Book Value
Fixed assets			
Club premises	18,000	-	18,000
Furniture and equipment	39,000	17,900	21,100
	£57,000	£17,900	39,100
Current assets			
Stocks	1,500		
Prepayments : Insurance	200		
Members' subscriptions in arrears	7,000		
Building society account (£2,500 + 200)	2,700		
Cash	500		
	11,900		

	£ Cost	£ Accumulated Depreciation	£ Net Book Value
Less : **Current liabilities**			
Trade creditors	2,000		
Members' subscriptions paid in advance	800		
Accruals (£250 + 300 + 700)	1,250	4,050	7,850
			£46,950

Accumulated Fund

Balance at 1 April 19X4 (Wkg3)	51,600
Less : Excess of expenditure over income for the year	(4,650)
	£46,950

Workings

1. Members' Subscriptions :

	£	£
Cash received during the year		35,000
Add : Paid in advance at 1 4 X4	1,000	
Amounts in arrears at 31 3 X5	7,000	8,000
		43,000
Less : Amounts in arrears at 1 4 X4	6,000	
Paid in advance at 31 3 X5	800	6,800
Members' subscriptions for the year to 31 3 X5		£36,200

2. Depreciation of Furniture and Equipment :

	£
10% x £35,000	3,500
10% x £4,000	400
	£3,900

3. Opening Accumulated Fund :

	£
Club premises	18,000
Furniture and equipment (net)	21,000
Bar stock	7,000
Sundry prepayments (£300 + 6,000)	6,300
Building society account	2,500
Cash	500
	55,300
Less : Accruals and creditors (£200 + 1,500 + 400 +1,000 + 600)	3,700
Accumulated Fund Balance at 1 April 19X4	£51,600

SOLUTIONS TO CHAPTER 28 EXERCISES

EXERCISE 28.1   PAGE 219

(a)

GRAHAM, HARVEY, RUTHERFORD AND MILES
Appropriation Account for the year ended 31 December 19X6

Net profit :   £85,550
Appropriation :

	Graham	Harvey	Rutherford	Miles	Total
	£	£	£	£	£
Interest on capital	7,500	7,000	6,000	6,000	26,500
Salary	10,000	10,000	8,000	8,000	36,000
Interest on drawings	(1,729)	(1,100)	(832)	(789)	(4,450)
Share of balance	9,625	9,625	5,500	2,750	27,500
	£25,396	£25,525	£18,668	£15,961	£85,550

(b)

The solution to this part is on the following page.

EXERCISE 28.2   PAGE 220

(a)   (i)   Interest to be allowed on Capital Accounts at 12% per annum.

(ii)   The partners to receive salaries as follows :

	£
Grahame	7,000
Margo	6,500
Raj	5,500

(iii)   The balance of profits and losses to be shared in the ratio Grahame : Margo : Raj - 5 : 3 : 2.

(iv)   No interest is to be charged on drawings.

(b)   Net profit for the year was £30,000 calculated as follows :

	Grahame	Margo	Raj	Total
	£	£	£	£
Interest on capital	6,000	3,600	1,800	11,400
Salary	7,000	6,500	5,500	19,000
Share of balance	(200)	(120)	(80)	(400)
	£12,800	£9,980	£7,220	£30,000

The solution to the remainder of this question follows after the next page.

Solution to EXERCISE 28.1(b)

Current Accounts

		Graham £	Harvey £	Ruther-ford £	Miles £
1 1 X6	Balances b/d	-	-	1,240	-
31 12 X6	Drawings	23,050	21,980	16,640	17,300
31 12 X6	Interest on drawings	1,729	1,100	832	789
31 12 X6	Balances c/d	4,446	6,915	788	-
		£29,225	£29,995	£19,500	£18,089
1 1 X7	Balances b/d	-	-	-	359

		Graham £	Harvey £	Ruther-ford £	Miles £
1 1 X6	Balances b/d	2,100	3,370	-	980
31 12 X6	Interest on capital	7,500	7,000	6,000	6,000
31 12 X6	Salary	10,000	10,000	8,000	8,000
31 12 X6	Share of profits	9,625	9,625	5,500	2,750
31 12 X6	Balances c/d	-	-	359	-
		£29,225	£29,995	£19,500	£18,089
1 1 X7	Balances b/d	4,446	6,915	788	-

EXERCISE 28.2 (continued)

(c)   The partners would have shared the profit of £30,000 equally as follows:

	£
Grahame	10,000
Margo	10,000
Raj	10,000
	£30,000

(d)   The partners' shares in profit would have been as follows :

	Grahame £	Margo £	Raj £	Total £
Interest on capital	6,000	3,600	1,800	11,400
Salary	7,000	6,500	5,500	19,000
Share of balance	14,800	8,880	5,920	29,600
	£27,800	£18,980	£13,220	£60,000

EXERCISE 28.3   PAGE 221

FIELDING AND SPENCE
Profit and Loss Account for the year ended 31 December 19X6

	£	£
Fees invoiced to clients		104,900
Less : Expenses -		
Rent of office premises (£12,100 + 1,100)	13,200	
Depreciation on computer equipment (50% x £8,400)	4,200	
Depreciation on motor vehicles (25% x £18,400)	4,600	
Salaries	45,217	
Stationery (£2,094 - 211)	1,883	
Insurances (£2,620 - 390)	2,230	
Telephone	1,020	
Heat and light	2,938	
Motor vehicle running costs	5,134	
Interest on bank overdraft	224	
Staff training costs	1,994	82,640
Net profit for the year		£22,260
Appropriation :		
Interest on capital :		
Fielding	1,200	
Spence	640	
Balance of profits :		
Fielding (50%)	10,210	
Spence (50%)	10,210	20,420
		£22,260

Balance Sheet at 31 December 19X6

	£ Cost	£ Accumulated Depreciation	£ Net Book Value
Fixed assets			
Motor vehicles	18,400	9,200	9,200
Computer equipment	8,400	4,200	4,200
	£26,800	£13,400	13,400
Current assets			
Stocks of stationery		211	
Client accounts unpaid		16,900	
Prepayment		390	
		17,501	
Less : Current liabilities			
Creditors	912		
Accrual	1,100		
Bank	2,940	4,952	12,549
			£25,949
Capital accounts :			
Fielding		15,000	
Spence		8,000	23,000
Current accounts :			
Fielding (£680 + 1,200 +10,210 - 10,620)		1,470	
Spence (£740 + 640 + 10,210 - 10,111)		1,479	2,949
			£25,949

EXERCISE 28.4   PAGE 222

(a)

DOBBINSON AND SPENCER
Trading, Profit and Loss Account
for the year ended 31 October 19X6

	£	£	£
Sales		36,360	
Less : Sales returns		480	35,880
Less : Cost of sales :			
Opening stock		3,840	
Purchases	18,250		
Less : Purchase returns	270	17,980	
		21,820	
Less : Closing stock		5,160	16,660
Gross Profit			19,220
Add : Income -			
Discounts received			370
			19,590

Less: Expenses -		
Wages and salaries (£7,320 + 100)	7,420	
Rent, rates and insurance	2,100	
Discounts allowed	580	
Sundry expenses	175	
Motor vehicle expenses	815	
Depreciation : Motor vehicle (20% x £7,000)	1,400	12,490
Net profit for the year		£7,100

Appropriation :		
Interest on capital :		
Dobbinson	350	
Spencer	250	600
Balance of profits :		
Dobbinson (50%)	3,250	
Spencer (50%)	3,250	6,500
		£7,100

(b)

Balance Sheet at 31 October 19X6

	£ Cost	£ Accumulated Depreciation	£ Net Book Value
Fixed assets			
Fixtures and fittings	1,200	-	1,200
Office furniture	820	-	820
Motor vehicles	7,000	1,400	5,600
	£9,020	£1,400	7,620
Current assets			
Stock		5,160	
Debtors		6,800	
Bank balance		3,950	
Cash in hand		260	
		16,170	
Less : **Current liabilities**			
Creditors	7,900		
Accrual	100	8,000	8,170
			£15,790
Capital accounts :			
Dobbinson		7,000	
Spencer		5,000	12,000
Current accounts :			
Dobbinson (£1,230 + 350 +3,250 - 3,100)		1,730	
Spencer (£1,160 + 250 +3,250 -2,600)		2,060	3,790
			£15,790

EXERCISE 28.5 PAGE 223

SEA AND BREEZE
Profit and Loss Account for the year ended 31 October 19X7

	£	£	£
Fees invoiced to clients			110,000
Commission from insurance companies			2,750
Building society agency commissions			6,200
			118,950
Less : Expenses -			
Stationery (£1,850 - 190)		1,660	
Insurance		1,400	
Staff salaries		52,000	
Light and heat		2,800	
Rates (£1,400 - 200)		1,200	
Telephone (£1,600 + 60)		1,660	
Vehicles expenses		4,800	
Office expenses		2,800	
Bad debt		100	
Depreciation : Office machinery	1,800		
Motor vehicles	4,500	6,300	74,720
Net profit for the year			£44,230
Appropriations :			
Salary :			
Breeze			4,000
Interest on capital :			
Sea		3,000	
Breeze		2,000	5,000
Balance of profit :			
Sea (60%)		21,138	
Breeze (40%)		14,092	35,230
			£44,230

Current Accounts

	Sea £	Breeze £			Sea £	Breeze £
1 11 X6 Balance b/d	1,000	-	1 11 X6	Balance b/d	-	3,000
31 10 X6 Drawings	9,750	8,250	31 10 X6	Salary	-	4,000
31 10 X6 Balances c/d	13,388	14,842	31 10 X6	Int. on cap.	3,000	2,000
			31 10 X6	Balance of profit	21,138	14,092
	£24,138	£23,092			£24,138	£23,092
			1 11 X6	Balances b/d	13,388	14,842

EXERCISE 28.6   PAGE 224
S
(a)

NEW CASTLE ANTIQUES
Trading, Profit and Loss Account for the year ended 31 March 19X7

	£	£	£
Sales			20,000
Less : Cost of sales :			
Opening stock		1,100	
Purchases		7,900	
		9,000	
Less : Closing stock		1,000	8,000
Gross Profit			12,000
Less : Expenses -			
Rates		1,100	
Insurance (£220 - 54)		166	
Electricity (£310 + 80)		390	
Telephone		260	
Motor expenses (£640 - 100 - 150)		390	
General expenses		170	
Depreciation : Furniture & fittings			
(10% x £3,300)	330		
Motor vehicles (20% x £3,200)	640	970	
Interest on loan : Jean Phillips (10% x £5,000/2)		250	3,696
Net profit for the year			**£8,304**

	£	£
Appropriation :		
Salary :		
Jean Phillips		2,500
Interest on capital :		
Jean Phillips	1,200	
Peter Phillips	800	2,000
Balance of profits :		
Jean Phillips (2/3)	2,536	
Peter Phillips (1/3)	1,268	3,804
		£8,304

(b)

Balance Sheet at 31 March 19X7

	£ Cost	£ Accumulated Depreciation	£ Net Book Value
Fixed assets			
Freehold property	30,000	-	30,000
Furniture and fittings	3,300	990	2,310
Motor vehicles	4,000	1,440	2,560
	£37,300	£2,430	34,870

Current assets

Stock	1,000	
Trade debtors	140	
Prepayment	54	
Bank	210	
Cash	60	
	1,464	

Less : **Current liabilities**

Trade creditors	250		
Accrual	80	330	1,134
			£36,004

Capital accounts :

Jean Phillips	15,000	
Peter Phillips	10,000	25,000

Current accounts :

Jean Phillips	5,336	
Peter Phillips	668	6,004
		31,004

Loan account :

Jean Phillips		5,000
		£36,004

Current Accounts

		Jean Phillips £	Peter Phillips £			Jean Phillips £	Peter Phillips £
31 3 X7	Drawings	3,500	2,000	1 4 X6	Balances b/d	2,450	750
31 3 X7	Drawings –			31 3 X7	Int, on loan	250	-
	motor exps.	100	150	31 3 X7	Salary	2,500	-
31 3 X7	Balance c/d	5,336	668	31 3 X7	Int. on cap.	1,200	800
				31 3 X7	Balance of profit	2,536	1,268
		£8,936	£2,818			£8,936	£2,818
				1 4 X7	Balances b/d	5,336	668

EXERCISE 28.7   PAGE 225

DEGG AND SANT
Trading, Profit and Loss Account
for the year ended 31 December 19X4

	£	£	£
Sales			35,366
Less : Sales returns			687
			34,679
Less : Cost of sales :			
Opening stock		5,316	

	£	£	£
Purchases	21,135		
Less : Purchase returns	351		
	20,784		
Carriage inwards	192	20,976	
		26,292	
Less : Closing stock		7,860	
		18,432	
Wages and salaries (75% x £8,416)		6,312	24,744
Gross Profit			9,935
Add : Income -			
Discounts received		284	
Bank interest		205	489
			10,424
Less : Expenses -			
Wages and salaries (25% x £8,416)		2,104	
Discounts allowed		336	
Insurance (£184 - 42)		142	
General expenses		1,480	
Carriage outwards (£483 + 51)		534	
Reduction in value of furniture and fittings (1,880 - 1,600)		280	4,876
Net profit for the year			**£5,548**

	£	£
Appropriation :		
Salary :		
Sant		4,000
Interest on capital :		
Degg	720	
Sant	900	1,620
Balance of loss :		
Degg (3/4)	(54)	
Sant (1/4)	(18)	(72)
		£5,548

Balance Sheet at 31 December 19X4

	£	£	£
Fixed assets			
Premises at cost			12,000
Furniture and fittings at revaluation			1,600
			13,600
Current assets			
Stocks		7,860	
Debtors		2,217	
Prepayment		42	
Bank deposit account		8,400	
Cash in hand		42	
		18,561	

Less : **Current liabilities**

Creditors	4,148		
Accrual	51		
Bank overdraft	214	4,413	14,148
			£27,748

Capital accounts :

Degg	12,000	
Sant	15,000	27,000

Current accounts :

Degg (£720 - 54 - 1,800)	(1,134)	
Sant (£4,000 + 900 - 18 - 3,000)	1,882	748
		£27,748

EXERCISE 28.8   PAGE 226

(a)

BOTTLE AND GLASS
Appropriation Account for the year to 31 May 19X5

	£	£
Net profit for the year		82,000
Add : Interest on drawings (5% p.a. = 2.5% for the half year) :		
Bottle	500	
Glass	125	625
		82,625
Less : Salary :		
Glass	10,000	
Interest on capital (10%) :		
Bottle	4,000	
Glass	1,000	15,000
		67,625
Less : Balance apportioned :		
Bottle (3/5)	40,575	
Glass (2/5)	27,050	67,625

(b)

Capital Accounts for the year to 31 May 19X5

		Bottle £	Glass £			Bottle £	Glass £
31 5 X5	Drawings	20,000	5,000	1 6 X4	Balances b/d	40,000	10,000
31 5 X5	Int. on draw.	500	125	31 5 X5	Salary	-	10,000
31 5 X5	Balances c/d	64,075	42,925	31 5 X5	Int. on cap.	4,000	1,000
				31 5 X5	Balance of profit	40,575	27,050
		£84,575	£48,050			£84,575	£48,050
				1 6 X5	Balances b/d	64,075	42,925

(c)

Balance Sheet at 31 May 19X5

	£ Cost	£ Accumulated Depreciation	£ Net Book Value
Fixed assets			
Vehicles	12,000	3,000	9,000
Furniture and fittings	65,000	10,000	55,000
	£77,000	£13,000	64,000
Current assets			
Stocks		80,000	
Debtors		116,000	
Bank		2,000	
		198,000	
Less : **Current liabilities**			
Creditors		130,000	68,000
			£132,000
Capital accounts :			
Bottle		64,075	
Glass		42,925	107,000
Loan account :			
Bottle			25,000
			£132,000

EXERCISE 28.9   PAGE 227

(a)

PETER JAMES AND ANGUS VICTOR
Profit and Loss Account for the year ended 30 September 19X6

	£	£
Gross profit : October 19X5 to March 19X6	13,000	
April to September 19X6	26,000	39,000
Less : Expenses -		
Establishment and administrative expenses (£9,100 + 360)	9,460	
Sales and distribution expenses	13,000	
Depreciation : Freehold property	1,500	
Fixtures and fittings	1,800	
Loan interest	500	
Sales commission (2% x £26,000)	520	26,780
Net profit for the year		£12,220

Appropriation :
Partner's salary :
Angus Victor   5,000

	£	£
Interest on capital accounts:		
Peter James	1,250	
Angus Victor	750	2,000
Balance of profits:		
Peter James	2,610	
Angus Victor	2,610	5,220
		£12,220

(b)

Balance Sheet at 30 September 19X6

	£	£	£
	Cost	Accumulated Depreciation	Net Book Value
Fixed assets			
Freehold property	30,000	7,500	22,500
Fixtures and fittings	18,000	11,400	6,600
	£48,000	£18,900	29,100
Current assets			
Stocks		11,000	
Debtors		4,600	
Balance at bank		2,700	
		18,300	
Less : **Current liabilities**			
Creditors	5,800		
Accrued charges (£500 + 360 +520)	1,380	7,180	11,120
			£40,220
Capital accounts:			
Peter James		25,000	
Angus Victor		15,000	40,000
Current accounts:			
Peter James (Wkg)		(5,840	
Angus Victor (Wkg)		(3,940)	(9,780)
			30,220
Loan account :			
Peter James			10,000
			£40,220

(c) Reference should be made to (i) the level of partners' drawings and (ii) the debit balances as at 30 September 19X6 on the partners' current accounts.

Workings

Partners' Current Accounts :

	Peter James £	Angus Victor £
As at 30 September 19X5	6,000	(2,300)
Partner's salary	-	5,000
Interest on capital accounts	1,250	750
Balance of net profit	2,610	2,610
	9,860	6,060
Drawings	(15,700)	(10,000)
	£(5,840)	£(3,940)

EXERCISE 28.10 PAGE 228

EDDY AND DALE
Partnership Journal

		Dr £	Cr £
Freehold premises	Dr	60,000	
Motor vehicles	Dr	6,000	
Fixtures and fittings	Dr	5,000	
Stock	Dr	3,500	
Debtors	Dr	5,500	
Bank	Dr	5,250	
Goodwill	Dr	6,000	
To : Sundry creditors			3,450
To : Capital			87,800
		£91,250	£91,250
Motor vehicles	Dr	7,000	
Fixtures and fittings	Dr	8,000	
Stock	Dr	6,000	
Debtors	Dr	7,000	
Bank	Dr	3,400	
Goodwill	Dr	5,700	
To : Sundry creditors			3,200
To : Capital			33,900
		£37,100	£37,100
Capital : D Eddy (2/3 x £11,700)	Dr	7,800	
P Dale (1/3 x £11,700)	Dr	3,900	
To : Goodwill			11,700
		£11,700	£11,700

Balance Sheet as at 1 January 19X8

	£	£
Fixed assets		
Freehold Premises		60,000
Motor vehicles		13,000
Fixtures and fittings		13,000
		86,000
Current assets		
Stock	9,500	
Debtors	12,500	
Cash at bank	8,650	
	30,650	
Less : **Current liabilities**		
Sundry creditors	6,650	24,000
		£110,000
Capital accounts		
D Eddy (£87,800 - 7,800)		80,000
P Dale (£33,900 - 3,900)		30,000
		£110,000

EXERCISE 28.11   PAGE 229

(a)

ELSIE AND CIAH

Appropriation of profit for the year to 31 December 19X8

	£	£
Net profit for the year		
before allowing for the following adjustments :		19,480
Depreciation : Plant and machinery (14% x £4,000/2)	280	
Interest on bank loan	260	540
Net profit for the year		£18,940
Appropriation :		
Interest on capital :		
Elsie [(12% x £17,000) + (12% x £7,000 x 1/3)]	2,320	
Ciah [(12% x £13,000) + (12% x £3,000 x 1/6)]	1,620	3,940
Balance of profit :		
Elsie (3/5)	9,000	
Ciah (2/5)	6,000	15,000
		£18,940

(b)

Capital Accounts

	Elsie £	Ciah £			Elsie £	Ciah £
			1 1 X8	Balances b/d	17,000	13,000
			1 9 X8	Cash	7,000	-
31 12 X8 Balances c/d	24,000	16,000	1 11 X8	Cash	-	3,000
	£24,000	£16,000			£24,000	£16,000
			1 1 X9	Balances b/d	24,000	16,000

Current Accounts

	Elsie £	Ciah £			Elsie £	Ciah £
31 12 X8 Drawings	8,000	5,000	31 12 X8	Int. on cap.	2,320	1,620
31 12 X8 Balances c/d	3,320	2,620	31 12 X8	Balance of profit	9,000	6,000
	£11,320	£7,620			£11,320	£7,620
			1 1 X9	Balances b/d	3,320	2,620

(c)

Cash Position : Net Effect

	£	£	£
Capital received from partners :			
1 9 X8 Elsie		7,000	
1 11 X8 Ciah		3,000	10,000
Less : Purchase of land		10,000	
Purchase of plant and machinery		4,000	
Drawings : Elsie	8,000		
Ciah	5,000	13,000	
Bank interest		260	27,260
Net decrease in cash			£(17,260)

SOLUTIONS TO CHAPTER 29 EXERCISES

EXERCISE 29.1 PAGE 233

(a)

FRANK AND LOUIS
Frank's Books
Joint Venture with Louis Account

		£			£
1 1 X1	Dobson - delivery van	7,000	7 1 X1	Cash - sales	1,000
5 1 X1	Cash - purchases	65,000	31 1 X1	Debtors - sales	20,000
31 1 X1	Cash - office expenses	1,000	28 2 X1	Debtors - sales	45,000
4 2 X1	Creditors - purchases	16,000	31 3 X1	Debtors - sales	10,000
15 2 X1	Cash - van expenses	1,800	31 3 X1	Cash - van sold	5,000
31 3 X1	Cash - office expenses	3,000	31 3 X1	Cash - Louis	24,800
31 3 X1	Debtors - bad debt	4,000			
31 3 X1	Net profit	8,000			
		£105,800			£105,800

Louis' Books
Joint Venture with Frank Account

		£			£
1 1 X1	Cash - purchases	15,000	31 1 X1	Debtors - sales	40,000
5 1 X1	Cash - purchases	20,000	28 2 X1	Debtors - sales	50,000
7 1 X1	Bank - storage room rent	2,000	31 3 X1	Cash - sales	19,000
31 1 X1	Cash - office expenses	2,500			
4 2 X1	Creditors - purchases	30,000			
31 3 X1	Cash - office expenses	6,000			
31 3 X1	Cash - travelling expenses	700			
31 3 X1	Net profit	8,000			
31 3 X1	Cash - Frank	24,800			
		£109,000			£109,000

(b)

FRANK AND LOUIS
Memorandum Joint Venture Account for the period
11 January 19X1 to 31 March 19X1

	£	£
Sales (£1,000+20,000+45,000+10,000+40,000+50,000+19,000)		185,000
Less : Purchases (£65,000+16,000+15,000+20,000+30,000)		146,000
Gross profit		39,000
Less : Expenses -		
Office expenses (£1,000+3,000+2,500+6,000)	12,500	
Storage room rent	2,000	
Van expenses	1,800	

	£	£
Loss on disposal of delivery van (£7,000-5,000)	2,000	
Travelling expenses	700	
Bad debt	4,000	23,000
Net profit		16,000

Divided :		
Frank	8,000	
Louis	8,000	16,000

EXERCISE 29.2   PAGE 234

THUNDER AND LIGHTNING LTD AND HIPPO LTD

(a)   **Calculation of Hippo Ltd's premium**

		PROFITS			WEIGHTED		
Year	Weighting	Thunder Ltd	Lightning Ltd	Total	Thunder Ltd	Lightning Ltd	Total
		£	£	£	£	£	£
19X3	1	72,000	24,000	96,000	72,000	24,000	96,000
19X4	2	(15,000)	(21,000)	(36,000)	(30,000)	(42,000)	(72,000)
19X5	3	40,000	60,000	100,000	120,000	180,000	300,000
					£162,000	£162,000	£324,000

	Thunder	Lightning	Total
Average (divided by 6)	27,000	27,000	54,000
Premium payable by Hippo Ltd = 20% thereon	£5,400	£5,400	£10,800

(b)   **Division of Joint Venture profit for 19X6**

	£
19X5 profits	100,000
20% increase	20,000
19X6 profits	120,000
Less : Commission (0.5% x £2,400,000)	12,000
	108,000
Less : Hippo's share of profits (£108 x 8/108)	8,000
Profit to be shared between Thunder and Lightning	£100,000

Workings

Calculation of Thunder and Lightning's share of net profit based on sales value of goods produced and sold by each company.

	Thunder Ltd		Lightning Ltd		Total
	£		£		£
19X5	480,000	(40%)	720,000	(60%)	1,200,000
Division (%)	40		60		100
19X6	1,680,000		720,000		*2,400,000
Division (%)	70		30		100

*(100% increase)

Therefore division of Joint Venture profit :

	£	£
Net profit before division		108,000
Hippo Ltd	8,000	
Balance : Thunder Ltd (70% x £100,000)	70,000	
Lightning Ltd	30,000	108,000

EXERCISE 29.3   PAGE 235

(a)

JOHNSON AND BEATON
Hew Johnson's Books
Joint Venture with Beaton Account

	£			£
17 11 X3 Bank - purchases of wine	6,000	17 11 X3 Bank - amount received from Beaton		5,100
- duty thereon	4,200	2 2 X4 Sales (to self) (50x£26)		1,300
17 11 X3 Bank - landing and dock charges	402	2 2 X4 Sales (to self) (50x£26)		1,300
- carriage	326	2 2 X4 Amount due from Beaton c/d		5,179
- insurance	155			
- warehousing	217			
2 2 X4 Profit on venture	1,579			
	£12,879			£12,879
3 2 X4 Balance b/d	5,179			

Margaret Beaton's Books
Joint Venture with Johnson Account

	£		£
17 11 X3 Bank - amount sent to Johnson	5,100	2 2 X4 Sales (to self) (20x£26)	520
21 1 X4 Northern Globe Hotels bill discounted (£7,448x5%)	372	10 1 X3 Sales - Hawk Hotels (35x£28x95%)	931
		12 12 X3 Silver Inns Group (85x£28x95%)	2,261

		£			£
2 2 X4	Bank - telephone	110	17 12 X3	Tornish Hotels (65x£28x95%)	1,729
	- printing and stationery	78	14 1 X4	Glen Allan Lodge (8x£28)	224
	- delivery and insurance	892	21 1 X4	Northern Globe Hotels (280x£28x95%)	7,448
2 2 X4	Profit on venture	1,578	1 2 X4	Ancorn Guest House (7x£28)	196
2 2 X4	Balance c/d	5,179			
		£13,309			£13,309
			3 2 X4	Balance b/d	5,179

(b)

Memorandum Joint Venture Account for the period 17 November 19X3 to 2 February 19X4

	£	£
Sales : Johnson	2,600	
: Beaton	13,309	15,909
Less : Purchases		10,200
Gross profit		5,709
Less : Expenses -		
Landing and dock charges	402	
Carriage	326	
Insurance	155	
Warehousing	217	
Telephone	110	
Printing and stationery	78	
Delivery and insurance	892	
Discount on bill	372	2,552
Net profit		3,157
Appropriation :		
Johnson	1,579	
Beaton	1,578	3,157

SOLUTIONS TO CHAPTER 30 EXERCISES

EXERCISE 30.1   PAGE 240

(a)

ALAN, BRIAN AND COLIN
Goodwill Account

	£		£
Balance b/d	2,000	Capital :	
Capital (Wkg : £34,000-2,000) :		Alan (5/17)	10,000
Alan (5/8 x £32,000)	20,000	Brian (6/17)	12,000
Brian (3/8 x £32,000)	12,000	Colin (6/17)	12,000
	£34,000		£34,000

(b)

Capital Accounts

	Alan £	Brian £	Colin £		Alan £	Brian £	Colin £
Goodwill	10,000	12,000	12,000	Balances b/d	80,000	116,000	-
Balances c/d	90,000	116,000	48,000	Goodwill	20,000	12,000	-
				Cash	-	-	50,000
				Cars	-	-	10,000
	£100,000	£128,000	£60,000		£100,000	£128,000	£60,000
				Balances b/d	90,000	116,000	48,000

(c)

ALAN, BRIAN AND COLIN
Balance Sheet as at 1 May 19X5

	£000	£000
Fixed assets		
Tangible assets (£148+10)		158
Current assets		
Sundry	74	
Cash at bank (£6+50)	56	
	130	
Less : **Current liabilities**	34	96
		£254
Capital accounts		
Alan		90
Brian		116
Colin		48
		£254

Working

Calculation of weighted average profits :

Year	Profits £	Weighting	Weighted Profits £
19X2/3	25,000	1	25,000
19X3/4	34,000	2	68,000
19X4/5	37,000	3	111,000
		6	£204,000

Therefore average weighted profits $= \dfrac{£204,000}{6} = £34,000$

EXERCISE 30.2   PAGE 241

(a)

CHAIR AND TABLE
Realisation Account

	£		£
Furniture : Decrease in value (£9,000-8,000)	1,000	Goodwill (£12,000-10,000)	2,000
Provision for bad debts :		Discounts received	300
Leeds (8%x£10,000)	800	Balance :	
Manchester (8%x£5,000)	400	Chair (2/3)	2,800
Redecoration (£2,500+700)	3,200	Table (1/3)	1,400
Dissolution costs	1,100		
	£6,500		£6,500

(b)

Bank Account

	£		£
Balance b/d	40,000	Dissolution costs	1,100
Capital - cash introduced by Table	300	Capital - cash paid out to Chair	39,200
	£40,300		£40,300

(c)

Capital Accounts

	Chair £	Table £		Chair £	Table £
Goodwill	7,000	5,000	Balances b/d	50,000	13,000
Furniture	5,000	3,000	Creditors		-
Debtors (at B.V.-8%)	9,200	4,600	(£11,000-300)	10,700	
Revaluation	2,800	1,400	Redecoration	2,500	700
Bank	39,200	-	Bank	-	300
	£63,200	£14,000		£63,200	£14,000

EXERCISE 30.3   PAGE 242

EXERCISE 30.3 PAGE 242

(a)

ADAMS, BARTRAM, CHARLTON and DIXON
Capital Accounts - 1 January 19X8

	Adams £	Bartram £	Charlton £	Dixon £		Adams £	Bartram £	Charlton £	Dixon £
Current A/c	-	1,000	-	-	Balances				
Motor car	-	2,800	-	-	b/d	10,000	8,000	4,000	-
Cash	-	2,500	-	-	Bank - cash				
Loan	-	4,500	-	-	introduced	-	-	-	7,000
Balances					Goodwill	3,000	2,000	1,000	-
c/d	14,200	-	5,400	7,000	Realisation -				
					premises	1,200	800	400	-
	£14,200	£10,800	£5,400	£7,000		£14,200	£10,800	£5,400	£7,000
					Balances				
					b/d	14,200	-	5,400	7,000

(b)

ADAMS, CHARLTON AND DIXON
Balance Sheet at 1 January 19X8

	£	£	£
Fixed assets			
Goodwill			6,000
Premises			9,700
Motor vehicles at net book value (£11,100-2,800)			8,300
			24,000
Current assets			
Stock in trade		2,960	
Debtors		10,976	
		13,936	
Less : **Current liabilities**			
Creditors	3,700		
Bank overdraft (£7,000-2,500-4,636)	136	3,836	10,100
			£34,100
Capital accounts :			
Adams			14,200
Charlton			5,400
Dixon			7,000
			26,600
Current accounts :			
Adams		2,000	
Charlton		1,000	3,000
			29,600
Loan account			
Bartram			4,500
			£34,100

EXERCISE 30.4   PAGE 243

(a)

RACHEL, ANDREW, WILLIAM AND GEORGE
Trading and Profit and Loss Account
for the year ended 31 December 19X5

	Half-year to 30 June 19X5 £000	Half-year to 31 December 19X5 £000	Year ended 31 December 19X5 £000
Sales	175	175	350
Less : Cost of goods sold :			
Opening stock	31	32.5	31
Purchases	92.5	92.5	185
	123.5	125	216
Less : Closing stock	32.5	34	34
	91	91	182
Gross profit	84	84	168
Less : Expenses :			
General overheads	16	16	32
Depreciation	25	25	50
	41	41	82
Net profit	£43	£43	£86
Appropriation :			
Salaries :			
Andrew	-	8	8
William	-	4	4
Commission on sales :			
Andrew	7	-	7
William	-	14	14
George	-	7	7
Balance of profit :			
Rachel	18	3	21
Andrew	12	3	15
William	6	2	8
George	-	2	2
	£43	£43	£86

(b)

Capital Accounts

	Rachel £000	Andrew £000	William £000	George £000		Rachel £000	Andrew £000	William £000	George £000
Goodwill	7.8	7.8	5.2	5.2	Balance b/d	36.0	30.0	17.0	-
Drawings	5.0	7.0	10.0	2.0	Goodwill	3.0	2.0	1.0	-
					Cash	-	-	-	15.0
					Salaries	-	8.0	4.0	-
					Commission	-	7.0	14.0	7.0
Balances c/d	47.2	47.2	28.8	16.8	Balance of profit	21.0	15.0	8.0	2.0
	£60	£62	£44	£24		£60	£62	£44	£24
					Balances b/d	47.2	47.2	28.8	16.8

(c)

Balance Sheet at 31 December 19X5

	£000	£000
Fixed assets		
At cost		200
Less : Depreciation		108
		92
Current assets		
Stock	34	
Debtors	39	
Bank balance	7	
	80	
Less : **Current liabilities**		
Creditors	32	48
		£140
Capital accounts		
Rachel		47.2
Andrew		47.2
William		28.8
George		16.8
		£140

EXERCISE 30.5   PAGE 244

(a)

MARK AND LUKE
Realisation Account

	£		£
Loss on sale of fixed assets (£25,000-21,000)	4,000	Capital accounts (loss on realisation) :	
Loss on sale of stock (£64,000-41,000)	23,000	Mark (1/2)	21,325
		Luke (1/2)	21,325

544

	£		£
Bad debts	6,500		
Redundancy pay	3,500		
Dissolution expenses	650		
Goodwill	5,000		
	£42,650		£42,650

(b)

Cash Account

	£		£
Fixed assets	21,000	Balance b/d	15,700
Stock	41,000	Creditors (£41,200+3,500)	44,700
Debtors	36,500	Dissolution expenses	650
		Balance :	
		Mark	24,675
		Luke	12,775
	£98,500		£98,500

(c)

Capital Accounts

	Mark	Luke		Mark	Luke
	£	£		£	£
Realisation	21,325	21,325	Balances b/d	46,000	34,100
Cash	24,675	12,775			
	£46,000	£34,100		£46,000	£34,100

EXERCISE 30.6   PAGE 244

(a)

TESS, MAX AND HENRIETTA
Cash Book

	£		£
Balance b/d	20,000	Creditors (£41-1.5)	39,500
Freehold property	110,000	Dissolution expenses	2,000
Equipment	24,000	Balance of cash :	
Stock	27,000	Tess	76,450
Debtors (£32-4)	28,000	Max	97,400
Cash - Henrietta	6,350		
	£215,350		£215,350

(b)

Realisation Account

	£		£
Loss on sale of equipment (£35-24)	11,000	Profit on sale of freehold property (110-100)	10,000
Loss on sale of stock (£40-27)	13,000	Discount from creditors	1,500

	£		£
Discount to debtors	4,000	Capital accounts (loss on	
Dissolution expenses	2,000	realisation) :	
		Tess (3/10)	5,550
		Max (6/10)	11,100
		Henrietta (1/10)	1,850
	£30,000		£30,000

(c)

Capital Accounts

	Tess	Max	Henrietta		Tess	Max	Henrietta
	£	£	£		£	£	£
Current A/c	-	-	5,500	Balances b/d	46,000	75,000	1,000
Realisation	5,550	11,100	1,850	Current A/c	36,000	2,000	-
Cash	76,450	97,400	-	Loan	-	31,500	-
				Cash	-	-	6,350
	£82,000	£108,500	£7,350		£82,000	£108,500	£7,350

EXERCISE 30.7   PAGE 245

(a)

APPLE AND ORANGE AND PEAR AND PLUM
Realisation Accounts

	Apple & Orange	Pear & Plum		Apple & Orange	Pear & Plum
	£	£		£	£
Property :			Property :		
(£30,000-25,000)	5,000	-	(£85,000-50,000)	-	35,000
Fixtures and fittings :			Goodwill	8,000	25,000
(£8,000-5,000)	3,000	-	Capital accounts :		
(£14,000-10,000)	-	4,000	Apple (1/2)	2,700	-
Motor vehicle :			Orange (1/2)	2,700	-
(£7,000-2,000)	5,000	-			
(£10,000-6,000)	-	4,000			
Debtors :					
(£1,000-600)	400	-			
(£1,500-500)	-	1,000			
Capital accounts :					
Pear (2/3)	-	34,000			
Plum (1/3)	-	17,000			
	£13,400	£60,000		£13,400	£60,000

(b)

Capital Accounts

	Apple £	Orange £	Pear £	Plum £		Apple £	Orange £	Pear £	Plum £
Realisation	2,700	2,700	-	-	Balances b/d	20,000	20,000	50,000	25,000
Motor vehicles	-	2,000	-	-	Realisation	-	-	34,000	17,000
Goodwill	8,250	8,250	8,250	8,250	Bank	30,950	32,950	-	6,250
Bank	-	-	35,750	-					
Balances c/d	40,000	40,000	40,000	40,000					
	£50,950	£52,950	£84,000	£48,250		£50,950	£52,950	£84,000	£48,250
					Balances b/d	40,000	40,000	40,000	40,000

(c)

FRUIT AND COMPANY
Balance Sheet as at 1 January 19X9

	£	£
Fixed assets		
Property		110,000
Fixtures and fittings		15,000
Motor vehicles		6,000
		131,000
Current assets		
Stocks	7,000	
Debtors	600	
Bank and cash (£500+1,500+30,950+32,950+6,250-35,750)	36,400	
	44,000	
Less : **Current liabilities**		
Creditors	15,000	29,000
		£160,000
Capital accounts :		
Apple		40,000
Orange		40,000
Pear		40,000
Plum		40,000
		£160,000

EXERCISE 30.8   PAGE 246

(a)

SWALE AND AIRE
Realisation Account

	£		£
Plant and equipment (£10,000-8,000)	2,000	Property (£40,000-24,500)	15,500
Debtors and prepayments (£12,000-11,000)	1,000	Stocks (£13,000-10,000)	3,000
		Goodwill	42,000

	£		£
Creditors and accruals			
(£10,500-7,000)	3,500		
Balance :			
Swale	36,000		
Aire	18,000		
	£60,500		£60,500

(b) Partners' Capital Accounts

	Swale £	Aire £	Wharfe £
Balances b/d	30,000	5,000	-
Current accounts	2,000	3,500	-
Revaluation account	36,000	18,000	-
	68,000	26,500	-
Motor car	(3,000)	-	
	65,000	26,500	-
Bank	(32,500)	-	45,000
Loan	(32,500)	-	-
Goodwill written back	-	(21,000)	(21,000)
Balances at 1 October 19X5	-	£5,500	£24,000

(c)

AIRE AND WHARFE
Balance Sheet as at 1 October 19X5

	£	£
Fixed assets		
Property at cost		40,000
Plant and equipment (£8,000-3,000)		5,000
		45,000
Current assets		
Stocks	13,000	
Debtors and prepayments	11,000	
Cash at bank (Wkg)	3,500	
	27,500	
Less : **Current liabilities**		
Creditors and accruals	10,500	17,000
		£62,000
Capital accounts :		
Aire		5,500
Wharfe		24,000
		29,500
Loan account		
Swale		32,500
		£62,000

Working : Cash at bank

	£
Balance at 30 9 X5	1,000
Wharfe's capital contribution	45,000
	46,000
Swale's loan repaid	(10,000)
Swale's capital repaid (half)	(32,500)
Balance at 1 October 19X5	£3,500

EXERCISE 30.9   PAGE 248

(a)

PROUDIE, SLOPE AND THORNE
Revaluation Account

	£000		£000
Furniture - decrease in valuation (£12-5)	7	Land and buildings - increase in valuation (£200-160)	40
Motor vehicles - decrease in valuation [£20-(10+4)]	6	Goodwill (Wkg)	150
Stock write-off	5		
Bad debt	2		
Increase in doubtful debts provision [(£42-2)x5% - 1]	1		
Office expenses - accrual	3		
Professional charges	1		
Partners' capital accounts :			
Proudie (3/5)	99		
Slope (1/5)	33		
Thorne (1/5)	33		
	£190		£190

(b)

Partners' Capital Accounts

	Proudie £000	Slope £000	Thorne £000		Proudie £000	Slope £000	Thorne £000
Motor vehicle	4	-	-	Balances b/d	100	60	40
Goodwill w/b	-	75	75	Current A/cs	24	10	8
Cash	8	-	-	Revaluation A/c	99	33	33
Balance to Loan Account	219	-	-	Loan	8	-	-
Balances c/d	-	28	6				
	£231	£103	£81		£231	£103	£81
				Balances b/d	-	28	6

(c)

SLOPE AND THORNE
Balance Sheet at 1 June 19X6

	£000	£000	£000
Fixed assets			
Land and buildings			200
Furniture			5
Motor vehicles			10
			215
Current assets			
Stocks		18	
Trade debtors	40		
Less : Provision for doubtful debts	2	38	
Prepayments		2	
Cash (£10-8)		2	
		60	
Less : **Current liabilities**			
Trade creditors	15		
Accruals (£3+3+1)	7	22	38
			£253
Capital accounts :			
Slope			28
Thorne			6
			34
Loan account			
Proudie			219
			£253

Working - Calculation of goodwill

	£000	£000	£000
Profit for year to :			
31 May 19X4			130
31 May 19X5			150
31 May 19X6		181	
Less : Reduction in stock	5		
Accrual	3		
Bad debt written off	2		
Increase in provision for doubtful debts [(£42-2)x5% - 1]	1	11	170
			£450

	£
Average yearly profit = £450,000/3 =	£150,000

Apportioned :

Proudie (3/5)	90,000
Slope (1/5)	30,000
Thorne (1/5)	30,000
	£150,000

Written back :

Slope (1/2)	75,000
Thorne (1/2)	75,000
	£150,000

SOLUTIONS TO CHAPTER 31 EXERCISES

EXERCISE 31.1 PAGE 254

(a)

GRAIN AND SALT
Capital Accounts

	Grain	Salt		Grain	Salt
	£	£		£	£
Motor vehicles	-	2,300	Balances b/d	24,000	5,000
Shares	30,000	20,000	Current accounts	4,200	1,000
Bank	13,740	-	Realisation	15,540	10,360
			Bank	-	5,940
	£43,740	£22,300		£43,740	£22,300

(b)

Realisation Account

	£		£
Motor vehicle (3,000-2,300)	700	Freehold premises (£50-40)	10,000
Capital accounts :		Goodwill	16,600
Grain (3/5)	15,540		
Salt (2/5)	10,360		
	£26,600		£26,600

(c)

Bank Account

	£		£
Balance b/d	800	Loan account	18,000
Herbsbest Ltd	25,000	Capital : Grain	13,740
Capital : Salt	5,940		
	£31,740		£31,740

(d)

Herbsbest Ltd Account

	£		£
Freehold premises	50,000	Sundry creditors	13,600
Fixtures and fittings	2,000	Bank	25,000
Stock in trade	8,000	Shares :	
Sundry debtors	12,000	Grain (3/5)	30,000
Balance = Goodwill	16,600	Salt (2/5)	20,000
	£88,600		£88,600

EXERCISE 31.2   PAGE 255

(a)

BIRCH AND LARCH
Realisation Account

	£		£
Plant and machinery		Premises (£26,000-22,000)	4,000
(£8,120-6,600)	1,520	Goodwill (Wkg1)	430
Vehicles (£6,800-750-5,250)	800		
Stock (£3,600-3,570)	30		
Provision for bad debt	230		
Balance :			
Birch (3/5)	1,110		
Larch (2/5)	740		
	£4,430		£4,430

Capital Accounts

	Birch £	Larch £		Birch £	Larch £
Shares	22,500	15,000	Balances b/d	27,000	12,000
Bank	5,610	-	Realisation	1,110	740
			Bank	-	2,260
	£28,110	£15,000		£28,110	£15,000

(b)

OAK LTD
Balance Sheet at 1 January 19X2

	£	£
Fixed assets		
Preliminary expenses		880
Goodwill (Wkg1)		430
Premises		26,000
Plant and machinery		6,600
Motor vehicles		5,250
		39,160
Current assets		
Stock (£720+1,040+1,810)	3,570	
Debtors	4,510	
Bank(Wkg2)	94,120	
	102,200	
Less : **Current liabilities**		
Trade creditors	3,860	98,340
		£137,500

Capital	Authorised	Issued and fully paid
Ordinary shares of £0.50 each	£250,000	£137,500

(c)   Preliminary expenses should be written off either to the profit and loss account or against any share premium account.

Goodwill should either be written off against any reserve account or amortised through the profit and loss account.

Workings

(1)

Oak Ltd Account

	£		£
Premises	26,000	Trade creditors	3,860
Plant and machinery	6,600	Cash	5,000
Motor vehicles	5,250	Shares :	
Stock	3,570	Birch (3/5)	22,500
Debtors (£4,740-230)	4,510	Larch (2/5)	15,000
Balance = Goodwill	430		
	£46,360		£46,360

(2)

Oak Ltd's Bank Account

	£		£
Shares	100,000	Preliminary expenses	880
		Birch and Larch	5,000
		Balance c/d	94,120
	£100,000		£100,000
Balance b/d	94,120		

EXERCISE 31.3   PAGE 256

CROW AND NEST
Trading, Profit and Loss and
Profit and Loss Appropriation Account
for the year to 31 October 19X4

	£	£	£
Sales			500,000
Less : Cost of goods sold –			
Opening stock		30,000	
Purchases		260,000	
		290,000	
Less : Closing stock		40,000	250,000
Gross profit			250,000

	£	£	£
Less : Expenses -			
General expenses (£170,000+10,000)		180,000	
Vehicle depreciation (£40,000x25%)		10,000	
Rates (£20,000-5,000)		15,000	205,000
Net profit			45,000
Less : Appropriations -			
Nest - Salary		8,000	
Interest on capital (10%) : Crow	5,000		
Nest	2,000	7,000	
Balance : Crow	20,000		
Nest	10,000	30,000	45,000

(b)

Partner's Capital Accounts at 31 October 19X4

	Crow £	Nest £		Crow £	Nest £
Drawings	8,000	6,000	Balances b/d	50,000	20,000
Reduction in value of			Salary	-	8,000
the vehicles (£20,000-			Interest on capital	5,000	2,000
14,000), shared 2:1	4,000	2,000	Balance of profits	20,000	10,000
Balance, settled by the			Goodwill, shared 2:1	16,000	8,000
allotment of ordinary					
shares	79,000	40,000			
	£91,000	£48,000		£91,000	£48,000

(c)

Balance Sheet at 1 November 19X4

	£	£	£
Fixed assets			
Goodwill at cost			24,000
Vehicles at cost			14,000
Current assets			
Stock		40,000	
Trade debtors		80,000	
Prepayment		5,000	
Bank		1,000	
		126,000	
Less : **Current liabilities**			
Trade creditors	35,000		
Accrual	10,000	45,000	81,000
			£119,000

Financed by :

Capital	Authorised	Issued and fully paid
Ordinary shares of £1 each	£200,000	£119,000

EXERCISE 31.4   PAGE 257

(a)   (i)

AMIS, LODGE AND PYM
Trading, Profit and Loss and
Profit and Loss Appropriation Account
for the year to 31 March 19X8

	£	£	£
Sales			404,500
Less : Cost of goods sold -			
Opening stock		30,000	
Purchases	225,000		
Carriage inwards	4,000	229,000	
		259,000	
Less : Closing stock		35,000	224,000
Gross profit			180,500
Add : Income -			
Bank interest		750	
Discounts received		4,530	5,280
			185,780
Less : Expenses -			
Carriage outwards		12,000	
Depreciation :			
Motor vehicle [(£80-20)x25%]	15,000		
Plant and machinery (£100x20%)	20,000	35,000	
Discounts allowed		10,000	
Increase in provision for bad and doubtful debts [(£14,300x5%)-420]		295	
Office expenses (£30,400+405)		30,805	
Rent, rates, heat and light (£8,800-1,500)		7,300	95,400
Net profit			90,380
Add : Interest on drawings and current accounts :			
Amis		1,000	
Lodge		900	
Pym		720	2,620
			93,000
Less : Appropriations -			
Salary - Pym		13,000	
Interest on capital accounts :			
Amis	8,000		
Lodge	1,500		
Pym	500	10,000	23,000

	£	£	£
			70,000
Balance of profit :			
Amis (5/10)		35,000	
Lodge (3/10)		21,000	
Pym (2/10)		14,000	70,000

(ii)

Current Accounts

	Amis £	Lodge £	Pym £		Amis £	Lodge £	Pym £
Balances b/d	1,000	500	400	Salary	-	-	13,000
Drawings	25,000	22,000	15,000	Interest			
Interest on				on capital	8,000	1,500	500
drawings	1,000	900	720	Balance of			
Balances to				profit	35,000	21,000	14,000
Capital A/cs	16,000	-	11,380	Balance to			
				Capital A/c	-	900	-
	£43,000	£23,400	£27,500		£43,000	£23,400	£27,500

(b) (i)

Realisation Account

	£		£
Motor vehicles (£80,000-20,000 -15,000-5,000-30,000)	10,000	Stock (£38,500-35,000)	3,500
Plant and machinery (£100,000		Trade creditors (£16,500-16,000)	500
-36,600-20,000-35,000)	8,400	Goodwill (Wkg)	35,000
Trade debtors (£14,300			
-420-295-12,985)	600		
Profit on realisation transferred to Capital Accounts :			
Amis	10,000		
Lodge	6,000		
Pym	4,000		
	£39,000		£39,000

(ii)

Bank Account

	£		£
Balance b/d	4,900	Office expenses	405
Trade debtors	12,985	Trade creditors	16,000
Rent returned	1,500	Balance to Amis	76,000
Fowles Ltd	63,500		
Cash contributed by partners (to Capital) :			
Lodge	4,900		
Pym	4,620		
	£92,405		£92,405

(iii)

Capital Accounts

	Amis £	Lodge £	Pym £		Amis £	Lodge £	Pym £
Current A/cs	-	900	-	Balances b/d	80,000	15,000	5,000
Motor vehicles	5,000	-	-	Current A/cs	16,000	-	11,380
Shares	25,000	25,000	25,000	Realisation account	10,000	6,000	4,000
Bank	76,000	-	-	Bank	-	4,900	4,620
	£106,000	£25,900	£25,000		£106,000	£25,900	£25,000

Working

Fowles Ltd Account

	£		£
Motor vehicles	30,000	Bank	63,500
Plant and machinery	35,000	Shares at par :	
Stock	38,500	Amis	25,000
Balance = goodwill	35,000	Lodge	25,000
		Pym	25,000
	£138,500		£138,500

SOLUTIONS TO CHAPTER 32 EXERCISES

EXERCISE 32.1   PAGE 264

POTTERIES MANUFACTURING CO LTD
Profit and Loss Appropriation Account
for the year to 31 December 19X4

	£	£
Net profit for the year		35,700
Less : Dividends :		
Preference (8%×£40,000)	3,200	
Ordinary : interim	7,500	
Ordinary : final	12,500	23,200
Retained profit for the year		12,500
Less : Transfer to fixed assets replacement cost reserve		5,000
		7,500
Retained profits brought forward		4,000
Retained profits carried forward		£11,500

Balance Sheet at 31 December 19X4

	£	£	£
Fixed assets			
At cost			141,000
Less : Accumulated depreciation			55,200
			85,800
Current assets			
Raw materials stock	26,000		
Work in progress	36,000		
Finished goods stock	29,000	91,000	
Debtors		59,200	
		150,200	
Less : **Current liabilities**			
Trade creditors	40,400		
Dividends (£1,600+12,500)	14,100		
Bank overdraft	10,000	64,500	85,700
			£171,500

Capital and reserves	Authorised	Issued and fully paid
Ordinary shares of £0.50 each	150,000	100,000
8% preference shares of £1 each	75,000	40,000
	£225,000	140,000
Fixed assets replacement cost reserve (£15,000+5,000)		20,000
Profit and loss account		11,500
		£171,500

EXERCISE 32.2   PAGE 265

MAINSTREAM PLC
Profit and Loss and Profit and Loss Appropriation Account
for the year ended 31 March 19X8

	£	£
Gross profit b/d		69,000
Rent, rates and insurance (£2,600-500)	2,100	
General expenses	4,800	
Administration expenses (£10,000+300)	10,300	
Bad debt written off	147	
Provision for bad debts (2%x£18,800)	376	
Directors' fees	2,150	
Debenture interest (10%x£60,000)	6,000	
Depreciation of fixed assets (10%x£195,000)	19,500	45,373
Net profit for the year		23,627
Less : Dividends :		
Preference (10%x£40,000)	4,000	
Ordinary : interim (4p x £100,000)	4,000	
Ordinary : final (6p x £100,000)	6,000	14,000
Retained profit for the year		9,627
Retained profits brought forward		5,829
Retained profits carried forward		£15,456

Balance Sheet at 31 March 19X8

	£	£	£
Fixed assets			
At cost			195,000
Less : Accumulated depreciation (£15,000+19,500)			34,500
			160,500
Current assets			
Stocks		37,800	
Debtors	18,800		
Less : Provision for bad debts	376	18,424	
Prepayment		500	
Bank		16,132	
		72,856	
Less : **Current liabilities**			
Creditors	6,600		
Accruals	300		
Debenture interest	3,000		
Dividends (£2,000+6,000)	8,000	17,900	54,956
			£215,456

Capital and reserves	Authorised	Issued and fully paid
Ordinary shares of £1 each	100,000	100,000
10% preference shares of £1 each	40,000	40,000
	£140,000	140,000
Profit and loss account		15,456

Loans

10% debentures		60,000
		£215,456

EXERCISE 32.3 PAGE 266

PRIME PRODUCTS LTD
Corrected Balance Sheet at 31 September 19X6

	£ Cost	£ Aggregate Depreciation	£ Net Book Value
Fixed assets			
Plant and machinery	31,000	19,375	11,625
Motor vehicles	17,000	10,200	6,800
	£48,000	£29,575	18,425
Current assets			
Stock (£12,400+1,200)		13,600	
Trade debtors and prepayments (Wkg1)		8,110	
Balance at bank (£3,900-150)		3,750	
		25,460	
Less : **Current liabilities**			
Creditors and accrued charges (£5,100-64) (Wkg2)		5,036	20,424
			£38,849
Capital and reserves			
Ordinary shares of £1 each (£20,000+5,000)			25,000
General reserve			10,000
Profit and loss account (£4,225+300+64-150-400-190)			3,849
			£38,849

Workings

		£
(1)	Trade debtors per draft balance sheet as at 30 September 19X6 (£9,600-400)	9,200
	Less: Goods not sold but on sale or return basis (at selling price)	1,600
		7,600
	Less: Provision for doubtful debts (2.5% of trade debtors)	190
		7410
	Prepayments (£400+300)	700
		£8,110

		£
(2)	Correction of sales manager's bonus :	
	Reductions in gross profit for the year ended 30 September 19X6 :	
	Re : Goods not sold but on sale or return basis	400
	Re : Stock valuation error at 30 September 19X5	6,000
		£6,400

Reduction in sales manager's commission (1%x6,400)	£64

EXERCISE 32.4   PAGE 267

R HIGSON LTD
Balance Sheet (extracts) at 31 July 19X7

Capital and reserves	Authorised	Issued and fully paid
Ordinary shares of £1 each	260,000	200,000
10% preference shares of £1 each	80,000	60,000
	£340,000	260,000
General reserve (£14,600+1,730)		16,330
Profit and loss account [£21,760 + (68,800-6,000-22,000-1,730)]		60,830
		337,160
Loans		
12.5% debenture loan stock		50,000
Current liabilities		
Creditors	38,555	
Dividends (£6,000+22,000)	28,000	
Bank overdraft	31,900	98,455
		£485,615

EXERCISE 32.5   PAGE 268

BILSTON LTD

(a)

Penn's Books
Sale of Business Account

Reduction in value :	£	Increase in value :	£
Equipment (£28-20)	8,000	Stock (£68-62)	6,000
Vehicles (£31-4-15)	12,000	Goodwill	116,000
Debtors (£47-44)	3,000		
Capital account	99,000		
	£122,000		£122,000

Capital Account

	£		£
Premises	50,000	Balance b/d	161,000
Motor vehicle	4,000	Sale of business	99,000
Bank	26,000		
Shares (£50+130)	180,000		
	£260,000		£260,000

Bank Account

	£		£
Balance b/d	6,000	Capital	26,000
Bilston Ltd	20,000		
	£26,000		£26,000

(b)

Bilston Ltd's Books
Acquisition of Business Account

	£		£
Creditors	63,000	Equipment	20,000
Cash	20,000	Vehicles	15,000
Shares	50,000	Stock	68,000
Share premium	130,000	Debtors	44,000
		Goodwill	116,000
	£263,000		£263,000

Bilston Ltd
Balance Sheet at 1 April 19X5

	£	£	£
Fixed assets			
Premises			150
Equipment (£60+20)			80
Vehicles (£93+15)			108
			338
Current assets			
Stock (£104+68)		172	
Debtors (£90+44)		134	
		306	
Less : **Current liabilities**			
Creditors	140		
Accruals	30		
Bank overdraft (£8-20)	12	182	124
			£462

563

Capital and reserves

Ordinary shares of £1 each (£100+50)	150
Share premium	130
Reserves (£298-116)	182
	£462

EXERCISE 32.6   PAGE 269

(a)

MERGED PLC
C V Badge's Books
Realisation Account

	£000		£000
Decrease in value :		Increase in value :	
Plant and machinery	20	Freehold property	30
Vehicles	6	Goodwill (£365-350)	15
Equipment	6		
Stocks	6		
Debtors	5		
Capital (net increase in value)	2		
	£45		**£45**

Capital Account

	£000		£000
Merged plc (300,000 shares of £1 each + premium of £0.10 per share)	330	Balance b/d	336
		Realisation	2
Bank (£14+35-41)	8		
	£338		**£338**

Rupert plc's Books
Realisation Account

	£000		£000
Decrease in value :		Increase in value :	
Plant and machinery	25	Freehold property	10
Vehicles	4	Decrease in value :	
Stocks	5	Creditors	2
Debtors	1	Goodwill	97
Bank - expenses	10		
Capital (net increase in value)	64		
	£109		**£109**

Capital Account

	£000		£000
Rupert plc (300,000 shares of £1 each + premium of £0.50 per share)	450	Ordinary shares of £1 each	300
		Retained profits	130
Bank (£21+50-17-10)	44	Increase in value	64
	£494		£494

(b)

Balance Sheet at 1 July 19X5

	£000	£000
Fixed assets at cost :		
Intangible assets		
Goodwill (£15+97)		112
Tangible assets		
Freehold property (£150+250)	400	
Plant and machinery (£80+100)	180	
Vehicles (£10+16)	26	
Equipment (£25+10)	35	641
Current assets		
Stocks (£60+40)	100	
Debtors (£25+24)	49	
Bank (£200+100-35-50)	215	
	364	
Less : **Current liabilities**		
Creditors	37	327
		£1,080
Capital and reserves		
Ordinary shares of £1 each (£200+300+300)		800
Share premium (£30+150)		180
		980
Loans		
10% debentures of £1 each		100
		£1,080

Note : Goodwill should not be retained in the balance sheet. It should either be written off against reserves or amortised over its useful economic life.

SOLUTIONS TO CHAPTER 33 EXERCISES

EXERCISE 33.1   PAGE 279

BELL FOODS LTD
Journal

			Dr £	Cr £
27 10 X0	Bank	Dr	21,250	
	To: Ordinary share application and allotment			21,250
	Being amounts received on application			
31 10 X0	Ordinary share application and allotment	Dr	51,000	
	To: Ordinary share capital			34,000
	To: Share premium			17,000
	Being allotment of shares			
4 11 X0	Bank	Dr	29,750	
	To: Ordinary share application and allotment			29,750
	Being receipt of amounts due on allotment			
28 11 X0	First call	Dr	25,500	
	To: Ordinary share capital			25,500
	Being amount of the first call			
3 12 X0	Bank	Dr	25,500	
	To: First call			25,500
	Being receipt of the first call money due			
31 12 X0	Second call	Dr	25,500	
	To: Ordinary share capital			25,500
	Being amount of the second call			
5 1 X1	Bank	Dr	24,900	
	To: Second call			24,900
	Being receipt of the second call money due			
31 3 X1	Investments - own shares	Dr	600	
	To: Second call			600
	Being the forfeiture of 2,000 ordinary shares on second call			
14 11 X0	9% redeemable debenture stock	Dr	20,000	
	To: 9% redeemable debenture stock redemption			20,000
	Being 9% debentures to be redeemed			

		Dr £	Cr £
14 11 X0	9% redeemable debenture stock redemption	Dr 19,600	
	To : Bank		19,600
	Being payment to redeem the 9% redeemable debentures at 98 ex interest		
14 11 X0	9% redeemable debenture stock redemption	Dr 400	
	To : Share premium		400
	Being profit on the redemption of the 9% redeemable debentures		
28 11 X0	9% redeemable debenture stock interest	Dr 2,250	
	To : Bank		2,250
	Being the interest due on the 9% redeemable debentures (including £900 on debentures sold ex interest)		

EXERCISE 33.2   PAGE 279

(a)

PORTER INDUSTRIES PLC
Profit and Loss Appropriation Account
for the year ended 31 December 19X3

	£	£
Net profit for the year b/d (by deduction)		646,200
Less : Dividends :		
Preference (7% redeemable preference)	56,000	
Ordinary : interim dividend of 1p per share	80,000	
Ordinary : proposed final dividend of 4p per share	320,000	456,000
Retained profit for the year		190,200
Retained profits brought forward		1,700,000
Retained profits carried forward		£1,890,200

(b)

Journal

		Dr £	Cr £
15 3 X4	Bank	Dr 4,400,000	
	To : Ordinary share capital		2,000,000
	To : Share premium		2,400,000
	Being issue of 4,000,000 ordinary shares of £0.50 each at a premium of £0.60 per share		

31 3 X4	7% redeemable preference shares To: Bank Being the redemption of the 7% redeemable preference shares	Dr	800,000	800,000
31 3 X4	7% redeemable debentures To: Bank Being the redemption of the 7% redeemable debentures at par	Dr	3,000,000	3,000,000
31 3 X4	Preference dividend To: Bank Being the dividend payable on the 7% redeemable preference shares (3 months)	Dr	14,000	14,000
31 3 X4	Debenture interest Creditors To: Bank Being the interest due on the 7% debentures now repaid, including one month's interest accrued at 31 December 19X3	Dr Dr	52,500 17,500	70,000
31 3 X4	Buildings To: Bank Being investment of surplus cash on issue of ordinary shares in buildings (£4,400-800-3,000-14*-70*)	Dr	516,000	516,000

<u>Note</u> : *It is assumed that the surplus cash means after allowing for the preference dividend and the debenture interest.

EXERCISE 33.3 PAGE 280

REYLAP LTD
Journal

			Dr £	Cr £

1 3 X9	Bank
	   To: Ordinary share application and
	     allotment
	Being applications for 1,600,000 shares
	received at 5p per share
		Dr	80,000	80,000

16 3 X9	Ordinary share application and allotment To: Bank Being return of application money to unsuccessful subscribers	Dr	40,000	40,000

		Dr £	Cr £
16 3 X9	Ordinary share application and allotment	Dr 200,000	
	To : Ordinary share capital		200,000
	Being allotment of shares		
22 3 X9	Bank	Dr 160,000	
	To : Ordinary share application and allotment		160,000
	Being receipt of amounts due on allotment		
30 3 X9	Call	Dr 80,000	
	To : Share premium		80,000
	Being the amount of the call on shares, the final amount assumed to be the premium of 10p per share.		

Balance Sheet at 31 March 19X9

	£
Current assets	
Debtors : Called up share capital not paid	80,000
Cash at bank and in hand	200,000
	£280,000
Capital and reserves	
Called up share capital	200,000
Share premium account	80,000
	£280,000

EXERCISE 33.4   PAGE 280

(a)

NEWSTEAD TRADING ESTATE CO LTD
Journal

		Dr £	Cr £
25 2 X5	Bank	Dr 62,500	
	To : Ordinary share application and allotment		62,500
	Being the amount received on application		
1 3 X5	Ordinary share application and allotment	Dr 62,500	
	To : Ordinary shares		50,000
	To : Share premium		12,500
	Being the allotment of shares		

		Dr £	Cr £
25 3 X5	Bank	Dr 47,500	
	To : 8% debenture application and allotment		47,500
	Being the amount received on application		
1 4 X5	8% debenture application and allotment	Dr 50,000	
	To : 8% debentures		50,000
	Being the allotment of 8% debentures		
1 4 X5	Share premium	Dr 2,500	
	To : 8% debenture application and allotment		2,500
	Being the write-off of the 5% discount on the issue of debentures		
1 5 X5	8% redeemable cumulative preference shares	Dr 100,000	
	To : 8% preference share redemption		100,000
	Being the 8% redeemable cumulative preference shares to be redeemed		
1 5 X5	8% preference share redemption	Dr 100,000	
	To : Bank		100,000
	Being the payment made to redeem the shares		
	(Note : insufficient information is given to be able to deal with any accumulated dividend)		
1 9 X5	Ordinary shares interim dividend	Dr 4,000	
	To : Bank		4,000
	Being the interim dividend on ordinary shares at 2p per share		
1 10 X5	8% debenture interest	Dr 2,000	
	To : Bank		2,000
	Being the payment of the half year's interest on the 8% debentures		

(b)   The debenture interest will be charged against profits.

EXERCISE 33.5 PAGE 281

(i)

KAMMER PLC
Ordinary Share Capital Account

		£			£
1 6 X7	Balance c/d	600,000	1 10 X6	Balance b/d	500,000
			1 12 X6	Application and allotment	70,000
			1 6 X7	First and final call	30,000
		£600,000			£600,000
			2 6 X7	Balance b/d	600,000

(ii)

Share Premium Account

		£			£
1 9 X7	Balance c/d	52,500	1 12 X6	Application and allotment	50,000
			1 9 X7	Investment - own shares	2,500
		£52,500			£52,500
			2 9 X7	Balance b/d	52,500

(iii)

Application and Allotment Account

		£			£
1 12 X6	Bank - refunds in full (75,000 x £0.65)	48,750	1 11 X6	Bank (200,000 x £0.65)	130,000
1 12 X6	Bank - refunds : 3 for 4 only (25,000 x £0.65)	16,250	1 12 X6	Bank (100,00 x £0.55)	55,000
1 12 X6	Ordinary share capital	70,000			
1 12 X6	Share premium (100,000 x £0.50)	50,000			
		£185,000			£185,000

(iv)

First and Final Call Account

		£			£
1 6 X7	Ordinary share capital (100,000 x £0.30)	30,000	1 6 X7	Bank (95,000 x £0.30)	28,500
			1 6 X7	Investments - own shares (5,000 x £0.30)	1,500
		£30,000			£30,000

(v)

Investments - Own Shares

		£			£
1 6 X7	First and final call	1,500	1 9 X7	Bank	
1 9 X7	Share premium	2,500		(5,000 x £0.80)	4,000
		£4,000			£4,000

EXERCISE 33.6 PAGE 281

RUDOLPH LTD
Journal

			Dr £	Cr £
23 3 X4	Bank	Dr	30,000	
	To: Ordinary share application and allotment			30,000
	Being amounts received on application			
5 4 X4	Ordinary share application and allotment	Dr	90,000	
	To: Ordinary share capital			45,000
	To: Share premium			45,000
	Being allotment of shares			
5 4 X4	Bank	Dr	60,000	
	To: Ordinary share application and allotment			60,000
	Being receipt of amounts on allotment			
30 4 X4	First call	Dr	52,500	
	To: Ordinary share capital			52,500
	Being the amount of the first call			
4 5 X4	Bank	Dr	49,000	
	To: First call			49,000
	Being the receipt of the first call money			
25 6 X4	Second call	Dr	52,500	
	To: Ordinary share capital			52,500
	Being the amount of the second call			
29 6 X4	Bank	Dr	49,000	
	To: Second call			49,000
	Being the receipt of the second call money			
31 7 X4	Investments - own shares	Dr	7,000	
	To: First call			3,500
	To: Second call			3,500
	Being the forfeiture of the shares			

		Dr £	Cr £

31 7 X4	7% redeemable debenture stock
	    To : 7% redeemable debenture stock
	             redemption
	Being debentures to be redeemed
		Dr 40,000	40,000

31 7 X4	7% redeemable debenture stock redemption To : Bank Being the redemption of the 7% debentures at 96 ex interest	Dr 38,400	38,400
31 7 X4	7% redeemable debenture stock redemption To : Share premium Being the profit on the 7% debenture loan stock redeemed	Dr 1,600	1,600
15 8 X4	7% debenture interest To : Bank Being the half-year's interest payable on the 7% debentures (including the debentures redeemed at 96 ex interest)	Dr 2,800	2,800

EXERCISE 33.7   PAGE 282

JONES PLC
Journal

		Dr £	Cr £

31 3 X4	Bank
	    To : Ordinary share application and
	             allotment
	Being amounts received on application
		Dr 15,000	15,000

29 4 X4	Ordinary share application and allotment
	    To : Ordinary share capital
	    To : Share premium
	Being allotment of shares, including the
	premium of 7p per share
		Dr 34,000	20,000
			14,000

29 4 X4	Bank (£19,000-38)
	    To : Ordinary share application and
	             allotment
	Being receipt of amounts due on allotment
	[John Smith failing to pay 400 x 12p
	   = 48 - (200x5p) = 38]
		Dr 18,962	18,962

			Dr £	Cr £
30 6 X4	First call	Dr	20,000	
	To : Ordinary share capital			20,000
	Being the amount due on first call			
30 6 X4	Bank	Dr	19,900	
	To : First call			19,900
	Being the amount received on first call			
31 8 X4	Second call	Dr	10,000	
	To : Ordinary share capital			10,000
	Being the amount of the call to make			
	them fully paid			
31 8 X4	Bank	Dr	9,950	
	To : Second call			9,950
	Being the amount received on second call			
31 8 X4	Investments - own shares	Dr	10	
	Share premium	Dr	28	
	To : Ordinary share application			
	and allotment			38
	Being forfeiture of shares, including premium			
	of 7p per share (it is assumed that John Smith			
	applied for 600 shares)			
31 8 X4	Investments - own shares	Dr	150	
	To : First call			100
	To : Second call			50
	Being forfeiture of shares by John Smith			
	and James Brown			
30 9 X4	Bank (1000 x 22p)	Dr	220	
	To : Investments - own shares			220
	Being proceeds of re-issue of shares			
30 9 X4	Investments - own shares	Dr	60	
	To : Share premium			60
	Being the transfer of the premium on			
	re-issued shares [£220 - (£10 + 150)]			

EXERCISE 33.8   PAGE 282

(i)

JOHN POTTER LTD
Cash Account (extract)

	£		£
1 1 X2 8% debentures	3,000	31 12 X2 Debenture interest	240
31 12 X3 Debenture sinking fund	82	31 12 X2 Sinking fund	
31 12 X4 Debenture sinking fund	173	investments	915
31 12 X4 Sinking fund		31 12 X3 Debenture interest	240
investments	1,912	31 12 X3 Sinking fund	
		investments (£915+82)	997
		31 12 X4 Debenture interest	240
		31 12 X4 8% debentures	3,000

(ii)

8% Debentures Account

	£		£
31 12 X4 Cash	3,000	1 1 X2 Cash	3,000

(iii)

Debenture Sinking Fund Account

	£		£
		31 12 X2 Profit and loss	
		appropriation	915
		31 12 X3 Cash : interest	82
		31 12 X3 Profit and loss	
		appropriation	915
		31 12 X4 Cash : interest	173
		31 12 X4 Profit and loss	
31 12 X4 General reserve	3,000	appropriation	915
	£3,000		£3,000

(iv)

Appropriation Account (extract)

	£
31 12 X2 Debenture sinking fund	915
31 12 X3 Debenture sinking fund	915
31 12 X4 Debenture sinking fund	915

(v)

Profit and Loss Account (extract)

	£
31 12 X2 Debenture interest	240
31 12 X3 Debenture interest	240
31 12 X4 Debenture interest	240

SOLUTIONS TO CHAPTER 34 EXERCISES

EXERCISE 34.1   PAGE 290

THOMAS MINTON
Branch stock accounts

	TUNSTALL Mem. Selling Price £	TUNSTALL Cost £	LONGTON Mem. Selling Price £	LONGTON Cost £
Opening balances	7,200	4,800	14,400	9,600
Goods sent to branches	36,000	24,000	115,200	76,800
Branches profit and loss	-	10,880	-	36,040
	£43,200	£39,680	£129,600	£122,440

	TUNSTALL Mem. Selling Price £	TUNSTALL Cost £	LONGTON Mem. Selling Price £	LONGTON Cost £
Goods returned from branches	3,600	2,400	5,760	3,840
Branch debtors - credit sales	3,000	3,000	10,000	10,000
Branch cash - cash sales	29,880	29,880	100,000	100,000
Closing stock c/d	6,600	4,400	12,900	8,600
Stock loss	120	-	940	-
	£43,200	£39,680	£129,600	£122,440

EXERCISE 34.2   PAGE 290

(a)

BRITTEN, HOLST AND BAX
Branch Stock Accounts

	A £	B £		A £	B £
Purchases	184,000	192,000	Branch debtors	146,400	168,220
Returns from branch customers (cash refunds given)	960	820	Branch stock c/d	38,560	24,600
	£184,960	£192,820		£184,960	£192,820
Branch stock b/d	38,560	24,600			

Branch Stock Adjustment Accounts

	A £	B £		A £	B £
Branch stock c/d	9,640	6,150	Purchases	46,000	48,000
Branch profit & loss	36,360	41,850			
	£46,000	£48,000		£46,000	£48,000
			Branch stock b/d	9,640	6,150

Branch Profit and Loss Accounts
for the year to 31 December 19X1

	A £	B £		A £	B £
Rent	5,400	6,800	Branch stock adjustment (gross profit)	36,360	41,850
Expenses (branches)	17,475	26,785			
Expenses (head office)	12,175	12,175			
Depreciation - motor vehicle (20%x£15,000) (40 : 60)	1,200	1,800			
Leasehold admin. (10%x£42,000) (50 : 50)	2,100	2,100	Net loss c/d	1,990	7,810
	£38,350	£49,660		£38,350	£49,660

(b)

**Profit and Loss Appropriation Account
for the year to 31 December 19X1**

	£	£	£
Net loss b/d :			
Branch A			(1,990)
Branch B			(7,810)
			(9,800)
Appropriation :			
Interest on capital (8%) :			
Britten	3,520		
Holst	2,480		
Bax	960	6,960	
Balance of loss :			
Britten (1/2)	(8,380)		
Holst (1/4)	(4,190)		
Bax (1/4)	(4,190)	(16,760)	(9,800)

EXERCISE 34.3   PAGE 291

(i)

**DELITY PLC
Branch Stock Accounts**

	Aville £	Betown £		Aville £	Betown £
Balances b/d	60,000	90,000	Goods returned		
Goods sent to			to head office	20,000	30,000
branch	810,000	1,222,000	Branch debtors –		
Transfer from			credit sales	750,700	1,178,000
Aville	–	38,400	Branch stock –		
			damaged	–	2,000
			Transfer to		
			Betown	36,000	–
			Balances c/d	63,300	140,400
	£870,000	£1,350,400		£870,000	£1,350,400
Balances b/d	63,300	140,400			

(ii)

Branch Stock Adjustment Accounts

	Aville £	Betown £		Aville £	Betown £
Goods returned			Balances b/d	12,000	22,500
to head office	4,000	7,500	Goods sent to		
Branch stock –			branch	162,000	305,500
damaged	–	500	Transfer from		
Transfers to			Aville	–	9,600
Betown	7,200	–			

	Aville £	Betown £		Aville £	Betown £
Profit and loss	150,140	294,500			
Balances c/d	12,660	35,100			
	£174,000	£337,600		£174,000	£337,600
			Balances b/d	12,660	35,100

(iii)

Debtors Accounts

	Aville £	Betown £		Aville £	Betown £
Balances b/d	49,100	72,000	Discounts allowed	32,400	41,500
Sales = balancing			Bad debt	-	3,000
figure	750,700	1,178,500	Cash	714,000	1,112,000
			Balances c/d	53,400	94,000
	£799,800	£1,250,500		£799,800	£1,250,500
Balances b/d	53,400	94,000			

(iv)

Cash Accounts

	Aville £	Betown £		Aville £	Betown £
Debtors	714,000	1,112,000	Remitted to head office	690,000	1,083,500
			Expenses	24,000	28,500
	£714,000	£1,112,000		£714,000	£1,112,000

(v)

Profit and Loss Accounts for the year 19X4

	Aville £	Betown £		Aville £	Betown £
Discounts allowed	32,400	41,500	Branch stock adjustment	150,140	294,500
Bad debt	-	3,000			
Local expenses	24,000	28,500			
Other expenses	43,740	120,125			
Net profit for the year	50,000	101,375			
	£150,140	£294,500		£150,140	£294,500

EXERCISE 34.4 PAGE 292
(a)

PAPER PRODUCTS
Branch Stock Account

	£000		£000
Balance b/d	75	Goods sent to branch (returns)	30
Goods sent to branch	600	Branch bank (cash sales)	120
Branch debtors	8	Branch debtors	437
		Balance c/d	90
		Branch stock adjustment (balancing figure)	6
	£683		£683
Balance b/d	90		

Goods Sent to Branch Account

	£000		£000
Branch stock adjustment (1/3 x £600,000)	200	Branch stock	600
Branch stock	30	Branch stock adjustment	10
Head office trading	380		
	£610		£610

Branch Stock Adjustment Account

	£000		£000
Goods sent to branch (1/3 x £30,000)	10	Balance b/d (1/3 x £75,000)	25
Branch stock (stock loss)	6	Goods sent to branch	200
Balance c/d (1/3 x £90,000)	30		
Branch profit and loss	179		
	£225		£225
		Balance b/d	30

Branch Debtors Account

	£000		£000
Balance b/d	66	Branch stock (returns)	8
Branch stock	437	Branch bank	390
		Discounts allowed	9
		Bad debts	15
		Balance c/d	81
	£503		£503
Balance b/d	81		

Branch Bank Account

	£000		£000
Balance b/d	3	General expenses	42
Branch stock (cash sales)	120	Transfer to head office bank account	459
Branch debtors	390	Balance c/d	12
	£513		£513
Balance b/d	12		

(b)

PAPER PRODUCTS
Trading and Profit and Loss Account for the year to 31 March 19X6

| | WORKINGS | | |
	£000	Head office £000	Branch £000
Sales :			
Cash	1,620	1,500	120
Credit (Wkg1)	2,389	1,960	429
	4,009	3,460	549
Less : Cost of goods sold :			
Opening stock	230	180	50
Purchases (Wkg2)	2,780	2,400	380
	3,010	2,580	430
Less : Closing stock	280	220	60
	2,730	2,360	370
Gross profit	1,279	1,100	179
Less : Expenses :			
Bad debts	39	24	15
Discounts allowed	38	29	9
General expenses	452	410	42
	529	463	66
Net profit	£750	£637	£113

Workings

		Head office £000	Branch £000
(1)	Credit sales :		
	Sales	2,000	437
	Less : Returns	40	8
		£1,960	£429
(2)	Purchases :		
	As per question	2,780	–
	Less : Transfer to branch 600		
	Returns 30		
	570 x 2/3	380	380
		£2,400	£380

SOLUTIONS TO CHAPTER 35 EXERCISES

EXERCISE 35.1   PAGE 297

IRENE
Trading and Profit and Loss Account for the year to 31 March 19X1

	Ayr £000	Perth £000
Sales	510	100
Transferred to branch	70	-
	580	100
Less : Cost of goods sold		
Opening stock	20	6
Purchases	415	-
Transferred from head office	-	70
	435	76
Less : Closing stock	25	8
	410	68
Gross profit	170	32
Less : Expenses :		
Administrative expenses	130	40
Depreciation of fixed assets (10% x £90/20)	9	2
	139	42
Net profit/loss for the year	£31	£(10)

Balance Sheet at 31 March 19X1

	£000	£000
Fixed assets at cost (£90+20)		110
Less : Accumulated depreciation (£36+6+9+2)		53
		57
Current assets		
Stocks (£25+8)	33	
Debtors (£65+8)	73	
Bank (£5+1)	6	
	112	
Less : **Current liabilities**		
Creditors (£32+5)	37	75
		£132
Capital		
At 1 April 19X0		111
Add : Net profit for the year (£31-10)		21
		£132

Head Office Books
Perth Current Account

	£000		£000
Balance b/d	34	Net loss for the year	10
		Balance c/d	24
	£34		£34
Balance b/d	24		

Branch Books
Head Office Current Account

	£000		£000
Net loss for the year	10	Balance b/d	34
Balance c/d	24		
	£34		£34
		Balance b/d	24

EXERCISE 35.2   PAGE 297

SONG
Trading and Profit and Loss Account
for the year to 31 December 19X1

	Dave £000	Mana £000
Sales	350	210
Transferred to branch	125	-
	475	210
Less : Cost of goods sold		
Opening stock	30	20
Purchases	400	-
Transferred from head office	-	125
	430	145
Less : Closing stock	40	30
	390	115
Gross profit	85	95
Less : Expenses :		
Administrative expenses	50	20
Depreciation of plant and machinery (25% x £80/20)	20	5
Increase in provision for unrealised profit on stock [(1/5 x £30) - 4]	2	-
	72	25
Net profit for the year	£13	£70

Balance Sheet at 31 December 19X1

	£000	£000
Fixed assets		
Plant and machinery, at cost (£80+20)		100
Less : Accumulated depreciation (£40+5+20+5)		70
		30
Current assets		
Stocks (£40+30-6)	64	
Debtors (£60+65)	125	
Cash (£16+5)	21	
	210	
Less : **Current liabilities**		
Creditors (£35+2)	37	173
		£203
Capital		
At 1 January 19X1		132
Add : Net profit for the year (£13+70)	83	
Less : Drawings	12	71
		£203

EXERCISE 35.3   PAGE 298

(a)

SCOTT
Trading and Profit and Loss Account
for the year to 30 June 19X3

	Arbroath £000	Montrose £000
Sales	300	120
Transferred to branch (£99-11)	88	-
	388	120
Less : Cost of goods sold		
Opening stock	35	33
Purchases	280	-
Transferred from head office	-	88
	315	121
Less : Closing stock [£40 + (11 x 10/11)] = 50	50	55
	265	66
Gross profit	123	54
Less : Expenses :		
Delivery expenses	18	6
Shop expenses	17	12

	Arbroath £000	Montrose £000
Depreciation of furniture and fittings [10% x (£30-20)] [10% x (£15-5)]	1	1
Increase in provision for unrealised profit on stock [(1/11 x £55) - 3]	2	-
	38	19
Net profit for the year	£85	£35

Balance Sheet at 30 June 19X3

	£000	£000
Fixed assets		
Furniture and fittings, at cost (£30+15)		45
Less : Accumulated depreciation (£20+5+1+1)		27
		18
Current assets		
Stocks [£40+(100/110 x 11)+55-5]	100	
Debtors (£5+3)	8	
Cash and bank (£6+4+9)	19	
	127	
Less : **Current liabilities**		
Creditors (£20+2)	22	105
		£123
Capital		
At 1 July 19X2		17
Add : Net profit for the year (£85+35)	120	
Less : Drawings	14	106
		£123

(b)

Head Office Books
Branch Current Account

	£000		£000
Balance b/d	54	Goods in transit c/d	11
Branch net profit	35	Cash in transit c/d	9
		Balance c/d	69
	£89		£89
Balance b/d	69		

Branch Books
Head Office Current Account

	£000		£000
Balance c/d	69	Balance b/d	34
		Net profit	35
	£69		£69
		Balance b/d	69

EXERCISE 35.4   PAGE 299

DEVON
Trading and Profit and Loss Account for the year to 30 April 19X4

	Exeter £000	Torquay £000	Combined £000
Sales	750	300	1,050
Transfers to branch (£75-15)	60	-	-
	810	300	1,050
Less : Cost of sales :			
Opening stock	20	50	61
Purchases	710	173	883
Transfers from head office	-	60	-
	730	283	944
Less : Closing stock (£40+10)	50	25	70
	680	258	874
Gross profit	130	42	176
Less : Expenses :			
General	65	16	81
Depreciation - equipment	35	12	47
Reduction in provision for unrealised stock profit [(50/150 x £15) - 9]	(4)	-	-
	96	28	128
Net profit for the year	£34	£14	£48

Balance Sheet at 30 April 19X4

	Exeter £000	Torquay £000	Combined £000
Fixed assets			
Equipment	175	60	235
Less : Accumulated depreciation	140	36	176
	35	24	59
Current assets			
Stocks (£50-5)	45	25	70
Debtors	250	35	285
Current account (£80-15-3+14)	76	-	-
Cash at bank and in hand (£8+3)	11	6	17
	382	66	372
Less : **Current liabilities**			
Creditors	(110)	(14)	(124)
Current account (£62+14)	-	(76)	-
	(110)	(90)	(124)
Net current assets	272	(24)	248
	£307	£0	£307

Capital

At 1 May 19X3	283	-	283
Add : Net profit for the year	48	-	48
Less : Drawings	(24)	-	(24)
	£307	£0	£307

EXERCISE 35.5   PAGE 300

MAPP LTD
Trading and Profit and Loss Account for the year to 30 June 19X8

	Head office £	Branch £	Combined £
Sales	350,000	215,000	565,000
Goods to branch	166,000	-	-
	516,000	215,000	565,000
Less : Cost of sales :			
Opening stock	15,000	9,000	22,500
Purchases	225,000	-	225,000
Goods from head office	-	154,000	-
	240,000	163,000	247,500
Less : Closing stock (Wkg1)	20,000	24,000	50,000
	220,000	139,000	197,500
Gross profit	296,000	76,000	367,500
Administration expenses	135,000	9,000	144,000
Distribution costs	30,000	12,000	42,000
Provision for unrealised profit (Wkg2)	4,500	-	-
	169,500	21,000	186,000
Net profit	£126,500	£55,000	£181,500

Balance Sheet at 30 June 19X8

	Head office £	Branch £	Combined £
Fixed assets :			
Plant and machinery at net book value	383,000	38,000	421,000
Current assets			
Stocks	20,000	24,000	40,000
Goods in transit	10,000	-	10,000
Debtors	15,000	20,000	35,000
Branch current account (Wkg3)	79,000	-	-
Cash at bank and in hand	19,000	2,000	21,000
Cash in transit	10,000	-	10,000
	153,000	46,000	116,000

Creditors : amounts falling due within one year

Creditors	(22,500)	(5,000)	(27,500)
Head office current account (Wkg3)	-	(79,000)	-
	(22,500)	(84,000)	(27,500)
Net current assets	130,500	(38,000)	88,500

Provisions for liabilities and charges

Provision for unrealised profit	(4,000)	-	-
	£509,500	£0	£509,500

Capital and reserves			
Called up share capital	300,000	-	300,000
Profit and loss account (£28,000 + 181,500)	209,500	-	209,500
	£509,500	-	£509,500

Workings

	£	£
1. Combined closing stocks :		
Head office stock		20,000
Branch stock	24,000	
Goods in transit	12,000	
	36,000	
Less : Provision for unrealised profit	6,000	30,000
		£50,000

2. Provision for unrealised profit :	Units
Price structure	100
Mark-up	20
Cost to branch	120

	£
On branch closing stock (£24,000 x 20/120)	4,000
Goods in transit (£12,000 x 20/120)	2,000
	6,000
Provision brought forward	1,500
Additional provision required	£4,500

3. Head office books : Branch current account

	£
Balance b/d	46,000
Branch profit	55,000
Goods in transit c/d	(12,000)
Cash in transit c/d	(10,000)
Balance c/d	£79,000

4. Branch books : Head office current account

	£
Balance b/d	24,000
Branch profit	55,000
	£79,000

SOLUTIONS TO CHAPTER 36 EXERCISES

EXERCISE 36.1   PAGE 306

TROY
Van Account

		£			£
1 1 X1	Hire purchase	16,000			

Hire Purchase Loan Account

		£			£
1 1 X1	Bank - deposit	4,000	1 1 X1	Van	16,000
30 6 X1	Bank	3,200	30 6 X1	HP loan interest	2,057
31 12 X1	Bank	3,200	31 12 X1	HP loan interest	1,714
31 12 X1	Balance c/d	9,371			
		£19,771			£19,771
30 6 X2	Bank	3,200	1 1 X2	Balance b/d	9,371
31 12 X2	Bank	3,200	30 6 X2	HP loan interest	1,371
31 12 X2	Balance c/d	5,371	31 12 X2	HP loan interest	1,029
		£11,771			£11,771
30 6 X2	Bank	3,200	1 1 X3	Balance b/d	5,371
31 12 X2	Bank	3,200	30 6 X3	HP loan interest	686
			31 12 X3	HP loan interest	343
		£6,400			£6,400

Hire Purchase Loan Interest Account

		£			£
30 6 X1	HP loan	2,057	31 12 X1	Profit and loss	3,771
31 12 X1	HP loan	1,714			
		£3,771			£3,771
30 6 X2	HP loan	1,371	31 12 X2	Profit and loss	2,400
31 12 X2	HP loan	1,029			
		£2,400			£2,400
30 6 X3	HP loan	686	31 12 X3	Profit and loss	1,029
31 12 X3	HP loan	343			
		£1,029			£1,029

Workings

Sum of digits = [6 x (6+1)]/2 = 21
Apportionment of interest (6 x 3,200 = 19,200 - 12,000 = £7,200) :

Half year to		£
30 6 X1	6/21 x £7,200	2,057
31 12 X1	5/21 x £7,200	1,714
30 6 X2	4/21 x £7,200	1,371
31 12 X2	3/21 x £7,200	1,029
30 6 X3	2/21 x £7,200	686
31 12 X3	1/21 x £7,200	343
		£7,200

EXERCISE 36.2   PAGE 306

	£
Cash price	50,000
Less : deposit	12,500
Amount advanced	£37,500

$$\text{Annuity factor} = \frac{\text{Amount advanced}}{\text{Periodic rental}}$$

$$= \frac{£37,500}{11,454}$$

$$= 3.274$$

Using annuity tables (present value of an annuity of £1), for a five year period, 3.274 implies an interest rate of 16%.

EXERCISE 36.3   PAGE 307

JENNIE
Car Account

		£			£
1 4 X4	Hire purchase loan	9,000			

Car Depreciation Account

		£			£
			31 3 X5	Profit and loss	2,250

Hire Purchase Loan Account

		£			£
1 4 X4	Bank	3,000	1 4 X4	Car	9,000
30 4 X4	Bank	222	30 4 X4	HP interest	100
31 5 X4	Bank	222	31 5 X4	HP interest	98
30 6 X4	Bank	222	30 6 X4	HP interest	96
31 7 X4	Bank	222	31 7 X4	HP interest	94

		£			£
31 8 X4	Bank	222	31 8 X4	HP interest	92
30 9 X4	Bank	222	30 9 X4	HP interest	90
31 10 X4	Bank	222	31 10 X4	HP interest	87
30 11 X4	Bank	222	30 11 X4	HP interest	85
31 12 X4	Bank	222	31 12 X4	HP interest	83
31 1 X5	Bank	222	31 1 X5	HP interest	81
28 2 X5	Bank	222	28 2 X5	HP interest	78
31 3 X5	Bank	222	31 3 X5	HP interest	76
31 3 X5	Balance c/d	4,396			
		£10,060			£10,060
			1 4 X5	Balance b/d	4,396

Hire Purchase Loan Interest Account

		£			£
30 4 X4	HP loan	100			
31 5 X4	HP loan	98			
30 6 X4	HP loan	96			
31 7 X4	HP loan	94			
31 8 X4	HP loan	92			
30 9 X4	HP loan	90			
31 10 X4	HP loan	87			
30 11 X4	HP loan	85			
31 12 X4	HP loan	83			
31 1 X5	HP loan	81			
28 2 X5	HP loan	78			
31 3 X5	HP loan	76	31 3 X5	Profit and loss	1,060
		£1,060			£1,060

EXERCISE 36.4   PAGE 307

BULWELL AGGREGATES LTD
Lorries Account

		£			£
1 1 X1	Granby Garages	54,000			

Interest Account

		£			£
31 12 X1	Granby	11,250	31 12 X1	Profit and loss	11,250
31 12 X2	Granby	8,063	31 12 X2	Profit and loss	8,063
31 12 X3	Granby	4,078	31 12 X3	Profit and loss	4.078

Granby Garages Account

		£			£
1 1 X1	Cash	9,000	1 1 X1	Lorries	54,000
31 12 X1	Cash	24,000	1 1 X1	Interest	11,250
31 12 X1	Balance c/d	32,250			
		£65,250			£65,250
1 1 X2	Cash	24,000	1 1 X2	Balance b/d	32,250
31 12 X2	Balance c/d	16,313	31 12 X2	Interest	8,063
		£40,313			£40,313
1 1 X3	Cash	20,391	1 1 X3	Balance b/d	16,313
			31 12 X3	Interest	4,078
		£30,391			£20,391

Depreciation Account

	£			£
31 12 X1 Balance c/d	12,500	31 12 X1 Profit and loss		12,500
31 12 X2 Balance c/d	25,000	1 1 X2	Balance b/d	12,500
		31 12 X2	Profit and loss	12,500
	£25,000			£25,000
31 12 X3 Balance c/d	37,500	1 1 X3	Balance b/d	25,000
		31 12 X3	Profit and loss	12,500
	£37,500			£37,500
31 12 X4 Balance c/d	50,000	1 1 X4	Balance b/d	37,500
		31 12 X4	Profit and loss	12,500
	£50,000			£50,000

Balance Sheet at 31 December (extracts)

	19X1 £	19X2 £	19X3 £	19X4 £
Fixed assets				
Vehicles, at cost	54,000	54,000	54,000	54,000
Less : Accumulated depreciation	12,500	25,000	37,500	50,000
	41,500	29,000	16,500	4,000
Current liabilities				
Obligations under hire purchase contracts	15,937	16,313	-	-
Long term liabilities				
Obligations under hire purchase contracts	16,313	-	-	-

Charge against profit

	19X1	19X2	19X3	19X4
	£	£	£	£
Interest	11,250	8,063	4,078	-
Depreciation	12,500	12,500	12,500	12,500

Working

Calculation of interest :

19X1	25% x £45,000 = £11,250
19X2	25% x £32,250 = £8,063
19X3	25% x £16,313 = £4,078

EXERCISE 36.5   PAGE 307

(a)

MIDGE

Car Account

		£			£
1 5 X5	Hire purchase loan	20,000	31 10 X6	Car disposal	20,000

Car Depreciation Account

		£			£
31 10 X6	Car disposal	5,000	30 4 X6	Profit and loss	5,000

Hire Purchase Loan Account

		£			£
1 5 X5	Bank	5,000	1 5 X5	Car	20,000
30 4 X6	Bank	6,460	30 4 X6	HP interest	
30 4 X6	Balance c/d	10,640		(14% x £15,000)	2,100
		£22,100			£22,100
31 10 X6	Bank	14,000	1 5 X6	Balance b/d	10,640
			31 10 X6	HP interest	
				(14% x £10,640 x 1/2)	745
			30 4 X7	Profit and loss - loss on termination of loan	2,615
		£14,000			£14,000

Hire Purchase Loan Interest Account

		£			£
30 4 X6	HP loan	2,100	30 4 X6	Profit and loss	2,100
31 10 X6	HP loan	745	30 4 X7	Profit and loss	745

Car Disposal Account

	£			£
31 10 X6 Car	20,000	31 10 X6	Car depreciation	5,000
		31 10 X6	Bank - insurance	6,000
		30 4 X7	Profit and loss - loss on disposal	9,000
	£20,000			£20,000

(b)

MIDGE
Balance Sheet (extracts) at 30 April 19X6

	£
Fixed assets	
Car at cost	20,000
Less : Accumulated depreciation	5,000
	15,000
Current liabilities	
Obligations under hire purchase contracts	
(£6,460-1,490) (Wkg)	4,970
Long-term liabilities	
Obligations under hire purchase contracts	
(£6,460-790) (Wkg)	5,670

Working

30 4 19X7	14% x £10,640	£1,490
30 4 19X8	14% x (£10,640 + 1490 - 6460)	£790 (approx)

SOLUTIONS TO CHAPTER 37 EXERCISES

EXERCISE 37.1 PAGE 313

GRANBY
Bulwell Aggregates Account

		£			£
1 1 X1	HP Sales	54,000	1 1 X1	Bank (deposit)	9,000
31 12 X1	HP interest	11,250	31 12 X1	Bank (instalment)	24,000
			31 12 X1	Balance c/d	32,250
		£65,250			£65,250
1 1 X2	Balance b/d	32,250	31 12 X2	Bank (instalment)	24,000
31 12 X2	HP interest	8,063	31 12 X2	Balance c/d	16,313
		£40,313			£40,313
1 1 X3	Balance b/d	16,313	31 12 X3	Bank (instalment)	20,391
31 12 X3	HP interest	4,078			
		£20,391			£20,391

HP Interest Account

		£			£
31 12 X1	HP Trading	11,250	31 12 X1	Bulwell	11,250
31 12 X2	HP Trading	8,063	31 12 X2	Bulwell	8.063
31 12 X3	HP Trading	4,078	31 12 X3	Bulwell	4,078

HP Trading Account

		£			£
31 12 X1	General Trading	43,200	1 1 X1	HP sales	54,000
31 12 X1	Provision for unrealised profit c/d (Wkg)	6,450	31 12 X1	HP interest	11,250
31 12 X1	Gross profit	15,600			
		£65,250			£65,250
31 12 X2	Provision for unrealised profit c/d (Wkg)	3,263	1 1 X2	Provision for unrealised profit b/d	6,450
31 12 X2	Gross profit	11,250	31 12 X2	HP interest	8,063
		£14,513			£14,513
			1 1 X3	Provision for unrealised profit b/d	3,263
31 12 X3	Gross profit	7,341	31 12 X3	HP interest	4,078
		£7,341			£7,341

Working

Calculation of provision for unrealised profit :

$$\text{Profit margin} = \frac{10,800}{54,000} \times \frac{100}{1} = 20\%$$

20% on £32,250 = £6,450
20% on £16,313 = £3,263

EXERCISE 37.2   PAGE 313

(a)

BROMFORD LTD
Hire Purchase Trading Account
for the year ended 31 December 19X6

	£		£
General trading		HP sales	2,400
(100/133.33 x £2,400)	1,800	HP interest (Wkg3)	155
Provision for unrealised			
profit (Wkg1) .	502		
Gross profit	253		
	£2,555		£2,555

(b)

TILL AND CO'S BOOKS
Profit and Loss Account (extract) for the year to 31 March 19X7

	Dr
	£
Interest on hire purchase agreement (Wkg3)	216
Depreciation of photocopier (£2,400/3 x 3/4)	600

Balance Sheet (extract) at 31 March 19X7   £

	£
Fixed asset	
Office equipment, at cost	2,400
Less : Accumulated depreciation	600
	1,800
Current liabilities	
Obligation under hire purchase agreement	
[£2,400 - 480 + 216 - (9 x 95)]	1,281

Workings

1.   Profit margin = £600/1800 x 100 = <u>33.33%</u>

     Provision for unrealised profit = 33.33% x £1,505 (Wkg2) = <u>£502</u>

2.   Amount not yet due :

	£
List price	2,400
Less : deposit	480
	1,920
Add : interest (Wkg3)	155
	2,075
Less : instalments (6x95)	570
	£1,505

3.   <u>Note</u> :   The Examiner does not give any indication of how the interest charge is to be dealt with. The sum of digits method has, therefore, been chosen, but other methods would be acceptable.

Sum of digits = $n(n+1)/2$ = 24 (24+1)/2 = <u>300</u>

Apportionment of interest (£360) :

	£	
24/300 x 360 =	29	
23/300 x 360 =	28	
22/300 x 360 =	26	
21/300 x 360 =	25	
20/300 x 360 =	24	
19/300 x 360 =	23	£155 (for the six months to 31 December 19X6)
18/300 x 360 =	22	
17/300 x 360 =	20	
16/300 x 360 =	19	£216 (for the nine months to 31 March 19X7)

EXERCISE 37.3   PAGE 314

(a)

JOHN MURRAY
Saloon XY

Car ID Letter	Date sold (list price £3,850)	Deposit of 20% (£770) £	36 monthly payments (of £96)	Total instalments (£3,456) £	Total HP price (£4,226) £
A	2 1 X4	770	11	1,056	1,826
B	2 3 X4	770	9	864	1,634
C	4 4 X4	770	5	480	1,250
D	5 8 X4	770	4	384	1,154
E	6 10 X4	770	2	192	962
		£3,850	31	£2,976	£6,826

(b)

JOHN MURRAY
Trading Account for the year to 31 December 19X4

	£	£
Hire purchase sales at cash prices (4 x £3,850)		15,400
Hire purchase interest [(£31-5) x 10]		260
Deposit and instalments received on repossessions [£770 + (96 x 5)]		1,250
		16,910
Less : Cost of goods sold :		
Purchases (5 x £3,000)	15,000	
Less : Closing stock	2,000	13,000
Gross profit		**£3,910**

EXERCISE 37.4   PAGE 314

(a)

TAIN
Hire Purchase Trading Account for the year to 31 March 19X6

	£		£
Purchases (£450+750+ 200+1,000)	2,400	Cash (£600+1,000+600+150)	2,350
		Goods repossessed (Wkg)	100
Gross profit on HP (Wkg)	550	Stock on hire at 31 March 19X6	500
	£2,950		£2,950

Workings

Date	Cash received	£	Stock at cost £	Profit £
1 May 19X5	Deposit (25%x£600)	150		
	Instalments (6x£75)	450		
		600		
	Less : Cost price	450	-	150
1 July 19X5	Deposit (25%x£1,000)	250		
	Instalments (6x£125)	750		
		1,000		
	Less : Cost price	750	-	250
1 Jan 19X6	Deposit (25%x£1,200)	300		
	Instalments (2x£150)	300		
		600		

Stock

<u>Balance outstanding x Cost price</u>
         HP selling price

= (£1,200-600) x 1,000 / 1,200   500   -

Profit

<u>(Deposits + instalments) x Profit</u>
         HP selling price

= £600 x 200 / 1,200   -   100

                                                              £500

Repossession :

1 Dec 19X5   Deposit (25%x£300)   75
                        Instalments (2x£37.50)   75
                                                                        150

Stock

<u>Balance outstanding x Cost price</u>
         HP selling price

= £150 x 200 / 300   100   -

Profit

<u>(Deposits + instalments) x Profit</u>
         HP selling price

= £150 / 300 x 100   -   50

                                                              £100   £550

EXERCISE 37.5   PAGE 315

ROCK
Trading, Profit and Loss Account for the year to 31 August 19X4

	Televisions £	Videos £	Total £
Sales :			
Cash	180,000	-	180,000
Hire purchase (at cash prices)	-	380,000	380,000
Hire purchase (at hire purchase prices)	140,000	-	140,000
Hire purchase interest (Wkg1)	-	49,400	49,400
	320,000	429,400	749,400
Less : Cost of goods sold			
Purchases	150,000	140,000	290,000
Less : Closing stock	7,500	7,000	14,500
	142,500	133,000	275,500
Gross profit	£177,500	£296,400	473,900

	Televisions £	Videos £	Total £
Less : Expenses			
Retailing			179,275
Provision for unrealised profit (Wkg2)			65,625
Depreciation on fixed assets (20%)			9,000
			253,900
Net profit for the year			**£220,000**

ROCK
Balance Sheet at 31 August 19X4

	£	£	£
Fixed assets			
At cost			45,000
Less : Depreciation			9,000
			36,000
Current assets			
Stocks		14,500	
Debtors		1,000	
Hire purchase instalments not yet due on televisions	105,000		
Less : Provision for unrealised profit	65,625	39,375	
Hire purchase instalments not yet due on videos	342,000		
Less : Provision for unrealised profit	49,400	292,600	
		347,475	
Less : **Current liabilities**			
Creditors	121,000		
Bank overdraft	8,475	129,475	218,000
			£254,000
Financed by :			
Capital			
Amount introduced on 1 September 19X3			50,000
Add : Net profit for the year		220,000	
Less : Drawings		16,000	204,000
			£254,000

Workings

		£
1.	Videos - Hire purchase interest :	
	Total HP sales	478,800
	Less : Total cash sales revenue (380 x £1,000)	380,000
		98,800
	Apportioned equally over the two years of the respective agreements :	
	First year's interest	£49,400

		£
2.	Televisions - Provision for unrealised profit :	
	Total HP selling price (350 x £400)	140,000
	Less : Cost (350 x £150)	52,500
	Total gross profit on HP sales	87,500
	Apportioned pro rata to cash collected	
	Amount due = £105,000 (as per HP debtors)	
	Provision = (£105,000 x 87,500) / 140,000	£65,625

CHAPTER 38

EXERCISE 38.1 PAGE 323

PENNY
Forecasted Trading and Profit and Loss Account
for the year ended 31 May 19X6

	£	£
Sales [(£200,000 x 97%) x 105%]		203,700
Less : Cost of sales [(£150,000 x 97.5%) x 105%]		153,563
Gross profit		50,137
Less : Expenses :		
Fixed overhead (£20,000 + 1%)	20,200	
Wages (£24,000 - 5,000)	19,000	
Administration expenses (£12,000 - 1,500)	11,500	50,700
Forecasted net loss for the year		£(563)

<u>Note</u> :
No details of opening and closing stocks are given. A reduction of 2.5% in purchase prices would not necessarily apply to the cost of sales for the year to 31 May 19X5.

EXERCISE 38.2 PAGE 323

TRENT PLC

(a)

(i) **Finished stocks (Units)**

	Week			
	1	**2**	**3**	**4**
Opening stock	1,000	1,100	1,400	600
Production	900	1,100	-	
	1,900	2,200	1,400	
Less : Sales	800	800	800	
Closing stock	1,100	1,400	600	

Finished goods stock will run out in week 4, and assuming a five day working week, on the fourth day [600 < (4 x 800/5)].

(ii) Purchases of materials

	Weeks	
	1	2
	£	£
Budgeted production (900 x £35, 1,100 x £35)	31,500	38,500
Closing stock	40,000	25,000
	71,500	63,500
Less : Opening stock	36,000	40,000
Purchases of materials	£35,500	£23,500

(b) Cash budget of weeks 1 to 6

	Weeks					
	1	2	3	4	5	6
	£	£	£	£	£	£
Receipts						
Debtors (opening)	64,000	32,000	-	-	-	-
Debtors (weeks 1-6)	-	40,000	80,000	80,000	70,000	30,000
	64,000	72,000	80,000	80,000	70,000	30,000
Payments						
Wages (opening)	9,000	-	-	-	-	-
Creditors (opening)	21,000	-	-	-	-	-
Wages (weeks 1-6)	-	9,000	11,000	-	-	-
Creditors (weeks 1-6)	-	35,500	23,500	-	-	-
Manufacturing overheads	18,000	18,000	10,000	10,000	10,000	10,000
	48,000	62,500	44,500	10,000	10,000	10,000
Net cash flow	16,000	9,500	35,500	70,000	60,000	20,000
Opening cash	15,000	31,000	40,500	76,000	146,000	206,000
Closing cash	£31,000	£40,500	£76,000	£146,000	£206,000	£226,000

EXERCISE 38.3   PAGE 324

BRIAN PLC

(i)

**Budgeted Trading, Profit and Loss Account
for the year to 31 December 19X7**

	£000	£000
Sales (£30,000 + 10%)		33,000
Less : Cost of goods sold (by deduction)		20,350
Gross profit (33.33% + 5%)		12,650
Less : Expenses :		
Sales commissions (1% x £33,000)	330	
Loan interest (half year)	75	
Administration expenses (£3,500 + 5%)	3,675	
Directors' fees (£300 + 5%)	315	
Bank overdraft interest (£300 x 1/2)	150	
Depreciation (10% x £18,000)	1,800	6,345
Budgeted net profit for the year		£6,305

(ii)

**Summarised Budgeted Bank Account
for the year to 31 December 19X7**

	£000		£000
Debtors (£7,500+33,000-4,125)	36,375	Balance b/d	2,500
		Creditors	20,350
		Loan plus loan interest	1,575
		Sales commissions	330
		Administrative expenses	3,675
		Directors' fees	315
		Bank overdraft interest	150
		Balance c/d	7,480
	£36,375		£36,375
Balance b/d	7,480		

(iii)

Budgeted Balance Sheet as at 31 December 19X7

	£000	£000
Fixed assets (£18,000 - 1,800)		16,200
Current assets		
Stock	5,000	
Debtors (12.5% x £33,000)	4,125	
Cash at bank	7,480	
	16,605	
Less : **Current liabilities**		
Creditors	500	16,105
		£32,305

605

Capital and reserves

Ordinary shares	25,000
Reserves (£1,000 + 6,305)	7,305
	£32,305

EXERCISE 38.4　PAGE 325

RON BELT
**Budgeted Trading, Profit and Loss Account
for the year ended 31 December 19X8**

	£	£
Sales		160,000
Less : Cost of goods sold (£16,000 x 7)		
Purchases (£12,000 + 120,000)	132,000	
Less : Closing stock	20,000	112,000
Gross profit (30% of sales)		48,000
Less : Expenses :		
Sundry expenses	26,850	
Depreciation (20% x £22,750)	4,550	
Loan interest	600	32,000
Budgeted net profit for the year (10% of sales)		£16,000

Budgeted Balance Sheet as at 31 December 19X8

	£	£	£
Fixed assets at cost			22,750
Less : Accumulated depreciation			4,550
[(£160,000/2) - 61,800]			18,200
Current assets			
Stocks [(£16,000 x 2) - 12,000]		20,000	
Debtors (73/365 x £160,000)		32,000	
Prepayments		1,000	
Bank		8,800	
		61,800	
Less : **Current liabilities**			
Creditors (£120,000 x 54.75/365)	18,000		
Accruals (£2,000 + 600)	2,600	20,600	41,200
			£59,400
Capital			
Balance at 1 January 19X8			50,000
Add : Budgeted net profit for the year		16,000	
Less : Drawings		11,600	4,400
			54,400
Loan			5,000
			£59,400

Working

Bank Account (check)

	£		£
Capital	50,000	Fixed assets	22,750
Loan	5,000	Purchases of stock	12,000
Debtors (£160,000-32,000)	128,000	General expenses	
		(£26,850+1,000-2,000)	25,850
		Creditors (£120,000-18,000)	102,000
		Drawings	11,600
		Balance c/d	8,800
	£183,000		£183,000
Balance b/d	8,800		

SOLUTIONS TO CHAPTER 39 EXERCISES

EXERCISE 39.1 PAGE 331

CLIFF LTD
Statement of Source and Application of Funds
for the year to 31 December 19X5

	£000	£000
Source of funds		
Net loss for the year		(8)
Adjustments for items not involving the movement of funds :		
Depreciation	18	
Profit on sale of machinery	(4)	14
Total generated from operations		6
Funds from other sources :		
Sale of machinery (£12 + 4)	16	
Rights issue [(£300+60) x 1/6]	60	76
		82
Application of funds		
Purchase of machinery [(£42 - (37 - 12 - 18)]	(35)	
Purchase of property	(12)	(47)
		35
Increase in working capital		
Increase in stocks	10	
(Decrease) in debtors	(2)	
(Increase) in creditors, excluding taxation and proposed dividends	(14)	
Movement in net liquid funds :		
Increase in cash balances	41	35

EXERCISE 39.2 PAGE 332

A GREEN
Statement of Source and Application of Funds
for the year to 30 June 19X1

	£	£
Source of funds		
Net profit for the year		20,000
Adjustment for items not involving the movement of funds :		
Depreciation		1,600
Total generated from operations		21,600
Funds from other sources :		
Loan		10,000
		31,600
Application of funds		
Purchase of furniture and fittings	(1,000)	
Drawings	(22,600)	(23,600)
		8,000

Increase in working capital

Increase in stocks	1,000	
Increase in debtors	8,000	
(Increase) in creditors	(2,000)	
Movement in net liquid funds :		
Increase in cash balances	1,000	8,000

EXERCISE 39.3   PAGE 332

STONE
Statement of Source and Application of Funds
for the year to 30 April 19X5

	£000	£000
Source of funds		
Net profit for the year		35
Adjustments for items not involving the movement of funds :		
Depreciation	30	
Loss on disposal of plant (Wkg1)	7	37
Total generated from operations		72
Funds from other sources :		
Cash received from sale of plant		5
		77
Application of funds		
Purchase of plant, vehicles and equipment (Wkg2)	(52)	
Drawings	(55)	(107)
		(30)
Decrease in working capital		
Increase in stocks	17	
Increase in debtors	5	
(Increase) in creditors	(20)	
Movement in net liquid funds :		
(Decrease) in cash balances	(32)	(30)

Workings

		£000
(1)	Disposal of fixed assets :	
	Net book value [£30 - {25% x(£30 - 6) x 3}]	12
	Cash	(5)
	Loss on disposal	£7
(2)	Plant, vehicles and equipment :	
	1 5 X4 Balance b/d	80
	30 4 X5 Disposal (Wkg1)	(12)
	Depreciation	(30)
	Balance c/d	(90)
	Apparent purchases	£52

EXERCISE 39.4   PAGE 333

POOL
Statement of Source and Application of Funds
for the year to 31 May 19X2

	£	£
Source of funds		
Net profit for the year		12,150
Adjustments for items not involving the movement of funds :		
Depreciation [(Wkg2) + £150]	4,050	
Profit on disposal of vehicle (Wkg1)	(100)	3,950
Total generated from operations		16,100
Funds from other sources :		
Cash from sale of motor vehicle		600
		16,700
Application of funds		
Purchase of motor vehicles (Wkg3)	(10,000)	
Repayment of loan	(10,000)	
Drawings	(10,000)	(30,000)
		(13,300)
Decrease in working capital		
Increase in stocks	2,500	
Increase in debtors	1,200	
(Increase) in creditors	(400)	
Movement in net liquid funds :		
(Decrease) in cash balances	(16,600)	(13,300)

Workings

		£
(1)	Disposal of motor vehicle :	
	Cost	2,000
	Depreciation	1,500
		500
	Cash	600
	Profit	£100
(2)	Depreciation of motor vehicles :	
	Balance b/d	(3,900)
	Disposal	1,500
	Balance c/d	6,300
	To profit and loss account	£3,900
(3)	Purchase of motor vehicles :	
	Balance b/d	10,500
	Disposal	(2,000)
	Balance c/d	(18,500)
	Apparent purchases	£10,000

EXERCISE 39.5   PAGE 334
(a)

WINTER PLC
Statement of Source and Application of Funds
for the year to 31 October 19X7

	£	£
Source of funds		
Net profit for the year		42,200
Adjustments for items not involving the movement of funds :		
Depreciation [(£48 - 3) - 52]	7,000	
Profit on sale of fixed asset	(600)	6,400
Total generated from operations		48,600
Funds from other sources :		
Issue of shares at a premium (£40,000 + 9,800)		49,800
Sale of fixed asset		1,600
		100,000
Application of funds		
Dividends paid (£7,500 + 10,000)	(17,500)	
Purchase of fixed assets [(£280 - 4) - 282]	(6,000)	
Redemption of debentures	(80,000)	(103,500)
		(3,500)
Decrease in working capital		
Increase in stock	6,000	
Increase in debtors	3,500	
(Increase) in creditors, excluding taxation and		
proposed dividends	(3,000)	
Movement in net liquid funds :		
(Decrease) in cash balances	(10,000)	(3,500)

(b)   **Cash Flow Statement for the year to 31 October 19X7**

	£
Receipts	
Debtors (£12,500 + 250,000 - 16,000)	246,500
Issue of shares at a premium	49,800
Sale of fixed asset	1,600
	297,900
Payments	
Creditors (£12,000 + 186,000 - 15,000)	183,000
Operating expenses (£28,400 - 7,000)	21,400
Purchase of fixed assets	6,000
Redemption of debentures	80,000
Dividends paid	17,500
	307,900
Net cash flow	(10,000)
Opening cash	17,000
Closing cash	£7,000

Working

	£
Opening stock	16,000
Purchases (by deduction)	186,000
	202,000
Less : Closing stock	22,000
Cost of goods sold	£180,000

EXERCISE 39.6   PAGE 335

ALLEVO LTD
Statement of Source and Application of Funds
for the year to 31 December 19X0

	£	£
Source of funds		
Profit before tax		29,400
Adjustments for items not involving the movement of funds :		
Depreciation	4,620	
Goodwill (£9,240 - 8,400)	840	5,460
Total generated from operations		34,860
Funds from other sources :		
Issue of shares for cash	6,800	
Cash from sale of equipment (Wkg1)	800	
Cash from sale of investments (Wkg2)	3,700	11,300
		46,160
Application of funds		
Dividends paid	(10,590)	
Tax paid (Wkg3)	(12,260)	
Purchase of plant and equipment (Wkg4)	(10,500)	(33,350)
		12,810
Increase in working capital		
Increase in stock	23,100	
Increase in debtors	14,784	
(Increase) in creditors, excluding taxation and proposed dividends	(16,130)	
Movement in net liquid funds :		
(Decrease) in cash balances	(8,944)	12,810

Workings

	£
(1) Cash from sale of equipment :	
Disposal of equipment	1,680
Profit to profit and loss account	380
Accumulated depreciation	(1,260)
Cash received	£800
	£

(2)   Cash from sale of investments :

Balance b/d	8,400
Profit to profit and loss account	340
Balance c/d	(5,040)
Cash from sale of investments	£3,700

(3)   Tax paid :

Balance b/d	(1,260)
Balance b/d	(9,000)
To profit and loss account	(12,600)
Balance c/d	2,100
Balance c/d	8,500
Amount paid	£12,260

(4)   Purchase of plant and equipment :

Balance b/d	73,500
Balance c/d	(82,320)
Disposal	(1,680)
Apparent purchases	£10,500

SOLUTIONS TO CHAPTER 40 EXERCISES

EXERCISE 40.1   PAGE 340

CURRENT LTD
Statement of Value Added for the year to 31 December 19X1

	£000	£000
Turnover		760
Bought in materials and services		
[(£415-88-32) + (£247-40-26)]		(476)
Value added		**£284**

Applied the following way :		
To pay employees :		
Wages, pensions and other employment costs (£88+40)		128
To pay providers of capital		
Interest on loans	50	
Dividends to shareholders	19	69
To pay government		
Corporation tax payable		15
To provide for maintenance and expansion of assets		
Depreciation (£32+26)	58	
Retained profits	14	72
Value added		**£284**

EXERCISE 40.2   PAGE 341

TAY LTD
Statement of Value Added for the year to 31 January 19X2

	£000	£000
Turnover		2,820
Bought in materials and supplies		
(£1,407+55+110+18)		(1,590)
Value added		**£1,230**

Applied the following way :		
To pay employees :		
Salaries, wages and related employment costs (£270+450)		720
To pay providers of capital		
Interest on loans	30	
Dividends to shareholders (£15+45)	60	90
To pay government		
Local authority rates	75	
Corporation tax payable	120	195

	£000	£000
To provide for maintenance and expansion of assets		
Depreciation	95	
Retained profits	130	225
Value added		£1,230

EXERCISE 40.3   PAGE 341

DON LTD
Statement of Value Added for the year to 28 February 19X2

	£000	£000
Turnover		750
Bought in materials and services (£500+17+5)		(522)
		228
Interest received		20
Total value added		£248
Applied the following way :		
To pay employees :		
Wages, salaries and pension costs (£110+40)		150
To pay providers of capital		
Interest on loans	15	
Dividends to shareholders	30	45
To pay government		
Local authority rates	12	
Corporation tax payable	10	22
To provide for maintenance and expansion of assets		
Depreciation	21	
Retained profits	10	31
Total value added		£248

SOLUTIONS TO CHAPTER 41 EXERCISES

EXERCISE 41.1 PAGE 347

Using compound interest tables it can be ascertained that at an average rate of 5% per annum, Bill will have to pay £200 in about 15 years time (the compounded sum of £1 = 2.079 by the end of year 15).

EXERCISE 41.2 PAGE 347

CONTEXT PLC

	Historical cost profits before tax	Factor	Restated profits before tax
	£000		£(31 12 X5)'000
19X1	97	100/83	117
19X2	169	100/87	194
19X3	142	100/91	156
19X4	141	100/96	147
19X5	158	100/100	158

EXERCISE 41.3 PAGE 347

DEE PLC

(a) **Additional charges for cost of sales**

	£000	£000
Increase (£100 - 80)		20
Opening stock (£80 x 120/110)	87	
Closing stock (£100 x 120/125)	96	9
Due to price = additional charge		£11

(b) **Closing stock at current cost at 31 December 19X3**

£100 x 130/125 = £104,000

EXERCISE 41.4 PAGE 347

WEAVER PLC

(a) **Additional depreciation**

	£000
Historic cost (£50,000 x 20%)	10,000
Current cost (£80,000 x 20%)	16,000
Additional depreciation	£6,000

(b) **Current cost Balance Sheet (extract) at 31 December 19X3**

	£000
Fixed assets	
Machine at gross replacement cost	80,000
Less : Accumulated depreciation (2 x £16,000)	32,000
Net replacement cost	£48,000

SOLUTIONS TO CHAPTER 42 EXERCISES

EXERCISE 42.1   PAGE 354

(a)

(i) Current or working capital ratio :

$$\frac{\text{Current assets}}{\text{Current liabilities}}$$

(ii) Rate of stock turnover :

$$\frac{\text{Cost of goods sold}}{\text{Average stock}}$$

(iii) Time taken by debtors to pay bills (in weeks) :

$$\frac{\text{Average trade debtors}}{\text{Total credit sales}} \times 52$$

(iv) Gross profit as a % of sales :

$$\frac{\text{Gross profit}}{\text{Sales}} \times 100$$

(v) Net profit as a % of sales :

$$\frac{\text{Net profit}}{\text{Sales}} \times 100$$

(b)

	19X6	19X7

(i) **Current ratio**

$$\frac{1,460}{670}$$ $$\frac{1,850}{1,520}$$

$$= \underline{2.18 \text{ to } 1}$$ $$= \underline{1.22 \text{ to } 1}$$

(ii) **Stock turnover**

$$\frac{3,800 - 1,250}{0.5 \times (700 + 800)}$$ $$\frac{4,800 - 1,300}{0.5 \times (800 + 1,100)}$$

$$= \underline{3.4}$$ $$= \underline{3.68}$$

(iii) **Average debtor collection period**

$$\frac{0.5 \times (400 + 500)}{80\% \times 3,800} \times 52$$ $$\frac{0.5 \times (500 + 750)}{80\% \times 4,800} \times 52$$

$$= \underline{7.69 \text{ weeks}}$$ $$= \underline{8.46 \text{ weeks}}$$

(iv) **Gross profit ratio**

$$\frac{1250}{3800} \times 100$$ $$\frac{1300}{4800} \times 100$$

$$= \underline{32.89\%}$$ $$= \underline{27.08\%}$$

(v) **Net profit ratio**

$$\frac{340}{3800} \times 100 \qquad \frac{380}{4800} \times 100$$

$$= \underline{\underline{8.95\%}} \qquad = \underline{\underline{7.92\%}}$$

(c) **Comments on the results**

(1) The company appears to be increasing its sales by reducing its margin (note the gross profit ratio).

(2) Its net profit is increasing, although its return on sales is decreasing (note the net profit ratio).

(3) Check the liquidity position (note the current ratios and also check the acid test ratio) - especially the bank overdraft in 19X7.

(4) Note the increased amount of borrowing, and the interest (not given) needed to service it.

(5) Note the increase in share capital.

(6) Note that the increased share capital and the increase in loans still results in a bank overdraft by 19X7.

(d) **Courses of action to be taken**

(1) Improve the liquidity position : require debtors to pay more promptly, increase the stock turnover and consider the possibility of reducing the dividend.

(2) Examine the rise in overheads, and check whether the business is operating at the same level of efficiency that it achieved prior to the increase in sales.

(3) Examine its fixed assets to ascertain that it is utilising them efficiently at its new level of operation.

EXERCISE 42.2   PAGE 355

(a)

SHIRT PLC

(1) **Gross profit margin**

$$\frac{530 - 415}{530} \times 100 = \underline{\underline{22\%}}$$

(2) **Net profit margin**

$$\frac{13 + 7}{530} \times 100 = \underline{\underline{4\%}}$$

(3) **Return on shareholders' funds**

$$\frac{13 + 7}{260 + 359} \times 100 = \underline{\underline{3\%}}$$

(4) **Profit before interest to total assets**

$$\frac{13 + 7 + 12}{852} \times 100 = \underline{\underline{4\%}}$$

(5) **Current assets to current liabilities**

$$\frac{220 + 105 + 117}{50 + 20 + 13} = \underline{\underline{5.3 \text{ to } 1}}$$

(6) **Stock turnover**

$$\frac{220}{415} \times 52 = \underline{\underline{28 \text{ weeks}}}$$

(7) **Debtors turnover**

$$\frac{105}{530} \times 52 = \underline{\underline{10 \text{ weeks}}}$$

(8) **Creditors turnover**

$$*\frac{50}{415} \times 52 = \underline{\underline{6 \text{ weeks}}}$$

* credit purchases not disclosed

(b) **Significant differences**

(1) Shirt's gross profit is higher, but its net profit much lower, as is its return on shareholders' funds and profit before interest to total assets.
(2) A healthy liquidity ratio.
(3) A very low stock turnover.

(c) **Problems in making comparisons**

(1) Different entities not strictly comparable, e.g. manufacturing and selling differences.
(2) Inadequate information, e.g. purchases not disclosed.
(3) Problems of defining ratios, e.g. what is meant by gross profit margin.
(4) Use of an average for the trade.

EXERCISE 42.3   PAGE 355
CONE
(a) **Ratios**

(i) **Gross profit on sales :**

$$\frac{\text{gross profit}}{\text{sales}} \times 100$$

19X0 $\dfrac{80}{400} \times 100 = \underline{\underline{20.0\%}}$

19X1 $\dfrac{105}{630} \times 100 = \underline{\underline{16.7\%}}$

19X2 $\dfrac{130}{870} \times 100 = \underline{\underline{14.9\%}}$

(ii) **Gross profit on cost of goods sold :**

$$\frac{\text{gross profit}}{\text{cost of goods sold}} \times 100$$

19X0 $\dfrac{80}{320} \times 100 = \underline{\underline{25.0\%}}$

19X1 $\dfrac{105}{525} \times 100 = \underline{\underline{20.0\%}}$

19X2 $\dfrac{130}{740} \times 100 = \underline{\underline{17.6\%}}$

(iii) **Stock turnover :**

$$\frac{\text{cost of goods sold}}{0.5 \times (\text{opening} + \text{closing stock})}$$

19X0 $\dfrac{320}{0.5 \times (20 + 25)} = \underline{\underline{14.2}}$

19X1 $\dfrac{525}{0.5 \times (25 + 50)} = \underline{\underline{14.0}}$

19X2 $\dfrac{740}{0.5 \times (50 + 100)} = \underline{\underline{9.9}}$

Solutions to CHAPTER 42 Exercises

(iv) Return on capital employed :

$$\frac{\text{net profit}}{\text{capital}} \times 100$$

19X0 $\frac{40}{118} \times 100 = 33.9\%$

19X1 $\frac{55}{141} \times 100 = 39.0\%$

19X2 $\frac{60}{165} \times 100 = 36.4\%$

(v) Current ratio :

$$\frac{\text{current assets}}{\text{current liabilities}}$$

19X0 $\frac{85}{56} = 1.5 \text{ to } 1$

19X1 $\frac{160}{112} = 1.4 \text{ to } 1$

19X2 $\frac{340}{176} = 1.9 \text{ to } 1$

(vi) Liquidity (or quick) ratio :

$$\frac{\text{current assets - stock}}{\text{current liabilities}}$$

19X0 $\frac{85 - 25}{56} = 1.1 \text{ to } 1$

19X1 $\frac{160 - 50}{112} = 1.0 \text{ to } 1$

19X2 $\frac{340 - 100}{176} = 1.4 \text{ to } 1$

(vii) Debtors collection period :

$$\frac{\text{closing debtors}}{\text{credit sales}} \times 365$$

19X0 $\frac{50}{400} \times 365 = 46 \text{ days}$

19X1 $\frac{105}{630} \times 365 = 61 \text{ days}$

19X2 $\frac{240}{870} \times 365 = 101 \text{ days}$

(b) Review of the business : Points to be examined and commented upon.

(1) Cone appears to be cutting his margin on sales to stimulate sales. As a result there is an absolute increase in net profit, but not a proportionate one. This is probably due to the increase in fixed costs and interest on the loan.

(2) Note the changes in the return on capital employed, but these are year-end balances. The return on the average amount of capital invested in each year might be more appropriate (if profits are earned steadily throughout the year).

(3) Note the healthy current and liquidity ratios, but at the same time note the increasing amount of time the debtors are taking to settle their debts along with the decline in stock turnover.

(4) Note that Cone's liquidity position would have been more worrying if he had not taken out a loan.

EXERCISE 42.4   PAGE 357
(a)

CLAREGATE LTD

(i) **Debtors average credit time**

$$\frac{250}{1,000} \times 360 = \underline{90 \text{ days}}$$

(ii) **Profit to all long term capital employed**

$$\frac{124}{200 + 175 + 400} \times 100 = \underline{16\%}$$

(iii) **Return on shareholders' equity**

$$\frac{84}{375} \times 100 = \underline{22\%}$$

(iv) **Net profit after interest to turnover**

$$\frac{84}{1000} \times 100 = \underline{8.4\%}$$

(v) **Turnover to fixed assets**

$$\frac{1,000}{500} \times 100 = \underline{200\%}$$

(b) (i) Worse
  (ii) Worse
  (iii) Worse
  (iv) Better
  (v) Worse

(c)   (i)   (a)   Longer credit period given to encourage greater sales.
               (b)   More inefficient collection of debts.
       (ii)   (a)   Greater administrative costs.
               (b)   Reduced profit margins on sales.
     (iii)   (a)   Issue of debentures and consequent interest payment.
               (b)   Reduction in gross profit.
     (iv)   (a)   Selling prices may have been reduced.
               (b)   Administrative costs may have been reduced.
      (v)   (a)   Sales not risen in proportion to increasing amount of assets.
               (b)   Selling prices may have been reduced.

EXERCISE 42.5   PAGE 357

(a)   **Suggested ratios**

	19X5	19X6
(i) Gross profit ratio $\dfrac{\text{Gross profit}}{\text{Sales}} \times 100$	$\dfrac{1,850}{7,650} \times 100$ $= 24.2\%$	$\dfrac{2,070}{11,500} \times 100$ $= 18.0\%$
(ii) Return on capital employed $\dfrac{(\text{Profit before tax} + \text{long-term interest})}{(\text{Share capital} + \text{reserves} + \text{loans and other borrowings})} \times 100$	$\dfrac{(1,650+50)}{(5,900+5,000 +350)} \times 100$ $= 15.1\%$	$\dfrac{(1,550+350)}{(5,900+5,700 +3,350)} \times 100$ $= 12.7\%$
(iii) Acid test or quick assets or liquidity ratio $\dfrac{\text{Current assets} - \text{stock}}{\text{Current liabilities}}$	$\dfrac{3,600 - 1,500}{2,400}$ $= 0.9 \text{ to } 1$	$\dfrac{6.300 - 2,450}{2,700}$ $= 1.4 \text{ to } 1$
(iv) Trade debtor collection period $\dfrac{\text{Trade debtors}}{\text{Credit sales}} \times 365$	$\dfrac{1,200}{7,650} \times 365$ $= 58 \text{ days}$	$\dfrac{3,800}{11,500} \times 365$ $= 121 \text{ days}$

(v) Stock turnover ratio

$$\frac{\text{Stock}}{\text{Cost of sales}} \times 365 \qquad \frac{1{,}500}{5{,}800} \times 365 \qquad \frac{2{,}450}{9{,}430} \times 365$$

$$= \underline{\underline{95 \text{ days}}} \qquad = \underline{\underline{95 \text{ days}}}$$

(vi) Gearing

$$\frac{\text{Long-term borrowings}}{\text{Proprietor's interest} + \text{long-term borrowings}} \times 100 \qquad \frac{350}{10{,}900+350} \times 100 \qquad \frac{3{,}350}{11{,}600+3{,}350} \times 100$$

$$= \underline{\underline{3.1\%}} \qquad = \underline{\underline{22.4\%}}$$

(b) **Comments : Points to note**
Liquidity
(1) Note the movement downwards in the cash position.
(2) Note the improvement in the acid test ratio (perhaps because of the increase in trade debtors not matched by a similar increase in trade creditors).

Profitability
(1) Note the reduction in gross profit as part of an attempt to stimulate sales.
(2) Note the decrease in profit before taxation, and check its causes, e.g. increase in loan interest. Note also the effect on the return on capital employed.

Efficiency
(1) Note the large increase in the trade debtor collection period, in part, perhaps because of a deliberate policy decision, but there may be in-built inefficiencies.
(2) Note the stock turnover has remained static.

Shareholders' interests
(1) Note that the dividend payment was maintained.
(2) Note the increase in borrowing and the servicing of the loan interest.

(c) **Additional information**

(1) inflation rates
(2) number of new customers
(3) the changes in the sales product mix
(4) more details of the increased credit terms
(5) the level of bad debts
(6) changes in other costs
(7) the extra wear and tear on fixed assets
(8) short and long term financing arrangements.

EXERCISE 42.6   PAGE 358

CHAN, LING AND WONG

(a)

Profit and Loss Accounts for the year to 31 March 19X8

	Chan plc £000	Ling plc £000	Wong plc £000
Operating profit	300	300	300
Interest payable	-	-	(10)
Profit on ordinary activities before tax	300	300	290
Taxation	(90)	(90)	(87)
Profit on ordinary activities after tax	210	210	203
Dividends : Preference		(20)	(30)
Ordinary	(100)	(60)	(40)
	(100)	(80)	(70)
Retained profit for the year	£110	£130	£133

(b)

	Chan plc	Ling plc	Wong plc

(i) Earnings per share

$$\frac{\text{Net profit after tax and preference dividend}}{\text{Number of ordinary shares in issue}}$$

$\frac{210}{500}$	$\frac{210 - 20}{300}$	$\frac{203 - 30}{200}$
= 42p	= 63.3p	= 86.5p

(ii) Price/earnings ratio

$$\frac{\text{Market price of ordinary shares}}{\text{Earnings per share}}$$

$\frac{840}{42}$	$\frac{950}{63.3}$	$\frac{1,038}{86.5}$
= 20	= 15	= 12

(iii) Gearing ratio

$$\frac{\text{Loan capital+preference shares}}{\text{Shareholders' funds}} \times 100$$

Nil	$\frac{200}{300+100+130}$	$\frac{100+300}{200+100+133}$
	= 37.7%	= 92.4%

(c)   **The importance of gearing : Points to be made**

(1)   Define and explain the nature of gearing.

(2)   Note the earnings per share in Chan, Ling and Wong. If the profits are <u>rising</u>, the debenture interest and preference dividends are already covered. For an ordinary shareholder in both Ling and Wong, therefore, there is a good chance that the dividend will be increased. Chan's earnings per share are much lower because there are more shares on which the company has to pay a dividend.

(3)   If profits fluctuate, however, an investment in either Ling or Wong is more risky because a higher proportion of the profit will have to be paid to the debenture and preference share holders. Thus in these circumstances, it may be better to invest in Chan.

SOLUTIONS TO CHAPTER 43 TASKS

CASE STUDY 1   PAGE 363

BOB, KATE AND WAYNE

Tutor Guidelines

Task 1

No solution is provided. The main objective of the task is to encourage the student to study the details given in the case study, and then to arrive at a reasoned decision.

Task 2

No solution is provided. The main objective of the task is to encourage the student to research the considerable literature available on "starting your own business", and to concentrate on the accounting and legal considerations, as well as on the sources of finance available to small businesses.

Task 3

No solution is provided. The main objective of the task is to test the student's ability to consider the facts, and then to arrive at a sensible conclusion.

SOLUTIONS TO CHAPTER 44 TASKS

CASE STUDY 2   PAGE 365

ROSS PUMPS

Tutor Guidelines

Task 1

Receipts and Payments Account for the year to 31 March 19X4

	£000
Receipts	
Cash sales	220
Credit sales	100
	320
Payments	
Raw materials (£100 + 250)	350
Wages	51
Salaries	25
Rent	30
Rates	10
Insurances	4
Heat, light and power	15
Office expenses	12
Van expenses	6
	503
Net payments for the year	£(183)

Balance Sheet at 31 March 19X4

	£000	£000
Fixed assets		
Factory equipment		45
Office furniture		10
Delivery vans		30
		85
Current asset		
Cash at bank and in hand		42
		127
Long-term loan		(100)
		£27

Capital

Introduced at 1 April 19X3		230
Net payments over receipts for the year	(183)	
Add : Drawings	(20)	(203)
		£27

Task 2

No solution is provided, as the results will depend upon the student's own researches.

Task 3

An outline solution only is given, as the detailed results will depend upon the decisions taken in Task 2.

ROSS
Manufacturing, Trading and Profit and Loss Account
for the year to 31 March 19X4

	£000	£000
Direct materials :		
Purchases		400
Less : Closing stock		80
Direct materials consumed		320
Direct labour		
Manufacturing overhead :		
Depreciation : Factory equipment		
Heat, light and power	19	
Insurances	1	
Rates	27	
Rent	9	
Total manufacturing overhead incurred		
Less : Closing work in progress		
Manufacturing cost of goods produced		£
Sales		420
Less : Cost of goods sold :		
Manufacturing cost of goods produced		
Less : Closing stock		
Gross profit		
Less : General overhead expenses :		
Depreciation : Delivery vans		
: Office furniture		
Heat, light and power	1	
Insurances	1	
Loan interest		

	£000	£000
Office expenses	12	
Rates	1	
Rent	3	
Salaries	25	
Van expenses	6	
Net profit/loss for the year		£

Balance Sheet at 31 March 19X4

	£000 Cost	£000 Depreciation	£000 NBV
Fixed assets			
Factory equipment	45		
Office furniture	10		
Delivery vans	30		
	£85		
Current assets			
Raw materials	80		
Work in progress			
Finished goods	—		
Trade debtors		100	
Prepayments		2	
Cash at bank and in hand		42	
***Less* : Current liabilities**			
Trade creditors	50		
Accruals	—	—	
Long-term loan			(100)
			£
Capital and reserves			
Introduced at 1 April 19X3			230
Net profit/loss for the year			
Add/(Less) : Drawings		20	
			£

Task 4

Outline solution :

Balance Sheet at 31 March 19X4
using net realisable values

	£000	£000	£000
Fixed assets			
Factory equipment			15
Office furniture			1
Delivery vans			15
			31
Current assets			
Raw materials	60		
Finished goods	40	100	
Trade debtors		90	
Prepayments		1	
Cash at bank and in hand		42	
		233	
Less : **Current liabilities**			
Trade creditors	50		
Accruals			
Long-term loan			(100)
			£
Capital and reserves			
Introduced at 1 April 19X3			230
Net profit/loss for the year *			
Add : Drawings		(20)	
			£

* balancing figure

Task 5

No solution is given as the students should be encouraged to find out this information for themselves.

SOLUTIONS TO CHAPTER 45 TASKS

CASE STUDY 3   PAGE 369

CLYDE, FORTH AND TAY

Tutor Guidelines

Task 1

No specific solution is provided, as individual research should be encouraged.

Task 2

No specific solution is provided, as the students should be able to work out their own partnership agreement.

Task 3

No specific solution is provided, as the students should be encouraged to work out their own accounting treatment for the cars bought on hire purchase.

Task 4

Outline solution :

CLYDE AND FORTH

Trading, Profit and Loss Account for the year to 31 December 19X7

	£000	£000
Sales		
Less : Cost of goods sold :		
Purchases		
Less : Closing stock		
	—	
Gross profit		250
Less : Expenses :		
Car expenses		
Electricity		
Depreciation : Buildings		
: Shop furniture and equipment		
Insurances		
Interest on hire purchase loan		
Rates		
Rent		
Shop expenses		
	—	—
Net profit for the year		
Less : Appropriations		
Balance of profit :		
Clyde		
Forth		
	—	═

Balance Sheet at 31 December 19X7

	£000 Cost	£000 Depreciation	£000 NBV
Fixed assets			
Land and buildings	20		
Shop furniture and equipment	40		
Cars	28	—	—
	£88		
Current assets			
Stocks			
Trade debtors		30	
Prepayments			
Cash at bank		36	
Cash in hand		10	
Less : **Current liabilities**			
Obligation under hire purchase agreement			
Trade creditors	70		
Accruals			
	—	—	
Long-term liability			
Obligation under hire purchase agreement			
			—
			£
Capital accounts			
Clyde			60
Forth			20
			80
Capital accounts			
Clyde			
Forth		—	—
			£

Task 5

No specific solution is provided, as the students should be encouraged to incorporate their own ideas into the report for Tay.

SOLUTIONS TO CHAPTER 46 TASKS

CASE STUDY 4   PAGE 372

NOVELTIES LIMITED

Tutor Guidelines

Task 1

NOVELTIES LIMITED
Statements of Source and Application of Funds
for the year to 31 December

	19X2 £000	19X3 £000	19X4 £000	19X5 £000
Source of funds				
Profit/(loss) before taxation	710	1,000	700	(790)
Issue of shares for cash (including the premium)	250	-	1,125	-
	960	1,000	1,825	(790)
Application of funds				
Tax paid	(10)	(10)	(50)	(100)
Dividends paid	(100)	(200)	(400)	(800)
Movement in net book value of fixed assets	(800)	(1,220)	(1,015)	(1,560)
	(910)	(1,430)	(1,465)	(2,460)
	50	(430)	360	(3,250)
Movement in working capital				
Increase in stocks	200	100	5,600	500
Increase in trade debtors	600	900	2,100	4,700
Increase/(decrease) in prepayments	10	(10)	100	-
Increase in trade creditors	(750)	(1,400)	(6,450)	(5,600)
Increase in accruals	-	(20)	(20)	
Decrease in net liquid funds	(10)	-	(970)	(2,850)
	50	(430)	360	(3,250)

635

Task 2

Selected Accounting Ratios

	19X1	19X2	19X3	19X4	19X5
Profitability ratios					
Return on capital employed : Net profit before tax x 100 Shareholders' funds	16.1%	21.5%	26.0%	14.7%	(19.9%)
Gross profit ratio : Gross profit x 100 Sales	34.1%	32.8%	26.7%	21.5%	12.9%
Net profit ratio : Net profit before tax x 100 Sales	5.0%	5.5%	5.3%	2.7%	(1.7%)
Liquidity ratios					
Current assets ratio : Current assets Current liabilities	1.2:1	1.2:1	0.95:1	0.97:1	0.86:1
Acid test ratio : Current assets - stocks Current liabilities	0.43:1	0.51:1	0.52:1	0.36:1	0.46:1
Efficiency ratios					
Stock turnover ratio : Closing stock x 365 Cost of goods sold	109 days	77 days	51 days	137 days	73 days
Trade debtors collection period : Trade debtors x 365 Credit sales	32 days	38 days	43 days	72 days	71 days
Trade creditors payment period : Trade creditors x 365 Credit purchases	114 days	106 days	105 days	148 days	143 days

Task 3

Selected Trend Ratios

	19X1	19X2	19X3	19X4	19X5
Sales	100	156	228	312	566
Cost of goods sold	100	159	254	372	748
Gross profit	100	150	179	196	214
Distribution costs	100	150	162	195	281
Administrative costs	100	121	207	241	307
Net profit/(loss) before taxation	100	173	244	171	(193)

	19X1	19X2	19X3	19X4	19X5
Fixed assets (net book value)	100	139	198	247	322
Current assets	100	133	174	494	708
Current liabilities	100	144	229	632	1,020

Vertical analysis : selected items
As a percentage of sales :

	19X1	19X2	19X3	19X4	19X5
Cost of goods sold	66	67	73	78	87
Gross profit	34	33	27	22	13
Distribution costs	26	25	18	16	13
Administrative expenses	3	3	4	3	2
Net profit/(loss) before taxation	5	5	5	3	(2)

As a percentage of net assets :

	19X1	19X2	19X3	19X4	19X5
Fixed assets at net book value	81	87	106	107	168
Current assets	95	98	110	251	432
Current liabilities	76	85	116	258	500

Task 4

No solution is provided, as the key statistics depend upon the student's own judgement.

Task 5

No set solution is provided, as the students have to use some judgement in deciding what is the main data.

Task 6

No solution is provided, as the content and conclusion will depend upon the student's selection of data, and on individual interpretation..

INDEX